Taste of Home
Light&Tasty
Annual Recipes 2007

PICTURED ABOVE AND ON THE FRONT COVER: Makeover Traditional Cheesecake (page 211) and Maple-Orange Pot Roast (page 106).

Taste of Home
Light&Tasty
Annual Recipes 2007

Senior Editor/Books: Mark Hagen
Art Director: Gretchen Trautman
Vice President/Books: Heidi Reuter Lloyd
Layout Designers: Emma Acevedo, Kathy Crawford, Julie Stone
Proofreader: Linne Bruskewitz
Editorial Assistant: Barb Czysz

Taste of Home
Light&Tasty

Managing Editor: Mary Spencer
Associate Editors: Mary C. Hanson, John McMillan
Food Director: Diane Werner RD
Food Editor: Peggy Woodward RD
Senior Art Director: Sandra L. Ploy
Creative Director: Ardyth Cope
Copy Editor: S.K. Enk
Recipe Editors: Christine Rukavena, Sue A. Jurack, Mary King
Test Kitchen Manager: Karen Scales
Test Kitchen Home Economists: Tina Johnson, Ann Liebergen, Marie Parker,
Annie Rose, Pat Schmeling, Wendy Stenman, Amy Welk-Thieding RD
Contributing Home Economist: Jackie Josetti
Test Kitchen Assistants: Rita Krajcir, Kris Lehman, Sue Megonigle,
Julie Meyers, Megan Taylor
Editorial Assistant: Marilyn Iczkowski
Graphic Art Associate: Ellen Lloyd
Photographers: Rob Hagen (Senior), Dan Roberts, Jim Wieland
Associate Photographer: Lori Foy
Food Stylists: Joylyn Trickel (Senior), Sarah Thompson
Contributing Food Stylists: Diane Armstrong, Susan Breckenridge,
Sue Draheim, Mary Franz, Julie Herzfeldt, Jennifer Janz, Jim Rude
Food Stylists' Assistants: Kate Baumann, Kaitlyn Besasie
Set Stylist: Jennifer Bradley Vent
Contributing Set Stylists: Stephanie Marchese, Julie Ferron,
Grace Natoli Sheldon
Executive Editor, Digital Media: Bob Ottum
President: Barbara Newton
Senior Vice President/Editor in Chief: Catherine Cassidy
Vice President/Advertising Sponsorship Director: J.P. Perkins
Founder: Roy Reiman

Taste of Home Books
© 2007 Reiman Media Group, Inc.
5400 S. 60th Street, Greendale WI 53129

International Standard Book Number (10): 0-89821-521-8
International Standard Book Number (13): 978-089821-521-2
International Standard Serial Number: 1537-3134

To order additional copies of this book, write: Taste of Home Books,
P.O. Box 908, Greendale WI 53129; call toll-free 1-800/344-2560 to order
with a credit card. Or visit our Web site at www.reimanpub.com.

Contents

505 Home-Style Dishes For Healthy Families

COMFORTING casseroles, thick stews and decadent desserts. These are just some of the items people *think* they have to leave behind when eating right. After all, beefy entrees, rich cheese sauces, creamy cheesecakes and frosty treats aren't usually considered the anchors of a good-for-you recipe box.

The more that family cooks experiment in their kitchens, however, the more they realize trimmed-down foods can satisfy the heartiest appetites and please the pickiest palates. From coast to coast, folks are finding delicious ways to lighten up dinnertime staples with mouth-watering results.

They're re-creating scrumptious delights with only a fraction of the calories and fat usually found in those dishes. Luckily, these health-conscious cooks happily share their secrets in every issue of *Light & Tasty* magazine.

Unlike other food magazines, *Light & Tasty* takes a commonsense approach to eating. It suggests simple options with lighter ingredients that the whole family will enjoy. The recipes in *Light & Tasty* are lean on calories, fat, sodium and/or carbohydrates, but most importantly, they are loaded with flavor!

Page through *2007 Light & Tasty Annual Recipes*, and you'll find all 505 recipes from last year's issues. Many of the dishes are family favorites of our readers, so they're guaranteed to offer plenty of great, home-style flavor.

The recipes are lightened up, yet they don't leave you hungry. Discover incredible delights such as Chicken and Dumpling Soup (p. 37), Tenderloin with Herb Sauce (p. 264), Warm Chocolate Cakes (p. 241) and so much more.

In addition, each recipe was reviewed by a Registered Dietitian and includes Nutrition Facts, plus Diabetic Exchanges where appropriate.

So get ready to dig into all of the foods you and your family crave most. With *2007 Light & Tasty Annual Recipes*, eating right has never been easier or more delicious.

Diane Werner, R.D.

Food Director, *Light & Tasty*

What's Inside These Recipe-Packed Pages?

AS IF the 505 great-tasting recipes isn't enough reason to love *2007 Light & Tasty Annual Recipes*, the following features will certainly make this book a valued reference in your kitchen for years to come.

At-a-Glance Information. If you are on a special diet—or someone you cook for is—finding suitable recipes is a breeze. That's because low-fat, low-sodium, low-carb and meatless dishes are clearly labeled next to the recipe title. (Turn the page for an explanation of these special diet indicators.) As an added bonus, preparation times are provided for *every* recipe in the book.

User-Friendly Chapters. To assist in your menu planning, we've compiled all 505 recipes into 15 convenient chapters, such as Light Bites & Beverages, Beefed-Up Main Dishes, Chicken & Turkey Entrees, Meatless Main Dishes, From the Bread Basket and Dazzling Desserts. (For a complete listing of chapters, turn back to page 3.)

Mouth-Watering Meals. You'll find 12 complete meals (including pictures!), which are perfect for either weekday family dining (page 239) or weekend entertaining (page 261).

De-Light-Ful Dinner Planner. In addition to the meal chapters mentioned above, we've created 27 menu plans. (See the De-Light-Ful Dinner Planner on page 7.) Each meal features recipes found inside the book, as well as suggestions for "appealing partners" (side dishes, desserts or beverages) and meal-preparation pointers.

Hundreds of Color Photos. *More than half* of the recipes in this timeless collection are shown in full color. So you can be sure these satisfying foods not only taste terrific but are eye-appealing as well.

Easy-to-Use Indexes. Finding all 505 recipes is a snap with two simple-to-use indexes. The general index lists every recipe by food category, major ingredient and/or cooking technique. The alphabetical recipe listing is perfect for anyone looking for a specific family favorite. And, starting with this edition, both indexes highlight which recipes are table-ready in just 30 minutes or less.

Nutrition Facts Nuggets

Our Nutritional Guidelines

EVERY RECIPE in 2007 *Light & Tasty Annual Recipes* fits the lifestyle of health-conscious cooks. The recipe collection represents a variety of foods that will easily fit into any meal plan that is within the standards of the USDA's Daily Nutrition Guide (see box below). The target nutritional content of recipes, on a per serving basis, is:

- 400 calories (or less)
- 12 grams of fat (or less)
- 1,000 mg sodium (or less)
- 100 mg cholesterol (or less)

How we calculated the Nutrition Facts

- Whenever a choice of ingredients is given in a recipe (such as 1/3 cup of sour cream or plain yogurt), the first ingredient listed is the one calculated in the Nutrition Facts.
- When a range is given for an ingredient (such as 2 to 3 teaspoons), we calculate the first amount given.
- Only the amount of marinade absorbed during preparation is calculated.
- Garnishes listed in recipes are generally included in our calculations.

Diabetic Exchanges

ALL recipes in this book have been reviewed by a Registered Dietitian. Diabetic Exchanges are assigned to recipes in accordance with guidelines from the American Diabetic and American Dietetic Associations. The majority of recipes in 2007 *Light & Tasty Annual Recipes* are suitable for diabetics.

Special Diet Indicators

TO HELP folks on restricted diets easily find dishes to suit their needs, we clearly indicate recipes that are low in carbohydrates, fat or sodium or that contain no meat. You'll find these colored, special diet indicators after the recipe title where appropriate:

FAT One serving contains 3 grams or less of fat

SALT One serving contains 140 milligrams or less of sodium

CARB One serving contains 15 grams or less of carbohydrates

MEAT LESS Appetizers, salads, savory breads, side dishes and entrees that contain no meat

Your Serving Size Guide

This list is a general guide for healthy eating for most adults.

Grains
1 bread slice, pancake or waffle
Half of an average bagel (the size of a hockey puck)
1 cup dry cereal
1/2 cup cooked cereal, rice or pasta

Vegetables
1 cup raw leafy greens
1/2 cup of any chopped vegetable, raw or cooked
6-ounce glass of vegetable juice
1 small potato

Fruits
1 medium piece of fruit
1/2 cup sliced fruit
6-ounce glass of orange juice or any 100% fruit juice

Dairy
8-ounce container of yogurt
1/2 cup cottage cheese
1-1/2 ounces cheese (size of two dominoes)
8-ounce glass of milk

Meat and Beans
3 ounces cooked lean meat, poultry or fish (size of a deck of cards)
2 tablespoons peanut butter
1/2 cup beans

Daily Nutrition Guide

	Women 25-50	Women over 50	Men over 24
Calories	2,200	1,900 or less	2,900
Fat	73 g or less	63 g or less	96 g or less
Saturated Fat	24 g or less	21 g or less	32 g or less
Cholesterol	300 mg or less	300 mg or less	300 mg or less
Sodium	2,400 mg or less	2,400 mg or less	2,400 mg or less
Carbohydrates	335 g	283 g	446 g
Fiber	20-30 g	20-30 g	20-30 g
Protein	50 g	50 g or less	63 g

This chart is only a guide. Calorie requirements vary, depending on size, weight and amount of activity. Children's calorie and protein needs vary as they grow.

De-Light-Ful Dinner Planner

Setting a healthy meal on the table just became easier! Featuring recipes from this book, the 27 menus that follow make meal planning a breeze. In addition, dozens of "appealing partners" help round out the dinners and "practical tips" offer ideas for substitutions and finishing up leftovers.

Cranberry-Mustard
Pork Medallions and
Herb-Crusted Potatoes, p. 15

Stir-Fry Is a Swift Supper

From Penn Valley, California, Elaine Norgaard shares **Beef 'n' Asparagus Pasta** (p. 96). Ready in just 30 minutes, the family-friendly entree is loaded with sirloin steak, mushrooms, tomato and asparagus. The satisfying stir-fry makes a healthy meal-in-one any night of the week.

Cap off the dinner with Sheri Erickson's low-fat **Raspberry Angel Cake** (p. 226). The Montrose, Iowa cook likes to jazz up a convenient cake mix with almond and vanilla extracts for a bit of homemade flair. She tops the sweet specialty with colorful raspberries right before serving.

APPEALING PARTNERS

- Hot tea
- Tossed salad

PRACTICAL TIPS

- To prepare the pasta dish quickly, Elaine does all of the cutting and chopping first and keeps the ingredients near her stovetop.

- Eliminate the salt called for in the main course, and you'll shave 295 mg of sodium from each serving.

- If you're watching your sugar intake, Sheri suggests sweetening the dessert's raspberries with sugar substitute.

Timeless Tastes Get Easy Updates

Hot off the grill, juicy burgers are a sure sign of summer at Vicki Schurk's home. She puts a sizzling twist on these American staples when she whips up tasty **Turkey Burgers with Jalapeno Cheese Sauce** (p. 122). The burgers help her set dinner on her Hamden, Connecticut table in a matter of minutes.

Cucumbers with Dill (p. 56) make a refreshing accompaniment to the burgers...or most any entree. The *Light & Tasty* Test Kitchen staff created the no-fuss salad with time in mind.

APPEALING PARTNERS

- Baked beans
- Frozen yogurt

PRACTICAL TIPS

- If you usually top your burgers with ketchup, try swapping it out with salsa when enjoying the turkey patties.

- Remember the stovetop cheese sauce the next time you're looking to dress up baked potatoes or even scrambled eggs.

- Use a kitchen mandoline or a food processor attachment to thinly slice the cucumbers in the salad.

Casserole Makes Carefree Meal

When it comes to meal-in-one convenience, there's nothing more comforting than a piping-hot casserole—and Theresa Smith's **Italian Hot Dish** (p. 100) is no exception. The Sheboygan, Wisconsin reader says the filling pasta supper is one that her family requests time and again.

Complete the dinner with **Devil's Food Cookies** (p. 32). From Rock Rapids, Iowa, Melanie Van Den Brink notes that the rich, chocolaty treats are easy to calculate for point-based weight-loss programs.

APPEALING PARTNERS

- Romaine salad
- Herbed Soft Breadsticks (recipe on p. 267)

PRACTICAL TIPS

- You'll need one medium-sized green pepper to yield the amount called for in the entree.

- To save time, assemble the casserole the night before. Then all you have to do the following evening is pop it in the oven.

- Store extra cookies in a resealable storage bag in the freezer. They're a guilt-free way to curb anyone's chocolate cravings.

Grilled Salmon Stars in Salad

A fast marinade lends Oriental flair to fish fillets in **Salmon Caesar Salad** (p. 155). Ann Bagdonas from Antioch, California grills the fish before setting it over fresh greens that are topped with bottled salad dressing, Parmesan cheese and almonds.

End the meal with a nutritious treat that will keep your gang asking for more. **Custard Berry Parfaits** (p. 229), from Eagle, Idaho's Trisha Kruse, are a welcomed dessert, particularly during spring and summer when berries are at their best.

APPEALING PARTNERS

- Lemonade
- Biscuits

PRACTICAL TIPS

- Because the salmon is so flavorful and moist, Ann often serves the salad dressing on the side.

- The *L&T* home economists used a combination of strawberries, blackberries and raspberries in the parfaits. Feel free to prepare them with your favorite berries or whatever fruit you happen to have on hand.

- Top servings of angel food cake with the dessert's vanilla custard. Add sliced melon for a substantial garnish.

Soup and Bread Are a Satisfying Pair

Turkey sausage, pasta and a host of vegetables make **Tortellini Minestrone** (p. 42) a filling dinner-in-one. Pamela Smith sent the details behind the hearty soup from her home in Flushing, New York. After one taste, you'll see why it's a favorite at her house.

Warm slices of **Herb Quick Bread** (p. 196) complement the soup perfectly. In Shumway, Illinois, Donna Roberts relies on caraway seeds, nutmeg and thyme to flavor the rustic loaf. It's wonderful served alongside stew and pasta entrees as well.

APPEALING PARTNERS

- Light herbed butter
- Baked apples

PRACTICAL TIPS

- You'll need six medium carrots and three medium zucchini for the cup measurements that are called for in the minestrone.

- For extra fiber and bulk, add a can of kidney or butter beans (rinsed and drained) to the savory soup.

- Double the ingredients for the quick bread and bake two loaves at once. Handy for busy nights, the second loaf can be stored in the freezer for up to 2 months.

Weeknight Dinner Is Colorful, Casual

Broccoli, carrot and sweet red pepper make an eye-appealing combination in this one-dish main course from Sharon Allen. **Stir-Fried Walnut Chicken** (p. 125) is the perfect solution to the busy days she faces in Allentown, Pennsylvania.

For a fun treat, pour cups of ruby-red **Cranberry Herbal Tea Cooler** (p. 29). Our Test Kitchen staff members outdid themselves when they created the lip-smacking thirst quencher. It's a super change of pace from soft drinks and other beverages that you can enjoy anytime of the day.

APPEALING PARTNERS

- Baked egg rolls
- Fortune cookies

PRACTICAL TIPS

- Increase the entree's gingerroot or stir in some crushed red pepper flakes for a little extra kick.

- For a nutrition boost, toss a handful of frozen corn kernels into the stir-fry as the sauce thickens. Cook until these veggies are tender.

- Surprise your family by serving the tea in frosty glasses that you set in the freezer before you began preparing dinner.

A Chicken Dinner In No Time at All

Turn a weeknight meal into a dressy affair by serving Kim Pettipas' **Chicken with Cranberry Sauce** (p. 123). The Oromocto, New Brunswick reader tops juicy chicken breast halves with a wonderfully sweet berry sauce. Best of all, the picture-perfect main dish comes together in a pinch.

Gingered Butternut Squash (p. 69), shared by Fran Swartzentruber of Sebring, Ohio, is an ideal match to the chicken. Perfect for fall dinners, the squash is blended with candied ginger and ground nutmeg for a tongue-tingling taste.

APPEALING PARTNERS

- Apple cider
- Sesame Broccoli (recipe on p. 79)

PRACTICAL TIPS

- For a change of pace, Kim recommends an easy variation to her recipe. She sometimes serves the cranberry sauce over pork.

- One 12-ounce package of fresh cranberries yields 3 cups, but you only need 2 cups for the entree's sauce. Blend the extra berries with fat-free yogurt for a healthy smoothie.

- Fran often garnishes the squash with additional candied ginger.

Handheld Supper Earns Raves

Pork Cabbage Sandwiches (p. 140) will end the day on a flavorful note. A time-easing yet tangy marinade makes an appetizing seasoning for juicy pork tenderloin. The simple sandwich was sent by Lisa Gross of Janesville, Wisconsin, who says it's an all-time favorite for both her mother and herself.

Fire up the grill for Doris Sowers' **Apple Skewers** (p. 212). The Hutchinson, Kansas reader lightly spices the apples for a stress-free accompaniment that makes cleanup a cinch. The special kabobs are an easy idea that will surely grab your family's attention at the dinner table.

APPEALING PARTNERS

- Three-bean salad
- Vanilla wafers

PRACTICAL TIPS

- Start this recipe the night before by marinating the pork to hurry along the sandwiches the next day.

- Serve the apples with a side of reduced-fat or fat-free frozen yogurt for a sweet treat.

- For a light bite, sprinkle the apples' cinnamon-sugar mixture onto other grilled and non-grilled fruits.

Menu Offers Classic Comfort Quickly

In her Marwayne, Alberta kitchen, Kari Johnston puts leftover poultry to excellent use in **Turkey Fettuccine Skillet** (p. 132). The creamy pasta and turkey dish is topped with cheese, then it's quickly broiled for a mouthwatering finishing touch.

As a sweet ending to the meal, whip up **Cran-Apple Oatmeal Cookies** (p. 25). Sent by Theresa Smith of Rome, Georgia, the guilt-free treats make a big batch, so they're just right for sharing with drop-in guests, adding to brown-bag lunches during the week and snacking after school.

APPEALING PARTNERS

- Spinach salad
- Garlic bread

PRACTICAL TIPS

- Instead of leftover turkey, consider adding cubed cooked chicken, pork tenderloin or ham to the pasta dish. Feel free to mix in a handful of frozen peas as the skillet dish simmers.

- To boost nutrition, Kari likes to use whole wheat fettuccine in the main course.

- When at the grocery store, remember that you'll need two 6-ounce packages of dried cranberries for the cookies.

Traditional Meal Made Easy

In Houston, Texas, Bonnie Brown-Watson quickly dresses up dinner with mouth-watering results. **Pork Chops with Dijon Sauce** (p. 137) is a no-fuss meal that's as suitable for fast, family suppers as it is for weekend guests. Ready in just 30 minutes, the savory recipe relies on kitchen staples.

Serve the pork alongside Terri McKay's chilled **Sesame Green Bean Salad** (p. 48). Terri serves the low-fat side dish in her New Bern, North Carolina home. Try it yourself and you'll find that it's a refreshing change-of-pace from steamed green beans and tossed salads.

APPEALING PARTNERS

- Roasted potatoes
- Sliced peaches

PRACTICAL TIPS

- Bonnie sometimes replaces the Dijon mustard with spicy brown or honey mustard.

- Refrigerate any leftover beans, and toss them into a green salad for a fast lunch or dinner accompaniment later in the week.

- For a tasty twist, try replacing the green beans in the salad recipe with asparagus.

Spice Up Weeknights Southwestern Style

A savory combination of ingredients makes for a tongue-tingling supper-in-one with Jenny Kniesly's **Chipotle Chicken and Beans** (p. 127).

From Dover, Ohio, Jenny sent the south-of-the-border recipe that deliciously combines long grain rice, tender strips of chicken, black and white beans, bacon and finely chopped chipotle peppers. The stovetop supper also includes a hint of lime juice, cranberry sauce and a dash of cinnamon. It's bound to become a new favorite with your family.

APPEALING PARTNERS

- Cut green beans
- Corn bread

PRACTICAL TIPS

- Look for canned chipotle peppers in adobo sauce in the ethnic aisle of large supermarkets.

- Use strips of turkey bacon to reduce the fat even further.

- Preparing the dinner on the stovetop saves time, but Jenny suggests another option: She cooks the bacon before combining it with the other ingredients in her slow cooker. She then simmers everything for 6-7 hours or until the rice is tender and the chicken juices run clear.

Healthy Pitas Make for Fun

For a casual supper that's big on nutrition and timed right for busy families, give **Garbanzo Bean Pitas** a try (p. 180). Susan LeBrun of Sulphur, Louisiana treats pitas to a swift and satisfying bean spread before stuffing them with juicy cucumber slices and chopped tomato.

Crushed pineapple, citrus flavors, bananas and maraschino cherries make LeAnn Kane's **Icy Fruit Pops** a favorite summer dessert (p. 226). The Forsyth, Illinois cook relies on a sugar substitute for the healthy treats that are the perfect way to cool off when the mercury rises. Kids of all ages just can't seem to get enough of the frosty dinner finales.

APPEALING PARTNERS

- Pretzels
- Creamy Veggie Salad (recipe on p. 58)

PRACTICAL TIPS

- For extra zing, substitute lemon juice for the water in the pitas' bean spread.

- Susan sometimes adds Greek olives and feta cheese to the sandwiches.

- Don't have any cherries or strawberries for the pops? Use seedless grapes.

Stovetop Specialty Is a Surefire Hit

30-Minute Meal Can't Be Beat

Simple Menu Is Big on Flavor

Beat the suppertime doldrums with an exotic dish that's good for you, too. **Chinese Pork 'n' Noodles** (p. 138) offers colorful, well-seasoned produce and ribbons of tender pork that perfectly complement noodles. The speedy, mouth-watering stir-fry was sent by Jennifer Enzer of Manchester, Michigan.

Cap off the skillet supper with Robert Daggit's **Vanilla Tapioca Pudding** (p. 29). The Shoreview, Minnesota cook relies on just five ingredients for his pared-down take on the classic treat.

When it comes to cooking light, Kay Shimonek doesn't waste time. She sets low-carb **Lemon Thyme Chicken** (p. 115) on her Corsicana, Texas supper table in moments. A thick lemon and onion sauce tops lightly breaded chicken breasts in the easy dinner mainstay.

With only a hint of fat, pretty **Rice with Summer Squash** (p. 76) is a scrumptious addition to the chicken dinner...or any entree for that matter. It's great alongside grilled foods, too. Heather Ratigan of Kaufman, Texas hopes the buttery side dish will be as popular in your home as it is in hers.

When Marietta, Georgia's Beverly Little fixes her **Veggie Cheese Sandwiches** (p. 174), no one even misses the meat. Each satisfying bite features melted cheese, green pepper, tomato and mushrooms for a taste sensation that's tough to beat.

Serve the sandwiches with hearty helpings of **Black-Eyed Pea Salad** (p. 51) shared by Olive Foemmel from Chili, Wisconsin. Her cool combination of celery, black-eyed peas and tangy dressing brings an end to any recipe fatigue the health-conscious cook might face. Remember the recipe the next time you need to contribute to a bring-a-dish event.

APPEALING PARTNERS

- Vegetable soup
- Lemon scones

PRACTICAL TIPS

■ You can turn the stir-fry into a meatless main course or hearty side dish by simply leaving out the pork. Or, consider substituting it with vegetarian meat crumbles.

■ Don't have all of the veggies for the entree? Try using a bag of frozen stir-fry vegetables.

■ Layer the pudding in parfait glasses with fresh berries for an impressive, heart-smart dessert.

APPEALING PARTNERS

- Steamed broccoli
- Strawberry shortcake

PRACTICAL TIPS

■ The chicken recipe serves four, but if you're cooking for two, simply divide the ingredients in half. Just remember that half a tablespoon equals 1-1/2 teaspoons.

■ You only need a cup of broth for the side dish. Freeze the rest in a storage container for up to 3 months.

■ Feel free to substitute the zucchini in the rice with chopped green or sweet red pepper.

APPEALING PARTNERS

- Carrot sticks
- Chicken noodle soup

PRACTICAL TIPS

■ To cut the fat from the sandwiches even further, Beverly relies on slices of fat-free cheese.

■ For extra flair, add sliced olives or lean turkey bacon to the sandwiches if you like.

■ Consider mixing up the side dish's dressing and stirring it into your favorite chilled pasta or rice salad.

Go Italian In a Half Hour

Thirty minutes are all Paula Marchesi needs for her popular **Creamy Turkey Fettuccine** (p. 117). The Lenhartsville, Pennsylvania contributor simply relies on a light cheese spread to speed up the heartwarming sauce that's loaded with comforting goodness.

From her home in Kenai, Alaska, Gwen Klawunder sends a sensational accompaniment. **Yogurt-Herb Salad Dressing** (p. 52) comes together in no time and has only a trace of fat. Gwen likes it over baby spinach greens with tomatoes and cottage cheese, but try it over the mixed salad of your choice.

APPEALING PARTNERS

- Breadsticks
- Low-fat brownies

PRACTICAL TIPS

- Paula enjoys the pasta with slices of pumpkin or cranberry nut bread.

- Swap out the main course's turkey with cooked chicken, ham or even shrimp if that is what you have in the refrigerator.

- Instead of topping greens with croutons, Gwen likes to sprinkle healthy soy nuts over her salads.

Seafood Dinner Easily Impresses

Dorothy Bateman of Carver, Massachusetts has a surefire way to jazz up fish fillets. A little sherry and cream of shrimp soup make her **Easy Haddock Bake** (p. 159) an indulgent main course that's also low in calories, fat and carbohydrates.

Serve the golden fish and creamy sauce with **Savory Green Beans** (p. 77) from Carol Ann Hayden. The Everson, Washington cook likes to season the nutritious side dish with a delightful combination of savory, chives and garlic. Bits of sweet red pepper add a nice hint of color to the versatile recipe.

APPEALING PARTNERS

- Baked potatoes
- Lime gelatin

PRACTICAL TIPS

- For the main course, substitute cod fillets in place of the haddock if that's what your family prefers.

- Occasionally, Dorothy replaces the dry bread crumbs in her fish recipe with cracker crumbs.

- For extra flavor, Carol Ann suggests stirring a little bit of grated Parmesan cheese into the green beans right before serving.

Hearty Casserole Cuts Kitchen Time

From the *Light & Tasty* Test Kitchen, **Seafood 'n' Shells Casserole** (p. 151) is a heartwarming addition to any menu. Evaporated fat-free milk and a zesty cheese blend create a mouth-watering sauce that offers the oven-baked hot dish just the right amount of richness.

For a special ending, surprise your gang with **Pineapple Poke Cake** (p. 236). Ishpeming, Michigan's Sandra Etelamaki turns to store-bought cake and pudding mixes as well as canned pineapple to quickly put together the crowd-pleasing dessert.

APPEALING PARTNERS

- Dinner rolls
- Brussels sprouts

PRACTICAL TIPS

- Tuna makes a good replacement for the cod in the casserole, but you can also skip the fish altogether to make it a yummy meatless meal.

- The hot bake is a great way to use up any leftover pasta you might have on hand. If you're preparing pasta early in the week, be sure to make a little extra to trim prep time from this dish.

- For refreshing flavor, add 1/2 teaspoon of coconut extract to the pudding in the cake's frosting.

Ease Evenings with Slow-Cooked Stew

Festive Fare Is Ready in a Flash

Simple Salmon's Full of Benefits

You'll arrive home to a heartwarming sensation when you have Regina Stock's **Southwestern Beef Stew** (p. 97) simmering in the slow cooker. With a few minutes of prep in the morning, the Topeka, Kansas cook treats her gang to this jazzed-up beef-and-veggie combo at the end of the work day. Beef stew meat and picante sauce make it a no-stress specialty.

Warm slices of **Maple Syrup Corn Bread** (p. 192) complement the spicy stew perfectly. Roger Hickum of Plymouth, New Hampshire created the golden bread that offers a hint of sweet maple syrup in every bite.

Want a speedy entree with spicy flair? **Santa Fe Chicken** (p. 131) from Jon Carole Gilbreath of Tyler, Texas won't disappoint. The chicken-and-rice dish boasts a zippy sauce for a bright burst of color and Southwestern flavor. Topped with low-fat shredded cheese and a little cilantro, it's one entree that's sure to shake up routine meals at your home.

In Nashville, Tennessee, Ann Bassett counts on time-saving **Herbed Green Beans** (p. 71) to round out many of her meals. Seasoned with basil, oregano and marjoram, the beans and onion make a pleasing addition to just about any workweek menu you might serve.

Sensational Spiced Salmon (p. 161) has all of the mealtime benefits you're looking for. Low in saturated fat and carbohydrates, the main course features a sweet-spicy rub that offers phenomenal flavor. In addition, the entree is table-ready in less than half an hour, so it's easy enough for busy weeknights yet it is impressive enough for weekend entertaining. Michele Doucette of Stephenville, Newfoundland sent the recipe.

Peyton, Colorado's Sonya Fox shares her quick-cooking **Quinoa Pilaf** (p. 71). Tossed with carrots, onion and a hint of garlic, the great grain is as superb with beef and chicken as it is with salmon.

APPEALING PARTNERS

- Apple slices with cinnamon
- Hot chocolate

PRACTICAL TIPS

- To perk up the stew's flavor, use a spicy or hot picante sauce.

- Regina often adds a 6-ounce can of small pitted ripe olives to the entree for extra taste. Or, consider adding a can or two of sliced mushrooms to the slow cooker.

- Combine the dry ingredients for the corn bread ahead of time to beat the kitchen clock.

APPEALING PARTNERS

- Salsa
- Lime sherbet

PRACTICAL TIPS

- For extra flavor, use shredded reduced-fat Mexican cheese blend for the chicken dish.

- Experiment with whatever herbs or seasonings you enjoy when preparing Herbed Green Beans.

- Try fresh green beans in the side dish when they are in season.

APPEALING PARTNERS

- Vegetable soup
- Steamed carrots

PRACTICAL TIPS

- Try the salmon's herb rub on other types of meat and fish.

- For extra color and crunch, add broccoli or other vegetables of your choosing to the quinoa dish.

- Look for quinoa in the health food or baking section of your supermarket. Not a fan of quinoa? Prepare the recipe with 1 cup white rice instead.

Menu's as Easy As It Is Elegant

On rushed-for-time weeknights, hosting friends for dinner will be a breeze, thanks to Tami Morrison's lovely **Cranberry-Mustard Pork Medallions** (p. 148). In Kent, Washington, she dresses up lean pork tenderloin slices with a tangy cranberry sauce for a sensational main dish that comes together in mere moments.

Herb-Crusted Potatoes (p. 83) are a great match for the pork and many other entrees as well. Our team of home economists relied on an assortment of herbs to give the simple oven-roasted potatoes a distinctively bold taste. After just a few minutes of preparation, they bake in the oven to golden perfection.

APPEALING PARTNERS

- Peas
- Pumpkin Mousse (recipe on p. 209)

PRACTICAL TIPS

- To save time in the entree's preparation, combine the juice mixture, slice and flatten the pork and refrigerate it all the night before.

- For a special touch, add some grated orange peel to the pork's sauce.

- You can substitute 1 teaspoon of dried, crushed rosemary for the fresh rosemary in the potatoes.

Heat Up Nights With Enchiladas

Donna Roberts knows that nothing adds excitement like south-of-the-border fare. That's why the Shumway, Illinois cook kicks off suppertime with her delectable **Seafood Enchiladas** (p. 163). Filled with crabmeat that's set in a creamy cheese sauce, each generous serving seems anything but light.

While the main dish is baking, you'll have plenty of time to whip up a batch of **Home-Style Refried Beans** (p. 75) from Myra Innes. A little lime juice makes them a hit in her Auburn, Kansas home.

APPEALING PARTNERS

- Rice with Chilies 'n' Veggies (recipe on p. 68)
- Fruit smoothies

PRACTICAL TIPS

- Tortillas are easier to work with when they've been heated briefly in an oven or microwave.

- Cut into small cubes, cooked chicken makes a delicious replacement for the enchilada's crabmeat.

- Serve the beans on top of baked tortilla chips for a fast and tasty appetizer. With salsa and light sour cream, it makes a fat-savvy snack.

Menu Consists of Summer Sensations

In Harrison, Ohio, Dawn Sowders heads to the grill for her unbeatable **Herbed Barbecued Chicken** (p. 119). Much to the delight of her family, the finger-licking entree gets its must-try flavor from a savory marinade that includes oregano, rosemary, sage, thyme and more.

For a no-stress side dish that keeps healthy-eating commitments, give **Corn 'n' Red Pepper Medley** a try (p. 81). Gainesville, Florida's Lillian Julow livens up fresh corn with chili powder and garlic to easily round out menus any night of the week.

APPEALING PARTNERS

- Baked potatoes
- Fruit salad

PRACTICAL TIPS

- Slice and refrigerate any of the leftover chicken. Topped with salsa and wrapped in a fat-free flour tortilla, it makes a tasty lunch the following day.

- Add a little spice to the corn by stirring in a can of diced green chilies when adding the seasonings.

- To save time, use kitchen shears to mince the fresh parsley for Corn 'n' Red Pepper Medley. Save on cleanup by cutting it right into the skillet.

Relax Over An Entree Salad

You need only 25 minutes to toss together refreshing **Shrimp Romaine Salad** (p. 44). The *L&T* Test Kitchen staff turned to tarragon and a little garlic to season the light dressing that ideally complements the orange segments and shrimp.

Cherry tomatoes and slices of red onion add color to the nutritious meal-in-one, while brown rice lends enough bulk to fill you up fast.

APPEALING PARTNERS

- Iced tea
- Onion Poppy Seed Biscuits (recipe on p. 189)

PRACTICAL TIPS

- Remember this salad the next time you're looking to use up leftover shrimp or brown rice.

- You can use flaked imitation crabmeat in place of the shrimp if that's more readily available.

- Replace the orange segments with canned mandarin oranges if you like.

- If you purchase fresh, uncooked shrimp for the salad, immediately rinse it in cold water. Drained and refrigerated, it should be prepared within a day of purchase. Cooked shrimp can be stored in a sealed bag in the refrigerator for up to 3 days.

Hearty Combo Is a Welcomed Supper

Chock-full of veggies, **Beef and Wild Rice Medley** (p. 101) from Janelle Christensen begins evenings on a bright note in her Big Lake, Minnesota kitchen. The beefy dish provides meal-in-one ease with the delicious home-style flavor you and your family crave.

Luscious Fudgy Brownies (p. 232) make a delectable finish to the rice dish...or just about any other main course. They're so tasty, in fact, that no one suspects they are light. The chocolaty treats are a favorite of Krista Frank's gang in Rhododendron, Oregon.

APPEALING PARTNERS

- Tossed side salad
- Steamed cauliflower

PRACTICAL TIPS

- For a change, you can also whip up the rice medley with chicken or shrimp instead of beef.

- Assemble extra garlic powder, thyme and cayenne in a resealable plastic bag to make seasoning the meat even handier next time.

- Krista often prepares the brownies with raspberry instead of vanilla yogurt for an additional burst of flavor.

Sizzle Up a Surefire Winner

Celebrate the end of the day by calling your family to the table and serving sizzling **Sausage Fajitas** (p. 141). In addition to peppers, onion and mushrooms, Janie McClellan of Ocean Isle Beach, North Carolina uses smoked kielbasa in her fajitas for a tasty change from the chicken and beef varieties.

The host of vegetables keeps the flavorful fajitas lean, but it's the herbed marinade that truly pumps up the taste in this zesty, casual supper.

APPEALING PARTNERS

- Fat-free refried beans
- Cumin Rice with Avocado (recipe on p. 73)

PRACTICAL TIPS

- Janie sometimes adds zucchini and yellow squash to the fajitas. Add sliced tomatoes, olives or whatever other fixings your family prefers.

- If the weather cooperates, grill the sausage and veggies outdoors in a grill wok or a disposable aluminum pan.

- Use a colorful combination of sweet peppers such as red or yellow or even orange or purple. You'll need about four medium peppers for the fajitas.

Light Bites & Beverages

Just because you're watching what you eat doesn't mean you have to forgo enticing appetizers or special snacks. Whether looking for a savory hors d'oeuvre for a party or a sweet treat to stash in a lunch bag, you've come to the right spot. Just consider the 48 delicious ideas in this chapter!

BLT Bites, p. 28
Spinach Phyllo Triangles, p. 24

Spicy Peanut Chicken Kabobs

 FAT CARB

(PICTURED ABOVE)

PREP: 20 Min. + Marinating   **GRILL:** 10 Min.   **YIELD:** 8 Appetizers

These spicy skewers are marinated in a sweet-and-sour mixture that's loaded with flavor.
—Nancy Zimmerman, Cape May Court House, New Jersey

   1/4 cup reduced-fat creamy peanut butter
    3 tablespoons reduced-sodium soy sauce
4-1/2 teaspoons lemon juice
    1 tablespoon brown sugar
1-1/2 teaspoons ground coriander
    1 teaspoon ground cumin
  3/4 teaspoon salt
  1/4 teaspoon pepper
  1/4 to 1/2 teaspoon cayenne pepper
    1 garlic clove, minced
    1 large onion, finely chopped
    1 pound boneless skinless chicken breasts, cut into 1-inch cubes

In a small bowl, combine the first 10 ingredients. Pour 3/4 cup marinade into a large resealable plastic bag; add onion and chicken. Seal bag and turn to coat; refrigerate overnight. Cover and refrigerate remaining marinade.

If grilling the chicken, coat grill rack with nonstick cooking spray before starting the grill. Drain and discard marinade. Thread chicken onto eight metal or soaked wooden skewers. Grill, uncovered, over medium heat or broil 4 in. from the heat for 8-10 minutes or until no longer pink, turning once. Brush with reserved marinade before serving.

NUTRITION FACTS: 1 kabob equals 94 calories, 3 g fat (1 g saturated fat), 31 mg cholesterol, 275 mg sodium, 4 g carbohydrate, 1 g fiber, 13 g protein. **DIABETIC EXCHANGES:** 2 very lean meat, 1/2 fat.

TASTY TIP

For an entree, thread red bell pepper strips onto the skewers when preparing Spicy Peanut Chicken Kabobs. Grill as directed and serve over hot cooked rice.

Warm Broccoli Spinach Dip

 CARB MEAT-LESS

PREP: 15 Min.   **BAKE:** 20 Min.   **YIELD:** 3 Cups

A few added ingredients make a traditional spinach dip a little tastier and more exciting. It's always a hit at gatherings.
—Deborah Williams, Wildwood, Missouri

    1 package (8 ounces) reduced-fat cream cheese
  1/4 cup mayonnaise
    2 tablespoons fat-free milk
    1 can (14 ounces) water-packed artichoke hearts, rinsed, drained and chopped
    5 ounces frozen chopped spinach, thawed and squeezed dry
    8 tablespoons grated Parmesan cheese, *divided*
  1/2 cup frozen chopped broccoli, thawed
    1 garlic clove, minced
  1/2 teaspoon dried basil
  1/4 teaspoon garlic salt
  1/4 teaspoon salt
  1/4 teaspoon pepper
  1/4 cup shredded part-skim mozzarella cheese
Baked tortilla chips *or* fresh vegetables

In a large mixing bowl, beat the cream cheese, mayonnaise and milk until smooth. Stir in the artichokes, spinach, 6 tablespoons Parmesan cheese, broccoli, garlic, basil, garlic salt, salt and pepper.

Transfer to a 9-in. pie plate coated with nonstick cooking spray. Sprinkle with mozzarella cheese and remaining Parmesan cheese. Bake, uncovered, at 350° for 20-25 minutes or until cheese is melted. Serve immediately with tortilla chips or vegetables.

NUTRITION FACTS: 1/4 cup (calculated without chips or vegetables) equals 118 calories, 9 g fat (4 g saturated fat), 19 mg cholesterol, 358 mg sodium, 4 g carbohydrate, trace fiber, 5 g protein. **DIABETIC EXCHANGES:** 2 fat, 1 vegetable.

Chicken Turnovers

 CARB

PREP/TOTAL TIME: 30 Min.   **YIELD:** 8 Servings

These warm appetizers take advantage of refrigerated crescent roll dough. They're also a great way to use up leftover chicken.
—Sandralee Herr, Stevens, Pennsylvania

    1 cup diced cooked chicken breast
    1 cup (4 ounces) shredded reduced-fat cheddar cheese
  1/4 cup chopped celery
    1 tablespoon finely chopped onion
  1/4 teaspoon salt
  1/4 teaspoon pepper
    1 tube (8 ounces) refrigerated reduced-fat crescent rolls

In a small bowl, combine the chicken, cheese, celery, onion, salt and pepper. Separate crescent dough into eight triangles; top each with chicken mixture. Fold dough over and seal edges. Place on an ungreased baking sheet. Bake at 375° for 13-17 minutes or until golden brown. Serve warm.

NUTRITION FACTS: 1 turnover equals 169 calories, 8 g fat (3 g saturated fat), 24 mg cholesterol, 338 mg sodium, 13 g carbohydrate, trace fiber, 11 g protein. **DIABETIC EXCHANGES:** 1 starch, 1 very lean meat, 1 fat.

Tangy Vegetable Dip

PREP/TOTAL TIME: 10 Min. **YIELD:** 3 Cups

When I couldn't find any veggie dips I liked, I blended my own ingredients until I came up with this creamy combination. I love it!
—Penelope Heiges, Otter Creek, Maine

  1 cup (8 ounces) 1% cottage cheese
  1 package (8 ounces) reduced-fat cream cheese, cubed
  1/3 cup fat-free mayonnaise
  1/3 cup reduced-fat sour cream
  1/3 cup reduced-fat plain yogurt
  2 garlic cloves, minced
  2 teaspoons cider vinegar
  2 teaspoons Dijon mustard
  1/2 teaspoon salt
  1/2 teaspoon dill weed
  1/4 teaspoon cayenne pepper
  4 green onions, finely chopped
Assorted vegetables

In a blender or food processor, combine the first 11 ingredients; cover and process until smooth. Transfer to a bowl; stir in the onions. Serve with vegetables.

NUTRITION FACTS: 2 tablespoons dip (calculated without vegetables) equals 39 calories, 2 g fat (1 g saturated fat), 7 mg cholesterol, 157 mg sodium, 2 g carbohydrate, trace fiber, 3 g protein. **DIABETIC EXCHANGE:** 1/2 starch.

Tempting Shrimp Phyllo Tarts

CARB

(PICTURED BELOW)

PREP: 15 Min. + Chilling **BAKE:** 10 Min. **YIELD:** 2-1/2 Dozen

These tempting tidbits have been popular at church receptions and family gatherings alike. With shrimp and a wine sauce, the tarts will make any get-together feel like a special event.
—Heather Melnick, Macedon, New York

  4 ounces reduced-fat cream cheese
  1/4 cup shredded reduced-fat cheddar cheese
  3 tablespoons white wine *or* fat-free milk
  1/2 cup chopped cooked peeled shrimp
  1/2 teaspoon onion powder
  1/2 teaspoon salt
  1/4 to 1/2 teaspoon dried thyme
  30 frozen miniature phyllo tart shells

In a small bowl, combine the cream cheese, cheddar cheese and wine or milk. Stir in the shrimp, onion powder, salt and thyme. Cover and refrigerate for at least 2 hours to allow flavors to blend.

Spoon filling by heaping teaspoonfuls into tart shells. Place on an ungreased baking sheet. Bake at 350° for 8-12 minutes or until shells are lightly browned. Serve warm. Refrigerate leftovers.

NUTRITION FACTS: 2 tarts equals 76 calories, 4 g fat (1 g saturated fat), 14 mg cholesterol, 150 mg sodium, 5 g carbohydrate, trace fiber, 3 g protein. **DIABETIC EXCHANGES:** 1/2 starch, 1/2 fat.

Mexican Cheesecake

CARB **MEAT-LESS**

PREP: 20 Min. **BAKE:** 30 Min. + Chilling **YIELD:** 24 Servings

I've made this super-easy appetizer several times for parties, and people were so surprised it was light.
—Sandy Burkett, Galena, Ohio

    2 packages (8 ounces *each*) reduced-fat cream cheese
1-1/4 cups reduced-fat sour cream, *divided*
    1 envelope taco seasoning
    3 eggs, lightly beaten
1-1/2 cups (6 ounces) shredded sharp cheddar cheese
    1 can (4 ounces) chopped green chilies
    1 cup chunky salsa, drained
Baked tortilla chips *or* fresh vegetables

In a large mixing bowl, beat cream cheese, 1/2 cup sour cream and taco seasoning until smooth. Add eggs; beat on low speed just until combined. Stir in cheddar cheese and chilies.

Transfer to a 9-in. springform pan coated with nonstick cooking spray. Place pan on a baking sheet. Bake at 350° for 25-30 minutes or until center is almost set. Spread remaining sour cream evenly over top. Bake 5-8 minutes longer or until topping is set. Cool on a wire rack for 10 minutes. Carefully run a knife around edge of pan to loosen; cool 1 hour longer. Refrigerate overnight.

Just before serving, remove sides of pan. Spread salsa over cheesecake. Serve with tortilla chips or vegetables.

NUTRITION FACTS: 1 slice (calculated without tortilla chips or vegetables) equals 107 calories, 8 g fat (5 g saturated fat), 52 mg cholesterol, 338 mg sodium, 4 g carbohydrate, trace fiber, 5 g protein. **DIABETIC EXCHANGES:** 1 lean meat, 1 fat.

MAKE IT EASY
The cheesecake makes party planning a breeze because you can prepare it the day before, then quickly spread on the salsa topping just before guests arrive.

Smoked Salmon Pinwheels

CARB

PREP: 25 Min. + Chilling   **YIELD:** 3 Dozen

These salmon and arugula bites are delightful. The recipe's a snap to double for no-mess finger food that feeds a crowd.
—Rachelle Rodwell, New York, New York

     1 package (8 ounces) reduced-fat cream cheese
     2 green onions, cut into 1-inch pieces
 1/2 teaspoon grated lemon peel
 1/4 teaspoon kosher salt
 1/8 teaspoon white pepper
     1 cup chopped smoked salmon
     4 flour tortillas (10 inches)
 1/2 cup fresh arugula *or* baby spinach
     1 teaspoon olive oil
 1/2 teaspoon lemon juice

In a food processor, combine the cream cheese, onions, lemon peel, salt and pepper; cover and process until smooth. Transfer to a small bowl; stir in salmon. Spread over tortillas.

In a small bowl, toss arugula with olive oil and lemon juice; place over salmon mixture. Roll up tortillas tightly and wrap in plastic wrap. Refrigerate for 2-3 hours. Cut each roll-up into nine slices.

NUTRITION FACTS: 2 appetizers equals 90 calories, 4 g fat (2 g saturated fat), 11 mg cholesterol, 226 mg sodium, 8 g carbohydrate, 1 g fiber, 4 g protein. **DIABETIC EXCHANGES:** 1/2 starch, 1/2 fat.

Apple-Goat Cheese Bruschetta

MEAT-LESS

(PICTURED BELOW)

PREP/TOTAL TIME: 20 Min.   **YIELD:** 16 Appetizers

It takes just six ingredients and 20 minutes to put together this beautiful bruschetta. Crunchy apple and warm goat cheese give the fancy treats their mouth-watering flavor.
—Laura Perry, Exton, Pennsylvania

 16 slices French bread (1/2 inch thick)
     1 medium Fuji apple, chopped
 1/4 cup crumbled goat cheese
 3/4 teaspoon minced fresh thyme

 1/2 teaspoon minced fresh oregano
 1/4 teaspoon coarsely ground pepper

Place bread slices on an ungreased baking sheet. Broil 3-4 in. from the heat for 1-2 minutes or until golden brown. Combine the apple, goat cheese, thyme, oregano and pepper; sprinkle over bread. Broil 1 minute longer or until cheese is softened.

NUTRITION FACTS: 2 appetizers equals 157 calories, 5 g fat (2 g saturated fat), 6 mg cholesterol, 206 mg sodium, 24 g carbohydrate, 2 g fiber, 4 g protein. **DIABETIC EXCHANGES:** 1-1/2 starch, 1/2 fat.

Crab-Stuffed Deviled Eggs

FAT CARB

PREP/TOTAL TIME: 20 Min.   **YIELD:** 8 Servings

Whether served as an appetizer or alongside an entree, these deviled eggs offer a welcomed, less-fat twist. That's because they're filled with a creamy combination that includes crabmeat, hot pepper sauce and a dash of cayenne pepper.
—Karen Conklin, Santee, South Carolina

     8 hard-cooked eggs
     3 tablespoons fat-free mayonnaise
     2 tablespoons lemon juice
     4 teaspoons minced fresh tarragon
     1 tablespoon chopped green onion
 1/4 teaspoon salt
 1/4 teaspoon hot pepper sauce
 1/8 teaspoon cayenne pepper
     1 can (6 ounces) crabmeat, drained, flaked and cartilage removed

Cut eggs in half lengthwise. Remove yolks; set aside egg whites and four yolks (discard remaining yolks or save for another use). In a bowl, mash reserved yolks. Stir in the mayonnaise, lemon juice, tarragon, onion, salt, hot pepper sauce and cayenne. Add crab; mix well. Stuff or pipe into egg whites. Refrigerate until serving.

NUTRITION FACTS: 2 stuffed egg halves equals 73 calories, 3 g fat (1 g saturated fat), 126 mg cholesterol, 249 mg sodium, 2 g carbohydrate, trace fiber, 9 g protein. **DIABETIC EXCHANGE:** 1 lean meat.

Watermelon Salsa

FAT SALT CARB MEAT-LESS

PREP: 15 Min. + Chilling   **YIELD:** 3 Cups

On hot days, this sweet salsa with watermelon, orange juice, pineapple and fresh cilantro is sure to hit the spot. I toss it together in a matter of minutes.   —Betsy Hanson, Tiverton, Rhode Island

     2 cups chopped seedless watermelon
     1 can (8 ounces) unsweetened crushed pineapple, drained
 1/4 cup chopped sweet onion
 1/4 cup minced fresh cilantro
     3 tablespoons orange juice
 1/8 teaspoon hot pepper sauce
Baked tortilla chips

In a small bowl, combine the first six ingredients. Cover and refrigerate for at least 1 hour. Serve with tortilla chips.

NUTRITION FACTS: 1/4 cup salsa (calculated without chips) equals 23 calories, trace fat (trace saturated fat), 0 cholesterol, 1 mg sodium, 5 g carbohydrate, trace fiber, trace protein. **DIABETIC EXCHANGE:** 1/2 fruit.

Favorite Recipe Made Lighter

HOLIDAY TRADITIONS come in all shapes and sizes. For *Light & Tasty* magazine's editor, Mary Spencer, an annual party is the perfect opportunity to start the festivities off right.

"My sister hosts a Christmas Eve, Eve party every year," Mary writes. "We always look forward to her decadent artichoke dip. She received the recipe from a friend, and it's loaded with cheese, artichokes and just the right amount of jalapenos for a crowd-pleasing flavor."

Unfortunately, all of the creamy goodness and cheese also makes Mary's favorite appetizer high in calories and fat. Our home economists wanted to maintain the dip's buttery texture and phenomenal flavor as they set out to slim it down.

They began by replacing some ingredients with low-fat counterparts and cut back on others to trim fat. To make up for the volume lost when they decreased the mayonnaise, they increased the amount of plain yogurt that the recipe originally called for. They also scaled back the mozzarella cheese, adding reduced-fat ricotta to give the hors d'oeuvre the rich texture that made it a staple with Mary's family.

What was the final outcome? Makeover Creamy Artichoke Dip is an ooey-gooey sensation that packs all of the comforting goodness of the original.

With 50% less fat than the submission Mary sent, it's sure to star on the holiday table for many years to come.

Makeover Creamy Artichoke Dip

 CARB   MEAT-LESS

(PICTURED ABOVE)

PREP: 20 Min. COOK: 1 Hour YIELD: 5 Cups

    2 cans (14 ounces *each*) water-packed artichoke hearts, rinsed, drained and coarsely chopped
    1 package (8 ounces) reduced-fat cream cheese, cubed
    1 carton (6 ounces) plain yogurt
    1 cup (4 ounces) shredded part-skim mozzarella cheese
    1 cup reduced-fat ricotta cheese
  3/4 cup shredded Parmesan cheese, *divided*
  1/2 cup shredded reduced-fat Swiss cheese
  1/4 cup reduced-fat mayonnaise
    2 tablespoons lemon juice
    1 tablespoon chopped seeded jalapeno pepper
    1 teaspoon garlic powder
    1 teaspoon seasoned salt
Baked tortilla chips

In a 3-qt. slow cooker, combine the artichokes, cream cheese, yogurt, mozzarella, ricotta, 1/2 cup Parmesan, Swiss, mayonnaise, lemon juice, jalapeno, garlic powder and seasoned salt. Cover and cook on low for 1 hour or until heated through. Sprinkle with remaining Parmesan cheese. Serve with tortilla chips.

NUTRITION FACTS: 1/4 cup (calculated without tortilla chips) equals 104 calories, 6 g fat (3 g saturated fat), 20 mg cholesterol, 348 mg sodium, 5 g carbohydrate, trace fiber, 7 g protein. DIABETIC EXCHANGES: 1 fat, 1/2 starch.

Editor's Note: When cutting or seeding hot peppers, use rubber or plastic gloves to protect your hands. Avoid touching your face.

Creamy Artichoke Dip

CARB   MEAT-LESS

PREP: 20 Min. COOK: 1 Hour YIELD: 5 Cups

    2 cans (14 ounces *each*) water-packed artichoke hearts, rinsed, drained and coarsely chopped
    2 cups (8 ounces) shredded part-skim mozzarella cheese
    1 package (8 ounces) cream cheese, cubed
    1 cup (4 ounces) shredded Parmesan cheese
  1/2 cup mayonnaise
  1/2 cup shredded Swiss cheese
    2 tablespoons lemon juice
    2 tablespoons plain yogurt
    1 tablespoon seasoned salt
    1 tablespoon chopped seeded jalapeno pepper
    1 teaspoon garlic powder
Tortilla chips

In a 3-qt. slow cooker, combine the first 11 ingredients. Cover and cook on low for 1 hour or until heated through. Serve with tortilla chips.

NUTRITION FACTS: 1/4 cup (calculated without tortilla chips) equals 152 calories, 12 g fat (5 g saturated fat), 27 mg cholesterol, 519 mg sodium, 4 g carbohydrate, trace fiber, 7 g protein.

Editor's Note: When cutting or seeding hot peppers, use rubber or plastic gloves to protect your hands. Avoid touching your face.

> **MAKEOVER TIP**
> When reducing mayonnaise to cut calories in creamy dips, add plain yogurt to maintain the volume.

In a blender or food processor, combine the sauce ingredients; cover and process until smooth. Serve with egg rolls.

NUTRITION FACTS: 2 egg rolls with 1-1/2 teaspoons sauce equals 108 calories, 3 g fat (trace saturated fat), 19 mg cholesterol, 222 mg sodium, 17 g carbohydrate, 1 g fiber, 4 g protein. **DIABETIC EXCHANGES:** 1 starch, 1/2 fat.

Veggie Shrimp Egg Rolls

(PICTURED ABOVE)

FAT ▼

PREP: 45 Min. + Standing   **COOK:** 10 Min. per Batch   **YIELD:** 38 Egg Rolls

These appetizers will be the hit of your cocktail party. The apricot dipping sauce comes together easily, and you can even replace the shrimp with cooked crab, lobster or chicken.

—Carole Resnick, Cleveland, Ohio

- 2 teaspoons minced fresh gingerroot
- 1 garlic clove, minced
- 3 tablespoons olive oil, *divided*
- 1/2 pound uncooked medium shrimp, peeled, deveined and chopped
- 2 green onions, finely chopped
- 1 medium carrot, finely chopped
- 1 medium sweet red pepper, finely chopped
- 1 cup canned bean sprouts, rinsed and finely chopped
- 2 tablespoons reduced-sodium soy sauce
- 2 tablespoons water
- 38 wonton wrappers

APRICOT-MUSTARD DIPPING SAUCE:
- 3/4 cup apricot spreadable fruit
- 1 tablespoon water
- 1 tablespoon lime juice
- 1 tablespoon reduced-sodium soy sauce
- 1-1/2 teaspoons Dijon mustard
- 1/4 teaspoon minced fresh gingerroot

In a large skillet, saute ginger and garlic in 1 tablespoon oil over medium heat until tender. Add shrimp, onions, carrot, red pepper, bean sprouts, soy sauce and water; cook for 2-3 minutes or until vegetables are crisp-tender and shrimp turn pink. Reduce heat to low; cook for 4-5 minutes or until most of the liquid has evaporated. Remove from the heat; let stand for 15 minutes.

Place a tablespoonful of shrimp mixture in the center of a

wonton wrapper. (Keep wrappers covered with a damp paper towel until ready to use.) Fold bottom corner over filling. Fold sides toward center over filling. Moisten remaining corner with water; roll up tightly to seal.

In a large skillet over medium heat, cook egg rolls, a few at a time, in remaining oil for 5-7 minutes on each side or until golden brown. Drain on paper towels.

In a blender or food processor, combine the sauce ingredients; cover and process until smooth. Serve with egg rolls.

NUTRITION FACTS: 2 egg rolls with 1-1/2 teaspoons sauce equals 108 calories, 3 g fat (trace saturated fat), 19 mg cholesterol, 222 mg sodium, 17 g carbohydrate, 1 g fiber, 4 g protein. **DIABETIC EXCHANGES:** 1 starch, 1/2 fat.

Blood Orange Berry Punch

(PICTURED BELOW)

FAT SALT
▼ ▼

PREP/TOTAL TIME: 15 Min.   **YIELD:** 8 Servings (2 Quarts)

For a sip of summer, regardless of the weather outside, try this refreshing beverage from the Light & Tasty home economists. Raspberries, blood oranges, pineapple and ginger ale blend well in the sparkling, pretty punch.

- 1 package (12 ounces) frozen unsweetened raspberries, thawed
- 1-3/4 cups blood orange juice (about 7 medium oranges)
- 2 cans (6 ounces *each*) unsweetened pineapple juice, chilled
- 4 cans (12 ounces *each*) diet ginger ale, chilled
- 1 medium blood orange, thinly sliced, optional

Mash raspberries; strain, reserving juice and discarding seeds. Just before serving, combine the raspberry juice, orange juice and pineapple juice in a punch bowl. Stir in ginger ale. Garnish with orange slices if desired.

NUTRITION FACTS: 1 cup equals 69 calories, trace fat (trace saturated fat), 0 cholesterol, 24 mg sodium, 16 g carbohydrate, 1 g fiber, 1 g protein. **DIABETIC EXCHANGE:** 1 fruit.

Sesame Pork

CARB

(PICTURED AT RIGHT)

PREP: 15 Min. + Marinating   **BAKE:** 30 Min.   **YIELD:** 12 Servings

This pork hors d'oeuvre is simple. Soy sauce, ginger and sesame seeds give the tenderloins a delicious Asian flair.

—Shirley Kula, San Diego, California

1/2 cup reduced-sodium soy sauce
1/3 cup honey
1/4 cup sherry *or* chicken broth
 1 tablespoon canola oil
1/4 teaspoon garlic powder
1/4 teaspoon ground ginger
 2 pork tenderloins (1 pound *each*)
SESAME COATING:
 2 tablespoons ground mustard
 3 tablespoons water
 1 tablespoon reduced-sodium soy sauce
1/4 cup sesame seeds, toasted

In a large resealable plastic bag, combine the first six ingredients. Add pork; seal bag and turn to coat. Refrigerate for 8 hours or overnight.

Drain and discard marinade. Place tenderloins on a rack in a shallow roasting pan lined with heavy-duty foil. Bake at 425° for 30-35 minutes or until a meat thermometer reads 160°. Let stand for 5 minutes.

In a small bowl, combine the mustard, water and soy sauce; brush over meat. Sprinkle with sesame seeds. Thinly slice and serve warm or cold.

NUTRITION FACTS: 2 ounces cooked pork equals 120 calories, 4 g fat (1 g saturated fat), 42 mg cholesterol, 145 mg sodium, 2 g carbohydrate, 1 g fiber, 16 g protein. **DIABETIC EXCHANGE:** 2 lean meat.

spoon, carefully scrape out the fuzzy center portions of artichokes and discard.

In a small bowl, combine the bread crumbs, cheese, parsley, garlic, Italian seasoning, lemon peel, pepper and salt. Add olive oil; mix well. Gently spread artichoke leaves apart; fill with bread crumb mixture.

Place in an 11-in. x 7-in. x 2-in. baking dish coated with nonstick cooking spray. Bake, uncovered, at 350° for 15-20 minutes or until filling is lightly browned.

NUTRITION FACTS: 1 stuffed artichoke equals 212 calories, 7 g fat (3 g saturated fat), 8 mg cholesterol, 596 mg sodium, 28 g carbohydrate, 9 g fiber, 11 g protein. **DIABETIC EXCHANGES:** 3 vegetable, 1 starch, 1 lean meat, 1/2 fat.

Italian Stuffed Artichokes

MEAT-LESS

PREP: 50 Min. + Standing   **BAKE:** 15 Min.   **YIELD:** 4 Servings

My mother made stuffed artichokes as a special treat on Easter, Thanksgiving and Christmas. We looked forward to them throughout the year. —Emma Magielda, Amsterdam, New York

 4 large artichokes
 2 teaspoons lemon juice
 2 cups soft Italian bread crumbs, toasted
1/2 cup grated Parmigiano-Reggiano cheese
1/2 cup minced fresh parsley
 2 garlic cloves, minced
 2 teaspoons Italian seasoning
 1 teaspoon grated lemon peel
1/2 teaspoon pepper
1/4 teaspoon salt
 1 tablespoon olive oil

Using a sharp knife, level the bottom of each artichoke and cut 1 in. from the tops. Using kitchen scissors, snip off tips of outer leaves; brush cut edges with lemon juice. Stand artichokes in a Dutch oven; add 1 in. of water. Bring to a boil. Reduce heat; cover and simmer for 30-35 minutes or until leaves near the center pull out easily.

Invert artichokes to drain; let stand for 10 minutes. With a

Cranberry Snack Mix

MEAT-LESS

PREP: 10 Min.   **BAKE:** 50 Min. + Cooling   **YIELD:** 6 Cups

Seasoned with cinnamon, ginger and nutmeg, this sweet mix is just perfect for fall. —Sarah Gerlach, Willmar, Minnesota

 2 cups *each* square oat cereal, Corn Chex and miniature pretzels
1/3 cup orange juice concentrate
1/4 cup butter, melted
 2 tablespoons brown sugar
 1 teaspoon ground cinnamon
3/4 teaspoon ground ginger
1/4 teaspoon ground nutmeg
2/3 cup dried cranberries

In a large bowl, combine cereals and pretzels. In a small bowl, combine concentrate, butter, brown sugar and spices. Pour over cereal mixture; toss to coat.

Spread in a foil-lined 15-in. x 10-in. x 1-in. baking pan. Bake at 250° for 50 minutes, stirring every 10 minutes. Stir in berries. Cool, stirring several times. Store in an airtight container.

NUTRITION FACTS: 1/2 cup equals 163 calories, 4 g fat (2 g saturated fat), 10 mg cholesterol, 273 mg sodium, 30 g carbohydrate, 2 g fiber, 3 g protein. **DIABETIC EXCHANGES:** 1-1/2 starch, 1 fat, 1/2 fruit.

Spinach Phyllo Triangles

(PICTURED ON PAGE 17)

FAT ▼ CARB ▼ MEAT-LESS

PREP: 30 Min. **BAKE:** 15 Min. **YIELD:** 2 Dozen

These crispy pockets of spinach and feta cheese with a hint of oregano look like a lot of work, but after assembling a few, you zip through them. —Jody McIntyre, Burns Lake, British Columbia

   1/2 cup chopped onion
     1 garlic clove, minced
     1 package (10 ounces) frozen chopped spinach, thawed and squeezed dry
   1/2 teaspoon dried oregano
 1-1/2 cups (6 ounces) crumbled feta cheese
    12 sheets phyllo dough (14 inches x 9 inches)
Butter-flavored nonstick cooking spray

In a nonstick skillet coated with nonstick cooking spray, cook onion and garlic until onion is tender. Stir in spinach and oregano; cook over medium-low heat just until spinach is warmed. Drain. Remove from the heat; stir in feta cheese and set aside.

Spray one sheet of phyllo dough with butter-flavored nonstick cooking spray. (Keep remaining phyllo covered with plastic wrap and a damp towel to prevent drying.) Fold dough in half lengthwise; spray with butter-flavored nonstick cooking spray. Cut dough in half lengthwise, forming two strips.

Place 1 tablespoon of spinach mixture on lower corner of each strip. Fold dough over filling, forming a triangle. Continue folding, like a flag, until you come to the end of each strip. Spray with butter-flavored nonstick cooking spray, making sure all edges are sprayed and sealed. Repeat with remaining phyllo and filling.

Place triangles on a baking sheet coated with nonstick cooking spray. Bake at 375° for 15-20 minutes or until golden brown. Remove to a wire rack. Serve warm.

NUTRITION FACTS: 2 appetizers equals 74 calories, 3 g fat (2 g saturated fat), 8 mg cholesterol, 199 mg sodium, 8 g carbohydrate, 2 g fiber, 4 g protein. **DIABETIC EXCHANGES:** 1/2 starch, 1/2 fat.

Refried Bean Nachos

(PICTURED AT LEFT)

PREP/TOTAL TIME: 25 Min.   **YIELD:** 4 Servings

Cumin and cayenne jazz up these homemade chips. Our Test Kitchen topped them with beans and cheese for a hearty snack.

     4 flour tortillas (8 inches)
Refrigerated butter-flavored spray
   1/2 teaspoon ground cumin
   1/4 teaspoon ground coriander
   1/4 teaspoon chili powder
   1/8 teaspoon cayenne pepper
     1 can (16 ounces) vegetarian refried beans
   1/2 cup shredded reduced-fat cheddar cheese
     1 large tomato, chopped
     4 green onions, chopped
   1/2 cup salsa

Spritz one side of each tortilla with refrigerated butter-flavored spray. Combine the cumin, coriander, chili powder and cayenne; sprinkle over tortillas. Cut each into 12 wedges. Place in a single layer in ungreased 15-in. x 10-in. x 1-in. baking pans. Bake at 425° for 5-7 minutes or until lightly browned.

Meanwhile, in a microwave-safe bowl, heat the refried beans on high for 1-2 minutes or until warm. Arrange baked tortillas on serving plates; top with the beans, cheese, tomato and onions. Serve with salsa.

NUTRITION FACTS: 1 serving equals 310 calories, 7 g fat (2 g saturated fat), 10 mg cholesterol, 959 mg sodium, 49 g carbohydrate, 9 g fiber, 16 g protein. **DIABETIC EXCHANGES:** 3 starch, 1 very lean meat, 1 vegetable, 1/2 fat.

Editor's Note: This recipe was tested with I Can't Believe It's Not Butter Spray.

Savory Popcorn Seasoning

 SALT ▼ CARB ▼

PREP/TOTAL TIME: 10 Min.   **YIELD:** 24 Batches (about 1/4 cup)

I love this combination of herbs and seasonings tossed with popcorn. Cayenne pepper adds a bit of heat to the late-night treat. —Janice Campbell, Elmendorf Air Force Base, Alaska

     1 tablespoon garlic powder
     1 tablespoon dried parsley flakes
 1-1/2 teaspoons *each* dried basil, marjoram and thyme
 1-1/2 teaspoons pepper
   3/4 teaspoon cayenne pepper
ADDITIONAL INGREDIENTS FOR POPCORN:
     2 cups air-popped popcorn
 1-1/2 teaspoons butter, melted

In a small bowl, combine the garlic powder, parsley, basil, marjoram, thyme, pepper and cayenne. Store in an airtight container for up to 6 months.

To prepare popcorn: In a small bowl, combine the popcorn, butter and 1/2 teaspoon seasoning; toss to coat.

NUTRITION FACTS: 2 cups popped popcorn with 1-1/2 teaspoons butter and 1/2 teaspoon seasoning equals 114 calories, 6 g fat (4 g saturated fat), 15 mg cholesterol, 59 mg sodium, 13 g carbohydrate, 3 g fiber, 2 g protein. **DIABETIC EXCHANGES:** 1 starch, 1 fat.

Cran-Apple Oatmeal Cookies

SALT

PREP: 20 Min.   BAKE: 15 Min. per Batch   YIELD: 5-1/2 Dozen

The original recipe for these delightful cookies called for raisins. Since we aren't raisin fans, I added dried cranberries instead. The results? Incredible! —Theresa Smith, Rome, Georgia

    3/4 cup reduced-fat butter, softened
1-1/4 cups packed brown sugar
      1 egg
    1/4 cup 2% milk
1-1/2 teaspoons vanilla extract
      1 cup all-purpose flour
1-1/4 teaspoons ground cinnamon
    1/2 teaspoon salt
    1/4 teaspoon baking soda
    1/4 teaspoon ground nutmeg
      3 cups quick-cooking oats
1-1/2 cups dried cranberries
      1 cup chopped peeled tart apple
    1/2 cup chopped walnuts

In a large mixing bowl, cream butter and brown sugar. Beat in the egg, milk and vanilla. Combine the flour, cinnamon, salt, baking soda and nutmeg; gradually add to creamed mixture. Stir in the oats, cranberries, apple and walnuts.

Drop by rounded tablespoonfuls 2 in. apart onto ungreased baking sheets. Bake at 375° for 12-15 minutes or until lightly browned. Cool for 2 minutes before removing to wire racks.

NUTRITION FACTS: 2 cookies equals 125 calories, 4 g fat (2 g saturated fat), 14 mg cholesterol, 77 mg sodium, 21 g carbohydrate, 1 g fiber, 3 g protein. **DIABETIC EXCHANGES:** 1 starch, 1 fat.

Editor's Note: This recipe was tested with Land O'Lakes light stick butter.

Italian Sausage-Stuffed Mushrooms

CARB

PREP: 35 Min.   BAKE: 25 Min.   YIELD: 32 Appetizers

With sausage, two types of cheese and bacon, these tasty bites will disappear fast! —Kelly McWherter, Houston, Texas

   32 large fresh mushrooms
  1/2 pound Italian turkey sausage links, casings removed
    4 ounces reduced-fat cream cheese
  1/2 cup shredded reduced-fat cheddar cheese
  1/4 cup thinly sliced green onions
    2 bacon strips, cooked and crumbled

Remove stems from mushrooms and chop; set mushroom caps aside. In a small nonstick skillet coated with nonstick cooking spray, cook mushroom stems and sausage until meat is no longer pink; drain. Cool to room temperature.

In a small mixing bowl, beat cream cheese until smooth. Add the cheddar cheese, onions and sausage mixture; mix well. Spoon into mushroom caps.

Place in a 15-in. x 10-in. x 1-in. baking pan coated with nonstick cooking spray. Bake at 400° for 20 minutes. Sprinkle with bacon. Bake 3-5 minutes longer or until heated through. Serve warm. Refrigerate leftovers.

NUTRITION FACTS: 2 stuffed mushrooms equals 68 calories, 4 g fat (2 g saturated fat), 16 mg cholesterol, 155 mg sodium, 3 g carbohydrate, 1 g fiber, 6 g protein. **DIABETIC EXCHANGES:** 1 vegetable, 1 fat.

Turkey Wonton Cups

CARB

(PICTURED BELOW)

PREP: 30 Min.   BAKE: 5 Min. per Batch   YIELD: 4 Dozen

Wonton wrappers make these hors d'oeuvres as fun to make as they are to eat. I tried them at a party and couldn't believe how tasty they were. No one suspected the bites were low-carb.
—Barbara Rafferty, Portsmouth, Rhode Island

   48 wonton wrappers
1-1/4 pounds lean ground turkey
    2 cups (8 ounces) shredded reduced-fat cheddar cheese
    1 cup fat-free ranch salad dressing
  1/2 cup chopped green onions
  1/4 cup chopped ripe olives

Press wonton wrappers into miniature muffin cups coated with nonstick cooking spray. (Keep wrappers covered with a damp paper towel until ready to bake.) Bake at 375° for 5 minutes or until lightly browned. Cool for 2 minutes before removing from pans to wire racks.

In a large nonstick skillet coated with nonstick cooking spray, cook the turkey over medium heat until no longer pink; drain. In a large bowl, combine the turkey, cheese, ranch dressing, onions and olives. Spoon by rounded tablespoonfuls into wonton cups.

Place on an ungreased baking sheet. Bake at 375° for 5-6 minutes or until heated through. Serve warm.

NUTRITION FACTS: 2 wonton cups equals 154 calories, 7 g fat (3 g saturated fat), 34 mg cholesterol, 366 mg sodium, 14 g carbohydrate, trace fiber, 11 g protein. **DIABETIC EXCHANGES:** 1 starch, 1 lean meat, 1/2 fat.

Favorite Recipe Made Lighter

COOKIES are tough to crumble in the makeover game. That's why we weren't sure we could help Connie Colgan. From Castle Rock, Colorado, she writes, "My recipe for peanut butter cookies is a favorite. Are you able to lighten it up for me?"

After just one bite, it was clear why Connie's treats are a hit…they're loaded with chocolate chips, peanuts, coconut and raisins. In fact, the only bad things about the cookies are the calories and fat grams they contain.

Due to high amounts of butter and sugar, cookie recipes are hard to revamp and often result in textures or flavors dissimilar from the original. Our staff eagerly tackled the challenge, though. They decreased the butter called for and replaced some of it with a reduced-fat variety. Light peanut butter was also used, but the team reached for a chunky version. This kept the cookies' crunch but meant that the peanuts originally called for could be eliminated altogether.

A sugar blend for baking replaced the granular sugar and kept the cookies golden brown. The coconut was reduced, and the chocolate chips were replaced with miniature chips. This guaranteed chocolate flavor in every bite but actually allowed the home economists to use less chocolate overall.

Makeover Chunky Peanut Butter Cookies are a success. Perfect for a snack, dessert or brown-bag treat, two cookies boast fewer calories and 31% less fat than the originals.

Chunky Peanut Butter Cookies

PREP: 25 Min. **BAKE:** 15 Min. per Batch **YIELD:** 6 Dozen

    1 cup butter, softened
    1 cup sugar
    1 cup packed brown sugar
    1 cup creamy peanut butter
    2 eggs
1-1/2 cups all-purpose flour
    1 cup quick-cooking oats
    1 teaspoon baking powder
    1 teaspoon salt
1/2 teaspoon baking soda
    1 cup semisweet chocolate chips
    1 cup raisins
    1 cup dry roasted peanuts, chopped
    1 cup flaked coconut

In a large mixing bowl, cream butter and sugars. Beat in peanut butter. Add eggs, one at a time, beating well after each addition. Combine the flour, oats, baking powder, salt and baking soda; gradually add to creamed mixture. Stir in the chocolate chips, raisins, peanuts and coconut.

Drop by rounded tablespoonfuls onto ungreased baking sheets. Bake at 350° for 12-14 minutes or until golden brown. Cool for 2 minutes before removing to wire racks.

NUTRITION FACTS: 2 cookies equals 234 calories, 13 g fat (6 g saturated fat), 25 mg cholesterol, 225 mg sodium, 27 g carbohydrate, 2 g fiber, 4 g protein.

Makeover Chunky Peanut Butter Cookies
(PICTURED ABOVE)

PREP: 25 Min. **BAKE:** 15 Min. per Batch **YIELD:** 5 Dozen

    1/3 cup butter, softened
    1/3 cup reduced-fat butter, softened
    1 cup packed brown sugar
    1/2 cup sugar blend for baking
    1 cup reduced-fat chunky peanut butter
    2 eggs
    2 cups all-purpose flour
1-1/2 cups quick-cooking oats
    1 teaspoon baking powder
    1 teaspoon salt
    1/2 teaspoon baking soda
    1 cup raisins
    3/4 cup flaked coconut
    1/2 cup miniature semisweet chocolate chips

In a large mixing bowl, cream butters, brown sugar and sugar blend. Beat in peanut butter. Add eggs, one at a time, beating well after each addition. Combine the flour, oats, baking powder, salt and baking soda; gradually add to creamed mixture. Stir in the raisins, coconut and chocolate chips.

Drop by rounded tablespoonfuls onto ungreased baking sheets. Bake at 350° for 12-14 minutes or until golden brown. Cool for 2 minutes before removing to wire racks.

NUTRITION FACTS: 2 cookies equals 209 calories, 9 g fat (4 g saturated fat), 23 mg cholesterol, 219 mg sodium, 30 g carbohydrate, 2 g fiber, 5 g protein. **DIABETIC EXCHANGES:** 2 starch, 1-1/2 fat.

Editor's Note: This recipe was tested with Land O'Lakes light stick butter and Splenda Sugar Blend for Baking.

Raspberry Sweet Tea

FAT ▼ SALT ▼ CARB ▼

(PICTURED BELOW)

PREP: 20 Min. + Chilling   **YIELD:** 15 Servings

Stir together this refreshing, spring sipper with only a handful of ingredients. Our recipe editors think that its smile-fetching flavor will make it a popular thirst-quencher.

> 4 quarts water, *divided*
> Sugar substitute equivalent to 1 cup sugar
> 10 individual tea bags
> 1 package (12 ounces) frozen unsweetened raspberries, thawed and undrained
> 3 tablespoons lime juice

In a large saucepan, bring 2 qts. of water to a boil. Stir in sugar substitute until dissolved. Remove from the heat. Add tea bags; steep for 5-8 minutes. Discard tea bags.

In another saucepan, bring raspberries and remaining water to a boil. Reduce heat; simmer, uncovered, for 3 minutes.

Strain and discard pulp. Add raspberry juice and lime juice to the tea. Transfer to a large pitcher. Refrigerate until chilled.

NUTRITION FACTS: 1 cup equals 17 calories, trace fat (0 saturated fat), 0 cholesterol, trace sodium, 4 g carbohydrate, 1 g fiber, trace protein. **DIABETIC EXCHANGE:** Free food.

Editor's Note: This recipe was tested with Splenda No Calorie Sweetener.

Artichoke Rye Toasts

FAT ▼ CARB ▼ MEAT-LESS

PREP: 30 Min.   **BAKE:** 10 Min.   **YIELD:** 2 Dozen

Quick, light and savory, these mouth-watering artichoke bites make irresistible finger food for guests at any gathering.
> —Jo Ann Guzolik, West Leechburg, Pennsylvania

> 24 slices snack rye bread
> Refrigerated butter-flavored spray
> 1 can (14 ounces) water-packed artichoke hearts, rinsed, drained and chopped
> 1/2 cup grated Parmesan cheese
> 1/4 cup shredded cheddar cheese
> 1/8 teaspoon cayenne pepper
> 4 egg whites
> 1/4 teaspoon paprika

Place the bread on ungreased baking sheets; spritz with butter-flavored spray. In a small bowl, combine the artichokes, cheeses and cayenne. In a small mixing bowl, beat egg whites until stiff; fold into artichoke mixture.

Spread over bread; sprinkle with paprika. Bake at 400° for 10-12 minutes or until golden brown. Serve warm. Refrigerate leftovers.

NUTRITION FACTS: 2 pieces equals 78 calories, 2 g fat (1 g saturated fat), 5 mg cholesterol, 270 mg sodium, 9 g carbohydrate, 1 g fiber, 5 g protein. **DIABETIC EXCHANGE:** 1 starch.

Editor's Note: This recipe was tested with I Can't Believe It's Not Butter Spray.

Zesty Vegetable Dip

FAT ▼ CARB ▼

PREP: 10 Min. + Chilling   **YIELD:** 1 Cup

The flavors blend together so well in this creamy, fast dip. We especially love it with cauliflower. —Wanda Baugh, Mascoutah, Illinois

> 1 cup fat-free mayonnaise
> 1 teaspoon tarragon vinegar
> 1 teaspoon Worcestershire sauce
> 1 teaspoon prepared horseradish
> 1 teaspoon onion powder
> 1 teaspoon garlic powder
> 1 teaspoon curry powder
> Assorted fresh vegetables

In a small bowl, combine the mayonnaise, vinegar, Worcestershire sauce and horseradish. Stir in the onion powder, garlic powder and curry. Cover and refrigerate for at least 1 hour. Serve with vegetables.

NUTRITION FACTS: 2 tablespoons equals 26 calories, 1 g fat (trace saturated fat), 3 mg cholesterol, 249 mg sodium, 5 g carbohydrate, 1 g fiber, trace protein. **DIABETIC EXCHANGE:** Free food.

> **TASTY TIP**
> Can't get your gang to take to fat-free ingredients? Try mixing half of the fat-free item with it's reduced-fat counter-part. Over time, increase the fat-free portion for a tasty transition. Try it with the recipe for Zesty Vegetable Dip.

Spring Green Guacamole

(PICTURED BELOW)

FAT SALT CARB MEAT-
LESS

PREP: 15 Min. + Chilling   **YIELD:** 2-1/2 Cups

Love guacamole but hate the fat? Try this vibrant version that's made with heart-smart peas. We never feel guilty when we snack on this guacamole. —Carey Waterworth, Silvana, Washington

      1 package (10 ounces) frozen peas
      1 cup cubed peeled avocado
  1/2 cup fat-free sour cream
  1/4 cup chopped green onions
      2 tablespoons minced fresh cilantro
4-1/2 teaspoons lime juice
      1 tablespoon canned chopped green chilies, drained
      1 garlic clove, minced
  1/4 teaspoon salt
  1/8 teaspoon pepper
Baked tortilla chips

Cook peas according to package directions; drain and place in a food processor. Add the avocado, sour cream, onions, cilantro, lime juice, chilies, garlic, salt and pepper; cover and process until smooth.

   Transfer to a bowl. Cover and refrigerate for 1 hour or until chilled. Serve with tortilla chips.

NUTRITION FACTS: 1/4 cup guacamole (calculated without chips) equals 63 calories, 2 g fat (trace saturated fat), 2 mg cholesterol, 108 mg sodium, 8 g carbohydrate, 2 g fiber, 3 g protein. **DIABETIC EXCHANGES:** 1/2 starch, 1/2 fat.

TASTY TIP
To give the guacamole more kick, add a dash of cayenne pepper and extra cilantro.

Garlic Bean Dip

CARB MEAT-
LESS

PREP: 10 Min. + Chilling   **YIELD:** 6 Servings

I've contributed this thick dip to many get-togethers, and there's never any left to bring home.
—Kallee McCreery, Escondido, California

      1 can (15 ounces) garbanzo beans *or* chickpeas, rinsed and drained
  1/3 cup reduced-fat mayonnaise
      2 tablespoons minced fresh parsley
4-1/2 teaspoons lemon juice
      1 garlic clove, peeled
  1/4 teaspoon salt
Pita bread wedges

In a food processor or blender, combine the beans, mayonnaise, parsley, lemon juice, garlic and salt; cover and process until smooth. Transfer to a serving dish. Cover and refrigerate for 1 hour. Serve with pita bread.

NUTRITION FACTS: 1/4 cup (calculated without pita bread) equals 112 calories, 6 g fat (1 g saturated fat), 5 mg cholesterol, 297 mg sodium, 13 g carbohydrate, 3 g fiber, 3 g protein. **DIABETIC EXCHANGES:** 1 starch, 1 fat.

BLT Bites

FAT

(PICTURED ON PAGE 17)

PREP: 30 Min. + Chilling   **YIELD:** 28 Appetizers

Celery adds a nice crunch to these no-fuss appetizers. The delightful nibbles are always popular at parties and get-togethers.
—Beth Borgemenke, Mason, Ohio

    28 cherry tomatoes
      7 bacon strips, cooked and crumbled
  1/2 cup fat-free mayonnaise
  1/3 cup chopped green onions
      3 tablespoons grated Parmesan cheese
      2 tablespoons finely chopped celery
      2 tablespoons minced fresh parsley

Cut a thin slice off the top of each tomato. Scoop out and discard pulp; invert tomatoes onto paper towels to drain. In a small bowl, combine the bacon, mayonnaise, onions, cheese, celery and parsley. Spoon into tomatoes. Cover and refrigerate for at least 2 hours.

NUTRITION FACTS: 2 stuffed tomatoes equals 38 calories, 2 g fat (1 g saturated fat), 4 mg cholesterol, 144 mg sodium, 3 g carbohydrate, 1 g fiber, 2 g protein. **DIABETIC EXCHANGE:** Free food.

Granola Bars

FAT SALT

PREP: 10 Min.   **BAKE:** 15 Min. + Cooling   **YIELD:** 8 Bars

My family relies on these bars for a fast snack any time of day. For an easy "power breakfast," enjoy the bars with low-fat yogurt, fresh fruit and juice. —Angela Agarand, Regina, Saskatchewan

1-1/4 cups Mueslix cereal with raisins, dates and almonds
  1/4 cup Grape-Nuts
  1/4 cup whole wheat flour
      2 tablespoons raisins

2 tablespoons dried cranberries

2 tablespoons miniature semisweet chocolate chips

1/4 teaspoon ground cinnamon

1/3 cup honey

In a large bowl, combine the first seven ingredients. Add honey; mix well. Pour into an 8-in. square baking dish coated with nonstick cooking spray; pat down evenly. Bake at 300° for 15-20 minutes or until golden brown. Cool on a wire rack. Cut into squares.

NUTRITION FACTS: 1 bar equals 144 calories, 2 g fat (1 g saturated fat), 0 cholesterol, 40 mg sodium, 33 g carbohydrate, 2 g fiber, 2 g protein. **DIABETIC EXCHANGE:** 2 starch.

Cranberry Herbal Tea Cooler

 FAT SALT CARB

PREP: 25 Min. + Chilling   **YIELD:** 8 Servings

You only need a few ingredients for this flavorful take on traditional iced tea from our home economists. After just one sip, it's sure to become one of your summer favorites.

3-1/2 cups water

1/2 cup orange juice

2 tablespoons sugar

8 orange spice herbal tea bags

4 cups reduced-sugar cranberry juice

Orange slices

In a saucepan, bring the water, orange juice and sugar to a boil. Reduce heat; cover and simmer for 10 minutes. Remove from the heat; add tea bags. Let stand for 4 minutes.

Remove and discard tea bags. Transfer to a pitcher; stir in cranberry juice. Refrigerate until chilled. Garnish with orange slices.

NUTRITION FACTS: 1 cup equals 42 calories, trace fat (0 saturated fat), 0 cholesterol, 4 mg sodium, 10 g carbohydrate, trace fiber, trace protein. **DIABETIC EXCHANGE:** 1/2 fruit.

Vanilla Tapioca Pudding

FAT

PREP: 10 Min. + Chilling   **YIELD:** 4 Servings

As a widower, I've recently started to learn how to cook. I created this tapioca pudding that's not only low in fat, but easy to make, too. I hope you enjoy it as much as I do.
—Robert Daggit, Shoreview, Minnesota

3-1/4 cups fat-free milk

2 tablespoons quick-cooking tapioca

2 tablespoons sugar

1 package (.8 ounce) sugar-free cook-and-serve vanilla pudding mix

1/4 teaspoon vanilla extract

In a large saucepan, combine the milk, tapioca, sugar and pudding mix. Bring to a boil, stirring constantly. Remove from the heat; stir in vanilla. Spoon into four dessert dishes. Cover and refrigerate for 2 hours before serving.

NUTRITION FACTS: 3/4 cup equals 134 calories, trace fat (trace saturated fat), 4 mg cholesterol, 211 mg sodium, 26 g carbohydrate, trace fiber, 7 g protein. **DIABETIC EXCHANGES:** 1 starch, 1 fat-free milk.

Crab Asparagus Quesadillas
(PICTURED ABOVE)

PREP/TOTAL TIME: 20 Min.   **YIELD:** 6 Servings

Fresh asparagus and crabmeat make a decadent combination in this no-fuss appetizer.   —Curtis Gunnarson, Sycamore, Illinois

4 flour tortillas (8 inches)

2 cups (8 ounces) shredded reduced-fat Mexican cheese blend

1 cup chopped fresh asparagus, cooked

1/2 cup chopped imitation crabmeat

2 tablespoons plus 3/4 cup picante sauce, *divided*

2 teaspoons canola oil

6 tablespoons fat-free sour cream

12 large ripe olives, sliced

On two tortillas, layer each with 1/2 cup cheese, 1/2 cup asparagus, 1/4 cup crab, 1 tablespoon picante sauce and remaining cheese. Top with remaining tortillas; press down lightly.

In a skillet coated with nonstick cooking spray, cook one quesadilla at a time in oil for 2 minutes on each side or until cheese is melted. Cut each into six wedges. Serve with sour cream, olives and remaining picante sauce.

NUTRITION FACTS: 2 wedges equals 280 calories, 13 g fat (4 g saturated fat), 31 mg cholesterol, 778 mg sodium, 28 g carbohydrate, 1 g fiber, 17 g protein. **DIABETIC EXCHANGES:** 2 starch, 2 lean meat, 1 fat.

TASTY TIP

"For an easy meal, serve the Crab Asparagus Quesadillas with refried beans, corn mixed with diced green chilies and an avocado salad," suggests Curtis Gunnarson.

Flavorful Tomato Juice

FAT ⬇

PREP: 20 Min. **COOK:** 45 Min. + Chilling **YIELD:** 4 Servings

Jalapeno, horseradish and spicy pepper sauce are some of my favorite ingredients. I knew they were the perfect way to spice up this thick, homemade tomato juice. It may be a little work, but the bold flavor is well worth the effort.

—Jeannie Linsavage, Albuquerque, New Mexico

      8 medium tomatoes, chopped
1-1/2 cups water
      1 small onion, chopped
      3 garlic cloves, minced
      1 jalapeno pepper, seeded and chopped
      3 tablespoons sugar
      3 tablespoons lime juice
      2 teaspoons celery seed
      1 teaspoon salt
      1 teaspoon ground mustard
      1 teaspoon prepared horseradish
   1/8 teaspoon dried basil
   1/8 teaspoon dried parsley flakes
Dash hot pepper sauce

In a large saucepan, combine all ingredients. Bring to a boil. Reduce heat; simmer, uncovered, for 30 minutes or until tomatoes are tender. Cool to room temperature.

Transfer mixture to a blender; cover and process until blended. Strain and discard seeds. Return tomato juice to saucepan. Bring to a boil. Reduce heat; simmer, uncovered, for 12-18 minutes or until juice measures 3 cups. Cool. Transfer to a pitcher; cover and refrigerate until chilled.

NUTRITION FACTS: 3/4 cup equals 121 calories, 2 g fat (trace saturated fat), 0 cholesterol, 624 mg sodium, 27 g carbohydrate, 4 g fiber, 3 g protein. **DIABETIC EXCHANGES:** 2 vegetable, 1 starch.

Editor's Note: When cutting or seeding hot peppers, use rubber or plastic gloves to protect your hands. Avoid touching your face.

Fruity Cereal Bars

FAT SALT ⬇ ⬇

PREP/TOTAL TIME: 30 Min. **YIELD:** 20 Servings

With dried apple and cranberries, these crispy cereal bars are perfect for snacks or brown-bag lunches. Store the extras in plastic containers, that is, if you have any left!

—Giovanna Kranenberg, Cambridge, Minnesota

   3 tablespoons butter
   1 package (10 ounces) large marshmallows
   6 cups crisp rice cereal
1/2 cup dried chopped apple
1/2 cup dried cranberries

In a large saucepan, combine butter and marshmallows. Cook and stir over medium-low heat until melted. Remove from the heat; stir in the cereal, apple and cranberries.

Pat into a 13-in. x 9-in. x 2-in. pan coated with nonstick cooking spray; cool. Cut into squares.

NUTRITION FACTS: 1 bar equals 105 calories, 2 g fat (1 g saturated fat), 5 mg cholesterol, 102 mg sodium, 22 g carbohydrate, trace fiber, 1 g protein. **DIABETIC EXCHANGES:** 1-1/2 starch, 1/2 fat.

Crispy Caribbean Veggie Wraps

FAT MEAT-LESS ⬇ ⬇

(PICTURED BELOW)

PREP: 40 Min. **BAKE:** 15 Min. **YIELD:** 22 Appetizers

With their hearty sweet potato filling, these crunchy wraps are truly delicious. They always have friends and family asking for more.

—Mary Beth Harris-Murphree, Tyler, Texas

      1 medium sweet potato
   1/2 cup canned black beans, rinsed and drained
   1/4 cup chopped red onion
      2 tablespoons minced fresh cilantro
      1 tablespoon lime juice
      1 teaspoon *each* salt, ground cumin and chopped jalapeno pepper
      1 garlic clove, minced
   1/4 cup water
     22 wonton wrappers
1-1/2 cups salsa

Scrub sweet potato and pierce with a fork; place on a microwave-safe plate. Microwave, uncovered, on high for 12-14 minutes or until tender, turning once. Cool. Slit potato and scoop pulp into a small bowl. Mash pulp; stir in the next eight ingredients.

Lightly brush water over all four edges of one wonton wrapper. (Keep wrappers covered with a damp paper towel until ready to use.) Spread 1 tablespoon filling along one edge of wrapper; roll up tightly. Repeat with remaining wrappers and filling. Place on a baking sheet coated with nonstick cooking spray. Lightly spray wraps with nonstick cooking spray. Bake at 375° for 15 minutes or until golden brown. Serve with salsa.

NUTRITION FACTS: 2 wraps with about 2 tablespoons salsa equals 80 calories, trace fat (trace saturated fat), 1 mg cholesterol, 482 mg sodium, 17 g carbohydrate, 3 g fiber, 5 g protein. **DIABETIC EXCHANGE:** 1 starch.

Editor's Note: This recipe was tested in a 1,100-watt microwave. When cutting or seeding hot peppers, use rubber or plastic gloves to protect your hands. Avoid touching your face.

Favorite Recipe Made Lighter

COMFORTING, creamy and crowd-pleasing are just a few of the words that describe Susanne Nonekowski's sensational Warm Spinach Spread. "Served alongside bread cubes, crackers or even vegetables, it's an artichoke dip similar to those found on the appetizer menu at many restaurants," she writes from her home in Oak Harbor, Ohio. "The spread is sometimes served in a bread bowl.

"It's my all-time favorite, and I truly don't think that my husband could make it through football season without it," Susanne adds. "But if you could cut the fat without sacrificing the flavor, I'd really appreciate it. I've already tried using reduced-fat mayonnaise, but I would like to hear any other suggestions you may have."

No problem, Susanne! The *L&T* home economists lit up with smiles after trying this decadent recipe, so they couldn't wait to lend a hand and pare-down your dish. The team realized that the spread was high in artery-clogging fats so they quickly mapped out a game plan, put on their aprons and got to work.

Because reduced-fat mayonnaise still packs on calories, the team used it to replace only half of the 2 cups of full-fat mayonnaise originally called for. The remainder was replaced with a surprise ingredient that many home cooks often forget about…tofu. Soft tofu is smooth in consistency and mild in flavor so it kept the volume and texture of Susanne's spread without altering its wonderful taste. Best of all, it's much healthier than heavy mayonnaise, making it a great addition to nearly any light dip or spread.

After a test or two, our makeover experts found that they needed to decrease the amount of garlic in the recipe because the intensity of herbs sometimes increases when used in less-fat dishes.

Makeover Warm Spinach Spread is a bubbling-hot success that Susanne and her husband are sure to enjoy. Not only is it delicious, but it also boasts 60% less fat than Susanne's original with nearly half of the calories.

Warm Spinach Spread

 CARB MEAT-LESS

PREP: 25 Min.   YIELD: 5 Cups

- 2 cups mayonnaise
- 2 cups grated Parmesan cheese
- 1 can (14 ounces) water-packed artichoke hearts, rinsed, drained and chopped
- 2 packages (10 ounces *each*) frozen chopped spinach, thawed and squeezed dry
- 2 garlic cloves, minced

In a large bowl, combine all ingredients. Spoon into an ungreased 9-in. deep-dish pie plate. Bake, uncovered, at 350° for 20-25 minutes or until heated through. Serve warm.

NUTRITION FACTS: 1/4 cup equals 211 calories, 20 g fat (4 g saturated fat), 14 mg cholesterol, 340 mg sodium, 3 g carbohydrate, 1 g fiber, 5 g protein.

Makeover Warm Spinach Spread

 CARB MEAT-LESS

(PICTURED ABOVE)

PREP/TOTAL TIME: 30 Min.   YIELD: 5 Cups

- 1 package (16 ounces) soft tofu
- 2 cups grated Parmesan cheese
- 1 cup reduced-fat mayonnaise
- 1 can (14 ounces) water-packed artichoke hearts, rinsed, drained and chopped
- 2 packages (10 ounces *each*) frozen chopped spinach, thawed and squeezed dry
- 3 garlic cloves, minced

In a large bowl, combine all ingredients. Spoon into an ungreased 9-in. deep-dish pie plate. Bake, uncovered, at 350° for 20-25 minutes or until heated through. Serve warm.

NUTRITION FACTS: 1/4 cup equals 109 calories, 8 g fat (2 g saturated fat), 11 mg cholesterol, 317 mg sodium, 4 g carbohydrate, 1 g fiber, 7 g protein. **DIABETIC EXCHANGES:** 11/2 fat, 1/2 starch.

MAKEOVER TIP
An herb's flavor is often intensified when used in a low-fat casserole, so consider reducing the amount called for when trimming down a recipe.

Crab Rangoon

FAT CARB

PREP/TOTAL TIME: 25 Min.   **YIELD:** 14 Appetizers

Bite into our Test Kitchen's golden appetizers and you'll find a creamy crab filling that rivals that of restaurant fare. Best of all, the party starters are baked and not fried, so you don't have to feel guilty about enjoying them.

    3 ounces reduced-fat cream cheese
1/8 teaspoon garlic salt
1/8 teaspoon Worcestershire sauce
    1 pouch (3.53 ounces) premium crabmeat, drained
    1 green onion, chopped
  14 wonton wrappers

In a small bowl, combine the cream cheese, garlic salt and Worcestershire sauce until smooth. Stir in crab and onion. Place 2 teaspoonfuls in the center of each wonton wrapper. Moisten edges with water; bring corners to center over filling and press edges together to seal.

Place on a baking sheet coated with nonstick cooking spray. Lightly spray wontons with nonstick cooking spray. Bake at 425° for 8-10 minutes or until golden brown. Serve warm.

NUTRITION FACTS: 2 appetizers equals 83 calories, 3 g fat (2 g saturated fat), 19 mg cholesterol, 248 mg sodium, 10 g carbohydrate, trace fiber, 4 g protein. **DIABETIC EXCHANGES:** 1 starch, 1/2 fat.

Devil's Food Cookies

(PICTURED BELOW)

PREP: 15 Min.   **BAKE:** 10 Min. per Batch   **YIELD:** 28 Cookies

Most people don't realize that these cookies are low in fat. You get more than two dozen of the treats from a cake mix and just four other common ingredients.

—Melanie Van Den Brink, Rock Rapids, Iowa

1 package (18-1/4 ounces) devil's food cake mix
2 eggs
2 tablespoons butter, softened
3 tablespoons water
1/2 cup miniature semisweet chocolate chips

In a large mixing bowl, combine the cake mix, eggs, butter and water (batter will be thick). Fold in chocolate chips.

Drop by tablespoonfuls 2 in. apart onto baking sheets coated with nonstick cooking spray. Bake at 350° for 10-13 minutes or until set and edges are lightly browned. Cool for 2 minutes before removing to wire racks.

NUTRITION FACTS: 1 cookie equals 105 calories, 4 g fat (2 g saturated fat), 17 mg cholesterol, 155 mg sodium, 16 g carbohydrate, 1 g fiber, 1 g protein. **DIABETIC EXCHANGES:** 1 starch, 1/2 fat.

Terrific Tomato Tart

 CARB

PREP: 15 Min.   **BAKE:** 20 Min.   **YIELD:** 8 Servings

This recipe is fabulous! Fresh tomatoes, feta cheese and prepared pesto are delightful toppings for the crispy phyllo dough crust.

—Diane Halferty, Corpus Christi, Texas

12 sheets phyllo dough (14 inches x 9 inches)
  2 tablespoons olive oil
  2 tablespoons dry bread crumbs
  2 tablespoons prepared pesto
3/4 cup crumbled feta cheese, *divided*
  1 medium tomato, cut into 1/4-inch slices
  1 large yellow tomato, cut into 1/4-inch slices
1/4 teaspoon pepper
  5 to 6 fresh basil leaves, thinly sliced

Place one sheet of phyllo dough on a baking sheet lined with parchment paper; brush with 1/2 teaspoon oil and sprinkle with 1/2 teaspoon bread crumbs. (Keep remaining phyllo covered with plastic wrap and a damp towel to prevent it from drying out.) Repeat layers, being careful to brush oil all the way to edges.

Fold each side 3/4 in. toward center to form a rim. Spread with pesto and sprinkle with half of the feta cheese. Alternately arrange the red and yellow tomato slices over cheese. Sprinkle with the pepper and remaining feta.

Bake at 400° for 20-25 minutes or until crust is golden brown and crispy. Cool on a wire rack for 5 minutes. Remove parchment paper before cutting. Garnish with basil.

NUTRITION FACTS: 1 piece equals 135 calories, 7 g fat (2 g saturated fat), 7 mg cholesterol, 221 mg sodium, 13 g carbohydrate, 1 g fiber, 5 g protein. **DIABETIC EXCHANGES:** 1-1/2 fat, 1 starch.

Fried Green Tomatoes

MEAT-LESS

PREP: 30 Min.   **COOK:** 25 Min.   **YIELD:** 6 Servings

A quick, from-scratch salsa makes a mouth-watering addition to these tomato slices. The golden coating is so crispy, no one suspects they are light. —Ingrid Parker, Hattiesburg, Mississippi

1/2 cup all-purpose flour
  1 teaspoon sugar
  1 teaspoon salt
3/4 teaspoon cayenne pepper
  1 egg
  1 tablespoon fat-free milk
  1 cup cornflake crumbs
  4 medium green tomatoes, cut into 1/2-inch slices
1/4 cup canola oil

SALSA:

    5 medium red tomatoes, seeded and chopped
1/2 cup minced fresh cilantro
1/4 cup chopped onion
    2 jalapeno peppers, seeded and chopped
4-1/2 teaspoons lime juice
    2 teaspoons sugar
    1 garlic clove, minced
1/4 teaspoon salt
1/4 teaspoon pepper

In a shallow bowl, combine the flour, sugar, salt and cayenne. In another shallow bowl, beat egg and milk. Place cornflake crumbs in a third bowl. Pat green tomato slices dry. Coat with flour mixture, dip into egg mixture, then coat with crumbs.

In a large nonstick skillet, heat 4 teaspoons oil over medium heat. Fry tomato slices, four at a time, for 3-4 minutes on each side or until golden brown, adding more oil as needed. Drain on paper towels.

Place fried tomatoes on an ungreased baking sheet. Bake at 375° for 4-5 minutes or until tender. Meanwhile, in a bowl, combine the salsa ingredients. Serve with the fried tomatoes.

NUTRITION FACTS: 2 tomato slices with 1/3 cup salsa equals 207 calories, 11 g fat (1 g saturated fat), 35 mg cholesterol, 343 mg sodium, 25 g carbohydrate, 3 g fiber, 5 g protein. **DIABETIC EXCHANGES:** 2 vegetable, 2 fat, 1 starch.

Editor's Note: When cutting or seeding hot peppers, use rubber or plastic gloves to protect your hands. Avoid touching your face.

Oatmeal Raisin Cookies

PREP: 25 Min.   **BAKE:** 15 Min. per Batch   **YIELD:** About 3 Dozen

These sweet, cinnamon-flavored cookies are chock-full of oats. Best of all, they are loaded with old-fashioned flavor and only a bit of fat. Tuck a few extra into your lunch bag because you're sure to want them as an afternoon snack, too.

—Nancy Johnson, Laverne, Oklahoma

1/2 cup butter, softened
    1 cup sugar blend for baking
    2 eggs, lightly beaten
1/2 cup unsweetened applesauce
    1 tablespoon molasses
1-1/2 teaspoons vanilla extract
    3 cups old-fashioned oats
1-1/2 cups all-purpose flour
    1 teaspoon baking powder
    1 teaspoon ground cinnamon
1/4 teaspoon salt
3/4 cup raisins

In a large mixing bowl, cream butter and sugar blend for 2 minutes on medium speed. Beat in eggs. Add applesauce, molasses and vanilla. Combine the oats, flour, baking powder, cinnamon and salt; gradually add to creamed mixture and mix well. Fold in raisins.

Drop by rounded tablespoonfuls 2 in. apart onto baking sheets lightly coated with nonstick cooking spray. Bake at 350° for 11-13 minutes or until lightly browned. Cool for 2 minutes before removing to wire racks.

NUTRITION FACTS: 2 cookies equals 188 calories, 6 g fat (3 g saturated fat), 34 mg cholesterol, 104 mg sodium, 31 g carbohydrate, 2 g fiber, 4 g protein. **DIABETIC EXCHANGES:** 2 starch, 1 fat.

Editor's Note: This recipe was tested with Splenda Sugar Blend for Baking.

Fruit and Nut Trail Mix
(PICTURED ABOVE)

PREP: 15 Min.   **BAKE:** 1 Hour + Cooling   **YIELD:** 4 Cups

This mouth-watering mix is filled with familiar fall tastes. Watching weekend football games, we all enjoy snacking on this sweet and crunchy medley. Or, keep it on hand for late-night snacking or an on-the-go treat.   —Mary Ann Dell, Phoenixville, Pennsylvania

    1 package (6 ounces) dried apricots, quartered
3/4 cup walnut halves
3/4 cup golden raisins
1/2 cup salted cashew halves
1/2 cup sunflower kernels
1/3 cup dried cranberries
1/4 cup sugar
1-1/2 teaspoons Chinese five-spice powder
1/2 teaspoon salt
1/4 teaspoon ground cinnamon
    1 egg white
    1 teaspoon water

Coat a foil-lined 15-in. x 10-in. x 1-in. baking pan with nonstick cooking spray; set aside. In a large bowl, combine the first 10 ingredients.

In a small mixing bowl, beat egg white and water on high speed for 1 minute or until frothy; fold into fruit mixture.

Spread onto prepared pan. Bake at 250° for 1 hour, stirring every 15 minutes. Cool completely. Store in an airtight container.

NUTRITION FACTS: 1/3 cup equals 206 calories, 11 g fat (1 g saturated fat), 0 cholesterol, 182 mg sodium, 27 g carbohydrate, 3 g fiber, 4 g protein. **DIABETIC EXCHANGES:** 2 fat, 1 fruit, 1/2 starch.

Peppered Chicken Pizza
(PICTURED ABOVE)

PREP: 55 Min. + Rising   **BAKE:** 15 Min.   **YIELD:** 20 Appetizer Servings

A homemade crust is topped with chicken, red pepper flakes and broiled peppers in this crowd-pleasing appetizer. I prepare the vegetables in advance so I can quickly assemble the pizza and pop it in the oven. —Julie DeRuw, Oakville, Washington

    2 packages (1/4 ounce *each*) active dry yeast
    1 cup warm water (110° to 115°)
    2 cups bread flour
    1 cup all-purpose flour
    2 tablespoons olive oil
    2 teaspoons sugar
    1 teaspoon salt
TOPPING:
    2 tablespoons olive oil
    3 garlic cloves, minced
  3/4 teaspoon salt
    1 *each* medium green, sweet red and yellow pepper, julienned
  1/2 medium red onion, sliced and separated into rings
  1/2 pound boneless skinless chicken breast, cut into 1/4-inch strips
  1/4 teaspoon crushed red pepper flakes
  2/3 cup hickory smoke-flavored barbecue sauce
1-1/2 cups (6 ounces) shredded part-skim mozzarella cheese
1-1/2 cups (6 ounces) shredded reduced-fat Mexican cheese blend

In a large mixing bowl, dissolve yeast in warm water. Stir in the flours, oil, sugar and salt until smooth. Turn onto a lightly floured surface; knead until smooth and elastic, about 6 minutes. Place in a bowl coated with nonstick cooking spray, turning once to coat top. Cover and let rise in a warm place until doubled, about 45 minutes.

Punch down dough; let stand for 10 minutes. Roll out to a 15-in. x 10-in. rectangle. Place in a 15-in. x 10-in. x 1-in. pan coated with nonstick cooking spray. Let stand for 10 minutes.

Prick with a fork. Bake at 375° for 7 minutes. Meanwhile, in a small bowl, combine the oil, garlic and salt; let stand for 15 minutes.

Place peppers and onion on a baking sheet; drizzle with half of the oil mixture. Broil 4 in. from the heat for 5 minutes or until vegetables are tender and lightly browned. Toss chicken with pepper flakes and remaining oil mixture; place on a baking sheet. Broil 4 in. from heat for 5 minutes or until juices run clear.

Arrange vegetables and chicken over crust. Drizzle with barbecue sauce; sprinkle with cheeses. Bake for 15-20 minutes or until lightly browned.

NUTRITION FACTS: 1 piece equals 168 calories, 6 g fat (2 g saturated fat), 17 mg cholesterol, 437 mg sodium, 19 g carbohydrate, 1 g fiber, 10 g protein. **DIABETIC EXCHANGES:** 1 starch, 1 lean meat, 1 vegetable.

Pepper Steak Quesadillas

PREP/TOTAL TIME: 30 Min.   **YIELD:** 4 Servings

I came up with these savory quesadillas one day when my family needed a quick lunch before running off in several directions. —Barbara Moore, Farmington, New Mexico

  1/2 pound boneless beef sirloin steak
  1/2 *each* medium green, sweet red and yellow pepper, julienned
    1 tablespoon chopped red onion
    1 garlic clove, minced
    1 tablespoon minced fresh cilantro
  1/4 teaspoon dried rosemary, crushed
    4 flour tortillas (6 inches)
    6 cherry tomatoes, halved
  1/4 cup sliced fresh mushrooms
    1 cup (4 ounces) shredded part-skim mozzarella cheese

If grilling the steak, coat grill rack with nonstick cooking spray before starting the grill. Grill steak, covered, over medium heat or broil 4 in. from the heat for 4-6 minutes on each side or until meat reaches desired doneness (for medium-rare, a meat thermometer should read 145°; medium, 160°; well-done, 170°). Let stand for 10 minutes.

Meanwhile, in a large skillet coated with nonstick cooking spray, saute the peppers, onion and garlic for 5-6 minutes or until tender. Sprinkle with cilantro and rosemary.

Place two tortillas on a baking sheet coated with nonstick cooking spray. Cut steak into thin strips; place on tortillas. Using a slotted spoon, place pepper mixture over steak. Top with tomatoes, mushrooms, cheese and remaining tortillas; lightly spray top of tortillas with nonstick cooking spray.

Bake at 425° for 5-10 minutes or until golden brown and cheese is melted. Cut each quesadilla into four wedges.

NUTRITION FACTS: 2 wedges equals 252 calories, 10 g fat (4 g saturated fat), 48 mg cholesterol, 383 mg sodium, 19 g carbohydrate, 1 g fiber, 22 g protein. **DIABETIC EXCHANGES:** 2 lean meat, 1 starch, 1 vegetable.

> **MAKE IT EASY**
> Consider preparing the quesadillas the next time you have leftover beef in the refrigerator you'd like to finish.

Simmer Up A Souper Bowl!

Few foods chase the chill and warm the soul like bowls of steaming soup. Featuring good-for-you items, time-easing convenience and endless variety, it's no wonder why satisfying soups are staples in homes from coast to coast.

Shrimp and Black Bean Soup, p. 38

NUTRITION FACTS: 1-1/2 cups equals 218 calories, 5 g fat (1 g saturated fat), 3 mg cholesterol, 588 mg sodium, 35 g carbohydrate, 7 g fiber, 9 g protein. DIABETIC EXCHANGES: 2 vegetable, 1-1/2 starch, 1 lean meat.

Hearty Cheese Soup

PREP: 20 Min.   **COOK:** 30 Min.   **YIELD:** 10 Servings

This is a stick-to-the-ribs family pleaser. Creamy and cheesy, the soup is wonderful for winter.   —Cathy Smith, Amarillo, Texas

- 1 pound lean ground turkey
- 3/4 cup chopped onion
- 4 cups diced peeled potatoes
- 4 cups reduced-sodium chicken broth
- 3/4 cup shredded carrots
- 3/4 cup diced celery
- 1 teaspoon salt
- 1 teaspoon dried basil
- 1 teaspoon dried parsley flakes
- 1/2 teaspoon pepper
- 1/4 cup all-purpose flour
- 1-1/2 cups fat-free milk
- 6 ounces reduced-fat process cheese (Velveeta), cubed
- 1/4 cup reduced-fat sour cream

In a nonstick skillet, cook turkey and onion over medium heat until meat is no longer pink; drain. Add the potatoes, broth, carrots, celery, salt, basil, parsley and pepper. Bring to a boil. Reduce heat; cover and simmer for 8-10 minutes or until vegetables are tender.

In a small bowl, combine flour and milk until smooth; stir into soup. Bring to a boil; cook and stir for 1-2 minutes or until thickened. Reduce heat to low; add the cheese. Cook and stir until cheese is melted. Remove from the heat; stir in the sour cream.

NUTRITION FACTS: 1 cup equals 208 calories, 6 g fat (3 g saturated fat), 46 mg cholesterol, 833 mg sodium, 22 g carbohydrate, 2 g fiber, 16 g protein. DIABETIC EXCHANGES: 2 lean meat, 1 starch, 1 vegetable.

Mushroom Barley Soup

FAT MEAT-
↓ LESS

PREP: 30 Min.   **COOK:** 45 Min.   **YIELD:** 10 Servings

Looking for a filling, meatless meal in a bowl? Ladle up this delicious soup. It's a treasured favorite of my husband, five kids and grandkids—and guaranteed to warm the body.
                    —Darlene Wiese-Appleby, Creston, Ohio

- 1 medium leek (white portion only), thinly sliced and halved
- 1 cup chopped celery
- 4 garlic cloves, minced
- 2 teaspoons olive oil
- 3/4 pound sliced fresh mushrooms
- 1-1/2 cups chopped peeled turnips
- 1-1/2 cups chopped carrots
- 4 cans (14-1/2 ounces *each*) reduced-sodium beef broth *or* vegetable broth
- 1 can (14-1/2 ounces) diced tomatoes, undrained
- 1 bay leaf

Bean and Pasta Soup

MEAT-
LESS

(PICTURED ABOVE)

PREP: 20 Min.   **COOK:** 30 Min.   **YIELD:** 5 Servings

We're always on the lookout for filling, low-fat recipes, and this soup is right on target.   —Maria Gooding, St. Thomas, Ontario

- 1 cup uncooked small pasta
- 2 celery ribs, thinly sliced
- 2 medium carrots, thinly sliced
- 1 medium onion, chopped
- 1 garlic clove, minced
- 1 tablespoon olive oil
- 2 cups water
- 1 can (14-1/2 ounces) diced tomatoes, undrained
- 1-1/4 cups reduced-sodium chicken broth *or* vegetable broth
- 1 teaspoon dried basil
- 1/4 teaspoon dried rosemary, crushed
- 1/4 teaspoon salt
- 1/8 teaspoon pepper
- 1 can (15 ounces) white kidney *or* cannellini beans, rinsed and drained
- 2 cups shredded fresh spinach
- 1/4 cup shredded Parmesan cheese

Cook pasta according to package directions. Meanwhile, in a large nonstick saucepan, saute the celery, carrots, onion and garlic in oil for 5 minutes. Stir in the water, tomatoes, broth, basil, rosemary, salt and pepper. Bring to a boil. Reduce heat; cover and simmer for 10 minutes or until carrots are tender.

Drain pasta; stir into vegetable mixture. Add the beans; heat through. Stir in spinach; cook until spinach is wilted, about 2 minutes. Sprinkle with Parmesan cheese.

1/2 teaspoon salt
1/2 teaspoon dried thyme
1/4 teaspoon pepper
1/4 teaspoon caraway seeds
1 cup quick-cooking barley
4 cups fresh baby spinach, cut into thin strips

In a large saucepan coated with nonstick cooking spray, cook the leek, celery and garlic in oil for 2 minutes. Add the mushrooms, turnips and carrots; cook 4-5 minutes longer or until mushrooms are tender.

Stir in the broth, tomatoes and seasonings. Bring to a boil. Reduce heat; cover and simmer for 10-15 minutes or until turnips are tender. Add barley; simmer 10 minutes longer. Stir in spinach; cook 5 minutes more or until spinach and barley are tender. Discard bay leaf.

NUTRITION FACTS: 1-1/4 cups equals 126 calories, 2 g fat (trace saturated fat), 3 mg cholesterol, 517 mg sodium, 23 g carbohydrate, 6 g fiber, 6 g protein. **DIABETIC EXCHANGES:** 1 starch, 1 vegetable.

Easy Minestrone

FAT MEAT-
LESS

PREP: 20 Min.   **COOK:** 6 Hours   **YIELD:** 10 Servings

You can assemble this dish in a slow cooker in the morning and forget about it the rest of the day. I have three boys who are not big fans of veggies, but they enjoy this hearty soup.
—Yvonne Andrus, American Fork, Utah

4 medium tomatoes, chopped
2 medium carrots, chopped
2 celery ribs, chopped
1 medium zucchini, halved and sliced
1-1/2 cups shredded cabbage
1 can (16 ounces) kidney beans, rinsed and drained
1 can (15 ounces) garbanzo beans *or* chickpeas, rinsed and drained
6 cups reduced-sodium chicken broth *or* vegetable broth
1-1/4 teaspoons Italian seasoning
1 teaspoon salt
1/4 teaspoon pepper
2 cups cooked elbow macaroni
5 tablespoons shredded Parmesan cheese

In a 5-qt. slow cooker, combine the first 11 ingredients. Cover and cook on low for 6-8 hours or until vegetables are tender. Just before serving, stir in macaroni and heat through. Serve with Parmesan cheese.

NUTRITION FACTS: 1-1/3 cups equals 149 calories, 2 g fat (1 g saturated fat), 2 mg cholesterol, 798 mg sodium, 25 g carbohydrate, 6 g fiber, 9 g protein. **DIABETIC EXCHANGES:** 1 starch, 1 very lean meat, 1 vegetable.

SHOP SMART
You'll need about a fourth of a head of cabbage to yield the 1-1/2 cups shredded cabbage for the Easy Minestrone. Shred the rest of the cabbage to make coleslaw for another meal.

Chicken and Dumpling Soup
(PICTURED BELOW)

PREP: 25 Min.   **COOK:** 40 Min.   **YIELD:** 4 Servings

Like a security blanket for the soul, this chicken and dumpling soup is a true classic. My husband is not very fond of leftovers, but he likes this so much, he could eat it every day of the week.
—Morgan Byers, Berkley, Michigan

3/4 pound boneless skinless chicken breasts, cut into 1-inch cubes
1/4 teaspoon salt
1/8 teaspoon pepper
2 teaspoons olive oil
1/4 cup all-purpose flour
4 cups reduced-sodium chicken broth, *divided*
1 cup water
2 cups frozen French-cut green beans
1-1/2 cups sliced onions
1 cup coarsely shredded carrots
1/4 teaspoon dried marjoram
2/3 cup reduced-fat biscuit/baking mix
1/3 cup cornmeal
1/4 cup shredded reduced-fat cheddar cheese
1/3 cup fat-free milk

Sprinkle chicken with salt and pepper. In a nonstick skillet, saute chicken in oil until browned and juices run clear.

In a large saucepan, combine flour and 1/2 cup broth until smooth. Stir in water and remaining broth. Add the beans, onions, carrots, marjoram and chicken. Bring to a boil. Reduce heat; simmer, uncovered, for 10 minutes.

Meanwhile, in a small bowl, combine the biscuit mix, cornmeal and cheese. Stir in milk just until moistened. Drop batter in 12 mounds onto simmering soup. Cover and simmer for 15 minutes or until a toothpick inserted in a dumpling comes out clean (do not lift the cover while simmering).

NUTRITION FACTS: 1-1/4 cups soup with 3 dumplings equals 353 calories, 8 g fat (2 g saturated fat), 52 mg cholesterol, 1,111 mg sodium, 44 g carbohydrate, 5 g fiber, 28 g protein. **DIABETIC EXCHANGES:** 3 very lean meat, 2 starch, 2 vegetable, 1 fat.

Shrimp and Black Bean Soup

(PICTURED BELOW)

PREP: 20 Min.   **COOK:** 40 Min.   **YIELD:** 8 Servings

Packed with tomatoes, corn, beans and shrimp, this bold entree will definitely warm you up on cold days. My family likes spicy foods, and everyone loves this dish.   —Elizabeth Lewis, Hayden, Alabama

   1 large onion, chopped
   1 tablespoon olive oil
   2 cans (14-1/2 ounces *each*) reduced-sodium chicken broth
   2 cans (10 ounces *each*) diced tomatoes and green chilies, undrained
   2 cups frozen corn
   1 can (15 ounces) black beans, rinsed and drained
   1 can (14-1/2 ounces) diced tomatoes, undrained
4-1/2 teaspoons chili powder
   1 teaspoon sugar
1/2 teaspoon salt
   1 pound uncooked medium shrimp, peeled and deveined
1/4 cup minced fresh parsley

In a Dutch oven, saute onion in oil for 3-4 minutes or until tender. Add the broth, tomatoes and green chilies, corn, black beans, tomatoes, chili powder, sugar and salt. Bring to a boil, stirring occasionally. Reduce heat; cover and simmer for 20 minutes.

Stir in shrimp; cook 5-6 minutes longer or until shrimp turn pink. Stir in parsley.

NUTRITION FACTS: 1-1/2 cups equals 177 calories, 3 g fat (trace saturated fat), 84 mg cholesterol, 983 mg sodium, 25 g carbohydrate, 6 g fiber, 15 g protein. **DIABETIC EXCHANGES:** 2 very lean meat, 1 starch, 1 vegetable, 1/2 fat.

Beef Vegetable Soup

PREP: 10 Min.   **COOK:** 4 Hours   **YIELD:** 9 Servings

Here's a slow-cooked recipe that chases away winter's chill. It's nice to come home to a meal that's ready to eat.
—Colleen Juhl, Dayton, Ohio

1 pound lean ground beef
1 medium onion, chopped
2 garlic cloves, minced
4 cups picante V8 juice
2 cups coleslaw mix
1 can (14-1/2 ounces) Italian stewed tomatoes
1 package (10 ounces) frozen corn
1 package (9 ounces) frozen cut green beans
2 tablespoons Worcestershire sauce
1 teaspoon dried basil
1/4 teaspoon pepper

In a large nonstick skillet, cook the beef, onion and garlic over medium heat until meat is no longer pink; drain. Transfer to a 5-qt. slow cooker. Stir in the remaining ingredients. Cover and cook on high for 4-5 hours or until heated through.

NUTRITION FACTS: 1 cup equals 169 calories, 5 g fat (2 g saturated fat), 18 mg cholesterol, 578 mg sodium, 19 g carbohydrate, 3 g fiber, 14 g protein. **DIABETIC EXCHANGES:** 1 starch, 1 lean meat, 1 vegetable.

Salmon Chowder

PREP: 20 Min.   **COOK:** 25 Min.   **YIELD:** 6 Servings

This filling chowder makes a hearty meal. I serve it at many functions, and I'm always asked for the recipe. Loaded with salmon, zucchini and corn, it's a hit.
—Vicki Thompson, Bristol, New Brunswick

1 small onion, chopped
1 garlic clove, minced
1/4 teaspoon dried thyme
1/4 teaspoon dried basil
1 tablespoon butter
2 cups 1% milk
1 can (10-1/2 ounces) condensed chicken broth, undiluted
1/2 cup frozen corn
1/2 cup chopped carrot
1 medium red potato, cut into 1/2-inch cubes
3 tablespoons all-purpose flour
1/4 cup cold water
1/2 pound salmon fillet, cut into 1-inch pieces
1/2 cup chopped zucchini
1/2 teaspoon salt
1/4 teaspoon pepper
1/2 cup shredded reduced-fat cheddar cheese

In a large saucepan over medium heat, cook and stir the onion, garlic, thyme and basil in butter until onion is tender. Stir in the milk, broth, corn, carrot and potato. Bring to a boil. Reduce heat; cover and simmer for 6-8 minutes or until vegetables are tender.

Combine flour and water until smooth; stir into onion mixture. Bring to a boil; cook and stir for 2 minutes or until

In a Dutch oven, cook the onions, carrots and celery in oil for 6-8 minutes or until crisp-tender. Stir in the broth, potatoes, tomatoes, garlic, salt and pepper. Bring to a boil. Reduce heat; cover and simmer for 15-20 minutes or until vegetables are tender.

In a small bowl, combine flour and water until smooth; stir into vegetable mixture. Bring to a boil; cook and stir for 2 minutes or until thickened. Stir in cabbage and peas.

For dumplings, in a small bowl, combine baking mix, carrots and parsley. Stir in water until moistened. Drop in 10 mounds onto simmering soup. Cover and simmer for 15 minutes or until a toothpick inserted in a dumpling comes out clean (do not lift cover while simmering). Garnish with cheese.

NUTRITION FACTS: 1-1/4 cups soup with 1 dumpling equals 258 calories, 7 g fat (2 g saturated fat), 5 mg cholesterol, 826 mg sodium, 44 g carbohydrate, 5 g fiber, 8 g protein. **DIABETIC EXCHANGES:** 2 starch, 2 vegetable, 1 fat.

Lime Chicken Chili

PREP: 25 Min.   **COOK:** 40 Min.   **YIELD:** 6 Servings

Lime juice gives this chili a zesty twist, while canned tomatoes and beans make assembly a snap. I serve it with toasted tortilla strips.
> —Diane Randazzo, Sinking Spring, Pennsylvania

- 1 medium onion, chopped
- 1 *each* medium sweet yellow, red and green pepper, chopped
- 3 garlic cloves, minced
- 2 tablespoons olive oil
- 1 pound ground chicken
- 1 tablespoon all-purpose flour
- 1 tablespoon baking cocoa
- 1 tablespoon ground cumin
- 1 tablespoon chili powder
- 2 teaspoons ground coriander
- 1/2 teaspoon salt
- 1/2 teaspoon garlic pepper blend
- 1/4 teaspoon pepper
- 2 cans (14-1/2 ounces *each*) diced tomatoes, undrained
- 1/4 cup lime juice
- 1 teaspoon grated lime peel
- 1 can (15 ounces) white kidney *or* cannellini beans, rinsed and drained
- 2 flour tortillas (8 inches), cut into 1/4-inch strips
- 6 tablespoons reduced-fat sour cream

In a saucepan, saute onion, peppers and garlic in oil for 7-8 minutes or until crisp-tender. Add chicken; cook and stir over medium heat for 8-9 minutes or until no longer pink.

Stir in flour, cocoa and seasonings. Add tomatoes, lime juice and lime peel. Bring to a boil. Reduce heat; simmer, uncovered, for 20-25 minutes or until thickened, stirring frequently. Stir in beans; heat through.

Meanwhile, place tortilla strips on a baking sheet coated with nonstick cooking spray. Bake at 400° for 8-10 minutes or until crisp. Serve chili with sour cream and tortilla strips.

NUTRITION FACTS: 1 cup with 5 tortilla strips and 1 tablespoon sour cream equals 357 calories, 14 g fat (4 g saturated fat), 55 mg cholesterol, 643 mg sodium, 40 g carbohydrate, 8 g fiber, 21 g protein. **DIABETIC EXCHANGES:** 3 vegetable, 2 lean meat, 1-1/2 starch, 1 fat.

thickened. Reduce heat; add salmon and zucchini. Simmer, uncovered, for 3-5 minutes or until fish flakes easily with a fork. Stir in salt and pepper. Sprinkle with cheese before serving.

NUTRITION FACTS: 1 cup equals 214 calories, 10 g fat (4 g saturated fat), 38 mg cholesterol, 656 mg sodium, 16 g carbohydrate, 2 g fiber, 16 g protein. **DIABETIC EXCHANGES:** 1-1/2 fat, 1 starch, 1 lean meat.

Vegetable Soup with Dumplings
(PICTURED ABOVE)

MEAT-LESS

PREP: 25 Min.   **COOK:** 40 Min.   **YIELD:** 10 Servings

Not only is this soup my family's favorite meatless recipe, but it's a complete meal-in-one. It's full of vegetables, and the fluffy carrot dumplings are a great change of pace.
> —Karen Mau, Jacksboro, Tennessee

- 1-1/2 cups chopped onions
- 4 medium carrots, sliced
- 3 celery ribs, sliced
- 2 tablespoons canola oil
- 3 cups vegetable broth
- 4 medium potatoes, peeled and sliced
- 4 medium tomatoes, chopped
- 2 garlic cloves, minced
- 1/2 teaspoon salt
- 1/2 teaspoon pepper
- 1/4 cup all-purpose flour
- 1/2 cup water
- 1 cup chopped cabbage
- 1 cup frozen peas

CARROT DUMPLINGS:
- 2-1/4 cups reduced-fat biscuit/baking mix
- 1 cup shredded carrots
- 1 tablespoon minced fresh parsley
- 1 cup cold water
- 10 tablespoons shredded reduced-fat cheddar cheese

Zippy Chicken Soup
(PICTURED ABOVE)

 FAT

PREP/TOTAL TIME: 30 Min.   **YIELD:** 6 Servings

This spicy, satisfying soup is one of my husband's winter favorites. It's quick to make but tastes like it simmered all day.
—Linda Lashley, Redgranite, Wisconsin

- 1/2 pound boneless skinless chicken breasts, cut into 1-inch cubes
- 2 cans (14-1/2 ounces *each*) reduced-sodium chicken broth, *divided*
- 2 cups frozen corn
- 1 can (15 ounces) black beans, rinsed and drained
- 1 can (10 ounces) diced tomatoes and green chilies, undrained
- 1 jalapeno pepper, seeded and chopped
- 2 tablespoons minced fresh cilantro
- 3 teaspoons chili powder
- 1/2 teaspoon ground cumin
- 1 tablespoon cornstarch
- 18 baked tortilla chips

Shredded reduced-fat Mexican cheese blend, optional

In a large nonstick saucepan or Dutch oven coated with nonstick cooking spray, cook chicken over medium heat for 4-6 minutes or until juices run clear.

Set aside 2 tablespoons of broth; add remaining broth to pan. Stir in the corn, beans, tomatoes, jalapeno, cilantro, chili powder and cumin. Bring to a boil. Reduce heat; simmer, uncovered, for 15 minutes.

Combine the cornstarch and reserved broth until smooth; stir into soup. Bring to a boil; cook and stir for 2 minutes or until thickened. Top each serving with tortilla chips. Garnish with cheese if desired.

NUTRITION FACTS: 1-1/3 cups with 3 tortilla chips (calculated without cheese) equals 194 calories, 2 g fat (trace saturated fat), 24 mg cholesterol, 752 mg sodium, 29 g carbohydrate, 5 g fiber, 17 g protein. **DIABETIC EXCHANGES:** 2 starch, 2 very lean meat.

Editor's Note: When cutting or seeding hot peppers, use rubber or plastic gloves to protect your hands. Avoid touching your face.

Tomato Crab Soup

 CARB

PREP: 20 Min.   **COOK:** 30 Min.   **YIELD:** 10 Servings

With crab and bits of vegetables in every bite, this creation is sure to please all the seafood fans in your family.
—Clinton Liu, Edmonds, Washington

- 1 small onion, chopped
- 1/4 cup chopped sweet red pepper
- 4 garlic cloves, minced
- 3 tablespoons butter
- 4 plum tomatoes, finely chopped
- 1/4 cup all-purpose flour
- 1/2 teaspoon pepper
- 1/8 teaspoon salt
- 3 cans (14-1/2 ounces *each*) reduced-sodium chicken broth
- 1 can (6 ounces) tomato paste
- 2 cans (6 ounces *each*) crabmeat, drained, flaked and cartilage removed
- 3 tablespoons minced fresh basil
- 1 cup milk

In a large saucepan, saute the onion, red pepper and garlic in butter for 3 minutes. Stir in tomatoes; cook 2-3 minutes longer or until onion is tender.

Whisk in the flour, pepper and salt until blended. Gradually stir in the broth and tomato paste. Bring to a boil; cook and stir for 2 minutes or until thickened. Stir in crab and basil. Gradually stir in milk; heat through.

NUTRITION FACTS: 1 cup equals 126 calories, 5 g fat (3 g saturated fat), 43 mg cholesterol, 526 mg sodium, 11 g carbohydrate, 2 g fiber, 11 g protein. **DIABETIC EXCHANGES:** 1 very lean meat, 1 vegetable, 1/2 starch, 1/2 fat.

Lime Navy Bean Chili
FAT

PREP: 15 Min. + Soaking   **COOK:** 5 Hours   **YIELD:** 6 Servings

My slow cooker makes it easy to come home to a wonderful, warm dinner like this one—no matter how busy the day was.
—Connie Thomas, Jensen, Utah

- 1-1/4 cups dried navy beans
- 3 cups water
- 2 bone-in chicken breast halves (7 ounces *each*), skin removed
- 1 cup frozen corn
- 1 medium onion, chopped
- 1 can (4 ounces) chopped green chilies
- 4 garlic cloves, minced
- 1 tablespoon chicken bouillon granules
- 1 teaspoon ground cumin

1/2 teaspoon chili powder

2 tablespoons lime juice

Place beans in a large saucepan; add water to cover by 2 in. Bring to a boil; boil for 2 minutes. Remove from the heat; cover and let stand for 1 hour. Drain and rinse beans, discarding liquid.

In a 3-qt. slow cooker, combine the beans, water, chicken, corn, onion, chilies, garlic, bouillon, cumin and chili powder. Cover and cook on low for 5-6 hours or until beans are tender and chicken juices run clear.

Remove chicken breasts; remove meat from the bones and cut into bite-size pieces. Discard bones and return chicken to the chili. Stir in lime juice just before serving.

NUTRITION FACTS: 1 cup equals 250 calories, 2 g fat (1 g saturated fat), 30 mg cholesterol, 532 mg sodium, 37 g carbohydrate, 12 g fiber, 22 g protein. **DIABETIC EXCHANGES:** 2 starch, 2 very lean meat, 1 vegetable.

Easy Hamburger Soup

PREP: 10 Min.   **COOK:** 1-1/4 Hours   **YIELD:** 8 Servings

Brown-bag lunches will be a little tastier with this hot and hearty beef and barley soup. The recipe is very simple to prepare.
—Mary Prior, St. Paul, Minnesota

1-1/2 pounds lean ground beef

1 medium onion, chopped

1 can (28 ounces) diced tomatoes, undrained

2 cans (14-1/2 ounces *each*) beef broth

1 cup water

4 celery ribs, thinly sliced

4 large carrots, halved and thinly sliced

10 whole peppercorns

1 teaspoon dried thyme

1/2 teaspoon salt

1/2 cup quick-cooking barley

1/4 cup minced fresh parsley

In a large saucepan, cook beef and onion over medium heat until meat is no longer pink; drain. Stir in the tomatoes, broth and water. Add celery and carrots.

Place peppercorns on a double thickness of cheesecloth; bring up corners of cloth and tie with kitchen string to form a bag. Add to beef mixture. Stir in thyme and salt. Bring to a boil. Reduce heat; cover and simmer for 45 minutes or until vegetables are tender.

Return to a boil. Stir in barley. Reduce heat; cover and simmer for 10-12 minutes or until barley is tender. Remove from the heat; stir in parsley. Let stand for 5 minutes. Discard spice bag.

NUTRITION FACTS: 1-1/3 cups equals 227 calories, 7 g fat (3 g saturated fat), 42 mg cholesterol, 762 mg sodium, 20 g carbohydrate, 5 g fiber, 20 g protein. **DIABETIC EXCHANGES:** 2 lean meat, 2 vegetable, 1/2 starch.

MAKE IT EASY
"The Easy Hamburger Soup is excellent as a leftover," assures Mary Prior. Make it for tonight's dinner and enjoy it as heartwarming noontime fare tomorrow.

Anytime Turkey Chili
(PICTURED BELOW)

FAT

PREP: 15 Min.   **COOK:** 1-1/4 Hours   **YIELD:** 8 Servings

I created this dish to grab the voters' attention at a chili contest we held in our backyard. With pumpkin, brown sugar and cooked turkey, it's like an entire Thanksgiving dinner in one bowl.
—Brad Bailey, Cary, North Carolina

2/3 cup chopped sweet onion

1/2 cup chopped green pepper

1-1/2 teaspoons dried oregano

2 garlic cloves, minced

1 teaspoon ground cumin

1 teaspoon olive oil

1 can (16 ounces) kidney beans, rinsed and drained

1 can (15-1/2 ounces) great northern beans, rinsed and drained

1 can (15 ounces) solid-pack pumpkin

1 can (15 ounces) crushed tomatoes

1 can (14-1/2 ounces) reduced-sodium chicken broth

1/2 cup water

2 tablespoons brown sugar

2 tablespoons chili powder

1/2 teaspoon pepper

3 cups cubed cooked turkey breast

In a large saucepan, saute the onion, green pepper, oregano, garlic and cumin in oil until vegetables are tender. Stir in the beans, pumpkin, tomatoes, broth, water, brown sugar, chili powder and pepper; bring to a boil. Reduce heat; cover and simmer for 1 hour. Add turkey; heat through.

NUTRITION FACTS: 1 cup equals 241 calories, 2 g fat (trace saturated fat), 45 mg cholesterol, 478 mg sodium, 32 g carbohydrate, 10 g fiber, 25 g protein. **DIABETIC EXCHANGES:** 3 very lean meat, 1-1/2 starch, 1 vegetable.

Simple Chicken Soup

FAT ▼

PREP/TOTAL TIME: 20 Min.   **YIELD:** 6 Servings

I revised a recipe that my family loved so it would be lighter and easier to make. Accompanied by a green salad and fresh bread, this version makes a hearty meal. —Sue West, Alvord, Texas

- 2 cans (14-1/2 ounces *each*) reduced-sodium chicken broth
- 1 tablespoon dried minced onion
- 1 package (16 ounces) frozen mixed vegetables
- 2 cups cubed cooked chicken breast
- 2 cans (10-3/4 ounces *each*) reduced-fat reduced-sodium condensed cream of chicken soup, undiluted

In a large saucepan, bring the broth and onion to a boil. Reduce heat. Add the vegetables; cover and cook for 6-8 minutes or until crisp-tender. Stir in the chicken and soup; heat through.

NUTRITION FACTS: 1-1/3 cups equals 195 calories, 3 g fat (1 g saturated fat), 44 mg cholesterol, 820 mg sodium, 21 g carbohydrate, 3 g fiber, 19 g protein. **DIABETIC EXCHANGES:** 2 very lean meat, 2 vegetable, 1 starch.

Tortellini Minestrone

PREP: 20 Min.   **COOK:** 50 Min.   **YIELD:** 9 Servings

We take turns cooking meals at my church, and this recipe is always popular. It's a smart way to use zucchini, and people enjoy the cheese tortellini as well as the sausage. —Pamela Smith, Flushing, New York

- 1-1/4 pounds Italian turkey sausage links, casings removed
- 1 large onion, chopped
- 2 garlic cloves, minced
- 6-1/2 cups reduced-sodium beef broth
- 1 can (14-1/2 ounces) diced tomatoes, undrained
- 2 cups thinly sliced carrots
- 1 cup thinly sliced celery
- 1 cup ketchup
- 1 teaspoon Italian seasoning
- 2 cups sliced zucchini
- 1 medium green pepper, chopped
- 2 cups frozen cheese tortellini
- 1/4 cup minced fresh parsley
- 2 tablespoons grated Parmesan cheese

In a Dutch oven or large saucepan, cook the sausage, onion and garlic over medium heat until meat is no longer pink; drain. Add the broth, tomatoes, carrots, celery, ketchup and Italian seasoning. Bring to a boil. Reduce heat; simmer, uncovered, for 20-25 minutes or until vegetables are tender.

Add the zucchini and green pepper; cook 5-7 minutes longer or until green pepper is tender. Stir in tortellini and parsley. Bring to a boil. Reduce heat to medium; cook, uncovered, for 5 minutes or until tortellini is tender. Sprinkle with Parmesan cheese just before serving.

NUTRITION FACTS: 1-1/2 cups equals 247 calories, 8 g fat (3 g saturated fat), 43 mg cholesterol, 1,179 mg sodium, 27 g carbohydrate, 3 g fiber, 17 g protein. **DIABETIC EXCHANGES:** 2 lean meat, 2 vegetable, 1 starch.

Kielbasa Split Pea Soup

FAT ▼

(PICTURED ABOVE)

PREP: 15 Min.   **COOK:** 55 Min.   **YIELD:** 12 Servings

Turkey kielbasa brings great flavor to this simple split pea soup. It's been a hit with my entire family—even our picky toddler enjoys it. —Sandra Bonde, Brainerd, Minnesota

- 2 celery ribs, thinly sliced
- 1 medium onion, chopped
- 1 package (16 ounces) dried green split peas
- 9 cups water, *divided*
- 1 pound smoked turkey kielbasa, halved and sliced
- 4 medium carrots, halved and thinly sliced
- 2 medium potatoes, peeled and cubed
- 1 tablespoon minced fresh parsley
- 1 teaspoon dried basil
- 1-1/2 teaspoons salt
- 1/2 teaspoon pepper

In a soup kettle or Dutch oven coated with nonstick cooking spray, cook celery and onion until tender. Stir in split peas and 6 cups water. Bring to a boil. Reduce heat; cover and simmer for 25 minutes.

Stir in the kielbasa, carrots, potatoes, parsley, basil, salt, pepper and remaining water. Return to a boil. Reduce heat; cover and simmer for 20-25 minutes or until peas and vegetables are tender.

NUTRITION FACTS: 1 cup equals 208 calories, 2 g fat (trace saturated fat), 13 mg cholesterol, 635 mg sodium, 34 g carbohydrate, 11 g fiber, 15 g protein. **DIABETIC EXCHANGES:** 2 starch, 2 very lean meat.

TASTY TIP
Pair Kielbasa Split Pea Soup with breadsticks or rye rolls for a fast meal.

Step Up to the Salad Bar

Whether crisp and refreshing or cool and creamy, salads are a welcomed part of any meal. Dress up your table tonight with one of the green leaf specialties, pasta delights or tangy salad dressings found in this chapter. They're all heart-smart options you'll toss together time and again.

Grapefruit Avocado Salad, p. 60

Shrimp Romaine Salad
(PICTURED ABOVE)

PREP/TOTAL TIME: 25 Min.   **YIELD:** 4 Servings

A refreshing dinner awaits when this shrimp-topped salad from our home economists is on the menu. Brown rice increases the nutrition, and citrus flavors make it a delight any time of year.

    2 cups cooked brown rice
    2 cups torn romaine
1-1/2 cups orange segments
    1 cup halved cherry tomatoes
  1/2 cup sliced red onion
    3 tablespoons orange juice concentrate
    2 tablespoons cider vinegar
    1 tablespoon olive oil
  3/4 teaspoon dried tarragon
  1/2 teaspoon garlic powder
  1/2 teaspoon salt
  1/4 teaspoon pepper
  3/4 pound cooked medium shrimp, peeled and deveined

In a large bowl, combine the rice, romaine, oranges, tomatoes and onion. For dressing, in a small bowl, whisk the orange juice concentrate, vinegar, oil, tarragon, garlic powder, salt and pepper. Set aside 4 teaspoons. Pour remaining dressing over rice mixture and toss to coat. Divide among four plates; top with shrimp. Drizzle with the reserved dressing.

NUTRITION FACTS: 1 serving equals 301 calories, 6 g fat (1 g saturated fat), 166 mg cholesterol, 498 mg sodium, 41 g carbohydrate, 5 g fiber, 22 g protein. **DIABETIC EXCHANGES:** 2 very lean meat, 1-1/2 starch, 1 vegetable, 1 fruit, 1/2 fat.

Smoked Turkey Cranberry Salad

PREP/TOTAL TIME: 15 Min.   **YIELD:** 4 Servings

A trip to the deli and a stop at the produce department make this an easy dinner solution. It's a healthy salad with a bold, smoky flavor. And it's a surefire way to get your family to eat right.
—Lisa Renshaw, Kansas City, Missouri

  1/4 cup reduced-fat mayonnaise
  1/4 cup reduced-fat plain yogurt
    2 tablespoons cranberry juice
    1 tablespoon minced chipotle peppers in adobo sauce
  1/4 teaspoon ground cumin
    3 cups cubed deli smoked turkey
  1/4 cup sliced celery
    4 cups torn mixed salad greens
  1/2 cup dried cranberries

In a bowl, combine the first five ingredients. Stir in turkey and celery. Divide the salad greens among four plates; top each with 3/4 cup turkey mixture and 2 tablespoons cranberries.

NUTRITION FACTS: 1 serving equals 231 calories, 8 g fat (1 g saturated fat), 49 mg cholesterol, 1,236 mg sodium, 21 g carbohydrate, 2 g fiber, 21 g protein. **DIABETIC EXCHANGES:** 3 very lean meat, 1 vegetable, 1 fruit, 1 fat.

Heirloom Tomato Salad

(PICTURED BELOW)

CARB MEAT-LESS

PREP: 20 Min. + Chilling   **YIELD:** 6 Servings

This is a simple yet elegant combination that always pleases guests. Not only is it tasty, but it's healthy, too. The more colorful the tomatoes, the prettier the salad will be.

—Jessie Apfel, Berkeley, California

2 cups torn fresh spinach
2 cups sliced multicolored heirloom tomatoes
1 cup red *and* yellow cherry tomatoes, halved
1 cup sliced red onion

DRESSING:
3 tablespoons olive oil
2 tablespoons white balsamic vinegar
1 garlic clove, minced
1/2 teaspoon salt
1/4 teaspoon *each* dried basil, oregano, thyme and sage
1/4 teaspoon dried rosemary, crushed
1/4 teaspoon pepper
1/8 teaspoon dried parsley flakes

In a large bowl, combine the spinach, tomatoes and onion. In a small bowl, whisk the dressing ingredients. Pour over salad and toss to coat. Cover and refrigerate for at least 2 hours. Serve with a slotted spoon.

NUTRITION FACTS: 2/3 cup equals 79 calories, 5 g fat (1 g saturated fat), 0 cholesterol, 165 mg sodium, 8 g carbohydrate, 2 g fiber, 1 g protein. **DIABETIC EXCHANGES:** 1 vegetable, 1 fat.

SHOP SMART
Flavorful heirloom tomatoes are grown in an assortment of shapes, colors and sizes. Look for them at specialty food and farmers markets. Or substitute your favorite tomatoes in this salad instead.

Broccoli Cauliflower Coleslaw

(PICTURED ABOVE)

FAT CARB

PREP: 20 Min. + Chilling   **YIELD:** 10 Servings

Most slaw has too much sugar and fat for us, so I came up with this lighter alternative. Everyone says it's the best slaw they've ever had. The refreshing side is assembled in a dash so it can chill until noontime.   —Becca Brasfield, Burns, Tennessee

3 cups shredded cabbage
1-1/2 cups shredded carrots
1 cup chopped red onion
2 cups fresh cauliflowerets
2 cups fresh broccoli florets

DRESSING:
1/2 cup fat-free mayonnaise
1/4 cup packed brown sugar
3 tablespoons lemon juice
2 tablespoons canola oil
1 teaspoon prepared mustard
1/2 teaspoon salt
1/8 teaspoon Worcestershire sauce

In a large bowl, combine the cabbage, carrots, onion, cauliflower and broccoli. In a small bowl, whisk the dressing ingredients. Add to coleslaw and toss to coat. Cover and refrigerate for at least 30 minutes before serving.

NUTRITION FACTS: 3/4 cup equals 83 calories, 3 g fat (trace saturated fat), 1 mg cholesterol, 242 mg sodium, 13 g carbohydrate, 2 g fiber, 1 g protein. **DIABETIC EXCHANGES:** 1 vegetable, 1/2 starch, 1/2 fat.

Asparagus Salad

(PICTURED BELOW)

FAT SALT CARB MEAT-LESS

PREP/TOTAL TIME: 15 Min.   **YIELD:** 6 Servings

A tangy, homemade dressing nearly steals the show from crisp-tender asparagus in this nutritious dish. You'll be happy to find that it's a lovely display that isn't a lot of work.

—Tammy Allison, Cape May Court House, New Jersey

    1 pound fresh asparagus, trimmed
    2 tablespoons water
    4 cups spring mix salad greens
1/3 cup balsamic vinegar
    2 tablespoons orange juice
    2 tablespoons *each* apricot and pineapple preserves
    1 tablespoon sesame seeds, toasted
    1 teaspoon minced fresh gingerroot
1/4 cup slivered almonds, toasted

Place the asparagus and water in a microwave-safe 11-in. x 7-in. x 2-in. baking dish. Cover and microwave on high for 2-3 minutes or until crisp-tender. Drain and immediately place asparagus in ice water. Drain and pat dry.

Place salad greens on a serving platter; top with asparagus. In a small bowl, whisk the vinegar, orange juice, preserves, sesame seeds and ginger. Drizzle over salad. Sprinkle with toasted almonds.

NUTRITION FACTS: 1 serving equals 93 calories, 3 g fat (trace saturated fat), 0 cholesterol, 27 mg sodium, 15 g carbohydrate, 2 g fiber, 3 g protein. **DIABETIC EXCHANGES:** 1 vegetable, 1/2 starch, 1/2 fat.

Strawberry Salad with Cinnamon Vinaigrette

SALT CARB MEAT-LESS

PREP/TOTAL TIME: 25 Min.   **YIELD:** 12 Servings

This is my husband's favorite. I've taken it to everything from fancy dinner parties to casual camping trips, and everyone lines up for seconds. The vinaigrette has a little kick to it.

—Nancy Tafoya, Fort Collins, Colorado

1/3 cup raspberry vinegar
1/3 cup olive oil
    3 tablespoons sugar
1/2 teaspoon salt
1/2 teaspoon ground cinnamon
1/2 teaspoon hot pepper sauce
1/4 teaspoon pepper
    6 cups torn romaine
    2 cups fresh strawberries, quartered
    1 medium ripe avocado, peeled and sliced
    1 can (11 ounces) mandarin oranges, drained
1/2 cup chopped red onion
1/2 cup chopped pecans, toasted

In a jar with a tight-fitting lid, combine first seven ingredients; shake well until sugar is dissolved. In a large bowl, combine romaine, strawberries, avocado, oranges, onion and pecans. Drizzle with vinaigrette and toss gently. Serve immediately.

NUTRITION FACTS: 2/3 cup equals 153 calories, 12 g fat (2 g saturated fat), 0 cholesterol, 104 mg sodium, 11 g carbohydrate, 2 g fiber, 2 g protein. **DIABETIC EXCHANGES:** 2 fat, 1/2 starch, 1/2 fruit.

Favorite Recipe Made Lighter

A TIME-HONORED tradition in Monika Rahn's home, Creamy French Dressing is an anticipated taste at family get-togethers. "This salad dressing has been a favorite for years," she writes from Dillsburg, Pennsylvania.

"My daughter-in-law and I particularly like it, but we feel it's too high in fat and sugar. I usually work on my own recipes, but can't seem to lighten this one successfully. Can you help?" asks Monika.

The zesty dressing relies on a substantial amount of oil to give it a rich, silky body and to mellow the acidic properties found in ingredients such as lemon juice and ketchup. The problem is that the oil is the main contributor where fat is concerned.

The L&T Test Kitchen staff began by removing half of the oil, and replacing it with a cooked combination of cornstarch and water. This mixture helped restore the texture of Monika's dressing and round out the flavors without adding fat.

After removing almost 40% of the fat from her submission and cutting back on the dressing's sugar content, we couldn't wait for Monika to sample Makeover Creamy French Dressing.

"I am so pleased with the results of this slimmed-down salad dressing," she happily writes. "We all like the new version. Not only was it just as easy to prepare, but it tastes good, too. Best of all it is a healthier way to top our greens at dinnertime."

Creamy French Dressing   CARB

PREP/TOTAL TIME: 20 Min.   **YIELD:** 2 Cups

- 1/2 cup lemon juice
- 1/2 cup sugar
- 1/2 cup ketchup
- 1/4 cup chopped onion
- 1-1/2 teaspoons salt
- 1-1/2 teaspoons Worcestershire sauce
- 1/8 teaspoon garlic powder
- 1 cup canola oil

In a blender or food processor, combine the first seven ingredients; cover and process until smooth. While processing, gradually add oil in a steady stream. Process until thickened. Transfer to a bowl or jar; cover and store in the refrigerator.

NUTRITION FACTS: 2 tablespoons equals 127 calories, 11 g fat (1 g saturated fat), 0 cholesterol, 253 mg sodium, 7 g carbohydrate, trace fiber, trace protein.

> ### MAKEOVER TIP
> Boil a combination of water and cornstarch to use as a replacement for some of the oil in your favorite homemade salad dressing.

Makeover Creamy French Dressing   CARB
(PICTURED ABOVE)

PREP/TOTAL TIME: 20 Min.   **YIELD:** 2 Cups

- 2 teaspoons cornstarch
- 1/2 cup water
- 1/2 cup lemon juice
- 1/2 cup ketchup
- 1/3 cup sugar
- 2 tablespoons chopped onion
- 1-1/2 teaspoons Worcestershire sauce
- 1/2 teaspoon salt
- 1/2 teaspoon prepared mustard
- 1/8 teaspoon onion powder
- 1/8 teaspoon garlic powder
- 1/2 cup canola oil

In a small saucepan, combine the cornstarch and water. Bring to a boil; cook and stir for 1-2 minutes or until thickened.

In a blender or food processor, combine the lemon juice, ketchup, sugar, onion, Worcestershire sauce, salt, mustard, onion powder and garlic powder; cover and process until smooth. While processing, gradually add oil in a steady stream. Process until thickened. Transfer to a bowl; stir in cornstarch mixture. Cover and store in the refrigerator.

NUTRITION FACTS: 2 tablespoons equals 90 calories, 7 g fat (1 g saturated fat), 0 cholesterol, 170 mg sodium, 7 g carbohydrate, trace fiber, trace protein. **DIABETIC EXCHANGES:** 1-1/2 fat, 1/2 starch.

Lentil Couscous Salad

MEAT-LESS

PREP: 20 Min.   **COOK:** 25 Min. + Chilling   **YIELD:** 5 Servings

This easy lentil salad won first place in a local cooking contest.
—Shannon Schunicht, College Station, Texas

    1 cup dried lentils, rinsed
    5 cups water, *divided*
  3/4 cup uncooked couscous
    1 medium sweet red pepper, chopped
    1 cup frozen corn, thawed
    4 green onions, thinly sliced
    2 tablespoons canola oil
    1 tablespoon red wine vinegar
    2 tablespoons minced fresh cilantro
    1 jalapeno pepper, seeded and chopped
    2 to 3 teaspoons hot pepper sauce
    1 teaspoon salt
    1 teaspoon ground cumin
  1/2 teaspoon pepper

In a large saucepan, bring lentils and 4 cups water to a boil. Reduce heat; cover and simmer for 18-22 minutes or until lentils are tender. Drain; transfer to a large bowl. Cover and refrigerate for at least 1 hour.

Meanwhile, in a small saucepan, bring remaining water to a boil. Stir in couscous. Cover and remove from the heat; let stand for 5-10 minutes or until water is absorbed. Fluff with a fork; cool.

Add the red pepper, corn, onions and couscous to lentils. In a small bowl, whisk the oil and vinegar. Whisk in the cilantro, jalapeno, hot pepper sauce, salt, cumin and pepper. Drizzle over salad and toss to coat. Cover and refrigerate for at least 1 hour.

NUTRITION FACTS: 1-1/2 cups equals 322 calories, 7 g fat (1 g saturated fat), 0 cholesterol, 495 mg sodium, 53 g carbohydrate, 15 g fiber, 16 g protein. **DIABETIC EXCHANGES:** 2-1/2 starch, 1 very lean meat, 1 vegetable, 1 fat.

Editor's Note: When cutting or seeding hot peppers, use rubber or plastic gloves to protect your hands. Avoid touching your face.

Sesame Green Bean Salad

FAT ▼ CARB ▼ MEAT-LESS

(PICTURED ABOVE)

PREP/TOTAL TIME: 20 Min.   **YIELD:** 5 Servings

Someone asks for the recipe every time I make this bean salad. It's a refreshing dish that's great for potlucks and other get-togethers.

—Terri McKay, New Bern, North Carolina

    1 pound fresh green beans, trimmed
    1 tablespoon reduced-sodium soy sauce
    2 teaspoons canola oil
    1 teaspoon sugar
    1 teaspoon cider vinegar
    1 teaspoon sesame oil
  1/4 teaspoon salt
    2 teaspoons sesame seeds, toasted

Place the beans in a large saucepan and cover with water. Bring to a boil. Cook, uncovered, for 8-10 minutes or until the beans are crisp-tender. Drain and rinse in cold water; pat dry. Place in a serving bowl.

In a small bowl, whisk the soy sauce, canola oil, sugar, vinegar, sesame oil and salt. Pour over beans and toss to coat. Sprinkle with sesame seeds; toss again. Serve at room temperature.

NUTRITION FACTS: 3/4 cup equals 65 calories, 3 g fat (trace saturated fat), 0 cholesterol, 238 mg sodium, 7 g carbohydrate, 3 g fiber, 1 g protein. **DIABETIC EXCHANGES:** 1 vegetable, 1/2 fat.

TASTY TIP

It's easy to add a splash of color to Sesame Green Bean Salad. Simply slice a few cherry tomatoes in half and gently toss them with the beans right before serving.

Delicious Apple Salad

MEAT-LESS

PREP/TOTAL TIME: 15 Min.   **YIELD:** 6 Servings

This yummy fruit salad was a favorite of my great-grandmother's. My family always enjoys it, and I'm happy knowing it's good for them, too.   —Sue Gronholz, Beaver Dam, Wisconsin

    3 cups cubed Golden *and* Red Delicious apples (1/2-inch cubes)
    2 tablespoons lemon juice
    1 cup chopped celery
    1 cup miniature marshmallows
  2/3 cup fat-free mayonnaise
  1/2 cup chopped pecans *or* walnuts

In a large bowl, toss apples with lemon juice. Add celery and marshmallows. Stir in mayonnaise. Just before serving, stir in nuts. Serve immediately or refrigerate.

NUTRITION FACTS: 3/4 cup equals 152 calories, 8 g fat (1 g saturated fat), 3 mg cholesterol, 233 mg sodium, 21 g carbohydrate, 3 g fiber, 1 g protein. **DIABETIC EXCHANGES:** 1 starch, 1 fat, 1/2 fruit.

Garden Shell Salad

FAT ↓ MEAT-LESS

(PICTURED BELOW)

PREP: 30 Min. + Chilling   YIELD: 8 Servings

Fresh basil marries the flavors of this splendid salad. I lightly dress the dish so it's versatile enough to complement most any meal.
— Kathy Glasgow, Marysville, California

- 8 ounces uncooked small pasta shells
- 2 cups frozen peas
- 1 cup thinly sliced celery
- 1/2 cup chopped sweet red pepper
- 1/4 cup chopped onion
- 2/3 cup fat-free mayonnaise
- 1 tablespoon white balsamic vinegar
- 1 tablespoon minced fresh basil *or* 1 teaspoon dried basil
- 1 teaspoon Dijon mustard
- 1/4 teaspoon salt
- 1/4 teaspoon pepper

Cook pasta according to package directions, adding the peas during the last 2-3 minutes of cooking time. Drain and rinse in cold water.

In a large bowl, combine the pasta, peas, celery, red pepper and onion. In a small bowl, whisk the mayonnaise, vinegar, basil, mustard, salt and pepper. Pour over pasta mixture and toss to coat. Cover and refrigerate for at least 1 hour before serving.

NUTRITION FACTS: 3/4 cup equals 157 calories, 1 g fat (trace saturated fat), 2 mg cholesterol, 380 mg sodium, 31 g carbohydrate, 3 g fiber, 6 g protein. DIABETIC EXCHANGE: 2 starch.

TASTY TIP
To turn Garden Shell Salad into a healthy main course, Kathy Glasgow likes to stir in a can of drained tuna.

Asian Cabbage Slaw

SALT ↓ CARB ↓ MEAT-LESS

(PICTURED ABOVE)

PREP/TOTAL TIME: 25 Min.   YIELD: 4 Servings

Never one to stick to tradition, I experimented with a recipe I had for Asian slaw by adding fruit and nuts. I hope you like it as much as I do.
— Lillian Julow, Gainesville, Florida

- 3 cups shredded napa *or* Chinese cabbage
- 1 large navel orange, peeled and sectioned
- 1 cup julienned peeled jicama
- 1/4 cup chopped watercress
- 2 tablespoons canola oil
- 2 tablespoons rice wine vinegar
- 2 teaspoons sugar
- 3/4 teaspoon grated fresh gingerroot
- 3/4 teaspoon reduced-sodium soy sauce

Dash pepper
- 1 tablespoon chopped walnuts

In a large bowl, combine the cabbage, orange, jicama and watercress. In a small bowl, whisk the oil, vinegar, sugar, ginger, soy sauce and pepper. Pour over cabbage mixture and toss to coat. Sprinkle with walnuts. Serve immediately.

NUTRITION FACTS: 3/4 cup equals 132 calories, 8 g fat (1 g saturated fat), 0 cholesterol, 48 mg sodium, 13 g carbohydrate, 4 g fiber, 2 g protein. DIABETIC EXCHANGES: 1-1/2 fat, 1 vegetable, 1/2 fruit.

TASTY TIP
"I often add some cherries to the Asian Cabbage Slaw for extra sweetness," notes Lillian Julow.

Favorite Recipe Made Lighter

EVERY YEAR *Light & Tasty* home economist Pat Schmeling creates the perfect holiday menu for her family. "I ask each of my family members for their favorite food," Pat explains from her home in Wisconsin. "Holiday Salad is always requested by my daughter. It's a menu item that she and my entire family looks forward to having at Christmas."

With the delightful salad's pretty presentation and tangy taste, it's easy to see why it's become a holiday staple at Pat's house. "There's just enough sweetness from the apples to appeal to the younger people at my table, and yet the mustard and nutmeg give the salad a unique flavor that adults enjoy," she relates.

Though the recipe is fairly straightforward, lightening the vinaigrette proved to be a little complex. The makeover team knew they'd have to maintain a certain proportion of oil to vinegar to create a pleasing mouthfeel, yet they wanted to skim back the oil to make the dressing a bit healthier.

They rolled up their sleeves and began by decreasing the oil in the vinaigrette and adding a small amount of water to restore volume. They also cut back on vinegar to prevent the dressing from tasting too tart.

To save calories and fat, the original salad's cheese and nuts were pared down. With these changes, the teammates cut 182 calories and almost half of the fat. Now Pat's favorite salad is a healthy option on her Christmas menu.

Makeover Holiday Salad
(PICTURED ABOVE)

SALT CARB MEAT-LESS

PREP: 25 Min. + Chilling   **YIELD:** 12 Servings

    1/4 cup white wine vinegar
      3 tablespoons water
      1 tablespoon Dijon mustard
    3/4 teaspoon dill weed
    3/4 teaspoon ground nutmeg
    1/4 teaspoon salt
    1/4 teaspoon pepper
    1/3 cup olive oil
      4 large Red Delicious apples, cored and thinly sliced
    1/3 cup crumbled blue cheese
      3 tablespoons coarsely chopped walnuts, toasted
      9 cups torn romaine
      3 cups chopped watercress (about 1-1/2 bunches)

In a small bowl, whisk the vinegar, water, mustard, dill, nutmeg, salt and pepper. Slowly add oil while whisking. In a large bowl, combine the apples, blue cheese, walnuts and 3 tablespoons dressing; toss to coat. Cover and refrigerate for up to 4 hours. Cover and refrigerate remaining dressing.

Just before serving, combine romaine and watercress in a large salad bowl; drizzle with remaining dressing and toss to coat. Divide among salad plates; top with apple mixture.

NUTRITION FACTS: 1 serving equals 129 calories, 9 g fat (2 g saturated fat), 3 mg cholesterol, 130 mg sodium, 13 g carbohydrate, 3 g fiber, 2 g protein. **DIABETIC EXCHANGES:** 1-1/2 fat, 1 vegetable, 1 fruit.

Holiday Salad

CARB MEAT-LESS

PREP: 25 Min. + Chilling   **YIELD:** 12 Servings

    1/3 cup white wine vinegar
      1 tablespoon Dijon mustard
    3/4 teaspoon dill weed
    3/4 teaspoon ground nutmeg
    1/4 teaspoon salt
    1/4 teaspoon pepper
    3/4 cup olive oil
      4 large Red Delicious apples, cored and thinly sliced
    1/2 cup crumbled blue cheese
    1/3 cup walnut halves
      9 cups torn romaine
      3 cups chopped watercress (about 1-1/2 bunches)

In a small bowl, whisk the vinegar, mustard, dill, nutmeg, salt and pepper. Slowly add oil while whisking. In a large bowl, combine the apples, blue cheese, walnuts and 3 tablespoons dressing; toss to coat. Cover and refrigerate for up to 4 hours. Cover and refrigerate remaining dressing.

Just before serving, combine romaine and watercress in a large salad bowl; drizzle with remaining dressing and toss to coat. Divide among 12 salad plates; top with apple mixture.

NUTRITION FACTS: 1 serving equals 211 calories, 17 g fat (3 g saturated fat), 4 mg cholesterol, 156 mg sodium, 13 g carbohydrate, 3 g fiber, 3 g protein.

MAKEOVER TIP
When you cut back on oil and vinegar, add a small amount of water to make up the difference in a vinaigrette.

Spinach with Hot Bacon Dressing

CARB ▼

PREP/TOTAL TIME: 30 Min. **YIELD:** 6 Servings

This warm and hearty spinach-and-bacon salad offers cold-weather comfort at any meal. The L&T staff created a glossy dressing with a hint of celery seed for a special touch.

> 8 cups torn fresh spinach
> 3 bacon strips, diced
> 1/2 cup chopped red onion
> 2 tablespoons brown sugar
> 2 tablespoons cider vinegar
> 1/4 teaspoon salt
> 1/4 teaspoon ground mustard
> 1/8 teaspoon celery seed
> 1/8 teaspoon pepper
> 1 teaspoon cornstarch
> 1/3 cup cold water

Place spinach in a large salad bowl; set aside. In a small nonstick skillet, cook bacon over medium heat until crisp. Using a slotted spoon, remove to paper towels to drain.

In the drippings, saute onion until tender. Stir in the brown sugar, vinegar, salt, mustard, celery seed and pepper. Combine cornstarch and water until smooth; stir into skillet. Bring to a boil; cook and stir for 1-2 minutes or until thickened.

Remove from the heat; pour over the spinach and toss to coat. Sprinkle with the bacon. Serve immediately.

NUTRITION FACTS: 3/4 cup equals 97 calories, 7 g fat (2 g saturated fat), 8 mg cholesterol, 215 mg sodium, 8 g carbohydrate, 1 g fiber, 2 g protein. **DIABETIC EXCHANGES:** 1-1/2 fat, 1 vegetable.

Buffet Rice Salad

PREP: 30 Min. + Cooling **YIELD:** 12 Servings

This chilled dish goes well with grilled foods. The green pepper, radishes and cucumber add color and crunch while complementing the cubed ham and the from-scratch vinaigrette.
—Josie Varro, Coquitlam, British Columbia

> 1 cup uncooked instant rice
> 1/3 cup canola oil
> 3 tablespoons white vinegar
> 1/2 teaspoon dried oregano
> 1/2 teaspoon Dijon mustard
> 1 garlic clove, minced
> 1/4 teaspoon salt
> 1/8 teaspoon pepper
> 1 can (16 ounces) kidney beans, rinsed and drained
> 1-1/2 cups frozen peas, thawed
> 1 cup cubed fully cooked lean ham
> 1 cup sliced radishes
> 1 small green pepper, diced
> 1/2 cup chopped cucumber
> 1/2 cup chopped green onions
> 1/4 cup minced fresh parsley
> 10 cherry tomatoes, halved

Cook rice according to package directions. Cool to room temperature. For dressing, in a small bowl, combine the oil, vinegar, oregano, mustard, garlic, salt and pepper.

In a large bowl, combine the rice, beans, peas, ham, radishes, green pepper, cucumber, onions and parsley. Just before serving, add dressing and toss to coat. Top with tomatoes.

NUTRITION FACTS: 2/3 cup equals 155 calories, 7 g fat (1 g saturated fat), 4 mg cholesterol, 287 mg sodium, 17 g carbohydrate, 3 g fiber, 6 g protein. **DIABETIC EXCHANGES:** 1-1/2 fat, 1 starch.

Black-Eyed Pea Salad

MEAT-LESS

(PICTURED BELOW)

PREP/TOTAL TIME: 15 Min. **YIELD:** 4 Servings

A homemade dressing helps marry the flavors of this creamy salad. It is a wonderful contribution to a spring luncheon or barbecue buffet in the summertime. —Olive Foemmel, Chili, Wisconsin

> 1 can (15-1/2 ounces) black-eyed peas, rinsed and drained
> 1 celery rib, chopped
> 1 tablespoon finely chopped onion
> 1 tablespoon canola oil
> 1 tablespoon cider vinegar
> 1 tablespoon reduced-fat mayonnaise
> 1/4 teaspoon salt
> Dash cayenne pepper
> 1 medium tomato, seeded and diced

In a bowl, combine the peas, celery and onion. In another bowl, whisk the oil, vinegar, mayonnaise, salt and cayenne. Stir into vegetable mixture. Refrigerate until serving. Stir in tomato just before serving.

NUTRITION FACTS: 3/4 cup equals 133 calories, 5 g fat (trace saturated fat), 1 mg cholesterol, 321 mg sodium, 17 g carbohydrate, 3 g fiber, 6 g protein. **DIABETIC EXCHANGES:** 1 starch, 1 fat.

Shrimp 'n' Shells Salad

(PICTURED BELOW)

FAT

PREP: 20 Min. + Chilling   **YIELD:** 9 Servings

I received this recipe from a friend. It can even be served as a light dinner with toasted garlic bread. I serve the low-fat salad on a bed of fresh greens. —Heather Richardson, St. Paul, Virginia

> 8 ounces uncooked small pasta shells
> 1 cup fat-free mayonnaise
> 1/4 cup grated Parmesan cheese
> 1/4 cup 1% buttermilk
> 1/3 cup finely chopped onion
> 2 tablespoons minced fresh parsley
> 1-1/2 teaspoons minced fresh basil
> 1/2 teaspoon salt
> 1/2 teaspoon pepper
> 1 pound cooked medium shrimp, peeled and deveined
> 1/4 cup frozen peas, thawed
> 1/4 cup diced pimientos
> 1 medium tomato, seeded and chopped
> 2 green onions, thinly sliced

Cook pasta according to package directions. Meanwhile, for dressing, combine the mayonnaise, Parmesan cheese, buttermilk, onion, parsley, basil, salt and pepper in a blender or food processor; cover and process until blended.

Drain the pasta and rinse in cold water. In a large bowl, combine the pasta, shrimp, peas, pimientos, tomato and onions. Add dressing and toss to coat. Cover and refrigerate until chilled.

NUTRITION FACTS: 3/4 cup equals 191 calories, 3 g fat (1 g saturated fat), 81 mg cholesterol, 477 mg sodium, 26 g carbohydrate, 2 g fiber, 15 g protein. **DIABETIC EXCHANGES:** 1-1/2 starch, 1 lean meat, 1/2 fat.

Tomato Artichoke Salad

FAT CARB MEAT-LESS

PREP: 15 Min. + Chilling   **YIELD:** 4 Servings

Here's a salad with the rich flavor of artichokes, olives and summer-ripe tomatoes. It makes a nutritious accompaniment for nearly any entree. —Clara Coulston, Washington Court House, Ohio

> 1/4 cup lemon juice
> 1/4 cup chopped seeded peeled cucumber
> 2 tablespoons fat-free plain yogurt
> 1/2 teaspoon dried oregano
> 1/4 teaspoon salt
> 1/4 teaspoon pepper
> 1 can (14 ounces) water-packed artichoke hearts, rinsed, drained and halved
> 1 can (2-1/4 ounces) sliced ripe olives, drained
> 2 medium tomatoes, seeded and chopped
> 1/2 cup julienned firm silken tofu
> 1/2 cup chopped red onion

For dressing, in a blender or food processor, combine the lemon juice, cucumber, yogurt, oregano, salt and pepper; cover and process until blended.

In a bowl, combine the artichokes, olives, tomatoes, tofu and onion. Add dressing and toss to coat. Cover and refrigerate for at least 30 minutes before serving.

NUTRITION FACTS: 1 cup equals 102 calories, 3 g fat (trace saturated fat), trace cholesterol, 555 mg sodium, 15 g carbohydrate, 2 g fiber, 6 g protein. **DIABETIC EXCHANGES:** 2 vegetable, 1/2 starch, 1/2 fat.

Yogurt-Herb Salad Dressing

FAT SALT CARB

PREP: 10 Min. + Chilling   **YIELD:** 1 Cup

We enjoy this tasty dressing with baby spinach greens, sliced tomatoes and onions. It's even wonderful drizzled over fat-free cottage cheese. —Gwen Klawunder, Kenai, Alaska

> 1 cup (8 ounces) fat-free plain yogurt
> 1 tablespoon white vinegar
> 1 tablespoon cider vinegar
> 1 teaspoon honey
> 1 tablespoon dried minced onion
> 1-1/2 teaspoons Dijon mustard
> 3/4 teaspoon dill weed
> 3/4 teaspoon Italian seasoning
> 3/4 teaspoon prepared mustard
> 1/4 teaspoon seasoned salt
> 1/8 teaspoon pepper

In a small bowl, whisk the yogurt, vinegars and honey. Stir in the remaining ingredients. Cover and refrigerate for at least 1 hour before serving.

NUTRITION FACTS: 2 tablespoons equals 19 calories, trace fat (trace saturated fat), 1 mg cholesterol, 94 mg sodium, 4 g carbohydrate, trace fiber, 1 g protein. **DIABETIC EXCHANGE:** Free food.

TASTY TIP

When preparing Yogurt-Herb Salad Dressing you can swap out the dill for your favorite herb or seasoning.

Sweet-Sour Spinach Salad

(PICTURED ABOVE)

PREP/TOTAL TIME: 20 Min. **YIELD:** 6 Servings

When I tasted this tangy salad at a cookout, I immediately asked for the recipe. Even though I pared it down and added more veggies, it's still a hit. —Jennifer Cain, Bel Air, Maryland

  1 package (10 ounces) fresh spinach, torn
  1 can (8 ounces) sliced water chestnuts, drained and halved
1/2 cup thinly sliced yellow summer squash
1/2 cup sliced fresh mushrooms
1/3 cup garbanzo beans *or* chickpeas, rinsed and drained
1/4 cup chopped onion
  2 tablespoons sugar
  2 tablespoons canola oil
  2 tablespoons ketchup
  1 tablespoon water
  1 tablespoon cider vinegar
  1 garlic clove, minced
1/4 teaspoon salt
  3 bacon strips, cooked and crumbled

In a large bowl, combine the spinach, water chestnuts, squash, mushrooms, garbanzo beans and onion. In a small bowl, whisk the sugar, oil, ketchup, water, vinegar, garlic and salt. Pour over spinach mixture and toss to coat evenly. Sprinkle with bacon. Serve immediately.

NUTRITION FACTS: 1-1/3 cups equals 133 calories, 7 g fat (1 g saturated fat), 3 mg cholesterol, 247 mg sodium, 17 g carbohydrate, 4 g fiber, 4 g protein. **DIABETIC EXCHANGES:** 1 starch, 1 fat.

Veggie Pasta Salad

PREP: 20 Min. **COOK:** 15 Min. + Chilling **YIELD:** 10 Servings

This colorful pasta salad with fresh vegetables has a pleasant balsamic vinegar dressing. Fix it ahead of time and you can enjoy sensational meatless meals all week.
 —Melissa Marsh, Bethlehem, Pennsylvania

  8 ounces uncooked tricolor spiral pasta
  3 small tomatoes, chopped
  1 cup thinly sliced green onions
  1 cup *each* chopped celery, sweet red pepper, zucchini and carrots
  3 tablespoons balsamic vinegar
  2 tablespoons minced fresh basil *or* 2 teaspoons dried basil
  2 tablespoons olive oil
  1 tablespoon sugar
  1 tablespoon minced fresh oregano *or* 1 teaspoon dried oregano
  2 garlic cloves, minced
  1 teaspoon salt
1/8 teaspoon pepper
1/2 cup grated Parmesan cheese

Cook pasta according to package directions. Meanwhile, in a large bowl, combine the vegetables, vinegar, basil, oil, sugar, oregano, garlic, salt and pepper. Drain pasta and rinse in cold water; stir into vegetable mixture. Add Parmesan cheese; toss to coat. Cover and refrigerate for at least 2 hours before serving.

NUTRITION FACTS: 1 cup equals 108 calories, 5 g fat (1 g saturated fat), 4 mg cholesterol, 352 mg sodium, 13 g carbohydrate, 2 g fiber, 4 g protein. **DIABETIC EXCHANGES:** 1 starch, 1/2 fat.

Greens and Roasted Beets

(PICTURED ABOVE)

SALT CARB MEAT-LESS

PREP: 10 Min. **BAKE:** 1 Hour + Cooling **YIELD:** 4 Servings

A refreshing from-scratch dressing is the ideal topping to this colorful salad with bright beets, mixed greens and mandarin oranges. Our home economists think the salad would be a dressy accompaniment to any Thanksgiving menu.

- 2 whole fresh beets
- 3 cups torn mixed salad greens
- 1 can (11 ounces) mandarin oranges, drained
- 2 tablespoons cider vinegar
- 2 teaspoons orange juice concentrate
- 1/4 teaspoon ground mustard
- 1/4 teaspoon dried thyme
- 1/8 teaspoon pepper
- 5 teaspoons canola oil
- 1 teaspoon sesame oil

Spray beets with nonstick cooking spray. Place in an ungreased 8-in. square baking dish. Cover and bake at 350° for 60-70 minutes or until tender; cool. Peel and cut into 1/2-in. cubes.

In a large salad bowl, combine greens, beets and oranges. In a blender, combine the vinegar, orange juice concentrate, mustard, thyme and pepper; cover and process until blended. While processing, gradually add canola oil and sesame oil. Drizzle over salad and toss to coat. Serve immediately.

NUTRITION FACTS: 1-1/4 cups equals 122 calories, 7 g fat (1 g saturated fat), 0 cholesterol, 30 mg sodium, 14 g carbohydrate, 2 g fiber, 2 g protein. **DIABETIC EXCHANGES:** 1-1/2 fat, 1 vegetable, 1/2 fruit.

Wild Rice Turkey Salad

PREP: 20 Min. **COOK:** 20 Min. + Chilling **YIELD:** 6 Servings

This tasty turkey dish offers a wonderful blend of flavors. With sweet grapes and apple, a dash of cinnamon and crunchy vegetables, it'll appeal to young and old alike.

—Meredith Berg, Hudson, Wisconsin

- 2 cups cubed cooked turkey breast
- 2 cups cooked long grain rice
- 1-1/2 cups cooked wild rice
- 1-1/2 cups green grapes, halved
- 1/2 cup thinly sliced celery
- 1/2 cup chopped water chestnuts
- 1/2 cup fat-free mayonnaise
- 3/4 teaspoon salt
- 1/4 teaspoon ground cinnamon
- 1 cup chopped red apple
- 6 lettuce leaves
- 6 tablespoons slivered almonds, toasted

In a large bowl, combine the first six ingredients. In a small bowl, combine the mayonnaise, salt and cinnamon; stir into turkey mixture until combined. Cover and refrigerate for at least 1 hour.

Just before serving, stir in apple. Serve in a lettuce-lined bowl; sprinkle with almonds.

NUTRITION FACTS: 1-1/3 cups equals 279 calories, 5 g fat (1 g saturated fat), 42 mg cholesterol, 494 mg sodium, 40 g carbohydrate, 4 g fiber, 19 g protein. **DIABETIC EXCHANGES:** 2 very lean meat, 1-1/2 starch, 1 fruit, 1/2 fat.

Cran-Orange Gelatin Salad
(PICTURED BELOW)

PREP: 45 Min. + Chilling   YIELD: 15 Servings

When I saw this gelatin salad in a flyer, I decided to make it lighter. I like to serve it as a fruit salad, but others may like it for a sweet treat after supper.   —Eva DeWolf, Erwin, Tennessee

       1 can (15 ounces) mandarin oranges
       2 packages (.3 ounce *each*) sugar-free cranberry gelatin
1-1/2 cups boiling water
       1 can (16 ounces) whole-berry cranberry sauce
1-1/2 cups crushed salt-free pretzels
       6 tablespoons butter, melted
Sugar substitute equivalent to 5 tablespoons sugar, *divided*
       1 package (8 ounces) fat-free cream cheese
       1 carton (8 ounces) frozen reduced-fat whipped topping, thawed

Drain oranges, reserving juice in a 2-cup measuring cup; set oranges and juice aside.

In a large bowl, dissolve the gelatin in boiling water. Stir in cranberry sauce until melted. Add enough cold water to the reserved juice to measure 1-1/2 cups; add to gelatin mixture. Stir in the oranges. Chill until partially set.

Meanwhile, in a large bowl, combine the pretzels, butter and 2 tablespoons sugar substitute. Press into an ungreased 13-in. x 9-in. x 2-in. dish; chill.

In a small mixing bowl, beat cream cheese and remaining sugar substitute until smooth. Fold in whipped topping. Spread over crust. Spoon gelatin mixture over cream cheese layer. Chill for at least 3 hours or until set.

NUTRITION FACTS: 1 piece equals 183 calories, 7 g fat (5 g saturated fat), 13 mg cholesterol, 185 mg sodium, 26 g carbohydrate, 1 g fiber, 4 g protein. **DIABETIC EXCHANGES:** 2 starch, 1 fat.

Editor's Note: This recipe was tested with Splenda No Calorie Sweetener.

Shrimp Orzo Salad
(PICTURED ABOVE)

PREP/TOTAL TIME: 30 Min.   YIELD: 16 Servings

A half hour is all you need for this delightful crowd-pleaser. Offering plenty of shrimp, artichoke hearts, olives and a host of herbs, it's a tasty alternative to typical shrimp salads. It completes any buffet.
    —Ginger Johnson, Pottstown, Pennsylvania

       1 package (16 ounces) orzo pasta
    3/4 pound cooked medium shrimp, peeled, deveined and cut into thirds
       1 cup finely chopped green pepper
       1 cup finely chopped sweet red pepper
       1 can (14 ounces) water-packed artichoke hearts, rinsed, drained and quartered
    3/4 cup finely chopped red onion
    1/2 cup minced fresh parsley
    1/3 cup chopped fresh dill
    1/3 cup chopped pimiento-stuffed olives
    1/2 cup white wine vinegar
       3 garlic cloves, minced
       1 teaspoon salt
    1/2 teaspoon dried basil
    1/2 teaspoon dried oregano
    1/2 teaspoon pepper
    1/4 cup olive oil

Cook pasta according to package directions; drain and rinse in cold water. Place in a large bowl; add the shrimp, peppers, artichokes, onion, parsley, dill and olives.

In a small bowl, combine the vinegar, garlic, salt, basil, oregano and pepper. Slowly whisk in oil. Pour over pasta mixture and toss to coat. Refrigerate until serving.

NUTRITION FACTS: 3/4 cup equals 179 calories, 5 g fat (1 g saturated fat), 32 mg cholesterol, 297 mg sodium, 25 g carbohydrate, 2 g fiber, 9 g protein. **DIABETIC EXCHANGES:** 1-1/2 starch, 1 lean meat, 1 vegetable.

Jicama Romaine Salad

(PICTURED ABOVE)

FAT SALT CARB MEAT-LESS

PREP/TOTAL TIME: 15 Min.   YIELD: 8 Servings

My family and I are real fans of jicama. It's juicy, sweet and adds crunch and heat to this wonderful salad with feisty Mexican flair.
—Stephanie Homme, Baton Rouge, Louisiana

    4 cups torn romaine
    4 cups julienned peeled jicama
    2 medium tomatoes, cut into thin wedges
  1/2 cup shredded reduced-fat cheddar cheese
CHILI PEPPER DRESSING:
    2 tablespoons fat-free mayonnaise
    1 tablespoon fat-free milk
    1 tablespoon sour cream
    1 garlic clove, minced
    1 teaspoon dried oregano
  1/2 teaspoon ground cumin
  1/8 teaspoon hot pepper sauce
  1/4 cup chopped green chilies

In a large salad bowl, combine the romaine, jicama, tomatoes and cheese. In a small bowl, combine the mayonnaise, milk, sour cream, garlic, oregano, cumin and hot sauce; stir in chilies. Pour over salad and toss to coat. Serve immediately.

NUTRITION FACTS: 3/4 cup equals 67 calories, 2 g fat (1 g saturated fat), 7 mg cholesterol, 114 mg sodium, 10 g carbohydrate, 4 g fiber, 3 g protein. DIABETIC EXCHANGES: 2 vegetable, 1/2 fat.

Broccoli Grape Salad

SALT MEAT-LESS

PREP: 15 Min. + Chilling   YIELD: 9 Servings

This fresh and lovely broccoli salad turns ordinary luncheons into dressy affairs. —Nancy Warman, Centerville, Ohio

    4 cups fresh broccoli florets, cut into small pieces
1-1/2 cups seedless red *or* green grapes, halved
    1 cup chopped celery
    1 cup raisins
  1/3 cup reduced-fat mayonnaise
  1/4 cup fat-free plain yogurt
    2 tablespoons sugar
    1 tablespoon cider vinegar
  1/4 cup sunflower kernels

In a large bowl, combine the broccoli, grapes, celery and raisins. In a small bowl, combine the mayonnaise, yogurt, sugar and vinegar. Pour over broccoli mixture and mix well. Cover and refrigerate for at least 1 hour. Just before serving, stir in sunflower kernels.

NUTRITION FACTS: 3/4 cup equals 145 calories, 5 g fat (1 g saturated fat), 3 mg cholesterol, 120 mg sodium, 24 g carbohydrate, 2 g fiber, 3 g protein. DIABETIC EXCHANGES: 1 vegetable, 1 fruit, 1 fat.

Cucumbers with Dill

FAT CARB MEAT-LESS

(PICTURED BELOW)

PREP: 20 Min. + Chilling   YIELD: 6 Servings

Our Test Kitchen sprinkled these cucumber slices with salt and let them stand in a colander to draw out excess water so they stay crisp when set on a buffet. Try them with grilled entrees.

    2 medium cucumbers, sliced 1/8 inch thick
    1 tablespoon kosher salt
  1/2 cup white vinegar
  1/4 cup snipped fresh dill
    3 tablespoons sugar
  1/2 teaspoon coarsely ground pepper

Place cucumber slices in a colander over a plate; sprinkle with salt and toss. Let stand for 15 minutes, stirring once. Rinse and drain well.

In a large bowl, combine the vinegar, dill, sugar and pepper. Add cucumbers and toss to coat. Cover and refrigerate for at least 15 minutes before serving.

NUTRITION FACTS: 2/3 cup equals 40 calories, trace fat (0 saturated fat), 0 cholesterol, 941 mg sodium, 9 g carbohydrate, 1 g fiber, 1 g protein. DIABETIC EXCHANGES: 1 vegetable, 1/2 starch.

Honey-Mustard Salad Dressing

SALT CARB ▼ ▼

(PICTURED ABOVE)

PREP: 10 Min. + Chilling   **YIELD:** About 1 Cup

No one believes this thick, creamy dressing is actually light. Ground mustard and red wine vinegar make it tangy, while honey sweetens it a little bit.   —Jill Smith, Irmo, South Carolina

  1/2 cup reduced-fat mayonnaise
  1/2 cup reduced-fat sour cream
    3 tablespoons honey
    2 tablespoons red wine vinegar
    2 tablespoons fat-free milk
    2 teaspoons lime juice
    1 teaspoon ground mustard
  1/8 teaspoon garlic powder
  1/8 teaspoon dried thyme
  1/8 teaspoon dried savory
  1/8 teaspoon pepper
Dash celery salt

In a small bowl, whisk all ingredients until blended. Cover and refrigerate for at least 2 hours before serving.

NUTRITION FACTS: 2 tablespoons equals 86 calories, 6 g fat (2 g saturated fat), 9 mg cholesterol, 128 mg sodium, 8 g carbohydrate, trace fiber, 1 g protein. **DIABETIC EXCHANGES:** 1 fat, 1/2 starch.

White and Black Bean Salad

FAT MEAT-▼ LESS

PREP/TOTAL TIME: 15 Min.   **YIELD:** 8 Servings

Filled with beans, this colorful salad makes a good-for-you addition to any meal. I like to keep dishes like this one on hand for my growing teenage son.   —Darlene Strommer, Avon, Minnesota

    1 cup chopped red onion
    2 teaspoons olive oil
  1/3 cup red wine vinegar
  1/4 cup chopped green pepper
  1/4 cup chopped sweet red pepper
    2 tablespoons minced fresh parsley
Sugar substitute equivalent to 1 teaspoon sugar
  1/4 teaspoon salt
  1/4 teaspoon pepper
    1 can (15-1/2 ounces) great northern beans, rinsed and drained
    1 can (15 ounces) black beans, rinsed and drained

In a small nonstick skillet, cook onion in oil until tender. In a large bowl, combine the vinegar, peppers, parsley, sugar substitute, salt, pepper and onion. Stir in beans. Chill until serving.

NUTRITION FACTS: 2/3 cup equals 110 calories, 1 g fat (trace saturated fat), 0 cholesterol, 305 mg sodium, 19 g carbohydrate, 5 g fiber, 6 g protein. **DIABETIC EXCHANGES:** 1 starch, 1 very lean meat.

Editor's Note: This recipe was tested with Splenda No Calorie Sweetener.

2 green onions
3/4 cup loosely packed cilantro leaves
2 garlic cloves, minced
3 tablespoons honey
2 teaspoons sesame seed oil
2 teaspoons reduced-sodium soy sauce
1/2 to 3/4 teaspoon crushed red pepper flakes
1/2 teaspoon salt
1-1/2 cups soft tofu (about 10 ounces)
1/2 cup rice wine vinegar

Thinly slice one green onion; set aside. Cut the other onion into pieces; place in a blender. Add the cilantro, garlic, honey, oil, soy sauce, red pepper flakes and salt; cover and process until blended. Add tofu and vinegar; cover and process until smooth.

Transfer to a small bowl; stir in the sliced onion. Cover and refrigerate for at least 1 hour before serving.

NUTRITION FACTS: 2 tablespoons equals 29 calories, 1 g fat (trace saturated fat), 0 cholesterol, 101 mg sodium, 4 g carbohydrate, trace fiber, 1 g protein. **DIABETIC EXCHANGE:** 1/2 fat.

Rice and Barley Salad

MEAT-LESS

PREP: 15 Min.   **COOK:** 15 Min. + Chilling   **YIELD:** 8 Servings

Chock-full of colorful veggies and loaded with fiber, this hearty, mouth-watering salad is almost a meal in itself.

—Lee Massa, Mulberry, Kansas

1 cup water
1/2 cup quick-cooking barley
1/2 cup boiling water
1/2 cup uncooked instant rice
1 can (15 ounces) black beans, rinsed and drained
1 *each* large green and sweet yellow pepper, chopped
1 jar (2 ounces) diced pimientos, drained
1/3 cup chopped sweet onion
1/4 cup minced fresh parsley
3 tablespoons olive oil
2 tablespoons red wine vinegar
2 garlic cloves, minced
1/2 teaspoon sugar
1/2 teaspoon salt
1/2 teaspoon ground cumin
1/4 teaspoon pepper
1/8 teaspoon cayenne pepper

In a small saucepan, bring water and barley to a boil. Reduce heat; cover and simmer for 10-12 minutes or until barley is tender. Meanwhile, in a small bowl, combine the boiling water and rice; cover and let stand for 5 minutes. Fluff with a fork.

In a large bowl, combine the beans, peppers, pimientos, onion, parsley, barley and rice.

In a small bowl, whisk the oil, vinegar, garlic, sugar and seasonings. Stir into barley mixture. Cover and refrigerate for at least 30 minutes before serving.

NUTRITION FACTS: 3/4 cup equals 170 calories, 6 g fat (1 g saturated fat), 0 cholesterol, 253 mg sodium, 26 g carbohydrate, 5 g fiber, 5 g protein. **DIABETIC EXCHANGES:** 1-1/2 starch, 1 vegetable, 1 fat.

Creamy Veggie Salad

CARB MEAT-LESS

(PICTURED ABOVE)

PREP: 10 Min. + Chilling   **YIELD:** 9 Servings

This delicious, light recipe with its hint of horseradish has been a favorite for years. It's so refreshing on a hot summer day and always receives compliments. —Gene Kelly, Fort Myers, Florida

4 cups fresh broccoli florets
4 cups fresh cauliflowerets
1 package (10 ounces) frozen peas, thawed
5 green onions, sliced
1/2 cup reduced-fat sour cream
1/2 cup reduced-fat mayonnaise
1 to 2 tablespoons prepared horseradish
1/4 teaspoon salt
1/8 teaspoon pepper

In a large bowl, combine the broccoli, cauliflower, peas and onions. In a small bowl, combine the remaining ingredients; mix well. Pour over vegetables and toss to coat. Cover and refrigerate for several hours or overnight.

NUTRITION FACTS: 1 cup equals 109 calories, 6 g fat (2 g saturated fat), 9 mg cholesterol, 235 mg sodium, 11 g carbohydrate, 4 g fiber, 4 g protein. **DIABETIC EXCHANGES:** 1 vegetable, 1 fat, 1/2 starch.

Creamy Cilantro Dressing

FAT SALT CARB

PREP: 10 Min. + Chilling   **YIELD:** 2 Cups

This thick dressing makes a healthy choice when topping an assortment of mixed greens. —Nancy Wherry, Chula Vista, California

Arugula Salad with Sugared Pecans
(PICTURED BELOW)

SALT CARB MEAT-
LESS

PREP/TOTAL TIME: 25 Min. **YIELD:** 6 Servings

Sugared pecans add a hint of sweetness to this picture-perfect salad from the L&T Test Kitchen. Keep a close eye on the nuts because they toast quickly.

- 3/4 teaspoon butter
- 1/3 cup chopped pecans
- 1 teaspoon sugar
- 4 cups torn leaf lettuce
- 2 cups fresh arugula *or* baby spinach
- 1 small fennel bulb, thinly sliced
- 1/2 cup grape tomatoes
- 2 tablespoons lemon juice
- 2 tablespoons olive oil
- 1 tablespoon water
- 1 tablespoon honey
- 1/8 teaspoon salt

In a small, heavy skillet, melt butter. Add pecans; cook over medium heat until toasted, about 4 minutes. Sprinkle with sugar; cook and stir for 2-4 minutes or until sugar is melted. Spread on foil to cool.

In a large salad bowl, combine the lettuce, arugula, fennel and tomatoes. In a jar with a tight-fitting lid, combine the remaining ingredients; shake well. Drizzle over salad and toss to coat. Top with sugared pecans. Serve immediately.

NUTRITION FACTS: 1 cup equals 127 calories, 10 g fat (1 g saturated fat), 1 mg cholesterol, 81 mg sodium, 10 g carbohydrate, 3 g fiber, 2 g protein. **DIABETIC EXCHANGES:** 2 fat, 1 vegetable.

TASTY TIP
The sugared nuts in the arugula salad make a sweet addition to other dishes, too. Sprinkle them over stir-fries, ice cream treats, sweet potatoes, French toast, or even poached or grilled fruit.

Grapefruit Avocado Salad

 SALT CARB MEAT-LESS

(PICTURED ABOVE)

PREP/TOTAL TIME: 20 Min.   YIELD: 8 Servings

I brighten lettuce greens with the fruity tartness of pink grapefruit and orange juice. This elegant citrus salad pairs well with most entrees.   —Mary Relyea, Canastota, New York

　　6　cups torn leaf lettuce
　　3　large pink grapefruit, peeled and sectioned
　　1　medium ripe avocado, peeled and sliced
　　1　small red onion, thinly sliced
　1/4　cup orange juice
　　3　tablespoons olive oil
　　1　tablespoon lemon juice
　3/4　teaspoon ground cumin
　　1　garlic clove, minced
Dash hot pepper sauce
　1/4　cup chopped pecans, toasted

Divide lettuce among eight salad plates. Arrange the grapefruit, avocado and onion over lettuce. In a small bowl, whisk the orange juice, oil, lemon juice, cumin, garlic and hot sauce; drizzle over salads. Sprinkle with pecans.

NUTRITION FACTS: 1 serving equals 165 calories, 12 g fat (2 g saturated fat), 0 cholesterol, 7 mg sodium, 15 g carbohydrate, 4 g fiber, 2 g protein. DIABETIC EXCHANGES: 2 fat, 1 vegetable, 1/2 fruit.

Caesar Dressing

 CARB

PREP: 15 Min. + Chilling   YIELD: 1-2/3 Cups

Looking for a new and different salad dressing to whisk up in minutes for special occasions? You can't miss with our home economists' light, savory Caesar blend. It really dresses up fresh greens!

　2/3　cup reduced-fat mayonnaise
　1/2　cup reduced-fat sour cream
　1/2　cup buttermilk
　　1　tablespoon red wine vinegar
　　1　tablespoon stone-ground mustard
　1-1/2　teaspoons lemon juice
　1-1/2　teaspoons Worcestershire sauce
　1/3　cup grated Parmigiano-Reggiano cheese
　　2　anchovy fillets, minced
　　2　garlic cloves, minced
　1/2　teaspoon coarsely ground pepper

In a small bowl, whisk the mayonnaise, sour cream, buttermilk, vinegar, mustard, lemon juice and Worcestershire sauce. Stir in the cheese, anchovies, garlic and pepper. Cover and refrigerate for at least 1 hour.

NUTRITION FACTS: 2 tablespoons equals 71 calories, 6 g fat (2 g saturated fat), 10 mg cholesterol, 205 mg sodium, 3 g carbohydrate, trace fiber, 2 g protein. DIABETIC EXCHANGE: 1 fat.

Side Dishes & More

Enhance tonight's menu with dinner accompaniments that not only complement the main course, but keep your healthy-eating commitments. Comforting rice and pasta specialties and colorful vegetable medleys are just some of the items offered here.

Greek-Style Squash, p. 70

Italian Broccoli with Peppers
(PICTURED ABOVE)

 FAT ↓ CARB ↓ MEAT-LESS

PREP/TOTAL TIME: 20 Min.   **YIELD:** 6 Servings

This cheese-topped vegetable medley goes with just about anything!
—Maureen McClanahan, St. Louis, Missouri

  6 cups water
  4 cups fresh broccoli florets
  1 medium sweet red pepper, julienned
  1 medium sweet yellow pepper, julienned
  1 tablespoon olive oil
  1 garlic clove, minced
  1 teaspoon dried oregano
1/2 teaspoon salt
1/4 teaspoon pepper
  1 medium ripe tomato, cut into wedges and seeded
  1 tablespoon grated Parmesan cheese

In a large saucepan, bring water to a boil. Add broccoli; cover and boil for 3 minutes. Drain and immediately place broccoli in ice water. Drain and pat dry.

In a large nonstick skillet, saute peppers in oil for 3 minutes or until crisp-tender. Add the broccoli, garlic, oregano, salt and pepper; saute 2 minutes longer. Add the tomato; heat through. Sprinkle with Parmesan cheese.

NUTRITION FACTS: 3/4 cup equals 55 calories, 3 g fat (1 g saturated fat), 1 mg cholesterol, 228 mg sodium, 7 g carbohydrate, 2 g fiber, 2 g protein. **DIABETIC EXCHANGES:** 1 vegetable, 1/2 fat.

SHOP SMART
You'll need about 2 pounds of fresh broccoli for the 4 cups of florets required of this side dish. And if you'd like to serve Italian Broccoli with Peppers for a main course, be sure to pick up a package of cooked chicken strips to stir into the medley.

Orange Ginger Carrots

FAT MEAT-LESS

PREP/TOTAL TIME: 20 Min.   YIELD: 4 Servings

Ginger and a splash of orange juice add extra zing to this colorful vegetable side dish. It comes together nicely on the stovetop, and, even though it's quite versatile, I think that it pairs especially well with baked ham.   —Joyce Guth, Mohnton, Pennsylvania

        3 cups sliced carrots
        1 tablespoon cornstarch
        1 tablespoon sugar
    1/2 teaspoon salt
    1/2 teaspoon ground ginger
    1/2 cup orange juice
        1 tablespoon butter

Place carrots and 1 in. of water in a small saucepan; bring to a boil. Reduce heat; cover and simmer for 8-10 minutes or until crisp-tender. Drain and keep warm.

In the same pan, combine the cornstarch, sugar, salt and ginger. Stir in orange juice until smooth. Bring to a boil; cook and stir for 1 minute or until thickened. Remove from the heat; stir in butter until melted. Add carrots and toss to coat.

NUTRITION FACTS: 3/4 cup equals 99 calories, 3 g fat (2 g saturated fat), 8 mg cholesterol, 355 mg sodium, 18 g carbohydrate, 3 g fiber, 1 g protein. DIABETIC EXCHANGES: 2 vegetable, 1/2 fruit, 1/2 fat.

Tabbouleh

FAT MEAT-LESS

PREP: 35 Min. + Chilling   YIELD: 10 Servings

This dish is so good and good for you that I have a special place in my garden for mint and parsley plants. This way, I can prepare it whenever I want to. It is best after it has chilled overnight.   —Marion Cosgrove, Fergus Falls, Minnesota

    1-1/4 cups bulgur
    1-1/2 cups boiling water
        2 medium tomatoes, diced
        1 cup chopped peeled cucumber
    3/4 cup minced fresh flat-leaf parsley
    1/2 cup thinly sliced green onions
        3 tablespoons minced fresh mint
    1-1/4 teaspoons salt
    1/2 teaspoon dill weed
    1/4 teaspoon celery salt
    1/3 cup lemon juice
        2 tablespoons olive oil

Place bulgur in a small bowl; cover with boiling water. Cover and let stand for 30 minutes or until water is absorbed.

In a large serving bowl, combine the tomatoes, cucumber, parsley, onions, mint, salt, dill and celery salt. Combine lemon juice and oil; pour over vegetable mixture and toss to coat. Stir in bulgur. Cover the tabbouleh and refrigerate at least 4 hours before serving.

NUTRITION FACTS: 3/4 cup equals 97 calories, 3 g fat (trace saturated fat), 0 cholesterol, 342 mg sodium, 16 g carbohydrate, 4 g fiber, 3 g protein. DIABETIC EXCHANGES: 1 starch, 1/2 fat.

Editor's Note: Look for bulgur in the cereal, rice or organic food aisle of your grocery store.

Lemon Roasted Potatoes

(PICTURED BELOW)

FAT

PREP: 10 Min.   BAKE: 35 Min.   YIELD: 6 Servings

These crispy potatoes are delicious with many meat and fish entrees. Tangy lemon permeates the entire side dish, giving the potatoes a marvelous flavor.   —Mitzi Sentiff, Alexandria, Virginia

        2 pounds small red potatoes, quartered
        1 medium lemon, halved and sliced
        1 tablespoon olive oil
        2 teaspoons minced fresh rosemary
    1/2 teaspoon salt
    1/8 teaspoon coarsely ground pepper

In a large bowl, combine all ingredients; toss to coat. Arrange in a single layer in a 15-in. x 10-in. x 1-in. baking pan coated with nonstick cooking spray. Bake at 425° for 35-40 minutes or until potatoes are golden and tender.

NUTRITION FACTS: 3/4 cup equals 132 calories, 2 g fat (trace saturated fat), 0 cholesterol, 207 mg sodium, 25 g carbohydrate, 3 g fiber, 3 g protein. DIABETIC EXCHANGES: 1-1/2 starch, 1/2 fat.

Roasted Dill Potatoes

(PICTURED BELOW)

MEAT-LESS

PREP: 15 Min. **BAKE:** 30 Min. **YIELD:** 4 Servings

Snipped dill breathes new life into red potatoes with this recipe. Zero cholesterol and only a few fat grams make it a heart-smart dinner accompaniment for everyday suppers.

—Kathrine Jimmie, Petersburg, Alaska

    2 pounds small red potatoes, thinly sliced
    1 tablespoon olive oil
    2 garlic cloves, minced
    2 tablespoons snipped fresh dill
1-1/4 teaspoons salt
  1/4 teaspoon pepper

Place the potatoes in a 15-in. x 10-in. x 1-in. baking pan coated with nonstick cooking spray. Drizzle with oil; sprinkle with garlic, dill, salt and pepper. Bake, uncovered, at 425° for 30-35 minutes or until golden brown, stirring every 10 minutes.

NUTRITION FACTS: 1 cup equals 196 calories, 4 g fat (1 g saturated fat), 0 cholesterol, 752 mg sodium, 37 g carbohydrate, 4 g fiber, 4 g protein. **DIABETIC EXCHANGES:** 2 starch, 1 fat.

Garlicky Kale

FAT MEAT-LESS

PREP: 20 Min. **COOK:** 15 Min. **YIELD:** 6 Servings

This warm and zippy side dish features fresh kale and sweet raisins. It tastes wonderful served hot or cold.

—Clara Coulston, Washington Court House, Ohio

1-1/2 pounds fresh kale
    3 cups water
    4 garlic cloves, minced
    1 teaspoon olive oil
  1/2 cup golden raisins
  1/4 cup pitted ripe olives, sliced
  1/4 teaspoon salt
  1/4 teaspoon crushed red pepper flakes

Cut out and discard the thick vein from each kale leaf. Coarsely chop kale. In a large saucepan or Dutch oven, bring water to a boil. Stir in kale. Cover and cook for 6-8 minutes or until almost tender; drain and set aside.

In a large nonstick skillet coated with nonstick cooking spray, cook garlic in oil for 1 minute. Stir in the raisins, olives, salt and pepper flakes; cook 1 minute longer. Stir in the kale; cook for 3-4 minutes or until tender.

NUTRITION FACTS: 2/3 cup equals 111 calories, 2 g fat (trace saturated fat), 0 cholesterol, 206 mg sodium, 22 g carbohydrate, 3 g fiber, 4 g protein. **DIABETIC EXCHANGES:** 2 vegetable, 1 fruit.

Grilled Pattypans

 FAT SALT CARB

PREP/TOTAL TIME: 15 Min. **YIELD:** 6 Servings

Just a few minutes and a handful of ingredients are all you'll need for a sweet, scrumptious side dish. Our Test Kitchen added hoisin sauce and rice wine vinegar for an Asian flair.

    6 cups pattypan squash (about 1-1/2 pounds)
  1/4 cup apricot spreadable fruit
    2 teaspoons hoisin sauce
    1 teaspoon rice wine vinegar
  1/2 teaspoon sesame oil
  1/4 teaspoon salt
  1/8 teaspoon ground ginger

Place squash in a grill wok or basket coated with nonstick cooking spray. Grill, covered, over medium heat for 5 minutes. Turn squash; grill 3-5 minutes longer or until tender.

Meanwhile, in a small bowl, combine the remaining ingredients. Transfer the squash to a serving bowl; add sauce and toss gently. Serve immediately.

NUTRITION FACTS: 3/4 cup equals 54 calories, trace fat (trace saturated fat), trace cholesterol, 127 mg sodium, 12 g carbohydrate, 1 g fiber, 1 g protein. **DIABETIC EXCHANGES:** 1 vegetable, 1/2 starch.

Editor's Note: If you do not have a grill wok or basket, use a disposable foil pan. Poke holes in the bottom of the pan with a meat fork to allow liquid to drain.

HEALTHY OUTLOOK
Yellow pattypan squash's skin has carotenoid pigments, which help protect against cataracts and age-related eye diseases.

Asian Vegetable Pasta

(PICTURED ABOVE)

PREP/TOTAL TIME: 20 Min. **YIELD:** 5 Servings

Peanut butter and a sprinkling of nuts give this dish plenty of taste. While red pepper flakes offer a little kick, brown sugar balances the flavors. —Mitzi Sentiff, Alexandria, Virginia

- 4 quarts water
- 8 ounces uncooked angel hair pasta
- 1 pound fresh asparagus, trimmed and cut into 1-inch pieces
- 3/4 cup julienned carrots
- 1/3 cup reduced-fat creamy peanut butter
- 3 tablespoons rice wine vinegar
- 3 tablespoons reduced-sodium soy sauce
- 2 tablespoons brown sugar
- 1/2 teaspoon crushed red pepper flakes
- 1/4 cup unsalted peanuts, chopped

In a Dutch oven, bring the water to a boil. Add pasta and asparagus; cook for 3 minutes. Stir in carrots; cook for 1 minute or until pasta is tender. Drain and keep warm.

In a small saucepan, combine the peanut butter, vinegar, soy sauce, brown sugar and pepper flakes. Bring to a boil over medium heat, stirring constantly. Pour over pasta mixture and toss to coat. Sprinkle with peanuts.

NUTRITION FACTS: 1 cup equals 358 calories, 10 g fat (2 g saturated fat), 0 cholesterol, 472 mg sodium, 54 g carbohydrate, 5 g fiber, 15 g protein. **DIABETIC EXCHANGES:** 3 starch, 1 lean meat, 1 vegetable, 1 fat.

TASTY TIP

"For a meatless main course, I like to serve the pasta with sesame breadsticks and fresh fruit," suggests Mitzi Sentiff. And if you're looking to shave a few more calories from Mitzi's recipe, skip the chopped peanuts and sprinkle some chopped green onion over the top of the dish instead.

Pattypan Saute
(PICTURED ABOVE)

PREP/TOTAL TIME: 25 Min.   **YIELD:** 4 Servings

Summer flavors like tomato and sweet red pepper pair well with sauteed pattypan squash in this lovely side dish created by the Light & Tasty home economists. A sprinkling of shredded Parmesan cheese makes it savory and special. Best of all, it's a terrific change of pace that comes together easily on the stovetop.

        2 cups halved pattypan squash
        1 medium onion, halved and sliced
        2 garlic cloves, minced
        2 teaspoons canola oil
        1 small sweet red pepper, cut into 1/2-inch pieces
        1 cup sliced fresh mushrooms
        1 medium tomato, chopped
    1/2 teaspoon salt
    1/2 teaspoon Italian seasoning
    1/8 teaspoon pepper
        2 tablespoons shredded Parmesan cheese

In a large nonstick skillet coated with nonstick cooking spray, saute the squash, onion and garlic in oil for 2 minutes. Add red pepper and mushrooms; saute for 5-7 minutes or until vegetables are crisp-tender.

Stir in the tomato, salt, Italian seasoning and pepper; heat through. Sprinkle with Parmesan cheese.

NUTRITION FACTS: 3/4 cup equals 73 calories, 3 g fat (1 g saturated fat), 2 mg cholesterol, 343 mg sodium, 9 g carbohydrate, 2 g fiber, 3 g protein. **DIABETIC EXCHANGES:** 2 vegetable, 1/2 fat.

Butternut Squash Apple Bake

PREP: 15 Min.   **BAKE:** 40 Min.   **YIELD:** 8 Servings

Even if you don't like squash, you'll enjoy this side dish. Sweet slices of butternut squash are topped with apples in a cinnamon-sugar glaze for an elegant accompaniment to any meal.
    —Ellie Klopping, Toledo, Ohio

        1 butternut squash (2 pounds), peeled and cut into 1/2-inch slices
        3 medium tart apples, peeled, cored and thinly sliced into rings
    1/3 cup packed brown sugar
    1-1/2 teaspoons all-purpose flour
    1/4 teaspoon ground cinnamon
        2 tablespoons butter, melted

Arrange squash in a 15-in. x 10-in. x 1-in. baking pan coated with nonstick cooking spray. Top with apple rings. Combine the brown sugar, flour and cinnamon; sprinkle over apples. Drizzle with butter.

Cover and bake at 350° for 40-50 minutes or until squash and apples are tender.

NUTRITION FACTS: 1 serving equals 120 calories, 3 g fat (2 g saturated fat), 8 mg cholesterol, 36 mg sodium, 25 g carbohydrate, 4 g fiber, 1 g protein. **DIABETIC EXCHANGES:** 1 starch, 1/2 fruit, 1/2 fat.

TASTY TIP

"I like to garnish the butternut squash with chopped walnuts or pecans," Ellie Klopping notes.

Favorite Recipe Made Lighter

TURNING CLASSIC RECIPES into light and lively fare is a goal for many health-minded family cooks. After all, it's hard to stick to heart-smart foods when you're longing for all of the old favorites that made meals special.

Gravies, butter sauces and other rich condiments are easy ways to turn the ordinary into the extraordinary and make menu items memorable. All too often, though, those items are loaded with calories, fat and sodium. That's why the staff of the *Light & Tasty* Test Kitchen decided to revamp a traditional recipe for Hollandaise sauce.

If you're not familiar with the lemon-flavored sauce, you may recognize it as a spring standby commonly used over eggs benedict and asparagus. Hollandaise is also a delicious way to dress up beef and poultry as well as fish and seafood.

Basic Hollandaise sauce requires only a few items, making it a bit of a challenge to lighten up. After all, there isn't much wiggle room for change when there are not many items to start with.

Two of the main ingredients (butter and egg yolks) add fat, but butter lends richness and egg yolks offer a smooth consistency for draping. Both characteristics have become hallmarks of this popular condiment. In addition, the yolks help to emulsify the sauce by keeping the butter and lemon juice from separating.

After a number of experiments, our kitchen specialists got the best result from combining a milk mixture with a small amount of a basic Hollandaise. The milk mixture added volume and thickening without extraneous flavor.

Makeover Hollandaise Sauce features half the calories, total fat and saturated fat found in a typical Hollandaise. It even boasts 59 fewer milligrams cholesterol than most versions. Best of all, Makeover Hollandaise Sauce is rich and silky enough to ladle over your all-time favorites.

Makeover Hollandaise Sauce

(PICTURED ABOVE)

PREP/TOTAL TIME: 25 Min.   YIELD: about 3/4 Cup

> 1 tablespoon all-purpose flour
> 1/4 teaspoon salt
> 1/8 teaspoon white pepper
> 1/2 cup fat-free milk
> 1 egg yolk
> 2 tablespoons lemon juice
> 1 tablespoon water
> 1/4 cup butter, melted

In a small saucepan, combine the flour, salt and pepper. Gradually stir in milk until smooth. Bring to a boil over medium heat; cook and stir for 1 minute or until thickened. Reduce heat to low; keep warm and stir occasionally.

In a double boiler over simmering water, constantly whisk the egg yolk, lemon juice and water until mixture begins to thicken and coats the back of a metal spoon. Reduce heat to low. Slowly drizzle in butter, whisking constantly. Whisk in milk mixture. Serve immediately.

NUTRITION FACTS: 2 tablespoons equals 68 calories, 6 g fat (4 g saturated fat), 42 mg cholesterol, 140 mg sodium, 2 g carbohydrate, trace fiber, 1 g protein. **DIABETIC EXCHANGE:** 1-1/2 fat.

Hollandaise Sauce

CARB

PREP/TOTAL TIME: 25 Min.   YIELD: about 3/4 Cup

> 3 egg yolks
> 3 tablespoons water
> 2 tablespoons lemon juice
> 3/4 cup butter, melted
> 1/8 teaspoon salt
> 1/8 teaspoon white pepper

In a double boiler over simmering water, constantly whisk the egg yolks, water and lemon juice until mixture begins to thicken and coats the back of a metal spoon. Reduce heat to low. Slowly drizzle in butter, whisking constantly. Whisk in salt and pepper. Serve immediately.

NUTRITION FACTS: 2 tablespoons equals 139 calories, 15 g fat (9 g saturated fat), 101 mg cholesterol, 170 mg sodium, trace carbohydrate, trace fiber, 1 g protein.

MAKE IT EASY
Use a double broiler when experimenting with a delicate egg-based sauce. Or, cook the sauce in a small metal bowl that's set over a saucepan of simmering water. However, don't let the water touch the bottom of the bowl.

Crunchy Yam Bake

(PICTURED BELOW)

FAT MEAT-
LESS

PREP: 30 Min.   **BAKE:** 30 Min.   **YIELD:** 8 Servings

This is one of my favorite recipes. The yummy yams are the perfect addition to a holiday ham or turkey and ideal for impressing a potluck crowd.   —Marian Moreman, Canyon Country, California

2-1/2 pounds yams *or* sweet potatoes, peeled and cubed
1/2 cup egg substitute
1/4 cup packed brown sugar
1/2 teaspoon salt
1/2 teaspoon ground cinnamon

TOPPING:

1 tablespoon butter
2 tablespoons finely chopped pecans
2 tablespoons brown sugar
1/4 cup Special K

Place yams in a large saucepan and cover with water. Bring to a boil. Reduce heat; cover and cook for 15-20 minutes or until tender.

Drain yams and place in a large mixing bowl; mash. Stir in the egg substitute, brown sugar, salt and cinnamon.

Transfer to a 1-qt. baking dish coated with nonstick cooking spray. Cover; bake at 350° for 15 minutes.

Meanwhile, in a saucepan, melt butter. Add pecans and brown sugar; cook and stir until sugar is melted. Stir in cereal until coated. Sprinkle over yam mixture. Bake, uncovered, 15-20 minutes longer or until a thermometer reads 160° and topping is golden brown.

NUTRITION FACTS: 1/2 cup equals 145 calories, 3 g fat (1 g saturated fat), 4 mg cholesterol, 211 mg sodium, 28 g carbohydrate, 2 g fiber, 3 g protein. **DIABETIC EXCHANGES:** 2 starch, 1/2 fat.

Rice with Chilies 'n' Veggies

(PICTURED ABOVE)

FAT MEAT-
LESS

PREP: 15 Min.   **COOK:** 30 Min.   **YIELD:** 8 Servings

I turned to a favorite dish when I wanted to use peppers from my garden. I added several other fresh vegetables, and this was the result. It's an ideal accompaniment to any menu.
        —Kate Selner, Lino Lakes, Minnesota

1/3 cup fat-free milk
1/2 cup frozen corn, thawed
1 cup uncooked long grain rice
2 teaspoons canola oil
1 large onion, chopped
1 medium zucchini, chopped
1 medium sweet red pepper, chopped
1/2 cup chopped carrot
1 can (4 ounces) chopped green chilies
1 garlic clove, minced
2 cups vegetable broth
1 bay leaf

In a food processor or blender, process milk and corn until smooth; set aside. In a large skillet, saute rice in oil for 5-6 minutes or until lightly browned. Stir in the onion, zucchini, red pepper, carrot, chilies, garlic and reserved corn mixture; cook for 1 minute.

Add broth and bay leaf; bring to a boil. Reduce heat; cover and simmer for 20 minutes or until rice is tender and liquid is absorbed. Discard the bay leaf before serving.

NUTRITION FACTS: 3/4 cup equals 134 calories, 2 g fat (trace saturated fat), trace cholesterol, 318 mg sodium, 27 g carbohydrate, 2 g fiber, 4 g protein. **DIABETIC EXCHANGES:** 1 starch, 1 vegetable, 1/2 fat.

TASTY TIP

"I often use spicy peppers from my garden instead of canned chilies," Kate Selner says. "I roast them in the oven before chopping them and adding them to a recipe."

Gingered Butternut Squash

(PICTURED BELOW)

MEAT-LESS

PREP: 30 Min.   **COOK:** 20 Min.   **YIELD:** 6 Servings

I found this recipe in a magazine years ago and thought it was the best squash dish I'd ever tasted. When I serve it to guests, they feel the same.   —Fran Swartzentruber, Sebring, Ohio

 2 medium butternut squash, peeled, seeded and cubed
 2 tablespoons butter
 1 tablespoon maple syrup
 2 tablespoons candied ginger
 3/4 teaspoon salt
 1/4 teaspoon pepper
 1/8 teaspoon ground nutmeg
 2 tablespoons half-and-half cream

Place squash in a large saucepan; cover with water. Bring to a boil. Reduce heat; cover and simmer for 12-16 minutes or until tender. Drain.

In a large mixing bowl, beat squash with butter and syrup. Beat in the ginger, salt, pepper and nutmeg. Gradually add cream until blended. Transfer to a serving bowl; serve immediately.

NUTRITION FACTS: 2/3 cup equals 180 calories, 5 g fat (3 g saturated fat), 13 mg cholesterol, 349 mg sodium, 36 g carbohydrate, 9 g fiber, 3 g protein. **DIABETIC EXCHANGES:** 2 starch, 1/2 fat.

SHOP SMART

Candied ginger, a sweetened dried ginger, is suitable for cooking and baking. It's often labeled "crystallized ginger" and can be found with the spices in the baking aisle. Also look for it in Asian markets or the international section of many grocery stores.

Greek-Style Squash

 CARB MEAT-LESS

(PICTURED ABOVE)

PREP: 15 Min.   **GRILL:** 30 Min.   **YIELD:** 4 Servings

What a great way to use up summer squash! You can almost taste the sunshine in this eye-fetching side dish. Grilling in foil packets makes cleanup a breeze.   —Betty Washburn, Reno, Nevada

   2 small yellow summer squash, thinly sliced
   2 small zucchini, thinly sliced
   1 medium tomato, seeded and chopped
1/4 cup pitted ripe olives
   2 tablespoons chopped green onion
   2 teaspoons olive oil
   1 teaspoon lemon juice
3/4 teaspoon garlic salt
1/4 teaspoon dried oregano
1/8 teaspoon pepper
   2 tablespoons grated Parmesan cheese

Place the yellow squash, zucchini, tomato, olives and onion on a double thickness of heavy-duty foil (about 17 in. x 18 in.). Combine the oil, lemon juice, garlic salt, oregano and pepper; pour over vegetables. Fold foil around mixture and seal tightly. Grill, covered, over medium heat for 30-35 minutes or until vegetables are tender. Carefully open foil; transfer vegetables to a serving bowl. Sprinkle with Parmesan cheese.

NUTRITION FACTS: 3/4 cup equals 80 calories, 5 g fat (1 g saturated fat), 2 mg cholesterol, 479 mg sodium, 8 g carbohydrate, 3 g fiber, 4 g protein. **DIABETIC EXCHANGES:** 2 vegetable, 1/2 fat.

Herbal Salt Substitute

 FAT SALT CARB

PREP/TOTAL TIME: 10 Min.   **YIELD:** 1/2 Cup

For those told to cut back on salt, this all-around handy blend can give herbal zest to recipes.   —Lorna Wall, Ottawa, Ontario

   1 tablespoon dried basil
   1 tablespoon dried thyme
   1 tablespoon ground coriander
   2 teaspoons onion powder
   2 teaspoons dried parsley flakes
   2 teaspoons ground cumin
   1 teaspoon garlic powder
   1 teaspoon ground mustard
   1 teaspoon cayenne pepper
   1 teaspoon paprika

In a small bowl, combine all ingredients. Store in an airtight container in a cool, dry place for up to 1 year.

NUTRITION FACTS: 1 teaspoon equals 5 calories, trace fat (trace saturated fat), 0 cholesterol, 1 mg sodium, 1 g carbohydrate, trace fiber, trace protein. **DIABETIC EXCHANGE:** Free food.

TASTY TIP
Put the salt substitute in decorative shakers to give as thoughtful stocking stuffers during the holidays!

Quinoa Pilaf

(PICTURED BELOW)

PREP/TOTAL TIME: 30 Min. YIELD: 4 Servings

*I created this recipe after tasting quinoa at a local restaurant.
I really enjoy rice pilaf, but I don't usually have time to make it.
This time-saving side is a tasty and healthy alternative.*

—Sonya Fox, Peyton, Colorado

- 1 medium onion, chopped
- 1 garlic clove, minced
- 1 teaspoon olive oil
- 1 medium carrot, chopped
- 1 can (14-1/2 ounces) reduced-sodium chicken broth *or* vegetable broth
- 1/4 cup water
- 1/4 teaspoon salt
- 1 cup quinoa, rinsed

In a small nonstick saucepan coated with nonstick cooking spray, cook onion and garlic in oil for 2 minutes. Add carrot; cook 2 minutes longer. Stir in the broth, water and salt; bring to a boil.

Stir in quinoa; return to a boil. Reduce heat; cover and simmer for 12-15 minutes or until liquid is absorbed. Remove from the heat; let stand for 5 minutes. Fluff with a fork.

NUTRITION FACTS: 3/4 cup equals 198 calories, 4 g fat (trace saturated fat), 0 cholesterol, 434 mg sodium, 35 g carbohydrate, 4 g fiber, 8 g protein. DIABETIC EXCHANGES: 2 starch, 1/2 fat.

Editor's Note: If using vegetable broth, omit the salt.

Herbed Green Beans

(PICTURED ABOVE)

FAT CARB MEAT-
LESS

PREP/TOTAL TIME: 15 Min. YIELD: 4 Servings

An assortment of herbs adds a refreshing burst of flavor to green beans. You can serve this recipe in moments, and it goes so well with just about any menu. —Ann Bassett, Nashville, Tennessee

- 1 small onion, chopped
- 2 teaspoons butter
- 1 package (16 ounces) frozen cut green beans, thawed
- 1/2 teaspoon garlic salt
- 1/2 teaspoon dried basil
- 1/4 teaspoon salt
- 1/4 teaspoon dried oregano
- 1/4 teaspoon dried marjoram

In a large nonstick skillet coated with nonstick cooking spray, cook onion in butter over medium heat for 2 minutes. Stir in the green beans and seasonings. Cook and stir 6-8 minutes longer or until beans are tender.

NUTRITION FACTS: 3/4 cup equals 59 calories, 2 g fat (1 g saturated fat), 5 mg cholesterol, 524 mg sodium, 9 g carbohydrate, 3 g fiber, 2 g protein. DIABETIC EXCHANGES: 2 vegetable, 1/2 fat.

TASTY TIP
Quinoa (pronounced KEEN-wah) is prepared like rice, and makes for a fast and healthy side dish when mixed with fresh herbs and low-salt seasonings.

Favorite Recipe Made Lighter

LOOKING for a sensational new side dish to set on the table? Sandy Moyer has just the recipe for you. Perfect for Easter Sunday, special meals and spring bring-a-dish events, her golden Pineapple Casserole is one that will have people for talking for days.

"It is a wonderful side dish with any main course, but it's particularly tasty when featured alongside ham," she writes from her kitchen in Gilbertsville, Pennsylvania.

"Although it's truly one of my family's all-time favorites, I was hoping that you could come up with a lighter version. The recipe I use is very delicious and rich, but I'm sorry to say that it also calls for an awful lot of fattening ingredients such as butter."

No problem, Sandy! In fact, after taking just one bite of Sandy's phenomenal Pineapple Casserole, our makeover gurus completely understood why it was important to trim down the dish...something so tasty needs to be enjoyed regularly without any guilt!

The original submission was so buttery and sweet, that our home economists decided to reduce the butter by two-thirds and cut the sugar in half. This change seemed drastic but, thankfully, the reductions didn't affect the unbeatable flavor or creamy texture found in Sandy's bubbling specialty.

The dish also called for a total of four whole eggs. As such, the team substituted two of the eggs with two egg whites. In making this change, however, the casserole lost a bit of its thick, creamy quality so our staff headed back to the drawing board. To rectify the situation, they added a few tablespoons of flour to the recipe and the texture was quickly restored.

Boasting 106 fewer calories and almost 60% less fat, Makeover Pineapple Casserole is a smart addition to any spring lineup. Try it yourself and see how quickly it becomes a mainstay in your home.

Pineapple Casserole

MEAT-LESS

PREP: 15 Min.   **BAKE:** 35 Min.   **YIELD:** 8 Servings

- 1 cup butter, softened
- 1 cup sugar
- 4 eggs
- 1 can (20 ounces) unsweetened crushed pineapple, drained
- 5 slices white bread, cubed

In a large mixing bowl, cream butter and sugar. Add eggs, one at a time, beating well after each addition. Stir in pineapple. Gently fold in bread cubes.

Spoon into a greased 2-qt. baking dish. Bake, uncovered, at 350° for 35-40 minutes or until top is lightly golden. Serve warm.

NUTRITION FACTS: 1/2 cup equals 335 calories, 21 g fat (12 g saturated fat), 134 mg cholesterol, 278 mg sodium, 35 g carbohydrate, 1 g fiber, 4 g protein.

Makeover Pineapple Casserole

MEAT-LESS

(PICTURED ABOVE)

PREP: 15 Min.   **BAKE:** 35 Min.   **YIELD:** 8 Servings

- 1 can (20 ounces) unsweetened crushed pineapple
- 1/3 cup butter, softened
- 1/2 cup sugar
- 2 eggs
- 2 egg whites
- 2 tablespoons all-purpose flour
- 5 slices white bread, cubed

Drain pineapple, reserving 1 cup juice; set pineapple and juice aside. In a large mixing bowl, cream butter and sugar. Add eggs, one at a time, beating well after each addition. Beat in egg whites. Stir in flour, then reserved pineapple and juice. Gently fold in bread cubes.

Spoon into a 2-qt. baking dish coated with nonstick cooking spray. Bake, uncovered, at 350° for 35-40 minutes or until top is lightly golden. Serve warm.

NUTRITION FACTS: 1/2 cup equals 229 calories, 9 g fat (5 g saturated fat), 74 mg cholesterol, 191 mg sodium, 33 g carbohydrate, 1 g fiber, 4 g protein. **DIABETIC EXCHANGES:** 2 fat, 1 starch, 1 fruit.

MAKEOVER TIP
Adding a little flour can replace the thickening agent that is sometimes lost when egg yolks are removed from a recipe.

Cumin Rice with Avocado

(PICTURED BELOW)

PREP: 10 Min.   **COOK:** 35 Min.   **YIELD:** 6 Servings

Cumin, picante sauce and avocado do a terrific job of jazzing up long grain rice in this light, versatile recipe. It's great with extra-spicy food. —Margaret Allen, Abingdon, Virginia

2-1/4 cups water
   1 tablespoon butter
   2 teaspoons reduced-sodium chicken bouillon granules
3/4 teaspoon ground cumin
   1 cup uncooked long grain rice
1/3 cup picante sauce
   1 medium ripe avocado, peeled and cubed
   2 green onions, sliced

In a large saucepan, bring water to a boil. Add the butter, bouillon and cumin; stir until butter is melted. Add rice. Reduce heat; cover and simmer for 20-25 minutes or until rice is tender. Stir in picante sauce; heat through. Stir in avocado and onions.

NUTRITION FACTS: 2/3 cup equals 191 calories, 7 g fat (2 g saturated fat), 5 mg cholesterol, 187 mg sodium, 29 g carbohydrate, 2 g fiber, 3 g protein. **DIABETIC EXCHANGES:** 1-1/2 starch, 1-1/2 fat.

Red Pepper Bean Medley

CARB ▼ MEAT-LESS

PREP/TOTAL TIME: 20 Min.   **YIELD:** 8 Servings

I turn to this light favorite when spring is in the air. The bright dish doubles as a salad when served cold.
—Louise Watkins, Long Key, Florida

   1 pound fresh green beans, trimmed
   2 large sweet red peppers, cut into thin strips
   2 green onions, sliced
   2 tablespoons lemon juice
   2 tablespoons olive oil
   2 teaspoons grated lemon peel
1/2 teaspoon salt
1/8 teaspoon pepper

Place green beans in a steamer basket; place in a saucepan over 1 in. of water. Bring to a boil; cover and steam for 5 minutes. Add red peppers; cover and steam 5-6 minutes longer or until vegetables are crisp-tender.

In a small bowl, combine the remaining ingredients. Transfer beans and peppers to a serving bowl; add onion mixture and toss to combine.

NUTRITION FACTS: 3/4 cup equals 63 calories, 4 g fat (trace saturated fat), 0 cholesterol, 152 mg sodium, 8 g carbohydrate, 3 g fiber, 2 g protein. **DIABETIC EXCHANGES:** 1 vegetable, 1 fat.

Cranberry Cornmeal Dressing
(PICTURED ABOVE)

PREP: 30 Min. **BAKE:** 40 Min. **YIELD:** 8 Servings

This moist dressing is perfect when paired with poultry or even pork. The sweet-tart flavor of the dried cranberries really complements the dish's turkey sausage.

—Corinne Portteus, Albuquerque, New Mexico

3 cups reduced-sodium chicken broth, *divided*
1/2 cup yellow cornmeal
1/2 teaspoon salt
1/2 teaspoon white pepper
1/2 pound Italian turkey sausage links, casings removed
1 large onion, diced
1 large fennel bulb, diced (about 1 cup)
1 garlic clove, minced
1 egg yolk
3/4 cup dried cranberries
4 cups soft French *or* Italian bread crumbs
2 tablespoons minced fresh parsley
1 tablespoon balsamic vinegar
1 teaspoon minced fresh sage
1 teaspoon minced fresh savory
1/2 teaspoon ground nutmeg

In a small bowl, whisk 1 cup broth, cornmeal, salt and pepper until smooth. In a large saucepan, bring remaining broth to a boil. Add cornmeal mixture, stirring constantly. Return to a boil; cook and stir for 3 minutes or until thickened. Remove from the heat; set aside.

Crumble the sausage into a large nonstick skillet, add onion, fennel and garlic. Cook over medium heat until sausage is no longer pink; drain. Stir in egg yolk and cornmeal mixture. Add the cranberries, bread crumbs, parsley, vinegar, sage, savory and nutmeg.

Transfer to a 1-1/2-qt. baking dish coated with nonstick cooking spray. Cover and bake at 350° for 40-45 minutes or until heated through.

NUTRITION FACTS: 2/3 cup equals 205 calories, 4 g fat (1 g saturated fat), 42 mg cholesterol, 695 mg sodium, 33 g carbohydrate, 3 g fiber, 9 g protein. **DIABETIC EXCHANGES:** 2 starch, 1 lean meat.

Home-Style Refried Beans

(PICTURED BELOW)

FAT MEAT-
LESS

PREP/TOTAL TIME: 15 Min.   YIELD: 2-2/3 Cups

Cumin, cayenne pepper and lime juice make these beans so tasty, particularly when compared to the canned variety. I like to dress them up with reduced-fat cheese and salsa.

—Myra Innes, Auburn, Kansas

    2/3 cup finely chopped onion
      4 teaspoons canola oil
      4 garlic cloves, minced
      1 teaspoon ground cumin
    1/2 teaspoon salt
    1/4 teaspoon cayenne pepper
      2 cans (15 ounces *each*) pinto beans, rinsed and drained
    1/2 cup water
      4 teaspoons lime juice

In a large saucepan, saute onion in oil until tender. Stir in the garlic, cumin, salt and cayenne; cook and stir for 1 minute. Add beans and mash. Add water; cook and stir until heated through and water is absorbed. Remove from the heat; stir in lime juice.

NUTRITION FACTS: 1/3 cup equals 123 calories, 3 g fat (trace saturated fat), 0 cholesterol, 290 mg sodium, 19 g carbohydrate, 5 g fiber, 5 g protein. DIABETIC EXCHANGES: 1 starch, 1 very lean meat, 1/2 fat.

HEALTHY OUTLOOK
Refried beans are common at ethnic restaurants, but order carefully since most are made with lots of oil. Home-Style Refried Beans offer all the taste without the guilt.

Caramelized Onion Mashed Potatoes

(PICTURED ABOVE)

PREP: 15 Min.   COOK: 45 Min.   YIELD: 6 Servings

Caramelized onions give a sweet taste to this side dish from our Test Kitchen. Prepared with red potatoes, low-fat cheese and crumbled bacon, it makes a heartwarming accompaniment to a variety of dinners.

      1 tablespoon canola oil
      2 large onions, thinly sliced
      1 teaspoon salt, *divided*
  1-1/2 pounds medium red potatoes, quartered
      3 garlic cloves, peeled and halved
    1/3 cup reduced-fat sour cream
      3 tablespoons fat-free milk
    1/4 teaspoon pepper
      1 tablespoon butter, melted
    1/2 cup shredded reduced-fat cheddar cheese
      2 bacon strips, cooked and crumbled

Heat oil in a large nonstick skillet over medium heat; add onions and 1/2 teaspoon salt. Cook and stir for 15 minutes or until moisture has evaporated and onions are completely wilted. Reduce heat to medium-low. Cook and stir for 30-40 minutes or until onions are caramelized. (If necessary, add water, 1 tablespoon at a time, if onions begin to stick to the pan.)

Meanwhile, place potatoes and garlic in a large saucepan; cover with water. Bring to a boil. Reduce heat; cover and simmer for 18-22 minutes or until tender.

Drain potatoes; place in a large bowl and mash. Add the sour cream, milk, pepper and remaining salt; mash until blended. Stir in caramelized onions. Transfer to a serving bowl. Drizzle with butter; sprinkle with cheese and bacon.

NUTRITION FACTS: 2/3 cup equals 200 calories, 9 g fat (4 g saturated fat), 18 mg cholesterol, 528 mg sodium, 25 g carbohydrate, 3 g fiber, 7 g protein. DIABETIC EXCHANGES: 1-1/2 starch, 1-1/2 fat.

Rice with Summer Squash

(PICTURED AT LEFT)

FAT MEAT-LESS ▼

PREP: 15 Min.   **COOK:** 25 Min.   **YIELD:** 4 Servings

I don't usually create my own recipes, but this one passed my palate test. It offers a buttery flavor that those of us who are watching our weight miss.   —Heather Ratigan, Kaufman, Texas

    1 cup chopped carrots
1/2 cup chopped onion
    1 tablespoon butter
    1 cup reduced-sodium chicken broth *or* vegetable broth
1/3 cup uncooked long grain rice
1/4 teaspoon salt
1/4 teaspoon pepper
    1 medium yellow summer squash, chopped
    1 medium zucchini, chopped

In a saucepan coated with nonstick cooking spray, cook carrots and onion in butter until tender. Stir in the broth, rice, salt and pepper. Bring to a boil. Reduce heat; cover and simmer for 13 minutes.

Stir in the yellow squash and zucchini. Cover and simmer 6-10 minutes longer or until rice and vegetables are tender.

NUTRITION FACTS: 3/4 cup equals 123 calories, 3 g fat (2 g saturated fat), 8 mg cholesterol, 346 mg sodium, 21 g carbohydrate, 3 g fiber, 4 g protein. **DIABETIC EXCHANGES:** 1 starch, 1 vegetable, 1/2 fat.

Braised Winter Vegetables

FAT MEAT-LESS ▼

PREP: 25 Min.   **COOK:** 35 Min.   **YIELD:** 8 Servings

Simmered in a seasoned broth, this down-home medley is perfect on chilly nights. Our Test Kitchen team hopes you enjoy it.

    1 medium onion, coarsely chopped
    2 garlic cloves, coarsely chopped
4-1/2 teaspoons canola oil
    1 medium sweet potato, peeled and cut into 1-1/2-inch cubes
    1 medium potato, peeled and cut into 1-1/2-inch cubes
    1 small rutabaga, peeled and cut into 1-1/2-inch cubes
    2 medium carrots, cut into 1-inch pieces
    1 medium parsnip, peeled and cut into 1-1/2-inch pieces
    2 teaspoons minced fresh thyme *or* 3/4 teaspoon dried thyme
    1 teaspoon salt
1/2 teaspoon pepper
    1 bay leaf
1/2 cup reduced-sodium chicken broth *or* vegetable broth

In a large heavy saucepan or Dutch oven coated with nonstick cooking spray, saute onion and garlic in oil until tender. Stir in the vegetables and seasonings. Add broth. Bring to a boil. Reduce heat; cover and simmer for 20-25 minutes or until vegetables are tender.

Uncover and increase the heat to medium-high; cook until most of the liquid has evaporated. Discard the bay leaf before serving.

NUTRITION FACTS: 1 cup equals 92 calories, 3 g fat (trace saturated fat), 0 cholesterol, 349 mg sodium, 16 g carbohydrate, 3 g fiber, 2 g protein. **DIABETIC EXCHANGES:** 1 vegetable, 1/2 starch, 1/2 fat.

Parsnip Carrot Bake

CARB MEAT-LESS

PREP: 10 Min.   **BAKE:** 30 Min.   **YIELD:** 4 Servings

No one will suspect that this unbeatable recipe is healthy. The Light & Tasty home economists used a hint of dill to season the carb-smart side dish. We're sure you'll agree that it's a colorful way to get your gang to eat their vegetables.

1-1/2 cups julienned carrots
1-1/2 cups julienned peeled parsnips
   1 tablespoon water
   1/2 teaspoon salt
   1/4 teaspoon dill seed
   1/4 teaspoon dried parsley flakes
   2 tablespoons butter

Place the carrots and parsnips in a 1-qt. baking dish coated with nonstick cooking spray. Sprinkle with water, salt, dill seed and parsley. Dot with butter. Cover and bake at 375° for 30-35 minutes or until vegetables are tender.

NUTRITION FACTS: 3/4 cup equals 108 calories, 6 g fat (4 g saturated fat), 15 mg cholesterol, 374 mg sodium, 14 g carbohydrate, 4 g fiber, 1 g protein. **DIABETIC EXCHANGES:** 3 vegetable, 1 fat.

Lentil Rice Medley

FAT MEAT-LESS

PREP: 25 Min.   **COOK:** 35 Min.   **YIELD:** 12 Servings

This combination pairs well with chicken or fish. I often serve it to my family as well as guests, and it's always enjoyed.
                    —Dee Fifer, Commerce City, Colorado

   1 medium onion, chopped
   2 garlic cloves, minced
   1 tablespoon olive oil
   3 medium carrots, chopped
   1 cup dried lentils, rinsed
   1/2 cup uncooked brown rice
3-1/4 cups water
1-1/2 teaspoons salt
   1 teaspoon dried basil
   1 teaspoon dried oregano
   1 teaspoon ground cumin
   1/4 teaspoon pepper
   3 cups fresh broccoli florets
   1 small zucchini, chopped
   1 can (8 ounces) tomato sauce
   1 medium tomato, chopped

In a large nonstick skillet coated with nonstick cooking spray, saute onion and garlic in oil for 1 minute. Add carrots; cook 2 minutes longer. Add lentils and rice; cook and stir for 2 minutes. Stir in the water and seasonings. Bring to a boil. Reduce heat; cover and simmer for 10 minutes.

Stir in broccoli and zucchini; return to a boil. Reduce heat; simmer, uncovered, for 15-20 minutes or until lentils and rice are tender, stirring occasionally. Stir in tomato sauce and tomato; heat through.

NUTRITION FACTS: 2/3 cup equals 120 calories, 2 g fat (trace saturated fat), 0 cholesterol, 396 mg sodium, 21 g carbohydrate, 7 g fiber, 7 g protein. **DIABETIC EXCHANGES:** 1 starch, 1 vegetable.

Savory Green Beans

FAT CARB MEAT-LESS

(PICTURED ABOVE)

PREP/TOTAL TIME: 30 min.   **YIELD:** 6 Servings

This was my mother's favorite way to fix green beans. She grew savory in her garden, giving the recipe fresh flavor. It is low in fat and goes well with any main course.
                    —Carol Ann Hayden, Everson, Washington

   3/4 cup chopped sweet red pepper
   1 garlic clove, minced
   1 tablespoon canola oil
1-1/2 pounds fresh green beans, trimmed and cut into 2-inch pieces
   1/2 cup water
   2 tablespoons minced fresh savory *or* 2 teaspoons dried savory
   1 tablespoon minced chives
   1/2 teaspoon salt

In a large skillet, saute red pepper and garlic in oil for 2-3 minutes or until tender. Add the green beans, water, savory, chives and salt. Bring to a boil. Reduce heat; cover and simmer for 8-10 minutes or until beans are crisp-tender.

NUTRITION FACTS: 3/4 cup equals 59 calories, 3 g fat (trace saturated fat), 0 cholesterol, 203 mg sodium, 9 g carbohydrate, 4 g fiber, 2 g protein. **DIABETIC EXCHANGES:** 2 vegetable, 1/2 fat.

HEALTHY OUTLOOK
Not only are green beans high in fiber, but they're a great source of folate...a B vitamin that can help prevent heart disease.

Pineapple Cranberry Relish

PREP/TOTAL TIME: 30 Min.   **YIELD:** 3 Cups

This refreshing relish features three kinds of fruit and a splash of cilantro. Serve it atop grilled chicken or pork to perk up the taste.
—Sue Dannahower, Fort Pierce, Florida

> 1 cup fresh *or* frozen cranberries
> 1/2 cup water
> 1/2 cup sugar
> 2 cups cubed fresh pineapple
> 1 cup coarsely chopped fresh strawberries
> 1 jalapeno pepper, seeded and chopped
> 2 tablespoons lime juice
> 1 to 2 tablespoons minced fresh cilantro
> 1/8 teaspoon salt

In a small saucepan, combine the cranberries, water and sugar. Cook and stir over medium heat until the berries pop, about 15 minutes. Cool.

Transfer to a bowl; stir in the remaining ingredients. Store in the refrigerator.

NUTRITION FACTS: 1/4 cup equals 54 calories, trace fat (trace saturated fat), 0 cholesterol, 25 mg sodium, 14 g carbohydrate, 1 g fiber, trace protein. **DIABETIC EXCHANGES:** 1/2 starch, 1/2 fruit.

Editor's Note: *When cutting or seeding hot peppers, use rubber or plastic gloves to protect your hands. Avoid touching your face.*

Rice Pilaf

PREP/TOTAL TIME: 30 Min.   **YIELD:** 6 Servings

A combination of egg noodles and rice makes this side dish a savory change of pace. I season the pilaf with minced garlic, fresh parsley and a little butter.   —Judy Barry, West Milford, New Jersey

> 1/2 cup uncooked fine egg noodles, broken
> 2 teaspoons canola oil
> 1 tablespoon butter
> 1 cup uncooked long grain rice
> 3 garlic cloves, minced
> 2 cups water
> 2 teaspoons very low sodium chicken bouillon granules
> 1/4 teaspoon salt
> 1/4 teaspoon pepper
> 1/4 cup minced fresh parsley

In a large saucepan, cook and stir noodles in oil and butter until lightly browned. Stir in the rice and garlic; cook 2 minutes longer. Add the water, bouillon, salt and pepper. Bring to a boil. Reduce heat; cover and simmer for 13 minutes. Stir in parsley; cover and cook 2-5 minutes longer or until rice is tender.

NUTRITION FACTS: 2/3 cup equals 161 calories, 4 g fat (1 g saturated fat), 8 mg cholesterol, 123 mg sodium, 28 g carbohydrate, 1 g fiber, 3 g protein. **DIABETIC EXCHANGES:** 2 starch, 1/2 fat.

HEALTHY OUTLOOK
Garlic can help reduce LDL cholesterol and blood pressure and increase heart-smart HDL cholesterol. So the garlic in Rice Pilaf not only heightens the dish's flavor, but it improves its health benefits as well.

Stuffed Sweet Onions
(PICTURED BELOW)

PREP: 30 Min.   **COOK:** 5 Min.   **YIELD:** 4 Servings

Looking for an impressive addition to a menu? Consider this eye-appealing idea. A filling of savory ham and herbed bread crumbs makes the onions a decadent accompaniment to meals.
—Jeanne Allen, Rye, Colorado

> 3 quarts water
> 4 medium sweet onions, peeled
> 1 tablespoon chopped green onion
> 1-1/2 teaspoons minced fresh parsley
> 6 teaspoons butter, *divided*
> 1/2 cup chopped fully cooked lean ham
> 1/4 teaspoon salt
> 1/4 teaspoon pepper
> 1/4 teaspoon celery seed
> 1/8 teaspoon garlic powder
> 1/2 cup soft bread crumbs, *divided*

In a large saucepan, bring water to a boil. Add onions; cover and boil for 9-11 minutes or until tender. Drain; cool for 5 minutes. Cut a thin slice off the top of each onion; carefully hollow out, leaving a 1/2-in. shell. Chop removed onion.

In a nonstick skillet coated with nonstick cooking spray, cook the chopped onion, green onion and parsley in 4 teaspoons butter for 3 minutes. Add the ham, salt, pepper, celery seed and garlic powder; cook until onions are tender and ham is lightly browned. Stir in 1/4 cup bread crumbs; heat through. Stuff into onion shells.

Melt remaining butter; toss with remaining bread crumbs. Sprinkle over stuffing. Broil 6 in. from the heat for 3-4 minutes or until crumbs are lightly browned and onions are heated through.

NUTRITION FACTS: 1 serving equals 158 calories, 7 g fat (4 g saturated fat), 26 mg cholesterol, 597 mg sodium, 16 g carbohydrate, 3 g fiber, 8 g protein. **DIABETIC EXCHANGES:** 2 vegetable, 1 lean meat, 1 fat.

Stir-Fried Vegetables

(PICTURED ABOVE)

PREP/TOTAL TIME: 25 Min. **YIELD:** 6 Servings

I need less than 30 minutes to prepare this veggie stir-fry for my family. It tastes just as garden-fresh as it looks.
—Jane Shapton, Tustin, California

   2 tablespoons cornstarch
   1 teaspoon sugar
   1 teaspoon minced fresh gingerroot
   1 cup reduced-sodium chicken broth *or* vegetable broth
1/4 cup cold water
   3 tablespoons reduced-sodium soy sauce
   3 tablespoons white wine vinegar
   2 medium carrots, julienned
   2 cups fresh broccoli florets
   4 teaspoons canola oil
   2 medium sweet red peppers, julienned
   2 medium green peppers, julienned
   1 cup sliced green onions, *divided*

In a small bowl, combine the cornstarch, sugar, ginger, broth, water, soy sauce and vinegar until smooth; set aside. In a large nonstick skillet or wok, stir-fry the carrots and broccoli in oil for 2 minutes. Add peppers; stir-fry 6-8 minutes longer or until vegetables are crisp-tender.

Stir cornstarch mixture and add to the skillet. Bring to a boil; cook and stir for 2 minutes or until thickened. Add 3/4 cup onions; cook 2 minutes longer. Garnish with remaining onions.

NUTRITION FACTS: 2/3 cup equals 93 calories, 3 g fat (trace saturated fat), 0 cholesterol, 424 mg sodium, 14 g carbohydrate, 3 g fiber, 3 g protein. **DIABETIC EXCHANGES:** 2 vegetable, 1/2 fat.

HEALTHY OUTLOOK
The peppers in Stir-Fried Vegetables may have you seeing red…and that's a good thing! Sweet red peppers are an excellent source of vitamin A, which promotes strong vision.

Sesame Broccoli

PREP/TOTAL TIME: 25 Min. **YIELD:** 6 Servings

This tasty broccoli has become a favorite at our house. It's quick and easy, and it adds a colorful presentation to any menu.
—Janice Cawman, Yakima, Washington

      1 pound fresh broccoli, cut into spears
      1 tablespoon reduced-sodium soy sauce
      2 teaspoons olive oil
      2 teaspoons balsamic vinegar
1-1/2 teaspoons honey
      2 teaspoons sesame seeds, toasted

Place broccoli in a steamer basket; place in a saucepan over 1 in. of water. Bring to a boil; cover and steam for 10-15 minutes or until crisp-tender. Meanwhile, in a small saucepan, combine the soy sauce, oil, vinegar and honey; cook and stir over medium-low heat until heated through.

Transfer broccoli to a serving bowl; drizzle with soy sauce mixture. Sprinkle with sesame seeds.

NUTRITION FACTS: 3/4 cup equals 48 calories, 2 g fat (trace saturated fat), 0 cholesterol, 127 mg sodium, 6 g carbohydrate, 2 g fiber, 3 g protein. **DIABETIC EXCHANGES:** 1 vegetable, 1/2 fat.

Quinoa Squash Pilaf
(PICTURED ABOVE)

FAT ▼ MEAT-LESS

PREP: 30 Min.　**COOK:** 20 Min.　**YIELD:** 8 Servings

This is a wonderful side dish with a variety of flavors and good-for-you ingredients.　　—Annette Spiegler, Arlington Heights, Illinois

　　1 cup quinoa, rinsed and drained
　　1 can (14-1/2 ounces) vegetable broth
1/4 cup water
　　2 medium zucchini, halved lengthwise and sliced
　　1 medium yellow summer squash, halved lengthwise and sliced
　　1 cup chopped leeks (white portion only)
　　2 garlic cloves, minced
　　1 tablespoon olive oil
　　1 large tomato, chopped
　　1 tablespoon minced fresh cilantro
1/2 teaspoon salt
1/2 teaspoon dried oregano
1/2 teaspoon ground cumin
1/2 teaspoon chili powder
1/4 teaspoon pepper
1/8 teaspoon crushed red pepper flakes
　　2 cups fresh baby spinach, chopped

In a large nonstick skillet coated with nonstick cooking spray, toast the quinoa over medium heat until lightly browned, stirring occasionally.

　　In a small saucepan, bring broth and water to a boil. Add quinoa. Reduce heat; simmer, uncovered, for 15 minutes or until liquid is absorbed; set aside.

　　In a large nonstick skillet, saute the zucchini, yellow squash, leeks and garlic in oil until tender. Stir in the tomato, cilantro, seasonings and quinoa; heat through. Add spinach; cook and stir until spinach is wilted.

NUTRITION FACTS: 3/4 cup equals 126 calories, 3 g fat (trace saturated fat), 0 cholesterol, 377 mg sodium, 21 g carbohydrate, 3 g fiber, 5 g protein. **DIABETIC EXCHANGES:** 1 starch, 1 vegetable, 1/2 fat.

STORAGE SMARTS
Store uncooked quinoa in an airtight container in a cool, dry place. If you live in a warm climate, refrigerate or freeze quinoa.

Mushroom Veggie Couscous

PREP/TOTAL TIME: 30 Min.   YIELD: 9 Servings

I dress up couscous with mushrooms, onions and carrot. Seasoned with white wine and thyme, the light dish is a nice change of pace.
—Ann Berger, Howell, Michigan

   1 can (14-1/2 ounces) reduced-sodium chicken broth
1/4 cup white wine *or* additional reduced-sodium chicken broth
   1 package (10 ounces) couscous
1/3 cup chopped onion
   2 garlic cloves, minced
   2 tablespoons olive oil
1/2 pound fresh mushrooms, chopped
   1 medium carrot, shredded
   2 green onions, thinly sliced
   2 tablespoons minced fresh parsley
1/2 teaspoon salt
1/4 teaspoon dried thyme
1/8 teaspoon pepper
1/4 cup slivered almonds, toasted

In a small saucepan, bring broth and wine or additional broth to a boil. Stir in couscous. Cover and remove from the heat; let stand for 5 minutes.

Meanwhile, in a large nonstick skillet, saute onion and garlic in oil for 2 minutes. Add mushrooms; cook and stir 2 minutes longer. Add the carrot, green onions, parsley, salt, thyme and pepper; cook and stir for 2 minutes or until vegetables are tender.

Fluff couscous with a fork; stir into vegetable mixture. Sprinkle with almonds.

NUTRITION FACTS: 3/4 cup equals 184 calories, 5 g fat (1 g saturated fat), 0 cholesterol, 258 mg sodium, 28 g carbohydrate, 3 g fiber, 6 g protein. **DIABETIC EXCHANGES:** 1-1/2 starch, 1 vegetable, 1 fat.

parsley pointers

Want to give your side dish extra style? Consider leafy greens of parsley! The pretty herb adds flavorful flair and healthy doses of vitamin A and C to recipes…without an ounce of fat.

With more than 30 types of parsley to choose from, jazzing up a dish is easier than ever. Just consider these varieties:

• Curly-Leaf. This is the most common type of parsley and is found in most supermarkets. It offers a slightly peppery flavor.

• Flat-Leaf. A parsley that resembles cilantro and offers a stronger flavor than curly-leaf parsley.

• Chervil or French. Darker in color than other types of parsley, this version features delicate leaves and a taste of anise.

• Cilantro or Chinese. A zesty flavor is the hallmark of this parsley. Its flat leaves are bright green.

Corn 'n' Red Pepper Medley

MEAT-LESS

(PICTURED BELOW)

PREP/TOTAL TIME: 25 Min.   YIELD: 4 Servings

I think this fresh-tasting idea is a fun treatment for corn. It's colorful, comes together quickly on the stovetop and goes well with grilled foods such as chicken or steak.
—Lillian Julow, Gainesville, Florida

   2 cups fresh corn
   1 tablespoon olive oil
   2 large sweet red peppers, chopped
1/2 cup chopped onion
   1 garlic clove, minced
1/4 cup minced fresh parsley
1/2 teaspoon salt
1/2 teaspoon chili powder
1/4 teaspoon pepper

In a large nonstick skillet, cook corn in oil for 2 minutes. Add the red peppers, onion and garlic; cook and stir for 4-6 minutes or until peppers are crisp-tender. Stir in the parsley, salt, chili powder and pepper; cook 1-2 minutes longer.

NUTRITION FACTS: 3/4 cup equals 130 calories, 5 g fat (1 g saturated fat), 0 cholesterol, 314 mg sodium, 22 g carbohydrate, 4 g fiber, 4 g protein. **DIABETIC EXCHANGES:** 1 starch, 1 vegetable, 1 fat.

Favorite Recipe Made Lighter

GOLDEN, crumb-topped entrees fresh from the oven are the quintessential image of comfort food. And Lisa Eldridge's Summer Squash Casserole fits the picture perfectly. "A friend gave me the recipe," she says from Topeka, Kansas. "It's excellent, but it's very high in fat and calories."

Crushed saltine crackers, eggs, heavy cream and lots of cheese are the side dish's main culprits. Our makeover staff began by decreasing the eggs and substituting heavier ingredients with their less-fattening counterparts. The saltine crackers in the casserole were eliminated and reduced-fat butter-flavored crackers were substituted to replicate the original's buttery topping.

To boost taste, garlic was added. And the cheese called for in the original recipe was replaced with a smaller amount of more flavorful sharp cheddar cheese.

With the changes, the casserole needed help holding its shape, so flour was added. As a result, Makeover Summer Squash Casserole has 233 fewer calories, 65% less fat and 284 mg less sodium per serving!

After tasting the revised recipe, Lisa confirms, "The makeover has the same great flavor as the original, but now I can feel better about fixing it for my family."

Summer Squash Casserole

PREP: 30 Min.   **BAKE:** 45 Min. + Standing   **YIELD:** 15 Servings

    3 pounds yellow summer squash, cut into 1/4-inch slices
    2 medium onions, sliced
    1 cup butter, melted, *divided*
    5 eggs
    2 cups heavy whipping cream
    5 cups (20 ounces) shredded cheddar cheese, *divided*
2-1/2 cups crushed saltines, *divided*
    1/2 teaspoon salt
    1/4 teaspoon pepper

Place squash in a large saucepan or Dutch oven; add 1 in. of water. Bring to a boil. Reduce heat; cover and simmer for 5-6 minutes or until crisp-tender. Drain well. In a large skillet, saute onions in 1/4 cup butter until tender; add squash and gently combine. Transfer to a large bowl.

In another large bowl, combine eggs, cream, 4-1/2 cups cheese, 2 cups saltine crumbs, salt, pepper and remaining butter. Pour over squash mixture; stir gently to combine. Transfer to a greased 13-in. x 9-in. x 2-in. baking dish.

Bake, uncovered, at 350° for 35 minutes. Sprinkle with remaining cheese and saltine crumbs. Bake 5 minutes longer or until cheese is melted and crumbs are golden brown. Let stand for 10 minutes before serving.

NUTRITION FACTS: 1 serving equals 443 calories, 37 g fat (24 g saturated fat), 187 mg cholesterol, 594 mg sodium, 15 g carbohydrate, 2 g fiber, 13 g protein.

Makeover Summer Squash Casserole

(PICTURED ABOVE)

PREP: 30 Min.   **BAKE:** 45 Min. + Standing   **YIELD:** 15 Servings

    3 pounds yellow summer squash, cut into 1/4-inch slices
    2 medium onions, sliced
    2 tablespoons butter, *divided*
    2 garlic cloves, minced
    6 tablespoons all-purpose flour
    4 eggs
    4 egg whites
    2 cups 2% milk
    4 cups (16 ounces) shredded sharp cheddar cheese
    1/4 teaspoon salt
    1/8 teaspoon pepper
    12 reduced-fat butter-flavored crackers, crushed

Place squash in a large saucepan or Dutch oven; add 1 in. of water. Bring to a boil. Reduce heat; cover and simmer for 5-6 minutes or until crisp-tender. Drain and set aside.

In a large nonstick skillet, saute onions in 1 tablespoon butter until tender. Add garlic; saute 1 minute longer. Add squash; stir gently to combine. Transfer to a 13-in. x 9-in. x 2-in. baking dish coated with nonstick cooking spray.

In a large bowl, combine the flour, eggs, egg whites, milk, cheese, salt and pepper. Pour over squash mixture. Bake, uncovered, at 350° for 40 minutes.

Melt remaining butter; toss with cracker crumbs. Sprinkle over casserole; bake 5 minutes longer or until crumbs are golden brown and a knife inserted near the center comes out clean. Let stand for 10 minutes before serving.

NUTRITION FACTS: 1 serving equals 210 calories, 13 g fat (8 g saturated fat), 95 mg cholesterol, 310 mg sodium, 13 g carbohydrate, 2 g fiber, 12 g protein.

Herb-Crusted Potatoes

(PICTURED ABOVE)

FAT MEAT-LESS

PREP: 10 Min.   **BAKE:** 40 Min.   **YIELD:** 4 Servings

With just a few minutes of prep, you can toss these potatoes into the oven to bake. Our Test Kitchen seasoned them with rosemary, oregano and thyme, to bring a pleasantly bold flavor to any meal.

 1-1/2 pounds Yukon Gold potatoes, cut into wedges
     1 tablespoon olive oil
     1 tablespoon minced fresh rosemary
     1 teaspoon dried thyme
     1 teaspoon dried oregano
   1/2 teaspoon salt
   1/4 to 1/2 teaspoon pepper

In a large bowl, toss potatoes with oil. Combine the seasonings; sprinkle over potatoes and toss to coat. Arrange in a single layer in a 15-in. x 10-in. x 1-in. baking pan coated with nonstick cooking spray. Bake at 425° for 40-45 minutes or until tender, stirring once.

NUTRITION FACTS: 1 cup equals 174 calories, 3 g fat (trace saturated fat), 0 cholesterol, 306 mg sodium, 31 g carbohydrate, 2 g fiber, 4 g protein. **DIABETIC EXCHANGES:** 2 starch, 1/2 fat.

Hot Fruit Compote

FAT SALT MEAT-LESS

PREP: 10 Min.   **BAKE:** 45 Min.   **YIELD:** 12 Servings

I threw this together once when I needed another side dish. It was a success!   —Lisa Sharman, Helena, Alabama

     2 medium tart apples, peeled and cubed
     1 can (20 ounces) unsweetened pineapple chunks, drained
     1 can (15 ounces) reduced-sugar sliced pears, drained
     1 can (15 ounces) reduced-sugar sliced peaches, drained
     1 can (16 ounces) whole-berry cranberry sauce
   1/4 cup packed brown sugar
     1 teaspoon ground cinnamon
   1/4 teaspoon ground ginger
   1/4 teaspoon ground cloves

In a 2-qt. baking dish coated with nonstick cooking spray, combine the apples, pineapple, pears and peaches. In a small bowl, combine the cranberry sauce, brown sugar, cinnamon, ginger and cloves. Stir into fruit mixture. Cover and bake at 350° for 45-55 minutes or until bubbly.

NUTRITION FACTS: 2/3 cup equals 125 calories, trace fat (trace saturated fat), 0 cholesterol, 17 mg sodium, 32 g carbohydrate, 2 g fiber, trace protein. **DIABETIC EXCHANGES:** 1 starch, 1 fruit.

Veggies from the Grill

(PICTURED BELOW)

CARB MEAT-LESS

PREP/TOTAL TIME: 25 Min.   **YIELD:** 6 Servings

Yellow summer squash, bright asparagus and other vegetables get flame-broiled treatment in this versatile idea. Our home economists gave the grilled specialty a flavor boost with red wine vinegar, basil and a sprinkling of Parmesan cheese.

- 2 tablespoons olive oil
- 1/2 teaspoon salt
- 1/4 teaspoon pepper
- 1/2 pound fresh asparagus, trimmed and cut into 2-inch pieces
- 1 medium yellow summer squash, cut into 1-inch pieces
- 1 medium sweet red pepper, cut into 1-inch pieces
- 1 medium sweet onion, cut into 1-inch pieces
- 1 cup quartered fresh mushrooms
- 2 tablespoons red wine vinegar
- 2 tablespoons minced fresh basil
- 1/4 cup shredded Parmesan cheese

In a large resealable plastic bag, combine the oil, salt and pepper. Add the asparagus, squash, red pepper, onion and mushrooms; seal bag and turn to coat.

Transfer the vegetables to a grill wok or basket. Grill, uncovered, over medium heat for 8-12 minutes or until tender, stirring frequently.

Place vegetables in a serving bowl. Add vinegar and basil; toss to coat. Sprinkle with Parmesan cheese. Serve warm.

NUTRITION FACTS: 3/4 cup equals 81 calories, 6 g fat (1 g saturated fat), 2 mg cholesterol, 258 mg sodium, 6 g carbohydrate, 2 g fiber, 3 g protein. **DIABETIC EXCHANGES:** 1 vegetable, 1 fat.

Stuffing from the Slow Cooker

MEAT-LESS

(PICTURED ABOVE)

PREP: 30 Min.   **COOK:** 3 Hours   **YIELD:** 12 Servings

If you're hosting a big Thanksgiving dinner this year, add this simple, slow-cooked stuffing to your menu to ease entertaining duties. It comes in handy when you run out of oven space at large family gatherings. —Mrs. Donald Seiler, Macon, Mississippi

- 1 cup chopped onion
- 1 cup chopped celery
- 1/4 cup butter
- 6 cups cubed day-old white bread
- 6 cups cubed day-old whole wheat bread
- 1 teaspoon salt
- 1 teaspoon poultry seasoning
- 1 teaspoon rubbed sage
- 1/2 teaspoon pepper
- 1 can (14-1/2 ounces) reduced-sodium chicken broth *or* vegetable broth
- 1/2 cup egg substitute

In a small nonstick skillet over medium heat, cook onion and celery in butter until tender. In a large bowl, combine the bread cubes, salt, poultry seasoning, sage and pepper. Stir in onion mixture. Combine broth and egg substitute; add to bread mixture and toss to coat.

Transfer to a 3-qt. slow cooker coated with nonstick cooking spray. Cover and cook on low for 3-4 hours or until heated through.

NUTRITION FACTS: 2/3 cup equals 141 calories, 5 g fat (3 g saturated fat), 10 mg cholesterol, 548 mg sodium, 19 g carbohydrate, 2 g fiber, 5 g protein. **DIABETIC EXCHANGES:** 1-1/2 starch, 1/2 fat.

Breakfast & Brunch

Rise and shine! The most important meal of the day is tastier than ever. Begin each morning on a healthy note as you whip up these sunny specialties. You're sure to find that there's no better way to jump start your day.

French Omelet, p. 88

Egg 'n' Potato Burritos

(PICTURED BELOW)

PREP: 20 Min.   **COOK:** 25 Min.   **YIELD:** 6 Servings

This is my husband's favorite breakfast. The dish adds zip to meals on the fly. —Ann Yarber, Washington, Oklahoma

- 1 cup frozen shredded hash brown potatoes
- 3 green onions, chopped
- 1 tablespoon olive oil
- 8 eggs, beaten
- 1 can (14-1/2 ounces) diced tomatoes with mild green chilies, drained
- 1/2 teaspoon salt
- 1/2 teaspoon pepper
- 6 fat-free flour tortillas (8 inches), warmed
- 1 cup (4 ounces) shredded reduced-fat cheddar cheese

In a large nonstick skillet, cook potatoes and onions in oil over medium heat for 8-10 minutes or until potatoes are tender, stirring occasionally. In a large bowl, combine the eggs, tomatoes, salt and pepper. Pour over potato mixture. Reduce heat to medium-low. Cook and stir until eggs are completely set.

Remove from the heat. Spoon about 1/2 cup of egg mixture down the center of each tortilla; sprinkle with cheese. Fold sides and ends of each tortilla over filling and roll up.

NUTRITION FACTS: 1 burrito equals 317 calories, 13 g fat (5 g saturated fat), 297 mg cholesterol, 905 mg sodium, 33 g carbohydrate, 2 g fiber, 17 g protein. **DIABETIC EXCHANGES:** 2 starch, 11/2 fat, 1 lean meat, 1 vegetable.

Pumpkin Pancakes

(PICTURED ABOVE)

PREP/TOTAL TIME: 20 Min.   **YIELD:** 6 Servings

I created these light pumpkin-flavored pancakes with two kinds of flour and a blend of spices for a delightful taste. Serve them as a change of pace or for a fun meat-free dinner.
—Vicki Floden, Story City, Iowa

- 1-1/2 cups all-purpose flour
- 1/2 cup whole wheat flour
- 2 tablespoons brown sugar
- 2 teaspoons baking powder
- 1 teaspoon ground cinnamon
- 1/2 teaspoon salt
- 1/2 teaspoon ground ginger
- 1/2 teaspoon ground nutmeg
- 1-1/2 cups fat-free milk
- 1/2 cup canned pumpkin
- 1 egg white
- 2 tablespoons canola oil

In a large bowl, combine the first eight ingredients. Combine the milk, pumpkin, egg white and oil; stir into dry ingredients just until moistened.

Pour batter by 1/4 cupfuls onto a hot griddle coated with nonstick cooking spray; turn when bubbles form on top. Cook each until second side is golden brown.

NUTRITION FACTS: 2 pancakes equals 240 calories, 5 g fat (1 g saturated fat), 1 mg cholesterol, 375 mg sodium, 41 g carbohydrate, 3 g fiber, 8 g protein. **DIABETIC EXCHANGES:** 2-1/2 starch, 1 fat.

Meatless Sausage Egg Bake

(PICTURED ABOVE)

MEAT-
LESS

PREP: 25 Min.   **BAKE:** 35 Min. + Standing   **YIELD:** 8 Servings

Our hot bake pleases all palates. The Test Kitchen staff used vege-
tarian breakfast patties to create a satisfying casserole that doesn't
pack on pounds.

  1 small onion, chopped
  1 small green pepper, chopped
  1 small sweet red pepper, chopped
  2 teaspoons canola oil
12 egg whites
  6 eggs
  1 cup fat-free milk
  1 package (16 ounces) frozen shredded hash brown
     potatoes, thawed

  1 cup (4 ounces) shredded reduced-fat cheddar cheese
  1 package (8 ounces) frozen vegetarian breakfast
     sausage patties, thawed and crumbled
  1 teaspoon salt
1/2 teaspoon pepper

In a small nonstick skillet, saute onion and peppers in oil until tender. In a large bowl, beat the egg whites, eggs and milk.
Stir in hash browns, cheese, crumbled sausage, salt, pepper
and onion mixture.

Transfer to a 13-in. x 9-in. x 2-in. baking dish coated with
nonstick cooking spray. Bake, uncovered, at 350° for 35-45
minutes or until a knife inserted near the center comes out
clean. Let stand for 10 minutes before cutting.

NUTRITION FACTS: 1 piece equals 256 calories, 11 g fat (3 g saturated fat),
170 mg cholesterol, 733 mg sodium, 19 g carbohydrate, 4 g fiber, 22 g
protein. **DIABETIC EXCHANGES:** 3 lean meat, 1 starch, 1/2 fat.

French Omelet

CARB

(PICTURED ABOVE)

PREP/TOTAL TIME: 20 Min.   **YIELD:** 2 Servings

This cheesy omelet is modeled after one I tried in a restaurant. Mine is so hearty and rich-tasting that no one suspects it's light.
—Bernice Morris, Marshfield, Missouri

    2 eggs, lightly beaten
1/2 cup egg substitute
1/4 cup fat-free milk
1/8 teaspoon salt
1/8 teaspoon pepper
1/4 cup cubed fully cooked lean ham
    1 tablespoon chopped onion
    1 tablespoon chopped green pepper
1/4 cup shredded reduced-fat cheddar cheese

In a small bowl, combine the eggs, egg substitute, milk, salt and pepper. Coat a 10-in. nonstick skillet with nonstick cooking spray and place over medium heat. Add egg mixture. As eggs set, lift edges, letting uncooked portion flow underneath.

When eggs are set, sprinkle ham, onion, green pepper and cheese over one side; fold omelet over filling. Cover and let stand for 1 minute or until cheese is melted.

NUTRITION FACTS: 1/2 omelet equals 180 calories, 9 g fat (4 g saturated fat), 230 mg cholesterol, 661 mg sodium, 4 g carbohydrate, trace fiber, 20 g protein. **DIABETIC EXCHANGES:** 3 lean meat, 1 fat.

Chili-Cheese Breakfast Bake

MEAT-LESS

PREP: 20 Min. + Chilling   **BAKE:** 1 Hour   **YIELD:** 4 Servings

Here's a Southwest-flavored breakfast casserole that will get 'em out of bed on nippy mornings.   —Kathy Mead, Surprise, Arizona

    6 slices whole wheat bread, cubed
1/2 cup shredded reduced-fat Mexican cheese blend
    1 can (4 ounces) chopped green chilies
    4 eggs
    4 egg whites
    2 cups fat-free milk
    1 teaspoon ground mustard
1/2 teaspoon salt
Dash pepper

In a 1-1/2-qt. baking dish coated with nonstick cooking spray, layer half of the bread cubes, cheese and chilies. Repeat layers. In a large bowl, whisk the eggs, egg whites, milk, mustard, salt and pepper; pour over top. Cover and refrigerate overnight.

Remove from the refrigerator 30 minutes before baking. Bake, uncovered, at 350° for 60-70 minutes or until a knife inserted near the center comes out clean and a thermometer reads 160°. Let stand for 5 minutes before cutting.

NUTRITION FACTS: 1-1/2 cups equals 287 calories, 10 g fat (4 g saturated fat), 225 mg cholesterol, 910 mg sodium, 28 g carbohydrate, 3 g fiber, 22 g protein. **DIABETIC EXCHANGES:** 2 lean meat, 1-1/2 starch, 1/2 fat-free milk, 1/2 fat.

Favorite Recipe Made Lighter

SWEET SUCCESS is certain with Valma Devall's Crumb Coffee Cake. "The recipe is delightful," writes the Kennewick, Washington baker, "but I'd like a lighter version."

Our home economists replaced some of the butter with canola oil and unsweetened applesauce. Butter flavoring helped capture the buttery taste of Valma's cake.

The makeover professionals halved the sugar and replaced it with a sugar blend for baking. Using low-fat ingredients and less icing helped our staff cut 60% of the saturated fat from Makeover Crumb Coffee Cake as well as 43% of the cholesterol.

Crumb Coffee Cake

PREP: 35 Min. **BAKE:** 25 Min. + Cooling **YIELD:** 18 Servings

    1 cup butter, softened
1-1/2 cups sugar
    2 eggs, lightly beaten
1-1/2 teaspoons vanilla extract
    2 cups cake flour
    1 teaspoon baking powder
    1 teaspoon baking soda
    1 cup (8 ounces) sour cream
FILLING:
    1/2 cup chopped walnuts
    1/4 cup packed brown sugar
    2 tablespoons sugar
    1 teaspoon ground cinnamon
TOPPING:
    7 tablespoons all-purpose flour
    1/4 cup packed brown sugar
    3 tablespoons sugar
    2 teaspoons ground cinnamon
    5 tablespoons cold butter
    1 cup chopped walnuts
ICING:
    1/4 cup confectioners' sugar
1-1/2 teaspoons milk
    1/4 teaspoon vanilla extract

In a bowl, cream butter and sugar. Beat in eggs and vanilla. Combine the flour, baking powder and baking soda; add to creamed mixture alternately with sour cream. Pour half of the batter into a greased 13-in. x 9-in. x 2-in. baking pan. Combine filling ingredients; sprinkle over batter. Carefully top with remaining batter. For the topping, combine the flour, sugars and cinnamon in a bowl; cut in butter until crumbly. Stir in walnuts. Sprinkle over batter. Bake at 350° for 45-50 minutes or until a toothpick inserted near the center comes out clean. Cool on a wire rack. Combine icing ingredients; drizzle over cake.

NUTRITION FACTS: 1 piece equals 391 calories, 22 g fat (10 g saturated fat), 68 mg cholesterol, 244 mg sodium, 44 g carbohydrate, 1 g fiber, 5 g protein.

Makeover Crumb Coffee Cake
(PICTURED AT RIGHT)

PREP: 35 Min.
BAKE: 25 Min. + Cooling
YIELD: 18 Servings

    1/4 cup butter, softened
    3/4 cup sugar
    1/3 cup sugar blend for
        baking
    2 eggs, lightly beaten
    1/2 cup unsweetened applesauce
    1/4 cup canola oil
1-1/2 teaspoons vanilla extract
    1/4 teaspoon butter flavoring
    2 cups cake flour
    1 teaspoon baking powder
    1 teaspoon baking soda
    1/4 teaspoon salt
    1 cup (8 ounces) reduced-fat sour cream
FILLING:
    1/2 cup chopped walnuts
    1/4 cup packed brown sugar
    2 tablespoons sugar
    1 teaspoon ground cinnamon
TOPPING:
    3 tablespoons plus 1-1/2 teaspoons all-purpose flour
    2 tablespoons brown sugar
4-1/2 teaspoons sugar
    1 teaspoon ground cinnamon
    2 tablespoons plus 1-1/2 teaspoons cold butter
    1/2 cup chopped walnuts
ICING:
    1/4 cup confectioners' sugar
1-1/2 teaspoons milk
    1/4 teaspoon vanilla extract

In a bowl, beat butter, sugar and sugar blend on medium speed for 2 minutes or until crumbly. Add the next five ingredients; mix well. Combine flour, baking powder, baking soda and salt; add to butter mixture alternately with sour cream. Pour half of the batter into a 13-in. x 9-in. x 2-in. baking pan coated with nonstick cooking spray. Combine filling ingredients; sprinkle over batter. Carefully top with remaining batter.

For the topping, combine the flour, sugars and cinnamon in a bowl; cut in butter until crumbly. Stir in walnuts. Sprinkle over batter. Bake at 350° for 25-30 minutes or until a toothpick inserted near the center comes out clean. Cool on a wire rack. Combine icing ingredients; drizzle over cake.

NUTRITION FACTS: 1 piece equals 278 calories, 13 g fat (4 g saturated fat), 39 mg cholesterol, 185 mg sodium, 36 g carbohydrate, 1 g fiber, 5 g protein. **DIABETIC EXCHANGES:** 2-1/2 fat, 2 starch.

Editor's Note: This recipe was tested with Splenda Sugar Blend for Baking.

Place tomatoes in a small bowl. Cover with 1/4 cup water; let stand for 30 minutes. Meanwhile, in a large bowl, whisk the eggs, egg whites, cilantro, butter, salt, pepper and the remaining water.

Heat an 8-in. nonstick skillet coated with nonstick cooking spray; pour about 1/2 cup egg mixture into center of skillet. Lift and tilt pan to evenly coat bottom. Cook for 1-1/2 to 2 minutes or until top appears dry; turn and cook 30-45 seconds longer or until set. Remove from the pan and press into a 1-cup baking dish or ramekin coated with nonstick cooking spray. Repeat with remaining egg mixture, making three more omelet cups (coat skillet with nonstick cooking spray as needed). Sprinkle provolone cheese into cups.

Drain tomatoes; chop and set aside. In a large nonstick skillet, saute leeks and onions in oil until tender. Stir in the tomatoes, olives and oregano; cook over medium heat for 2-3 minutes. Spoon into omelet cups. Sprinkle with Parmesan cheese; drizzle with honey. Bake at 350° for 10-12 minutes or until heated through.

NUTRITION FACTS: 1 filled omelet cup equals 246 calories, 16 g fat (6 g saturated fat), 178 mg cholesterol, 764 mg sodium, 12 g carbohydrate, 1 g fiber, 15 g protein. **DIABETIC EXCHANGES:** 2 lean meat, 2 fat, 1 vegetable.

Pepper Cheese Omelet

 CARB MEAT-LESS

PREP/TOTAL TIME: 25 Min. **YIELD:** 2 Servings

Featuring red pepper, onion and cheese, this savory omelet is as scrumptious for dinner as it is for brunch.
—Susan Rekerdres, Dallas, Texas

      2 eggs
      4 egg whites
      2 teaspoons fat-free milk
      1 teaspoon paprika
    1/4 teaspoon salt
    1/4 teaspoon pepper
      2 tablespoons finely chopped onion
      2 tablespoons finely chopped sweet red pepper
    1/4 cup shredded part-skim mozzarella cheese

In a small bowl, beat the eggs, egg whites, milk, paprika, salt and pepper. Coat an 8-in. nonstick skillet with nonstick cooking spray and place over medium heat. Add half of the egg mixture. As eggs set, lift edges, letting uncooked portion flow underneath.

When eggs are set, sprinkle half of the onion, red pepper and cheese over one side; fold omelet over filling. Cover and let stand for 1 minute or until cheese is melted. Repeat with remaining ingredients.

NUTRITION FACTS: 1 omelet equals 156 calories, 7 g fat (3 g saturated fat), 221 mg cholesterol, 537 mg sodium, 4 g carbohydrate, 1 g fiber, 17 g protein. **DIABETIC EXCHANGES:** 2 lean meat, 1/2 fat.

> **TASTY TIP**
> For extra heat, use Hungarian paprika in the Pepper Cheese Omelet. It is known for being stronger and richer than traditional or Spanish paprika.

Savory Omelet Cups
(PICTURED ABOVE)

 CARB MEAT-LESS

PREP: 40 Min. **BAKE:** 10 Min. **YIELD:** 4 Servings

I replaced the pastry portion of a different recipe with crepe-like cups. Baked in ovenproof dishes, each cup is filled with cheese, leeks, olives and sun-dried tomatoes.
—Joan Churchill, Dover, New Hampshire

    1/4 cup sun-dried tomatoes (not packed in oil)
    1/2 cup water, *divided*
      3 eggs
      6 egg whites
      2 tablespoons minced fresh cilantro
      4 teaspoons butter, melted
    1/2 teaspoon salt
    1/4 teaspoon pepper
    1/3 cup shredded provolone cheese
      1 cup chopped leeks (white portion only)
      2 green onions, chopped
      1 tablespoon olive oil
      2 tablespoons chopped Greek olives
      2 teaspoons minced fresh oregano *or* 1/2 teaspoon dried oregano
    1/4 cup grated Parmesan cheese
      1 tablespoon honey

Chicken Club Brunch Ring

CARB

(PICTURED ABOVE)

PREP: 20 Min.   **BAKE:** 20 Min.   **YIELD:** 16 Servings

A few tubes of low-fat crescent rolls make this impressive recipe a snap. The ring is filled with chicken salad, and I serve warm slices with a mustard-flavored mayonnaise.

—Rebecca Clark, Warrior, Alabama

 1/2 cup fat-free mayonnaise
   1 tablespoon minced fresh parsley
   2 teaspoons Dijon mustard
 1-1/2 teaspoons finely chopped onion
 1-3/4 cups cubed cooked chicken breast (1/2-inch cubes)
   2 bacon strips, cooked and crumbled
   1 cup (4 ounces) reduced-fat shredded Swiss cheese, *divided*
   2 tubes (8 ounces *each*) refrigerated reduced-fat crescent rolls
   2 plum tomatoes
   2 cups shredded lettuce

In a large bowl, combine the mayonnaise, parsley, mustard and onion. Stir in the chicken, bacon and 3/4 cup cheese.

Unroll crescent dough; separate into 16 triangles. Arrange on an ungreased 12-in. round pizza pan, forming a ring with pointed ends facing outer edge of pan and wide ends overlapping. Spoon chicken mixture over wide ends; fold points over filling and tuck under wide ends (filling will be visible). Chop half of a tomato; set aside. Slice remaining tomatoes; place over filling and tuck into dough.

Bake at 375° for 20-25 minutes or until golden brown. Sprinkle with remaining cheese. Let stand for 5 minutes. Place lettuce in center of ring; sprinkle with chopped tomato.

NUTRITION FACTS: 1 piece equals 153 calories, 6 g fat (2 g saturated fat), 17 mg cholesterol, 368 mg sodium, 14 g carbohydrate, trace fiber, 9 g protein. **DIABETIC EXCHANGES:** 1 starch, 1 very lean meat, 1 fat.

Kiwi Smoothies

FAT SALT

PREP/TOTAL TIME: 10 Min.   **YIELD:** 4 Servings

These fresh-flavored smoothies can start a day out right or perk up an afternoon. My daughter created the recipe, and we all love it.

—Cindy Reams, Philipsburg, Pennsylvania

   3 kiwifruit, peeled and cut into chunks
   2 medium ripe bananas, cut into 4 pieces and frozen
   1 cup frozen blueberries
   1 cup (8 ounces) fat-free plain yogurt
   3 tablespoons honey
 1/4 teaspoon almond extract, optional
 1-1/2 cups crushed ice

Place the fruit, yogurt, honey and extract if desired in a blender; cover and process until combined. Add ice; cover and process until blended. Stir if necessary. Pour into chilled glasses; serve immediately.

NUTRITION FACTS: 1 cup equals 196 calories, 1 g fat (trace saturated fat), 1 mg cholesterol, 48 mg sodium, 46 g carbohydrate, 5 g fiber, 5 g protein. **DIABETIC EXCHANGES:** 2-1/2 fruit, 1/2 fat-free milk.

Favorite Recipe Made Lighter

BUTTERY quiches filled with fresh vegetables and a blend of eggs and cheese are perfect for bright and sunny brunches as well as chilly fall evenings. And Pam Pressly's Monterey Quiche is no exception.

The Beachwood, Ohio reader relies on eggs, butter, cottage cheese and plenty of Monterey Jack cheese to give the dish its rich flavor and a light texture that's a hit with everyone who tries it. With its creamy goodness and Southwestern flair, it is certainly no wonder the savory specialty won over the *Light & Tasty* testing panel after just one bite.

Unfortunately, Pam's brunch favorite is high in total fat as well as saturated fat. It also offers a whopping 239 mg of cholesterol, so our home economists knew they had their work cut out for them. After a thorough review of the ingredients, they began by replacing certain items with common, low-fat alternates. They also decreased the amount of butter, eggs and cheese. Because so much fat was cut, the team members realized they needed to boost the flavor a bit, so they decided to add a a little sauteed onion and garlic to the golden, early-morning eye-opener.

While cutting back on eggs slashed cholesterol, it also robbed the dish of its delicate texture. That's when the makeover pros increased the volume by beating two egg whites until stiff before adding them to the casserole. They also sprinkled some shredded cheese on top to give the lighter version the golden brown look of the original.

Trimmed of 187 calories and 151 mg of cholesterol, Makeover Monterey Quiche has all the comforting taste of Pam's original. Try it yourself and see. It's ideal for a special brunch or lunch with fresh fruit on the side.

Monterey Quiche

MEAT-LESS

PREP: 25 Min. **BAKE:** 45 Min. + Standing **YIELD:** 2 Quiches (6 servings each)

- 10 eggs
- 4 cups (16 ounces) shredded Monterey Jack cheese
- 2 cups (16 ounces) small-curd cottage cheese
- 2 cans (4 ounces *each*) chopped green chilies
- 1/2 cup butter, melted
- 1/2 cup all-purpose flour
- 1 teaspoon baking powder

Dash salt

- 2 unbaked deep-dish pastry shells (9 inches)

In a large mixing bowl, combine the first eight ingredients. Pour into pastry shells.

Bake at 400° for 10 minutes. Reduce heat to 350°; bake 30 minutes longer or until a knife inserted near the center comes out clean. Let stand for 10 minutes before cutting.

NUTRITION FACTS: 1 piece equals 452 calories, 32 g fat (16 g saturated fat), 239 mg cholesterol, 692 mg sodium, 22 g carbohydrate, trace fiber, 21 g protein.

Makeover Monterey Quiche

MEAT-LESS

(PICTURED ABOVE)

PREP: 25 Min. **BAKE:** 45 Min. + Standing **YIELD:** 2 Quiches (6 servings each)

- 1/2 cup chopped onion
- 1 tablespoon butter
- 2 garlic cloves, minced
- 8 egg whites, *divided*
- 4 eggs
- 2 cups (16 ounces) 1% small-curd cottage cheese
- 2 cups (8 ounces) shredded reduced-fat Monterey Jack cheese *or* Mexican cheese blend, *divided*
- 2 cans (4 ounces *each*) chopped green chilies
- 1/3 cup all-purpose flour
- 3/4 teaspoon baking powder
- 1/4 teaspoon salt
- 2 unbaked deep-dish pastry shells (9 inches)

In a small nonstick skillet, cook onion in butter over medium-low heat until tender, stirring occasionally. Add garlic; cook 2 minutes longer.

In a large mixing bowl, combine 6 egg whites, eggs, cottage cheese, 1-1/2 cups shredded cheese, chilies, flour, baking powder, salt and onion mixture. In a small mixing bowl, beat remaining egg whites until stiff peaks form. Fold into cheese mixture. Pour into pastry shells.

Bake at 400° for 10 minutes. Reduce heat to 350°; bake for 30 minutes. Sprinkle with remaining cheese; bake 5 minutes longer or until a knife inserted near each center comes out clean and cheese is melted. Let stand for 10 minutes before cutting.

NUTRITION FACTS: 1 piece equals 265 calories, 14 g fat (5 g saturated fat), 88 mg cholesterol, 610 mg sodium, 21 g carbohydrate, 1 g fiber, 16 g protein.

MAKEOVER TIP
Reduced-fat Monterey Jack cheese is sometimes hard to find. Look for reduced-fat Mexican cheese blend as an alternative.

Omelet Lorraine

CARB

PREP/TOTAL TIME: 20 Min.   YIELD: 2 Servings

This easy eye-opener is something to crow about. It's like Quiche Lorraine without the crust. It also makes a smart, late-night meal.
—Diane Hixon, Niceville, Florida

  2 eggs, lightly beaten
1/2 cup egg substitute
  2 tablespoons fat-free milk
  1 tablespoon dried minced onion
1/8 teaspoon salt
1/8 teaspoon pepper
  2 bacon strips, cooked and crumbled
1/4 cup reduced-fat shredded Swiss cheese
  1 teaspoon dried parsley flakes

In a small bowl, beat the eggs, egg substitute, milk, onion, salt and pepper. Coat a 10-in. nonstick skillet with nonstick cooking spray and place over medium heat. Add egg mixture. As eggs set, lift edges, letting uncooked portion flow underneath.

    When eggs are set, sprinkle bacon, cheese and parsley over one side; fold omelet over filling. Cover and let stand for 1 minute or until cheese is melted.

NUTRITION FACTS: 1/2 omelet equals 183 calories, 9 g fat (3 g saturated fat), 224 mg cholesterol, 489 mg sodium, 5 g carbohydrate, trace fiber, 20 g protein. DIABETIC EXCHANGES: 3 lean meat, 1 fat.

Spiced Oatmeal Mix

FAT SALT MEAT-LESS

(PICTURED BELOW)

PREP/TOTAL TIME: 15 Min.   YIELD: 18 Servings

Here's a comforting oatmeal that's a quick treat any time.
—Loretta Kleinjan, Volga, South Dakota

  8 cups quick-cooking oats
1-1/2 cups chopped mixed dried fruit
1/2 cup sugar
1/2 cup packed brown sugar
2-1/2 teaspoons ground cinnamon
  1 teaspoon salt
1/2 teaspoon ground nutmeg

In a large bowl, combine all of the ingredients. Store in an airtight container for up to 1 month.

To prepare oatmeal: In a deep microwave-safe bowl, combine 1/2 cup oatmeal mix and 1 cup water. Microwave, uncovered, on high for 1-2 minutes or until bubbly, stirring every 30 seconds. Let stand for 1-2 minutes before serving.

NUTRITION FACTS: 1 cup prepared oatmeal equals 210 calories, 3 g fat (trace saturated fat), 0 cholesterol, 137 mg sodium, 42 g carbohydrate, 4 g fiber, 6 g protein. DIABETIC EXCHANGES: 2 starch, 1/2 fruit.

Editor's Note: This recipe was tested in a 1,100-watt microwave.

Orange Strawberry Smoothies

FAT SALT

(PICTURED ABOVE)

PREP/TOTAL TIME: 5 Min.   YIELD: 6 Servings

My family and friends were so surprised when I told them that this refreshing, healthy drink has a secret ingredient...tofu! My dad even requests it for dessert. —Jan Gilreath, Winnebago, Minnesota

2-1/4 cups orange juice
  1 package (12.3 ounces) silken reduced-fat firm tofu, drained
  3 cups halved frozen unsweetened strawberries
1-1/2 cups sliced ripe bananas

In a food processor, combine the orange juice, tofu, strawberries and bananas; cover and pulse until blended. Transfer to chilled glasses; serve immediately.

NUTRITION FACTS: 1 cup equals 120 calories, 1 g fat (trace saturated fat), 0 cholesterol, 51 mg sodium, 25 g carbohydrate, 3 g fiber, 5 g protein. DIABETIC EXCHANGES: 1-1/2 fruit, 1 very lean meat.

Asparagus Tart

(PICTURED BELOW)

PREP: 20 Min.   **BAKE:** 25 Min. + Standing   **YIELD:** 8 Servings

This golden crust is filled with a creamy egg mixture that includes Gruyere cheese and asparagus spears. Serve it as a meatless main course or an elegant side dish.

—Mary Relyea, Canastota, New York

    1 pound fresh asparagus, trimmed
    3 cups water
Pastry for single-crust pie (9 inches)
    2/3 cup shredded Gruyere *or* Swiss cheese, *divided*
    1/2 cup minced fresh flat-leaf parsley
    4 eggs, lightly beaten
    3/4 cup half-and-half cream
    1/2 teaspoon salt
    1/8 teaspoon cayenne pepper
    1/8 teaspoon ground nutmeg

Cut 2 in. from the top of each asparagus spear; set tops aside. Cut stem ends into 3/4-in. pieces. In a small saucepan, bring water to a boil. Add the 3/4-in. asparagus pieces; cover and boil for 3-4 minutes. Drain and immediately place asparagus in ice water. Drain and pat dry.

On a lightly floured surface, roll out pastry into a 13-in. circle. Press onto the bottom and up the sides of an un-greased 11-in. tart pan with removable bottom; trim edges. Place the blanched asparagus, 1/3 cup cheese and parsley in crust. In a small bowl, combine the eggs, cream, salt, cayenne and nutmeg; pour into crust. Arrange asparagus tops over egg mixture. Sprinkle with remaining cheese.

Place pan on a baking sheet. Bake at 400° for 25-30 minutes or until a knife inserted near the center comes out clean. Let stand for 10 minutes before cutting.

NUTRITION FACTS: 1 piece equals 233 calories, 15 g fat (7 g saturated fat), 132 mg cholesterol, 326 mg sodium, 16 g carbohydrate, 1 g fiber, 8 g protein. **DIABETIC EXCHANGES:** 2-1/2 fat, 1 starch, 1 lean meat.

Mixed Berry French Toast Bake

PREP: 20 Min. + Chilling   **BAKE:** 45 Min.   **YIELD:** 8 Servings

I love this recipe! Perfect for fuss-free holiday breakfasts or company, it's scrumptious and such a cinch to put together the night before.

—Amy Berry, Poland, Maine

    1 loaf (1 pound) French bread, cubed
    6 egg whites
    3 eggs
1-3/4 cups fat-free milk
    1 teaspoon sugar
    1 teaspoon ground cinnamon
    1 teaspoon vanilla extract
    1/4 teaspoon salt
    1 package (12 ounces) frozen unsweetened mixed berries
    2 tablespoons cold butter
    1/3 cup packed brown sugar

Place bread cubes in a 13-in. x 9-in. x 2-in. baking dish coat-ed with nonstick cooking spray. In a bowl, combine the egg whites, eggs, milk, sugar, cinnamon, vanilla and salt; pour over bread. Cover and refrigerate for 8 hours or overnight.

Thirty minutes before baking, remove the berries from the freezer and set aside, and remove the baking dish from the refrigerator. Bake, covered, at 350° for 30 minutes.

In a small bowl, cut butter into brown sugar until crumbly. Sprinkle berries and brown sugar mixture over French toast. Bake, uncovered, for 15-20 minutes or until a knife inserted near the center comes out clean.

NUTRITION FACTS: 1 serving equals 297 calories, 7 g fat (3 g saturated fat), 88 mg cholesterol, 545 mg sodium, 46 g carbohydrate, 3 g fiber, 12 g protein.

Strawberry Banana Smoothies

PREP/TOTAL TIME: 5 Min.   **YIELD:** 3 Servings

Frozen berries and fruit keep these frosty smoothies extra thick. Best of all, the easy recipe is a great way to use up the last banana of the bunch.   —Christy Adkins, Martinez, Georgia

    3/4 cup fat-free milk
    3/4 cup ice cubes, crushed
    1/2 cup reduced-fat strawberry yogurt
    1/2 cup frozen unsweetened strawberries
    1 small firm banana, chopped and frozen
Sugar substitute equivalent to 1/2 cup sugar

In a blender, combine all of the ingredients; cover and process for 30-45 seconds or until smooth. Stir if necessary. Pour into chilled glasses; serve immediately.

NUTRITION FACTS: 1 cup equals 110 calories, 1 g fat (trace saturated fat), 3 mg cholesterol, 55 mg sodium, 23 g carbohydrate, 1 g fiber, 4 g protein. **DIABETIC EXCHANGES:** 1/2 fruit, 1/2 reduced-fat milk.

Editor's Note: This recipe was tested with Splenda No Calorie Sweetener.

Beefed-Up Main Courses

It's easy to keep meat-and-potato lovers running to the table…even if they're cutting back on fat, sodium or carbohydrates. Let these hearty, reader recipes bulk up your weekly menu and show your gang how satisfying healthy eating can be.

Ginger Pepper Steak, p. 102

Beef 'n' Asparagus Pasta
(PICTURED ABOVE)

PREP/TOTAL TIME: 30 Min.   **YIELD:** 4 Servings

I like to serve this stir-fry over penne pasta, but feel free to use whatever variety you have on hand. The recipe also makes a filling meatless entree without the beef.
—Elaine Norgaard, Penn Valley, California

- 3 cups uncooked bow tie pasta
- 1 tablespoon cornstarch
- 3/4 cup reduced-sodium beef broth, *divided*
- 1 boneless beef sirloin steak (1 pound), cut into 2-inch strips
- 1 tablespoon olive oil
- 1 pound fresh asparagus, trimmed and cut into 1-inch pieces
- 4 green onions, chopped
- 4 garlic cloves, minced
- 1 cup sliced fresh mushrooms
- 1 large tomato, diced
- 1 teaspoon dried basil
- 1/2 teaspoon dried oregano
- 1/2 cup dry red wine *or* additional reduced-sodium beef broth
- 2 tablespoons sliced ripe olives, drained
- 1/2 teaspoon salt
- 1/4 teaspoon pepper

Cook pasta according to package directions. In a small bowl, combine cornstarch and 1/4 cup broth until smooth; set aside.

Meanwhile, in a large nonstick skillet or wok, stir-fry beef in oil for 1 minute. Add the asparagus, onions and garlic; stir-fry for 2 minutes. Add the mushrooms, tomato, basil and oregano; stir-fry 2 minutes longer.

Add the wine or additional broth, olives, salt, pepper and remaining broth. Stir cornstarch mixture and stir into skillet.

Bring to a boil; cook and stir for 2 minutes or until thickened. Drain pasta; top with beef mixture.

NUTRITION FACTS: 1 cup beef mixture with 1 cup pasta equals 348 calories, 11 g fat (3 g saturated fat), 64 mg cholesterol, 478 mg sodium, 31 g carbohydrate, 3 g fiber, 29 g protein. **DIABETIC EXCHANGES:** 3 lean meat, 1-1/2 starch, 1 vegetable, 1 fat.

Ground Beef Potpie

PREP: 25 Min.   **BAKE:** 30 Min. + Standing   **YIELD:** 6 Servings

A must-try for the meat-and-potato lover in your home, slices of this hearty meal-in-one are sure to satisfy. The Light & Tasty home economists used refrigerated pastry crust to make it easy as pie.

- 1 pound lean ground beef
- 2 medium onions, chopped
- 1-1/2 cups finely chopped carrots
- 2 cups mashed potatoes (without added milk and butter)
- 1/4 cup beef broth
- 1 teaspoon rubbed sage
- 3/4 teaspoon salt
- 1/2 teaspoon dried thyme
- 1/2 teaspoon dried marjoram
- 1/2 teaspoon pepper
- 1 sheet refrigerated pie pastry

In a large nonstick skillet, cook the beef, onions and carrots over medium heat until beef is no longer pink; drain if necessary. Stir in the potatoes, broth and seasonings. Spoon into an ungreased 9-in. pie plate.

Place pastry over filling; crimp edges to seal. Cut slits in top. Bake at 400° for 30-35 minutes or until crust is golden brown. Let stand for 10 minutes before cutting.

NUTRITION FACTS: 1 piece equals 358 calories, 15 g fat (6 g saturated fat), 44 mg cholesterol, 539 mg sodium, 35 g carbohydrate, 4 g fiber, 18 g protein. **DIABETIC EXCHANGES:** 2 starch, 2 lean meat, 2 fat, 1 vegetable.

Southwestern Beef Stew

(PICTURED BELOW)

PREP: 30 Min.   **COOK:** 8-1/4 Hours   **YIELD:** 7 Servings

This zippy stew seasoned with picante sauce is great on cold winter evenings. The preparation is so easy…it's ready in minutes after a busy day at work. —Regina Stock, Topeka, Kansas

   2 pounds beef stew meat, cut into 1-inch cubes
   1 jar (16 ounces) picante sauce
   2 medium potatoes, peeled and cut into 1/2-inch cubes
   4 medium carrots, cut into 1/2-inch slices
   1 large onion, chopped
   1 teaspoon chili powder
1/4 teaspoon salt
1/4 teaspoon ground cumin
   1 tablespoon cornstarch
1/4 cup cold water

In a large nonstick skillet coated with nonstick cooking spray, brown beef on all sides; drain. Transfer to a 3-qt. slow cooker. Stir in the picante sauce, potatoes, carrots, onion, chili powder, salt and cumin. Cover and cook on low for 8-9 hours or until meat and vegetables are tender.

In a small bowl, combine cornstarch and water until smooth; stir into stew. Cover and cook on high for 15 minutes or until gravy is thickened.

NUTRITION FACTS: 1 cup equals 266 calories, 9 g fat (3 g saturated fat), 81 mg cholesterol, 436 mg sodium, 18 g carbohydrate, 2 g fiber, 26 g protein. **DIABETIC EXCHANGES:** 3 lean meat, 2 vegetable, 1/2 starch.

Grilled Meat Loaves

(PICTURED ABOVE)

PREP: 15 Min.   **GRILL:** 20 Min.   **YIELD:** 4 Servings

A craving for meat loaf combined with a hesitancy to turn on the oven led me to create this grilled entree. It's a huge time-saver, and the scrumptious sauce keeps the lean loaves moist.
—Jennifer Sheller, Lebanon, Pennsylvania

   1 egg white
1/3 cup fat-free milk
   1 tablespoon prepared horseradish
   1 slice rye bread, crumbled
1/4 cup grated carrot
1-1/2 teaspoons dried minced onion
   1 teaspoon minced fresh parsley
1/2 teaspoon salt
1/8 teaspoon pepper
   1 pound lean ground beef
SAUCE:
   2 tablespoons ketchup
4-1/2 teaspoons brown sugar
   1 tablespoon prepared mustard

In a large bowl, combine the egg white, milk and horseradish. Stir in the bread, carrot, onion, parsley, salt and pepper. Crumble beef over mixture and mix well. Shape into four small loaves.

Grill loaves, covered, over medium-hot heat or broil 4-6 in. from the heat for 8 minutes. Turn; cook 8 minutes longer. Combine the sauce ingredients; spoon over loaves. Cook for 2-3 minutes or until a meat thermometer reads 160°.

NUTRITION FACTS: 1 meat loaf equals 241 calories, 9 g fat (4 g saturated fat), 70 mg cholesterol, 569 mg sodium, 14 g carbohydrate, 1 g fiber, 24 g protein. **DIABETIC EXCHANGES:** 3 lean meat, 1 starch.

Teriyaki Flank Steak
(PICTURED AT RIGHT)

CARB

PREP: 10 Min. + Marinating   GRILL: 15 Min.   YIELD: 6 Servings

Warm spring days are the perfect time to get out the grill. And this marinade of teriyaki sauce, ginger and orange peel, makes a perfectly tender steak.   —Sandi Poznanski, St. Howard Beach, New York

    2/3 cup reduced-sodium teriyaki sauce
    1/4 cup water
    1/4 cup honey
      1 tablespoon cider vinegar
  1-3/4 teaspoons ground ginger
  1-1/2 teaspoons grated orange peel
    1/8 teaspoon pepper
      4 garlic cloves, minced
      4 teaspoons sesame oil
      1 beef flank steak (1-1/2 pounds)
      1 green onion, chopped

In a small bowl, combine the first seven ingredients. Transfer 3/4 cup marinade to a large resealable plastic bag; add garlic and sesame oil. Score surface of flank steak, making diamond shapes 1/4 in. deep; place in bag. Seal and turn to coat; refrigerate for 8 hours or overnight. Cover and refrigerate remaining marinade for basting.

Coat grill rack with nonstick cooking spray before starting the grill. Drain and discard marinade from steak. Grill, uncovered, over medium heat for 7-10 minutes on each side or until meat reaches desired doneness (for medium-rare, a meat thermometer should read 145°; medium, 160°; well-done, 170°), basting occasionally with 3 tablespoons of the reserved marinade. Let stand for 5 minutes; slice across the grain. Heat remaining marinade; serve over beef. Sprinkle with green onion.

NUTRITION FACTS: 3 ounces cooked beef equals 220 calories, 10 g fat (4 g saturated fat), 54 mg cholesterol, 352 mg sodium, 9 g carbohydrate, trace fiber, 23 g protein. **DIABETIC EXCHANGES:** 3 lean meat, 1/2 starch.

Vegetable Beef Stir-Fry
CARB

PREP/TOTAL TIME: 30 Min.   YIELD: 4 Servings

My husband, Jerry, has made this entree for years. Even those who don't usually like Chinese food give this low-carb main dish rave reviews.   —Mary Loeffler, Imperial, Pennsylvania

      1 teaspoon cornstarch
      2 tablespoons reduced-sodium soy sauce
      1 teaspoon minced fresh gingerroot
    1/2 teaspoon sugar
    1/4 teaspoon pepper
      1 boneless beef sirloin steak (1 pound), cut into thin
        strips
SAUCE:
      1 teaspoon cornstarch
    1/2 cup reduced-sodium chicken broth
      2 tablespoons ketchup
      1 tablespoon reduced-sodium soy sauce
      2 teaspoons sesame oil
      2 teaspoons canola oil, *divided*
      1 medium sweet onion, cut into chunks

      1 medium green pepper, cut into chunks
      3 plum tomatoes, cut into chunks

In a large bowl, combine the first five ingredients; add beef and toss to coat. Refrigerate for 15 minutes. For sauce, in a small bowl, combine the cornstarch, broth, ketchup, soy sauce and sesame oil until smooth; set aside.

In a large nonstick skillet or wok coated with nonstick cooking spray, stir-fry the beef mixture in 1 teaspoon canola oil until no longer pink. Remove and keep warm. Stir-fry the onion in remaining canola oil for 2 minutes. Add green pepper; stir-fry for 2 minutes. Add tomatoes; stir-fry 1 minute longer.

Return beef to the pan. Stir sauce; add to beef and vegetables. Bring to a boil; cook and stir for 2 minutes or until thickened.

NUTRITION FACTS: 1 cup equals 240 calories, 11 g fat (3 g saturated fat), 63 mg cholesterol, 673 mg sodium, 12 g carbohydrate, 2 g fiber, 24 g protein. **DIABETIC EXCHANGES:** 3 lean meat, 1 vegetable, 1/2 starch, 1/2 fat.

secrets behind the sizzle

Cut from the well-exercised flank section of the steer (just below the loin and sirloin), flank steak is lean, flat and boneless with visible striated muscle fibers and connective tissue. To keep the tasty cut tender:

• Marinate for several hours or overnight before grilling or broiling.

• Score the meat on both sides for increased absorption of the marinade.

• Cook it to just the right temperature to prevent it from getting tough.

• Cut it into thin slices across the grain before serving.

If you have trouble finding flank steak at your grocery store, ask the butcher. Sometimes it is labeled as London broil or jiffy steak.

Mushroom Pepper Steak

(PICTURED BELOW)

CARB

PREP: 15 Min. + Marinating   **COOK:** 15 Min.   **YIELD:** 4 Servings

A fast marinade flavors and tenderizes the sirloin steak in this colorful stir-fry. Garlic and ginger do a terrific job of rounding out the savory flavor. —Billie Moss, El Sobrante, California

   6 tablespoons reduced-sodium soy sauce, *divided*
1/8 teaspoon pepper
   1 pound boneless beef sirloin steak, cut into thin strips
   1 tablespoon cornstarch
1/2 cup reduced-sodium beef broth
   1 garlic clove, minced
1/2 teaspoon minced fresh gingerroot
   3 teaspoons canola oil, *divided*
   1 cup julienned sweet red pepper
   1 cup julienned green pepper
   2 cups sliced fresh mushrooms
   2 medium tomatoes, cut into wedges
   6 green onions, cut into 1/2-inch pieces

In a large resealable plastic bag, combine 3 tablespoons soy sauce and pepper; add beef. Seal bag and turn to coat; refrigerate for 30-60 minutes. In a small bowl, combine the cornstarch, broth and remaining soy sauce until smooth; set aside.

Drain and discard marinade from beef. In a large nonstick skillet or wok, stir-fry the garlic and ginger in 2 teaspoons oil for 1 minute. Add the beef; stir-fry for 4-6 minutes or until no longer pink. Remove beef and keep warm.

Stir-fry the peppers in remaining oil for 1 minute. Add mushrooms; stir-fry 2 minutes longer or until peppers are crisp-tender. Stir broth mixture and add to vegetable mixture. Bring to a boil; cook and stir for 2 minutes or until thickened. Return beef to pan; add tomatoes and onions. Cook for 2 minutes or until heated through.

NUTRITION FACTS: 1-1/4 cups beef mixture equals 241 calories, 10 g fat (3 g saturated fat), 64 mg cholesterol, 841 mg sodium, 13 g carbohydrate, 3 g fiber, 25 g protein. **DIABETIC EXCHANGES:** 3 lean meat, 2 vegetable, 1 fat.

Burrito Pita Pockets

PREP/TOTAL TIME: 30 Min.   **YIELD:** 4 Servings

Quick, delicious and kid-friendly is how I describe my solution to busy, weeknight meals. The handheld pockets are filled with flavor and make an easy, on-the-go addition to summer outings. —Laura Mahaffey, Annapolis, Maryland

   1 pound lean ground beef
   1 envelope burrito seasoning
   1 cup water
   1 can (2-1/4 ounces) sliced ripe olives, drained
   2 pita breads (6 inches), halved
   1 cup shredded lettuce
   1 medium tomato, seeded and chopped
3/4 cup shredded reduced-fat cheddar cheese

In a large nonstick skillet coated with nonstick cooking spray, cook beef over medium heat until no longer pink; drain. Stir in burrito seasoning and water. Bring to a boil. Reduce heat; simmer, uncovered, for 3-5 minutes or until thickened. Stir in olives.

Fill pita bread halves with beef mixture, lettuce, tomato and cheese.

NUTRITION FACTS: 1 filled pita half equals 375 calories, 15 g fat (7 g saturated fat), 71 mg cholesterol, 1,108 mg sodium, 28 g carbohydrate, 3 g fiber, 32 g protein. **DIABETIC EXCHANGES:** 4 lean meat, 2 starch.

Spinach Meatball Subs
(PICTURED BELOW)

PREP: 20 Min.   COOK: 30 Min.   YIELD: 6 Servings

I often make spaghetti and meatballs from this recipe. Use the meatballs for your favorite pasta dish and you'll have supper in a hurry. —Susan Corpman, Newhall, Iowa

   2 large fresh mushrooms, quartered
   2 tablespoons Worcestershire sauce
   6 garlic cloves, minced
   2 tablespoons Italian seasoning
   1 teaspoon pepper
1/2 teaspoon salt
   2 egg whites
   1 package (10 ounces) frozen chopped spinach, thawed and squeezed dry
1/4 cup grated Parmesan cheese
   1 pound lean ground beef
   1 jar (14 ounces) marinara *or* spaghetti sauce
   6 Italian rolls *or* submarine buns, split
   6 tablespoons shredded part-skim mozzarella cheese

In a food processor, combine the first six ingredients; cover and process until blended. Add the egg whites, spinach and Parmesan cheese; cover and process until blended. Transfer to a large bowl; crumble beef over mixture and mix well.

Shape into 1-1/2-in. balls. Line a 15-in. x 10-in. x 1-in. baking pan with heavy-duty foil; place meatballs in pan. Bake at 400° for 10-13 minutes or until meat is no longer pink.

Place the marinara sauce in a large saucepan; add meatballs. Bring to a boil. Reduce heat; cover and simmer for 15 minutes. Spoon meatballs and sauce onto rolls. Sprinkle with mozzarella cheese. Broil for 5-8 minutes or until the cheese is melted.

NUTRITION FACTS: 1 sandwich equals 355 calories, 9 g fat (4 g saturated fat), 53 mg cholesterol, 769 mg sodium, 40 g carbohydrate, 4 g fiber, 27 g protein. DIABETIC EXCHANGES: 2 starch, 2 lean meat, 2 vegetable.

Italian Hot Dish
(PICTURED ABOVE)

PREP: 30 Min.   BAKE: 40 Min.   YIELD: 4 Servings

My husband had a poor perception of healthy food until he tried this beefy casserole. The combination of pasta, mushrooms, green pepper and oregano makes it a favorite in our house.
—Theresa Smith, Sheboygan, Wisconsin

1-1/2 cups uncooked small pasta shells
   1 pound lean ground beef
   1 cup sliced fresh mushrooms, *divided*
1/2 cup chopped onion
1/2 cup chopped green pepper
   1 can (15 ounces) tomato sauce
   1 teaspoon dried oregano
1/2 teaspoon garlic powder
1/4 teaspoon onion powder
1/8 teaspoon pepper
1/2 cup shredded part-skim mozzarella cheese, *divided*
   4 teaspoons grated Parmesan cheese, *divided*

Cook pasta according to package directions. Meanwhile, in a large nonstick skillet coated with nonstick cooking spray, cook the beef, 1/2 cup mushrooms, onion and green pepper until meat is no longer pink; drain. Stir in the tomato sauce, oregano, garlic powder, onion powder and pepper. Bring to a boil. Reduce heat; cover and simmer for 15 minutes.

Drain pasta; place in an 8-in. square baking dish coated with nonstick cooking spray. Top with meat sauce and remaining mushrooms. Sprinkle with 1/4 cup mozzarella and 2 teaspoons Parmesan.

Cover and bake at 350° for 35 minutes. Uncover; sprinkle with remaining cheeses. Bake 5-10 minutes longer or until heated through and cheese is melted.

NUTRITION FACTS: 1 serving equals 391 calories, 12 g fat (5 g saturated fat), 65 mg cholesterol, 663 mg sodium, 36 g carbohydrate, 3 g fiber, 33 g protein. DIABETIC EXCHANGES: 3 lean meat, 2 starch, 2 vegetable, 1/2 fat.

Roast Beef Wrapsody in Blue

PREP/TOTAL TIME: 25 Min.   **YIELD:** 4 Servings

While packing lunch one day, I realized we were out of bread, so I used flour tortillas instead. I added crispy vegetables, our favorite type of dressing and some roast beef, and the results were absolutely delightful!   —Sherry Little, Sherwood, Arkansas

    1/2 cup shredded napa *or* Chinese cabbage
    1/2 cup chopped seeded peeled cucumber
    1/2 cup chopped seeded tomato
      3 tablespoons fat-free ranch salad dressing
      4 flour tortillas (6 inches), warmed
    1/4 cup crumbled blue cheese
    1/4 cup cubed peeled jicama
      2 tablespoons sliced ripe olives, drained
    1/4 pound thinly sliced deli roast beef

In a small bowl, combine the cabbage, cucumber and tomato. Drizzle with dressing and toss to coat. Divide among the tortillas; top with blue cheese, jicama, olives and beef. Roll up tightly and secure with toothpicks. Serve immediately or refrigerate. Remove toothpicks before serving.

NUTRITION FACTS: 1 wrap equals 190 calories, 7 g fat (2 g saturated fat), 17 mg cholesterol, 769 mg sodium, 22 g carbohydrate, 1 g fiber, 10 g protein. **DIABETIC EXCHANGES:** 1-1/2 starch, 1 very lean meat, 1/2 fat.

Weekday Lasagna

PREP: 35 MIN.   **BAKE:** 1 HOUR + STANDING   **YIELD:** 9 SERVINGS

This is my husband's favorite dish. I love it because it's low-fat and a real time-saver since you don't cook the noodles before baking.   —Karen McCabe, Provo, Utah

      1 pound lean ground beef
    1/2 cup chopped onion
      1 can (28 ounces) crushed tomatoes
  1-3/4 cups water
      1 can (6 ounces) tomato paste
      1 envelope spaghetti sauce mix
      1 egg, lightly beaten
      2 cups (16 ounces) fat-free cottage cheese
      2 tablespoons grated Parmesan cheese
      6 uncooked lasagna noodles
      1 cup (4 ounces) shredded part-skim mozzarella cheese

In a large saucepan, cook beef and onion over medium heat until meat is no longer pink; drain. Stir in the tomatoes, water, tomato paste and spaghetti sauce mix. Bring to a boil. Reduce the heat; cover and simmer for 15-20 minutes, stirring occasionally.

In a small bowl, combine the egg, cottage cheese and Parmesan cheese. Spread 2 cups meat sauce into a 13-in. x 9-in. x 2-in. baking dish coated with nonstick cooking spray. Layer with three noodles, half of the cottage cheese mixture and half of the remaining meat sauce. Repeat layers.

Cover and bake at 350° for 50 minutes. Uncover; sprinkle with mozzarella. Bake 10-15 minutes longer or until cheese is melted and lasagna is bubbly. Let stand for 15 minutes before cutting.

NUTRITION FACTS: 1 piece equals 280 calories, 7 g fat (3 g saturated fat), 65 mg cholesterol, 804 mg sodium, 29 g carbohydrate, 4 g fiber, 25 g protein. **DIABETIC EXCHANGES:** 3 lean meat, 2 vegetable, 1 starch.

Beef and Wild Rice Medley

(PICTURED BELOW)

PREP: 15 Min.   **COOK:** 25 Min.   **YIELD:** 4 Servings

A packaged rice mix speeds up preparation of this meal-in-one entree. Cayenne pepper gives the beef a little kick, and an assortment of veggies adds color and crunch.   —Janelle Christensen, Big Lake, Minnesota

    1/2 teaspoon garlic powder
    1/2 teaspoon dried thyme
    1/8 teaspoon cayenne pepper
      1 pound boneless beef sirloin steak, cut into 3/4-inch cubes
      1 tablespoon canola oil
    1/4 cup sliced celery
    1/4 cup julienned green pepper
  2-1/4 cups water
      1 package (6 ounces) long grain and wild rice mix
      1 small tomato, chopped
      2 tablespoons chopped green onion

In a small bowl, combine the garlic powder, thyme and cayenne. Sprinkle over beef cubes.

In a large saucepan coated with nonstick cooking spray, cook beef in oil until no longer pink; drain. Stir in celery and green pepper; cook 2 minutes longer. Stir in the water and rice mix with contents of seasoning packet.

Bring to a boil. Reduce heat; cover and simmer for 23-28 minutes or until rice is tender. Stir in tomato; heat through. Sprinkle with onion.

NUTRITION FACTS: 1 cup equals 327 calories, 10 g fat (2 g saturated fat), 63 mg cholesterol, 626 mg sodium, 33 g carbohydrate, 1 g fiber, 26 g protein. **DIABETIC EXCHANGES:** 3 lean meat, 2 starch, 1/2 fat.

Gingered Pepper Steak

(PICTURED BELOW)

PREP: 15 Min. + Marinating   **COOK:** 15 Min.   **YIELD:** 4 Servings

Seasoned with just the right amount of ginger, this colorful stir-fry is a quick favorite. I got the recipe from my best friend after she made it for me years ago. I loved it then...and still do!

—Tracy Youngman, Post Falls, Idaho

1/3 cup reduced-sodium soy sauce
2 tablespoons cider vinegar
1 tablespoon sugar
3/4 teaspoon ground ginger
1 tablespoon cornstarch
1 beef flank steak (1 pound), cut into thin strips
1 *each* large green and sweet red pepper, julienned
1 teaspoon canola oil

Hot cooked rice, optional

In a small bowl, combine the soy sauce, vinegar, sugar and ginger. In another small bowl, combine the cornstarch and half of the soy sauce mixture until smooth; cover and refrigerate. Pour remaining soy sauce mixture into a large resealable plastic bag; add flank steak. Seal bag and turn to coat; refrigerate for 1-2 hours.

In a large nonstick skillet or wok coated with nonstick cooking spray, stir-fry peppers for 2-3 minutes or until crisp-tender; remove and keep warm.

Drain and discard marinade. In the same pan, stir-fry beef in hot oil for 3-4 minutes or until no longer pink. Stir reserved soy sauce mixture and stir into skillet. Bring to a boil; cook and stir for 2 minutes or until thickened. Return peppers to the pan; heat through. Serve over rice if desired.

NUTRITION FACTS: 1 cup (calculated without rice) equals 235 calories, 10 g fat (4 g saturated fat), 54 mg cholesterol, 875 mg sodium, 12 g carbohydrate, 2 g fiber, 24 g protein. **DIABETIC EXCHANGES:** 3 lean meat, 1 vegetable, 1/2 starch, 1/2 fat.

Orange Beef Stir-Fry

PREP/TOTAL TIME: 30 Min.   **YIELD:** 4 Servings

With its citrusy splash of flavor, this has become a Chinese New Year tradition at our house. As a college student, our son frequently fixed it when it was his turn to cook.

—Marguerite Shaeffer, Sewell, New Jersey

2 tablespoons cornstarch, *divided*
2 teaspoons plus 2 tablespoons sugar, *divided*
4 tablespoons reduced-sodium soy sauce, *divided*
1 egg white
1 beef flank steak (1 pound), cut into thin slices
1/4 cup water
1/4 cup orange juice concentrate
1 tablespoon ketchup
1 teaspoon grated orange peel
1/2 teaspoon hoisin sauce
1 tablespoon canola oil
2 cups hot cooked long grain rice

In a large bowl, combine 1 tablespoon cornstarch and 2 teaspoons sugar. Stir in 2 tablespoons soy sauce until smooth. Add egg white and beat until blended. Add beef and toss to coat. Let stand for 5 minutes.

In a small bowl, combine remaining cornstarch with water until smooth. Add the orange juice concentrate, ketchup, orange peel, hoisin sauce and remaining sugar and soy sauce; set aside.

In a large nonstick skillet or wok, stir-fry beef mixture in hot oil for 2-4 minutes or until meat is no longer pink. Stir orange juice mixture and stir into skillet. Bring to a boil; cook and stir for 2 minutes or until thickened. Serve with rice.

NUTRITION FACTS: 3/4 cup stir-fry with 1/2 cup rice equals 390 calories, 13 g fat (4 g saturated fat), 48 mg cholesterol, 725 mg sodium, 44 g carbohydrate, 1 g fiber, 24 g protein. **DIABETIC EXCHANGES:** 3 lean meat, 2 starch, 1/2 fruit, 1/2 fat.

Chili Sauce Meat Loaf

CARB

(PICTURED ABOVE)

PREP: 20 Min.   **BAKE:** 55 Min. + Standing   **YIELD:** 6 Servings

This meat loaf with a zesty chili sauce is a sure way to please a family. My son-in-law is in his glory when I serve this tasty main course. —Averleen Ressie, Rice Lake, Wisconsin

- 1/3 cup plus 2 tablespoons chili sauce, *divided*
- 1 egg white
- 1 tablespoon Worcestershire sauce
- 3/4 cup quick-cooking oats
- 3/4 cup finely chopped onion
- 2 garlic cloves, minced
- 1 teaspoon dried thyme
- 1/2 teaspoon salt
- 1/2 teaspoon pepper
- 1-1/2 pounds lean ground beef

In a large bowl, combine 1/3 cup chili sauce, egg white, Worcestershire sauce, oats, onion, garlic, thyme, salt and pepper. Crumble beef over mixture and mix.

Shape into a 9-in. x 4-in. loaf; place in an 11-in. x 7-in. x 2-in. baking dish coated with nonstick cooking spray.

Bake, uncovered, at 350° for 50 minutes. Brush with remaining chili sauce. Bake 5-10 minutes longer or until a meat thermometer reads 160°. Let stand for 10 minutes before slicing.

NUTRITION FACTS: 2 slices equals 244 calories, 10 g fat (4 g saturated fat), 69 mg cholesterol, 565 mg sodium, 14 g carbohydrate, 2 g fiber, 24 g protein. **DIABETIC EXCHANGES:** 3 lean meat, 1 starch.

HEALTHY OUTLOOK

In addition to giving Chili Sauce Meat Loaf extra bulk, the quick-cooking oats offer healthful benefits, too. They're a good source of beta-glucan, a soluble fiber that helps you feel full longer.

Stuffed Steak Spirals

CARB

(PICTURED BELOW)

PREP: 35 Min.   **BAKE:** 30 Min. + Standing   **YIELD:** 6 Servings

When looking for an entree for guests, I rely on this appealing recipe. Swirled with a tangy stuffing, the steak has an impressive presentation and taste. —Margaret Pach, Mesa, Arizona

- 1/4 cup chopped sun-dried tomatoes (not packed in oil)
- 1/2 cup boiling water
- 1/2 cup grated Parmesan cheese
- 1/4 cup minced fresh parsley
- 1 tablespoon prepared horseradish, drained
- 1 to 1-1/2 teaspoons coarsely ground pepper
- 1 beef flank steak (1-1/2 pounds)
- 2 teaspoons canola oil

Place tomatoes in a small bowl; add water. Cover and let stand for 5 minutes; drain. Stir in the Parmesan cheese, parsley, horseradish and pepper; set aside.

Cut steak horizontally from a long side to within 1/2 in. of opposite side. Open meat so it lies flat; cover with plastic wrap. Flatten to 1/4 in. thickness. Remove plastic; spoon tomato mixture over meat to within 1/2 in. of edges. Roll up tightly jelly-roll style, starting with a long side. Tie with kitchen string.

Line a shallow roasting pan with heavy-duty foil; coat the foil with nonstick cooking spray. In a large nonstick skillet coated with nonstick cooking spray, brown meat in oil on all sides. Place in prepared pan.

Bake, uncovered, at 400° for 30-40 minutes or until meat reaches desired doneness (for medium-rare, a meat thermometer should read 145°; medium, 160°; well-done, 170°). Let stand for 10-15 minutes. Remove string and cut into slices.

NUTRITION FACTS: 1 serving equals 214 calories, 12 g fat (5 g saturated fat), 53 mg cholesterol, 229 mg sodium, 2 g carbohydrate, 1 g fiber, 22 g protein. **DIABETIC EXCHANGES:** 3 lean meat, 1 fat.

Cut green peppers in half lengthwise; remove seeds. In a large kettle, cook peppers in boiling water for 3-5 minutes. Drain and rinse in cold water. Spoon about 1/3 cup beef mixture into each pepper half.

Place in a 13-in. x 9-in. x 2-in. baking dish coated with non-stick cooking spray. Cover and bake at 350° for 25-30 minutes or until peppers are crisp-tender and filling is heated through.

Top with the remaining chopped tomatoes. Garnish with sour cream, cheese, green onions and grape tomatoes if desired.

NUTRITION FACTS: 2 stuffed pepper halves equals 268 calories, 11 g fat (5 g saturated fat), 62 mg cholesterol, 137 mg sodium, 18 g carbohydrate, 5 g fiber, 26 g protein. **DIABETIC EXCHANGES:** 3 lean meat, 2 vegetable, 1 fat.

Baked Flank Steak

CARB

PREP: 20 Min.   **BAKE:** 50 Min.   **YIELD:** 6 Servings

I've been whipping up this wonderfully satisfying dish for my family for some 15 years now. It's low in calories, and it always brings me raves. —Susan Tannahill, Westford, Massachusetts

   1 beef flank steak (1-1/2 pounds)
   2 medium tomatoes, cut into eighths
   1 medium green pepper, sliced into rings
   1 large onion, thinly sliced and separated into rings
   2 cups sliced fresh mushrooms
   3 tablespoons chili sauce
   3 tablespoons ketchup
   1 tablespoon Worcestershire sauce
1/2 teaspoon salt
1/2 teaspoon pepper
   2 tablespoons cornstarch
   3 tablespoons cold water

Score surface of steak, making shallow diagonal cuts. Place in a 13-in. x 9-in. x 2-in. baking pan coated with nonstick cooking spray. Place tomatoes, green pepper, onion and mushrooms around meat. Combine the chili sauce, ketchup, Worcestershire sauce, salt and pepper; drizzle over meat and vegetables.

Cover and bake at 350° for 50-60 minutes or until meat and vegetables are tender. Remove and keep warm. Pour pan juices into a measuring cup; skim fat.

In a saucepan, combine cornstarch and water until smooth. Gradually stir in 1-1/2 cups pan juices. Bring to a boil; cook and stir for 2 minutes or until thickened. Thinly slice steak across the grain; serve with vegetables and gravy.

NUTRITION FACTS: 3 ounces cooked beef with vegetables and 1/4 cup gravy equals 233 calories, 9 g fat (4 g saturated fat), 54 mg cholesterol, 628 mg sodium, 15 g carbohydrate, 2 g fiber, 24 g protein. **DIABETIC EXCHANGES:** 3 lean meat, 1 vegetable, 1/2 starch.

South-of-the-Border Stuffed Peppers
(PICTURED ABOVE)

SALT

PREP: 25 Min.   **BAKE:** 25 Min.   **YIELD:** 4 Servings

Our Test Kitchen staff put a fun twist on a dinnertime staple with this colorful main course. Garlic, chili powder, cumin and more season the ground beef so well, you won't even miss the salt.

   1 pound lean ground beef
  2/3 cup chopped sweet red pepper
  1/2 cup chopped onion
   2 garlic cloves, minced
1-3/4 cups chopped seeded tomatoes, *divided*
   4 teaspoons chili powder
   1 teaspoon cornstarch
   1 teaspoon ground cumin
  1/2 teaspoon dried oregano
  1/4 teaspoon cayenne pepper
  1/2 cup water
   4 medium green peppers
   2 tablespoons reduced-fat sour cream
   2 tablespoons shredded cheddar cheese
   2 green onions, chopped
   4 grape tomatoes, halved, optional

In a large nonstick skillet, cook the beef, red pepper, onion and garlic over medium heat until meat is no longer pink; drain. Stir in 1/2 cup tomatoes, chili powder, cornstarch, cumin, oregano and cayenne. Gradually stir in water. Bring to a boil. Reduce heat; simmer, uncovered, for 5 minutes.

TASTY TIP
Be sure not to discard any leftover cooked flank steak. Chilled slices are a tasty way to beef up green salads. Or, use the extra meat in no-fuss fajitas.

Spaghetti with Italian Meatballs
(PICTURED BELOW)

PREP: 20 Min.   **COOK:** 1-1/4 Hours   **YIELD:** 10 Servings

This hearty dinner is one of my family's favorites. We enjoy the sauce and beefy meatballs with a variety of pasta.
—Sharon Crider, St. Robert, Missouri

      3/4 cup chopped onion
        1 garlic clove, minced
        1 tablespoon olive oil
        1 can (28 ounces) Italian crushed tomatoes, undrained
        1 can (6 ounces) tomato paste
        1 cup water
  1-1/2 teaspoons dried oregano
      1/2 teaspoon salt
      1/2 teaspoon pepper
MEATBALLS:
        4 slices white bread, torn
      1/2 cup water
        2 eggs, lightly beaten
      1/2 cup grated Parmesan cheese
        1 garlic clove, minced
        1 teaspoon dried basil
        1 teaspoon dried parsley flakes
      1/2 teaspoon salt
        1 pound lean ground beef
        2 teaspoons olive oil
        1 package (16 ounces) spaghetti

In a large saucepan coated with nonstick cooking spray, cook onion and garlic in oil until tender. Stir in the tomatoes, tomato paste, water, oregano, salt and pepper. Bring to a boil. Reduce heat; cover and simmer for 30 minutes.

Meanwhile, in a small bowl, soak bread in water for 5 minutes. Squeeze out excess liquid. In a large bowl, combine the eggs, Parmesan cheese, garlic, basil, parsley, salt and bread. Crumble beef over mixture and mix well. Shape into 1-in. balls.

In a large nonstick skillet coated with nonstick cooking spray, brown meatballs in batches in oil over medium heat.

Add meatballs to sauce; return to a boil. Reduce heat; simmer, uncovered, for 30 minutes or until meatballs are no longer pink. Cook spaghetti according to package directions; drain. Serve with meatballs and sauce.

NUTRITION FACTS: 3 meatballs and 1/2 cup sauce with 2/3 cup spaghetti equals 368 calories, 9 g fat (3 g saturated fat), 73 mg cholesterol, 661 mg sodium, 50 g carbohydrate, 3 g fiber, 20 g protein. **DIABETIC EXCHANGES:** 2-1/2 starch, 2 lean meat, 2 vegetable, 1/2 fat.

portion pointers

Try these tips to better control serving sizes:

- Ask for a to-go container at restaurants and pack the food you will take home before you start eating.
- Avoid serving meals "family style." Portion food onto a plate and bring it to the table.
- Use smaller dinner plates.
- Don't eat directly from bags or cartons. Set the food on a plate or napkin and put the rest away.

Maple-Orange Pot Roast
(PICTURED BELOW)

PREP: 25 Min. **BAKE:** 3 Hours **YIELD:** 8 Servings

Served with fresh bread, this easy-to-prepare, tender roast is a wonderful reminder of autumn flavors. It always brings back memories of a friend's maple sap house in New Hampshire, where I'm originally from. —Christina Marquis, Orlando, Florida

  1 boneless beef rump roast (3 pounds)
1/2 cup orange juice
1/4 cup sugar-free maple-flavored syrup
1/4 cup white wine *or* chicken broth
  2 tablespoons balsamic vinegar
  1 tablespoon Worcestershire sauce
  1 teaspoon grated orange peel
  1 bay leaf
1/2 teaspoon salt
1/4 teaspoon pepper
1-1/2 pounds red potatoes, cut into large chunks
  5 medium carrots, cut into 2-inch pieces
  2 celery ribs, cut into 2-inch pieces
  2 medium onions, cut into wedges
  4 teaspoons cornstarch
1/4 cup cold water

In a large nonstick skillet coated with nonstick cooking spray, brown roast on all sides; drain. Place in a roasting pan coated with nonstick cooking spray.

In the same skillet, combine the orange juice, syrup, wine or broth, vinegar, Worcestershire sauce, orange peel, bay leaf, salt and pepper. Bring to a boil, stirring frequently; pour over meat. Place the potatoes, carrots, celery and onions

around roast. Cover and bake at 325° for 3 hours or until meat is tender.

Remove meat and vegetables and keep warm. Pour pan juices into a measuring cup. Discard bay leaf and skim fat. Pour into a saucepan. In a small bowl, combine cornstarch and water until smooth. Gradually stir into juices. Bring to a boil; cook and stir for 2 minutes or until thickened. Serve with pot roast and vegetables.

NUTRITION FACTS: 3 ounces cooked beef with 3/4 cup vegetables and 2 tablespoons gravy equals 335 calories, 8 g fat (3 g saturated fat), 102 mg cholesterol, 264 mg sodium, 27 g carbohydrate, 4 g fiber, 36 g protein. **DIABETIC EXCHANGES:** 3 lean meat, 2 vegetable, 1 starch.

Slow Cooker Fajitas
(PICTURED ABOVE)

PREP: 25 Min. **COOK:** 8 Hours **YIELD:** 8 Servings

I love the fajitas they serve in Mexican restaurants, but when I prepared them at home, the meat was always chewy. Then I tried this recipe in my slow cooker, and my husband and I savored every last bite. —Katie Urso, Seneca, Illinois

  1 *each* medium green, sweet red and yellow pepper, cut into 1/2-inch strips
  1 medium onion, thinly sliced
  2 pounds boneless beef sirloin steaks, cut into thin strips
3/4 cup water
  2 tablespoons red wine vinegar
  1 tablespoon lime juice
  1 teaspoon ground cumin

- 1 teaspoon chili powder
- 1/2 teaspoon salt
- 1/2 teaspoon garlic powder
- 1/2 teaspoon pepper
- 1/2 teaspoon cayenne pepper
- 8 flour tortillas (8 inches), warmed
- 1/2 cup salsa
- 1/2 cup shredded reduced-fat cheddar cheese
- 8 teaspoons minced fresh cilantro

Place peppers and onion in a 5-qt. slow cooker. Top with beef. Combine the water, vinegar, lime juice and seasonings; pour over meat. Cover and cook on low for 8-9 hours or until meat is tender.

Using a slotted spoon, place about 3/4 cup meat mixture down the center of each tortilla. Top each with 1 tablespoon salsa, 1 tablespoon cheese and 1 teaspoon cilantro; roll up.

NUTRITION FACTS: 1 fajita equals 335 calories, 10 g fat (3 g saturated fat), 69 mg cholesterol, 564 mg sodium, 33 g carbohydrate, 2 g fiber, 30 g protein. **DIABETIC EXCHANGES:** 3 lean meat, 2 starch, 1 vegetable.

Texas Beef Barbecue
(PICTURED BELOW RIGHT)

PREP: 15 Min.   **COOK:** 8 Hours   **YIELD:** 16 Servings

A boneless beef roast simmers for hours in a slightly sweet sauce before it's shredded and tucked into rolls for filling sandwiches. This is a family favorite. —Jennifer Bauer, Lansing, Michigan

- 1 boneless beef sirloin tip roast (4 pounds)
- 1 can (5-1/2 ounces) spicy hot V8 juice
- 1/2 cup water
- 1/4 cup white vinegar
- 1/4 cup ketchup
- 2 tablespoons Worcestershire sauce
- 1/2 cup packed brown sugar
- 1 teaspoon salt
- 1 teaspoon ground mustard
- 1 teaspoon paprika
- 1/4 teaspoon chili powder
- 1/8 teaspoon pepper
- 16 kaiser rolls, split

Cut roast in half; place in a 5-qt. slow cooker. Combine the V8 juice, water, vinegar, ketchup, Worcestershire sauce, brown sugar and seasonings; pour over roast. Cover and cook on low for 8-10 hours or until meat is tender.

Remove meat and shred with two forks; return to slow cooker and heat through. Spoon 1/2 cup meat mixture onto each roll.

NUTRITION FACTS: 1 sandwich equals 339 calories, 8 g fat (2 g saturated fat), 60 mg cholesterol, 606 mg sodium, 39 g carbohydrate, 1 g fiber, 27 g protein. **DIABETIC EXCHANGES:** 3 lean meat, 2-1/2 starch.

MAKE IT EASY
Store any leftover Texas Beef Barbecue in the freezer for satisfying sandwiches anytime.

Grilled Beef Teriyaki

PREP: 20 Min. + Marinating   **GRILL:** 20 Min.   **YIELD:** 6 Servings

Pineapple juice and soy sauce combine for a delightful marinade in this sweet-savory main dish. —Lou Dubrule, El Paso, Texas

- 1 beef flank steak (1-1/2 pounds)
- 3/4 cup beef broth
- 1/2 cup unsweetened pineapple juice
- 1/4 cup reduced-sodium soy sauce
- 1 tablespoon lemon juice
- 1 tablespoon honey
- 1/4 teaspoon ground ginger
- 2 large onions, cut into 1/4-inch slices

Score surface of steak, making shallow diagonal cuts. In a bowl, combine the broth, pineapple juice, soy sauce, lemon juice, honey and ginger.

Pour 1 cup marinade into a resealable plastic bag; add steak. Seal bag and turn to coat; refrigerate for 8 hours or overnight, turning once or twice. Add onions to remaining marinade; cover and refrigerate for 4-6 hours, stirring several times.

Coat grill rack with nonstick cooking spray before starting the grill. Drain and discard marinade. Grill steak, covered, over medium heat for 8-10 minutes on each side or until meat reaches desired doneness (for medium-rare, a meat thermometer should read 145°; medium, 160°; well-done, 170°).

Meanwhile, place onion slices on a vegetable grill rack coated with nonstick cooking spray; grill for 6 minutes on each side or until tender. Thinly slice steak across the grain; serve with grilled onions.

NUTRITION FACTS: 1 serving equals 196 calories, 8 g fat (4 g saturated fat), 54 mg cholesterol, 210 mg sodium, 6 g carbohydrate, 1 g fiber, 23 g protein. **DIABETIC EXCHANGES:** 3 lean meat, 1 vegetable.

Favorite Recipe Made Lighter

"SAVORY crepes are a family specialty at Christmas," says L&T recipe editor Christine Rukavena, "but if they were lighter, I would serve them more often."

We reworked Christine's dish with delicious results. Consider preparing Makeover Manicotti Crepes tonight!

Manicotti Crepes

PREP: 1-1/2 Hours + Simmering **BAKE:** 35 Min. **YIELD:** 10 Servings

- 1 can (28 ounces) whole tomatoes, undrained
- 1-1/2 cups water
- 1 can (8 ounces) tomato sauce
- 1 tablespoon sugar
- 1 teaspoon dried oregano
- 1/2 teaspoon celery salt
- 6 eggs
- 1-3/4 cups water
- 1-1/2 cups all-purpose flour
- 1/4 teaspoon salt
- 3 slices white bread, cubed
- 1/2 cup milk
- 1 egg, lightly beaten
- 3 tablespoons minced fresh parsley
- 2 teaspoons salt
- 1 teaspoon pepper
- 1 pound ground beef
- 1/2 pound bulk mild Italian sausage
- 8 ounces part-skim mozzarella cheese, diced
- 2 tablespoons vegetable oil, *divided*
- 1/2 cup shredded Parmesan cheese

Place tomatoes in a food processor; cover and process until smooth. Transfer to a saucepan; add the next five ingredients. Bring to a boil. Reduce heat; simmer, uncovered, for 2 hours or until reduced to about 4-1/2 cups, stirring occasionally.

Beat eggs and water. Combine flour and salt; add to egg mixture and mix well. Cover and refrigerate for 1 hour.

Soak bread in milk for 5 minutes. Stir in egg, parsley, salt and pepper. Crumble beef and sausage over mixture; mix well. Stir in mozzarella. Cover and refrigerate until assembling.

Heat 3/4 teaspoon oil in an 8-in. nonstick skillet. Stir crepe batter; pour 3 tablespoons into center of skillet. Lift and tilt pan to coat bottom evenly. Cook until top appears dry; turn and cook 15-20 seconds longer. Remove to a wire rack. Repeat with remaining batter, using remaining oil as needed. When cool, stack crepes with waxed paper in between.

Spread about 1/4 cup filling down the center of each crepe; roll up and place in a greased 13-in. x 9-in. x 2-in. baking dish and 11-in. x 7-in. x 2-in. baking dish. Spoon sauce over top; sprinkle with Parmesan cheese. Cover and bake at 350° for 35-45 minutes or until a meat thermometer reads 165°.

NUTRITION FACTS: 2 crepes equals 448 calories, 25 g fat (10 g saturated fat), 213 mg cholesterol, 1,320 mg sodium, 26 g carbohydrate, 2 g fiber, 28 g protein.

Makeover Manicotti Crepes

PREP: 1-1/2 Hours + Simmering **BAKE:** 35 Min. **YIELD:** 10 Servings

- 1 can (28 ounces) whole tomatoes, undrained
- 1-1/2 cups water
- 1 can (8 ounces) tomato sauce
- 3 teaspoons sugar
- 1 teaspoon dried oregano
- 1/4 teaspoon celery salt
- 2 eggs
- 1 cup egg substitute
- 1-3/4 cups fat-free milk
- 1 teaspoon canola oil
- 1-1/2 cups all-purpose flour
- 1/4 teaspoon salt
- 3 slices whole wheat bread, cubed
- 1/2 cup fat-free milk
- 1/4 cup egg substitute
- 1 cup finely chopped green pepper
- 3 tablespoons minced fresh parsley
- 2 garlic cloves, minced
- 1 teaspoon salt
- 1 teaspoon pepper
- 1 pound lean ground beef
- 1/2 pound Italian turkey sausage links, casings removed
- 1 cup (4 ounces) shredded part-skim mozzarella cheese
- 1/4 cup shredded Parmesan cheese

For the sauce, place tomatoes in a food processor; cover and process until smooth. Transfer to a large saucepan; add the next five ingredients. Bring to a boil. Reduce heat; simmer gently, uncovered, for 2 hours or until reduced to about 4-1/2 cups, stirring occasionally.

Beat the next four ingredients. Combine flour and salt; add to egg mixture and mix well. Cover and refrigerate for 1 hour.

Soak bread in milk for 5 minutes. Stir in the egg substitute, green pepper, parsley, garlic, salt and pepper. Crumble beef and sausage over mixture; mix well. Stir in mozzarella. Cover and refrigerate until assembling.

Coat an 8-in. nonstick skillet with nonstick cooking spray; heat. Stir crepe batter; pour 3 tablespoons into center of skillet. Lift and tilt pan to coat bottom evenly. Cook until top appears dry; turn and cook 15-20 seconds longer. Remove to a wire rack. Repeat with remaining batter, coating skillet with cooking spray as needed. When cool, stack crepes with waxed paper in between. Spread 1/4 cup filling down the center of each crepe; roll up and place in a 13-in. x 9-in. x 2-in. baking dish and an 11-in. x 7-in. x 2-in. baking dish coated with nonstick cooking spray. Spoon sauce over top; sprinkle with Parmesan cheese. Cover and bake at 350° for 35-45 minutes or until a meat thermometer reads 165°.

NUTRITION FACTS: 2 filled crepes equals 319 calories, 10 g fat (4 g saturated fat), 91 mg cholesterol, 977 mg sodium, 30 g carbohydrate, 2 g fiber, 26 g protein. **DIABETIC EXCHANGES:** 3 lean meat, 1-1/2 starch, 1 vegetable.

Italian Pot Roast

CARB

(PICTURED ABOVE)

PREP: 15 Min.   **COOK:** 2-3/4 Hours   **YIELD:** 12 Servings

Not only will this tender roast and mouth-watering gravy fill your house with a wonderful aroma, but it will have your family running to the table. —Karen Schultz Breda, Needham, Massachusetts

 1 boneless beef bottom round roast (3 pounds)
1-1/2 cups water
 6 garlic cloves, minced
 2 bay leaves
 2 tablespoons dried basil
4-1/2 teaspoons dried oregano
1-1/2 teaspoons salt
 1/2 teaspoon crushed red pepper flakes
 1/2 teaspoon garlic powder
 1 tablespoon cornstarch
 3 tablespoons cold water

In a Dutch oven coated with nonstick cooking spray, brown roast on all sides; drain. Combine the water, garlic and seasonings; pour over roast. Bring to a boil. Reduce heat; cover and simmer for 2-3/4 to 3-1/4 hours or until the meat is tender.

Discard the bay leaves. Remove roast to a serving platter; let stand for 10 minutes.

Meanwhile, for gravy, pour pan drippings and loosened browned bits into a measuring cup; skim and discard fat. Transfer to a small saucepan. Combine cornstarch and cold water until smooth; gradually stir into drippings. Bring to a boil; cook and stir for 2 minutes or until thickened. Slice beef; serve with gravy.

NUTRITION FACTS: 3 ounces cooked beef with 4-1/2 teaspoons gravy equals 183 calories, 7 g fat (2 g saturated fat), 82 mg cholesterol, 398 mg sodium, 2 g carbohydrate, 1 g fiber, 27 g protein. **DIABETIC EXCHANGES:** 3 lean meat, 1/2 fat.

Colorful Beef Wraps

(PICTURED BELOW)

PREP/TOTAL TIME: 30 Min.   **YIELD:** 6 Servings

I saute sirloin steak, red onion and roasted peppers for these quick wraps. Spreading fat-free ranch salad dressing inside the tortillas jazzes up the taste nicely. —Robyn Cavallaro, Easton, Pennsylvania

 1 boneless beef sirloin steak (1 pound), cut into thin strips
 3 garlic cloves, minced
 1/4 teaspoon pepper
 3 tablespoons reduced-sodium soy sauce, *divided*
 3 teaspoons olive oil, *divided*
 1 medium red onion, cut into wedges
 1 jar (7 ounces) roasted sweet red peppers, drained and cut into strips
 1/4 cup dry red wine *or* reduced-sodium beef broth
 6 tablespoons fat-free ranch salad dressing
 6 flour tortillas (8 inches)
1-1/2 cups torn iceberg lettuce
 1 medium tomato, chopped
 1/4 cup chopped green onions

In a large nonstick skillet coated with nonstick cooking spray, saute the beef, garlic, pepper and 2 tablespoons soy sauce in 2 teaspoons oil until meat is no longer pink. Remove and keep warm.

Saute the onion in remaining oil for 2 minutes. Stir in the red peppers, wine or broth and remaining soy sauce; bring to a boil. Return beef to the pan; simmer for 5 minutes or until heated through.

Spread ranch dressing over one side of each tortilla; sprinkle with lettuce, tomato and green onions. Spoon about 3/4 cup beef mixture down the center of each tortilla; roll up.

NUTRITION FACTS: 1 wrap equals 325 calories, 9 g fat (2 g saturated fat), 43 mg cholesterol, 830 mg sodium, 39 g carbohydrate, 1 g fiber, 20 g protein. **DIABETIC EXCHANGES:** 2 starch, 2 lean meat, 1 vegetable, 1 fat.

Brisket with Cranberry Gravy

(PICTURED ABOVE)

 SALT

PREP: 15 Min.   COOK: 5-1/2 Hours   YIELD: 12 Servings

With just a few minutes of preparation, this tender beef brisket simmers into a delectable entree. The meat and gravy are great for sandwiches and leftovers the next day.
—Noelle LaBrecque, Round Rock, Texas

    1 medium onion, sliced
    1 fresh beef brisket (3 pounds), halved
    1 can (16 ounces) jellied cranberry sauce
  1/2 cup cranberry juice concentrate
    2 tablespoons cornstarch
  1/4 cup water

Place onion in a 5-qt. slow cooker; top with brisket. Combine the cranberry sauce and juice concentrate; pour over beef. Cover and cook on low for 5-1/2 to 6 hours or until meat is tender.

Remove brisket and keep warm. Strain cooking juices, discarding onion; skim fat. In a small saucepan, combine cornstarch and water until smooth; stir in the cooking juices. Bring to a boil over medium heat, stirring constantly. Cook and stir for 2 minutes or until thickened. Thinly slice brisket across the grain; serve with gravy.

NUTRITION FACTS: 3 ounces cooked beef with 3 tablespoons gravy equals 301 calories, 14 g fat (5 g saturated fat), 68 mg cholesterol, 57 mg sodium, 23 g carbohydrate, 1 g fiber, 20 g protein. **DIABETIC EXCHANGES:** 3 lean meat, 1-1/2 starch, 1 fat.

Editor's Note: This is a fresh beef brisket, not corned beef. The meat comes from the first cut of the brisket.

Yummy Pizza Bake

PREP: 25 Min.   BAKE: 40 Min.   YIELD: 8 Servings

After a friend served this filling pizza to my husband and me, it quickly became one of our favorite meals. I always come home with an empty dish and recipe requests when I take it to an event.
—Rita McCullough, New Knoxville, Ohio

1-1/2 pounds lean ground beef
    1 medium onion, chopped
    1 medium green pepper, chopped

    1 cup sliced fresh mushrooms
    1 can (15 ounces) pizza sauce
  1/4 teaspoon garlic powder
  1/4 teaspoon dried oregano
    1 cup (4 ounces) shredded part-skim mozzarella cheese
    2 eggs, lightly beaten
    1 cup fat-free milk
    1 tablespoon canola oil
    1 cup all-purpose flour
  1/2 teaspoon salt
  1/2 cup grated Parmesan cheese
  10 slices pepperoni, chopped

In a large skillet, cook the beef, onion, green pepper and mushrooms over medium heat until meat is no longer pink and vegetables are tender; drain. Stir in the pizza sauce, garlic powder and oregano. Transfer to a 13-in. x 9-in. x 2-in. baking dish coated with nonstick cooking spray; sprinkle with mozzarella cheese.

In a small bowl, combine the eggs, milk, oil, flour and salt; pour over meat mixture. Sprinkle with Parmesan cheese and pepperoni. Bake, uncovered, at 350° for 40-45 minutes or until golden brown.

NUTRITION FACTS: 1 piece equals 331 calories, 14 g fat (6 g saturated fat), 110 mg cholesterol, 589 mg sodium, 21 g carbohydrate, 2 g fiber, 28 g protein. **DIABETIC EXCHANGES:** 3 lean meat, 1-1/2 starch, 1 fat.

Mushroom-Beef Spaghetti Sauce

FAT CARB

PREP: 20 Min.   COOK: 6 Hours   YIELD: 12 Servings

I found this sauce in a recipe exchange and wish I could credit the person who gave it to me. My children love it! I added mushrooms, but if you'd like it chunkier, add some bell pepper or whatever vegetables you have on hand.
—Meg Fisher, Marietta, Georgia

    1 pound lean ground beef
  1/2 pound sliced fresh mushrooms
    1 small onion, chopped
    2 cans (14-1/2 ounces *each*) whole tomatoes, undrained and cut up
    1 can (12 ounces) tomato paste
    1 can (8 ounces) tomato sauce
    1 cup reduced-sodium beef broth
    2 tablespoons dried parsley flakes
    1 tablespoon brown sugar
    1 teaspoon dried basil
    1 teaspoon dried oregano
    1 teaspoon salt
  1/4 teaspoon pepper
Hot cooked spaghetti

In a large nonstick skillet, cook the beef, mushrooms and onion until meat is no longer pink; drain. Transfer to a 3-qt. slow cooker.

Stir in the tomatoes, tomato paste, tomato sauce, broth, parsley, brown sugar, basil, oregano, salt and pepper. Cover and cook on low for 6-8 hours. Serve over spaghetti.

NUTRITION FACTS: 1/2 cup sauce (calculated without spaghetti) equals 115 calories, 3 g fat (1 g saturated fat), 19 mg cholesterol, 493 mg sodium, 12 g carbohydrate, 3 g fiber, 10 g protein. **DIABETIC EXCHANGES:** 2 vegetable, 1 lean meat.

Chicken & Turkey Entrees

When it comes to healthy fare, poultry is natural choice. Not only do chicken and turkey dishes offer the comforting flavors families crave, but they are low in calories, fat and carbohydrates. In addition, chicken is a quick-cooking staple for busy cooks, making it a great option for any meal.

Sherried Artichoke Chicken, p. 130

Curry Chicken

(PICTURED BELOW)

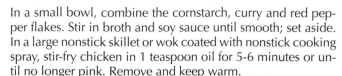

PREP: 20 Min.   COOK: 15 Min.   YIELD: 4 Servings

A little curry powder makes this meal-in-one a super change of pace from weeknight staples. I like how the dash of red pepper flakes adds extra spice and how the carrots, broccoli and green onions lend so much color to the stir-fry.

—Judie White, Florien, Louisiana

> 1 tablespoon cornstarch
> 2 teaspoons curry powder
> 1/8 teaspoon crushed red pepper flakes
> 1 cup reduced-sodium chicken broth
> 1 tablespoon reduced-sodium soy sauce
> 1 pound boneless skinless chicken breasts, cut into cubes
> 2 teaspoons canola oil, *divided*
> 1 cup sliced fresh carrots
> 2 garlic cloves, minced
> 3 cups fresh broccoli florets
> 4 green onions, thinly sliced

In a small bowl, combine the cornstarch, curry and red pepper flakes. Stir in broth and soy sauce until smooth; set aside. In a large nonstick skillet or wok coated with nonstick cooking spray, stir-fry chicken in 1 teaspoon oil for 5-6 minutes or until no longer pink. Remove and keep warm.

In the same pan, stir-fry carrots and garlic in remaining oil for 1 minute. Stir in broccoli; cook 2 minutes longer. Add onions; cook 1-2 minutes longer.

Stir broth mixture and stir into vegetables. Bring to a boil; cook and stir for 2 minutes or until thickened. Return chicken to the pan; heat through.

NUTRITION FACTS: 1 cup equals 194 calories, 5 g fat (1 g saturated fat), 63 mg cholesterol, 389 mg sodium, 10 g carbohydrate, 3 g fiber, 26 g protein. DIABETIC EXCHANGES: 3 very lean meat, 1 vegetable, 1/2 fat.

SHOP SMART

Save time when preparing the chicken stir-fry with sliced carrots from the produce department. The deeper the orange color, the more healthy beta-carotene the carrots are likely to contain.

Jamaican Jerk Turkey Wraps

(PICTURED BELOW)

PREP: 20 Min.   **GRILL:** 20 Min.   **YIELD:** 4 Servings

I received this recipe after tasting the spicy wraps at a neighborhood party. The grilled turkey tenderloins and easy jalapeno dressing make them tops with my gang.

—Mary Ann Dell, Phoenixville, Pennsylvania

> 2 cups broccoli coleslaw mix
> 1 medium tomato, seeded and chopped
> 3 tablespoons reduced-fat coleslaw dressing
> 1 jalapeno pepper, seeded and chopped
> 1 tablespoon prepared mustard
> 1-1/2 teaspoons Caribbean jerk seasoning
> 2 turkey breast tenderloins (8 ounces *each*)
> 4 fat-free flour tortillas (8 inches)

In a large bowl, toss the coleslaw mix, tomato, coleslaw dressing, jalapeno and mustard; set aside. Rub the seasoning over turkey tenderloins.

Coat grill rack with nonstick cooking spray before starting the grill. Grill tenderloins, covered, over medium heat for 8-10 minutes on each side or until a meat thermometer reads 170°. Let stand for 5 minutes.

Grill tortillas, uncovered, over medium heat for 45-55 seconds on each side or until warmed. Thinly slice turkey; place down the center of tortillas. Top with the coleslaw mixture and roll up.

NUTRITION FACTS: 1 wrap equals 295 calories, 4 g fat (1 g saturated fat), 59 mg cholesterol, 658 mg sodium, 34 g carbohydrate, 3 g fiber, 31 g protein. **DIABETIC EXCHANGES:** 3 very lean meat, 2 starch, 1 vegetable, 1/2 fat.

Editor's Note: When cutting or seeding hot peppers, use rubber or plastic gloves to protect your hands. Avoid touching your face.

Chicken Lettuce Wraps

CARB

(PICTURED ABOVE)

PREP/TOTAL TIME: 25 Min.   **YIELD:** 6 Servings

Filled with chicken, mushrooms, water chestnuts and carrot, these wraps are healthy and yummy. They get delicious, Asian flair from gingerroot, rice wine vinegar and teriyaki sauce.

—Kendra Doss, Smithville, Missouri

> 1-1/2 pounds boneless skinless chicken breasts, cubed
> 1 tablespoon plus 1-1/2 teaspoons peanut oil, *divided*
> 3/4 cup chopped fresh mushrooms
> 1 can (8 ounces) water chestnuts, drained and diced
> 1 tablespoon minced fresh gingerroot
> 2 tablespoons rice wine vinegar
> 2 tablespoons reduced-sodium teriyaki sauce
> 1 tablespoon reduced-sodium soy sauce
> 1/2 teaspoon garlic powder
> 1/4 teaspoon crushed red pepper flakes
> 1-1/2 cups shredded carrots
> 1/2 cup julienned green onions
> 12 Bibb *or* Boston lettuce leaves
> 1/3 cup sliced almonds, toasted

In a large nonstick skillet coated with nonstick cooking spray, cook chicken in 1 tablespoon oil for 3 minutes; drain. Add the mushrooms, water chestnuts and ginger; cook 4-6 minutes longer or until chicken juices run clear. Drain and set aside.

In a small bowl, whisk the vinegar, teriyaki sauce, soy sauce, garlic powder, red pepper flakes and remaining oil. Stir in the carrots, onions and chicken mixture. Spoon onto lettuce leaves; sprinkle with almonds. If desired, fold sides of lettuce over filling and roll up.

NUTRITION FACTS: 2 wraps equals 230 calories, 9 g fat (2 g saturated fat), 63 mg cholesterol, 278 mg sodium, 12 g carbohydrate, 3 g fiber, 26 g protein. **DIABETIC EXCHANGES:** 3 very lean meat, 2 vegetable, 1 fat.

Favorite Recipe Made Lighter

A COMFORTING DINNER is sure to be had with Melanie Dalbec's down-home casserole. Featuring chicken, spinach and cheese, her Greek Spaghetti is a real crowd pleaser.

"The hot dish is good, but it's not at all healthy," writes Melanie. "I would love it if you could make it over."

Eager to serve the casserole to their own families, the *L&T* cooks rolled up their sleeves and dissected Melanie's meal-in-one. They decreased the mayonnaise, sour cream and canned soup and took advantage of the ingredients' lighter counterparts. Part-skim mozzarella cheese was used to replace the Monterey Jack cheese that was originally called for.

To replicate the creaminess of the original and boost the flavor, a mixture of fat-free milk, flour and chicken bouillon granules was added to the recipe.

Makeover Greek Spaghetti offers all of the hearty goodness you'd expect from a casserole. Best of all, nearly 60% of the fat was cut from the original submission, 159 calories were removed and the sodium content decreased by one-third.

Makeover Greek Spaghetti
(PICTURED ABOVE)

PREP: 30 Min.   BAKE: 25 Min.   YIELD: 10 Servings

- 1 package (16 ounces) spaghetti, broken into 2-inch pieces
- 4 cups cubed cooked chicken breast
- 2 packages (10 ounces *each*) frozen chopped spinach, thawed and squeezed dry
- 1 can (10-3/4 ounces) reduced-fat, reduced-sodium condensed cream of chicken soup, undiluted
- 3/4 cup reduced-fat mayonnaise
- 3/4 cup reduced-fat sour cream
- 3 celery ribs, chopped
- 1 small onion, chopped
- 1/2 cup chopped green pepper
- 1 jar (2 ounces) diced pimientos, drained
- 1/2 teaspoon salt-free lemon-pepper seasoning
- 3 tablespoons all-purpose flour
- 1-1/3 cups fat-free milk
- 1 teaspoon chicken bouillon granules
- 1 cup (4 ounces) shredded part-skim mozzarella cheese
- 1/2 cup soft bread crumbs
- 1/4 cup shredded Parmesan cheese

Cook spaghetti according to package directions; drain. Return spaghetti to saucepan. Stir in the chicken, spinach, soup, mayonnaise, sour cream, celery, onion, green pepper, pimientos and lemon-pepper.

In a small saucepan, whisk flour and milk until smooth. Bring to a boil over medium heat; cook and stir for 2 minutes or until thickened. Stir in bouillon. Pour over spaghetti mixture and mix well.

Transfer to a 13-in. x 9-in. x 2-in. baking dish coated with nonstick cooking spray (dish will be full). Top with mozzarella cheese, bread crumbs and Parmesan cheese. Bake, uncovered, at 350° for 25-30 minutes or until heated through.

NUTRITION FACTS: 1-1/3 cups equals 442 calories, 13 g fat (5 g saturated fat), 67 mg cholesterol, 565 mg sodium, 49 g carbohydrate, 3 g fiber, 31 g protein. **DIABETIC EXCHANGES:** 3 very lean meat, 21/2 starch, 2 fat, 1 vegetable.

Greek Spaghetti

PREP: 30 Min.   BAKE: 25 Min.   YIELD: 10 Servings

- 1 package (16 ounces) spaghetti, broken into 2-inch pieces
- 4 cups cubed cooked chicken breast
- 2 packages (10 ounces *each*) frozen chopped spinach, thawed and squeezed dry
- 2 cans (10-3/4 ounces *each*) condensed cream of chicken soup, undiluted
- 1 cup mayonnaise
- 1 cup (8 ounces) sour cream
- 3 celery ribs, chopped
- 1 small onion, chopped
- 1/2 cup chopped green pepper
- 1 jar (2 ounces) diced pimientos, drained
- 1/2 teaspoon lemon-pepper seasoning
- 1 cup (4 ounces) shredded Monterey Jack cheese
- 1/2 cup soft bread crumbs
- 1/2 cup shredded Parmesan cheese

Cook spaghetti according to package directions; drain. Return spaghetti to saucepan. Stir in the chicken, spinach, soup, mayonnaise, sour cream, celery, onion, green pepper, pimientos and lemon-pepper.

Transfer to a greased 13-in. x 9-in. x 2-in. baking dish (dish will be full). Top with Monterey Jack cheese, bread crumbs and Parmesan cheese. Bake, uncovered, at 350° for 25-30 minutes or until heated through.

NUTRITION FACTS: 1-1/3 cups equals 601 calories, 32 g fat (10 g saturated fat), 85 mg cholesterol, 850 mg sodium, 44 g carbohydrate, 4 g fiber, 31 g protein.

Lemon Thyme Chicken

CARB

(PICTURED BELOW)

PREP: 10 Min. **COOK:** 25 Min. **YIELD:** 4 Servings

Chopped onions are a great addition to the lemon sauce in this supper. Best of all, it takes only a few minutes to brown the lightly breaded chicken on your stovetop.

—Kay Shimonek, Corsicana, Texas

       3 tablespoons all-purpose flour
     1/2 teaspoon salt
     1/4 teaspoon pepper
       4 boneless skinless chicken breast halves (4 ounces *each*)
       2 teaspoons olive oil
       1 medium onion, chopped
       1 tablespoon butter
     1/2 teaspoon dried thyme
       1 cup chicken broth
       3 tablespoons lemon juice
       2 tablespoons minced fresh parsley

In a small bowl, combine the flour, salt and pepper. Set aside 4-1/2 teaspoons for sauce. Sprinkle the remaining flour mixture over both sides of chicken. In a large nonstick skillet coated with nonstick cooking spray, cook chicken in oil over medium heat for 7-9 minutes on each side or until juices run clear. Remove and keep warm.

In the same pan, saute onion in butter until tender. Add the thyme and reserved flour mixture; stir until blended. Gradually stir in the broth and lemon juice, scraping up any browned bits from the bottom of the pan. Bring to a boil; cook and stir for 2 minutes or until thickened. Serve over chicken. Sprinkle with parsley.

NUTRITION FACTS: 1 chicken breast half with 3 tablespoons sauce equals 213 calories, 8 g fat (3 g saturated fat), 70 mg cholesterol, 614 mg sodium, 10 g carbohydrate, 1 g fiber, 25 g protein. **DIABETIC EXCHANGES:** 3 very lean meat, 1 fat, 1/2 starch.

Honey-Lime Roasted Chicken

SALT CARB

(PICTURED ABOVE)

PREP: 10 Min. **BAKE:** 2-1/2 Hours + Standing **YIELD:** 10 Servings

It's hard to believe this finger-licking main course starts with only five ingredients. The chicken is easy, light and so good.

—Lori Carbonell, Springfield, Vermont

       1 whole roasting chicken (5 to 6 pounds)
     1/2 cup lime juice
     1/4 cup honey
       1 tablespoon stone-ground mustard *or* spicy brown mustard
       1 teaspoon ground cumin

Carefully loosen the skin from the entire chicken. Place breast side up on a rack in a roasting pan. In a small bowl, whisk the lime juice, honey, mustard and cumin. Using a turkey baster, baste under the chicken skin with 1/3 cup lime juice mixture. Tie drumsticks together. Pour remaining lime juice mixture over chicken.

Bake, uncovered, at 350° for 2-1/2 to 3 hours or until a meat thermometer reads 180°, basting every 30 minutes with drippings (cover loosely with foil after 1 to 1-1/2 hours or when golden brown). Let stand for 10 minutes before carving. Remove and discard skin before serving.

NUTRITION FACTS: 3 ounces cooked chicken equals 197 calories, 7 g fat (2 g saturated fat), 77 mg cholesterol, 95 mg sodium, 8 g carbohydrate, trace fiber, 25 g protein. **DIABETIC EXCHANGES:** 3 lean meat, 1/2 starch.

Barbecued Chicken Breasts
(PICTURED BELOW)

PREP: 10 Min. + Marinating   **GRILL:** 40 Min.   **YIELD:** 6 Servings

I make large batches of this marinade and freeze it so it's on hand when we're in the mood to grill. There's a real zip to this chicken that kicks up flavor without much fat. I'm sure you'll like it as much as we do.   —Margaret Wilson, Hemet, California

  1-1/2 cups chili sauce
   1/2 cup red wine vinegar
  4-1/2 teaspoons prepared horseradish
     2 garlic cloves, minced
     6 bone-in chicken breast halves (9 ounces *each*)

In a small bowl, combine the chili sauce, vinegar, horseradish and garlic. Remove 1 cup to another bowl for basting; cover and refrigerate.

Carefully loosen chicken skin on one side to form a pocket. Place in a 13-in. x 9-in. x 2-in. baking dish. Spread some of the remaining marinade under the skin; spread the rest over the chicken. Cover and refrigerate for 1 hour.

Coat grill rack with nonstick cooking spray before starting the grill. Prepare grill for indirect heat. Place chicken skin side down on grill rack. Grill, covered, over indirect medium heat for 20 minutes. Turn; grill 20-25 minutes longer or until the juices run clear, basting occasionally with the reserved marinade.

NUTRITION FACTS: 1 chicken breast half (with skin removed) equals 261 calories, 4 g fat (1 g saturated fat), 102 mg cholesterol, 1,022 mg sodium, 17 g carbohydrate, trace fiber, 37 g protein. **DIABETIC EXCHANGES:** 5 very lean meat, 1 starch.

TASTY TIP
The vents on a charcoal grill help regulate temperature. Open vents circulate air, heating the coals. Closed vents eliminate air circulation, eventually extinguishing coals.

Apricot Orange Chicken
(PICTURED ABOVE)

PREP/TOTAL TIME: 30 Min.   **YIELD:** 4 Servings

A lot of lip-smacking apricot flavor makes this sweet stir-fry Sunday-worthy. It goes together so quickly, and I get rave reviews whenever I serve it.   —Sharon Warner, Ada, Oklahoma

  1-1/2 cups reduced-sodium chicken broth
   3/4 cup uncooked long grain rice
     1 tablespoon cornstarch
   1/2 cup cold water
     1 pound boneless skinless chicken breasts, cut into
        1-inch pieces
     2 teaspoons canola oil
   1/2 cup 100% orange marmalade spreadable fruit
   1/3 cup dried apricots, cut into thirds
   1/2 to 1 teaspoon Chinese five-spice powder
     1 teaspoon reduced-sodium soy sauce

In a small saucepan, bring broth and rice to a boil. Reduce heat; cover and simmer for 15 minutes or until rice is tender.

Meanwhile, in a small bowl, combine cornstarch and water until smooth; set aside. In a large nonstick skillet or wok coated with nonstick cooking spray, stir-fry chicken in hot oil for 5 minutes or until lightly browned. Stir in the marmalade, apricots, five-spice powder and soy sauce. Bring to a boil.

Stir cornstarch mixture and stir into chicken mixture. Bring to a boil; cook and stir for 2 minutes or until thickened. Serve over rice.

NUTRITION FACTS: 2/3 cup chicken mixture with 1/2 cup rice equals 391 calories, 5 g fat (1 g saturated fat), 63 mg cholesterol, 340 mg sodium, 57 g carbohydrate, 1 g fiber, 27 g protein. **DIABETIC EXCHANGES:** 3 very lean meat, 2 starch, 2 fruit, 1/2 fat.

Creamy Turkey Fettuccine

PREP/TOTAL TIME: 30 Min. **YIELD:** 6 Servings

This is one of my family's favorite turkey dishes. There are never any leftovers. I like it because it's quick, light and delicious.
—Paula Marchesi, Lenhartsville, Pennsylvania

  12 ounces uncooked fettuccine
3/4 cup fat-free milk
   4 ounces fat-free cream cheese, cubed
1/2 cup reduced-fat garlic-herb cheese spread
   2 cups cubed cooked turkey breast
   1 package (10 ounces) frozen chopped broccoli, thawed
1/2 cup chopped roasted sweet red peppers
1/2 cup shredded Parmesan cheese, *divided*
1/4 teaspoon pepper

Cook fettuccine according to package directions. Meanwhile, in a large saucepan, combine the milk, cream cheese and cheese spread. Cook and stir over medium heat until cheeses are melted and mixture is smooth. Stir in the turkey, broccoli, roasted peppers, 1/4 cup Parmesan cheese and pepper; heat through.

Drain fettuccine and place in a serving bowl. Top with turkey mixture; toss gently to coat. Sprinkle with remaining Parmesan cheese.

NUTRITION FACTS: 1-1/3 cups equals 376 calories, 7 g fat (4 g saturated fat), 59 mg cholesterol, 461 mg sodium, 46 g carbohydrate, 4 g fiber, 32 g protein. **DIABETIC EXCHANGES:** 3 very lean meat, 2-1/2 starch, 1 vegetable, 1 fat.

Chicken Orzo Skillet

PREP/TOTAL TIME: 30 Min. **YIELD:** 6 Servings

As a busy wife and mom with a home-based business, I try to make quick dinners that are healthy for my family. This all-in-one meal is always appreciated. —Kathleen Farrell, Rochester, New York

   1 cup uncooked orzo pasta
   1 pound boneless skinless chicken breasts, cubed
   3 teaspoons olive oil, *divided*
   3 garlic cloves, minced
   2 cans (14-1/2 ounces *each*) stewed tomatoes, cut up
   1 can (15 ounces) white kidney *or* cannellini beans, rinsed and drained
1-1/2 teaspoons Italian seasoning
1/2 teaspoon salt
   1 package (16 ounces) frozen broccoli florets, thawed

Cook orzo according to package directions. Meanwhile, in a large nonstick skillet coated with nonstick cooking spray, cook chicken in 2 teaspoons oil for 6-7 minutes or until no longer pink. Remove and keep warm.

In the same skillet, cook garlic in remaining oil until tender. Stir in the tomatoes, beans, Italian seasoning and salt. Bring to a boil. Stir in broccoli and chicken; heat through. Drain orzo; stir into chicken mixture.

NUTRITION FACTS: 1-1/2 cups equals 342 calories, 5 g fat (1 g saturated fat), 42 mg cholesterol, 589 mg sodium, 49 g carbohydrate, 7 g fiber, 25 g protein. **DIABETIC EXCHANGES:** 3 vegetable, 2 starch, 2 very lean meat, 1/2 fat.

Italian-Style Cabbage Rolls
(PICTURED ABOVE)

PREP: 45 Min. **BAKE:** 50 Min. **YIELD:** 5 Servings

Here's a great way to get your family to eat vegetables. Not only is this one of my gang's favorite dinners, but my 8-year-old son loves to help me roll the turkey mixture into the cabbage leaves.
—Erika Niehoff, Eveleth, Minnesota

1/3 cup uncooked brown rice
   1 medium head cabbage
1/2 cup shredded carrot
1/4 cup finely chopped onion
1/4 cup egg substitute
   1 can (10-3/4 ounces) reduced-fat reduced-sodium condensed tomato soup, undiluted, *divided*
   1 can (10-3/4 ounces) reduced-fat reduced-sodium condensed vegetable beef soup, undiluted, *divided*
1/4 teaspoon cayenne pepper
1/4 teaspoon pepper
   2 tablespoons Italian seasoning, *divided*
   1 pound lean ground turkey

Cook rice according to package directions. Meanwhile, cook cabbage in boiling water just until leaves fall off head. Set aside 10 large leaves for rolls (refrigerate remaining cabbage for another use). Cut out the thick vein from the bottom of each reserved leaf, making a V-shaped cut.

In a large bowl, combine the carrot, onion, egg substitute, 2 tablespoons tomato soup, 2 tablespoons vegetable soup, cayenne, pepper, 1 tablespoon Italian seasoning and rice. Crumble turkey over mixture and mix well. Place about 1/3 cupful on each cabbage leaf. Overlap cut ends of leaf; fold in sides, beginning from the cut end. Roll up completely to enclose filling.

Place rolls seam side down in an 11-in. x 7-in. x 2-in. baking dish coated with nonstick cooking spray. Combine the remaining soups; pour over cabbage rolls. Sprinkle with remaining Italian seasoning. Cover and bake at 350° for 50-60 minutes or until the cabbage is tender and a meat thermometer reads 165°.

NUTRITION FACTS: 2 cabbage rolls equals 293 calories, 10 g fat (3 g saturated fat), 74 mg cholesterol, 582 mg sodium, 29 g carbohydrate, 4 g fiber, 22 g protein. **DIABETIC EXCHANGES:** 3 lean meat, 1-1/2 starch, 1 vegetable.

Peppery Grilled Turkey Breast

(PICTURED BELOW)

PREP: 15 Min.   **GRILL:** 1-1/4 Hours + Standing   **YIELD:** 15 Servings

This is a combination of several favorite family recipes. People who try it for the first time are amazed to find that it's not only flavorful, but healthy as well.

—Mary Elizabeth Relyea, Canastota, New York

    2 tablespoons light brown sugar
    1 tablespoon salt
    2 teaspoons ground cinnamon
    1 teaspoon cayenne pepper
  1/2 teaspoon ground mustard
    1 bone-in turkey breast (5 pounds)
    1 cup reduced-sodium chicken broth
  1/4 cup white vinegar
  1/4 cup jalapeno pepper jelly
    2 tablespoons olive oil

In a small bowl, combine the brown sugar, salt, cinnamon, cayenne and mustard. With fingers, carefully loosen the skin from both sides of turkey breast. Spread half of spice mixture under turkey skin; secure skin to underside of breast with wooden toothpicks. Spread the remaining spice mixture over the skin.

Coat grill rack with nonstick cooking spray before starting the grill. Prepare grill for indirect heat, using a drip pan. Place turkey over drip pan. Grill, covered, over indirect medium heat for 30 minutes.

In a small saucepan, combine the broth, vinegar, jelly and oil. Cook and stir over medium heat for 2 minutes or until jelly is melted. Set aside 1/2 cup. Baste turkey with some of the remaining jelly mixture. Grill 45-60 minutes longer or until a meat thermometer reads 170° and juices run clear, basting every 15 minutes.

Cover and let stand for 10 minutes. Remove and discard turkey skin if desired. Brush with reserved jelly mixture before slicing.

NUTRITION FACTS: 4 ounces cooked turkey (with skin removed) equals 167 calories, 3 g fat (trace saturated fat), 78 mg cholesterol, 565 mg sodium, 6 g carbohydrate, trace fiber, 29 g protein. **DIABETIC EXCHANGES:** 4 very lean meat, 1/2 fat.

Two-Cheese Turkey Enchiladas

(PICTURED ABOVE)

PREP: 25 Min.   **BAKE:** 20 Min.   **YIELD:** 8 Servings

Cream cheese and sour cream create an incredible filling for these yummy turkey enchiladas. The comforting entree is always a huge hit with my gang.   —Shelly Platten, Amherst, Wisconsin

    1 pound extra-lean ground turkey
    1 large onion, chopped
  1/2 cup chopped green pepper
    1 teaspoon brown sugar
    1 teaspoon garlic powder
    1 teaspoon ground cumin
    1 teaspoon chili powder
    1 can (28 ounces) crushed tomatoes, *divided*
    1 package (8 ounces) reduced-fat cream cheese
  1/4 cup fat-free sour cream
    1 can (4 ounces) chopped green chilies
    1 cup salsa
    8 fat-free flour tortillas (8 inches), warmed
  1/2 cup shredded reduced-fat cheddar cheese

Crumble turkey into a large nonstick skillet; add onion, green pepper, brown sugar, garlic powder, cumin and chili powder. Cook and stir over medium heat until turkey is no longer pink. Stir in 1 cup crushed tomatoes. Reduce heat; simmer, uncovered, for 10 minutes, stirring occasionally.

In a small mixing bowl, beat the cream cheese, sour cream and chilies until blended; set aside. Combine salsa and remaining tomatoes; spread 1 cup into a 13-in. x 9-in. x 2-in. baking dish coated with nonstick cooking spray.

Spoon about 3 tablespoons cream cheese mixture and 1/3 cup turkey mixture down the center of each tortilla. Roll up and place seam side down in baking dish. Top with remaining salsa mixture; sprinkle with cheddar cheese. Bake, uncovered, at 350° for 20-25 minutes or until bubbly.

NUTRITION FACTS: 1 enchilada equals 329 calories, 9 g fat (5 g saturated fat), 49 mg cholesterol, 776 mg sodium, 41 g carbohydrate, 6 g fiber, 26 g protein. **DIABETIC EXCHANGES:** 2 starch, 2 very lean meat, 2 vegetable, 1-1/2 fat.

Greek Pasta Bake
(PICTURED BELOW)

PREP: 20 Min.   BAKE: 25 Min.   YIELD: 8 Servings

Whenever I bring this casserole to potlucks, it receives rave reviews. There's never anything left. Best of all, it's a healthy and hearty supper made with easy-to-find ingredients.
—Anne Taglienti, Kennett Square, Pennsylvania

- 1 package (12 ounces) whole wheat penne pasta
- 4 cups cubed cooked chicken breast
- 1 can (29 ounces) tomato sauce
- 1 can (14-1/2 ounces) diced tomatoes, drained
- 1 package (10 ounces) frozen chopped spinach, thawed and squeezed dry
- 2 cans (2-1/4 ounces *each*) sliced ripe olives, drained
- 1/4 cup chopped red onion
- 2 tablespoons chopped green pepper
- 1 teaspoon dried basil
- 1 teaspoon dried oregano
- 1/2 cup shredded part-skim mozzarella cheese
- 1/2 cup crumbled feta cheese

Cook pasta according to package directions; drain. In a large bowl, combine the pasta, chicken, tomato sauce, tomatoes, spinach, olives, onion, green pepper, basil and oregano.

Transfer to a 13-in. x 9-in. x 2-in. baking dish coated with nonstick cooking spray. Sprinkle with cheeses. Bake, uncovered, at 400° for 25-30 minutes or until heated through and cheese is melted.

NUTRITION FACTS: 1-1/2 cups equals 366 calories, 7 g fat (2 g saturated fat), 62 mg cholesterol, 847 mg sodium, 43 g carbohydrate, 6 g fiber, 32 g protein. DIABETIC EXCHANGES: 3 very lean meat, 2-1/2 starch, 1 vegetable, 1/2 fat.

TASTY TIP
"I serve Greek Pasta Bake with a crispy, field-green salad and crusty, artisan bread for a fast workweek meal," explains Anne Taglienti.

Herbed Barbecued Chicken
(PICTURED ABOVE)

 CARB

PREP: 10 Min. + Marinating   GRILL: 10 Min.   YIELD: 4 Servings

Garlic, rosemary, sage and thyme help season the marinade for my moist, tender chicken. A friend gave me the recipe years ago, and my family never tires of it.   —Dawn Sowders, Harrison, Ohio

- 2 tablespoons olive oil
- 2 tablespoons reduced-sodium soy sauce
- 2 tablespoons Worcestershire sauce
- 1 garlic clove, minced
- 1 tablespoon dried parsley flakes
- 1/2 teaspoon dried rosemary, crushed
- 1/2 teaspoon rubbed sage
- 1/4 teaspoon dried oregano
- 1/4 teaspoon dried thyme
- 1/4 teaspoon pepper
- 4 boneless skinless chicken breast halves (4 ounces *each*)

In a large resealable plastic bag, combine the first 10 ingredients; add chicken. Seal bag and turn to coat; refrigerate for 8 hours or overnight.

Coat grill rack with nonstick cooking spray before starting the grill. Drain and discard marinade. Grill chicken, covered, over medium heat for 5-8 minutes on each side or until juices run clear.

NUTRITION FACTS: 1 chicken breast half equals 159 calories, 6 g fat (1 g saturated fat), 63 mg cholesterol, 248 mg sodium, 1 g carbohydrate, trace fiber, 23 g protein. DIABETIC EXCHANGES: 3 very lean meat, 1/2 fat.

TASTY TIP
"We like leftover barbecued chicken sliced over a bed of fresh greens," explains Dawn Sowders.

Good Neighbor Chicken Pizza

PREP: 15 Min. + Marinating   **BAKE:** 10 Min.   **YIELD:** 6 Servings

I call this 'Good Neighbor' pizza because I got the recipe from a dear neighbor. Marinated in a scrumptious soy sauce mixture, grilled chicken gives the delicious dish an Asian flair.
—Connie Staal, Greenbrier, Arkansas

- 2 tablespoons cider vinegar
- 2 tablespoons reduced-sodium soy sauce
- 1 tablespoon olive oil
- 2 garlic cloves, minced
- 1/4 teaspoon cayenne pepper
- 1-3/4 cups cubed cooked chicken breast
- 1 prebaked thin Italian bread shell crust (10 ounces)
- 1/2 cup pizza sauce
- 1 cup sliced fresh mushrooms
- 1/2 cup sliced green onions
- 1/2 teaspoon Italian seasoning
- 1/2 cup shredded part-skim mozzarella cheese
- 1/2 cup shredded reduced-fat cheddar cheese
- 2 tablespoons slivered almonds

In a small bowl, combine the vinegar, soy sauce, oil, garlic and cayenne; add chicken and toss to coat. Cover and refrigerate for 30 minutes.

Place crust on a baking sheet. Spread with pizza sauce. Drain chicken; spoon over sauce. Top with mushrooms, onions, Italian seasoning, cheeses and almonds. Bake at 400° for 8-10 minutes or until vegetables are crisp-tender and cheese is melted.

NUTRITION FACTS: 1 slice equals 308 calories, 11 g fat (3 g saturated fat), 44 mg cholesterol, 694 mg sodium, 28 g carbohydrate, 2 g fiber, 23 g protein. **DIABETIC EXCHANGES:** 2 starch, 2 lean meat, 1 fat.

Summer Squash Chicken Casserole   CARB

PREP: 20 Min.   **BAKE:** 30 Min.   **YIELD:** 6 Servings

From the L&T Test Kitchen comes a rich and saucy casserole that features tender pattypans in a comforting chicken and rice combination. Pair it with a salad for a family-friendly supper.

- 1/2 cup uncooked instant rice
- 1 can (10-3/4 ounces) condensed cream of chicken soup, undiluted
- 1/3 cup reduced-fat mayonnaise
- 1/3 cup fat-free milk
- 4 cups cubed cooked chicken breast
- 2 cups pattypan squash, halved
- 1 small onion, finely chopped
- 1 jar (2 ounces) diced pimientos, drained
- 1 teaspoon dried thyme
- 1/4 teaspoon garlic powder
- 1/4 teaspoon pepper
- 1/3 cup shredded Parmesan cheese

Cook the rice according to package directions. In a large bowl, combine the soup, mayonnaise and milk. Stir in the chicken, squash, onion, pimientos, thyme, garlic powder, pepper and the cooked rice.

Spoon into a 2-qt. baking dish coated with nonstick cooking spray. Sprinkle with Parmesan cheese. Bake, uncovered, at 350° for 30-40 minutes or until the edges are bubbly and the center is set.

NUTRITION FACTS: 1 cup equals 297 calories, 11 g fat (3 g saturated fat), 84 mg cholesterol, 633 mg sodium, 15 g carbohydrate, 2 g fiber, 32 g protein. **DIABETIC EXCHANGES:** 4 very lean meat, 2 fat, 1 starch.

Spicy Buffalo Chicken Wraps   CARB
(PICTURED BELOW)

PREP/TOTAL TIME: 25 Min.   **YIELD:** 2 Servings

These wraps have a real kick. They're one of my husband's favorite sandwiches.
—Jennifer Beck, Rio Rancho, New Mexico

- 1/2 pound boneless skinless chicken breasts, cubed
- 1/2 teaspoon canola oil
- 2 tablespoons Louisiana-style hot sauce
- 1 cup shredded lettuce
- 2 flour tortillas (6 inches), warmed
- 2 teaspoons prepared reduced-fat ranch salad dressing
- 2 tablespoons crumbled blue cheese

In a nonstick skillet coated with nonstick cooking spray, cook chicken in oil for 6 minutes; drain. Stir in hot sauce. Bring to a boil. Reduce heat; simmer, uncovered, for 3-5 minutes or until sauce is thickened and chicken juices run clear.

Place lettuce on tortillas; drizzle with ranch dressing. Top with chicken mixture and blue cheese; roll up.

NUTRITION FACTS: 1 wrap equals 273 calories, 11 g fat (3 g saturated fat), 70 mg cholesterol, 453 mg sodium, 15 g carbohydrate, 1 g fiber, 28 g protein. **DIABETIC EXCHANGES:** 3 very lean meat, 1-1/2 fat, 1 starch.

Favorite Recipe Made Lighter

BUBBLING casseroles get high ranks in Eleanor Hein's kitchen. "Hot Chicken Salad is one of our favorites," she writes from Kirkland, Illinois. "I have friends who particularly enjoy it, and it's always big at potlucks.

"I could use some help when it comes to decreasing its fat," says Eleanor. "I played with the recipe but haven't had much luck. I hope you can help."

With all of the cheese, mayonnaise and sour cream in Eleanor's recipe, it's evident why family and friends clear their plates and run back for seconds. Eleanor is right to be concerned about the fat, though. Just one serving contains 42 grams.

Our makeover team took out many of the heavy ingredients and replaced them with smaller amounts of less-fat counterparts. Because light items don't always produce a particularly creamy texture, the ingredients were combined with a thickened milk mixture and plain yogurt.

In addition, the almonds were decreased and toasted for maximum flavor, and reduced-fat butter and cheese brought the numbers down even further.

Makeover Hot Chicken Salad is a mouth-watering success. It boasts 64% fewer fat grams than the original, and 253 less calories per serving. Best of all, it has all the satisfying comfort of Eleanor's most-requested dish.

Hot Chicken Salad

PREP: 25 Min. BAKE: 30 Min. YIELD: 6 Servings

  3/4 cup mayonnaise
  3/4 cup sour cream
    2 tablespoons lemon juice
    2 teaspoons grated onion
  1/2 teaspoon salt
    3 cups cubed cooked chicken breast
    1 cup chopped celery
    1 can (8 ounces) sliced water chestnuts, drained and coarsely chopped
    1 cup seasoned salad croutons
  1/2 cup slivered almonds
    1 cup soft bread crumbs
    1 tablespoon butter, melted
    1 cup (4 ounces) shredded cheddar cheese

In a large bowl, whisk the mayonnaise, sour cream, lemon juice, onion and salt until smooth. Stir in the chicken, celery, water chestnuts, croutons and almonds.

Spoon into a greased 11-in. x 7-in. x 2-in. baking dish. Cover and bake at 350° for 25 minutes.

Combine bread crumbs and butter; stir in cheese. Sprinkle over casserole. Bake, uncovered, 5-10 minutes longer or until heated through and cheese is melted.

NUTRITION FACTS: 3/4 cup equals 576 calories, 42 g fat (13 g saturated fat), 110 mg cholesterol, 682 mg sodium, 17 g carbohydrate, 3 g fiber, 29 g protein.

Makeover Hot Chicken Salad
(PICTURED ABOVE)

PREP: 25 Min. BAKE: 30 Min. YIELD: 6 Servings

1-1/2 teaspoons all-purpose flour
  1/2 cup fat-free milk
  1/2 cup plain yogurt
  1/4 cup reduced-fat mayonnaise
  1/4 cup reduced-fat sour cream
    1 tablespoon lemon juice
    2 teaspoons grated onion
  1/2 teaspoon salt
    3 cups cubed cooked chicken breast
    1 cup chopped celery
    1 can (8 ounces) sliced water chestnuts, drained and coarsely chopped
    1 cup seasoned salad croutons
  1/4 cup slivered almonds, chopped and toasted
    1 cup soft bread crumbs
    1 tablespoon reduced-fat butter, melted
  3/4 cup shredded reduced-fat cheddar cheese

In a small saucepan, whisk flour and milk until smooth. Bring to a boil over medium heat; cook and stir for 2 minutes or until thickened. Remove from the heat.

In a large bowl, whisk the yogurt, mayonnaise, sour cream, lemon juice, onion and salt until smooth. Whisk in the milk mixture. Stir in the chicken, celery, water chestnuts, croutons and almonds.

Spoon into a 2-qt. baking dish coated with nonstick cooking spray. Cover and bake at 350° for 25 minutes.

Combine bread crumbs and butter; stir in cheese. Sprinkle over casserole. Bake, uncovered, 5-10 minutes longer or until heated through and cheese is melted.

NUTRITION FACTS: 3/4 cup equals 323 calories, 15 g fat (5 g saturated fat), 78 mg cholesterol, 592 mg sodium, 19 g carbohydrate, 2 g fiber, 29 g protein. DIABETIC EXCHANGES: 3 very lean meat, 2-1/2 fat, 1 starch, 1 vegetable.

Editor's Note: This recipe was tested with Land O'Lakes light stick butter.

Sun-Dried Tomato Chicken

(PICTURED BELOW)

CARB ▼

PREP: 30 Min.   **BAKE:** 40 Min.   **YIELD:** 4 Servings

My husband likes to order a similar chicken dish at a local restaurant, so I created a lighter version for home. The sun-dried tomatoes are wonderful with the goat cheese.

—Anna Rhyne, Anderson, South Carolina

    3/4 cup finely chopped onion
      1 garlic clove, minced
      1 tablespoon butter
    1/2 cup sun-dried tomatoes (not packed in oil), chopped
    1/2 cup white wine *or* reduced-sodium chicken broth
    1/4 cup lemon juice
    1/4 cup minced fresh basil *or* 4 teaspoons dried basil
      4 boneless skinless chicken breast halves (6 ounces *each*)
    1/4 cup goat cheese
    1/2 teaspoon salt
    1/4 teaspoon pepper

In a large skillet, saute onion and garlic in butter for 3-4 minutes or until tender. Stir in the tomatoes, wine or broth and lemon juice; bring to a boil. Reduce heat; simmer, uncovered, for 10-15 minutes or until liquid is absorbed, stirring occasionally. Remove from the heat; stir in basil.

Flatten chicken to 1/4-in. thickness. Spread each with 1/4 cup tomato mixture to within 1/2 in. of edges. Crumble goat cheese over tomato mixture. Roll up each jelly-roll style, starting with a short side; secure with a toothpick or small metal skewer. Sprinkle with salt and pepper.

Place chicken in an 11-in. x 7-in. x 2-in. baking dish coated with nonstick cooking spray. Bake, uncovered, at 350° for 40-45 minutes or until juices run clear. Spoon pan juices over chicken and remove toothpicks before serving.

NUTRITION FACTS: 1 serving equals 299 calories, 11 g fat (6 g saturated fat), 113 mg cholesterol, 622 mg sodium, 9 g carbohydrate, 2 g fiber, 39 g protein. **DIABETIC EXCHANGES:** 5 very lean meat, 1-1/2 fat, 1 vegetable.

TASTY TIP
Anna Rhyne suggests replacing the goat cheese with feta cheese or light sour cream in her chicken entree.

Turkey Burgers with Jalapeno Cheese Sauce

(PICTURED ABOVE)

PREP/TOTAL TIME: 25 Min.   **YIELD:** 6 Servings

This is a lighter version of a burger that people enjoyed where I once worked. I substituted the beef with turkey and used low-fat cheese, but the results are tastier than the original crowd-pleaser.

—Vicki Schurk, Hamden, Connecticut

      3 slices whole wheat bread, torn
      1 cup fat-free milk, *divided*
      1 tablespoon minced garlic
  1-1/2 teaspoons ground mustard
    1/4 teaspoon salt
    1/4 teaspoon pepper
  1-1/2 pounds lean ground turkey
  1-1/4 teaspoons all-purpose flour
    3/4 cup shredded reduced-fat cheddar cheese
      1 jalapeno pepper, seeded and chopped
      6 whole wheat hamburger buns, split
      6 lettuce leaves
      6 slices tomato

In a large bowl, soak bread in 1/2 cup milk for 1 minute. Add the garlic, mustard, salt and pepper. Crumble turkey over mixture and mix well. Shape into six patties; set aside.

In a small saucepan, combine flour and remaining milk until smooth. Bring to a boil; cook and stir for 1-2 minutes or until thickened. Remove from the heat. Add cheese and jalapeno; stir until cheese is melted. Keep warm.

Coat grill rack with nonstick cooking spray before starting the grill. Grill patties, covered, over medium heat for 5-6 minutes on each side or until a meat thermometer reads 165°. Serve on buns with the lettuce, tomato and jalapeno cheese sauce.

NUTRITION FACTS: 1 burger equals 387 calories, 15 g fat (5 g saturated fat), 100 mg cholesterol, 599 mg sodium, 33 g carbohydrate, 5 g fiber, 30 g protein. **DIABETIC EXCHANGES:** 3 lean meat, 2 starch, 1 fat.

Editor's Note: When cutting or seeding hot peppers, use rubber or plastic gloves to protect your hands. Avoid touching your face.

Turkey Roulades

(PICTURED BELOW)

CARB

PREP: 40 Min.   BAKE: 40 Min.   YIELD: 8 Servings

The filling in this recipe goes so well with turkey. I love the combination of apple, mushrooms and spinach with a hint of lemon.
—Kari Wheaton, Beloit, Wisconsin

   1 cup diced peeled tart apple
   1 cup diced fresh mushrooms
  1/2 cup finely chopped onion
   2 teaspoons olive oil
   5 ounces frozen chopped spinach, thawed and squeezed dry
   2 tablespoons lemon juice
   2 teaspoons grated lemon peel
  3/4 teaspoon salt, *divided*
Pinch ground nutmeg
   4 turkey breast tenderloins (8 ounces *each*)
  1/4 teaspoon pepper
   1 egg, beaten
  1/2 cup seasoned bread crumbs

In a large nonstick skillet coated with nonstick cooking spray, saute the apple, mushrooms and onion in oil until tender. Remove from the heat; stir in the spinach, lemon juice, lemon peel, 1/4 teaspoon salt and nutmeg.

Make a lengthwise slit down the center of each tenderloin to within 1/2 in. of bottom. Open tenderloins so they lie flat; cover with plastic wrap. Flatten to 1/4-in. thickness. Remove plastic; sprinkle turkey with pepper and remaining salt.

Spread spinach mixture over tenderloins to within 1 in. of edges. Roll up jelly-roll style, starting with a short side; tie with kitchen string. Place egg and bread crumbs in separate shallow bowls. Dip roulades in egg, then roll in crumbs.

Place in an 11-in. x 7-in. x 2-in. baking pan coated with nonstick cooking spray. Bake, uncovered, at 375° for 40-45

minutes or until a meat thermometer reads 170°. Let roulades stand for 5 minutes before slicing.

NUTRITION FACTS: 1/2 roulade equals 184 calories, 4 g fat (1 g saturated fat), 82 mg cholesterol, 405 mg sodium, 9 g carbohydrate, 1 g fiber, 29 g protein. **DIABETIC EXCHANGES:** 4 very lean meat, 1/2 starch.

Chicken with Cranberry Sauce

(PICTURED ABOVE)

PREP/TOTAL TIME: 30 Min.   YIELD: 6 Servings

Cranberries and maple syrup make a sweet sauce for these easy chicken breast halves. They're a quick but lovely main course.
—Kim Pettipas, Oromocto, New Brunswick

   2 cups fresh *or* frozen cranberries
  3/4 cup water
  1/3 cup sugar
   6 boneless skinless chicken breast halves (4 ounces *each*)
  1/2 teaspoon salt
  1/4 teaspoon pepper
   1 tablespoon canola oil
  1/4 cup maple syrup

In a small saucepan, combine the cranberries, water and sugar. Cook over medium heat until berries pop, about 15 minutes.

Meanwhile, sprinkle chicken with salt and pepper. In a large nonstick skillet, cook chicken in oil over medium heat for 4-5 minutes on each side or until juices run clear. Stir syrup into cranberry mixture; serve with chicken.

NUTRITION FACTS: 1 chicken breast half with 3 tablespoons sauce equals 236 calories, 5 g fat (1 g saturated fat), 63 mg cholesterol, 253 mg sodium, 24 g carbohydrate, 1 g fiber, 23 g protein. **DIABETIC EXCHANGES:** 3 very lean meat, 1-1/2 starch, 1/2 fat.

HEALTHY OUTLOOK
If you prepare Chicken with Cranberry Sauce, you're in for more than great flavor. Cranberries have proven to be a tasty way to cut cholesterol and fight infections.

Easy Chicken Potpie

(PICTURED BELOW)

PREP: 20 Min.   **BAKE:** 40 Min.   **YIELD:** 6 Servings

I rely on a light biscuit mix and canned soup for this comforting favorite. A new take on an old standby, the potpie is excellent when served with cranberry sauce on the side.

—Martha Evans, Omaha, Nebraska

- 1 can (10-3/4 ounces) reduced-fat reduced-sodium condensed cream of chicken soup, undiluted
- 1 can (10-3/4 ounces) reduced-fat reduced-sodium condensed cream of mushroom soup, undiluted
- 1-1/4 cups fat-free milk, *divided*
- 1/2 teaspoon dried thyme
- 1/4 teaspoon pepper
- 1/8 teaspoon poultry seasoning
- 2 packages (16 ounces *each*) frozen mixed vegetables, thawed
- 1-1/2 cups cubed cooked chicken breast
- 1-1/2 cups reduced-fat biscuit/baking mix
- 1/3 cup egg substitute

In a large bowl, combine the soups, 1/2 cup milk, thyme, pepper and poultry seasoning. Stir in vegetables and chicken. Transfer to a 13-in. x 9-in. x 2-in. baking dish coated with non-stick cooking spray.

In a small bowl, stir the biscuit mix, egg substitute and remaining milk just until blended. Drop by 12 rounded tablespoonfuls onto chicken mixture. Bake, uncovered, at 350° for 40-50 minutes or until filling is bubbly and biscuits are golden brown.

NUTRITION FACTS: 1-1/3 cups chicken mixture with 2 biscuits equals 342 calories, 5 g fat (2 g saturated fat), 36 mg cholesterol, 871 mg sodium, 53 g carbohydrate, 7 g fiber, 21 g protein. **DIABETIC EXCHANGES:** 3 vegetable, 2-1/2 starch, 2 very lean meat.

Mexican Turkey Skillet

PREP: 20 Min.   **BAKE:** 30 Min.   **YIELD:** 8 Servings

This family-friendly main dish has a rich Mexican flavor that may seem indulgent, but it's delightfully light. Created by our Test Kitchen, it cooks in one skillet, so it's a snap to clean up after a weeknight supper.

- 1 pound lean ground turkey
- 1 cup chopped zucchini
- 1/2 cup chopped sweet red pepper
- 2 teaspoons canola oil
- 2 cups cooked rice
- 1 can (15 ounces) black beans, rinsed and drained
- 1 can (14-1/2 ounces) Mexican stewed tomatoes
- 1 can (8 ounces) tomato sauce
- 1/2 teaspoon ground cumin
- 1/4 teaspoon salt
- 1/4 teaspoon pepper
- 1 cup (4 ounces) shredded reduced-fat Mexican cheese blend

Chopped avocado, optional

In a large nonstick ovenproof skillet, cook turkey over medium heat until no longer pink; drain. Set turkey aside. In the same skillet, saute the zucchini and red pepper in oil for 2 minutes or until crisp-tender.

Stir in the turkey, rice, beans, tomatoes, tomato sauce, cumin, salt and pepper. Cover and bake at 350° for 30 minutes. Sprinkle with cheese. Let stand for 5 minutes before serving. Garnish with avocado if desired.

NUTRITION FACTS: 1 cup (calculated without avocado) equals 254 calories, 9 g fat (3 g saturated fat), 55 mg cholesterol, 616 mg sodium, 25 g carbohydrate, 4 g fiber, 19 g protein. **DIABETIC EXCHANGES:** 2 lean meat, 1 starch, 1 vegetable, 1/2 fat.

Special Turkey Sandwiches
(PICTURED ABOVE)

PREP/TOTAL TIME: 25 Min.   **YIELD:** 4 Servings

Every Saturday night, my family loves to have sandwiches for dinner. With their rich cream cheese spread, these have become a popular request. They don't taste at all light.
— Maria Bertram, Waltham, Massachusetts

      4 ounces reduced-fat cream cheese
  1/2 cup finely chopped fresh spinach
  1/2 cup minced fresh basil
  1/3 cup shredded Parmesan cheese
      1 garlic clove, minced
  1/2 large red onion, sliced
      2 tablespoons dry red wine *or* reduced-sodium beef broth
      8 slices whole wheat bread, toasted
  3/4 pound sliced deli turkey
      8 slices tomato
      8 lettuce leaves

In a small mixing bowl, beat the cream cheese, spinach, basil, Parmesan cheese and garlic until blended; set aside. In a small skillet, cook the onion in wine or broth until tender; set aside.

Place four slices of toast on a broiler pan; top with turkey. Place remaining toast on broiler pan; spread with cream cheese mixture. Broil for 2-3 minutes or until heated through. Layer onion, tomato and lettuce over turkey. Top with remaining toast.

NUTRITION FACTS: 1 sandwich equals 348 calories, 11 g fat (6 g saturated fat), 63 mg cholesterol, 1,426 mg sodium, 36 g carbohydrate, 5 g fiber, 29 g protein. **DIABETIC EXCHANGES:** 3 very lean meat, 2 starch, 1-1/2 fat.

Stir-Fried Walnut Chicken
(PICTURED BELOW)

PREP: 20 Min. + Marinating   **COOK:** 20 Min.   **YIELD:** 6 Servings

I prepare this simple stir-fry often because I love tasting the results. The meal-in-one recipe is just perfect for busy weeknights.
— Sharon Allen, Allentown, Pennsylvania

      1 teaspoon plus 3 tablespoons cornstarch, *divided*
      2 teaspoons plus 3 tablespoons reduced-sodium soy sauce, *divided*
      1 pound boneless skinless chicken breasts, cut into strips
  1-1/2 cups reduced-sodium chicken broth
  1-1/2 teaspoons grated fresh gingerroot
      5 teaspoons canola oil, *divided*
      1 medium onion, quartered
      1 garlic clove, minced
      1 medium sweet red pepper, julienned
  1/2 cup fresh broccoli florets
  1/2 cup chopped carrot
      1 can (8 ounces) sliced water chestnuts, drained
      3 cups cooked long grain rice
  1/4 cup chopped walnuts, toasted

In a small bowl, combine 1 teaspoon cornstarch and 2 teaspoons soy sauce until smooth. Place the chicken in a large resealable plastic bag; add soy sauce mixture. Seal bag and turn to coat; refrigerate for 30 minutes.

In another bowl, combine the remaining cornstarch and soy sauce until smooth. Stir in the broth and ginger; set aside.

In a large nonstick skillet or wok, stir-fry chicken in 2 teaspoons hot oil until no longer pink; remove and keep warm. In the same pan, stir-fry onion and garlic in remaining oil until tender. Add the red pepper, broccoli, carrot and water chestnuts; cook and stir until vegetables are crisp-tender.

Stir broth mixture and stir into vegetables. Bring to a boil; cook and stir for 1-2 minutes or until thickened. Return chicken to the pan; heat through. Serve over rice. Sprinkle with walnuts.

NUTRITION FACTS: 3/4 cup chicken mixture with 1/2 cup rice equals 318 calories, 9 g fat (1 g saturated fat), 42 mg cholesterol, 572 mg sodium, 38 g carbohydrate, 3 g fiber, 21 g protein. **DIABETIC EXCHANGES:** 2 very lean meat, 2 vegetable, 1-1/2 starch, 1-1/2 fat.

Greek Turkey Burgers
(PICTURED BELOW)

PREP/TOTAL TIME: 30 Min.   **YIELD:** 6 Servings

I pared down the recipe for these mouth-watering burgers after it was given to me by a dear friend. Cumin and cayenne pepper add to the turkey's wonderful taste.

—Marianne Shira, Osceola, Wisconsin

    1/3 cup fat-free plain yogurt
    1/3 cup reduced-fat mayonnaise
    1/4 cup chopped seeded peeled cucumber
    1/4 teaspoon Worcestershire sauce
    1/4 teaspoon garlic powder
    1/8 teaspoon salt
    1/8 teaspoon pepper
Dash dried thyme
BURGERS:
    1/2 cup finely chopped sweet onion
    1/2 cup finely chopped green pepper
      1 teaspoon ground cumin
    1/4 teaspoon salt
    1/4 teaspoon pepper
    1/4 teaspoon cayenne pepper
  1-1/2 pounds extra-lean ground turkey
    1/2 cup thinly sliced cucumber
      6 slices tomato
      6 hamburger buns, split

For cucumber sauce, in a small bowl, combine the first eight ingredients. Cover and refrigerate until serving.

In a large bowl, combine the onion, green pepper, cumin, salt, pepper and cayenne. Crumble turkey over mixture and mix well. Shape into six patties.

If grilling the burgers, coat grill rack with nonstick cooking spray before starting the grill. Grill, covered, over medium heat or broil 4 in. from the heat for 5-7 minutes on each side or

Italian Sausage with Polenta
(PICTURED ABOVE)

PREP/TOTAL TIME: 30 Min.   **YIELD:** 6 Servings

The turkey-and-broccoli mixture I serve over polenta is quick, easy and tastes great. Nutritious and delicious, it makes a comforting meal on a weeknight.   —Mary Bilyeu, Ann Arbor, Michigan

      1 package (20 ounces) Italian turkey sausage links, casings removed
    1/2 cup chopped red onion
      4 garlic cloves, minced
  2-1/2 cups fresh broccoli florets
      2 cans (15 ounces *each*) crushed tomatoes
      2 tablespoons prepared pesto
    1/2 teaspoon crushed red pepper flakes
    1/4 teaspoon pepper
      3 cups reduced-sodium chicken broth
      1 cup cornmeal
Shaved Parmesan cheese, optional

In a large nonstick skillet coated with nonstick cooking spray, cook the sausage, onion and garlic over medium heat until meat is no longer pink. Stir in the broccoli. Reduce heat; cover and cook for 5-7 minutes or until broccoli is tender.

Stir in the tomatoes, pesto, pepper flakes and pepper; bring to a boil. Reduce the heat; simmer, uncovered, for 10 minutes.

Meanwhile, for polenta, bring broth to a boil in a small saucepan. Slowly whisk in cornmeal; cook and stir for 1 minute or until thickened. Spoon onto plates; top with sausage mixture. Garnish with Parmesan cheese if desired.

NUTRITION FACTS: 1 cup sausage mixture with 1/2 cup polenta equals 337 calories, 12 g fat (4 g saturated fat), 52 mg cholesterol, 1,131 mg sodium, 35 g carbohydrate, 6 g fiber, 24 g protein.

TASTY TIP
For a change of pace, you could also serve the Italian turkey sausage mixture over pasta instead of polenta.

until a meat thermometer reads 165°.

Place cucumber and tomato slices on buns; top each bun with a burger and about 2 tablespoons cucumber sauce.

NUTRITION FACTS: 1 burger equals 316 calories, 9 g fat (1 g saturated fat), 51 mg cholesterol, 586 mg sodium, 28 g carbohydrate, 2 g fiber, 33 g protein. **DIABETIC EXCHANGES:** 4 very lean meat, 1-1/2 starch, 1 vegetable, 1 fat.

Cranberry Chicken Salad Sandwiches
(PICTURED AT RIGHT)

PREP/TOTAL TIME: 25 Min.   **YIELD:** 4 Servings

Cubed cooked chicken speeds assembly of these cute and filling chicken salad sandwiches. Dressed up with cranberries and served in dinner rolls, they're ready in no time.
—Sandra Sprinkle, Anniston, Alabama

     2 cups cubed cooked chicken breast
     6 tablespoons reduced-fat salad dressing
     1/2 cup dried cranberries
     1/4 cup finely chopped onion
     1/4 cup chopped celery
     1/2 teaspoon salt
     1/4 teaspoon pepper
     8 dinner rolls
     8 lettuce leaves

In a small bowl, combine the chicken, salad dressing, cranberries, onion, celery, salt and pepper. Cut tops off rolls; hollow out each roll, leaving a 1/2-in. shell. Line each with a lettuce leaf; fill with chicken salad. Replace tops.

NUTRITION FACTS: 2 sandwiches equals 354 calories, 10 g fat (2 g saturated fat), 83 mg cholesterol, 796 mg sodium, 41 g carbohydrate, 3 g fiber, 25 g protein. **DIABETIC EXCHANGES:** 3 very lean meat, 2 starch, 1 fruit, 1 fat.

Editor's Note: This recipe was tested with Miracle Whip Light salad dressing.

TASTY TIP
Sandra Sprinkle often mixes some chopped nuts into her cranberry chicken salad for extra crunch.

Chipotle Chicken and Beans

PREP: 15 Min.   **COOK:** 30 Min.   **YIELD:** 6 Servings

I was skeptical about this recipe due to its unique combination of ingredients, but it immediately became one of our all-time favorites.
—Jenny Kniesly, Dover, Ohio

     3/4 cup water, *divided*
     1/2 cup reduced-sodium chicken broth
     1/2 cup uncooked long grain rice
     6 boneless skinless chicken breast halves (4 ounces *each*)
     1/4 teaspoon salt
     3 bacon strips, diced
     1 cup chopped onion
     3 garlic cloves, minced
     1 cup chopped plum tomatoes
     1/2 teaspoon ground cumin
     1/4 teaspoon ground cinnamon
     1/2 cup whole-berry cranberry sauce
  4-1/2 teaspoons finely chopped chipotle peppers in adobo sauce
  1-1/2 teaspoons lime juice
     1 can (15 ounces) black beans, rinsed and drained
     1 can (15 ounces) white kidney *or* cannellini beans, rinsed and drained

In a small saucepan, bring 1/2 cup water and broth to a boil. Stir in rice. Reduce heat; cover and simmer for 15-18 minutes or until rice is tender.

Meanwhile, cut each chicken breast half widthwise into six strips. Sprinkle with salt. In a large nonstick skillet coated with nonstick cooking spray, cook chicken for 5 minutes on each side or until lightly browned. Remove and keep warm.

In the same skillet, cook bacon over medium heat until crisp. Using a slotted spoon, remove to paper towels; drain, reserving 1/2 teaspoon drippings. In the drippings, saute onion and garlic until tender. Add the tomatoes, cumin and cinnamon; cook for 2 minutes. Stir in the cranberry sauce, chipotle peppers, lime juice and remaining water. Bring to a boil.

Return chicken to the pan. Reduce heat; cover and simmer for 6-10 minutes or until chicken juices run clear. Remove and keep warm. Add rice and beans to the skillet; heat through. Serve chicken over bean mixture; sprinkle with bacon.

NUTRITION FACTS: 1 serving equals 366 calories, 5 g fat (2 g saturated fat), 66 mg cholesterol, 501 mg sodium, 46 g carbohydrate, 7 g fiber, 32 g protein. **DIABETIC EXCHANGES:** 3 very lean meat, 2-1/2 starch, 1 vegetable, 1/2 fat.

Favorite Recipe Made Lighter

"ABSOLUTELY WONDERFUL" is how Debra Hibbs describes her recipe for Creamy Chicken 'n' Artichokes. "It's excellent for company or special family dinners," she notes from Beaumont, California.

After sampling the artichoke-topped chicken in a lovely wine sauce, our makeover team couldn't agree more; however, they wanted to capture the flavor of Debra's original main course in a lighter form.

Since the recipe called for just a few ingredients, lightening it was a straightforward task. The team began by decreasing the overall amount of butter, browning the chicken in just one tablespoon instead of two. They also felt that the original sauce was rich and flavorful enough without adding any extra butter, so they eliminated it in the sauce altogether.

Substituting half-and-half cream for heavy whipping cream made the sauce even more calorie conscious, and to give it a similar consistency to Debra's submission, they added a little bit of flour.

With an unbelievable savings of 68% less fat and 220 calories, Makeover Creamy Chicken 'n' Artichokes is just as decadent as Debra's favorite dish. Serve it for the next special occassion or friendly get-together that you host. No one will be disappointed!

Makeover Creamy Chicken 'n' Artichokes
(PICTURED ABOVE)

PREP: 10 Min.   **COOK:** 30 Min.   **YIELD:** 4 Servings

- 4 boneless skinless chicken breast halves (4 ounces *each*)
- 1/2 teaspoon salt
- 1/4 teaspoon pepper
- 1 tablespoon butter
- 1 cup white wine *or* reduced-sodium chicken broth
- 1 cup uncooked instant rice
- 1 tablespoon all-purpose flour
- 2/3 cup half-and-half cream
- 1 package (9 ounces) frozen artichoke hearts, cooked, drained and quartered
- 1 can (2-1/4 ounces) sliced ripe olives, drained

Sprinkle chicken with the salt and pepper. In a large nonstick skillet coated with nonstick cooking spray, cook the chicken in butter for 3-4 minutes on each side or until browned. Remove and keep warm.

Add wine or broth to the skillet, stirring to loosen any browned bits. Bring to a boil. Return chicken to skillet. Reduce heat; simmer, uncovered, for 6-9 minutes or until chicken juices run clear. Remove chicken and keep warm.

Cook rice according to package directions. Meanwhile, in a small bowl, combine flour and cream; gradually stir into wine in skillet. Bring to a boil; cook and stir for 1-2 minutes or until thickened. Divide rice among four plates; top with chicken, sauce, artichokes and olives.

NUTRITION FACTS: 1 serving equals 373 calories, 12 g fat (6 g saturated fat), 90 mg cholesterol, 575 mg sodium, 31 g carbohydrate, 4 g fiber, 29 g protein. **DIABETIC EXCHANGES:** 3 very lean meat, 2 fat, 1-1/2 starch, 1 vegetable.

Creamy Chicken 'n' Artichokes

PREP: 10 Min.   **COOK:** 30 Min.   **YIELD:** 4 Servings

- 4 boneless skinless chicken breast halves (4 ounces *each*)
- 1/2 teaspoon salt
- 1/4 teaspoon pepper
- 4 tablespoons butter, *divided*
- 1 cup white wine *or* chicken broth
- 1 cup heavy whipping cream
- 1 cup uncooked instant rice
- 1 package (9 ounces) frozen artichoke hearts, cooked and drained
- 1 can (2-1/4 ounces) sliced ripe olives, drained

Sprinkle chicken with salt and pepper. In a large skillet, cook chicken in 2 tablespoons butter for 3-4 minutes on each side or until browned. Remove and keep warm.

Add wine or broth to the skillet, stirring to loosen any browned bits. Stir in cream; bring to a boil. Reduce heat; simmer, uncovered, for 5 minutes. Return chicken to the pan; simmer 6-8 minutes longer or until chicken juices run clear. Remove chicken; keep warm. Add remaining butter to cream mixture; bring to a boil. Reduce heat; simmer, uncovered, for 5-7 minutes or until sauce is reduced to 1 cup. Meanwhile, cook rice according to package directions. Divide the rice among four plates; top with the chicken, sauce, artichoke hearts and olives.

NUTRITION FACTS: 1 serving equals 593 calories, 38 g fat (22 g saturated fat), 175 mg cholesterol, 664 mg sodium, 30 g carbohydrate, 4 g fiber, 28 g protein.

Phyllo Chicken Potpie
(PICTURED ABOVE)

PREP: 35 Min.   **BAKE:** 10 Min.   **YIELD:** 6 Servings

Ribbons of buttery phyllo dough provide a crispy topping for this impressive entree. Pearl onions, mushrooms, asparagus and chicken are treated to a creamy sauce that our home economists gently flavored with thyme and sherry.

        6 cups water
        2 cups fresh pearl onions
    1-1/2 pounds boneless skinless chicken breasts, cubed
        2 tablespoons canola oil, *divided*
        2 medium red potatoes, peeled and chopped
        1 cup sliced fresh mushrooms
        1 can (14-1/2 ounces) reduced-sodium chicken broth
      1/2 pound fresh asparagus, trimmed and cut into 1-inch pieces
        3 tablespoons sherry *or* additional reduced-sodium chicken broth
        3 tablespoons cornstarch
      1/2 cup fat-free milk
    1-1/2 teaspoons minced fresh thyme
      1/2 teaspoon salt
      1/4 teaspoon pepper
       10 sheets phyllo dough (14 inches x 9 inches)
Refrigerated butter-flavored spray

In a Dutch oven, bring water to a boil. Add pearl onions; boil for 3 minutes. Drain and rinse in cold water; peel and set aside.

In a large skillet, cook chicken in 1 tablespoon oil over medium heat until juices run clear; remove and keep warm. In the same pan, saute potatoes in remaining oil for 5 minutes. Add onions and mushrooms; saute 3 minutes longer. Add the broth, asparagus and sherry or additional broth. Bring to a boil. Reduce heat; cover and simmer for 5 minutes or until potatoes are tender.

Combine cornstarch and milk until smooth; stir into skillet. Bring to a boil; cook and stir for 2 minutes or until thickened. Drain chicken; add to onion mixture. Stir in the thyme, salt and pepper. Transfer to an 8-in. square baking dish coated with nonstick cooking spray.

Stack all 10 phyllo sheets. Roll up, starting at a long side; cut into 1/2-in. strips. Place in a large bowl and toss to separate strips. Spritz with butter-flavored spray. Arrange over chicken mixture; spritz again. Bake, uncovered, at 425° for 10-15 minutes or until golden brown.

NUTRITION FACTS: 1 serving equals 325 calories, 8 g fat (1 g saturated fat), 63 mg cholesterol, 542 mg sodium, 33 g carbohydrate, 2 g fiber, 29 g protein. **DIABETIC EXCHANGES:** 3 very lean meat, 2 vegetable, 1-1/2 starch, 1 fat.

Editor's Note: This recipe was tested with I Can't Believe It's Not But-

HEALTHY OUTLOOK
Phyllo dough makes an ideal topping for a potpie. Not only is it low in calories and fat, but it lacks any saturated fat or cholesterol. Sometimes labeled "Filo," it can be purchased in fresh sheets, but the frozen variety is more popular.

Sherried Artichoke Chicken

(PICTURED BELOW)

CARB

PREP: 25 Min. **BAKE:** 25 Min. **YIELD:** 4 Servings

With a savory, no-fuss gravy, here's an entree that's perfect for weekend dinner parties and work-night suppers alike. I think that it's elegant but oh-so easy to toss together.

—Kathy Peters, North Versailles, Pennsylvania

- 1/2 teaspoon paprika
- 1/2 teaspoon salt
- 1/4 teaspoon pepper
- 4 boneless skinless chicken breast halves (4 ounces *each*)
- 2 tablespoons butter, *divided*
- 1 can (14 ounces) water-packed artichoke hearts, rinsed, drained and halved
- 1/2 pound sliced fresh mushrooms
- 1 cup reduced-sodium chicken broth
- 1/8 teaspoon dried tarragon
- 2 tablespoons all-purpose flour
- 1/2 cup sherry *or* additional reduced-sodium chicken broth

Combine the paprika, salt and pepper; sprinkle over both sides of chicken. In a large nonstick skillet, cook chicken in 1 tablespoon butter until browned on both sides. Transfer to a 2-qt. baking dish coated with nonstick cooking spray. Top with artichokes; set aside.

In the same skillet, saute mushrooms in remaining butter until tender. Stir in the broth and tarragon. Bring to a boil. Combine the flour and sherry or additional broth until smooth; stir into mushroom mixture. Bring to a boil; cook and stir for 2 minutes or until thickened.

Pour over chicken. Cover and bake at 350° for 25-30 minutes or until chicken juices run clear.

NUTRITION FACTS: 1 serving equals 263 calories, 9 g fat (4 g saturated fat), 78 mg cholesterol, 815 mg sodium, 12 g carbohydrate, 1 g fiber, 28 g protein. DIABETIC EXCHANGES: 3 very lean meat, 2 vegetable, 1 fat.

Ginger Chicken with Green Onions

CARB

PREP/TOTAL TIME: 30 Min. **YIELD:** 4 Servings

Fresh gingerroot, garlic and cayenne come together in a pleasant sauce for chicken in this simple skillet recipe. Every time I serve this to company, I receive compliments.

—Deborah Anderson, Willow Street, Pennsylvania

- 4 boneless skinless chicken breast halves (4 ounces *each*)
- 1/4 teaspoon salt
- 1/4 teaspoon pepper
- 3 teaspoons olive oil, *divided*
- 3 garlic cloves, minced
- 2 teaspoons minced fresh gingerroot
- 1 teaspoon grated lemon peel
- 3/4 cup reduced-sodium chicken broth, *divided*
- 1/2 teaspoon sugar
- 1/8 teaspoon cayenne pepper
- 1/2 medium lemon, cut into thin slices
- 1 tablespoon cornstarch
- 1/2 cup thinly sliced green onions

Sprinkle chicken with salt and pepper. In a large nonstick skillet coated with nonstick cooking spay, cook chicken in 2 teaspoons oil for 3 minutes on each side or until lightly browned. Remove and keep warm.

In the same skillet, cook the garlic, ginger and lemon peel in remaining oil for 1 minute. Stir in 1/2 cup broth, sugar and cayenne. Bring to a boil. Return chicken to the pan; top with lemon slices. Reduce heat; cover and simmer for 7-9 minutes or until chicken juices run clear.

Remove chicken and keep warm. Combine cornstarch and remaining broth until smooth; gradually stir into pan juices. Bring to a boil; cook and stir for 2 minutes or until thickened. Stir in green onions; cook 1-2 minutes longer. Serve over chicken.

NUTRITION FACTS: 1 chicken breast half with 2 tablespoons sauce equals 175 calories, 6 g fat (1 g saturated fat), 63 mg cholesterol, 322 mg sodium, 5 g carbohydrate, 1 g fiber, 24 g protein. DIABETIC EXCHANGES: 3 very lean meat, 1/2 starch, 1/2 fat.

Turkey Wild Rice Casserole

(PICTURED ABOVE RIGHT)

PREP: 1 Hour **BAKE:** 1 Hour **YIELD:** 6 Servings

This truly is a comforting meal-in-one. Featuring onion, carrot and celery, the wild rice mixture bakes in the same dish as the turkey breast tenderloins. —Lois Kinneberg, Phoenix, Arizona

- 3 cups water
- 1 cup uncooked wild rice
- 1/2 cup chopped onion
- 1/2 cup chopped carrot
- 1/2 cup chopped celery
- 1 tablespoon butter
- 1 tablespoon canola oil
- 3 tablespoons all-purpose flour

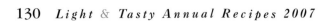

1/2 teaspoon rubbed sage
1/2 teaspoon salt, *divided*
1/8 teaspoon pepper
3/4 cup reduced-sodium chicken broth
1/2 cup fat-free milk
2 turkey breast tenderloins (3/4 pound *each*)
1 teaspoon dried parsley
1/8 teaspoon paprika

In a small saucepan, bring the water, wild rice and onion to a boil. Reduce heat; cover and simmer for 55-60 minutes or until rice is tender. Meanwhile, in another saucepan, saute carrot and celery in butter and oil until tender.

Combine the flour, sage, 1/4 teaspoon salt and pepper; stir into carrot mixture until blended. Gradually add broth and milk. Bring to a boil; cook and stir for 1 minute or until thickened. Remove from the heat. Stir in rice. Transfer to a 2-qt. baking dish coated with nonstick cooking spray.

Place turkey over rice mixture. Combine the parsley, paprika and remaining salt; sprinkle over turkey. Cover and bake at 350° for 60-70 minutes or until a meat thermometer inserted into turkey reads 170°. Slice turkey; serve over rice.

NUTRITION FACTS: 3 ounces cooked turkey with 2/3 cup rice mixture equals 313 calories, 5 g fat (2 g saturated fat), 87 mg cholesterol, 371 mg sodium, 29 g carbohydrate, 3 g fiber, 36 g protein. **DIABETIC EXCHANGES:** 3 lean meat, 1-1/2 starch, 1 vegetable.

Santa Fe Chicken
(PICTURED AT RIGHT)

PREP/TOTAL TIME: 30 Min.   **YIELD:** 4 Servings

Garnished with fresh cilantro, chicken and rice are turned into a complete supper that's ready in a dash.
—Jon Carole Gilbreath, Tyler, Texas

1 large onion, chopped
1 to 2 tablespoons chopped seeded jalapeno pepper
1 garlic clove, minced
1 tablespoon olive oil
1-1/4 cups reduced-sodium chicken broth
1 can (10 ounces) diced tomatoes and green chilies, undrained
1 cup uncooked long grain rice
4 boneless skinless chicken breast halves (4 ounces *each*)
1/2 teaspoon salt
1/4 teaspoon pepper
1/4 teaspoon ground cumin
3/4 cup shredded reduced-fat cheddar cheese
Minced fresh cilantro, optional

In a large skillet, saute the onion, jalapeno and garlic in oil until tender. Add broth and tomatoes; bring to a boil. Stir in rice.

Sprinkle chicken with salt, pepper and cumin; place over rice mixture. Cover and simmer for 10 minutes. Turn chicken; cook 5-10 minutes longer or until juices run clear.

Remove from the heat. Sprinkle with cheese; cover and let stand for 5 minutes. Garnish with cilantro if desired.

NUTRITION FACTS: 1 chicken breast half with 1 cup rice mixture equals 412 calories, 11 g fat (4 g saturated fat), 78 mg cholesterol, 966 mg sodium, 44 g carbohydrate, 2 g fiber, 33 g protein. **DIABETIC EXCHANGES:** 3 very lean meat, 2 starch, 2 fat, 1 vegetable.

Editor's Note: When cutting or seeding hot peppers, use rubber or plastic gloves to protect your hands. Avoid touching your face.

Turkey Fettuccine Skillet

(PICTURED BELOW)

PREP: 10 Min.   **COOK:** 30 Min.   **YIELD:** 6 Servings

I came up with a simple dish as a way to use leftover turkey after Thanksgiving and Christmas dinners. My children really enjoy it.
—Kari Johnston, Marwayne, Alberta

    8 ounces uncooked fettuccine
1/2 cup chopped onion
1/2 cup chopped celery
    4 garlic cloves, minced
    1 teaspoon canola oil
    1 cup sliced fresh mushrooms
    2 cups fat-free milk
    1 teaspoon salt-free seasoning blend
1/4 teaspoon salt
    2 tablespoons cornstarch
1/2 cup fat-free half-and-half
1/3 cup grated Parmesan cheese
    3 cups cubed cooked turkey breast
3/4 cup shredded part-skim mozzarella cheese

Cook fettuccine according to package directions. Meanwhile, in a large ovenproof skillet coated with nonstick cooking spray, saute the onion, celery and garlic in oil for 3 minutes. Add mushrooms; cook and stir until vegetables are tender. Stir in the milk, seasoning blend and salt. Bring to a boil.

Mix cornstarch and half-and-half until smooth; stir into skillet. Cook and stir for 2 minutes or until thickened and bubbly. Stir in Parmesan cheese just until melted.

Stir in turkey. Drain fettuccine; add to turkey mixture. Heat through. Sprinkle with mozzarella cheese. Broil 4-6 in. from the heat for 2-3 minutes or until cheese is melted.

NUTRITION FACTS: 1 cup equals 361 calories, 7 g fat (3 g saturated fat), 76 mg cholesterol, 343 mg sodium, 38 g carbohydrate, 2 g fiber, 34 g protein. **DIABETIC EXCHANGES:** 4 very lean meat, 2-1/2 starch, 1/2 fat.

Chicken Rice Casserole

PREP: 30 Min.   **BAKE:** 50 Min.   **YIELD:** 10 Servings

Tuck last night's chicken or turkey into this creamy, comforting casserole. Chopped celery and nuts add flavor and a fun crunch.
—Shirley Robb, Republic, Washington

    2 cups uncooked long grain rice
    2 cans (14-1/2 ounces *each*) reduced-sodium chicken broth
1/2 cup water
    2 cans (10-3/4 ounces *each*) reduced-fat reduced-sodium condensed cream of chicken soup, undiluted
    2 cups fat-free milk
    1 tablespoon dried minced onion
    1 teaspoon Worcestershire sauce
1/2 teaspoon salt
    4 cups cubed cooked chicken breast
    2 cups chopped celery
3/4 cup sliced almonds, *divided*

In a large saucepan, bring the rice, broth and water to a boil. Reduce heat; cover and simmer for 15-18 minutes or until the liquid is absorbed and the rice is tender.

Meanwhile, in a large bowl, combine the soup, milk, onion, Worcestershire sauce and salt. Stir in the chicken, celery, 1/2 cup almonds and rice. Transfer to a 13-in. x 9-in. x 2-in. baking dish coated with nonstick cooking spray.

Cover and bake at 350° for 45 minutes. Uncover; sprinkle with remaining almonds. Bake 5-10 minutes longer or until heated through.

NUTRITION FACTS: 1-1/4 cups equals 334 calories, 7 g fat (1 g saturated fat), 49 mg cholesterol, 660 mg sodium, 41 g carbohydrate, 2 g fiber, 25 g protein. **DIABETIC EXCHANGES:** 3 starch, 2 very lean meat, 1 fat.

Taco Oven-Fried Chicken

CARB

PREP: 10 Min.   **BAKE:** 35 Min.   **YIELD:** 4 Servings

Looking for a new low-carb sensation? Sink your teeth into this moist chicken. The zesty main course comes together in only 10 minutes, making it the perfect way to spice up weeknight menus.
—Peggy Campbell, Welch, Texas

1/2 cup fat-free milk
    1 tablespoon spicy brown mustard
    1 teaspoon reduced-sodium soy sauce
1/2 teaspoon hot pepper sauce
1/2 teaspoon Worcestershire sauce
    1 garlic clove, minced
1/2 cup all-purpose flour
    1 tablespoon reduced-sodium taco seasoning
1/2 teaspoon salt

Turkey Quesadillas with Cranberry Salsa

(PICTURED BELOW)

PREP: 10 Min.   **COOK:** 15 Min. + Cooling   **YIELD:** 4 Servings

A sweet-tart cranberry salsa is the ideal accompaniment to turkey in this easy quesadilla. With a hint of lemon and pear, the salsa is also good with chicken or pork.

—Jodi Kristensen, Macomb, Michigan

3/4 cup fresh *or* frozen cranberries
2 tablespoons sugar
1/4 cup water
1 small pear, chopped
1/4 cup chopped red onion
3 tablespoons chopped celery
1 tablespoon lemon juice
1 jalapeno pepper, seeded and chopped
2 teaspoons grated lemon peel
1/2 teaspoon ground cumin
4 flour tortillas (6 inches)
2 cups cubed cooked turkey breast
1 cup (4 ounces) shredded reduced-fat cheddar cheese

In a small saucepan, combine the cranberries, sugar and water. Cook over medium heat until the berries pop, about 10 minutes. Remove from the heat; cool to room temperature. Stir in the pear, onion, celery, lemon juice, jalapeno, lemon peel and cumin. Set aside.

Place tortillas on a griddle coated with nonstick cooking spray. Spoon turkey and sprinkle cheese over half of each tortilla; fold over. Cook over low heat for 1-2 minutes on each side or until cheese is melted. Serve with cranberry salsa.

NUTRITION FACTS: 1 quesadilla with 1/3 cup salsa equals 321 calories, 10 g fat (4 g saturated fat), 80 mg cholesterol, 449 mg sodium, 27 g carbohydrate, 2 g fiber, 32 g protein. **DIABETIC EXCHANGES:** 3 very lean meat, 1-1/2 starch, 1 fat, 1/2 fruit.

Editor's Note: When cutting or seeding hot peppers, use rubber or plastic gloves to protect your hands. Avoid touching your face.

1/2 teaspoon pepper
4 boneless skinless chicken breast halves (6 ounces *each*)

In a shallow bowl, combine the first six ingredients. In another shallow bowl, combine the flour, taco seasoning, salt and pepper. Dip chicken in milk mixture, then roll in flour mixture.

Place in a 15-in. x 10-in. x 1-in. baking pan coated with nonstick cooking spray. Bake, uncovered, at 350° for 35-40 minutes or until chicken juices run clear.

NUTRITION FACTS: 1 chicken breast half equals 218 calories, 4 g fat (1 g saturated fat), 94 mg cholesterol, 323 mg sodium, 7 g carbohydrate, trace fiber, 35 g protein. **DIABETIC EXCHANGES:** 5 very lean meat, 1/2 starch.

Cranberry Turkey Wraps

(PICTURED ABOVE)

PREP/TOTAL TIME: 15 Min.   **YIELD:** 8 Servings

These hefty grab-and-go wraps are speedy to assemble and low in calories. We often take them to the local stock show in a cooler and eat them in the stands. Everyone seems to love them!

—Bobbie Keefer, Byers, Colorado

1 can (11 ounces) reduced-sugar mandarin oranges, drained
1 medium tart apple, peeled and diced
3 tablespoons dried cranberries
1 carton (6 ounces) fat-free plain yogurt
2 tablespoons fat-free mayonnaise
8 flour tortillas (8 inches)
8 lettuce leaves
1-1/2 pounds thinly sliced deli turkey
8 slices (1 ounce *each*) part-skim mozzarella cheese
2 tablespoons chopped pecans, toasted

In a small bowl, combine the oranges, apple and cranberries. In another bowl, combine yogurt and mayonnaise; spread over tortillas. Layer each with lettuce, turkey, cheese, fruit mixture and pecans. Roll up tightly.

NUTRITION FACTS: 1 wrap equals 374 calories, 12 g fat (4 g saturated fat), 54 mg cholesterol, 1,477 mg sodium, 40 g carbohydrate, 1 g fiber, 27 g protein. **DIABETIC EXCHANGES:** 3 lean meat, 2 starch, 1 fat, 1/2 fruit.

Southwestern Stuffed Turkey Breast

FAT ⬇ CARB ⬇

(PICTURED BELOW)

PREP: 40 Min. **BAKE:** 1-1/4 Hours + Standing **YIELD:** 8 Servings

This luscious turkey breast is a sure hit with family and friends. The moist stuffing gives it a hint of Southwestern flair.
—Bernice Janowski, Stevens Point, Wisconsin

  1/3 cup sun-dried tomatoes (not packed in oil)
  2/3 cup boiling water
1-1/2 teaspoons dried oregano
    1 teaspoon salt
  3/4 teaspoon ground cumin
  1/2 teaspoon ground coriander
  1/4 teaspoon crushed red pepper flakes
    1 small onion, chopped
    1 small green pepper, diced
    1 garlic clove, minced
    1 tablespoon olive oil
    1 cup frozen corn, thawed
  1/2 cup dry bread crumbs
1-1/2 teaspoons grated lime peel
    1 boneless skinless turkey breast half (2 pounds)

Place tomatoes in a small bowl; cover with boiling water. Cover and let stand for 5 minutes. Drain, reserving 3 tablespoons liquid; set aside. Meanwhile, combine seasonings in a small bowl.

In a large skillet, saute tomatoes, onion, green pepper and garlic in oil until tender. Stir in corn and 2 teaspoons seasonings; remove from heat. Stir in bread crumbs and reserved tomato liquid. Add lime peel to remaining seasonings; set aside.

Cover turkey with plastic wrap. Flatten to 1/2-in. thickness; remove plastic. Sprinkle turkey with half of lime-seasoning mixture; spread vegetable mixture to within 1 in. of edges. Roll up jelly-roll style, starting with a short side; tie with kitchen string. Sprinkle with remaining lime-seasoning mixture. Place on a rack in a shallow roasting pan; cover loosely with foil.

Bake at 350° for 1 hour. Uncover; bake 15-30 minutes longer or until a meat thermometer reads 170°, basting occasionally with pan drippings. Let stand for 15 minutes before slicing.

NUTRITION FACTS: 1 slice equals 200 calories, 3 g fat (1 g saturated fat), 70 mg cholesterol, 458 mg sodium, 12 g carbohydrate, 2 g fiber, 30 g protein. **DIABETIC EXCHANGES:** 4 very lean meat, 1 starch.

Turkey Alfredo Pizza

(PICTURED ABOVE)

PREP/TOTAL TIME: 25 Min. **YIELD:** 6 Servings

A longtime family favorite, this thin-crust pizza is chock-full of flavor and nutrition—and an excellent way to use up leftover poultry.
—Edie DeSpain, Logan, Utah

    1 prebaked thin Italian bread shell crust (10 ounces)
    1 garlic clove, peeled and halved
  3/4 cup reduced-fat Alfredo sauce, *divided*
    1 package (10 ounces) frozen chopped spinach, thawed and squeezed dry
    2 teaspoons lemon juice
  1/4 teaspoon salt
  1/8 teaspoon pepper
    2 cups shredded cooked turkey breast
  3/4 cup shredded Parmesan cheese
  1/2 teaspoon crushed red pepper flakes

Place the crust on a baking sheet; rub with cut sides of garlic. Discard garlic. Spread 1/2 cup Alfredo sauce over crust.

In a small bowl, combine the spinach, lemon juice, salt and pepper; spoon evenly over sauce. Top with turkey; drizzle with remaining Alfredo sauce. Sprinkle with Parmesan cheese and pepper flakes. Bake at 425° for 11-13 minutes or until heated through and cheese is melted.

NUTRITION FACTS: 1 slice equals 300 calories, 9 g fat (4 g saturated fat), 60 mg cholesterol, 823 mg sodium, 27 g carbohydrate, 2 g fiber, 25 g protein. **DIABETIC EXCHANGES:** 3 lean meat, 2 starch.

Pork & Lamb Favorites

Today's pork is a delicious staple in homes from coast to coast. Whether stir-fried, roasted or pan-broiled, pork leads to swift, satisfying suppers. Similarly, lean cuts of lamb and varieties of sausage also make meal planning a snap, so turn the page for 27 new, mouth-watering mainstays.

Tarragon Chops with Mushrooms, p. 144

Pork in Orange Sauce
(PICTURED ABOVE)

PREP/TOTAL TIME: 25 Min.   **YIELD:** 3 Servings

A splash of citrus flavors this tender, pork stir-fry with crunchy cashews. Created by our Test Kitchen, it's a colorful combination that makes an everyday meal seem like a special occasion.

   2 teaspoons sugar
   1 teaspoon cornstarch
1/2 cup orange juice
   2 teaspoons grated fresh gingerroot
   2 teaspoons reduced-sodium soy sauce
   1 teaspoon grated orange peel
   1 pork tenderloin (1 pound), cut into 1/4-inch slices
   2 large carrots, julienned
   1 cup sliced celery
   2 tablespoons salted cashew halves

In a small bowl, combine sugar and cornstarch. Stir in the orange juice, ginger, soy sauce and orange peel until blended; set aside.

In a nonstick skillet or wok lightly coated with nonstick cooking spray, stir-fry the pork for 4-5 minutes or until no longer pink; remove and keep warm. Add carrots and celery; stir-fry for 2-3 minutes or until crisp-tender.

Stir orange juice mixture; add to vegetables. Bring to a boil; cook and stir for 1 minute or until thickened. Return pork to the pan; heat through. Stir in cashews.

NUTRITION FACTS: 1-1/4 cups equals 282 calories, 9 g fat (2 g saturated fat), 98 mg cholesterol, 292 mg sodium, 16 g carbohydrate, 1 g fiber, 34 g protein. **DIABETIC EXCHANGES:** 4 lean meat, 1 vegetable, 1/2 starch.

HEALTHY OUTLOOK

Not only is the tangy stir-fry low in fat and carbs, but it calls for tomatoes, which offer protective benefits from many types of cancers.

Asian Pork Roast

(PICTURED BELOW)

CARB

PREP: 25 Min.   **COOK:** 4-1/2 Hours   **YIELD:** 12 Servings

Slow-cooked dishes are a favorite in our home, and this one is perfect for fall and winter evenings. The pork roast cooks all afternoon with onions, honey, soy sauce and ginger for fabulous flavor.
—Sheree Shown, Junction City, Oregon

- 2 large onions, thinly sliced
- 3 garlic cloves, minced
- 1/2 teaspoon salt
- 1/2 teaspoon pepper
- 1 boneless whole pork loin roast (3 pounds)
- 1 tablespoon canola oil
- 3 bay leaves
- 1/4 cup hot water
- 1/4 cup honey
- 1/4 cup reduced-sodium soy sauce
- 2 tablespoons rice wine vinegar
- 1 teaspoon ground ginger
- 1/2 teaspoon ground cloves
- 3 tablespoons cornstarch
- 1/4 cup cold water
- 2 tablespoons sesame seeds, toasted

Hot cooked rice and sliced green onion tops, optional

Place onions in a 5-qt. slow cooker. In a small bowl, combine the garlic, salt and pepper. Cut roast in half; rub with garlic mixture. In a large nonstick skillet coated with nonstick cooking spray, brown pork in oil on all sides. Transfer to the slow cooker; add bay leaves.

In a small bowl, combine hot water and honey; stir in the soy sauce, vinegar, ginger and cloves. Pour over pork. Cover and cook on low for 4-5 hours or until a meat thermometer reads 160°.

Remove meat and onions from slow cooker; keep warm. Discard bay leaves. In a small bowl, combine cornstarch and cold water until smooth. Gradually stir into slow cooker.

Cover and cook on high for 30 minutes or until thickened, stirring twice. Slice pork; top with onions, sauce and sesame seeds. If desired, serve with rice and garnish with green onion tops.

NUTRITION FACTS: 3 ounces cooked pork with 3 tablespoons onions and 3 tablespoons sauce (calculated without optional ingredients) equals 203 calories, 7 g fat (2 g saturated fat), 56 mg cholesterol, 342 mg sodium, 11 g carbohydrate, 1 g fiber, 23 g protein. **DIABETIC EXCHANGES:** 3 lean meat, 1 starch.

Pork Chops with Dijon Sauce

(PICTURED ABOVE)

CARB

PREP/TOTAL TIME: 30 Min.   **YIELD:** 4 Servings

Here's a main course that tastes rich but isn't high in saturated fat. It's easy for weekdays, but the creamy sauce makes it fancy enough for weekends.   —Bonnie Brown-Watson, Houston, Texas

- 4 boneless pork loin chops (3/4 inch thick and 6 ounces each)
- 1/4 teaspoon salt
- 1/4 teaspoon pepper
- 2 teaspoons canola oil
- 1/3 cup reduced-sodium chicken broth
- 2 tablespoons Dijon mustard
- 1/3 cup fat-free half-and-half

Sprinkle pork chops with salt and pepper. In a large nonstick skillet coated with nonstick cooking spray, cook chops in oil for 5-7 minutes on each side or until a meat thermometer reads 160°. Remove and keep warm.

Stir broth into skillet, scraping up any browned bits. Stir in the mustard until blended. Stir in the half-and-half. Bring to a boil. Reduce heat; simmer, uncovered, for 5-6 minutes or until thickened. Serve with pork chops.

NUTRITION FACTS: 1 pork chop with 2 tablespoons sauce equals 272 calories, 13 g fat (4 g saturated fat), 82 mg cholesterol, 452 mg sodium, 3 g carbohydrate, trace fiber, 34 g protein. **DIABETIC EXCHANGES:** 5 lean meat, 1/2 fat.

Pork Tenderloin Stew

(PICTURED BELOW)

PREP: 20 Min. **COOK:** 40 Min. **YIELD:** 8 Servings

This thick, creamy stew is one dinner that my family requests often. It does an especially good job of warming us up on cold, winter days. —Janet Allen, Decatur, Illinois

    2 pork tenderloins (1 pound *each*), cut into 1-inch cubes
    1 tablespoon olive oil
    1 medium onion, chopped
    1 garlic clove, minced
    1 can (14-1/2 ounces) reduced-sodium chicken broth
    2 pounds red potatoes, peeled and cubed
    1 cup sliced fresh carrots
    1 cup sliced celery
  1/2 pound sliced fresh mushrooms
    2 tablespoons cider vinegar
    2 teaspoons sugar
1-1/2 teaspoons dried tarragon
    1 teaspoon salt
    2 tablespoons all-purpose flour
  1/2 cup fat-free milk
  1/2 cup reduced-fat sour cream

In a large nonstick skillet, cook pork in oil until no longer pink; remove and keep warm. In the same pan, saute onion and garlic until crisp-tender. Add the broth, vegetables, vinegar, sugar, tarragon and salt; bring to a boil. Reduce heat; cover and simmer for 25-30 minutes or until vegetables are tender.

Combine flour and milk until smooth; gradually stir into vegetable mixture. Bring to a boil; cook and stir for 2 minutes or until thickened. Add pork and heat through. Reduce heat; stir in sour cream just before serving.

NUTRITION FACTS: 1-1/4 cups equals 293 calories, 7 g fat (3 g saturated fat), 68 mg cholesterol, 521 mg sodium, 28 g carbohydrate, 3 g fiber, 28 g protein. **DIABETIC EXCHANGES:** 3 lean meat, 1 starch, 1 vegetable, 1/2 fat.

Chinese Pork 'n' Noodles

(PICTURED ABOVE)

PREP: 20 Min. **COOK:** 15 Min. **YIELD:** 4 Servings

I based the recipe for these noodles on a similar dish I found in a magazine. I changed a few things around, and my husband and I loved it. It's just as good when the pork is replaced with seafood. —Jennifer Enzer, Manchester, Michigan

    6 ounces uncooked angel hair pasta
    3 tablespoons hoisin sauce
    2 tablespoons reduced-sodium soy sauce
    2 teaspoons sesame oil
    1 pork tenderloin (1 pound), thinly sliced and halved
    3 teaspoons canola oil, *divided*
  3/4 cup julienned sweet red pepper
  3/4 cup halved fresh snow peas
  1/2 cup sliced onion
    1 cup sliced cabbage
  1/4 cup minced fresh cilantro

Cook pasta according to package directions. Meanwhile, in a small bowl, combine the hoisin sauce, soy sauce and sesame oil; set aside.

In a large nonstick skillet or wok, stir-fry pork in 2 teaspoons canola oil for 3 minutes or until no longer pink. Remove and keep warm. In the same skillet, stir-fry the red pepper, peas and onion in remaining oil for 3 minutes. Add cabbage; stir-fry 2 minutes longer or until vegetables are crisp-tender.

Stir the reserved hoisin sauce mixture and stir into skillet. Return the pork to the pan; heat through. Drain the pasta and add to the skillet; toss to coat. Sprinkle each serving with 1 tablespoon cilantro.

NUTRITION FACTS: 1-1/2 cups equals 398 calories, 11 g fat (2 g saturated fat), 64 mg cholesterol, 550 mg sodium, 43 g carbohydrate, 3 g fiber, 30 g protein. **DIABETIC EXCHANGES:** 3 lean meat, 2-1/2 starch, 1 vegetable, 1 fat.

Chops with Mixed Fruit

(PICTURED BELOW)

PREP: 10 Min.   **COOK:** 30 Min.   **YIELD:** 4 Servings

Apricots and pineapple lend fruity flavor to my longtime mainstay. It's a tasty, colorful and easy dinner.   —Phyllis Leslie, Toledo, Ohio

> 4 boneless pork loin chops (4 ounces *each*)
> 3/4 cup chopped onion
> 3/4 cup thinly sliced celery
> 8 pitted prunes
> 3/4 cup pineapple tidbits
> 1/3 cup dried apricots
> 1/3 cup plus 2 tablespoons water, *divided*
> 4 teaspoons reduced-sodium soy sauce

Dash dried marjoram

In a large nonstick skillet coated with nonstick cooking spray, cook pork chops over medium heat for 4-5 minutes on each side or until browned. Remove and keep warm.

In the same skillet, saute onion and celery for 3 minutes. Stir in the prunes, pineapple, apricots, 1/3 cup water, soy sauce and marjoram. Bring to a boil. Reduce heat; cover and simmer for 15 minutes.

Return pork to the pan. Stir in remaining water; return to a boil. Reduce heat; cover and simmer for 7-11 minutes or until meat is tender.

NUTRITION FACTS: 1 chop with 1/2 cup fruit mixture equals 232 calories, 7 g fat (2 g saturated fat), 55 mg cholesterol, 180 mg sodium, 19 g carbohydrate, 0 fiber, 23 g protein. **DIABETIC EXCHANGES:** 3 lean meat, 1 fruit.

Pork Tenderloin Fajitas

PREP/TOTAL TIME: 25 Min.   **YIELD:** 4 Servings

This recipe offers loads of appeal. Sizzling pork tenderloin and veggies are seasoned with cumin, chili powder and cilantro before being tucked into warm tortillas. Feel free to add red and yellow pepper strips for extra color if you'd like.

—Rachel Hozey, Pensacola, Florida

> 1/4 cup minced fresh cilantro
> 1/2 teaspoon garlic powder
> 1/2 teaspoon chili powder
> 1/2 teaspoon ground cumin
> 1 pork tenderloin (1 pound), thinly sliced
> 1 tablespoon canola oil
> 1 small onion, sliced and separated into rings
> 1 medium green pepper, julienned
> 4 flour tortillas (8 inches), warmed

Shredded cheddar cheese and sour cream, optional

In a small bowl, combine cilantro, garlic powder, chili powder and cumin; set aside. In a large skillet, saute pork in oil until no longer pink. Add onion and green pepper; cook until crisp-tender.

Sprinkle with seasoning mixture; toss to coat. Spoon onto tortillas; serve with cheese and sour cream if desired.

NUTRITION FACTS: 1 fajita (calculated without cheese and sour cream) equals 327 calories, 11 g fat (2 g saturated fat), 63 mg cholesterol, 299 mg sodium, 29 g carbohydrate, 1 g fiber, 28 g protein. **DIABETIC EXCHANGES:** 3 lean meat, 1-1/2 starch, 1 vegetable, 1/2 fat.

Corn-Stuffed Pork Chops
(PICTURED ABOVE)

PREP: 15 Min. **BAKE:** 35 Min. **YIELD:** 4 Servings

Here's a main course that's impressive enough for guests but simple enough for weeknights. The moist stuffing only takes a few moments to prepare. —Kimberly Andresen, Revere, Massachusetts

- 1/4 cup chopped onion
- 1/4 cup chopped green pepper
- 1 tablespoon butter
- 3/4 cup corn bread stuffing mix
- 1/2 cup frozen corn, thawed
- 2 tablespoons diced pimientos
- 1/4 teaspoon salt
- 1/8 teaspoon ground cumin
- 1/8 teaspoon pepper
- 4 bone-in pork loin chops (7 ounces *each*)

In a large skillet, saute onion and green pepper in butter for 3-4 minutes or until tender. Stir in the stuffing mix, corn, pimientos, salt, cumin and pepper. Cut a pocket in each pork chop by making a horizontal slice almost to the bone; fill with stuffing. Secure with toothpicks if necessary.

Place in an 11-in. x 7-in. x 2-in. baking dish coated with nonstick cooking spray. Bake, uncovered, at 375° for 35-40 minutes or until meat juices run clear. Discard toothpicks before serving.

NUTRITION FACTS: 1 serving equals 297 calories, 12 g fat (5 g saturated fat), 94 mg cholesterol, 433 mg sodium, 14 g carbohydrate, 1 g fiber, 32 g protein. **DIABETIC EXCHANGES:** 4 lean meat, 1 starch.

Pork Cabbage Sandwiches
(PICTURED AT RIGHT)

PREP: 25 Min. + Marinating **COOK:** 15 Min. **YIELD:** 4 Servings

Several years ago, my mom and I took a light-cooking course at a local technical college. We both loved this recipe from the class and still make it often today. —Lisa Gross, Janesville, Wisconsin

- 1/4 cup reduced-sodium soy sauce
- 3 tablespoons beer *or* nonalcoholic beer
- 2 tablespoons diced onion
- 1 garlic clove, minced
- 1/2 teaspoon minced fresh gingerroot
- 1 pork tenderloin (3/4 pound), cut into 1/4-inch slices
- 2 tablespoons olive oil
- 1 tablespoon white wine vinegar
- 1 teaspoon Dijon mustard
- 1/2 teaspoon sugar
- 1/8 teaspoon pepper
- 2 cups shredded red cabbage
- 1 loaf (8 ounces) French bread, halved lengthwise

Refrigerated butter-flavored spray
- 1/3 cup fat-free mayonnaise

In a small bowl, combine the first five ingredients. Remove 2 tablespoons to another bowl; set aside. Place pork in a large resealable plastic bag; add remaining marinade. Seal bag and turn to coat; refrigerate for 30 minutes.

Meanwhile, combine olive oil, vinegar, mustard, sugar and pepper. Add cabbage; toss to coat. Cover and refrigerate.

Hollow out 1/2 in. from top and bottom halves of bread (discard removed bread or save for another use). Spritz with butter-flavored spray. Broil 3-4 in. from the heat for 1-2 minutes or until toasted. Combine mayonnaise and reserved marinade; spread over bread.

Drain pork; discard marinade. In a large nonstick skillet coated with nonstick cooking spray, cook pork in batches until no longer pink. Spoon cabbage mixture onto bottom half of bread; top with pork. Replace bread top. Cut into four sandwiches.

NUTRITION FACTS: 1 sandwich equals 363 calories, 13 g fat (2 g saturated fat), 49 mg cholesterol, 962 mg sodium, 36 g carbohydrate, 3 g fiber, 23 g protein. **DIABETIC EXCHANGES:** 2-1/2 starch, 2 lean meat, 1-1/2 fat.

Editor's Note: This recipe was tested with I Can't Believe It's Not Butter Spray.

Sausage Fajitas
(PICTURED ABOVE)

PREP: 25 Min. + Marinating   **COOK:** 10 Min.   **YIELD:** 4 Servings

The secret to great fajitas is a quick, herb marinade. To save time, I like to marinate everything the night before.
—Janie McClellan, Ocean Isle Beach, North Carolina

   1 cup reduced-sodium chicken broth
1/4 cup olive oil
1/4 cup red wine vinegar
1/4 cup reduced-sodium soy sauce
1/4 cup Worcestershire sauce
   1 tablespoon *each* dried basil, oregano and thyme
1/4 teaspoon pepper
3/4 pound reduced-fat smoked kielbasa *or* Polish sausage, sliced
   3 cups julienned mixed sweet peppers
   1 medium red onion, thinly sliced
   1 cup sliced fresh mushrooms
   4 whole wheat tortillas (8 inches), warmed
   4 tablespoons fat-free sour cream
   1 small tomato, chopped

In a large resealable plastic bag, combine the first seven ingredients; add the sausage, peppers, onion and mushrooms. Seal bag and turn to coat; refrigerate for at least 2 hours.

Drain marinade, reserving 1/2 cup. In a large nonstick skillet, cook the sausage and vegetables in reserved marinade for 9-11 minutes or until sausage is heated through and vegetables are tender. Spoon sausage mixture over half of each tortilla; top with sour cream and tomato. Fold over.

NUTRITION FACTS: 1 fajita equals 329 calories, 10 g fat (2 g saturated fat), 33 mg cholesterol, 1,374 mg sodium, 48 g carbohydrate, 6 g fiber, 18 g protein. **DIABETIC EXCHANGES:** 2 starch, 2 lean meat, 2 vegetable, 1 fat.

TASTY TIP
In addition to the sour cream and chopped tomatoes, try topping the fajita mixture with some reduced-fat shredded cheddar cheese.

Skillet Pork Chops

CARB

PREP: 10 Min.   **COOK:** 25 Min.   **YIELD:** 4 Servings

It's hard to believe that tender pork chops and honey-mustard sauce are so low in carbohydrates. It's an easy meal that doesn't involve a lot of fat.   —Susan Taul, Birmingham, Alabama

   4 bone-in pork loin chops (3/4 inch thick and 6 ounces each)
1/4 teaspoon salt
1/8 teaspoon pepper
   1 tablespoon butter
   1 cup chopped onion
   1 cup water, *divided*
   2 teaspoons honey
   2 teaspoons prepared mustard
   2 teaspoons Worcestershire sauce
   1 teaspoon beef bouillon granules
   2 teaspoons cornstarch

Sprinkle pork chops with salt and pepper. In a large nonstick skillet coated with nonstick cooking spray, cook pork in butter for 4-6 minutes on each side or until browned. Remove and keep warm.

In the same pan, saute onion in drippings until tender. Add 3/4 cup water; stir to loosen browned bits from pan. Stir in the honey, mustard, Worcestershire sauce and bouillon. Bring to a boil. Return pork to the pan. Reduce heat; cover and simmer for 6-10 minutes or until meat is tender. Remove and keep warm.

In a small bowl, combine cornstarch and remaining water until smooth. Gradually stir into skillet. Bring to a boil; cook and stir for 2 minutes or until thickened. Serve over pork chops.

NUTRITION FACTS: 1 pork chop with 1/4 cup sauce equals 237 calories, 10 g fat (4 g saturated fat), 81 mg cholesterol, 503 mg sodium, 8 g carbohydrate, 1 g fiber, 27 g protein. **DIABETIC EXCHANGES:** 3 lean meat, 1/2 starch, 1/2 fat.

pork pointers

Today's pork is more popular than ever before. Not only is pork satisfying and versatile, but breeding and feeding changes have reduced pork's fat content to create leaner products. Consider keeping a pork tenderloin in the freezer for last-minute meals, and remember the following tips for perfect pork dishes.

- Ounce for ounce, pork tenderloin is almost as lean as boneless, skinless chicken breast. Other lean cuts include boneless loin roasts or chops, boneless sirloin roasts or chops and bone-in pork loin chops.

- Unlike beef, pork cuts vary little in tenderness. Use dry-heat cooking methods (broiling, grilling, roasting, stir-frying and pan-broiling) for a firm texture.

- Pork cooks quickly and is done at 160°. The internal color may be a faint pink. Juices may have a hint of pink or be clear. Pork will become dry and tough if overcooked.

Pork with Apple-Cinnamon Rice

PREP/TOTAL TIME: 30 Min. **YIELD:** 4 Servings

My mother always had a way of making every dish she served special. This pork tenderloin with apple, raisins, cinnamon and maple-flavored syrup is just one example. —Edie DeSpain, Logan, Utah

- 1-1/4 cups water
- 1/4 cup unsweetened apple juice
- 1 cup chopped peeled apple (about 1 medium)
- 3/4 cup uncooked long grain rice
- 1/4 cup raisins
- 1/2 teaspoon ground cinnamon
- 1/2 teaspoon salt, *divided*
- 1 pork tenderloin (1 pound)
- 1/4 teaspoon coarsely ground pepper
- 1 tablespoon butter
- 1/3 cup sugar-free maple-flavored syrup
- 1 tablespoon Dijon mustard
- 1/4 cup minced fresh parsley

In a saucepan, combine the water, apple juice, apple, rice, raisins, cinnamon and 1/4 teaspoon salt. Bring to a boil. Reduce heat; cover and simmer for 15-18 minutes or until liquid is absorbed.

Meanwhile, cut pork diagonally into 3/4-in. slices; sprinkle with pepper and remaining salt. In a large nonstick skillet, cook pork in butter over medium heat until no longer pink. Remove and keep warm.

In the same skillet, combine syrup and mustard. Bring to a boil; cook and stir for 1 minute. Stir parsley into the rice. Serve pork over rice; drizzle with sauce.

NUTRITION FACTS: 3 ounces cooked pork with 3/4 cup rice and 1 tablespoon sauce equals 350 calories, 7 g fat (3 g saturated fat), 71 mg cholesterol, 500 mg sodium, 46 g carbohydrate, 2 g fiber, 26 g protein. **DIABETIC EXCHANGES:** 3 lean meat, 2 starch, 1/2 fruit.

Herb-Rubbed Pork Roast

(PICTURED AT LEFT)

PREP: 10 Min. **BAKE:** 1-3/4 Hours + Standing **YIELD:** 12 Servings

A flavorful herb rub seasons this moist pork roast that's perfect for special meals. —Joyce Dubois, Wolsey, South Dakota

- 1-1/2 teaspoons salt
- 1-1/2 teaspoons celery salt
- 1 teaspoon onion powder
- 1 teaspoon garlic powder
- 1 teaspoon paprika
- 1 teaspoon pepper
- 1/2 teaspoon dill weed
- 1/2 teaspoon dried rosemary, crushed
- 1/2 teaspoon rubbed sage
- 1 boneless rolled pork loin roast (4 pounds)

In a small bowl, combine the seasonings; rub over roast. Place on a rack in a shallow roasting pan coated with nonstick cooking spray. Bake, uncovered, at 350° for 1-3/4 to 2 hours or until a meat thermometer reads 160°. Let stand for 10 minutes before slicing.

NUTRITION FACTS: 4 ounces cooked pork equals 190 calories, 7 g fat (3 g saturated fat), 75 mg cholesterol, 524 mg sodium, 1 g carbohydrate, trace fiber, 29 g protein. **DIABETIC EXCHANGE:** 4 lean meat.

Pork 'n' Napa Cabbage

PREP/TOTAL TIME: 30 Min. **YIELD:** 4 Servings

I've been making this one-dish pork dinner for more than 20 years. It's fast and flavorful. —Lisa Thomason, Ingleside, Illinois

- 1-1/4 cups water, *divided*
- 3 tablespoons reduced-sodium soy sauce
- 3 tablespoons reduced-fat chunky peanut butter
- 1 teaspoon ground ginger
- 1/2 teaspoon browning sauce, optional
- 1/4 teaspoon crushed red pepper flakes
- 2 tablespoons cornstarch
- 1 pork tenderloin (1 pound), cut into 1-inch cubes
- 5 teaspoons canola oil, *divided*
- 1 medium onion, chopped
- 2 garlic cloves, minced
- 5 cups thinly sliced napa *or* Chinese cabbage
- 1 cup thinly sliced carrots

In a small bowl, combine 1 cup water, soy sauce, peanut butter, ginger, browning sauce if desired and red pepper flakes; set aside. In another bowl, combine cornstarch and remaining water until smooth; set aside.

In a nonstick skillet or wok, stir-fry pork in 2 teaspoons oil until browned. Remove and keep warm. In the same pan, saute onion and garlic in remaining oil for 2 minutes. Add cabbage and carrots; stir-fry until crisp-tender.

Return pork to the pan. Stir in peanut butter mixture. Stir cornstarch mixture and gradually stir into pork mixture. Bring to a boil; cook and stir for 2 minutes or until thickened.

NUTRITION FACTS: 1 cup equals 328 calories, 14 g fat (3 g saturated fat), 63 mg cholesterol, 606 mg sodium, 20 g carbohydrate, 4 g fiber, 28 g protein. **DIABETIC EXCHANGES:** 3 lean meat, 2 vegetable, 2 fat, 1/2 starch.

Lemon-Basil Pork Chops

(PICTURED BELOW)

PREP: 10 Min. **BAKE:** 30 Min. **YIELD:** 4 Servings

My husband just loves these lovely lemon-flavored chops. I've made them many times and have always received good reviews.
—Linda Senuta, Oakdale, Pennsylvania

- 1 egg, lightly beaten
- 1 teaspoon lemon juice
- 1/2 cup seasoned bread crumbs
- 1 tablespoon butter, melted
- 2 teaspoons grated lemon peel
- 1 teaspoon dried basil
- 4 boneless pork loin chops (1-1/4 inches thick and 6 ounces *each*)

In a shallow dish, combine the egg and lemon juice. In another shallow dish, combine the bread crumbs, butter, lemon peel and basil. Dip pork chops in egg mixture, then coat with crumb mixture.

Place in a 13-in. x 9-in. x 2-in. baking dish coated with nonstick cooking spray. Bake, uncovered, at 375° for 30-35 minutes or until a meat thermometer reads 160° and juices run clear.

NUTRITION FACTS: 1 pork chop equals 280 calories, 12 g fat (5 g saturated fat), 121 mg cholesterol, 180 mg sodium, 5 g carbohydrate, trace fiber, 35 g protein. **DIABETIC EXCHANGES:** 4 lean meat, 1/2 fat.

> **TASTY TIP**
>
> "I usually serve my pork chops with buttered rice or noodles and a salad," Linda Senuta notes.

Pork with Sweet Pepper Relish

PREP: 20 Min. **COOK:** 35 Min. **YIELD:** 4 Servings

I'm happy to share my meal-in-one. Red wine, balsamic vinegar and brown sugar season a relish that's a smarter choice than gravy.
—Lillian Julow, Gainesville, Florida

- 2 large sweet red peppers, cut into thin rings
- 1 large green pepper, cut into thin rings
- 1 large red onion, thinly sliced and separated into rings
- 2 tablespoons olive oil, *divided*
- 1/2 cup dry red wine *or* reduced-sodium beef broth
- 2 tablespoons brown sugar
- 2 teaspoons balsamic vinegar
- 4 bone-in pork loin chops (1/2 inch thick and 7 ounces *each*)
- 1/2 teaspoon salt
- 1/4 teaspoon pepper

For pepper relish, in a large nonstick skillet coated with nonstick cooking spray, cook the peppers and onion in 1 tablespoon oil for 7 minutes or until onion is tender; drain. Stir in the wine or broth, brown sugar and vinegar. Reduce heat to low; cook until liquid evaporates, about 13 minutes. Remove vegetable mixture and keep warm.

Sprinkle pork chops with salt and pepper. In the same skillet, brown pork in remaining oil for 3 minutes on each side. Reduce heat; cover and cook for 5-6 minutes or until meat juices run clear. Serve with pepper relish.

NUTRITION FACTS: 1 pork chop with 3/4 cup relish equals 360 calories, 15 g fat (4 g saturated fat), 86 mg cholesterol, 366 mg sodium, 19 g carbohydrate, 3 g fiber, 32 g protein. **DIABETIC EXCHANGES:** 4 lean meat, 2 vegetable, 1 fat, 1/2 starch.

Tarragon Chops with Mushrooms

 SALT CARB

(PICTURED ABOVE)

PREP: 10 Min.   **COOK:** 30 Min.   **YIELD:** 4 Servings

Though I reduced the sodium in this delicious pork entree, it's just as flavorful. —Sherri Halloran, Colonial Heights, Virginia

> 4 boneless pork loin chops (3/4 inch thick and 6 ounces each)
> 1/8 teaspoon pepper
> 4-1/2 teaspoons butter, *divided*
> 3/4 pound sliced fresh mushrooms
> 1/2 cup white wine *or* reduced-sodium chicken broth
> 2 to 3 teaspoons minced fresh tarragon

Sprinkle pork chops with pepper. In a large nonstick skillet coated with nonstick cooking spray, cook chops in 1-1/2 teaspoons butter for 8-11 minutes on each side or until juices run clear. Remove and keep warm.

In the same skillet, saute mushrooms in remaining butter for 3-5 minutes or until almost tender. Add wine or broth, stirring to loosen browned bits. Stir in tarragon. Bring to a boil. Reduce heat; simmer, uncovered, for 7-10 minutes or until liquid is reduced by half. Serve over pork chops.

NUTRITION FACTS: 1 pork chop with 1/3 cup mushroom mixture equals 306 calories, 14 g fat (6 g saturated fat), 93 mg cholesterol, 96 mg sodium, 4 g carbohydrate, 1 g fiber, 35 g protein. **DIABETIC EXCHANGES:** 5 lean meat, 1 fat.

Sweet 'n' Sour Pork Stir-Fry

PREP/TOTAL TIME: 30 Min.   **YIELD:** 8 Servings

Here's a time-saving meal the whole family will love. Our Test Kitchen combined pork, pineapple, carrots, pepper, onion and a hint of ginger in a tasty sweet-and-sour sauce. Cleanup's as easy as the prep!

> 1 can (20 ounces) unsweetened pineapple tidbits
> 2 tablespoons cornstarch
> 2 tablespoons brown sugar
> 1/4 cup soy sauce
> 2 tablespoons rice wine vinegar
> 1 teaspoon ground ginger
> 2 garlic cloves, minced
> 1 small onion, sliced
> 1 large sweet red pepper, julienned
> 3 tablespoons canola oil, *divided*
> 1-1/2 pounds boneless pork loin chops, cut into thin strips
> 1-1/2 cups shredded carrots
> Hot cooked rice, optional

Drain pineapple, reserving juice; set pineapple aside. In a small bowl, combine the cornstarch, brown sugar, soy sauce, vinegar, ginger, garlic and reserved pineapple juice until blended; set aside.

In a large nonstick skillet or wok, stir-fry onion and red pepper in 2 tablespoons oil for 5 minutes or until crisp-tender. Remove and keep warm. In the same pan, stir-fry pork in remaining oil for 3-4 minutes or until no longer pink.

Stir soy sauce mixture and add to the pan. Bring to a boil; cook and stir for 2 minutes or until thickened.

Stir in the carrots, onion mixture and reserved pineapple; heat through. Serve with rice if desired.

NUTRITION FACTS: 1 cup (calculated without rice) equals 246 calories, 10 g fat (2 g saturated fat), 41 mg cholesterol, 500 mg sodium, 22 g carbohydrate, 2 g fiber, 18 g protein. **DIABETIC EXCHANGES:** 2 lean meat, 1 vegetable, 1 fat, 1/2 starch, 1/2 fruit.

Marinated Pork Roast
(PICTURED BELOW)

 CARB

PREP: 10 Min. + Marinating   **BAKE:** 50 Min. + Standing   **YIELD:** 9 Servings

I turn to honey, white wine and lemon juice to season this low-carb specialty. The marinade has a light, flavorful taste that works well with any cut of pork.   —Andrea Schumann, Moberly, Missouri

  1/4 cup reduced-sodium soy sauce
  1/4 cup grated onion
    1 tablespoon canola oil
    1 teaspoon lemon juice
    3 garlic cloves, minced
  3/4 teaspoon ground ginger
    1 boneless whole pork loin roast (2-1/2 pounds)
  1/4 cup white wine *or* chicken broth
  1/4 cup honey
    1 tablespoon brown sugar

In a large resealable plastic bag, combine the first six ingredients; add pork roast. Seal bag and turn to coat; refrigerate for 8 hours or overnight, turning several times.

Drain and discard marinade. Place roast on a rack in a shallow, foil-lined roasting pan. Bake, uncovered, at 350° for 25 minutes.

In a small bowl, combine the wine or broth, honey and brown sugar. Brush half over the meat. Bake 15 minutes longer. Brush with remaining honey mixture. Bake 10-20 minutes longer or until a meat thermometer reads 160°. Let stand for 10 minutes before slicing.

NUTRITION FACTS: 3 ounces cooked pork equals 227 calories, 9 g fat (3 g saturated fat), 70 mg cholesterol, 195 mg sodium, 10 g carbohydrate, trace fiber, 25 g protein. **DIABETIC EXCHANGES:** 3 lean meat, 1/2 starch.

Tangy Pulled Pork Sandwiches
(PICTURED ABOVE)

PREP: 10 Min.   **COOK:** 4 Hours   **YIELD:** 4 Servings

The slow cooker not only makes this a no-fuss meal, but it keeps the pork tender, moist and loaded with flavor. The sandwiches are so comforting, they seem anything but light.
    —Beki Kosydar-Krantz, Clarks Summit, Pennsylvania

    1 pork tenderloin (1 pound)
    1 cup ketchup
    2 tablespoons plus 1-1/2 teaspoons brown sugar
    2 tablespoons plus 1-1/2 teaspoons cider vinegar
    1 tablespoon plus 1-1/2 teaspoons Worcestershire sauce
    1 tablespoon spicy brown mustard
  1/4 teaspoon pepper
    4 kaiser rolls, split

Cut the tenderloin in half; place in a 3-qt. slow cooker. Combine the ketchup, brown sugar, vinegar, Worcestershire sauce, mustard and pepper; pour over pork. Cover and cook on low for 4-5 hours or until meat is tender.

Remove meat; shred with two forks. Return to the slow cooker; heat through. Serve on rolls.

NUTRITION FACTS: 1 sandwich equals 402 calories, 7 g fat (2 g saturated fat), 63 mg cholesterol, 1,181 mg sodium, 56 g carbohydrate, 2 g fiber, 29 g protein. **DIABETIC EXCHANGES:** 3-1/2 starch, 3 very lean meat, 1/2 fat.

Mediterranean Pork and Orzo
(PICTURED ABOVE)

PREP/TOTAL TIME: 30 Min.   YIELD: 6 Servings

Every food group is represented in this fabulous, stovetop meal-in-one. It's a wholesome favorite with our family.
—Mary Relyea, Canastota, New York

- 2 pork tenderloins (3/4 pound *each*)
- 1 teaspoon coarsely ground pepper
- 2 tablespoons olive oil
- 3 quarts water
- 1-1/4 cups uncooked orzo pasta
- 1/4 teaspoon salt
- 1 package (6 ounces) fresh baby spinach
- 1 cup grape tomatoes, halved
- 3/4 cup crumbled feta cheese

Rub pork with pepper; cut into 1-in. cubes. In a large nonstick skillet, cook pork in oil over medium heat for 8-10 minutes or until no longer pink.

Meanwhile, in a large saucepan, bring water to a boil. Stir in orzo and salt; cook, uncovered, for 8 minutes. Stir in spinach; cook 45-60 seconds longer or until orzo is tender and spinach is wilted.

Add tomatoes to the pork; cook and stir for 1 minute or until heated through. Drain orzo mixture; toss with pork mixture and feta cheese.

NUTRITION FACTS: 1 cup equals 372 calories, 11 g fat (4 g saturated fat), 71 mg cholesterol, 306 mg sodium, 34 g carbohydrate, 3 g fiber, 31 g protein. DIABETIC EXCHANGES: 3 lean meat, 2 starch, 1 fat.

Zippy Raspberry Roast Pork
(PICTURED AT RIGHT)

PREP: 20 Min.   BAKE: 1-1/4 Hours + Standing   YIELD: 12 Servings

Rosemary, sage, thyme and garlic make a mouth-watering rub for my pork dinner. The raspberry sauce gets a slight kick from chipotle peppers, marrying the flavors well.
—Kim Pettipas, Oromocto, New Brunswick

- 1 boneless whole pork loin roast (3-1/2 pounds)
- 4 teaspoons olive oil, *divided*
- 1 tablespoon minced fresh rosemary *or* 1 teaspoon dried rosemary, crushed
- 1 tablespoon minced fresh sage *or* 1 teaspoon rubbed sage
- 1 tablespoon minced fresh thyme *or* 1 teaspoon dried thyme
- 4 garlic cloves, peeled
- 1 teaspoon salt
- 1/2 teaspoon pepper

SAUCE:
- 1/2 cup chopped onion
- 3 garlic cloves, minced
- 2 teaspoons olive oil
- 4 cups fresh raspberries
- 3/4 cup sugar
- 1/2 cup raspberry vinegar
- 2 teaspoons chipotle peppers in adobo sauce
- 1/2 teaspoon salt

In a large nonstick skillet, brown roast on all sides in 3 teaspoons oil. Place on a rack in a shallow roasting pan. In a food processor, combine the rosemary, sage, thyme, garlic, salt, pepper and remaining oil; cover and process until smooth. Rub over roast. Bake, uncovered, at 350° for 70 minutes.

Meanwhile, in a large saucepan, saute onion and garlic in oil until tender. Add the raspberries, sugar, vinegar, chipotle peppers and salt. Bring to a boil. Reduce heat; simmer, uncovered, for 10 minutes or until sauce is reduced to 2 cups. Press through a sieve; discard seeds.

Brush 2 tablespoons of sauce over pork. Bake 5-15 minutes longer or until a meat thermometer reads 160°. Let stand for 10 minutes before slicing. Serve with remaining sauce.

NUTRITION FACTS: 3 ounces cooked pork with 3-1/2 teaspoons sauce equals 262 calories, 9 g fat (3 g saturated fat), 66 mg cholesterol, 341 mg sodium, 19 g carbohydrate, 3 g fiber, 26 g protein. DIABETIC EXCHANGES: 3 lean meat, 1 starch, 1/2 fat.

Artichoke-Lamb Sandwich Loaves

CARB ▼

(PICTURED AT RIGHT)

PREP: 50 Min. + Marinating   **BAKE:** 80 Min. + Chilling   **YIELD:** 24 Servings

These tender sandwiches will surely become the talk of your get-to-gether. I hollow out sourdough baguettes before filling them with cucumber, goat cheese and marinated lamb.

—Helen Hassler, Denver, Pennsylvania

    1/2 cup lemon juice
    1/2 cup olive oil
      6 garlic cloves, minced
      2 tablespoons minced fresh rosemary
      1 teaspoon salt
    1/4 teaspoon cayenne pepper
      1 boneless leg of lamb (2-1/2 pounds)
      2 cans (14 ounces *each*) water-packed artichoke hearts, rinsed and drained
    2/3 cup plus 6 tablespoons reduced-fat balsamic vinaigrette, *divided*
      2 sourdough baguettes (1 pound *each*)
      1 medium cucumber, thinly sliced
      2 medium tomatoes, thinly sliced
      6 ounces goat cheese, sliced

In a large resealable plastic bag, combine the first six ingredients; add lamb. Seal bag and turn to coat. Refrigerate for 8 hours or overnight.

Drain and discard marinade. Place lamb on a rack in a shallow roasting pan. Bake, uncovered, at 325° for 80-90 minutes or until meat reaches desired doneness (for medium-rare, a meat thermometer should read 145°; medium, 160°; well-done, 170°). Cool to room temperature. Cover and refrigerate for at least 2 hours.

Place artichokes in a resealable plastic bag; add 2/3 cup vinaigrette. Seal bag and turn to coat; let stand for 10 minutes. Drain and discard marinade.

Cut lamb into thin slices. Cut each baguette in half horizontally. Carefully hollow out top and bottom, leaving a 3/4-in. shell. Brush the bottom half of each loaf with 2 tablespoons vinaigrette. Layer with cucumber, tomatoes, lamb and artichokes; drizzle with remaining vinaigrette. Top with goat cheese. Replace bread tops and press down firmly; wrap tightly in plastic wrap. Refrigerate for at least 2 hours. Cut into slices.

NUTRITION FACTS: 2 slices equals 156 calories, 9 g fat (3 g saturated fat), 32 mg cholesterol, 302 mg sodium, 7 g carbohydrate, 1 g fiber, 11 g protein. **DIABETIC EXCHANGES:** 1 lean meat, 1 fat, 1/2 starch.

Pork Roast with Mango Salsa

CARB ▼

PREP: 25 Min. + Marinating   **GRILL:** 1-1/4 Hours + Standing   **YIELD:** 8 Servings

When my son and his wife were married in our backyard, I served a summery roast at the rehearsal dinner. It can be prepared on the grill or in the oven, but grilling truly enhances the flavors.

—B.J. Wall, Lanexa, Virginia

      3 tablespoons paprika
      1 tablespoon garlic powder
      2 teaspoons dried oregano
      2 teaspoons dried thyme
    3/4 teaspoon cayenne pepper
    1/2 teaspoon salt
    1/2 teaspoon ground cumin
    1/2 teaspoon pepper
    1/4 teaspoon ground nutmeg
      1 boneless pork top loin roast (2-1/2 pounds)
SALSA:
      1 medium mango, peeled and chopped
    1/2 cup chopped seeded plum tomatoes
    1/2 cup chopped red onion
    1/2 cup chopped peeled cucumber
    1/4 cup lime juice
      2 tablespoons minced fresh cilantro
      1 tablespoon olive oil
      1 tablespoon dry red wine *or* cider vinegar
      1 teaspoon ground cumin

In a small bowl, combine the first nine ingredients. Rub over the roast. Place in a shallow baking dish; cover and refrigerate for 3 hours or overnight. In a bowl, combine the salsa ingredients; cover and refrigerate until serving.

If grilling the roast, coat grill rack with nonstick cooking spray before starting the grill. Prepare grill for indirect heat. If baking the roast, place on a rack in a shallow roasting pan.

Grill pork, covered, over indirect medium heat for 1-1/4 hours or bake, uncovered, at 350° for 1-1/2 hours or until a meat thermometer reads 160°. Cover loosely with foil and let stand for 15 minutes before slicing. Serve with salsa.

NUTRITION FACTS: 3 ounces cooked pork with 1/4 cup salsa equals 256 calories, 11 g fat (4 g saturated fat), 79 mg cholesterol, 218 mg sodium, 10 g carbohydrate, 2 g fiber, 29 g protein. **DIABETIC EXCHANGES:** 4 lean meat, 1/2 fruit.

Saucy Mushroom Pork Chops

CARB

PREP/TOTAL TIME: 30 Min.   **YIELD:** 6 Servings

I came up with this easy way to dress up ordinary pork chops one night. My husband loved them. The sauce was even great over our mashed potatoes.   —Karlene Lantz, Felton, California

- 6 boneless pork loin chops (4 ounces *each*)
- 1/4 teaspoon salt
- 1/4 teaspoon pepper
- 2 teaspoons olive oil, *divided*
- 1 cup sliced fresh mushrooms
- 1/3 cup chopped onion
- 1 garlic clove, minced
- 1/2 cup white wine *or* reduced-sodium chicken broth
- 1 can (10-3/4 ounces) reduced-fat reduced-sodium condensed cream of mushroom soup, undiluted
- 1/2 cup reduced-sodium chicken broth

Sprinkle pork chops with salt and pepper. In a large nonstick skillet, brown chops on both sides in 1 teaspoon oil; remove and keep warm.

In the same skillet, saute the mushrooms, onion and garlic in remaining oil until tender.

Add wine or broth, stirring up any browned bits; cook for 4-6 minutes or until liquid is reduced by half. Stir in soup and broth. Bring to a boil. Return pork chops to the pan. Reduce heat; simmer, uncovered, for 8-10 minutes or until meat juices run clear.

NUTRITION FACTS: 1 pork chop with 1/4 cup sauce equals 217 calories, 9 g fat (3 g saturated fat), 59 mg cholesterol, 380 mg sodium, 6 g carbohydrate, trace fiber, 23 g protein. **DIABETIC EXCHANGES:** 3 lean meat, 1/2 starch.

Jalapeno-Glazed Pork Medallions

PREP/TOTAL TIME: 25 Min.   **YIELD:** 4 Servings

I rely on a spicy meal to shake up weekday menus. My easy jalapeno sauce perfectly complements savory pork. For something different, serve the pork slices with Asian rice noodles.   —Kathleen Smith, Pittsburgh, Pennsylvania

- 1/2 teaspoon garlic powder
- 1/2 teaspoon crushed red pepper flakes
- 1/2 teaspoon ground cumin
- 2 pork tenderloins (3/4 pound *each*), thinly sliced
- 1 tablespoon canola oil
- 1/4 cup jalapeno pepper jelly
- 3 tablespoons orange juice
- 4-1/2 teaspoons Worcestershire sauce
- 1-1/2 teaspoons Dijon mustard

Combine the garlic powder, pepper flakes and cumin; sprinkle over pork. In a large nonstick skillet, brown pork on both sides in oil. Remove and keep warm.

In the same skillet, combine the jalapeno jelly, orange juice, Worcestershire sauce and mustard. Cook and stir over medium heat for 3-4 minutes or until thickened. Return pork to the pan; cook and stir for 2-3 minutes or until pork juices run clear.

NUTRITION FACTS: 1 serving equals 296 calories, 10 g fat (2 g saturated fat), 95 mg cholesterol, 183 mg sodium, 16 g carbohydrate, trace fiber, 34 g protein. **DIABETIC EXCHANGES:** 4 lean meat, 1 starch.

Cranberry-Mustard Pork Medallions
(PICTURED ABOVE)

PREP: 15 Min.   **COOK:** 20 Min.   **YIELD:** 4 Servings

This pretty entree makes a great holiday dish. Served with a cranberry sauce, the pork medallions are light and filling, but they're so delicious, guests always want more.   —Tami Morrison, Kent, Washington

- 2/3 cup water
- 1/3 cup unsweetened apple juice concentrate
- 1/3 cup cranberry juice concentrate
- 1/3 cup port wine *or* 1 tablespoon additional cranberry juice concentrate plus 1/4 cup water
- 1 pork tenderloin (1 pound)
- 1/4 teaspoon garlic salt
- 1/8 teaspoon pepper
- 1 tablespoon olive oil
- 1 tablespoon butter
- 2 to 3 tablespoons Dijon mustard
- 1/3 cup dried cranberries

In a bowl, combine the first four ingredients; set aside. Cut pork into 1-in. slices; flatten to 1/4-in. thickness. Sprinkle with garlic salt and pepper. In a large nonstick skillet, saute pork in batches in oil and butter for 2-3 minutes on each side or until juices run clear. Remove and keep warm.

Add reserved juice mixture to the skillet; bring to a boil. Reduce heat; simmer for 3 minutes. Stir in mustard; cook and stir for 6-8 minutes or until slightly thickened. Add cranberries. Return pork to the pan; cover and simmer for 5 minutes or until heated through.

NUTRITION FACTS: 3 ounces cooked pork with 1/4 cup sauce equals 332 calories, 11 g fat (4 g saturated fat), 71 mg cholesterol, 419 mg sodium, 34 g carbohydrate, 1 g fiber, 23 g protein. **DIABETIC EXCHANGES:** 3 lean meat, 1 starch, 1 fruit, 1 fat.

Fish & Seafood Fare

You don't have to live on the coast to hook your family on seafood. Orange roughy, halibut, shrimp, crab and other denizens of the deep are low in fat, big on taste and available at most supermarkets. So cast a wide net and make one of the following recipes your catch of the day.

Dijon-Crusted Fish, p. 158

Raspberry-Chili Tuna on Greens
(PICTURED ABOVE)

PREP: 15 Min. + Marinating   **GRILL:** 10 Min.   **YIELD:** 4 Servings

I turn fresh tuna steaks into something sensational with my zippy marinade. Served on romaine lettuce with fresh veggies, this entree is special enough for guests.   —Kathy Hawkins, Ingleside, Illinois

> 6 tablespoons seedless raspberry preserves
> 1/4 cup balsamic vinegar
> 2 teaspoons Thai chili sauce
> 2 teaspoons minced fresh basil *or* 1/2 teaspoon dried basil
> 1/2 teaspoon salt
> 1/4 teaspoon pepper
> 4 tuna steaks (6 ounces *each*)
> 1 package (10 ounces) torn romaine
> 1/2 cup shredded carrot
> 1/2 cup thinly sliced cucumber

In a small bowl, combine the first six ingredients. Pour 1/4 cup marinade into a large resealable plastic bag; add tuna steaks.

Seal bag and turn to coat; refrigerate for 30 minutes, turning occasionally. Cover and refrigerate remaining marinade for dressing.

Coat grill rack with nonstick cooking spray before starting the grill. Drain and discard marinade. Grill tuna, covered, over medium-hot heat for 4-5 minutes on each side or until fish flakes easily with a fork.

In a large bowl, combine the romaine, carrot and cucumber; drizzle with reserved marinade and toss to coat. Divide among four plates. Top with grilled tuna.

NUTRITION FACTS: 1 tuna steak with 1-1/2 cups salad equals 282 calories, 2 g fat (trace saturated fat), 77 mg cholesterol, 390 mg sodium, 23 g carbohydrate, 1 g fiber, 41 g protein. **DIABETIC EXCHANGES:** 5 very lean meat, 1 starch, 1 vegetable.

SHOP SMART
The Thai chili sauce used in the tuna's marinade is a spicy staple in Thai cuisine. Look for it in the ethnic food section of your grocery store.

Herbed Orange Roughy

CARB

PREP/TOTAL TIME: 20 Min.   **YIELD:** 4 Servings

A host of seasonings flavors these delightful orange roughy fillets. They're so good, I rarely prepare fish any other way.
—Elaine Anderson, New Galilee, Pennsylvania

    2 tablespoons dry bread crumbs
    1 teaspoon dried parsley flakes
    1 teaspoon dried thyme
    1/4 teaspoon garlic powder
    1/4 teaspoon pepper
    1/8 teaspoon salt
    4 orange roughy fillets (6 ounces each)
    1 tablespoon butter
    1/4 cup white wine *or* reduced-sodium chicken broth
    1 tablespoon reduced-sodium soy sauce
    1 tablespoon finely chopped onion

In a small bowl, combine the first six ingredients. Sprinkle over both sides of orange roughy. In a large nonstick skillet coated with nonstick cooking spray, cook fillets in butter over medium heat for 5 minutes. Turn; stir in the wine or broth, soy sauce and onion. Cook 4-6 minutes longer or until fish flakes easily with a fork.

NUTRITION FACTS: 1 fillet equals 172 calories, 4 g fat (2 g saturated fat), 42 mg cholesterol, 392 mg sodium, 4 g carbohydrate, trace fiber, 26 g protein. **DIABETIC EXCHANGES:** 4 very lean meat, 1/2 fat.

Salmon with Tarragon Sauce

PREP/TOTAL TIME: 30 Min.   **YIELD:** 4 Servings

As graduate students with two young children, my husband and I enjoy this fast and easy seafood entree.
—Shannon Beck, Laredo, Texas

    4 salmon fillets (4 ounces each)
    1/2 cup chopped green onions
    1 tablespoon butter
    3 tablespoons all-purpose flour
    1-1/2 cups fat-free milk
    1 cup frozen peas, thawed
    3/4 cup fat-free sour cream
    1 teaspoon dried tarragon
    1/2 teaspoon salt
    1/4 teaspoon white pepper
    1/8 teaspoon ground turmeric
    1/8 teaspoon cayenne pepper

In a large skillet, bring 1 in. of water to a boil. Carefully add the salmon. Reduce heat; cover and simmer for 5-10 minutes or until fish flakes easily with a fork.

Meanwhile, in a large saucepan, saute the onions in butter until tender. Stir in flour until blended; gradually add milk. Bring to a boil over medium heat; cook and stir for 1-2 minutes or until thickened. Reduce heat to low. Stir in the peas, sour cream and seasonings; heat through. Serve over salmon.

NUTRITION FACTS: 1 fillet with 2/3 cup sauce equals 373 calories, 16 g fat (4 g saturated fat), 84 mg cholesterol, 519 mg sodium, 24 g carbohydrate, 2 g fiber, 32 g protein. **DIABETIC EXCHANGES:** 3 lean meat, 1-1/2 starch, 1-1/2 fat, 1 vegetable.

Seafood 'n' Shells Casserole

(PICTURED BELOW)

PREP: 25 Min.   **BAKE:** 25 Min.   **YIELD:** 6 Servings

With pasta and vegetables, this satisfying dish will warm you up on chilly nights. Our Test Kitchen staff poached the cod first to prevent it from watering out the comforting casserole.

    6 cups water
    1 teaspoon lemon-pepper seasoning
    1 bay leaf
    2 pounds cod fillets, cut into 1-inch pieces
    1 cup uncooked small pasta shells
    1 *each* medium green and sweet red pepper, chopped
    1 medium onion, chopped
    1 tablespoon butter
    3 tablespoons all-purpose flour
    2-1/2 cups fat-free evaporated milk
    3/4 teaspoon salt
    1/2 teaspoon dried thyme
    1/4 teaspoon pepper
    1 cup (4 ounces) shredded Mexican cheese blend

In a large skillet or Dutch oven, bring the water, lemon-pepper and bay leaf to a boil. Reduce heat; carefully add cod. Cover and simmer for 5-8 minutes or until fish flakes easily with a fork; drain and set aside. Discard bay leaf.

Cook pasta according to package directions. Meanwhile, in a large saucepan, saute peppers and onion in butter over medium heat until tender. Stir in flour until blended. Gradually stir in milk. Bring to a boil; cook and stir for 2 minutes or until thickened. Stir in the salt, thyme and pepper. Remove from the heat; stir in cheese until melted.

Drain pasta. Stir fish and pasta into sauce. Transfer to a 2-qt. baking dish coated with nonstick cooking spray. Cover and bake at 350° for 25-30 minutes or until heated through.

NUTRITION FACTS: 1 cup equals 389 calories, 9 g fat (6 g saturated fat), 83 mg cholesterol, 732 mg sodium, 35 g carbohydrate, 2 g fiber, 39 g protein. **DIABETIC EXCHANGES:** 3 very lean meat, 1-1/2 fat, 1 starch, 1 veg-

etable, 1 fat-free milk.

Crab-Stuffed Artichokes

(PICTURED BELOW)

PREP: 50 Min. **BAKE:** 20 Min. **YIELD:** 4 Servings

For an impressive presentation, consider this recipe that my mother passed on to me. The artichokes are wonderful for brunch.
—Suzanne Strocsher, Bothell, Washington

- 4 medium artichokes
- 2 tablespoons plus 2 teaspoons lemon juice, *divided*
- 4 pouches (3.53 ounces *each*) premium crabmeat, drained
- 1/2 cup reduced-fat shredded Swiss cheese
- 1/2 cup soft bread crumbs
- 1/3 cup reduced-fat mayonnaise
- 1/3 cup chopped green pepper
- 1/4 cup finely chopped onion
- 1/2 teaspoon salt

Using a sharp knife, level the bottom of each artichoke and cut 3/4 in. from the top. Using kitchen scissors, snip off tips of outer leaves; brush cut edges with 2 tablespoons lemon juice. Stand artichokes in a Dutch oven; add 2 in. of water. Bring to a boil. Reduce heat; cover and simmer for 25-30 minutes or until leaves near the center almost pull out easily.

Invert artichokes to drain. With a spoon, carefully scrape out the fuzzy center portion of artichokes and discard. In a large bowl, combine the crab, cheese, bread crumbs, mayonnaise, green pepper, onion, salt and remaining lemon juice. Gently

spread artichoke leaves apart; fill with stuffing.

Place in an ungreased 8-in. square baking dish; add 1/2 in. of warm water. Cover and bake at 350° for 20-25 minutes or until heated through and leaves near the outer edge pull out easily.

NUTRITION FACTS: 1 stuffed artichoke equals 221 calories, 8 g fat (2 g saturated fat), 73 mg cholesterol, 1,142 mg sodium, 22 g carbohydrate, 7 g fiber, 19 g protein. **DIABETIC EXCHANGES:** 3 vegetable, 2 very lean meat, 1-1/2 fat.

Crab Pasta Salad

PREP: 30 Min. + Chilling **YIELD:** 6 Servings

After enjoying this salad for years, I substituted fat-free mayonnaise and reduced-fat dressing one day. It had the same wonderful taste.
—Heather O'Neill, Dudley, Massachusetts

- 8 ounces uncooked spiral pasta
- 1 package (8 ounces) imitation crabmeat, chopped
- 1 cup frozen peas, thawed
- 1 cup fresh broccoli florets
- 1/2 cup chopped green pepper
- 1/4 cup sliced green onions
- 3/4 cup fat-free mayonnaise
- 1/3 cup reduced-fat Italian salad dressing
- 3 tablespoons grated Parmesan cheese

Cook pasta according to package directions; drain and rinse in cold water. In a large bowl, combine the pasta, crab, peas, broccoli, green pepper and onions. Combine the mayonnaise, salad dressing and Parmesan cheese; pour over pasta mixture and toss to coat. Cover and refrigerate for 2 hours or until well chilled.

NUTRITION FACTS: 1-1/3 cups equals 251 calories, 5 g fat (1 g saturated fat), 10 mg cholesterol, 746 mg sodium, 42 g carbohydrate, 3 g fiber, 12 g protein. **DIABETIC EXCHANGES:** 3 starch, 1 lean meat.

Cucumber Crab Bites

FAT SALT CARB

PREP/TOTAL TIME: 20 Min. **YIELD:** 4 Dozen

Hints of pineapple and cucumber add fresh flavor to these delicate hors d'oeuvres. —Jeannie Klugh, Lancaster, Pennsylvania

- 1/4 cup reduced-fat mayonnaise
- 1 teaspoon dill weed
- 1 teaspoon ground mustard
- 1/8 teaspoon seafood seasoning
- 1-1/4 cups canned crabmeat, drained, flaked and cartilage removed *or* imitation crabmeat
- 1 can (8 ounces) unsweetened crushed pineapple, drained
- 1 large English cucumber, cut into 1/4-inch slices
- 3 tablespoons thinly sliced green onions

In a large bowl, combine the mayonnaise, dill, mustard and seafood seasoning. Stir in the crab and pineapple. Spread over cucumber slices. Sprinkle with onions. Cover and refrigerate until serving.

NUTRITION FACTS: 4 appetizers equals 47 calories, 2 g fat (trace saturated fat), 14 mg cholesterol, 96 mg sodium, 4 g carbohydrate, trace fiber, 3 g protein. **DIABETIC EXCHANGE:** Free food.

Brown Sugar-Glazed Salmon
(PICTURED ABOVE)

CARB

PREP/TOTAL TIME: 25 Min.   **YIELD:** 4 Servings

I set protein-packed salmon fillets in the oven before stirring up a sweet basting sauce. Made in moments, the tangy entree is perfect for workweek suppers and weekend entertaining.

—Debra Martin, Belleville, Michigan

- 1 salmon fillet (1 pound)
- 1/4 teaspoon salt
- 1/4 teaspoon pepper
- 3 tablespoons brown sugar
- 1 tablespoon reduced-sodium soy sauce
- 4 teaspoons Dijon mustard
- 1 teaspoon rice wine vinegar

Cut salmon widthwise into four pieces. Place in a foil-lined 15-in. x 10-in. x 1-in. baking pan; sprinkle with salt and pepper. Bake, uncovered, at 425° for 10 minutes.

Meanwhile, in a small saucepan, combine the brown sugar, soy sauce, mustard and vinegar. Bring to a boil. Brush evenly over salmon. Broil 6 in. from the heat for 1-2 minutes or until fish flakes easily with a fork.

NUTRITION FACTS: 1 serving equals 256 calories, 13 g fat (2 g saturated fat), 67 mg cholesterol, 496 mg sodium, 11 g carbohydrate, trace fiber, 23 g protein. **DIABETIC EXCHANGES:** 3 lean meat, 1 starch, 1/2 fat.

MAKE IT LIGHTER
Watching your salt intake? Skip the salt in the Brown Sugar-Glazed Salmon recipe, and you'll slash 147 mg of sodium from each serving.

Shrimp and Feta Linguine

PREP/TOTAL TIME: 30 Min.   **YIELD:** 4 Servings

Delight your family and friends with this easy-to-prepare entree from our home economists. Featuring loads of shrimp, it's topped with feta cheese and laced with a hint of wine. Its appealing aroma is sure to make mouths water!

- 6 ounces uncooked linguine
- 1 pound uncooked medium shrimp, peeled and deveined
- 1/2 cup chopped onion
- 1 garlic clove, minced
- 1 tablespoon olive oil
- 3 cups sliced plum tomatoes
- 1/2 cup white wine *or* reduced-sodium chicken broth
- 1 tablespoon tomato paste
- 1 teaspoon dried oregano
- 1/2 teaspoon salt
- 1/4 teaspoon crushed red pepper flakes
- 1/4 cup crumbled feta cheese
- 2 tablespoons minced fresh parsley

Cook linguine according to package directions. Meanwhile, in a large nonstick skillet, saute the shrimp, onion and garlic in oil for 3-5 minutes or until shrimp turn pink.

Add the tomatoes, wine or broth, tomato paste, oregano, salt and pepper flakes. Bring to a boil. Reduce heat; simmer, uncovered, for 10 minutes. Drain linguine; top with shrimp mixture. Sprinkle with feta cheese and parsley.

NUTRITION FACTS: 1 cup shrimp mixture with 3/4 cup linguine equals 348 calories, 7 g fat (2 g saturated fat), 172 mg cholesterol, 576 mg sodium, 41 g carbohydrate, 4 g fiber, 27 g protein. **DIABETIC EXCHANGES:** 3 very lean meat, 2 starch, 2 vegetable, 1 fat.

Shrimp in Herbs
(PICTURED ABOVE)

 CARB

PREP: 25 Min.   COOK: 10 Min.   YIELD: 4 Servings

With a classic blend of herbs, this rich and elegant shrimp entree makes a special weeknight meal. —Iola Egle, Bella Vista, Arkansas

    2 pounds uncooked medium shrimp, peeled and
        deveined
    2 tablespoons olive oil
    3 garlic cloves, minced
1-1/2 cups chopped fresh tomatoes
    1 tablespoon minced chives
    1 tablespoon minced fresh flat-leaf parsley
    1 tablespoon minced fresh tarragon *or* 1 teaspoon dried
        tarragon
    1 teaspoon dried chervil
  3/4 teaspoon salt
  1/4 teaspoon pepper
    2 tablespoons butter, cubed

In a large nonstick skillet coated with nonstick cooking spray, cook shrimp in oil for 2 minutes. Add garlic; cook 2 minutes longer. Stir in the tomatoes and seasonings. Cook 3-5 minutes longer or until shrimp turn pink. Stir in butter until melted.

NUTRITION FACTS: 1 cup equals 304 calories, 15 g fat (5 g saturated fat), 351 mg cholesterol, 894 mg sodium, 5 g carbohydrate, 1 g fiber, 37 g protein. DIABETIC EXCHANGES: 5 very lean meat, 2-1/2 fat.

Orange Roughy Italiano

CARB

PREP/TOTAL TIME: 30 Min.   YIELD: 4 Servings

I'm not a big fan of fish, but this recipe is so simple and healthy with sliced zucchini and tomato. It's become a favorite at my house! —Sherry Fletcher, Highland, Illinois

    2 cups sliced zucchini
  1/2 cup thinly sliced onion
    1 teaspoon dried oregano
    1 tablespoon olive oil
    4 orange roughy fillets (4 ounces *each*)
  1/4 teaspoon salt
  1/8 teaspoon pepper
    1 medium tomato, chopped
  1/2 cup shredded part-skim mozzarella cheese

In a large nonstick skillet coated with nonstick cooking spray, saute the zucchini, onion and oregano in oil for 5 minutes or until onion is tender.

Sprinkle the fillets with salt and pepper; place over zucchini mixture. Sprinkle with tomato. Reduce heat; cover and simmer for 10 minutes or until fish flakes easily with a fork. Sprinkle with cheese; cover and let stand for 2 minutes or until cheese is melted.

NUTRITION FACTS: 1 serving equals 167 calories, 7 g fat (2 g saturated fat), 31 mg cholesterol, 290 mg sodium, 5 g carbohydrate, 2 g fiber, 21 g protein. DIABETIC EXCHANGES: 3 very lean meat, 1 vegetable, 1 fat.

Crab Linguine

PREP: 10 Min. **COOK:** 40 Min. **YIELD:** 6 Servings

I lightened up the creamy sauce for this delicious pasta dish after seeing it in a cookbook. My entire family loves it. In fact, they always ask for second helpings.

—Becky Moldenhauer, La Crescent, Minnesota

- 8 ounces uncooked linguine
- 1 cup reduced-sodium chicken broth
- 1 cup 2% milk
- 1/2 cup fat-free evaporated milk
- 2 tablespoons butter, *divided*
- 1 tablespoon all-purpose flour
- 2 packages (8 ounces *each*) imitation crabmeat, flaked
- 2 tablespoons finely chopped green onion
- 1 tablespoon lemon juice
- 1/2 teaspoon salt
- 1/8 teaspoon white pepper
- 2 tablespoons grated Parmesan cheese

Cook linguine according to package directions. Meanwhile, in a small saucepan, bring broth to a boil; cook until reduced to 1/3 cup. Stir in milk and evaporated milk; return to a boil. Reduce heat; simmer until reduced to about 1-1/3 cups, stirring constantly. Remove from the heat.

In a skillet, melt 1 tablespoon butter; stir in flour until smooth. Gradually stir in milk mixture. Bring to a boil; cook and stir for 2 minutes or until slightly thickened. Add the crab, onion, lemon juice, salt and pepper; heat through.

Drain linguine; place in a serving bowl. Toss with Parmesan cheese and remaining butter. Add sauce and toss to coat.

NUTRITION FACTS: 1 cup equals 293 calories, 6 g fat (3 g saturated fat), 24 mg cholesterol, 835 mg sodium, 43 g carbohydrate, 1 g fiber, 17 g protein. **DIABETIC EXCHANGES:** 3 starch, 1 very lean meat, 1/2 fat.

Pineapple-Tuna Salad Sandwiches

FAT ↓

PREP/TOTAL TIME: 15 Min. **YIELD:** 4 Servings

Here's a tasty twist on a brown-bag classic. I mix crushed pineapple and applesauce into tuna salad for a refreshing treat that's a perfect way to break up my day. —Maida Knox, Weirton, West Virginia

- 1/4 cup unsweetened applesauce
- 2 tablespoons fat-free mayonnaise
- 1/2 cup chopped celery
- 1/2 cup chopped green pepper
- 1/2 cup unsweetened crushed pineapple, drained
- 1/4 cup finely chopped onion
- 1/2 teaspoon salt-free herb seasoning blend
- 1/4 teaspoon garlic powder
- 1/8 teaspoon pepper
- 2 cans (6 ounces *each*) light water-packed tuna, drained and flaked
- 8 slices Italian bread
- 4 slices tomato
- 4 lettuce leaves

In a small bowl, combine the applesauce and mayonnaise. Stir in the celery, green pepper, pineapple, onion, seasoning blend, garlic powder and pepper. Add tuna; mix well. Spread over four slices of bread; top with tomato, lettuce and remaining bread.

NUTRITION FACTS: 1 sandwich equals 310 calories, 3 g fat (1 g saturated fat), 26 mg cholesterol, 715 mg sodium, 42 g carbohydrate, 3 g fiber, 28 g protein. **DIABETIC EXCHANGES:** 3 very lean meat, 2 starch, 1 vegetable, 1/2 fruit.

Salmon Caesar Salad

(PICTURE BELOW)

PREP/TOTAL TIME: 30 Min. **YIELD:** 4 Servings

This main course was invented out of a need to serve my family a balanced meal when time was limited. Even my young son likes it!

—Ann Bagdonas, Antioch, California

- 2 garlic cloves, minced
- 4 salmon fillets (4 ounces *each*)
- 1/2 cup teriyaki sauce
- 1 package (10 ounces) hearts of romaine salad mix
- 3/4 cup fat-free Caesar salad dressing
- 2 tablespoons grated Parmesan cheese
- 1/4 cup slivered almonds, toasted

Rub garlic over salmon; place in a large resealable plastic bag. Add teriyaki sauce. Seal bag and turn to coat; refrigerate for 10 minutes.

Drain and discard marinade. If grilling the salmon, coat grill rack with nonstick cooking spray before starting the grill. If broiling, place salmon on a broiler pan. Grill, covered, over high heat or broil 4 in. from the heat for 4-6 minutes on each side or until fish flakes easily with a fork.

In a large bowl, toss salad mix with Caesar dressing. Divide among four plates. Slice salmon into pieces; arrange over salads. Sprinkle with Parmesan cheese and almonds.

NUTRITION FACTS: 1 fillet with 2 cups salad equals 342 calories, 17 g fat (3 g saturated fat), 69 mg cholesterol, 794 mg sodium, 21 g carbohydrate, 4 g fiber, 28 g protein. **DIABETIC EXCHANGES:** 3 lean meat, 2 vegetable, 1-1/2 fat, 1 starch.

Open-Faced Swordfish Sandwiches
(PICTURED BELOW)

PREP: 20 Min. + Chilling   **GRILL:** 10 Min.   **YIELD:** 4 Servings

Topped with blue cheese salad dressing and a festive combination of carrots, red onion and lime juice, these warm sandwiches are a special way to welcome dinnertime.
— Alicia Montalvo Pagan, New Bedford, Massachusetts

- 1 cup canned bean sprouts, rinsed and drained
- 3/4 cup julienned carrots
- 1/4 cup thinly sliced red onion
- 1 tablespoon lime juice
- 1 teaspoon sugar
- 1/2 teaspoon minced fresh gingerroot
- 4 swordfish steaks (5 ounces *each*)
- 1 tablespoon olive oil
- 1/2 teaspoon salt
- 1/8 teaspoon cayenne pepper
- 4 slices sourdough bread (1/2 inch thick), toasted
- 8 teaspoons fat-free blue cheese salad dressing

In a small bowl, combine the bean sprouts, carrots and onion. Combine the lime juice, sugar and ginger; stir into vegetable mixture. Cover and refrigerate for 30 minutes.

Brush both sides of swordfish steaks with oil; sprinkle with salt and cayenne. If grilling the fish, coat grill rack with nonstick cooking spray before starting the grill. Grill fish, uncovered, over medium-hot heat or broil 4-6 in. from the heat for 6 minutes. Turn; grill or broil 4-7 minutes longer or until fish flakes easily with a fork.

Place a swordfish steak on each piece of toast; top with 2 teaspoons blue cheese dressing and about 1/2 cup bean sprout mixture.

NUTRITION FACTS: 1 sandwich equals 319 calories, 10 g fat (2 g saturated fat), 52 mg cholesterol, 749 mg sodium, 26 g carbohydrate, 3 g fiber, 30 g protein. **DIABETIC EXCHANGES:** 4 very lean meat, 1-1/2 starch, 1 vegetable, 1 fat.

Cilantro-Topped Salmon

PREP/TOTAL TIME: 30 Min.   **YIELD:** 6 Servings

This is a favorite with everyone who tries it. A tongue-tingling lime sauce complements tender salmon fillets in the pleasing main course.
— Nancy Culbert, Whitehorn, California

- 1-1/2 pounds salmon fillets
- 1/4 cup lime juice, *divided*
- 1/2 cup minced fresh cilantro
- 3 tablespoons thinly sliced green onions
- 1 tablespoon finely chopped jalapeno pepper
- 1 tablespoon olive oil
- 1/4 teaspoon salt
- 1/8 teaspoon pepper

Place salmon skin side down in a 13-in. x 9-in. x 2-in. baking dish coated with nonstick cooking spray. Drizzle with 1-1/2 teaspoons lime juice.

In a small bowl, combine the cilantro, onions, jalapeno, oil, salt, pepper and remaining lime juice. Spread over salmon. Bake, uncovered, at 350° for 20-25 minutes or until fish flakes easily with a fork.

NUTRITION FACTS: 1 serving equals 232 calories, 15 g fat (3 g saturated fat), 67 mg cholesterol, 166 mg sodium, 1 g carbohydrate, trace fiber, 23 g protein. **DIABETIC EXCHANGES:** 3 lean meat, 1 fat.

Editor's Note: When cutting or seeding hot peppers, use rubber or plastic gloves to protect your hands. Avoid touching your face.

Vegetable Crab Soup

PREP: 15 Min.   **COOK:** 35 Min.   **YIELD:** 8 Servings

Fresh crab is plentiful here in my town, so I like to feature it in an assortment of recipes. This chunky soup, for instance is one I turn to often.
— Emily Chaney, Penobscot, Maine

- 3/4 cup chopped onion
- 2 teaspoons canola oil
- 3/4 cup chopped celery
- 3 cans (14-1/2 ounces *each*) diced tomatoes, undrained
- 4 cups water
- 4 medium carrots, sliced
- 1 cup diced peeled potatoes
- 1 cup frozen corn
- 2 teaspoons reduced-sodium chicken bouillon granules
- 2-1/4 teaspoons seafood seasoning
- 3/4 teaspoon salt-free lemon-pepper seasoning
- 1 pound crabmeat
- 1 cup frozen peas, thawed

In a large saucepan, saute onion in oil for 1 minute. Add celery; saute until tender. Stir in the tomatoes, water, carrots, potatoes, corn, bouillon, seafood seasoning and lemon-pepper. Bring to a boil. Reduce heat; cover and simmer for 20-25 minutes or until vegetables are tender. Stir in crab and peas; heat through.

NUTRITION FACTS: 1-2/3 cups equals 167 calories, 2 g fat (trace saturated fat), 50 mg cholesterol, 691 mg sodium, 23 g carbohydrate, 5 g fiber, 15 g protein. **DIABETIC EXCHANGES:** 2 very lean meat, 2 vegetable, 1 starch.

Favorite Recipe Made Lighter

"RICH" AND "CREAMY" are two ways to describe Vonda Nixon's Velvet Shrimp. "Topped with seafood, a white sauce and cheese, this linguine dish is a fast, easy meal," Vonda says from Anchorage, Alaska.

After tasting a forkful of the pasta, the *L&T* staff was determined to capture the flavor of Vonda's entree while skimming back on the calories and fat.

A standard serving of pasta is 2 ounces, as opposed to the nearly 3-ounce servings the original recipe called for. As a result, our makeover experts slightly decreased the amount of pasta used.

Because half-and-half cream replaced the dish's heavy whipping cream, flour was added to thicken and stabilize the sauce. We substituted part-skim mozzarella cheese for the Muenster called for in the original recipe. These changes helped decrease the fat in Makeover Velvet Shrimp while offering all of the succulent taste.

The revised entree has 268 fewer calories and 69% less fat per serving than the original recipe. It also cut nearly half the cholesterol and over a fourth of the sodium, but it's still a seafood delight.

Velvet Shrimp

PREP: 15 Min.   **COOK:** 20 Min.   **YIELD:** 6 Servings

> 1 package (16 ounces) linguine
> 1/2 cup thinly sliced green onions
> 1 garlic clove, minced
> 3 tablespoons butter
> 4 teaspoons seafood seasoning
> 1 pound uncooked medium shrimp, peeled and deveined
> 1-1/2 cups heavy whipping cream
> 1 cup (4 ounces) shredded Muenster cheese

Cook linguine according to package directions. Meanwhile, in a large skillet, cook onions and garlic in butter for 1 minute. Stir in seafood seasoning; cook 1 minute longer. Add shrimp; cook for 3-4 minutes or until shrimp turn pink. Remove and keep warm.

Stir cream into skillet, scraping up any browned bits. Bring to a boil. Reduce heat; simmer, uncovered, for 5 minutes or until sauce is reduced to 1-1/4 cups. Add cheese; stir just until melted. Return shrimp to the pan; heat through. Drain linguine; top with shrimp mixture.

NUTRITION FACTS: 1-1/2 cups equals 656 calories, 36 g fat (21 g saturated fat), 227 mg cholesterol, 776 mg sodium, 58 g carbohydrate, 3 g fiber, 28 g protein.

MAKEOVER TIP
When slimming down a recipe that calls for Muenster cheese, remember that part-skim mozzarella cheese is a smart substitute.

Makeover Velvet Shrimp
(PICTURED ABOVE)

PREP: 15 Min.   **COOK:** 20 Min.   **YIELD:** 6 Servings

> 12 ounces uncooked linguine
> 1/2 cup thinly sliced green onions
> 1 garlic clove, minced
> 1 tablespoon butter
> 1 tablespoon seafood seasoning
> 1 pound uncooked medium shrimp, peeled and deveined
> 1 tablespoon all-purpose flour
> 1-1/2 cups half-and-half cream
> 3/4 cup shredded part-skim mozzarella cheese

Cook linguine according to package directions. Meanwhile, in a large nonstick skillet over medium heat, cook onions and garlic in butter for 1 minute. Stir in seafood seasoning; cook 1 minute longer. Add shrimp; cook for 3-4 minutes or until shrimp turn pink. Remove and keep warm.

Combine flour and cream until smooth; stir into skillet, scraping up any browned bits. Bring to a boil; cook and stir for 2 minutes or until thickened. Reduce heat; stir in cheese just until melted. Return shrimp to the pan and heat through. Drain linguine; top with shrimp mixture.

NUTRITION FACTS: 1-1/4 cups equals 388 calories, 11 g fat (6 g saturated fat), 150 mg cholesterol, 575 mg sodium, 45 g carbohydrate, 2 g fiber, 25 g protein. **DIABETIC EXCHANGES:** 3 starch, 2 very lean meat, 2 fat.

Dijon-Crusted Fish

(PICTURED ABOVE)

CARB

PREP/TOTAL TIME: 25 Min.   **YIELD:** 4 Servings

Parmesan cheese, Dijon and a hint of horseradish give this toasty fish lots of flavor. The preparation is so easy; it's ready in minutes.
—Scott Schmidtke, Chicago, Illinois

 3 tablespoons reduced-fat mayonnaise
 2 tablespoons grated Parmesan cheese, *divided*
 1 tablespoon lemon juice
 2 teaspoons Dijon mustard
 1 teaspoon horseradish
 4 tilapia fillets (5 ounces *each*)
 1/4 cup dry bread crumbs
 2 teaspoons butter, melted

In a small bowl, combine the mayonnaise, 1 tablespoon Parmesan cheese, lemon juice, mustard and horseradish. Place fillets on a baking sheet coated with nonstick cooking spray. Spread mayonnaise mixture evenly over fillets.

In a small bowl, combine the bread crumbs, butter and remaining Parmesan cheese; sprinkle over fillets. Bake at 425° for 13-18 minutes or until fish flakes easily with a fork.

NUTRITION FACTS: 1 fillet equals 214 calories, 8 g fat (3 g saturated fat), 80 mg cholesterol, 327 mg sodium, 7 g carbohydrate, trace fiber, 29 g protein. **DIABETIC EXCHANGES:** 4 very lean meat, 1-1/2 fat, 1/2 starch.

Tarragon Tuna Salad Wraps

PREP/TOTAL TIME: 25 Min.   **YIELD:** 4 Servings

These warm flour tortillas rolled around a cool and creamy tuna-vegetable mixture make super sandwiches year-round.
—Josephine Devereaux Piro, Easton, Pennsylvania

 1/2 cup reduced-fat mayonnaise
 4-1/2 teaspoons capers, drained
 4-1/2 teaspoons lime juice
 2 teaspoons minced fresh tarragon
 1 teaspoon salt-free lemon-pepper seasoning
 1/8 teaspoon cayenne pepper
 1 can (12 ounces) light water-packed tuna, drained
 2 tablespoons fat-free milk
 3 cups shredded lettuce
 3/4 cup coleslaw mix
 3/4 cup chopped green onions
 1 medium tomato, seeded and chopped
 4 flour tortillas (8 inches), warmed

In a large bowl, combine the mayonnaise, capers, lime juice, tarragon, lemon-pepper and cayenne. Place tuna in a small bowl; stir in 3 tablespoons mayonnaise mixture. Stir milk into the remaining mayonnaise mixture. Add the lettuce, coleslaw mix, onions and tomato; toss to coat.

Spoon the tuna mixture down center of each tortilla. Top with vegetables; roll up.

NUTRITION FACTS: 1 wrap equals 375 calories, 14 g fat (2 g saturated fat), 36 mg cholesterol, 888 mg sodium, 35 g carbohydrate, 2 g fiber, 28 g protein. **DIABETIC EXCHANGES:** 3 very lean meat, 2 starch, 2 fat, 1 vegetable.

Soft Fish Tacos
(PICTURED BELOW)

PREP/TOTAL TIME: 25 Min.   **YIELD:** 5 Servings

This combination of tilapia and cabbage may seem unusual, but after one bite, everyone's hooked!
—Carrie Billups, Florence, Oregon

>   4 cups coleslaw mix
>   1/2 cup fat-free tartar sauce
>   1/2 teaspoon salt
>   1/2 teaspoon ground cumin
>   1/4 teaspoon pepper
> 1-1/2 pounds tilapia fillets
>   2 tablespoons olive oil
>   1 tablespoon lemon juice
>   10 corn tortillas (6 inches), warmed
> Shredded cheddar cheese, chopped tomato and sliced avocado, optional

In a large bowl, toss the coleslaw mix, tartar sauce, salt, cumin and pepper; set aside. In a large nonstick skillet coated with nonstick cooking spray, cook tilapia in oil and lemon juice over medium heat for 4-5 minutes on each side or until fish flakes easily with a fork.

Place tilapia on tortillas; top with coleslaw mixture. Serve with cheese, tomato and avocado if desired.

NUTRITION FACTS: 2 tacos (calculated without optional toppings) equals 310 calories, 8 g fat (2 g saturated fat), 66 mg cholesterol, 542 mg sodium, 31 g carbohydrate, 4 g fiber, 29 g protein. **DIABETIC EXCHANGES:** 4 very lean meat, 2 starch, 1 fat.

Tuna-Stuffed Potatoes

PREP: 10 Min.   **COOK:** 25 Min.   **YIELD:** 4 Servings

Turn a baked potato into a light meal with this creamy and delicious tuna stuffing. Add a leafy green salad and it's a spur-of-the-moment lunch or late-night supper.
—Bobby Taylor, Michigan City, Indiana

>   4 medium baking potatoes
> 1/2 teaspoon salt
> 1/8 teaspoon pepper
>   1 can (6 ounces) light water-packed tuna, drained and flaked
>   2 tablespoons reduced-fat mayonnaise
> 1/2 cup shredded reduced-fat cheddar cheese, *divided*
>   2 green onions, finely chopped

Scrub and pierce potatoes; place on a microwave-safe plate. Microwave, uncovered, on high for 18-22 minutes or until tender, turning once. Let stand for 5 minutes. Cut a thin slice off the top of each potato and discard. Scoop out the pulp, leaving thin shells.

In a bowl, mash the pulp with salt and pepper. Stir in the tuna, mayonnaise, 1/4 cup cheese and onions. Spoon into potato shells. Sprinkle with remaining cheese. Microwave, uncovered, on high for 3-5 minutes or until heated through.

NUTRITION FACTS: 1 stuffed potato equals 285 calories, 6 g fat (3 g saturated fat), 25 mg cholesterol, 603 mg sodium, 40 g carbohydrate, 4 g fiber, 19 g protein. **DIABETIC EXCHANGES:** 2-1/2 starch, 2 very lean meat, 1 fat.

Editor's Note: This recipe was tested in a 1,100-watt microwave.

Easy Haddock Bake

PREP: 15 Min.   **BAKE:** 25 Min.   **YIELD:** 6 Servings

We call this recipe "Mock Lobster Casserole" because it turns haddock into something fancy. The canned soup lends a creamy touch, making the dinner seem indulgent even though it's actually light.
—Dorothy Bateman, Carver, Massachusetts

>   2 pounds fresh *or* frozen haddock fillets, thawed
>   1 can (10-3/4 ounces) condensed cream of shrimp soup, undiluted
>   2 tablespoons lemon juice
>   2 tablespoons sherry *or* reduced-sodium chicken broth
>   2 tablespoons finely chopped onion
>   2 garlic cloves, minced
> 4-1/2 teaspoons butter
>   1/4 cup dry bread crumbs
>   1/4 teaspoon Worcestershire sauce

Place the fillets in a 13-in. x 9-in. x 2-in. baking dish coated with nonstick cooking spray. In a small bowl, combine the soup, lemon juice and sherry or broth. Pour over fillets. Bake, uncovered, at 350° for 20 minutes.

In a small nonstick skillet, saute onion and garlic in butter for 2 minutes. Stir in bread crumbs and Worcestershire sauce. Sprinkle over fillets. Bake 5-10 minutes longer or until fish flakes easily with a fork.

NUTRITION FACTS: 1 serving equals 219 calories, 6 g fat (3 g saturated fat), 102 mg cholesterol, 569 mg sodium, 8 g carbohydrate, trace fiber, 30 g protein. **DIABETIC EXCHANGES:** 4 very lean meat, 1 fat, 1/2 starch.

Swordfish Skewers

PREP: 30 Min. + Marinating **GRILL:** 10 Min. **YIELD:** 4 Servings

I thread chunks of swordfish, fresh pineapple and green peppers onto skewers for a summer sensation. The kabobs offer a hint of citrus flavor. —Nancy Thome, Baraboo, Wisconsin

   1/4 cup rice wine vinegar
     1 jalapeno pepper, seeded and chopped
     1 tablespoon olive oil
     1 tablespoon lemon juice
   1/2 teaspoon grated lemon peel
   1/4 teaspoon chili powder
   1/4 teaspoon crushed red pepper flakes
   1/4 teaspoon cayenne pepper
 1-1/2 pounds swordfish steaks, cut into 1-inch pieces
     1 fresh pineapple, peeled and cut into 1-inch pieces
     2 medium green peppers, cut into 1-inch pieces

In a large resealable plastic bag, combine the first eight ingredients; add the swordfish, pineapple and green peppers. Seal bag and turn to coat; refrigerate for up to 1 hour.

Coat grill rack with nonstick cooking spray before starting the grill. Drain and discard marinade. On eight metal or soaked wooden skewers, alternately thread the swordfish, pineapple and green peppers. Grill, uncovered, over medium heat for 4-6 minutes on each side or until fish flakes easily with a fork.

NUTRITION FACTS: 2 skewers equals 280 calories, 8 g fat (2 g saturated fat), 62 mg cholesterol, 146 mg sodium, 19 g carbohydrate, 3 g fiber, 33 g protein. **DIABETIC EXCHANGES:** 5 very lean meat, 1 vegetable, 1 fruit, 1/2 fat.

Editor's Note: When cutting or seeding hot peppers, use rubber or plastic gloves to protect your hands. Avoid touching your face.

Grilled Tuna Steaks

CARB ▼

PREP: 5 Min. + Marinating **GRILL:** 5 Min. **YIELD:** 6 Servings

We love to grill these steaks, and this low-carb recipe is quick enough for weeknight meals. Simply make a salad and side dish while the steaks marinate, and dinner is ready in no time. —Michelle Armistead, Marlboro, New Jersey

   2/3 cup white wine *or* chicken broth
     2 tablespoons olive oil
     2 teaspoons dried oregano
     3 garlic cloves, minced
   1/2 teaspoon salt
   1/4 teaspoon pepper
     6 tuna steaks (6 ounces *each*)

In a bowl, combine the first six ingredients. Pour 1/2 cup marinade into a large resealable plastic bag; add tuna steaks. Seal bag and turn to coat. Refrigerate for 30 minutes, turning once or twice. Cover and refrigerate remaining marinade for basting.

Coat grill rack with nonstick cooking spray before starting the grill. Drain and discard marinade. Grill tuna, covered, over medium-hot heat for 3 minutes. Turn; baste with reserved marinade. Grill 2-4 minutes longer or until fish flakes easily with a fork. Before serving, brush tuna with remaining marinade.

NUTRITION FACTS: 1 serving equals 218 calories, 5 g fat (1 g saturated fat), 80 mg cholesterol, 202 mg sodium, 1 g carbohydrate, trace fiber, 38 g protein. **DIABETIC EXCHANGES:** 5 very lean meat, 1 fat.

Salmon Salad Pitas
(PICTURED BELOW)

PREP: 25 Min. + Chilling **YIELD:** 4 Servings

These salmon sandwiches are a healthy lunch. My husband and sons love them as leftovers.
  —Cheryl Bainbridge, Bloomington, Indiana

     1 salmon fillet (1 pound)
   1/4 cup chopped celery
   1/4 cup chopped seeded peeled cucumber
   1/4 cup reduced-fat sour cream
   1/4 cup fat-free mayonnaise
     1 tablespoon minced chives
     1 tablespoon minced fresh dill
     1 teaspoon Italian seasoning
   1/4 teaspoon salt
   1/8 teaspoon white pepper
     4 romaine leaves
     2 whole wheat pita breads (6 inches), halved

Place 2 in. of water in a large skillet; bring to a boil. Reduce heat; carefully add salmon. Poach, uncovered, for 6-12 minutes or until fish is firm and flakes easily with a fork. Remove salmon with a slotted spatula. Cool.

In a bowl, combine the celery, cucumber, sour cream, mayonnaise and seasonings. Flake the salmon; stir into salad mixture. Cover and refrigerate for at least 1 hour. Serve in lettuce-lined pita breads.

NUTRITION FACTS: 1 filled pita half equals 331 calories, 15 g fat (4 g saturated fat), 74 mg cholesterol, 522 mg sodium, 22 g carbohydrate, 3 g fiber, 27 g protein. **DIABETIC EXCHANGES:** 3 lean meat, 1-1/2 starch, 1 fat.

Sensational Spiced Salmon

(PICTURED ABOVE)

CARB

PREP/TOTAL TIME: 25 Min.   **YIELD:** 4 Servings

A sweet and spicy rub gives this quick salmon dish fantastic flavor. Paired with a green veggie and rice, it's a fantastic weeknight dinner that's special enough for company.

— Michele Doucette, Stephenville, Newfoundland

    2 tablespoons brown sugar
    4 teaspoons chili powder
    2 teaspoons grated lemon peel
  3/4 teaspoon ground cumin
  1/2 teaspoon salt
  1/4 teaspoon ground cinnamon
    4 salmon fillets (4 ounces *each*)

Combine the first six ingredients; rub over salmon. Place in an 11-in. x 7-in. x 2-in. baking dish coated with nonstick cooking spray. Bake, uncovered, at 350° for 15-20 minutes or until fish flakes easily with a fork.

NUTRITION FACTS: 1 fillet equals 244 calories, 13 g fat (3 g saturated fat), 67 mg cholesterol, 392 mg sodium, 9 g carbohydrate, 1 g fiber, 23 g protein. **DIABETIC EXCHANGES:** 3 lean meat, 1 fat, 1/2 starch.

Cod Florentine

CARB

PREP: 10 Min.   **COOK:** 25 Min.   **YIELD:** 4 Servings

My husband has high cholesterol, so I'm always looking for new fish recipes. I found this one in a cookbook. I hope you and your family like it, too.   — Lori Bolin, Soap Lake, Washington

  1/4 teaspoon salt
  1/4 teaspoon pepper
    4 cod fillets (6 ounces *each*)
    2 tablespoons lemon juice, *divided*
    2 packages (6 ounces *each*) fresh baby spinach
    2 tablespoons butter
  1/4 cup all-purpose flour
1-3/4 cups fat-free milk
    2 tablespoons shredded Parmesan cheese, *divided*

In a small bowl, combine salt and pepper. Sprinkle half over the cod; set remaining salt mixture aside. In a nonstick skillet coated with nonstick cooking spray, cook fillets until fish flakes easily with a fork. Remove from the heat. Drizzle with 1 tablespoon lemon juice; keep warm.

In another nonstick skillet coated with nonstick cooking spray, cook spinach for 3 minutes or until wilted. Drain and keep warm. In the same skillet, melt butter. Stir in flour and reserved salt mixture until blended. Gradually stir in milk until smooth. Bring to a boil; cook and stir for 2 minutes or until thickened. Stir in 1 tablespoon Parmesan cheese and remaining lemon juice. Set aside 1/2 cup sauce. Stir spinach into remaining sauce; heat through.

Divide spinach mixture among four plates; top with fish. Drizzle with reserved sauce and sprinkle with remaining Parmesan cheese.

NUTRITION FACTS: 1 serving equals 271 calories, 8 g fat (4 g saturated fat), 84 mg cholesterol, 463 mg sodium, 15 g carbohydrate, 3 g fiber, 35 g protein. **DIABETIC EXCHANGES:** 5 very lean meat, 1 vegetable, 1 fat, 1/2 fat-free milk.

Grilled Salmon with Nectarines

(PICTURED BELOW)

PREP/TOTAL TIME: 30 Min.   **YIELD:** 4 Servings

Everyone raves about this simple and elegant grilled salmon dish.
—Kerin Benjamin, Citrus Heights, California

> 1 tablespoon honey
> 1 tablespoon lemon juice
> 1 tablespoon olive oil
> 1/2 teaspoon salt, *divided*
> 3 medium nectarines, peeled and thinly sliced
> 1 tablespoon minced fresh basil *or* 1 teaspoon dried basil
> 4 salmon fillets (4 ounces *each*)
> 1/8 teaspoon pepper

In a bowl, combine the honey, lemon juice, oil and 1/4 teaspoon salt. Stir in nectarines and basil; set aside.

Coat grill rack with nonstick cooking spray before starting the grill. Rinse salmon and pat dry with paper towels. Sprinkle with pepper and remaining salt. Place salmon, skin side down, on grill. Grill, covered, over medium heat for 15-20 minutes or until fish flakes easily with a fork. Serve with nectarine mixture.

NUTRITION FACTS: 1 fillet with 1/3 cup nectarines equals 307 calories, 16 g fat (3 g saturated fat), 67 mg cholesterol, 507 mg sodium, 17 g carbohydrate, 2 g fiber, 23 g protein. **DIABETIC EXCHANGES:** 3 lean meat, 1-1/2 fat, 1 fruit.

Mini Tuna Loaves

PREP: 15 Min.   **BAKE:** 25 Min.   **YIELD:** 6 Servings

Our Test Kitchen has packed all the comfort of Mom's mouth-watering tuna casserole into six cute, individual-serving loaves topped with melted cheese. This simple, speedy recipe is sure to reel in raves.

> 1/2 cup chopped celery
> 1/3 cup chopped onion
> 2 teaspoons canola oil
> 3 cans (6 ounces *each*) solid white tuna, drained and chopped
> 2 cups soft bread crumbs
> 1/2 cup toasted wheat germ
> 2 eggs, lightly beaten
> 1/4 cup milk
> 2 tablespoons minced fresh parsley
> 1/2 teaspoon dried thyme
> 1/4 teaspoon salt
> 1/4 teaspoon pepper
> 1/3 cup shredded cheddar cheese

In a small skillet, saute celery and onion in oil for 5 minutes or until tender. In a large bowl, combine the tuna, bread crumbs, wheat germ, eggs, milk, parsley, thyme, salt and pepper. Stir in celery mixture. Shape into six oval loaves.

Place in a 15-in. x 10-in. x 1-in. baking pan coated with nonstick cooking spray. Bake at 350° for 20-25 minutes or

until lightly browned. Sprinkle with cheese. Bake 5 minutes longer or until cheese is melted.

NUTRITION FACTS: 1 loaf equals 257 calories, 10 g fat (3 g saturated fat), 116 mg cholesterol, 578 mg sodium, 14 g carbohydrate, 2 g fiber, 28 g protein. **DIABETIC EXCHANGES:** 3 very lean meat, 2 fat, 1 starch.

Seafood Enchiladas
(PICTURED AT RIGHT)

PREP: 30 Min.   **BAKE:** 35 Min.   **YIELD:** 8 Servings

I received this recipe from an old friend of the family many years ago, and my gang still loves it today. The crab makes it a wonderful change of pace from other weeknight suppers.
—Donna Roberts, Shumway, Illinois

1/2 **cup chopped onion**
  1 **garlic clove, minced**
  1 **tablespoon butter**
  1 **cup (8 ounces) reduced-fat sour cream**
  3 **tablespoons all-purpose flour**
  1 **cup reduced-sodium chicken broth**
  1 **can (4 ounces) chopped green chilies**
  1 **teaspoon ground coriander**
1/4 **teaspoon pepper**
  1 **cup (4 ounces) shredded reduced-fat Mexican cheese blend,** *divided*
  2 **cups coarsely chopped real** *or* **imitation crabmeat**
  8 **flour tortillas (6 inches), warmed**
1/2 **cup chopped tomato**
1/2 **cup chopped green onions**
1/4 **cup chopped ripe olives**

In a large saucepan, cook onion and garlic in butter over medium heat until tender. Combine sour cream and flour until smooth; gradually add to onion mixture. Stir in the broth, chilies, coriander and pepper.

Bring to a boil. Reduce heat; simmer, uncovered, for 2-3 minutes or until thickened. Remove from the heat; stir in 1/2 cup cheese.

Place crab in a bowl; stir in 1/2 cup cheese sauce. Spoon equal amounts on tortillas; roll up tightly. Place seam side down in an 11-in. x 7-in. x 2-in. baking dish coated with nonstick cooking spray. Top with remaining cheese sauce.

Cover and bake at 350° for 30 minutes. Uncover; sprinkle with remaining cheese. Bake 5 minutes longer or until cheese is melted. Let stand for 5 minutes. Top with tomato, green onions and olives.

NUTRITION FACTS: 1 enchilada equals 243 calories, 11 g fat (5 g saturated fat), 53 mg cholesterol, 662 mg sodium, 21 g carbohydrate, 1 g fiber, 16 g protein. **DIABETIC EXCHANGES:** 2 fat, 1-1/2 starch, 1 very lean meat.

Scallops with Sun-Dried Tomatoes

PREP/TOTAL TIME: 30 Min.   **YIELD:** 4 Servings

Thirty minutes is all the time you need for this stir-fry. I combine scallops with sun-dried tomatoes, pasta and a little lime juice.
—Jennifer Warzynak, Erie, Pennsylvania

  6 **ounces uncooked penne** *or* **medium tube pasta**
1/4 **cup chopped sun-dried tomatoes (not packed in oil)**

3/4 **cup hot water**
  4 **cups fresh broccoli florets**
1/2 **cup reduced-sodium chicken broth**
  3 **garlic cloves, minced**
  2 **tablespoons olive oil**
  1 **pound bay scallops**
  1 **teaspoon lime juice**
  1 **teaspoon minced fresh basil**
1/4 **teaspoon salt**
1/4 **cup shredded Parmesan cheese**

Cook pasta according to package directions. Meanwhile, in a small bowl, combine the sun-dried tomatoes and hot water. Let stand for 5 minutes; drain and set aside.

Place the broccoli and broth in a microwave-safe bowl. Cover and microwave on high for 2-4 minutes or until broccoli is crisp-tender; set aside.

In a large nonstick skillet coated with nonstick cooking spray, cook garlic in oil over medium heat for 1 minute. Add scallops; cook for 2 minutes. Stir in the lime juice, basil, salt, and reserved tomatoes and broccoli; cook 2-3 minutes longer or until scallops are firm and opaque.

Drain the pasta; stir into scallop mixture and heat through. Sprinkle with Parmesan cheese.

NUTRITION FACTS: 2 cups equals 367 calories, 10 g fat (2 g saturated fat), 41 mg cholesterol, 585 mg sodium, 40 g carbohydrate, 4 g fiber, 30 g protein. **DIABETIC EXCHANGES:** 3 very lean meat, 2 starch, 1-1/2 fat, 1 vegetable.

Editor's Note: This recipe was tested in a 1,100-watt microwave.

Zucchini-Wrapped Scallops
(PICTURED ABOVE)

CARB

PREP: 20 Min. + Marinating   **GRILL:** 10 Min.   **YIELD:** 4 Servings

Our home economists wanted to wrap seasoned scallops in zucchini strips before threading them onto skewers for grilling. The problem was finding a terrific scallop recipe to start with. When Hershey, Pennsylvania's Julie Gwinn shared her citrus marinade, they knew they had a hit on their hands.

2 tablespoons orange juice
1 tablespoon olive oil
1 teaspoon Caribbean jerk seasoning
1 teaspoon grated orange peel
1/8 teaspoon crushed red pepper flakes
1-1/2 pounds sea scallops (about 16)
2 medium zucchini

In a small bowl, combine the orange juice, oil, seasoning, orange peel and red pepper flakes; set aside 1 tablespoon for basting. Pour the remaining marinade into a large resealable plastic bag; add the scallops. Seal bag and turn to coat; refrigerate for 30 minutes.

Using a vegetable peeler or metal cheese slicer, cut zucchini into very thin lengthwise strips. Drain and discard marinade. Wrap a zucchini strip around each scallop. Secure by threading where the zucchini ends overlap onto metal or soaked wooden skewers.

Coat grill rack with nonstick cooking spray before starting the grill. Grill skewers, covered, over medium heat for 3-4 minutes on each side or until scallops are opaque, brushing once with reserved marinade.

NUTRITION FACTS: 1 serving equals 194 calories, 5 g fat (1 g saturated fat), 56 mg cholesterol, 346 mg sodium, 7 g carbohydrate, 1 g fiber, 29 g protein. **DIABETIC EXCHANGES:** 4 very lean meat, 1/2 starch, 1/2 fat.

Bacon Shrimp Creole
(PICTURED BELOW)

PREP: 25 Min.   **COOK:** 45 Min.   **YIELD:** 6 Servings

This dish is a compilation of two Creole recipes I found in my mom's New Orleans cookbooks.

—Jan Tucker, Virginia Beach, Virginia

3/4 cup chopped onion
2 celery ribs, chopped
1/2 cup chopped green pepper
2 tablespoons olive oil
3 garlic cloves, minced
1 can (14-1/2 ounces) diced tomatoes, undrained
1 can (8 ounces) tomato sauce
3/4 cup cold water, *divided*
1/4 cup crumbled cooked bacon
1 tablespoon dried parsley flakes
1 teaspoon sugar
1/2 teaspoon salt
1/2 teaspoon dried thyme
1/2 teaspoon curry powder
1/2 teaspoon pepper
1/4 teaspoon cayenne pepper
1 tablespoon all-purpose flour
1-1/2 pounds uncooked medium shrimp, peeled and deveined
3 cups hot cooked long grain rice

In a Dutch oven, saute the onion, celery and green pepper in oil until tender. Add garlic; saute 1 minute longer. Add the tomatoes, tomato sauce, 1/2 cup water, bacon, parsley, sugar, salt, thyme, curry powder, pepper and cayenne. Bring to a boil. Reduce heat; cover and simmer for 30 minutes.

Combine flour and remaining water until smooth; stir into tomato mixture. Bring to a boil; cook and stir for 1-2 minutes or until thickened. Reduce heat; add shrimp. Simmer, uncovered, for 5 minutes or until the shrimp turn pink. Serve with the rice.

NUTRITION FACTS: 3/4 cup shrimp creole with 1/2 cup rice equals 292 calories, 7 g fat (1 g saturated fat), 171 mg cholesterol, 814 mg sodium, 33 g carbohydrate, 3 g fiber, 24 g protein. **DIABETIC EXCHANGES:** 3 very lean meat, 2 vegetable, 1-1/2 starch, 1 fat.

Crumb-Topped Sole

 CARB

(PICTURED ABOVE)

PREP/TOTAL TIME: 15 Min. **YIELD:** 4 Servings

Looking for a low-carb supper that's ready in a pinch? Our Test Kitchen comes to your aid with buttery sole. The moist fillets are topped with pretty, golden bread crumbs, making them fit for weekend entertaining.

>   3 tablespoons reduced-fat mayonnaise
>   3 tablespoons grated Parmesan cheese, *divided*
>   2 teaspoons mustard seed
>   1/4 teaspoon pepper
>   4 sole fillets (6 ounces *each*)
>   1 cup soft bread crumbs
>   1 green onion, finely chopped
>   1/4 teaspoon ground mustard
>   2 teaspoons butter, melted

Combine the mayonnaise, 2 tablespoons Parmesan cheese, mustard seed and pepper; spread over tops of fillets. Place on a broiler pan coated with nonstick cooking spray. Broil 4 in. from the heat for 3-5 minutes or until fish flakes easily with a fork.

Meanwhile, in a small bowl, combine the bread crumbs, onion, ground mustard and remaining Parmesan cheese; stir in butter. Spoon over fillets; spritz topping with nonstick cooking spray. Broil 1-2 minutes longer or until golden brown.

NUTRITION FACTS: 1 fillet equals 267 calories, 10 g fat (3 g saturated fat), 94 mg cholesterol, 378 mg sodium, 8 g carbohydrate, 1 g fiber, 35 g protein. **DIABETIC EXCHANGES:** 5 lean meat, 1 fat, 1/2 starch.

Salmon Patties with Mustard Sauce

 CARB

PREP/TOTAL TIME: 25 Min. **YIELD:** 6 Servings

Featuring a creamy mustard sauce, these salmon patties put convenient canned salmon to scrumptious use. Serve them on a whole wheat bun with shredded lettuce if you'd like.

—Angie Philkill, Fort Gratiot, Michigan

>   2 egg whites, lightly beaten
>   1/4 cup dry bread crumbs
>   1/4 cup chopped green onions
>   1/4 cup fat-free mayonnaise
>   1 teaspoon blackening seasoning
>   2 cans (14-3/4 ounces *each*) salmon, drained, bones and skin removed
>   2 teaspoons butter

MUSTARD SAUCE:

>   6 tablespoons fat-free mayonnaise
>   1 tablespoon Dijon mustard

In a large bowl, combine the first five ingredients. Add salmon; mix well. Shape into six patties. In a large nonstick skillet, cook patties in butter over medium heat for 6 minutes on each side or until browned.

In a small bowl, combine the sauce ingredients. Serve with salmon patties.

NUTRITION FACTS: 1 patty with 1 tablespoon sauce equals 273 calories, 13 g fat (3 g saturated fat), 67 mg cholesterol, 1,119 mg sodium, 8 g carbohydrate, 1 g fiber, 31 g protein. **DIABETIC EXCHANGES:** 4 lean meat, 1/2 starch, 1/2 fat.

Asian Salmon Medallions
(PICTURED ABOVE)

 CARB

PREP: 35 Min.   **GRILL:** 10 Min.   **YIELD:** 4 Servings

Our home economists stuffed salmon rounds with herbs and basted them with a glossy sesame sauce during grilling.

  1/3 cup finely chopped onion
    2 tablespoons minced chives
    2 tablespoons minced fresh parsley
    1 garlic clove, minced
    4 salmon steaks (1 inch thick and 6 ounces *each*)
    3 tablespoons maple syrup
    2 tablespoons rice wine vinegar
    1 tablespoon hoisin sauce
    1 teaspoon sesame oil

In a small bowl, combine the onion, chives, parsley and garlic; set aside. Soak kitchen string in water.

Using tweezers or small pliers, remove pin bones from salmon by pulling the bones out at an angle.

To debone salmon for rolling, start at one end of the stomach flap and cut between the bones and all the way toward the backbone. Cut around the backbone and the small bone above it, cutting all the way up to, but not through, the skin holding the two sides together. Repeat on the other side so the center bones are completely separated from the salmon steak.

On each steak, trim off about 2 in. of skin from the end of the left stomach flap. Open steaks flat. Spoon onion mixture over salmon. Fold left side over filling.

Carefully roll up salmon to form a circle. Wrap soaked kitchen string around the salmon rolls and tie.

In a small bowl, combine the syrup, vinegar, hoisin sauce and sesame oil. Set aside 1 tablespoon sauce for serving.

Coat grill rack with nonstick cooking spray before starting the grill. Grill salmon, uncovered, over medium heat for 5 minutes; brush with sauce. Turn; grill for 3 minutes. Turn and brush with remaining sauce; grill 2-3 minutes longer or until fish flakes easily with a fork. Remove and discard string. Drizzle salmon with reserved sauce.

NUTRITION FACTS: 1 serving equals 380 calories, 20 g fat (4 g saturated fat), 100 mg cholesterol, 168 mg sodium, 14 g carbohydrate, trace fiber, 34 g protein. **DIABETIC EXCHANGES:** 5 lean meat, 1 starch, 1 fat.

HEALTHY OUTLOOK
Salmon is a strong fit for a healthy diet because it's high in heart-smart unsaturated fats which lower cholesterol.

Meatless Main Dishes

Whether you've made vegetarian meals a way of life or you're simply cutting back on red meat, the following pages offer plenty of sensational items to choose from. From pot-pies and pasta favorites to burgers and brunch basics, these entrees are so tasty, your family won't even miss the beef.

Harvest Vegetable Tart, p. 173

Hearty Lentil Spaghetti

(PICTURED ABOVE)

PREP: 15 Min.   **COOK:** 70 Min.   **YIELD:** 8 Servings

Packed full of lentils and Italian flavors, this entree is thick, zesty and satisfying.   —Marie Bender, Henderson, Nevada

> 3/4 cup chopped onion
>   2 garlic cloves, minced
>   1 tablespoon olive oil
> 1-1/2 cups dried lentils, rinsed
>   4 cups vegetable broth
> 1/2 teaspoon pepper
> 1/4 teaspoon cayenne pepper
>   1 can (14-1/2 ounces) Italian diced tomatoes
>   1 can (6 ounces) tomato paste
>   1 teaspoon white vinegar
> 1-1/2 teaspoons dried basil
> 1-1/2 teaspoons dried oregano
> 12 ounces uncooked spaghetti
> 1/4 cup shredded Parmesan cheese

In a large saucepan coated with nonstick cooking spray, cook onion and garlic in oil until tender. Stir in the lentils, broth, pepper and cayenne. Bring to a boil. Reduce heat; cover and simmer for 20-30 minutes or until lentils are tender.

Stir in the tomatoes, tomato paste, vinegar, basil and oregano. Return to a boil. Reduce heat; cover and simmer for 40-45 minutes.

Cook spaghetti according to package directions; drain. Serve with lentil sauce. Sprinkle with Parmesan cheese.

NUTRITION FACTS: 3/4 cup sauce with 3/4 cup spaghetti equals 353 calories, 3 g fat (1 g saturated fat), 2 mg cholesterol, 480 mg sodium, 63 g carbohydrate, 14 g fiber, 18 g protein.

Wholesome Veggie Burgers

PREP: 35 Min. + Chilling   **COOK:** 20 Min.   **YIELD:** 12 Servings

Chopped walnuts punch up the protein and taste of these budget-friendly patties. I freeze half of the burgers for nights when vegetarian friends drop by.
                    —Ellen Kosik Williams, Painted Post, New York

> 1 cup bulgur
> 1 cup boiling water
> 1 medium carrot, cut into 1/2-inch pieces
> 3 garlic cloves, halved
> 1/2 cup coarsely chopped sweet red pepper
> 1/4 cup coarsely chopped onion
> 1 can (16 ounces) kidney beans, rinsed and drained
> 2 eggs, lightly beaten
> 1 cup old-fashioned oats
> 1/3 cup chopped walnuts, toasted
> 2 tablespoons Italian seasoning
> 1 teaspoon salt
> 1/2 teaspoon pepper
> 1/2 cup cornmeal
> 6 teaspoons canola oil
> 12 whole wheat hamburger buns, split
> 12 lettuce leaves
> 12 slices tomato
> 12 slices sweet onion

Place bulgur in a bowl; stir in water. Cover and let stand for 30 minutes or until most of the liquid is absorbed. Drain and squeeze dry if needed.

Place carrot and garlic in a food processor; cover and process until carrot is chopped. Add red pepper and onion;

cover and pulse until red pepper is chopped. Add beans; cover and process until mixture is chunky.

In a large bowl, combine the eggs, oats, walnuts, Italian seasoning, salt, pepper, cornmeal, bulgur and carrot mixture; stir until mixture is firm (mixture will be sticky). Shape into 12 patties. Cover and refrigerate for at least 2 hours.

In a large nonstick skillet coated with nonstick cooking spray, cook four patties in 2 teaspoons oil for 3-4 minutes on each side or until lightly browned. Repeat with remaining patties and oil. Serve on buns with lettuce, tomato and onion.

NUTRITION FACTS: 1 burger equals 306 calories, 8 g fat (1 g saturated fat), 35 mg cholesterol, 481 mg sodium, 50 g carbohydrate, 10 g fiber, 12 g protein. **DIABETIC EXCHANGES:** 3 starch, 1 vegetable, 1 fat.

Editor's Note: Look for bulgur in the cereal, rice or organic food aisle of your grocery store.

Chili Potpies

(PICTURED BELOW RIGHT)

MEAT-LESS

PREP: 20 Min.   **BAKE:** 15 Min.   **YIELD:** 4 Servings

Welcome your family to the dinner table with these individual potpies. The L&T Test Kitchen staff created the simple, corn bread crust that perfectly complements a filling of tangy chili.

    1 medium onion, chopped
    1 medium green pepper, chopped
    2 teaspoons canola oil
    2 cans (14-1/2 ounces *each*) diced tomatoes, drained
    1 can (16 ounces) chili beans, undrained
1/4 cup tomato sauce
    2 tablespoons chili powder
    1 teaspoon brown sugar
1/2 teaspoon ground cumin
1/2 cup all-purpose flour
1/2 cup cornmeal
1/2 teaspoon baking powder
1/4 teaspoon salt
    1 tablespoon butter, melted
    3 to 4 tablespoons fat-free milk

In a large saucepan, saute onion and green pepper in oil until tender. Stir in the tomatoes, beans, tomato sauce, chili powder, brown sugar and cumin. Bring to a boil. Reduce heat to low; heat, uncovered, while preparing crust.

In a small bowl, combine the flour, cornmeal, baking powder and salt. Stir in butter and enough milk to form a ball. On a lightly floured surface, roll dough into a 12-in. circle. Using an inverted 10-oz. baking dish as a guide, score four circles. Cut out circles. Cut a small circle in the center of each pastry (discard the small cutouts or reroll the cutouts and use as decoration).

Coat four 10-oz. baking dishes with nonstick cooking spray. Fill with chili; top each with a dough circle. Tuck in edges of dough to seal. Bake at 375° for 13-17 minutes or until edges of crust are lightly browned.

NUTRITION FACTS: 1 potpie equals 354 calories, 7 g fat (3 g saturated fat), 8 mg cholesterol, 930 mg sodium, 67 g carbohydrate, 14 g fiber, 13 g protein. **DIABETIC EXCHANGES:** 3 starch, 3 vegetable, 1 very lean meat, 1 fat.

Spicy Beans and Rice

MEAT-LESS

PREP/TOTAL TIME: 25 Min.   **YIELD:** 6 Servings

For a fast meal when we're in a hurry, I microwave this zippy combination with rice and beans. It's nutritious and yummy.
—Sandra Castillo, Janesville, Wisconsin

    2 cups uncooked instant rice
    2 cups water
1/2 teaspoon garlic powder
1/2 teaspoon chili powder
1/2 teaspoon ground cumin
Dash pepper
    1 can (15-1/2 ounces) chili beans, undrained
    1 can (11 ounces) Mexicorn, drained
    1 can (10 ounces) diced tomatoes and green chilies, drained
1/2 cup salsa
    1 cup (4 ounces) shredded reduced-fat cheddar cheese

In a 2-qt. microwave-safe dish, combine the first six ingredients; cover and microwave on high for 5-7 minutes or until water is absorbed.

Stir in the beans, Mexicorn, tomatoes and salsa; top with cheese. Cover and microwave on high for 2-3 minutes or until heated through and cheese is melted.

NUTRITION FACTS: 1 cup equals 293 calories, 5 g fat (3 g saturated fat), 13 mg cholesterol, 903 mg sodium, 54 g carbohydrate, 8 g fiber, 14 g protein.

Editor's Note: This recipe was tested in a 1,100-watt microwave.

Kidney Bean Tostadas

MEAT-LESS

PREP/TOTAL TIME: 25 Min. **YIELD:** 6 Servings

I prepare healthful tostadas topped with beans for a meatless supper or lunch. Simmering the beans instead of frying them reduces the fat and enhances the flavor.
—Marguerite Shaeffer, Sewell, New Jersey

        1 can (16 ounces) kidney beans, rinsed and drained
1-1/2 teaspoons chili powder
    1/2 teaspoon ground cumin
        3 teaspoons canola oil, *divided*
    3/4 cup chunky salsa, *divided*
        6 corn tortillas (6 inches)
        1 cup shredded lettuce
        2 tablespoons reduced-fat sour cream

In a large nonstick skillet coated with nonstick cooking spray, cook the beans, chili powder and cumin in 1 teaspoon oil for 3 minutes. Stir in 1/2 cup salsa; bring to a boil. Reduce heat; simmer, uncovered, for 3-6 minutes or until thickened.

Meanwhile, brush both sides of tortillas with remaining oil. Place on an ungreased baking sheet. Bake at 400° for 5-8 minutes or until crisp. Spoon bean mixture over tortillas. Top with lettuce, sour cream and remaining salsa.

NUTRITION FACTS: 1 tostada equals 165 calories, 4 g fat (1 g saturated fat), 2 mg cholesterol, 314 mg sodium, 28 g carbohydrate, 7 g fiber, 9 g protein. **DIABETIC EXCHANGES:** 2 starch, 1 very lean meat, 1/2 fat.

Chili-Topped Sweet Potatoes

FAT ↓ MEAT-LESS

(PICTURED ABOVE)

PREP: 15 Min. **COOK:** 40 Min. **YIELD:** 8 Servings

After creating a thick and chunky chili, I realized it would make a fun topping for sweet potatoes. It really warms up cold winter nights.
—Jill Nerbas, St. Albert, Alberta

    8 medium sweet potatoes
    2 medium green peppers, chopped
    2 medium onions, chopped
    2 garlic cloves, minced
    1 tablespoon chili powder
    2 teaspoons ground cumin
    1 teaspoon ground coriander
1/2 teaspoon salt
1/4 teaspoon pepper
    1 teaspoon olive oil
    1 can (28 ounces) diced tomatoes, undrained
    1 can (15 ounces) black beans, rinsed and drained
    1 cup frozen corn, thawed
1/4 cup minced fresh parsley

Scrub sweet potatoes and pierce with a fork. Bake at 400° for 35-40 minutes or until tender.

Meanwhile, in a large nonstick skillet coated with nonstick cooking spray, cook the green peppers, onions, garlic, chili powder, cumin, coriander, salt and pepper in oil for 10 minutes. Stir in the tomatoes and beans. Bring to a boil. Reduce heat; simmer, uncovered, for 20 minutes. Stir in corn and parsley; simmer 5 minutes longer.

Cut sweet potatoes in half; top with chili.

NUTRITION FACTS: 1 sweet potato with 2/3 cup chili equals 233 calories, 1 g fat (trace saturated fat), 0 cholesterol, 400 mg sodium, 51 g carbohydrate, 10 g fiber, 7 g protein. **DIABETIC EXCHANGES:** 2-1/2 starch, 2 vegetable.

Quick Marinara

FAT ↓ CARB ↓ MEAT-LESS

PREP: 15 Min. **COOK:** 30 Min. **YIELD:** 9 Servings

I once tried a meat substitute in my marinara. The result was a classic, stick-to-your-ribs sauce I truly enjoyed.
—Thomas Licking, Green Lake, Wisconsin

        1 medium onion, chopped
        4 garlic cloves, minced
        1 tablespoon canola oil
    1/2 pound sliced fresh mushrooms
        1 can (28 ounces) Italian crushed tomatoes, undrained
        1 can (6 ounces) tomato paste
        1 tablespoon minced chives
1-1/2 teaspoons Italian seasoning
    3/4 teaspoon salt
    1/8 teaspoon crushed red pepper flakes
        2 cups frozen vegetarian meat crumbles
Hot cooked pasta, optional

In a large saucepan coated with nonstick cooking spray, cook onion and garlic in oil for 2 minutes. Add mushrooms; cook 3-4 minutes longer or until vegetables are tender.

Stir in the tomatoes, tomato paste, chives, Italian seasoning, salt and red pepper flakes. Bring to a boil. Reduce heat; simmer, uncovered, for 15 minutes. Stir in vegetarian meat crumbles; cook for 3-5 minutes or until heated through. Serve over pasta if desired.

NUTRITION FACTS: 1/2 cup sauce (calculated without pasta) equals 106 calories, 2 g fat (trace saturated fat), trace cholesterol, 562 mg sodium, 15 g carbohydrate, 3 g fiber, 7 g protein. **DIABETIC EXCHANGES:** 2 vegetable, 1 lean meat.

Tamale Veggie Pie

(PICTURED BELOW)

PREP: 25 Min.   **BAKE:** 20 Min.   **YIELD:** 6 Servings

This warm and comforting main course has a thick and zesty filling and a moist, tender corn bread topping. Serve it with a side salad and fruit for a great meatless meal.

—Deb Perry, Bluffton, Indiana

  1 cup chopped onion
  1 garlic clove, minced
  1 teaspoon canola oil
  1 can (14-1/2 ounces) Mexican diced tomatoes
  1 can (15 ounces) pinto beans, rinsed and drained
  1 cup (4 ounces) shredded reduced-fat cheddar cheese
  1 can (4 ounces) chopped green chilies
  1 jalapeno pepper, seeded and chopped
3/4 teaspoon ground cumin
3/4 teaspoon chili powder
TOPPING:
1/2 cup plus 1 tablespoon all-purpose flour
1/2 cup yellow cornmeal
1/2 teaspoon baking powder
1/4 teaspoon baking soda
1/4 teaspoon salt
  1 egg
1/2 cup plain yogurt
  2 teaspoons butter, melted

In a small nonstick skillet coated with nonstick cooking spray, cook onion and garlic in oil until tender. Transfer to a large bowl. Drain tomatoes, reserving 2 tablespoons juice; add tomatoes and juice to onion mixture.

Stir in the beans, cheese, chilies, jalapeno, cumin and chili powder. Transfer to an 8-in. square baking dish coated with nonstick cooking spray.

For topping, in a small bowl, combine the flour, cornmeal, baking powder, baking soda and salt. Whisk together the egg, yogurt and butter; stir into dry ingredients just until moistened. Spoon over filling; gently spread to cover top.

Bake, uncovered, at 375° for 20-25 minutes or until filling is bubbly and a toothpick inserted into the topping comes out clean.

NUTRITION FACTS: 1 piece equals 280 calories, 8 g fat (4 g saturated fat), 55 mg cholesterol, 746 mg sodium, 39 g carbohydrate, 6 g fiber, 13 g protein. **DIABETIC EXCHANGES:** 2 starch, 1 lean meat, 1 vegetable, 1 fat.

Editor's Note: When cutting or seeding hot peppers, use rubber or plastic gloves to protect your hands. Avoid touching your face.

Spinach-Stuffed Portobello Mushrooms

PREP: 15 Min.   **BAKE:** 40 Min.   **YIELD:** 4 Servings

Feta cheese and spinach lend Greek flair to these mushroom caps. Try them as a simple supper, no-fuss side dish or even a first course appetizer.

—Sandy Rossier, Brooksville, Florida

  4 large portobello mushrooms
1/4 cup chopped onion
  2 eggs, lightly beaten
1/2 cup reduced-fat sour cream
  1 package (10 ounces) frozen chopped spinach, thawed and squeezed dry
  1 cup crushed seasoned stuffing
1/2 cup crumbled feta cheese
1/2 teaspoon garlic salt
  3 tablespoons shredded Parmesan cheese

Line a baking sheet with heavy-duty foil; coat the foil with nonstick cooking spray and set aside. Remove stems from mushrooms; set caps aside and chop stems. In a microwave-safe bowl, combine the chopped mushrooms and onion. Cover and microwave at 50% power for 1-2 minutes or until tender, stirring every 30 seconds.

In a small bowl, combine the eggs and sour cream. Stir in the spinach, stuffing, feta cheese, garlic salt and onion mixture. Spoon into mushroom caps. Place on prepared baking sheet.

Bake at 350° for 35 minutes. Sprinkle with Parmesan cheese. Bake 5-10 minutes longer or until mushrooms are tender and cheese is melted.

NUTRITION FACTS: 1 stuffed mushroom equals 233 calories, 9 g fat (5 g saturated fat), 126 mg cholesterol, 735 mg sodium, 22 g carbohydrate, 5 g fiber, 15 g protein. **DIABETIC EXCHANGES:** 2 vegetable, 1 starch, 1 lean meat, 1 fat.

HEALTHY OUTLOOK

Vegetarian meat crumbles are a smart option for those cutting back on red meat. While the crumbles don't contain the amount of protein found in beef, they are virtually free of saturated fat and cholesterol.

The most popular variety are seasoned and precooked. Found in the freezer section, these crumbles offer the same texture as ground beef, making them ideal for pasta sauces, casseroles and soups.

Enchiladas Florentine

PREP: 25 Min. **BAKE:** 35 Min. **YIELD:** 10 Servings

After trying similar enchiladas at a Mexican restaurant, I created this tasty lighter version. Topped with a zesty lime-and-cilantro sauce, it's great with a side of reduced-fat refried beans or Spanish rice. —Debbie Purdue, Westland, Michigan

  1 carton (15 ounces) reduced-fat ricotta cheese
  1 package (10 ounces) frozen chopped spinach, thawed and squeezed dry
1-1/2 cups (6 ounces) shredded reduced-fat Mexican cheese blend, *divided*
  2 egg whites, lightly beaten
10 flour tortillas (8 inches)
  1 tablespoon cornstarch
  1 cup vegetable broth
  1 bottle (7 ounces) mild green taco sauce
1/4 cup minced fresh cilantro
  1 tablespoon lime juice
1/2 pound sliced fresh mushrooms
  2 teaspoons canola oil

In a large bowl, combine the ricotta, spinach, 1 cup cheese and egg whites. Spoon down the center of each tortilla. Roll up and place seam side down in a 13-in. x 9-in. x 2-in. baking dish coated with nonstick cooking spray.

In a small saucepan, combine the cornstarch and broth until smooth. Stir in taco sauce. Bring to a boil; cook and stir for 2 minutes or until thickened. Stir in cilantro and lime juice. Pour over enchiladas. In a nonstick skillet, saute mushrooms in oil until tender; arrange evenly over enchiladas.

Cover and bake at 350° for 30-35 minutes or until heated through. Uncover; sprinkle with remaining cheese. Bake 5 minutes longer or until cheese is melted.

NUTRITION FACTS: 1 enchilada equals 271 calories, 10 g fat (3 g saturated fat), 22 mg cholesterol, 674 mg sodium, 32 g carbohydrate, 1 g fiber, 15 g protein. **DIABETIC EXCHANGES:** 2 starch, 1 lean meat, 1 fat.

Black Bean Tortilla Pie
(PICTURED AT RIGHT)

PREP: 50 Min. **BAKE:** 15 Min. **YIELD:** 6 Servings

I found this Southwestern entree a while ago but decreased the amount of cheese and increased the herbs. It's one of my daughter's favorites. —Wendy Kelly, Voorheesville, New York

  1 medium onion, chopped
  1 medium green pepper, chopped
  3 garlic cloves, minced
  1 teaspoon ground cumin
1/4 teaspoon pepper
  1 tablespoon olive oil
  2 cans (15 ounces *each*) black beans, rinsed and drained
  1 can (14 ounces) vegetable broth
  1 package (10 ounces) frozen corn, thawed
  4 green onions, thinly sliced
  4 flour tortillas (8 inches)
  1 cup (4 ounces) shredded reduced-fat cheddar cheese, *divided*

In a large skillet, saute the onion, green pepper, garlic, cumin and pepper in oil. Add beans and broth. Bring to a boil; cook until liquid is reduced to about 1/3 cup. Stir in corn and green onions; remove from the heat.

Place one tortilla in a 9-in. springform pan coated with nonstick cooking spray. Layer with 1-1/2 cups bean mixture and 1/4 cup cheese. Repeat layers twice. Top with remaining tortilla. Place pan on a baking sheet.

Bake, uncovered, at 400° for 15-20 minutes or until heated through. Remove sides of pan. Sprinkle with remaining cheese. Cut into wedges.

NUTRITION FACTS: 1 wedge equals 353 calories, 9 g fat (3 g saturated fat), 14 mg cholesterol, 842 mg sodium, 53 g carbohydrate, 8 g fiber, 17 g protein. **DIABETIC EXCHANGES:** 3 starch, 1 very lean meat, 1 vegetable, 1 fat.

Artichoke Tomato Pasta

PREP/TOTAL TIME: 30 Min. **YIELD:** 6 Servings

I understand the meaning of a family-pleasing dish. Lightly flavored with artichoke hearts, my chunky pasta sauce is a hearty way to top off a busy day. It's an easy, vegetarian meal that's low in fat. —Diane Molberg, Emerald Park, Saskatchewan

  8 ounces uncooked spiral pasta
3/4 cup chopped onion
  1 garlic clove, minced
  1 tablespoon olive oil
  1 can (14-1/2 ounces) Italian stewed tomatoes, cut up
  1 can (8 ounces) tomato sauce
1/2 teaspoon dried basil
1/2 teaspoon dried oregano
1/8 teaspoon pepper
Dash ground cumin
  1 can (14 ounces) water-packed artichoke hearts, rinsed, drained and coarsely chopped
  4 tablespoons minced fresh parsley, *divided*
1/4 cup grated Parmesan cheese

Cook pasta according to package directions. Meanwhile, in a large nonstick skillet coated with nonstick cooking spray, saute onion and garlic in oil until tender. Stir in the tomatoes, tomato sauce, basil, oregano, pepper and cumin. Bring to a boil. Reduce heat; cover and simmer for 10 minutes.

Stir in artichokes and 2 tablespoons parsley. Simmer, uncovered, 5 minutes longer. Drain pasta; toss with artichoke mixture. Sprinkle with Parmesan cheese and remaining parsley.

NUTRITION FACTS: 1 cup equals 236 calories, 4 g fat (1 g saturated fat), 3 mg cholesterol, 634 mg sodium, 41 g carbohydrate, 3 g fiber, 9 g protein. **DIABETIC EXCHANGES:** 2 starch, 2 vegetable, 1/2 fat.

Harvest Vegetable Tart

MEAT-LESS

(PICTURED ABOVE)

PREP: 45 Min. + Chilling   **BAKE:** 30 Min.   **YIELD:** 6 Servings

When folks lay eyes on this lightened-up veggie tart, oohs of approval start circling. I've been serving it for 30 years. It always gets a warm reception. —Ruth Lee, Troy, Ontario

- 1/2 cup all-purpose flour
- 1/4 cup whole wheat flour
- 1/4 cup cornmeal
- 2 tablespoons grated Parmesan cheese
- 1/2 teaspoon salt
- 1/8 teaspoon cayenne pepper
- 1/4 cup cold butter, cubed
- 3 to 4 tablespoons cold water

FILLING:
- 1/2 cup thinly sliced green onions
- 2 garlic cloves, minced
- 1 tablespoon olive oil
- 5 slices peeled eggplant (3-1/2 inches x 1/4 inch)
- 2 tablespoons grated Parmesan cheese, *divided*
- 1 small tomato, cut into 1/4-inch slices
- 3 green pepper rings
- 3 sweet red pepper rings
- 1/2 cup frozen corn
- 2 eggs, lightly beaten
- 2/3 cup fat-free evaporated milk
- 3/4 teaspoon salt
- 1/4 teaspoon pepper

In a bowl, combine the first six ingredients. Cut in butter until crumbly. Gradually add water, tossing with a fork until dough forms a ball. Cover and refrigerate for at least 30 minutes.

Roll out pastry to fit a 9-in. tart pan with removable bottom. Transfer pastry to pan; trim even with edge of pan. Line unpricked pastry with a double thickness of heavy-duty foil. Bake at 450° for 8 minutes. Remove foil; bake 5 minutes longer.

In a large nonstick skillet coated with nonstick cooking spray, cook onions and garlic in oil for 2 minutes. Add eggplant; cook for 4-5 minutes or until softened. Cool for 5 minutes. Spoon into crust. Sprinkle with 1 tablespoon Parmesan cheese. Top with tomato slices and pepper rings. Sprinkle with corn.

In a small bowl, combine the eggs, milk, salt and pepper; pour over vegetables. Sprinkle with remaining Parmesan cheese. Bake at 350° for 30-35 minutes or until a knife inserted near the center comes out clean.

NUTRITION FACTS: 1 piece equals 256 calories, 13 g fat (6 g saturated fat), 95 mg cholesterol, 691 mg sodium, 27 g carbohydrate, 3 g fiber, 9 g protein. **DIABETIC EXCHANGES:** 2 fat, 1-1/2 starch, 1 vegetable.

Blushing Penne Pasta

(PICTURED ABOVE)

PREP/TOTAL TIME: 30 Min.   YIELD: 8 Servings

I call on Parmigiano-Reggiano for this rich, flavorful and creamy pasta dish. My friends and family have a hard time believing it's light, but it's actually low in saturated fat.
—Margaret Wilson, Hemet, California

      1 package (16 ounces) penne pasta
      1 cup thinly sliced onions
      2 tablespoons butter
      2 tablespoons minced fresh thyme *or* 2 teaspoons dried thyme
      2 tablespoons minced fresh basil *or* 2 teaspoons dried basil
      1 teaspoon salt
  1-1/2 cups half-and-half cream, *divided*
    1/2 cup white wine *or* reduced-sodium chicken broth
      1 tablespoon tomato paste
      2 tablespoons all-purpose flour
    1/2 cup shredded Parmigiano-Reggiano cheese, *divided*

Cook penne according to package directions. Meanwhile, in a large nonstick skillet over medium heat, cook onions in butter for 8-10 minutes or until lightly browned. Add thyme, basil and salt; cook 1 minute longer. Add 1 cup cream, wine or broth and tomato paste; cook and stir until blended.

Combine flour and remaining cream until smooth; gradually stir into onion mixture. Bring to a boil; cook and stir for 2 minutes or until thickened. Stir in 1/4 cup cheese. Drain penne; toss with sauce. Sprinkle with remaining cheese.

NUTRITION FACTS: 1 cup equals 336 calories, 10 g fat (6 g saturated fat), 34 mg cholesterol, 445 mg sodium, 46 g carbohydrate, 2 g fiber, 12 g protein.

Veggie Cheese Sandwiches

PREP/TOTAL TIME: 30 Min.   YIELD: 4 Servings

I keep the ingredients on hand for these toasted sandwiches. Add whatever vegetables fit your taste, or use this recipe the next time you need to clean out your refrigerator's produce drawer.
—Beverly Little, Marietta, Georgia

  1/2 cup sliced onion
  1/2 cup julienned green pepper
  2/3 cup chopped tomato
  1/2 cup sliced fresh mushrooms
    8 slices Italian bread (1/2 inch thick)
    4 slices reduced-fat process American cheese product
    4 teaspoons butter, softened

In a small nonstick skillet coated with nonstick cooking spray, cook onion and green pepper over medium heat for 2 minutes. Add tomato and mushrooms. Cook and stir until vegetables are tender; drain.

Divide the vegetable mixture over four slices of bread; top with cheese and remaining bread. Butter the top and bottom of each sandwich. In a skillet, toast sandwiches until lightly browned on both sides.

NUTRITION FACTS: 1 sandwich equals 168 calories, 6 g fat (3 g saturated fat), 15 mg cholesterol, 415 mg sodium, 20 g carbohydrate, 2 g fiber, 8 g protein. DIABETIC EXCHANGES: 1 starch, 1 vegetable, 1 fat.

Southwest Lasagna Rolls

(PICTURED BELOW)

MEAT-
LESS

PREP: 20 Min. **BAKE:** 35 Min. **YIELD:** 8 Servings

We love this south-of-the-border lasagna. The cheesy entree comes together easily with a can of vegetarian chili.

—Trisha Kruse, Eagle, Idaho

- 1 can (15 ounces) fat-free vegetarian chili
- 1 carton (15 ounces) reduced-fat ricotta cheese
- 1 cup (4 ounces) shredded reduced-fat Mexican cheese blend
- 1 can (4 ounces) chopped green chilies
- 1 teaspoon taco seasoning
- 1/4 teaspoon salt
- 8 lasagna noodles, cooked and drained
- 1 jar (16 ounces) salsa

In a large bowl, combine the first six ingredients. Spread about 1/2 cup on each noodle; carefully roll up. Place seam side down in a 13-in. x 9-in. x 2-in. baking dish coated with non-stick cooking spray. Cover and bake at 350° for 25 minutes. Uncover; top with salsa. Bake 10 minutes longer or until heated through.

NUTRITION FACTS: 1 lasagna roll equals 256 calories, 6 g fat (3 g saturated fat), 23 mg cholesterol, 645 mg sodium, 35 g carbohydrate, 8 g fiber, 19 g protein. **DIABETIC EXCHANGES:** 2 starch, 1 lean meat, 1 vegetable.

TASTY TIP
For a heart-smart dinner, prepare Southwest Lasagna Rolls, and consider one or two of these no-fuss, meatless side dishes:
- Marinated tomatoes
- Vegetable soup
- Tossed side salad
- Vegetarian refried beans
- Baked tortilla chips

Potato 'n' Roasted Pepper Quesadillas

MEAT-
LESS

PREP: 40 Min. **BAKE:** 10 Min. **YIELD:** 4 Servings

This is a nice alternative to other meatless meals. Using light cheese trims the fat without cutting the flavor.

—Jill Heatwole, Pittsville, Maryland

- 1 medium sweet red pepper
- 1 jalapeno pepper
- 3 medium potatoes, peeled, cooked and cut into 1/8-inch slices
- 1/2 cup chopped onion
- 2 teaspoons canola oil
- 1 tablespoon lime juice
- 1 tablespoon minced fresh cilantro
- 1/2 teaspoon salt
- 1/4 teaspoon pepper
- 1/2 cup shredded reduced-fat cheddar cheese
- 6 flour tortillas (6 inches)

Cut red pepper and jalapeno in half; remove and discard seeds. Place peppers cut side down on a foil-lined baking sheet. Broil 4 in. from the heat for 15-20 minutes or until skins are blistered and blackened. Immediately place peppers in a bowl; cover and let stand for 15-20 minutes. Peel off and discard charred skin. Chop peppers; set aside.

In a nonstick skillet coated with nonstick cooking spray, cook potatoes and onion in oil for 8 minutes or until potatoes are lightly browned and onion is tender. Remove from the heat.

Add the lime juice, cilantro, salt and pepper. Stir in cheese and roasted peppers.

Place three tortillas on a baking sheet coated with non-stick cooking spray. Spoon potato mixture onto each; top each with remaining tortillas and press down firmly.

Bake at 450° for 5 minutes. Spritz top of tortillas with non-stick cooking spray.

Carefully turn over; bake 5 minutes longer or until cheese is melted and tortillas are lightly browned. Cut each into four wedges.

NUTRITION FACTS: 3 wedges equals 262 calories, 7 g fat (2 g saturated fat), 10 mg cholesterol, 364 mg sodium, 40 g carbohydrate, 4 g fiber, 111 g protein. **DIABETIC EXCHANGES:** 2-1/2 starch, 1 lean meat, 1/2 fat.

Editor's Note: When cutting or seeding hot peppers, use rubber or plastic gloves to protect your hands. Avoid touching your face.

MAKE IT EASY
Need to speed things up? Buy a jar of roasted sweet red peppers and use leftover potatoes when preparing the Potato 'n' Roasted Pepper Quesadillas.

Heavenly Earth Burgers

MEAT-LESS

(PICTURED ABOVE)

PREP: 25 Min.　**COOK:** 10 Min.　**YIELD:** 6 Servings

Packed with nutrition, my rice-and-bean patties make a filling entree. Fresh parsley and carrots offer color and sunflower kernels add crunch. 　　　—Wendy McGowan, Poulsbo, Washington

　1-1/2　cups cooked brown rice
　　1/2　cup finely chopped onion
　　1/4　cup sunflower kernels
　　1/4　cup seasoned bread crumbs
　　1/2　cup shredded carrot
　　　3　tablespoons minced fresh parsley
　　　2　tablespoons reduced-sodium soy sauce
　　1/2　teaspoon dried thyme
　　　1　egg
　　　1　egg white
　　　1　cup garbanzo beans *or* chickpeas, rinsed and drained
　1-1/2　teaspoons canola oil
　　　6　whole wheat hamburger buns, split
　　　6　lettuce leaves
　　　6　slices tomato
　　　6　slices onion

In a large bowl, combine the first eight ingredients. In a food processor, combine the egg, egg white and garbanzo beans; cover and process until smooth. Stir into rice mixture. Shape into six patties.

In a nonstick skillet coated with nonstick cooking spray, cook patties in oil for 5-6 minutes on each side or until lightly browned and crisp. Serve on buns with lettuce, tomato and onion.

NUTRITION FACTS: 1 burger equals 320 calories, 9 g fat (1 g saturated fat), 35 mg cholesterol, 634 mg sodium, 49 g carbohydrate, 6 g fiber, 11 g protein. **DIABETIC EXCHANGES:** 3 starch, 1 fat.

Sweet Potato Bean Soup

FAT MEAT-LESS

PREP/TOTAL TIME: 30 Min.　**YIELD:** 4 Servings

I combine sweet potato, black beans and fresh cilantro for a fast and delicious soup. 　　　—Michelle Sweeny, Bloomington, Indiana

　　　1　medium sweet potato, peeled and cubed
　　　1　small green pepper, chopped
　　　1　small onion, chopped
　　　2　garlic cloves, minced
　　　1　teaspoon minced fresh cilantro
　　　1　teaspoon ground cumin
　　　1　can (15 ounces) black beans, rinsed and drained
　　　1　can (14-3/4 ounces) whole kernel corn, drained
　　　2　cups water
　　　1　can (8 ounces) tomato sauce
　　1/4　teaspoon salt
　　1/4　teaspoon pepper
　　　2　green onions, thinly sliced
　　　1　plum tomato, seeded and chopped

Place sweet potato in a small saucepan and cover with water. Bring to a boil. Reduce heat; cover and cook for 13-18 minutes or until tender. Drain, reserving 1/4 cup liquid. Cool slightly. Place sweet potato and reserved liquid in a blender or food processor; cover and process until smooth. Set aside.

In a small saucepan coated with nonstick cooking spray, cook the green pepper, onion and garlic until almost tender. Stir in cilantro and cumin; cook and stir until vegetables are tender. Add the beans, corn, water, tomato sauce, salt, pepper and reserved sweet potato puree; heat through. Garnish with green onions and tomato.

NUTRITION FACTS: 1-1/2 cups equals 224 calories, 1 g fat (trace saturated fat), 0 cholesterol, 901 mg sodium, 41 g carbohydrate, 8 g fiber, 9 g protein. **DIABETIC EXCHANGES:** 2-1/2 starch, 1 vegetable.

Saucy Bow Ties and Broccoli

FAT MEAT-LESS

PREP/TOTAL TIME: 30 Min.　**YIELD:** 8 Servings

Here's my secret to getting my kids to eat veggies. The tasty sauce and fun shape of the bow tie pasta bring them back for second servings of this yummy, meal-in-one every time.
　　　—Kris Capener, Ogden, Utah

　　　3　garlic cloves, minced
　　　1　tablespoon canola oil
　　　1　can (28 ounces) crushed tomatoes, undrained
　　1/4　cup vegetable broth *or* reduced-sodium chicken broth
　　　1　teaspoon dried basil
　　　1　teaspoon sugar
　　1/2　teaspoon salt
　　12　ounces uncooked bow tie pasta
　3-1/2　cups fresh broccoli florets

In a large nonstick skillet, saute garlic in oil until tender. Stir in the tomatoes, broth, basil, sugar and salt. Bring to a boil. Reduce heat; simmer, uncovered, for 13-15 minutes or until thickened, stirring frequently.

Meanwhile, cook pasta according to package directions, adding the broccoli during the last 5 minutes. Drain; top with tomato sauce.

NUTRITION FACTS: 1 cup pasta mixture with 1/2 cup sauce equals 213 calories, 3 g fat (trace saturated fat), 0 cholesterol, 309 mg sodium, 41 g carbohydrate, 4 g fiber, 8 g protein. DIABETIC EXCHANGES: 2 starch, 2 vegetable, 1/2 fat.

Four-Cheese Baked Ziti

MEAT-LESS

(PICTURED BELOW RIGHT)

PREP: 30 Min. **BAKE:** 10 Min. **YIELD:** 8 Servings

A day without pasta is like a day without sunshine! Beefed up with vegetables and cheese, my mouth-watering baked ziti will definitely make days brighter. —Diane Nemitz, Ludington, Michigan

- 1 cup diced onion
- 1/2 cup diced green pepper
- 1/2 cup shredded carrots
- 2 garlic cloves, minced
- 2 cans (14-1/2 ounces *each*) Italian diced tomatoes
- 1 can (15 ounces) crushed tomatoes
- 1 cup vegetable broth
- 1/8 teaspoon crushed red pepper flakes
- 8 ounces uncooked ziti *or* small tube pasta
- 1 cup (8 ounces) part-skim ricotta cheese
- 1/2 cup shredded provolone cheese
- 1/4 cup loosely packed basil leaves, thinly sliced
- 1 cup (4 ounces) shredded part-skim mozzarella cheese
- 1/4 cup grated Parmesan cheese

In a large nonstick skillet coated with nonstick cooking spray, saute the onion, green pepper, carrots and garlic until crisp-tender. Stir in the diced tomatoes, crushed tomatoes, broth and pepper flakes; bring to a boil. Reduce heat; simmer, uncovered, for 15 minutes.

Meanwhile, cook ziti according to package directions; drain and return to pan. Stir in the vegetable mixture, ricotta, provolone and basil.

Transfer to a 13-in. x 9-in. x 2-in. baking dish coated with nonstick cooking spray. Sprinkle with mozzarella and Parmesan. Bake, uncovered, at 425° for 10-15 minutes or until heated through and cheese is melted.

NUTRITION FACTS: 1 cup equals 286 calories, 8 g fat (5 g saturated fat), 24 mg cholesterol, 806 mg sodium, 39 g carbohydrate, 3 g fiber, 16 g protein. DIABETIC EXCHANGES: 3 vegetable, 1-1/2 starch, 1 lean meat, 1 fat.

Wild Mushroom Ravioli

MEAT-LESS

PREP: 35 Min. + Cooling **COOK:** 15 Min. **YIELD:** 4 Servings

From the Light & Tasty Test Kitchen staff, this recipe for home-made ravioli has a delicious twist. Instead of pasta, the creamy mushroom filling is served inside wonton wrappers for a meal that's both easy and satisfying.

- 1 cup water
- 1/2 ounce dried porcini mushrooms
- 1/4 cup finely chopped onion
- 1-1/2 cups sliced fresh shiitake mushrooms
- 3 teaspoons butter, *divided*
- 2 ounces reduced-fat cream cheese
- 1/4 teaspoon salt
- 1/8 teaspoon pepper
- 32 wonton wrappers
- 2 cups sliced fresh button mushrooms
- 2 garlic cloves, minced
- 1 cup Italian tomato sauce
- 2 tablespoons shredded Parmesan cheese
- 2 tablespoons minced fresh parsley

In a small saucepan, combine water and porcini mushrooms. Bring to a boil. Remove from the heat; let stand for 30 minutes. Drain, reserving liquid. Finely chop mushrooms; set aside.

In a small nonstick skillet, saute onion and shiitake mushrooms in 2 teaspoons butter until tender. Add porcini mushrooms and 1/4 cup soaking liquid. Bring to a boil. Reduce heat; simmer, uncovered, for 3-5 minutes or until liquid has evaporated. Remove from the heat. Stir in the cream cheese, salt and pepper. Cool to room temperature.

Spoon about 2 teaspoons of mushroom mixture in the center of a wonton wrapper. (Keep wrappers covered with a damp paper towel until ready to use.) Moisten edges with water, being sure to moisten wrapper all the way to the filling. Top with another wonton wrapper, pressing down around filling to seal. Trim about 1/4 in. from edges if desired. Repeat with remaining wrappers.

Bring a large saucepan or Dutch oven of water to a boil. Add ravioli. Reduce heat to a gentle simmer; cook for 1-2 minutes or until ravioli float to the top and are tender. Drain and keep warm.

In a small saucepan, saute button mushrooms and garlic in remaining butter. Add tomato sauce; heat through. Serve over ravioli. Sprinkle with Parmesan cheese and parsley.

NUTRITION FACTS: 4 ravioli with 1/3 cup sauce equals 331 calories, 8 g fat (4 g saturated fat), 25 mg cholesterol, 970 mg sodium, 54 g carbohydrate, 5 g fiber, 13 g protein.

Potato Gnocchi

MEAT-
LESS

PREP: 35 Min.   **COOK:** 10 Min.   **YIELD:** 8 Servings

My father was Italian and prepared this traditional dish when company visited. The pasta is as tantalizing today as it was when I was a child.   —Ruth Fiori Poyner, Boise, Idaho

    4 cups mashed potatoes (without added milk and butter)
    2 cups all-purpose flour
1-1/2 teaspoons salt
    2 eggs
    1 egg yolk
    4 teaspoons olive oil
    3 quarts water
    1 jar (26 ounces) meatless spaghetti sauce, warmed
  1/4 cup grated Parmesan cheese

In a large bowl, combine the mashed potatoes, flour and salt. In another bowl, whisk the eggs, yolk and olive oil; add to potato mixture. Turn onto a heavily floured surface; knead for 3-5 minutes or until smooth. Divide into fourths. On a floured surface, roll each portion into 3/4-in.-thick ropes; cut into 1-in. pieces.

    In a Dutch oven, bring water to a boil. Cook gnocchi in batches for 45-60 seconds or until they rise to the surface. Remove with a strainer. Serve spaghetti sauce over gnocchi; sprinkle with Parmesan cheese.

NUTRITION FACTS: 3/4 cup gnocchi with 1/3 cup sauce equals 283 calories, 5 g fat (1 g saturated fat), 82 mg cholesterol, 934 mg sodium, 47 g carbohydrate, 5 g fiber, 9 g protein. **DIABETIC EXCHANGES:** 2-1/2 starch, 1 vegetable, 1 fat.

Greek Pizzas
(PICTURED ABOVE)

MEAT-
LESS

PREP/TOTAL TIME: 30 Min.   **YIELD:** 4 Servings

Pita breads make crispy crusts for these individual pizzas. Topped with spinach, tomatoes and basil, as well as feta and ricotta cheeses, the fast pizzas are always a hit.
                    —Doris Allers, Portage, Michigan

    4 pita breads (6 inches)
    1 cup reduced-fat ricotta cheese
1/2 teaspoon garlic powder
    1 package (10 ounces) frozen chopped spinach, thawed and squeezed dry
    3 medium tomatoes, sliced
3/4 cup crumbled feta cheese
3/4 teaspoon dried basil

Place pita breads on a baking sheet. Combine the ricotta cheese and garlic powder; spread over pitas. Top with spinach, tomatoes, feta cheese and basil. Bake at 400° for 12-15 minutes or until bread is lightly browned.

NUTRITION FACTS: 1 pizza equals 320 calories, 7 g fat (4 g saturated fat), 26 mg cholesterol, 642 mg sodium, 46 g carbohydrate, 6 g fiber, 17 g protein. **DIABETIC EXCHANGES:** 2 starch, 2 vegetable, 1 lean meat, 1 fat.

> **TASTY TIP**
> Try replacing the basil in Greek Pizzas with a combination of rosemary and thyme. "Sliced mushrooms also make a good addition," says Doris Allers.

Grilled Veggie Wraps

MEAT-
LESS

PREP: 15 Min. + Marinating   **GRILL:** 15 Min.   **YIELD:** 4 Servings

My father is a meat-and-potatoes eater, but these wraps passed his test!   —Britani Sepanski, Indianapolis, Indiana

    2 tablespoons balsamic vinegar
1-1/2 teaspoons minced fresh basil
1-1/2 teaspoons olive oil
1-1/2 teaspoons molasses
  3/4 teaspoon minced fresh thyme
  1/8 teaspoon salt
  1/8 teaspoon pepper
    1 medium zucchini, cut lengthwise into 1/4-inch slices
    1 medium sweet red pepper, cut into 1-inch pieces
    1 medium red onion, cut into 1/2-inch slices
    4 ounces whole fresh mushrooms, cut into 1/2-inch pieces
    4 ounces fresh sugar snap peas
  1/2 cup crumbled feta cheese
    3 tablespoons reduced-fat cream cheese
    2 tablespoons grated Parmesan cheese
    1 tablespoon reduced-fat mayonnaise
    4 flour tortillas (8 inches)
    4 romaine leaves

In a large resealable plastic bag, combine the first seven ingredients; add vegetables. Seal bag and turn to coat; refrigerate for 2 hours, turning once.

Drain and reserve marinade. In a small bowl, combine cheeses and mayonnaise; set aside. Place vegetables in a grill basket or disposable foil pan with slits cut in the bottom. Grill, uncovered, over medium-high heat for 5 minutes.

Set aside 1 teaspoon marinade. Turn vegetables; baste with remaining marinade. Grill 5-8 minutes longer or until tender. Brush one side of each tortilla with reserved marinade. Grill tortillas, marinade side down, for 1-3 minutes or until lightly toasted. Spread 3 tablespoons of cheese mixture over ungrilled side of tortillas. Top with romaine and 1 cup vegetables; roll up.

NUTRITION FACTS: 1 wrap equals 332 calories, 14 g fat (6 g saturated fat), 26 mg cholesterol, 632 mg sodium, 39 g carbohydrate, 4 g fiber, 13 g protein. **DIABETIC EXCHANGES:** 2 starch, 2 vegetable, 2 fat.

Quinoa-Stuffed Peppers

(PICTURED BELOW)

MEAT-LESS

PREP: 35 Min. **BAKE:** 20 Min. **YIELD:** 6 Servings

Filled with quinoa, these peppers taste yummy. My family and I enjoy them regularly, and I always look forward to leftovers.
—Anna Engle, Streetsboro, Ohio

    1 can (14-1/2 ounces) vegetable broth
  1/4 cup water
    1 bay leaf
    1 cup quinoa, rinsed and drained
    2 *each* medium sweet red, yellow and orange peppers

    4 medium carrots, finely chopped
    2 medium onions, finely chopped
    1 tablespoon canola oil
    2 tablespoons sunflower kernels
    2 teaspoons dried parsley flakes
  1/2 teaspoon salt
  1/2 teaspoon dried basil
  1/2 teaspoon dried oregano
  1/2 teaspoon paprika
  1/8 teaspoon dried marjoram
  1/8 teaspoon dried thyme
  Dash cayenne pepper

In a small saucepan, bring the broth, water and bay leaf to a boil. Add quinoa. Reduce heat; simmer, uncovered, for 15-20 minutes or until liquid is absorbed. Discard bay leaf.

Cut peppers in half lengthwise and discard seeds. In a large kettle, cook peppers in boiling water for 3-5 minutes or until crisp-tender. Drain and rinse in cold water; invert onto paper towels.

In a large nonstick skillet, saute the carrots and onions in oil until tender. Add the quinoa, sunflower kernels and seasonings; cook and stir for 2 minutes or until heated through. Spoon into pepper halves.

Place in a 15-in. x 10-in. x 1-in. baking pan coated with nonstick cooking spray. Bake, uncovered, at 350° for 20-25 minutes or until peppers are tender.

NUTRITION FACTS: 2 stuffed pepper halves equals 221 calories, 6 g fat (1 g saturated fat), 0 cholesterol, 520 mg sodium, 38 g carbohydrate, 6 g fiber, 7 g protein. **DIABETIC EXCHANGES:** 3 vegetable, 1-1/2 starch, 1 fat.

Broccoli Tortellini Alfredo

MEAT-LESS

PREP/TOTAL TIME: 20 Min. **YIELD:** 4 Servings

Nutmeg is a pleasant addition to the creamy sauce for my pasta dish. It has great flavor without the guilt. Refrigerated tortellini, a sauce mix and a few kitchen staples help me get it on the table in no time. *—Mitzi Sentiff, Alexandria, Virginia*

      2 quarts water
      1 package (9 ounces) refrigerated cheese tortellini
    3/4 pound fresh broccoli florets
      1 envelope Alfredo sauce mix
  1-1/2 cups fat-free milk
      2 teaspoons reduced-fat butter
    1/8 teaspoon ground nutmeg
    1/4 cup shredded Parmesan cheese
    1/4 teaspoon pepper

In a large saucepan, bring water to a boil. Add tortellini and broccoli; cook until tender. Meanwhile, in a small saucepan, whisk the sauce mix and milk. Add butter and nutmeg; bring to a boil. Reduce heat; simmer, uncovered, for 2 minutes, stirring constantly.

Drain tortellini and broccoli; place in a large bowl. Stir in the Alfredo sauce, Parmesan cheese and pepper.

NUTRITION FACTS: 1-1/4 cups equals 262 calories, 8 g fat (4 g saturated fat), 23 mg cholesterol, 919 mg sodium, 35 g carbohydrate, 5 g fiber, 16 g protein. **DIABETIC EXCHANGES:** 2 starch, 1 vegetable, 1 fat, 1/2 fat-free milk.

Editor's Note: This recipe was tested with Land O'Lakes light stick butter.

Tofu Manicotti

(PICTURED BELOW)

MEAT-LESS

PREP: 25 Min.　**BAKE:** 50 Min.　**YIELD:** 5 Servings

To create a light main course, I borrowed ideas from different recipes. This pasta supper is easy to prepare, my toddlers love it and no one suspects that it includes tofu.
—Carolyn Diana, Scottsdale, Arizona

- 2 cups meatless spaghetti sauce
- 1 can (14-1/2 ounces) diced tomatoes, undrained
- 1/3 cup finely shredded zucchini
- 1/4 cup finely shredded carrot
- 1/2 teaspoon Italian seasoning
- 1 package (12.3 ounces) firm silken tofu
- 1 cup (8 ounces) 1% cottage cheese
- 1 cup (4 ounces) shredded part-skim mozzarella cheese
- 1 tablespoon grated Parmesan cheese
- 10 uncooked manicotti shells

Combine the spaghetti sauce, tomatoes, zucchini, carrot and Italian seasoning; spread 3/4 cup into a 13-in. x 9-in. x 2-in. baking dish coated with nonstick cooking spray. Combine the tofu and cheeses; stuff into uncooked manicotti shells. Place over spaghetti sauce; top with remaining sauce.

Cover and bake at 375° for 50-55 minutes or until noodles are tender. Let stand for 5 minutes before serving.

NUTRITION FACTS: 2 stuffed manicotti shells equals 319 calories, 7 g fat (3 g saturated fat), 16 mg cholesterol, 885 mg sodium, 42 g carbohydrate, 4 g fiber, 23 g protein. **DIABETIC EXCHANGES:** 3 vegetable, 2 lean meat, 1-1/2 starch, 1/2 fat.

TASTY TIP
The manicotti call for dressing up jarred spaghetti sauce, but feel free to use a homemade sauce if you would like.

Garbanzo Bean Pitas

MEAT-LESS

PREP/TOTAL TIME: 20 Min.　**YIELD:** 4 Servings

This is a super meatless recipe for informal dinners and quick lunches alike. I add a little horseradish to my pitas for extra flair.
—Susan LeBrun, Sulphur, Louisiana

- 1 can (15 ounces) garbanzo beans *or* chickpeas, rinsed and drained
- 1/2 cup fat-free mayonnaise
- 1 tablespoon water
- 2 tablespoons minced fresh parsley
- 2 tablespoons chopped walnuts
- 1 tablespoon chopped onion
- 1 garlic clove, minced
- 1/8 teaspoon pepper
- 2 whole wheat pita breads (6 inches), halved
- 4 lettuce leaves
- 1/2 small cucumber, thinly sliced
- 1 small tomato, seeded and chopped
- 1/4 cup fat-free ranch salad dressing, optional

In a blender or food processor, combine the first eight ingredients; cover and process until smooth. Spoon 1/3 cup bean mixture into each pita half. Top with lettuce, cucumber and tomato. Serve with ranch dressing if desired.

NUTRITION FACTS: 1 filled pita half (calculated without ranch dressing) equals 241 calories, 6 g fat (trace saturated fat), 3 mg cholesterol, 552 mg sodium, 41 g carbohydrate, 8 g fiber, 9 g protein. **DIABETIC EXCHANGES:** 2-1/2 starch, 1 very lean meat, 1/2 fat.

Egg Foo Yong

MEAT-LESS

PREP: 25 Min.　**COOK:** 25 Min.　**YIELD:** 4 Servings

This Chinese-American classic may require a little extra effort, but it's well worth it. Try it with cups of hot tea and fortune cookies for dessert.
—Karen Fitterer, Portland, Oregon

- 1-1/4 cups chopped celery
- 1-1/4 cups chopped fresh mushrooms
- 1-1/4 cups canned bean sprouts, chopped
- 1/3 cup chopped green onions
- 1/4 cup chopped onion
- 1/4 cup chopped water chestnuts
- 2 tablespoons canola oil
- 2-1/4 teaspoons reduced-sodium soy sauce
- 1/2 teaspoon garlic powder
- 1/4 teaspoon seasoned salt
- 4 eggs, beaten
- 2 egg whites, beaten
- 1/3 cup cracker meal

SAUCE:
- 1 tablespoon cornstarch
- 1 tablespoon sugar
- 1/4 cup cold water
- 1 cup vegetable broth
- 2 teaspoons cider vinegar
- 2 teaspoons reduced-sodium soy sauce
- 1 teaspoon browning sauce, optional

1/2 teaspoon garlic powder

1/2 teaspoon onion powder

1/2 teaspoon seasoned salt

In a large bowl, combine the first 10 ingredients. Stir in eggs, egg whites and cracker meal. Drop by 1/2 cupfuls into a large nonstick skillet coated with nonstick cooking spray. Cook for 3-4 minutes on each side or until browned.

Meanwhile, for sauce, combine cornstarch and sugar in a saucepan; stir in water until smooth. Add broth, vinegar, soy sauce, browning sauce if desired and seasonings. Bring to a boil; cook and stir for 2 minutes or until thickened. Serve with egg foo yong.

NUTRITION FACTS: 2 patties with 1/4 cup sauce equals 238 calories, 14 g fat (2 g saturated fat), 213 mg cholesterol, 939 mg sodium, 18 g carbohydrate, 3 g fiber, 11 g protein. **DIABETIC EXCHANGES:** 2 fat, 1 lean meat, 1 vegetable, 1/2 starch.

Spinach-Pine Nut Pasta

MEAT-LESS

PREP/TOTAL TIME: 20 Min.   **YIELD:** 5 Servings

This is a fantastic recipe. It's easy to prepare with a taste that rivals dishes served in fancy Italian restaurants.

—Katie Graczyk, Darien, Illinois

   8 ounces uncooked gemelli *or* spiral pasta

1/2 cup sun-dried tomatoes (not packed in oil), chopped

   8 ounces coarsely chopped fresh spinach

1-1/2 cups fat-free milk

   1 package (1.6 ounces) Alfredo sauce mix

1/2 cup pine nuts, *divided*

1/4 teaspoon salt

Cook pasta according to package directions, stirring in the tomatoes and spinach during the last 4 minutes of cooking time. Meanwhile, in a small saucepan, combine milk and Alfredo sauce mix. Bring to a boil; cook and stir for 1 minute or until thickened. Stir in 1/4 cup pine nuts and salt.

Drain pasta and vegetables; toss with Alfredo sauce. Sprinkle with remaining pine nuts.

NUTRITION FACTS: 1 cup equals 337 calories, 10 g fat (2 g saturated fat), 2 mg cholesterol, 618 mg sodium, 49 g carbohydrate, 4 g fiber, 15 g protein. **DIABETIC EXCHANGES:** 2-1/2 starch, 2 fat, 1 vegetable.

marvelous mushrooms

Once simply used to "beef up" side dishes and pasta sauces, mushrooms are now often key in replacing the meat found in many main courses. Keep these varieties in mind the next time you're looking to try something new.

- Portobello. Firm, large-capped mushrooms with robust flavor. They're great for marinating.

- Shiitake. Often used in Asian entrees. They are identified by umbrella-shaped caps.

- Crimini. Similar in appearance to button mushrooms but with a more pronounced flavor.

- Porcini. Woodsy mushrooms with thick stalks and reddish caps. Dried porcini mushrooms, as opposed

Portobello Pockets

MEAT-LESS

(PICTURED ABOVE)

PREP: 30 Min. + Marinating   **COOK:** 10 Min.   **YIELD:** 8 Servings

This recipe is one of my favorites. The sandwiches are easy and so loaded with fresh veggies, no one misses the meat.

—Elissa Armbruster, Medford, New Jersey

1/4 cup water

   3 tablespoons lime juice

   2 tablespoons canola oil

   1 tablespoon Italian seasoning

   1 teaspoon dried minced garlic

1/2 teaspoon dried celery flakes

1/4 teaspoon salt

1/4 teaspoon ground cumin

1/4 teaspoon ground nutmeg

1/4 teaspoon pepper

1/8 teaspoon cayenne pepper

   1 pound sliced baby portobello mushrooms

   1 *each* medium sweet yellow and red pepper, thinly sliced

   1 medium red onion, thinly sliced

   2 small zucchini, cut into 1/4-inch slices

   1 cup (4 ounces) shredded reduced-fat Mexican cheese blend

   8 pita breads (6 inches), cut in half

In a large resealable bag, combine the first 11 ingredients. Add the mushrooms, peppers, onion and zucchini; seal bag and turn to coat. Refrigerate overnight.

In a large nonstick skillet coated with nonstick cooking spray, cook and stir the vegetable mixture over medium-high heat for 6-8 minutes or until crisp-tender. Stir in cheese; cook 2-3 minutes longer or until cheese is melted. Stuff each pita half with 1/2 cup vegetable-cheese mixture. Serve immediately.

NUTRITION FACTS: 2 stuffed pita halves equals 272 calories, 8 g fat (2 g saturated fat), 10 mg cholesterol, 500 mg sodium, 41 g carbohydrate, 3 g fiber, 12 g protein. **DIABETIC EXCHANGES:** 2 starch, 1 lean meat, 1 vegetable, 1/2 fat.

Meatless Chili Mac

(PICTURED ABOVE)

FAT MEAT-LESS

PREP: 15 Min.   COOK: 25 Min.   YIELD: 8 Servings (2-1/2 quarts)

I came across this recipe in a newspaper years ago, and it's been a real hit at our house ever since. It's fast, filling and appealing to all ages. —Cindy Ragan, North Huntingdon, Pennsylvania

- 1 large onion, chopped
- 1 medium green pepper, chopped
- 1 garlic clove, minced
- 1 tablespoon olive oil
- 2 cups water
- 1-1/2 cups uncooked elbow macaroni
- 1 can (16 ounces) mild chili beans, undrained
- 1 can (15-1/2 ounces) great northern beans, rinsed and drained
- 1 can (14-1/2 ounces) diced tomatoes, undrained
- 1 can (8 ounces) tomato sauce
- 4 teaspoons chili powder
- 1 teaspoon salt
- 1 teaspoon ground cumin
- 1/2 cup fat-free sour cream

In a large saucepan or Dutch oven, saute the onion, green pepper and garlic in oil until tender. Stir in the water, macaroni, beans, tomatoes, tomato sauce and seasonings. Bring to a boil. Reduce heat; cover and simmer for 15-20 minutes or until macaroni is tender. Top each serving with 1 tablespoon sour cream.

NUTRITION FACTS: 1-1/4 cups equals 214 calories, 3 g fat (1 g saturated fat), 3 mg cholesterol, 857 mg sodium, 37 g carbohydrate, 8 g fiber, 10 g protein. **DIABETIC EXCHANGES:** 2 starch, 1 very lean meat, 1 vegetable.

Ginger Plum Stir-Fry

MEAT-LESS

PREP/TOTAL TIME: 30 Min.   YIELD: 4 Servings

Here's a great way to eat vegetables such as mushrooms, sweet red pepper and shredded cabbage. I serve this dish over cooked rice. —Evelyn Joan Brewer, Bluffton, Indiana

- 4 teaspoons cornstarch
- 1/2 teaspoon ground ginger
- 3/4 cup vegetable broth
- 1/4 cup reduced-sodium soy sauce
- 1/4 cup plum sauce
- 1 small sweet red pepper, cut into chunks
- 1 garlic clove, minced
- 2 teaspoons canola oil
- 1 cup sliced fresh mushrooms
- 1 package (16 ounces) coleslaw mix
- 1/4 cup thinly sliced green onions
- 1 package (12 ounces) frozen vegetarian meat crumbles

In a small bowl, combine cornstarch and ginger. Stir in the broth until smooth. Stir in the soy sauce and plum sauce until blended; set aside.

In a large nonstick skillet or wok coated with nonstick cooking spray, stir-fry red pepper and garlic in oil for 2 minutes. Add mushrooms; stir-fry 2 minutes longer. Add coleslaw mix and onions; stir-fry for 2 minutes.

Add vegetarian meat crumbles. Stir broth mixture; gradually stir into skillet. Bring to a boil; cook and stir for 1-2 minutes or until thickened and crumbles are heated through.

NUTRITION FACTS: 1-1/2 cups equals 247 calories, 6 g fat (1 g saturated fat), trace cholesterol, 1,264 mg sodium, 27 g carbohydrate, 7 g fiber, 20 g protein. **DIABETIC EXCHANGES:** 2 lean meat, 2 vegetable, 1 starch, 1/2 fat.

Southwestern Bean Patties
(PICTURED ABOVE)

PREP/TOTAL TIME: 30 Min.   **YIELD:** 6 Servings

I first made this recipe for a crowd of 11 people. Everyone loved the flavor and the guacamole topping. It was a real hit!
—Debby Chiorino, Oxnard, California

    1 small onion, chopped
1/4 cup finely chopped sweet red pepper
    1 garlic clove, minced
    5 teaspoons canola oil, *divided*
    1 can (16 ounces) fat-free refried beans
3/4 cup dry bread crumbs
    1 can (4 ounces) chopped green chilies, drained
    2 tablespoons minced fresh cilantro
1/4 teaspoon ground cumin
1/8 teaspoon pepper
1/3 cup cornmeal
    6 hamburger buns, split
1/2 cup guacamole
1/2 cup salsa

In a large nonstick skillet, saute the onion, red pepper and garlic in 1-1/2 teaspoons oil until tender. In a bowl, combine the refried beans, bread crumbs, chilies, cilantro, cumin, pepper and onion mixture; mix well. Shape into six patties; coat with cornmeal.

In the same skillet, cook patties in batches in remaining oil over medium-high heat for 2-3 minutes on each side or until lightly browned.

Place patties on bun bottoms (save bun tops for another use). Top each with 4 teaspoons of guacamole and 4 teaspoons of salsa.

NUTRITION FACTS: 1 serving equals 291 calories, 9 g fat (1 g saturated fat), 0 cholesterol, 760 mg sodium, 44 g carbohydrate, 9 g fiber, 11 g protein. **DIABETIC EXCHANGES:** 3 starch, 1 very lean meat, 1 fat.

Mushroom Pasta Medley
(PICTURED BELOW)

PREP: 15 Min.   **COOK:** 20 Min.   **YIELD:** 4 Servings

After trying something similar in a restaurant, I created this entree that features three types of mushrooms. My husband can't stop raving about it.   —Virginia Trent, Dayton, New Jersey

    6 ounces uncooked penne *or* medium tube pasta
    1 garlic clove, minced
    1 tablespoon butter
    1 tablespoon olive oil
    6 ounces fresh baby portobello mushrooms, sliced
    2 ounces fresh crimini mushrooms, sliced
    2 ounces fresh oyster mushrooms, sliced
    3 green onions, thinly sliced
    1 cup vegetable broth *or* reduced-sodium chicken broth
    2 tablespoons all-purpose flour
1/2 cup fat-free half-and-half
    2 tablespoons sherry *or* additional broth
    1 tablespoon shredded Parmesan cheese

Cook pasta according to package directions. Meanwhile, in a large nonstick skillet coated with nonstick cooking spray, cook garlic in butter and oil for 1 minute. Add portobello and crimini mushrooms; cook for 3 minutes. Add oyster mushrooms and onions; cook 3-4 minutes longer or until mushrooms are almost tender.

Add broth. Bring to a boil; boil for 2 minutes. Combine the flour and half-and-half until smooth; stir into skillet. Add sherry or additional broth. Bring to a boil; cook and stir for 2 minutes or until thickened.

Drain the pasta and stir into mushroom mixture; heat through. Sprinkle with Parmesan cheese.

NUTRITION FACTS: 1-1/4 cups equals 279 calories, 8 g fat (3 g saturated fat), 9 mg cholesterol, 242 mg sodium, 42 g carbohydrate, 3 g fiber, 11 g protein. **DIABETIC EXCHANGES:** 2-1/2 starch, 1-1/2 fat, 1 vegetable.

1/8 teaspoon salt

10 flour tortillas (6 inches)

1 cup (4 ounces) shredded reduced-fat cheddar cheese

In a large nonstick skillet coated with nonstick cooking spray, saute the yellow pepper, onion and garlic in oil for 2 minutes. Stir in the tomatoes and corn; cook 2 minutes longer. Add the black beans, pepper and salt. Cook until the vegetables are tender; drain.

Spritz one side of each tortilla with nonstick cooking spray; place plain side up on baking sheets coated with nonstick cooking spray. Spoon bean mixture onto half of each tortilla; sprinkle with cheese. Fold tortilla over filling.

Bake at 400° for 6 minutes. Carefully turn over; bake 4-7 minutes longer or until cheese is melted.

NUTRITION FACTS: 2 quesadillas equals 381 calories, 12 g fat (3 g saturated fat), 16 mg cholesterol, 820 mg sodium, 53 g carbohydrate, 6 g fiber, 18 g protein. **DIABETIC EXCHANGES:** 3-1/2 starch, 1 lean meat, 1 vegetable, 1 fat.

Curried Tofu Stir-Fry

MEAT-LESS

PREP: 25 Min.   **COOK:** 15 Min.   **YIELD:** 6 Servings

This Asian-inspired stir-fry will help you discover how tasty tofu can be. The blend of flavors makes this main dish appeal to folks who've never tried tofu. —Trisha Kruse, Eagle, Idaho

1 can (14 ounces) light coconut milk

1/4 cup reduced-sodium soy sauce

2 tablespoons cornstarch

1-1/2 teaspoons curry powder

1 teaspoon minced fresh gingerroot

1 teaspoon hoisin sauce

1/2 teaspoon salt

1/2 teaspoon brown sugar

1/2 teaspoon chili powder

1/2 teaspoon crushed red pepper flakes

1 package (16 ounces) firm tofu, cubed

2 teaspoons canola oil

1 medium sweet yellow pepper, julienned

1/2 pound sliced fresh mushrooms

8 green onions, cut into 1-inch pieces

4 cups shredded cabbage

4 plum tomatoes, chopped

3 cups hot cooked brown rice

In a small bowl, combine the first 10 ingredients; set aside. In a large nonstick skillet or wok coated with nonstick cooking spray, stir-fry tofu in oil for 2-3 minutes or until heated through. Remove and keep warm.

In the same pan, stir-fry yellow pepper for 1 minute. Add mushrooms and onions; stir-fry 2 minutes longer. Add cabbage and tomatoes; stir-fry for 2 minutes.

Stir coconut milk mixture and add to skillet; bring to a boil. Return tofu to skillet. Cook and stir for 1-2 minutes or until thickened and vegetables are crisp-tender. Serve with rice.

NUTRITION FACTS: 1-1/3 cups stir-fry with 1/2 cup rice equals 294 calories, 11 g fat (4 g saturated fat), trace cholesterol, 658 mg sodium, 38 g carbohydrate, 5 g fiber, 12 g protein. **DIABETIC EXCHANGES:** 2 starch, 2 vegetable, 1-1/2 fat, 1 lean meat.

Black Bean Quesadillas

MEAT-LESS

(PICTURED ABOVE)

PREP: 25 Min.   **BAKE:** 10 Min.   **YIELD:** 5 Servings

These savory bean and vegetable quesadillas are great for those who love Mexican flavors but can't handle too much heat. I serve them with salsa and fat-free sour cream.
—Cherylyn Radford, Fox Creek, Alberta

1 medium sweet yellow pepper, chopped

1 cup finely chopped onion

2 garlic cloves, minced

1 teaspoon canola oil

2 medium tomatoes, chopped

1 cup frozen corn, thawed

1 can (15 ounces) black beans, rinsed and drained

1/4 teaspoon pepper

From the
Bread Basket

Nothing beats the heartwarming aroma of freshly baked bread wafting through the house. All-time favorites such as golden loaves, sweet muffins and old-fashioned scones can be enjoyed without guilt. Just consider the heavenly baked goods that appear in this chapter.

Swedish Tea Ring, p. 192

Chocolate-Cherry Banana Bread
(PICTURED BELOW)

PREP: 30 Min.   **BAKE:** 45 Min. + Cooling   **YIELD:** 1 Loaf (16 slices)

I developed this sweet chocolate-and-banana bread after looking for ways to use extra dried tart cherries. It's so rich and moist, no one will guess it's lighter.   —Cindy Beberman, Orland Park, Illinois

- 1 cup boiling water
- 2/3 cup dried cherries
- 1/4 cup butter, softened
- 3/4 cup sugar
- 2 egg whites
- 1 egg
- 1 large ripe banana, mashed
- 1/2 cup fat-free sour cream
- 2 teaspoons vanilla extract
- 1-1/2 cups all-purpose flour
- 1/3 cup baking cocoa
- 1 teaspoon baking powder
- 1/2 teaspoon baking soda
- 1/2 teaspoon ground cinnamon
- 1/4 teaspoon salt
- 1/4 cup chopped pecans

In a small bowl, pour water over cherries; let stand for 15 minutes. Meanwhile, in a large mixing bowl, beat butter and sugar until crumbly, about 2 minutes. Add egg whites and egg, beating well after each addition.

Combine the banana, sour cream and vanilla. Combine the flour, cocoa, baking powder, baking soda, cinnamon and salt; add to creamed mixture alternately with banana mixture. Drain cherries and coarsely chop; fold into batter with pecans.

Pour into a 9-in. x 5-in. x 3-in. loaf pan coated with nonstick cooking spray. Bake at 350° for 45-50 minutes or until a toothpick inserted near the center comes out clean. Cool for 10 minutes before removing from pan to a wire rack to cool completely.

NUTRITION FACTS: 1 slice equals 164 calories, 5 g fat (2 g saturated fat), 22 mg cholesterol, 148 mg sodium, 27 g carbohydrate, 1 g fiber, 3 g protein. **DIABETIC EXCHANGES:** 2 starch, 1/2 fat.

Scottish Oat Scones
MEAT-LESS

PREP: 25 Min.   **BAKE:** 15 Min.   **YIELD:** 1-1/2 Dozen

Whether served for breakfast or afternoon tea, nothing beats cranberry-raisin scones. Spread with a little jam, they are a slice of heaven.   —Ruth Lee, Troy, Ontario

- 1-3/4 cups quick-cooking oats
- 1-1/2 cups all-purpose flour
- 1/3 cup sugar
- 3 teaspoons baking powder
- 3/4 teaspoon salt
- 1/2 cup fat-free milk
- 1/3 cup canola oil
- 1/4 cup butter, melted
- 1 egg
- 1 egg yolk
- 1/2 cup raisins
- 1/2 cup dried cranberries

TOPPING:
- 1 egg white
- 1 teaspoon water
- 1 teaspoon sugar

In a large bowl, combine the oats, flour, sugar, baking powder and salt. In a small bowl, combine the milk, oil, butter, egg and yolk; stir into oat mixture just until blended. Stir in raisins and cranberries (dough will be sticky).

Turn dough onto a well-floured surface; divide in half. With lightly floured hands, pat each portion of dough into a 6-3/4-in. circle, 1/2 in. thick. Cut each into nine wedges; place 2 in. apart on baking sheets coated with nonstick cooking spray.

In a small bowl, beat egg white and water; brush over tops of scones. Sprinkle with sugar. Bake at 400° for 12-15 minutes or until golden brown. Serve warm.

NUTRITION FACTS: 1 scone equals 175 calories, 8 g fat (2 g saturated fat), 31 mg cholesterol, 202 mg sodium, 23 g carbohydrate, 1 g fiber, 3 g protein. **DIABETIC EXCHANGES:** 1-1/2 fat, 1 starch, 1/2 fruit.

MAKE IT EASY
Always pat scone dough into a circle that meets the dimensions noted in the recipe. When cutting the wedges, flour the utensil often so the dough won't stick to it.

Delightful Holiday Bread
(PICTURED ABOVE)

FAT

PREP: 40 Min. + Rising   **BAKE:** 30 Min.   **YIELD:** 1 Loaf (24 slices)

The first time I made this braided bread for Christmas, everyone loved it. In fact, when my sister-in-law came for a visit the following July, she asked me to teach her how to make the impressive, almond-flavored loaf.
—Cheri Neustifter, Sturtevant, Wisconsin

2 packages (1/4 ounce *each*) active dry yeast
1-3/4 cups warm water (110° to 115°)
2 eggs
3 tablespoons sugar
2 tablespoons almond extract
2 tablespoons canola oil
1-1/2 teaspoons salt
5-3/4 to 6-1/4 cups all-purpose flour
TOPPING:
1 egg
1 tablespoon water
5 teaspoons sugar
3 tablespoons sliced almonds

In a mixing bowl, dissolve yeast in water. Add eggs, sugar, extract, oil, salt and 4 cups flour; beat until smooth. Stir in enough remaining flour to form a soft dough (dough will be sticky).

Turn onto a lightly floured surface; knead until smooth and elastic, about 6-8 minutes. Place in a bowl coated with nonstick cooking spray; turn once to coat top. Cover and let rise until doubled, about 1 hour.

Punch dough down; turn onto a lightly floured surface. Divide into thirds; shape each portion into a 20-in. rope. Place ropes on a large baking sheet coated with nonstick cooking spray; braid. Pinch ends together, forming a round loaf. Cover and let rise until doubled, about 40 minutes.

Beat egg and water; brush over loaf. Sprinkle with sugar and almonds. Bake at 350° for 30-35 minutes or until golden brown. Remove to a wire rack.

NUTRITION FACTS: 1 slice equals 147 calories, 2 g fat (trace saturated fat), 20 mg cholesterol, 154 mg sodium, 26 g carbohydrate, 1 g fiber, 4 g protein. **DIABETIC EXCHANGES:** 1-1/2 starch, 1/2 fat.

Favorite Recipe Made Lighter

SWEET, TENDER quick breads are a favorite of most bakers, but Joanne Jones of Salisbury, Maryland had a special request regarding her Poppy Seed Bread.

"A lot of my co-workers and I are on a weight-loss plan and would like to calculate how many points the bread has. Better yet," she shares, "could you do a makeover on the recipe?"

Loaded with butter, brown sugar and eggs and topped with a heavy glaze, the loaf posed several challenges for our makeover experts. They started by swapping out some of the whole eggs for egg whites and substituting half of the butter with applesauce.

Applesauce added sweetness, so the sugar was reduced. In addition, fat-free milk was used in the glaze and the amount of thick, heavy glaze was decreased overall.

With 113 fewer calories, half the cholesterol and 10 grams less sugar per slice, golden Makeover Poppy Seed Bread is a guilt-free treat Joanne can truly enjoy.

Poppy Seed Bread

PREP: 15 Min.   **BAKE:** 40 Min. + Cooling   **YIELD:** 12 Servings

        1 cup butter, softened
        1 cup packed brown sugar
        4 eggs
        1 teaspoon vanilla *or* almond extract
   1-1/3 cups all-purpose flour
        1/4 cup poppy seeds
   1-1/4 teaspoons baking powder
        1/4 teaspoon salt
        1 cup confectioners' sugar
        1 to 2 tablespoons milk

In a large mixing bowl, cream butter and brown sugar. Add eggs, one at a time, beating well after each addition. Beat in vanilla. Combine the flour, poppy seeds, baking powder and salt; gradually add to creamed mixture.

Spread into a greased 9-in. x 5-in. x 3-in. loaf pan. Bake at 350° for 40-45 minutes or until a toothpick inserted near the center comes out clean. Cool for 10 minutes before removing from pan to a wire rack to cool completely.

For glaze, combine confectioners' sugar and enough milk to achieve desired consistency; drizzle over bread.

NUTRITION FACTS: 1 slice equals 334 calories, 18 g fat (10 g saturated fat), 112 mg cholesterol, 275 mg sodium, 39 g carbohydrate, 1 g fiber, 4 g protein.

MAKEOVER TIP
A little glaze goes a long way. When topping baked goods, simply use less glaze to cut the calories, fat and sugar.

Makeover Poppy Seed Bread
(PICTURED ABOVE)

PREP: 15 Min.   **BAKE:** 40 Min. + Cooling   **YIELD:** 12 Servings

        1/2 cup butter, softened
        2/3 cup packed brown sugar
          2 eggs
          4 egg whites
        1/2 cup unsweetened applesauce
          1 teaspoon vanilla *or* almond extract
   1-1/3 cups all-purpose flour
        1/4 cup poppy seeds
   1-1/4 teaspoons baking powder
        1/4 teaspoon salt
        1/2 cup confectioners' sugar
   1-1/2 to 3 teaspoons fat-free milk

In a large mixing bowl, cream butter and brown sugar. Add eggs, one at a time, beating well after each addition. Beat in the egg whites, applesauce and vanilla (mixture will appear curdled). Combine the flour, poppy seeds, baking powder and salt; gradually add to creamed mixture.

Spread into a 9-in. x 5-in. x 3-in. loaf pan coated with nonstick cooking spray. Bake at 350° for 40-45 minutes or until a toothpick inserted near the center comes out clean. Cool for 10 minutes before removing from pan to a wire rack to cool completely.

For glaze, in a small bowl, combine confectioners' sugar and enough milk to achieve desired consistency; drizzle over bread.

NUTRITION FACTS: 1 slice equals 221 calories, 10 g fat (5 g saturated fat), 56 mg cholesterol, 203 mg sodium, 30 g carbohydrate, 1 g fiber, 4 g protein. **DIABETIC EXCHANGES:** 2 starch, 2 fat.

Onion Poppy Seed Biscuits

(PICTURED BELOW)

PREP/TOTAL TIME: 30 Min.   **YIELD:** 1 Dozen

Perfect alongside a salad or casserole, these buttermilk biscuits are ready in no time. Golden on the outside, tender on the inside, they offer a mild onion flavor with every bite. The L&T home economists hope you enjoy them.

        1 medium onion, finely chopped
        2 cups all-purpose flour
        1 teaspoon baking powder
        1 teaspoon brown sugar
    3/4 teaspoon poppy seeds
    1/2 teaspoon salt
    1/2 teaspoon baking soda
    1/4 cup cold butter
        1 cup 1% buttermilk

In a small nonstick skillet coated with nonstick cooking spray, saute the onion until tender; set aside. In a large bowl, combine the flour, baking powder, brown sugar, poppy seeds, salt and baking soda. Cut in butter until mixture resembles coarse crumbs. Stir in onions. Stir in buttermilk just until moistened.

Turn dough onto a lightly floured surface; knead 6-8 times. Pat to 1/2-in. thickness; cut with a floured 2-1/2-in. biscuit cutter. Place 2 in. apart on baking sheets coated with nonstick cooking spray. Bake at 450° for 9-12 minutes or until golden brown. Serve warm.

NUTRITION FACTS: 1 biscuit equals 125 calories, 4 g fat (3 g saturated fat), 11 mg cholesterol, 245 mg sodium, 18 g carbohydrate, 1 g fiber, 3 g protein. **DIABETIC EXCHANGES:** 1 starch, 1 fat.

Festive Poppy Seed Scones

(PICTURED ABOVE)

PREP: 20 Min.   **BAKE:** 15 Min.   **YIELD:** 1 Dozen

With their eye-opening citrus burst, these scones are perfect for breakfasts and brunches with friends. I like to serve them warm from the oven.   —Lisa Varner, Greenville, South Carolina

        2 cups all-purpose flour
    1/2 cup sugar
    1/2 cup quick-cooking oats
        1 tablespoon poppy seeds
        2 teaspoons baking powder
    1/2 teaspoon salt
    1/4 teaspoon baking soda
    1/3 cup cold butter
        1 egg
    1/2 cup orange juice
        3 tablespoons buttermilk
    1/2 cup dried cranberries
        1 teaspoon grated orange peel

In a large bowl, combine the first seven ingredients. Cut in butter until mixture resembles coarse crumbs. In a small bowl, whisk the egg, orange juice and buttermilk; add to crumb mixture just until moistened. Stir in cranberries and orange peel.

Turn onto a lightly floured surface; gently knead 6-8 times. Divide dough in half. Pat each portion into a 6-in. circle. Place circles on a baking sheet coated with nonstick cooking spray. Cut each circle into six wedges, but do not separate.

Bake at 375° for 15-20 minutes or until golden brown. Cool for 5 minutes before removing to a wire rack. Serve warm.

NUTRITION FACTS: 1 scone equals 197 calories, 6 g fat (3 g saturated fat), 31 mg cholesterol, 253 mg sodium, 32 g carbohydrate, 1 g fiber, 4 g protein. **DIABETIC EXCHANGES:** 2 starch, 1 fat.

Winter Squash Muffins
(PICTURED ABOVE)

PREP: 20 Min.   **BAKE:** 25 Min.   **YIELD:** 1 Dozen

Moist, scrumptious and studded with raisins, these easy muffins make a lovely breakfast treat, but they're also a delightful way to round out meals. —Mary Detweiler, West Farmington, Ohio

1-1/3 cups whole wheat flour
  1/2 cup raisins
    1 teaspoon baking powder
  3/4 teaspoon baking soda
  1/2 teaspoon ground cinnamon
  1/4 teaspoon salt
    1 egg
    1 cup pureed cooked winter squash
  1/2 cup buttermilk
  1/3 cup honey
  1/4 cup butter, melted

In a large bowl, combine the first six ingredients. In a small bowl, whisk the egg, squash, buttermilk, honey and butter. Stir into the dry ingredients just until moistened.

Coat muffin cups with nonstick cooking spray or use paper liners; fill half full. Bake at 350° for 25-30 minutes or until a toothpick comes out clean. Cool for 5 minutes before removing from pan to a wire rack.

NUTRITION FACTS: 1 muffin equals 144 calories, 5 g fat (3 g saturated fat), 28 mg cholesterol, 218 mg sodium, 25 g carbohydrate, 2 g fiber, 3 g protein. **DIABETIC EXCHANGES:** 1-1/2 starch, 1 fat.

Jalapeno Garlic Bread

(PICTURED AT LEFT, UPPER LEFT CORNER)

PREP: 30 Min. + Rising   **BAKE:** 40 Min. + Cooling
YIELD: 2 Loaves (12 slices each)

My mother loves spicy foods, so I created this crusty, rustic loaf just to suit her taste. Now my whole family enjoys it and asks for it regularly. —Natalie Ann Gallagher, Clovis, California

 1 cup warm fat-free milk (70° to 80°)
1/2 cup egg substitute
 2 tablespoons butter, melted
 1 teaspoon salt
 2 cups bread flour
 2 cups whole wheat flour
1/4 cup sugar
 2 teaspoons active dry yeast
FILLING:
3/4 cup chopped seeded jalapeno peppers
 3 garlic cloves, minced
 5 teaspoons butter, softened, *divided*
 1 teaspoon garlic salt
 3 tablespoons grated Parmesan cheese, *divided*

In bread machine pan, place the first eight ingredients in order suggested by manufacturer. Select dough setting (check dough after 5 minutes of mixing; add 1 to 2 tablespoons of water or flour if needed).

In a small bowl, combine the jalapenos and garlic; set aside. When cycle is completed, turn dough onto a lightly floured surface. Divide dough in half.

For each loaf, roll one portion of dough into a 14-in. x 9-in. rectangle. Spread with 1-1/2 teaspoons butter. Sprinkle with 1/2 teaspoon garlic salt, 1 tablespoon Parmesan cheese and 1/3 cup jalapeno mixture. Roll up jelly-roll style, starting with a short side; pinch seam to seal. Place in a 9-in. x 5-in. x 3-in. loaf pan coated with nonstick cooking spray. Cover and let rise in a warm place until doubled, about 40 minutes.

Melt remaining butter; brush over loaves. Sprinkle with remaining Parmesan cheese and jalapeno mixture. Bake at 350° for 40-50 minutes or until golden brown. Remove from pans to wire racks to cool.

NUTRITION FACTS: 1 slice equals 102 calories, 2 g fat (1 g saturated fat), 5 mg cholesterol, 220 mg sodium, 18 g carbohydrate, 2 g fiber, 4 g protein. **DIABETIC EXCHANGES:** 1 starch, 1/2 fat.

Editor's Note: When cutting or seeding hot peppers, use rubber or plastic gloves to protect your hands. Avoid touching your face.

Spiced Cranberry Wheat Bread

(PICTURED ABOVE LEFT, UPPER RIGHT CORNER)

PREP: 10 Min.   **BAKE:** 3-1/4 Hours   **YIELD:** 1 Loaf (16 slices)

Here's a healthy, hearty bread that's perfect for toasting or just snacking. The spices and orange flavor blend well with the cranberries to make this one of my seasonal favorites. —Trisha Kruse, Eagle, Idaho

1-1/4 cups water (70° to 80°)
1/3 cup honey
 2 tablespoons canola oil
1-1/2 teaspoons salt
2-1/4 cups bread flour

1-1/4 cups whole wheat flour
1/2 teaspoon ground cinnamon
1/4 teaspoon ground cloves
1/4 teaspoon ground nutmeg
 2 teaspoons active dry yeast
 1 cup dried cranberries
 1 tablespoon grated orange peel

In bread machine pan, place the first 10 ingredients in order suggested by manufacturer. Select whole grain bread setting. Choose crust color and 2-lb. loaf setting if available. Bake according to bread machine directions (check dough after 5 minutes of mixing; add 1 to 2 tablespoons of water or flour if needed).

Just before the final kneading (your machine may audibly signal this), add the cranberries and orange peel.

NUTRITION FACTS: 1 slice equals 150 calories, 2 g fat (trace saturated fat), 0 cholesterol, 222 mg sodium, 32 g carbohydrate, 2 g fiber, 4 g protein. **DIABETIC EXCHANGES:** 1-1/2 starch, 1/2 fruit.

Whole Wheat Buttermilk Rolls

(PICTURED AT FAR LEFT, LOWER RIGHT CORNER)

PREP: 35 Min. + Rising   **BAKE:** 10 Min.   **YIELD:** 1-1/2 Dozen

I'm always looking for recipes tailored to my husband's low-fat, low-sugar diet. These rolls are winners. —Irene Cliett, Cedar Bluff, Mississippi

1-1/2 cups self-rising flour
1-1/2 cups whole wheat flour, *divided*
1/3 cup sugar
 1 package (1/4 ounce) quick-rise yeast
 1 cup 1% buttermilk
1/4 cup canola oil

In a large mixing bowl, combine the self-rising flour, 3/4 cup whole wheat flour, sugar and yeast. In a small saucepan, heat buttermilk and oil to 120°-130° (mixture will appear curdled). Add to dry ingredients; beat just until smooth. Stir in remaining whole wheat flour.

Turn onto a lightly floured surface; knead until smooth and elastic, about 6-8 minutes. Cover the dough and rest for 10 minutes.

Roll dough to 1/2-in. thickness; cut with a floured 2-1/2-in. biscuit cutter. Place 2 in. apart on baking sheets coated with nonstick cooking spray. Cover and let rise in a warm place until doubled, about 35-40 minutes. Bake at 375° for 8-12 minutes or until golden brown. Serve warm.

NUTRITION FACTS: 1 roll equals 116 calories, 3 g fat (trace saturated fat), 1 mg cholesterol, 135 mg sodium, 19 g carbohydrate, 1 g fiber, 3 g protein. **DIABETIC EXCHANGES:** 1 starch, 1 fat.

Editor's Note: As a substitute for 1-1/2 cups self-rising flour, place 2-1/4 teaspoons baking powder and 3/4 teaspoon salt in a measuring cup. Add all-purpose flour to measure 1 cup. Combine with an additional

HEALTHY OUTLOOK
Whole wheat is chock-full of fiber as well as protein and B vitamins. Consider using whole wheat flour to replace some of the all-purpose flour in your favorite recipe.

Maple Syrup Corn Bread

(PICTURED BELOW)

MEAT-LESS

PREP/TOTAL TIME: 30 Min.　**YIELD:** 12 Servings

Here's a good old-fashioned recipe from New England. Flavored with a hint of maple syrup, this corn bread makes the perfect, change-of-pace companion to spicy chili or stew.

—Roger Hickum, Plymouth, New Hampshire

　1-1/4　cups all-purpose flour
　　　1　cup cornmeal
　　　2　teaspoons baking powder
　　　1　teaspoon salt
　　　1　egg
　　3/4　cup fat-free milk
　　1/2　cup maple syrup
　　　3　tablespoons butter, melted

In a large bowl, combine the flour, cornmeal, baking powder and salt. In a small bowl, whisk together the egg, milk, syrup and butter; stir into dry ingredients just until moistened.

Pour into a 9-in. square baking pan coated with nonstick cooking spray. Bake at 400° for 15-20 minutes or until a toothpick inserted near the center comes out clean. Serve warm.

NUTRITION FACTS: 1 piece equals 161 calories, 4 g fat (2 g saturated fat), 26 mg cholesterol, 307 mg sodium, 29 g carbohydrate, 1 g fiber, 3 g protein. **DIABETIC EXCHANGES:** 2 starch, 1/2 fat.

Swedish Tea Ring

(PICTURED AT RIGHT)

PREP: 30 Min. + Rising　**BAKE:** 20 Min. + Cooling
YIELD: 1 Ring (24 slices)

My mother used to prepare this delightful tea ring in the '40s, and it's still a favorite today. Maraschino cherries add a festive touch.

—Elsie Epp, Newton, Kansas

　　　1　tablespoon active dry yeast
　1-1/2　cups warm water (110° to 115°)
　　1/4　cup sugar
　　1/4　cup canola oil
　　　2　egg whites, beaten
　1-1/4　teaspoons salt
　5-1/2　to 6 cups all-purpose flour
　　1/2　cup chopped walnuts
　　1/2　cup chopped maraschino cherries, patted dry
　　1/4　cup packed brown sugar
　　　1　teaspoon ground cinnamon
　　　2　tablespoons butter, melted
ICING:
　　　1　cup confectioners' sugar
　　　1　to 2 tablespoons fat-free milk

In a large mixing bowl, dissolve yeast in warm water. Add sugar, oil, egg whites, salt and 1 cup flour; beat until smooth. Stir in enough remaining flour to form a soft dough. Knead on a floured surface until smooth, about 6-8 minutes. Place in a bowl coated with nonstick cooking spray; turn once to coat top. Cover and let rise until doubled, about 1 hour.

Combine the walnuts, cherries, brown sugar and cinnamon; set aside. Punch dough down; roll into an 18-in. x 12-in. rectangle. Brush with butter; sprinkle with nut mixture to within 1/2 in. of edges. Roll up tightly jelly-roll style, starting with a long side; seal ends.

Place seam side down on a 14-in. pizza pan coated with nonstick cooking spray; pinch ends together to form a ring. With scissors, cut from outside edge two-thirds of the way toward center of ring at scant 1-in. intervals. Separate strips slightly; twist so filling shows. Cover and let rise until doubled, about 40 minutes.

Bake at 400° for 20-25 minutes or until golden brown. Cool on a wire rack. Combine icing ingredients; drizzle over ring.

NUTRITION FACTS: 1 slice equals 196 calories, 5 g fat (1 g saturated fat), 3 mg cholesterol, 142 mg sodium, 34 g carbohydrate, 1 g fiber, 4 g protein. **DIABETIC EXCHANGES:** 2 starch, 1 fat.

Banana Nut Muffins

PREP/TOTAL TIME: 30 Min.　**YIELD:** 1 Dozen

If you have time for just a muffin, make it a good one. These fast-to-fix banana and spice-flavored treats from our Test Kitchen offer home-baked goodness any time of the day.

　　　2　cups all-purpose flour
　　2/3　cup packed brown sugar
　　　2　teaspoons baking powder
　　3/4　teaspoon ground cinnamon
　　1/4　teaspoon baking soda
　　1/4　teaspoon salt
　　1/4　teaspoon ground cloves

1 egg
1/4 cup egg substitute
1 cup mashed ripe bananas (2 to 3 medium)
1/4 cup unsweetened applesauce
3 tablespoons canola oil
1/3 cup chopped walnuts

In a large bowl, combine the first seven ingredients. Combine the egg, egg substitute, bananas, applesauce and oil; stir into dry ingredients just until moistened.

Coat muffin cups with nonstick cooking spray; fill two-thirds full. Sprinkle with nuts. Bake at 375° for 15-18 minutes or until muffins spring back when lightly touched.

Cool for 5 minutes before removing to a wire rack.

NUTRITION FACTS: 1 muffin equals 207 calories, 6 g fat (1 g saturated fat), 18 mg cholesterol, 177 mg sodium, 34 g carbohydrate, 1 g fiber, 4 g protein. **DIABETIC EXCHANGES:** 2 starch, 1 fat.

Nutcracker Bread

PREP: 20 Min.   **BAKE:** 35 Min. + Cooling   **YIELD:** 1 Loaf (16 slices)

This tender loaf, made in a springform pan, has a wonderful sweet and nutty flavor. Turkey, ham or velvety cream cheese and jelly sandwiches always taste better on slices of this bread.

—Jacqueline McComas, Paoli, Pennsylvania

1 cup chopped walnuts, toasted and cooled
3/4 cup packed brown sugar
2 cups all-purpose flour
1-1/4 teaspoons baking powder
1/2 teaspoon salt
1/4 teaspoon baking soda
3 eggs
1/2 cup reduced-fat sour cream
1/2 cup fat-free milk
1 tablespoon cider vinegar

In a food processor, combine walnuts and brown sugar; cover and pulse until finely chopped. Transfer to a large bowl.

Add the flour, baking powder, salt and baking soda; mix well. In a small bowl, beat the eggs, sour cream, milk and vinegar. Stir into dry ingredients just until moistened.

Transfer to an 8-in. springform pan coated with nonstick cooking spray. Bake at 350° for 35-40 minutes or until a toothpick inserted near the center comes out clean. Cool on a wire rack for 10 minutes.

Remove sides and bottom of pan; cool bread completely on a wire rack.

NUTRITION FACTS: 1 slice equals 170 calories, 6 g fat (1 g saturated fat), 42 mg cholesterol, 150 mg sodium, 24 g carbohydrate, 1 g fiber, 5 g protein. **DIABETIC EXCHANGES:** 1-1/2 starch, 1 fat.

Coconut-Glazed Orange Scones

(PICTURED ABOVE)

PREP/TOTAL TIME: 30 Min.   **YIELD:** 1-1/2 Dozen

Guaranteed to brighten winter afternoons, these warm treats from our Test Kitchen deliver tropical flair, complete with orange and coconut flavors.

    3-3/4 cups self-rising flour
    1/4 cup sugar
      2 teaspoons baking powder
    1/2 cup cold butter
      2 eggs
      1 cup plus 1 to 2 tablespoons fat-free milk, *divided*
      1 teaspoon grated orange peel
    1/2 cup confectioners' sugar
    1/4 teaspoon coconut extract

In a large bowl, combine the flour, sugar and baking powder. Cut in butter until mixture resembles coarse crumbs. In a small bowl, whisk eggs, 1 cup milk and orange peel; stir into crumb mixture just until moistened. Turn onto a floured surface; knead 10 times.

Roll into a 14-in. x 8-in. rectangle. Using a floured pizza cutter, cut widthwise into 2-in. strips, then cut diagonally into 2-in. strips, forming diamond shapes. Place 2 in. apart on baking sheets coated with nonstick cooking spray.

Bake at 400° for 8-10 minutes or until lightly browned. Remove to wire racks. For glaze, in a small bowl, combine the confectioners' sugar, coconut extract and enough remaining milk to achieve desired consistency; drizzle over scones. Serve warm.

NUTRITION FACTS: 1 scone equals 165 calories, 6 g fat (3 g saturated fat), 38 mg cholesterol, 410 mg sodium, 25 g carbohydrate, trace fiber, 4 g protein **DIABETIC EXCHANGES:** 1-1/2 starch, 1 fat.

Editor's Note: As a substitute for self-rising flour, place 5-1/2 teaspoons baking powder and 1-3/4 teaspoons salt in a measuring cup. Add all-purpose flour to measure 1 cup. Add another 2-3/4 cups all-purpose flour to the bowl.

Blueberry Quick Bread

(PICTURED BELOW)

PREP: 25 Min.   **BAKE:** 50 Min. + Cooling   **YIELD:** 2 Loaves (12 slices each)

This sweet bread recipe won a blue ribbon, perhaps because the crushed pineapple lends a delicious twist. It makes two loaves, so you can freeze one for a future treat if you like.

—Lois Everest, Goshen, Indiana

    2/3 cup butter, softened
    1-1/4 cups sugar blend for baking
      2 eggs
      4 egg whites
    1-1/2 teaspoons lemon juice
      3 cups all-purpose flour
    3-3/4 teaspoons baking powder
    1/2 teaspoon salt
    1/2 cup fat-free milk
      2 cups fresh *or* frozen blueberries
      1 cup canned unsweetened crushed pineapple, drained
    1/2 cup chopped pecans *or* walnuts
    1/2 cup flaked coconut

In a large mixing bowl, cream butter and sugar blend. Add the eggs, egg whites and lemon juice; mix well. Combine the flour, baking powder and salt; add to creamed mixture alternately with milk. Fold in the blueberries, pineapple, pecans and coconut.

Transfer to two 8-in. x 4-in. x 2-in. loaf pans coated with nonstick cooking spray. Bake at 350° for 50-60 minutes or until a toothpick inserted near the center comes out clean. Cool for 10 minutes before removing from pans to wire racks.

NUTRITION FACTS: 1 slice equals 193 calories, 8 g fat (4 g saturated fat), 31 mg cholesterol, 186 mg sodium, 27 g carbohydrate, 1 g fiber, 3 g protein. **DIABETIC EXCHANGES:** 1-1/2 starch, 1-1/2 fat.

Editor's Note: This recipe was tested with Splenda Sugar Blend for Baking. If using frozen blueberries, do not thaw before adding to batter.

Favorite Recipe Made Lighter

WE AGREE with Nita Cameron, who says that her Ultimate Corn Bread recipe is out of this world. Unlike others, her version is moist, buttery and offers a tender crumb with every bite.

"I think it's the tastiest corn bread I've ever had," says the Tacoma, Washington reader. "But as a diabetic and former heart patient, I carefully study all of my recipes. This one is too high in calories and fat. Maybe you can kick it down a notch."

Nita was correct in thinking that her corn bread recipe had a lot of calories and fat, but it's also big on cholesterol and sugar.

The butter in Nita's specialty enhanced the flavor and kept the bread tender. Realizing that they needed to decrease it, though, our home economists added butter flavoring to keep the taste of the original recipe. Buttermilk was then added to tenderize the bread.

Using honey and sugar substitute meant that the sugar could be decreased, and a reduced-fat baking mix replaced the full-fat version.

With an impressive 71% less cholesterol and 80% less fat, Makeover Ultimate Corn Bread is a heart-smart success. The sugar was cut in half and 190 calories were eliminated from each serving of Nita's recipe.

Ultimate Corn Bread

MEAT-LESS

PREP: 20 Min.   **BAKE:** 30 Min. + Cooling   **YIELD:** 12 Servings

  2-1/2 cups biscuit/baking mix
      1 cup sugar
    2/3 cup cornmeal
    1/4 teaspoon baking powder
    1/4 teaspoon ground nutmeg
      2 eggs
  1-1/4 cups milk
  1-1/4 cups butter, melted

In a large bowl, combine the first five ingredients. In another bowl, beat the eggs, milk and butter; stir into the dry ingredients just until moistened. Pour into a greased 9-in. square baking pan.

Bake at 350° for 30-35 minutes or until a toothpick inserted near the center comes out clean. Cool for 15 minutes before cutting. Serve warm.

NUTRITION FACTS: 1 piece equals 390 calories, 25 g fat (14 g saturated fat), 90 mg cholesterol, 541 mg sodium, 39 g carbohydrate, 1 g fiber, 4 g protein.

MAKEOVER TIP

Keep butter flavoring in mind when you want to cut down on butter, but don't want to lose the taste it offers.

Makeover Ultimate Corn Bread

MEAT-LESS

(PICTURED ABOVE)

PREP: 20 Min.   **BAKE:** 30 Min. + Cooling   **YIELD:** 12 Servings

  2-1/2 cups reduced-fat biscuit/baking mix
    3/4 cup cornmeal
Sugar substitute equivalent to 1/2 cup sugar
    1/4 cup sugar
    1/2 teaspoon baking soda
    1/4 teaspoon ground nutmeg
    1/4 teaspoon baking powder
      1 egg
      1 egg white
    3/4 cup 1% buttermilk
    1/2 cup fat-free milk
    1/2 cup unsweetened applesauce
      3 tablespoons butter, melted
      1 tablespoon honey
    1/2 teaspoon butter flavoring

In a large bowl, combine the first seven ingredients. In another bowl, beat the egg, egg white, buttermilk, milk, applesauce, butter, honey and butter flavoring; stir into dry ingredients just until moistened.

Pour into a 9-in. square baking pan coated with nonstick cooking spray. Bake at 350° for 30-35 minutes or until a toothpick inserted near the center comes out clean. Cool on a rack for 15 minutes before cutting. Serve warm.

NUTRITION FACTS: 1 piece equals 200 calories, 5 g fat (2 g saturated fat), 26 mg cholesterol, 419 mg sodium, 33 g carbohydrate, 1 g fiber, 5 g protein. **DIABETIC EXCHANGES:** 2 starch, 1 fat.

Editor's Note: This recipe was tested with Splenda No Calorie Sweetener.

Whole Wheat Blueberry Scones

PREP: 20 Min. **BAKE:** 30 Min. **YIELD:** 1 Dozen

No one will suspect that these moist scones are light. Featuring whole wheat flour and blueberries, golden wedges are tasty and nutritious delights that come from our Test Kitchen.

> 2 cups all-purpose flour
> 1-3/4 cups whole wheat flour
> 1/4 cup packed brown sugar
> 4 teaspoons baking powder
> 1/4 teaspoon baking soda
> 1/3 cup cold butter
> 1-3/4 cups 1% buttermilk
> 1-1/2 cups fresh blueberries
> 1 tablespoon sugar

In a large bowl, combine the flours, brown sugar, baking powder and baking soda. Cut in butter until mixture resembles coarse crumbs. Stir in buttermilk just until moistened. Stir in blueberries. Turn onto a floured surface; gently knead 10 times.

Transfer dough to a baking sheet coated with nonstick cooking spray. Pat into a 9-in. circle. Cut into 12 wedges, but do not separate. Sprinkle with sugar. Bake at 375° for 30-35 minutes or until golden brown. Serve warm.

NUTRITION FACTS: 1 scone equals 225 calories, 6 g fat (3 g saturated fat), 15 mg cholesterol, 253 mg sodium, 38 g carbohydrate, 3 g fiber, 6 g protein. **DIABETIC EXCHANGES:** 2-1/2 starch, 1 fat.

Apricot Nut Bread

PREP: 25 Min. **BAKE:** 55 Min. + Cooling **YIELD:** 1 Loaf (12 slices)

My family likes bread, apricots and nuts, so I put the three together to create this recipe. It's fairly easy to make, and everyone loves it. It never lasts long at our house.

—Robert Logan, Clayton, California

> 1 cup boiling water
> 1-1/4 cups chopped dried apricots
> 2 cups all-purpose flour
> 2/3 cup sugar
> 1-1/2 teaspoons baking powder
> 1 teaspoon salt
> 1/4 teaspoon baking soda
> 1 egg
> 3/4 cup apricot nectar
> 2 tablespoons butter, melted
> 1/4 cup chopped pecans
> 1 tablespoon grated orange peel

GLAZE:
> 2 tablespoons brown sugar
> 1 tablespoon butter
> 1-1/2 teaspoons fat-free milk
> 2 tablespoons finely chopped pecans

In a small bowl, pour water over apricots; set aside. In a large bowl, combine the flour, sugar, baking powder, salt and baking soda. Whisk together the egg, apricot nectar and butter; stir into dry ingredients just until moistened. Drain apricots; fold into batter with pecans and orange peel.

Transfer to an 8-in. x 4-in. x 2-in. loaf pan coated with

Herb Quick Bread

(PICTURED ABOVE)

PREP: 15 Min. **BAKE:** 40 Min. + Cooling **YIELD:** 1 Loaf (14 slices)

This loaf is especially good with soups and stews, but slices are also tasty alongside green salads. The herbs make it a treat any time of the year. —Donna Roberts, Shumway, Illinois

> 3 cups all-purpose flour
> 3 tablespoons sugar
> 1 tablespoon baking powder
> 1 tablespoon caraway seeds
> 1/2 teaspoon salt
> 1/2 teaspoon dried thyme
> 1/2 teaspoon ground nutmeg
> 1 egg
> 1 cup fat-free milk
> 1/3 cup canola oil

In a large bowl, combine the first seven ingredients. In a small bowl, whisk the egg, milk and oil; stir into dry ingredients just until moistened.

Transfer to a 9-in. x 5-in. x 3-in. loaf pan coated with nonstick cooking spray. Bake at 350° for 40-50 minutes or until a toothpick inserted near the center comes out clean. Cool for 10 minutes before removing from pan to a wire rack to cool completely.

NUTRITION FACTS: 1 slice equals 169 calories, 6 g fat (1 g saturated fat), 16 mg cholesterol, 184 mg sodium, 24 g carbohydrate, 1 g fiber, 4 g protein. **DIABETIC EXCHANGES:** 1-1/2 starch, 1 fat.

nonstick cooking spray. Bake at 350° for 55-65 minutes or until a toothpick comes out clean. Cool for 10 minutes before removing from pan to a wire rack.

For glaze, combine the brown sugar, butter and milk in a small saucepan. Cook and stir over medium heat until butter is melted and mixture is smooth. Cool to room temperature; drizzle over bread. Sprinkle with pecans.

NUTRITION FACTS: 1 slice equals 233 calories, 6 g fat (2 g saturated fat), 25 mg cholesterol, 320 mg sodium, 42 g carbohydrate, 2 g fiber, 3 g protein. **DIABETIC EXCHANGES:** 2 starch, 1 fruit, 1 fat.

Sweet Potato Scones

PREP: 25 Min.   **BAKE:** 20 Min.   **YIELD:** 8 Scones

It's a sure sign of autumn when I whip up these tender, tasty treats for friends in my home.   —Lillian Julow, Gainesville, Florida

  2-1/4 cups all-purpose flour
    1/4 cup packed brown sugar
      2 teaspoons baking powder
  1-1/2 teaspoons pumpkin pie spice
    3/4 teaspoon salt
    1/4 teaspoon baking soda
    1/3 cup cold butter
      1 egg, lightly beaten
      1 cup mashed sweet potatoes
    1/3 cup buttermilk

In a large bowl, combine the flour, brown sugar, baking powder, pumpkin pie spice, salt and baking soda. Cut in butter until mixture resembles coarse crumbs. In a small bowl, whisk the egg, sweet potatoes and buttermilk; add to dry ingredients just until moistened.

Turn onto a lightly floured surface; with lightly floured hands, knead dough 10-12 times. Pat into an 8-in. circle. Cut into eight wedges.

Separate wedges and place 1 in. apart on a baking sheet lightly coated with nonstick cooking spray. Bake at 400° for 16-21 minutes or until golden brown. Cool on a wire rack for 5 minutes. Serve warm.

NUTRITION FACTS: 1 scone equals 278 calories, 9 g fat (5 g saturated fat), 47 mg cholesterol, 465 mg sodium, 44 g carbohydrate, 2 g fiber, 6 g protein. **DIABETIC EXCHANGES:** 3 starch, 1-1/2 fat.

Hearty Sweet Potato Braids
(PICTURED AT RIGHT)

FAT MEAT-
LESS

PREP: 45 Min. + Rising   **BAKE:** 30 Min.   **YIELD:** 2 Loaves (12 slices each)

We make these delicious and nutritious loaves every Christmas. Thyme gives the pretty braids a lovely flavor. For a change, I often use safflower oil in this recipe.
                    —Suzanne Kesel, Cohocton, New York

      1 package (1/4 ounce) active dry yeast
    1/4 cup warm water (110° to 115°)
  1-1/2 cups mashed sweet potatoes, room temperature
      1 cup warm fat-free milk (110° to 115°)
    1/4 cup canola oil
      3 tablespoons honey
      1 cup all-purpose flour

    1/2 cup yellow cornmeal
      2 teaspoons salt
      1 teaspoon dried thyme
  2-3/4 to 3-1/4 cups whole wheat flour
      1 tablespoon cold fat-free milk

In a large mixing bowl, dissolve yeast in warm water. Add the sweet potatoes, milk, oil, honey, all-purpose flour, cornmeal, salt, thyme and 2 cups whole wheat flour; beat until smooth. Stir in enough of the remaining whole wheat flour to form a firm dough.

Turn onto a lightly floured surface. Knead until smooth and elastic, about 6-8 minutes. Place in a bowl coated with nonstick cooking spray; turn once to coat top. Cover and let rise in a warm place until doubled, about 1 hour.

Punch dough down; divide into six equal portions. Shape each into a 20-in. rope. Place three ropes on a baking sheet coated with nonstick cooking spray; braid. Pinch ends to seal and tuck under. Repeat with remaining ropes. Cover and let rise in a warm place until doubled, about 35 minutes.

Brush loaves with cold milk. Bake at 350° for 30-35 minutes or until golden brown. Remove to wire racks.

NUTRITION FACTS: 1 slice equals 131 calories, 3 g fat (trace saturated fat), trace cholesterol, 206 mg sodium, 24 g carbohydrate, 3 g fiber, 3 g protein. **DIABETIC EXCHANGES:** 1-1/2 starch, 1/2 fat.

Sun-Dried Tomato 'n' Basil Wreath

(PICTURED BELOW)

PREP: 50 Min. + Rising   **BAKE:** 20 Min.   **YIELD:** 1 Loaf (12 slices)

I added to a family recipe to create this bright and pretty wreath. Brushed with herb butter, it makes a special accompaniment to holiday meals.   —Teresa Morancie, Brewer, Maine

    1/2 cup boiling water
    1/4 cup sun-dried tomatoes (not packed in oil)
    1/2 cup fat-free milk
    1/4 cup grated Parmesan cheese
      3 tablespoons butter
      2 tablespoons sugar
  4-1/2 teaspoons minced fresh basil
    1/2 teaspoon salt
      1 package (1/4 ounce) active dry yeast
      2 tablespoons warm water (110° to 115°)
      1 egg, beaten
  2-1/4 to 2-1/2 cups all-purpose flour
HERB BUTTER:
      1 tablespoon butter
  2-1/4 teaspoons minced fresh basil
  1-1/2 teaspoons grated Parmesan cheese
  1-1/2 teaspoons olive oil

Pour boiling water over tomatoes; let stand 15 minutes. In a saucepan, combine the next six ingredients. Drain and chop tomatoes; add to pan. Cook and stir mixture over low heat until sugar is dissolved. Remove from heat; cool slightly.

In a large mixing bowl, dissolve yeast in warm water. Add tomato mixture, egg and 2 cups flour; beat until smooth. Stir in enough remaining flour to form a soft dough. Knead on a floured surface until smooth, about 6-8 minutes. Place in a bowl coated with nonstick cooking spray; turn once to coat top. Cover and let rise until doubled, about 1 hour.

In a saucepan, melt butter; add basil, Parmesan and oil. Keep warm. Punch dough down; divide into three portions. Shape each into an 18-in. rope. Brush with half of herb butter. Place ropes on a baking sheet coated with nonstick cooking spray; braid and shape into a wreath. Pinch ends to seal. Cover and let rise until doubled, about 40 minutes.

Brush with remaining herb butter. Bake at 350° for 20-25 minutes or until golden brown. Remove to a wire rack.

NUTRITION FACTS: 1 slice equals 155 calories, 6 g fat (3 g saturated fat), 30 mg cholesterol, 207 mg sodium, 21 g carbohydrate, 1 g fiber, 5 g protein. **DIABETIC EXCHANGES:** 1-1/2 starch, 1 fat.

Parmesan Sage Scones

(PICTURED ABOVE)

PREP/TOTAL TIME: 25 Min.   **YIELD:** 8 Scones

Prepared with only a handful of items, these savory wedges are ideal alongside soup, pasta or poultry. Our home economists dressed up the tops of the dinner accompaniments with whole sage leaves.

  2-1/4 cups biscuit/baking mix
    1/4 cup grated Parmesan cheese
  1-3/4 teaspoons minced fresh sage
    1/4 teaspoon pepper
    1/2 cup plus 1 tablespoon half-and-half cream, *divided*
      8 fresh sage leaves

In a large bowl, combine the biscuit mix, Parmesan cheese, minced sage and pepper. Stir in 1/2 cup cream. Turn onto a floured surface; knead 5 times. Transfer dough to a baking sheet coated with nonstick cooking spray. Pat into a 6-in. circle. Cut into eight wedges, but do not separate.

Brush remaining cream over dough. Press a sage leaf onto the top of each wedge. Bake at 375° for 10-15 minutes or until edges are until golden brown. Serve warm.

NUTRITION FACTS: 1 scone equals 172 calories, 8 g fat (3 g saturated fat), 10 mg cholesterol, 480 mg sodium, 22 g carbohydrate, 1 g fiber, 4 g protein. **DIABETIC EXCHANGES:** 1-1/2 starch, 1-1/2 fat.

Dazzling Desserts

Down-home pies, decadent chocolate bites and frosty favorites…with the right recipes you can indulge in these sensations without guilt. From no-fuss nibbles to impressive after-dinner delights, this expanded chapter features 78 sensational sweets that are perfect for every occasion.

Cranberry Pear Crisp Pie, p. 228

Cranberry-Nut Jelly Roll
(PICTURED ABOVE)

PREP: 40 Min. **BAKE:** 10 Min. + Cooling **YIELD:** 12 Servings

No one will believe a dessert this rich with nuts can be so light.
— Rose Mary Liptock, Uniontown, Pennsylvania

    4 **eggs,** *separated*
  3/4 **cup confectioners' sugar**
  1/2 **cup all-purpose flour**
  3/4 **teaspoon baking powder**
  1/4 **teaspoon baking soda**
  1/8 **teaspoon salt**
    1 **cup fresh** *or* **frozen cranberries, coarsely chopped**
  3/4 **cup finely chopped pecans**
FILLING:
    1 **package (8 ounces) fat-free cream cheese**
    2 **tablespoons butter, softened**
  1/2 **teaspoon almond extract**
    1 **cup confectioners' sugar**

Let eggs stand at room temperature for 30 minutes. Line a 15-in. x 10-in. x 1-in. baking pan with waxed paper; coat with nonstick cooking spray and set aside.

In a large mixing bowl, beat egg yolks on high speed for 3 minutes or until thickened. In a small mixing bowl with clean beaters, beat egg whites on medium speed until foamy. Gradually add confectioners' sugar, 1 tablespoon at a time, beating on high until soft peaks form. Fold into yolks. Combine the flour, baking powder, baking soda and salt; gently fold into egg mixture until combined. Fold in cranberries and pecans.

Spread batter into prepared pan. Bake at 350° for 7-10 minutes or until top springs back when lightly touched. Cool for 5 minutes. Invert cake onto a kitchen towel dusted with confectioners' sugar. Gently peel off waxed paper. Roll up cake in the towel jelly-roll style, starting with a short side. Cool on a wire rack.

For filling, in a small mixing bowl, combine the cream cheese, butter and extract. Set aside 1-1/2 teaspoons confectioners' sugar. Gradually beat remaining sugar into cream cheese mixture. Unroll cake; spread filling to within 1/2 in. of edges. Roll up again. Sprinkle with reserved confectioners' sugar. Store in the refrigerator.

NUTRITION FACTS: 1 slice equals 203 calories, 9 g fat (2 g saturated fat), 77 mg cholesterol, 219 mg sodium, 25 g carbohydrate, 1 g fiber, 6 g protein. **DIABETIC EXCHANGES:** 2 fat, 1-1/2 starch.

Lemon Cake

PREP: 15 Min.   **BAKE:** 35 Min. + Cooling   **YIELD:** 14 Servings

This recipe always turns out delicious. And because there are only a few grams of fat per serving, I can enjoy a slice without guilt.
—Pat Bertram, Attica, Michigan

  1 package (18-1/4 ounces) yellow cake mix
  1 package (.3 ounce) sugar-free lemon gelatin
  3/4 cup egg substitute
  1 can (5-1/2 ounces) apricot nectar
  1/2 cup unsweetened applesauce
  2 tablespoons canola oil
  1 teaspoon lemon extract
GLAZE:
  1 cup confectioners' sugar, *divided*
  1/4 cup lemon juice

In a large mixing bowl, combine the first seven ingredients. Beat on medium speed for 2 minutes. Coat a 10-in. fluted tube pan with nonstick cooking spray and dust with flour; carefully add the batter.

Bake at 350° for 35-40 minutes or until a toothpick inserted near the center comes out clean. Cool for 10 minutes before removing from the pan to a wire rack. With a meat fork or wooden skewer, poke holes in cake.

Set aside 2 tablespoons confectioners' sugar. In a small bowl, combine the remaining confectioners' sugar and lemon juice. Gradually pour over warm cake. Cool completely. Dust with reserved confectioners' sugar.

NUTRITION FACTS: 1 slice equals 227 calories, 5 g fat (1 g saturated fat), 0 cholesterol, 274 mg sodium, 41 g carbohydrate, 1 g fiber, 3 g protein. **DIABETIC EXCHANGES:** 2-1/2 starch, 1/2 fat.

Cherry Cheese Pie

PREP: 15 Min. + Chilling   **YIELD:** 8 Servings

Cooking foods that are satisfying but low-fat can be challenging. My health-conscious family loves this speedy, no-bake recipe, and I love that it gets me out of the kitchen so fast!
—Debbie Lucci, Salem, Virginia

  2 teaspoons unflavored gelatin
  1/4 cup cold water
  1 package (8 ounces) reduced-fat cream cheese
  1 teaspoon vanilla extract
Sugar substitute equivalent to 2 tablespoons sugar
  1 envelope whipped topping mix
  2 cups fat-free whipped topping
  1 reduced-fat graham cracker crust (8 inches)
  1 cup reduced-sugar cherry pie filling

In a small saucepan, sprinkle gelatin over cold water; let stand for 1 minute. Heat over low heat until gelatin is completely dissolved. Remove from the heat; set aside.

In a large mixing bowl, beat cream cheese and vanilla until blended. Gradually beat in sugar substitute. Gradually add whipped topping mix; beat on medium speed for 2 minutes. Gradually beat in gelatin mixture; beat 1 minute longer.

Mix in 1 cup whipped topping. Fold in remaining whipped topping. Spoon into crust; top with cherry pie filling. Cover and refrigerate for at least 1 hour before serving.

NUTRITION FACTS: 1 piece equals 259 calories, 10 g fat (6 g saturated fat), 20 mg cholesterol, 229 mg sodium, 33 g carbohydrate, trace fiber, 5 g protein. **DIABETIC EXCHANGES:** 2 starch, 2 fat.

Editor's Note: This recipe was tested with Splenda No Calorie Sweetener.

Orange Bundt Cake
(PICTURED BELOW)

PREP: 15 Min.   **BAKE:** 40 Min. + Cooling   **YIELD:** 14 Servings

This pretty cake comes together quickly with a boxed mix. Fat-free mayonnaise replaces the heavy oils, and the citrus glaze makes it special.
—Deborah Williams, Wildwood, Missouri

  1 package (18-1/4 ounces) yellow cake mix
  1 envelope whipped topping mix
  3/4 cup orange juice
  3/4 cup fat-free mayonnaise
  3 eggs
  1 tablespoon grated orange peel
GLAZE:
  1-1/2 cups confectioners' sugar
  2 tablespoons orange juice

In a large mixing bowl, combine the first six ingredients; beat on medium speed for 2 minutes. Coat a 10-in. fluted tube pan with nonstick cooking spray and dust with flour. Pour batter into pan.

Bake at 350° for 40-45 minutes or until a toothpick inserted near the center comes out clean. Cool for 10 minutes before removing from pan to a wire rack to cool completely. Combine the glaze ingredients; drizzle over cake.

NUTRITION FACTS: 1 piece equals 257 calories, 5 g fat (2 g saturated fat), 46 mg cholesterol, 353 mg sodium, 48 g carbohydrate, 1 g fiber, 3 g protein.

Lemon Meringue Cake
(PICTURED BELOW)

PREP: 15 Min.   **BAKE:** 45 Min. + Chilling   9 Servings

When my husband needed to watch his weight, I started looking for light recipes. With its fresh berries and meringue topping, this sponge cake became a favorite.

—Suzanne Premo, Sault Ste. Marie, Ontario

>   2 cups sliced fresh strawberries
> 1-1/4 cups sugar, *divided*
>   1/4 cup butter, softened
>   2 egg whites
>   1 teaspoon vanilla extract
> 1-1/4 cups all-purpose flour
> 1-1/2 teaspoons baking powder
> 1-1/2 teaspoons grated lemon peel
>   1/4 teaspoon salt
>   1/2 cup fat-free milk
> MERINGUE:
>   2 egg whites
>   1/4 cup sugar

In a small bowl, combine strawberries and 1/4 cup sugar. Refrigerate until serving. In a large mixing bowl, beat butter and remaining sugar until crumbly, about 2 minutes. Add egg whites and vanilla; beat well. Combine the flour, baking powder, lemon peel and salt; add to butter mixture alternately with milk.

Pour into an 8-in. square baking dish coated with nonstick cooking spray. Bake at 350° for 30-35 minutes or until a toothpick inserted near the center comes out clean.

For meringue, in a small mixing bowl, beat egg whites on medium speed until soft peaks form. Gradually beat in sugar, 1 tablespoon at a time, on high until stiff peaks form. Spread over hot cake, sealing meringue to edges.

Bake at 350° for 12-15 minutes or until meringue is golden brown. Cool on a wire rack for 1 hour. Refrigerate for 1-2 hours before serving. Cut into squares; top with refrigerated strawberry mixture.

NUTRITION FACTS: 1 piece with 1/4 cup strawberry mixture equals 261 calories, 5 g fat (3 g saturated fat), 14 mg cholesterol, 216 mg sodium, 50 g carbohydrate, 1 g fiber, 4 g protein.

Apricot Lemon Ice
(PICTURED ABOVE)

FAT SALT ▼▼

PREP: 15 Min. + Freezing   **YIELD:** 6 Servings

Frosty and full-flavored, this fruity treat melts any resistance to dessert. It's a great ice cream substitute for lactose-intolerant friends. And with only five ingredients, it couldn't be easier.

—Elizabeth Montgomery, Taylorville, Illinois

>   1 envelope unflavored gelatin
>   1/2 cup cold water
>   3 cups apricot nectar
>   1/2 cup light corn syrup
>   1/4 cup lemon juice

In a small saucepan, sprinkle gelatin over cold water; let stand for 1 minute. Cook over low heat, stirring until gelatin is completely dissolved. Remove from the heat; stir in the apricot nectar, corn syrup and lemon juice. Transfer to a shallow container. Cover and freeze for 2-3 hours or until firm.

Spoon into a large chilled metal mixing bowl; beat for 1-2 minutes or until light and creamy. Return to shallow container. Cover and freeze until firm.

NUTRITION FACTS: 2/3 cup equals 154 calories, trace fat (trace saturated fat), 0 cholesterol, 39 mg sodium, 40 g carbohydrate, 1 g fiber, 2 g protein. **DIABETIC EXCHANGE:** 2-1/2 starch.

Banana Split Cheesecake
(PICTURED ABOVE)

PREP: 35 Min. + Freezing **YIELD:** 8 Servings

Topped with chocolate syrup, caramel and pecans, here's an ooey-gooey dessert that's decadent but decidedly lighter than most.
—Cherie Sweet, Evansville, Indiana

- 1 can (8 ounces) unsweetened crushed pineapple
- 2 medium firm bananas, sliced
- 1 reduced-fat graham cracker crust (8 inches)
- 1 package (8 ounces) fat-free cream cheese
- 1-1/2 cups pineapple sherbet, softened
- 1 package (1 ounce) sugar-free instant vanilla pudding mix
- 1 carton (8 ounces) frozen reduced-fat whipped topping, thawed, *divided*
- 4 maraschino cherries, *divided*
- 1 tablespoon chocolate syrup
- 1 tablespoon caramel ice cream topping
- 1 tablespoon chopped pecans

Drain pineapple, reserving juice. In a small bowl, combine bananas and 2 tablespoons reserved juice; let stand for 5 minutes. Drain bananas, discarding juice. Arrange bananas over bottom of crust; set aside.

In a large mixing bowl, beat cream cheese and 2 tablespoons reserved pineapple juice. Gradually beat in sherbet. Gradually beat in pudding mix; beat 2 minutes longer. Refrigerate 1/3 cup pineapple until serving; fold remaining pineapple into cream cheese mixture. Fold in 2 cups whipped topping; spread evenly over banana slices. Cover and freeze until firm.

Remove from the freezer 10-15 minutes before serving. Chop three maraschino cherries and pat dry; arrange cherries and reserved pineapple around edge of pie. Drizzle with chocolate syrup and caramel topping. Dollop remaining whipped topping onto center of pie. Sprinkle with pecans; top with remaining cherry.

NUTRITION FACTS: 1 piece equals 310 calories, 8 g fat (5 g saturated fat), 4 mg cholesterol, 422 mg sodium, 52 g carbohydrate, 1 g fiber, 6 g protein.

Pecan Kisses

PREP: 15 Min.   **BAKE:** 15 Min. per Batch   **YIELD:** 4 Dozen

With just a few ingredients and a few minutes of prep time, these lighter-than-air meringue cookies make sweet snacks kids of all ages simply adore.
—Norlene Razak, Kyle, Texas

- 2 egg whites
- 1 teaspoon vanilla extract
- 1/4 teaspoon white vinegar
- 1/8 teaspoon salt
- 2 cups confectioners' sugar
- 1-1/2 cups chopped pecans

In a large mixing bowl, beat the egg whites, vanilla, vinegar and salt on medium speed until soft peaks form. Gradually add confectioners' sugar, 1 tablespoon at a time, beating on high until stiff glossy peaks form and sugar is dissolved. Fold in pecans.

Drop by rounded teaspoonfuls 1 in. apart onto baking sheets coated with nonstick cooking spray. Bake at 300° for 15-20 minutes or until firm to the touch and lightly browned. Remove to wire racks to cool. Store in an airtight container.

NUTRITION FACTS: 1 cookie equals 46 calories, 3 g fat (trace saturated fat), 0 cholesterol, 8 mg sodium, 6 g carbohydrate, trace fiber, trace protein.
DIABETIC EXCHANGES: 1/2 starch, 1/2 fat.

Granola Biscotti

(PICTURED ABOVE)

FAT SALT CARB

PREP: 20 Min. **BAKE:** 30 Min. + Cooling **YIELD:** 2-1/2 Dozen

These cranberry-studded snacks are low in fat but high in flavor.
—Lori Waites, Frankenmuth, Michigan

- 1/4 cup butter, softened
- 3/4 cup sugar
- 1 egg
- 1 egg white
- 1/4 teaspoon almond extract
- 1-1/3 cups all-purpose flour
- 1 teaspoon baking powder
- 1/2 teaspoon baking soda
- 1/4 teaspoon salt
- 3/4 cup reduced-fat granola
- 2/3 cup dried cranberries

In a small mixing bowl, beat butter and sugar until crumbly, about 2 minutes. Add the egg, egg white and extract; mix well. Combine the flour, baking powder, baking soda and salt; beat into butter mixture. Break apart any large pieces of granola; stir granola and cranberries into dough.

Divide dough in half. With lightly floured hands, shape each portion into a 12-in. x 1-1/2-in. rectangle; place each on a baking sheet coated with nonstick cooking spray. Bake at 350° for 20-25 minutes or until golden brown. Carefully remove to wire racks; cool for 5 minutes.

Transfer to a cutting board; cut with a serrated knife into 3/4-in. slices. Place cut side down on ungreased baking sheets. Bake for 5 minutes. Turn and bake 5-7 minutes longer or until firm.

Remove to wire racks to cool. Store in an airtight container.

NUTRITION FACTS: 1 cookie equals 75 calories, 2 g fat (1 g saturated fat), 11 mg cholesterol, 80 mg sodium, 14 g carbohydrate, trace fiber, 1 g protein. **DIABETIC EXCHANGE:** 1 starch.

Chocolate Raisin Biscotti

(PICTURED ABOVE)

FAT SALT CARB

PREP: 25 Min. **BAKE:** 30 Min. + Cooling **YIELD:** 3 Dozen

A drizzle of creamy frosting makes these chocolate treats from our Test Kitchen so special with coffee or tea.

- 3 tablespoons butter, softened
- 2/3 cup sugar
- 2 eggs
- 3/4 teaspoon vanilla extract, *divided*
- 1 cup all-purpose flour
- 1/4 cup baking cocoa
- 1 teaspoon baking powder
- 1/4 teaspoon baking soda
- 1/4 teaspoon salt
- 1/2 cup raisins
- 2/3 cup confectioners' sugar
- 4 to 5 teaspoons fat-free milk

In a small mixing bowl, beat butter and sugar until crumbly, about 2 minutes. Add eggs and 1/2 teaspoon vanilla; mix well. Combine the flour, cocoa, baking powder, baking soda and salt; beat into butter mixture. Stir in raisins (dough will be sticky).

Divide dough in half. With lightly floured hands, shape each portion into a 12-in. x 2-in. rectangle; place each on a baking sheet coated with nonstick cooking spray. Bake at 350° for 18-22 minutes or until set and tops begin to crack. Carefully remove to wire racks; cool for 5 minutes.

Transfer to a cutting board; cut with a serrated knife into scant 3/4-in. slices. Place cut side down on ungreased baking sheets. Bake for 5 minutes. Turn and bake 5-7 minutes longer or until firm. Remove to wire racks to cool.

In a small bowl, combine the confectioners' sugar, remaining vanilla and enough milk to achieve a drizzling consistency. Transfer to a small resealable plastic bag; cut a small hole in a corner of bag. Drizzle over biscotti. Let stand until set. Store in an airtight container.

NUTRITION FACTS: 1 cookie equals 56 calories, 1 g fat (1 g saturated fat), 14 mg cholesterol, 50 mg sodium, 11 g carbohydrate, trace fiber, 1 g protein. **DIABETIC EXCHANGE:** 1 starch.

Chocolate Swirl Cheesecake

PREP: 25 Min. **BAKE:** 40 Min. + Chilling **YIELD:** 12 Servings

Even Cupid couldn't resist this lovely dessert complete with an ambrosial chocolate topping. It's just perfect for Valentine's Day.
— Kathy Shan, Toledo, Ohio

>   2 cups (16 ounces) 2% cottage cheese
>   1 cup crushed chocolate wafers (20 cookies)
>   1 package (8 ounces) reduced-fat cream cheese, cubed
>   1/2 cup sugar
> Dash salt
>   3 teaspoons vanilla extract
>   2 eggs, lightly beaten
>   1 egg white
>   2 squares (1 ounce *each*) bittersweet chocolate, melted and cooled

Line a strainer with four layers of cheesecloth or one coffee filter; place over a bowl. Place cottage cheese in strainer; cover and refrigerate for 1 hour.

Coat the bottom and sides of a 9-in. springform pan with nonstick cooking spray; press cookie crumbs onto the bottom and 1 in. up the sides. Place pan on a double thickness of heavy-duty foil (about 16 in. square). Securely wrap foil around pan; set aside.

Transfer cottage cheese to a food processor (discard liquid from bowl); cover and process for 2-3 minutes or until smooth. Add cream cheese, sugar and salt; cover and process until smooth. Transfer to a large bowl; stir in the vanilla, eggs and egg white just until smooth. Remove 1 cup of batter; pour remaining batter into prepared pan. Combine the reserved batter with melted chocolate until well blended. Drop by spoonfuls over plain batter; cut through with a knife to swirl.

Place springform pan in a larger baking pan; add 1 in. of boiling water to larger pan. Bake at 350° for 40 minutes or until center is just set. Turn oven off and open door slightly. Cool cheesecake in oven for 30 minutes.

Remove pan from water bath. Remove foil from bottom of pan. Carefully run a knife around edge of pan to loosen; cool on a wire rack for 30 minutes. Chill 3-4 hours or overnight. Remove sides of pan. Refrigerate leftovers.

NUTRITION FACTS: 1 piece equals 186 calories, 8 g fat (4 g saturated fat), 51 mg cholesterol, 262 mg sodium, 21 g carbohydrate, 1 g fiber, 8 g protein. **DIABETIC EXCHANGES:** 1-1/2 starch, 1 lean meat, 1/2 fat.

Zucchini Chocolate Cake
(PICTURED BELOW)

PREP: 30 Min. **BAKE:** 30 Min. + Cooling **YIELD:** 18 Servings

As a confirmed chocoholic, I hope you enjoy this classic cake as much as I do. I modified the original recipe by using canola oil and applesauce. — Carleta Foltz, Sunrise Beach, Missouri

> 1-3/4 cups sugar
>   1/2 cup canola oil
>   2 eggs, lightly beaten
>   2/3 cup unsweetened applesauce
>   1 teaspoon vanilla extract
> 2-1/2 cups all-purpose flour
>   1/2 cup baking cocoa
>   1 teaspoon baking soda
>   1/2 teaspoon salt
>   1/2 cup 1% buttermilk
>   2 cups shredded zucchini
>   1 cup (6 ounces) miniature semisweet chocolate chips
>   1/2 cup chopped pecans, toasted

In a large mixing bowl, beat sugar and oil on medium speed for 1 minute. Add the eggs, applesauce and vanilla; beat 1 minute longer. Combine the flour, cocoa, baking soda and salt; add to sugar mixture alternately with buttermilk, beating just until blended. Stir in zucchini.

Transfer to a 13-in. x 9-in. x 2-in. baking pan coated with nonstick cooking spray. Bake at 350° for 20 minutes. Sprinkle with chocolate chips and pecans. Bake 10-15 minutes longer or until a toothpick inserted near the center comes out clean. Cool on a wire rack.

NUTRITION FACTS: 1 piece equals 286 calories, 13 g fat (3 g saturated fat), 24 mg cholesterol, 152 mg sodium, 42 g carbohydrate, 2 g fiber, 4 g protein. **DIABETIC EXCHANGES:** 2-1/2 starch, 2 fat.

Favorite Recipe Made Lighter

A CANDY-TOPPED TREAT was Kim Belcher's signature dessert, so she took matters into her own hands and lightened it up herself.

From Kingston Mines, Illinois, Kim sent her original recipe for Toffee Crunch Dessert that layered homemade angel food cake with sweetened whipped cream and crushed toffee bars. She also included a trimmed-down version. The L&T home economists were so impressed with her efforts, they made Kim an honorary member of the makeover team.

"Not only is the light dessert just as good as the original, but it's easier to prepare," Kim explains. "Instead of baking an angel food cake, I bought a prepared one. I was happy to learn that this saved calories as well as kitchen time."

The busy home baker once made the dessert's custard-like filling from whipped cream and egg yolks, both of which are high in fat and cholesterol. To bring these numbers down, Kim eliminated the eggs, and replaced the whipped cream with a no-fuss combination of fat-free milk, sugar-free instant pudding and prepared fat-free whipped topping.

Kim should be proud of Makeover Toffee Crunch Dessert. She cut 90% of the fat from her original recipe and all but 1 milligram of cholesterol. More than half the calories and 43% of the sugar are gone as well. Way to go, Kim!

Toffee Crunch Dessert

PREP: 20 Min. + Chilling   YIELD: 15 Servings

> 1 package (16 ounces) angel food cake mix
> 3 egg yolks
> 1 cup confectioners' sugar, *divided*
> 4 cups heavy whipping cream, *divided*
> 8 Butterfinger candy bars (2.1 ounces *each*), crushed

Prepare and bake cake according to package directions. Cool cake completely.

In a heavy saucepan, combine egg yolks and 3/4 cup confectioners' sugar. Gradually stir in 1/2 cup cream. Cook and stir over medium-low heat until mixture is thickened and reaches 160°. Transfer to a bowl. Cover and refrigerate for at least 30 minutes or until cooled.

In a large mixing bowl, beat the remaining cream and confectioners' sugar until stiff peaks form. Stir 3 cups whipped cream into the egg yolk mixture. Fold in the remaining whipped cream.

Cut cake into cubes. In a 13-in. x 9-in. x 2-in. dish coated with nonstick cooking spray, layer half of the cake, cream mixture and crushed candy bars. Repeat layers (dish will be full). Cover and refrigerate for at least 2 hours before serving.

NUTRITION FACTS: 3/4 cup equals 527 calories, 31 g fat (18 g saturated fat), 130 mg cholesterol, 311 mg sodium, 56 g carbohydrate, 1 g fiber, 9 g protein.

Makeover Toffee Crunch Dessert

FAT ↓

(PICTURED ABOVE)

PREP: 20 Min. + Chilling   YIELD: 15 Servings

> 1-1/2 cups cold fat-free milk
> 1 package (1 ounce) sugar-free instant vanilla pudding mix
> 2 cartons (8 ounces *each*) frozen fat-free whipped topping, thawed
> 1 prepared angel food cake (16 ounces), cubed
> 4 Butterfinger candy bars (2.1 ounces *each*), crushed

In a large bowl, whisk milk and pudding mix for 2 minutes. Let stand for 2 minutes or until soft-set. Stir in 2 cups whipped topping. Fold in the remaining whipped topping.

In a 13-in. x 9-in. x 2-in. dish coated with nonstick cooking spray, layer half of the cake cubes, pudding mixture and crushed candy bars. Repeat layers. Cover and refrigerate for at least 2 hours before serving.

NUTRITION FACTS: 3/4 cup equals 219 calories, 3 g fat (2 g saturated fat), 1 mg cholesterol, 366 mg sodium, 41 g carbohydrate, 1 g fiber, 5 g protein. DIABETIC EXCHANGES: 2-1/2 starch, 1/2 fat.

MAKEOVER TIP
Instead of preparing a heavy custard for refrigerated desserts, try combining milk, sugar-free pudding mix and fat-free whipped topping.

Gingerbread with Lemon Sauce

PREP: 25 Min. **BAKE:** 35 Min. + Cooling **YIELD:** 12 Servings

Our Test Kitchen updated a classic to create this moist and delicious cake with a delicate hint of ginger and a zippy lemon sauce. Served warm, it's the perfect ending to any holiday meal.

    2 cups cake flour
  1/2 cup packed brown sugar
    4 teaspoons ground ginger
1-1/2 teaspoons baking soda
  1/2 teaspoon salt
  1/2 teaspoon ground mace
    1 egg
  1/2 cup buttermilk
  1/2 cup unsweetened applesauce
  1/2 cup dark molasses
  1/4 cup butter, melted
SAUCE:
  1/2 cup sugar
    2 tablespoons cornstarch
  3/4 cup water
    1 tablespoon butter
  1/4 cup lemon juice
    1 tablespoon grated lemon peel
    2 drops yellow food coloring, optional

In a large bowl, combine the first six ingredients. In a small bowl, combine the egg, buttermilk, applesauce, molasses and butter; mix well. Stir into dry ingredients just until moistened.

Coat a 10-in. fluted tube pan with nonstick cooking spray and dust with flour; add batter. Bake at 350° for 35-40 minutes or until a toothpick inserted near the center comes out clean. Cool for 10 minutes before removing from pan to a wire rack to cool completely.

In a small saucepan, combine sugar and cornstarch. Stir in water until smooth. Bring to a boil; cook and stir for 2 minutes or until thickened. Remove from the heat. Stir in the butter until melted. Add the lemon juice, lemon peel and food coloring if desired; mix well. Serve with cake.

NUTRITION FACTS: 1 slice with 5 teaspoons sauce equals 251 calories, 6 g fat (3 g saturated fat), 31 mg cholesterol, 330 mg sodium, 48 g carbohydrate, 1 g fiber, 3 g protein.

Lemon Anise Biscotti

(PICTURED ABOVE RIGHT)

FAT SALT CARB

PREP: 25 Min. **BAKE:** 40 Min. + Cooling **YIELD:** 3 Dozen

With the popularity of gourmet coffee, I'm finding lots of people enjoy these classic Italian cookies for dipping.
—Carrie Sherrill, Forestville, Wisconsin

    2 eggs
    1 cup sugar
  1/4 cup canola oil
  1/2 teaspoon lemon extract
  1/4 teaspoon vanilla extract
    2 cups all-purpose flour
    1 teaspoon baking powder
  1/2 teaspoon salt

    4 teaspoons grated lemon peel
    2 teaspoons aniseed, crushed

In a small mixing bowl, beat eggs and sugar for 2 minutes or until thickened. Add oil and extracts; mix well. Combine the flour, baking powder and salt; beat into egg mixture. Stir in lemon peel and aniseed.

Divide dough in half. On a lightly floured surface, shape each portion into a 12-in. x 2-in. rectangle. Transfer to a baking sheet lined with parchment paper. Flatten to 1/2-in. thickness. Bake at 350° for 30-35 minutes or until golden and tops begin to crack. Carefully remove to wire racks; cool for 5 minutes.

Transfer to a cutting board; cut with a serrated knife into scant 3/4-in. slices. Place cut side down on ungreased baking sheets. Bake for 5 minutes. Turn and bake 5-7 minutes longer or until firm and golden brown. Remove to wire racks to cool. Store in an airtight container.

NUTRITION FACTS: 1 cookie equals 66 calories, 2 g fat (trace saturated fat), 12 mg cholesterol, 48 mg sodium, 11 g carbohydrate, trace fiber, 1 g protein. **DIABETIC EXCHANGES:** 1/2 starch, 1/2 fat.

biscotti basics

- Bake the dough in an oblong loaf. Cool slightly and cut into slices using a serrated knife.
- Store biscotti in airtight containers. If decorated with a coating, stack them between sheets of waxed or parchment paper.
- Biscotti also freeze well, but it's best to decorate, dip or drizzle them after removing them from the freezer.
- Because they're so sturdy and keep well, biscotti are ideal for mailing to family members and friends.

Sweet Potato Crisp

(PICTURED BELOW)

SALT ▼

PREP: 40 Min.   **BAKE:** 35 Min.   **YIELD:** 12 Servings

I like to share my not-too-sweet potato crisp with a wonderful buttery crumb topping. This is a welcome change from candied sweet potatoes. —Kathy Hamsher, Moon Township, Pennsylvania

- 4 medium sweet potatoes, cooked, peeled and cubed
- 1 package (8 ounces) fat-free cream cheese
- 1/4 teaspoon ground cinnamon
- 2 medium apples, quartered
- 1 cup fresh *or* frozen cranberries
- 1/2 cup all-purpose flour
- 1/2 cup quick-cooking oats
- 1/2 cup packed brown sugar
- 3 tablespoons cold butter
- 1/4 cup chopped pecans

In a large mixing bowl, beat the sweet potatoes, cream cheese and cinnamon until smooth. Spread evenly into an 11-in. x 7-in. x 2-in. baking dish coated with nonstick cooking spray. Place apples and cranberries in a food processor; cover and process until chopped. Spread over the sweet potato mixture.

In a small bowl, combine the flour, oats and brown sugar; cut in butter until mixture resembles coarse crumbs. Stir in pecans; sprinkle over filling. Bake, uncovered, at 350° for 35-40 minutes or until topping is golden brown and fruit is tender.

NUTRITION FACTS: 1 piece equals 180 calories, 5 g fat (2 g saturated fat), 9 mg cholesterol, 140 mg sodium, 29 g carbohydrate, 3 g fiber, 5 g protein. **DIABETIC EXCHANGES:** 2 starch, 1 fat.

Rocky Road Pudding

(PICTURED ABOVE)

SALT ▼

PREP: 30 Min. + Chilling   **YIELD:** 5 Servings

I'm always on the lookout for delicious things to fix my husband and my 89-year-old mother. This rich dessert is a winner with everyone. —Linda Foreman, Locust Grove, Oklahoma

Sugar substitute equivalent to 1/2 cup sugar
- 5 tablespoons baking cocoa
- 3 tablespoons cornstarch
- 1/8 teaspoon salt
- 2-1/2 cups fat-free milk
- 2 egg yolks, lightly beaten
- 2 teaspoons vanilla extract
- 1 cup miniature marshmallows
- 1/4 cup chopped walnuts, toasted

In a large saucepan, combine the sugar substitute, cocoa, cornstarch and salt. Stir in milk until smooth. Cook and stir over medium-high heat until thickened and bubbly. Reduce heat; cook and stir 2 minutes longer.

Remove from the heat. Stir a small amount of hot filling into egg yolks; return all to the pan, stirring constantly. Bring to a gentle boil; cook and stir for 2 minutes. Remove from the heat. Gently stir in the vanilla. Cool for 15 minutes, stirring occasionally.

Transfer to individual dessert dishes. Cover and refrigerate for 1 hour. Just before serving, top with the marshmallows and walnuts.

NUTRITION FACTS: 1/2 cup equals 183 calories, 6 g fat (1 g saturated fat), 88 mg cholesterol, 131 mg sodium, 25 g carbohydrate, 1 g fiber, 8 g protein. **DIABETIC EXCHANGES:** 1 starch, 1 fat, 1/2 fat-free milk.

Editor's Note: This recipe was tested with Splenda No Calorie Sweetener.

Apple Lasagna

(PICTURED AT RIGHT)

PREP: 25 Min.   **BAKE:** 45 Min. + Standing   **YIELD:** 15 Servings

With its apple filling, cinnamon-sugar topping and delectable drizzle, here's a unique dessert that's perfect for fall get-togethers.
—Pat Overlock, Concord, New Hampshire

    1 egg, lightly beaten
    2 cups (8 ounces) shredded reduced-fat cheddar cheese
    1 cup (8 ounces) part-skim ricotta cheese
    1/4 cup sugar
    1 teaspoon almond extract
    2 cans (21 ounces *each*) apple pie filling
    6 lasagna noodles, cooked, rinsed and drained
TOPPING:
    1/3 cup all-purpose flour
    1/3 cup packed brown sugar
    1/4 cup quick-cooking oats
    1/2 teaspoon ground cinnamon
Dash ground nutmeg
    3 tablespoons cold butter
SOUR CREAM SAUCE:
    3/4 cup reduced-fat sour cream
    3 tablespoons brown sugar

In a small bowl, combine the egg, cheeses, sugar and extract; set aside. Spread one can of pie filling into a 13-in. x 9-in. x 2-in. baking dish coated with nonstick cooking spray. Top with three lasagna noodles and cheese mixture. Layer with remaining noodles and pie filling.

In a small bowl, combine the flour, brown sugar, oats, cinnamon and nutmeg. Cut in butter until crumbly. Sprinkle over filling.

Bake, uncovered, at 350° for 45-50 minutes or until bubbly and heated through. Let stand for 15 minutes. Meanwhile, in a small bowl, combine the sauce ingredients. Serve with lasagna.

NUTRITION FACTS: 1 piece equals 280 calories, 8 g fat (5 g saturated fat), 40 mg cholesterol, 189 mg sodium, 44 g carbohydrate, 1 g fiber, 9 g protein. **DIABETIC EXCHANGES:** 3 starch, 1-1/2 fat.

Grilled Pear Sundaes

FAT SALT

PREP/TOTAL TIME: 15 Min.   **YIELD:** 6 Servings

Who says you can't make dessert on the grill? Our home economists whipped up this fast treat that's sure to turn heads…and keep healthy eating commitments. Sweetened with cinnamon-sugar, warm and tender pear slices are served alongside vanilla ice cream.

    4 medium slightly ripe pears, peeled and cored
    1 tablespoon sugar
    1/4 teaspoon ground cinnamon
Dash pepper
    2 cups reduced-fat no-sugar-added vanilla ice cream
    3 teaspoons honey

Coat grill rack with nonstick cooking spray before starting the grill. Prepare grill for indirect heat.

Cut each pear crosswise into six slices. Combine the sugar, cinnamon and pepper; sprinkle over pears. Transfer to a grill wok or basket. Grill pears, covered, over indirect medium heat for 2-3 minutes on each side or until tender.

For each serving, arrange four pear slices on a plate with 1/3 cup ice cream; drizzle with 1/2 teaspoon honey.

NUTRITION FACTS: 1 serving equals 150 calories, 3 g fat (2 g saturated fat), 7 mg cholesterol, 39 mg sodium, 30 g carbohydrate, 3 g fiber, 2 g protein. **DIABETIC EXCHANGES:** 1 starch, 1 fruit.

Pumpkin Mousse

FAT

PREP/TOTAL TIME: 15 Min.   **YIELD:** 4 Servings

Folks will never guess a dessert as delicious as this butterscotch-pumpkin blend could be so light!
—Patricia Sidloskas, Anniston, Alabama

1-1/2 cups cold fat-free milk
    1 package (1 ounce) sugar-free instant butterscotch pudding mix
    1/2 cup canned pumpkin
    1/2 teaspoon ground cinnamon
    1/4 teaspoon ground ginger
    1/4 teaspoon ground allspice
    1 cup fat-free whipped topping, *divided*

In a large bowl, whisk milk and pudding mix for 2 minutes. Let stand for 2 minutes or until soft-set. Combine the pumpkin, cinnamon, ginger and allspice; fold into pudding. Fold in 1/2 cup whipped topping. Transfer to individual serving dishes. Refrigerate until serving. Garnish with the remaining whipped topping.

NUTRITION FACTS: 2/3 cup mousse with 2 tablespoons whipped topping equals 96 calories, trace fat (trace saturated fat), 2 mg cholesterol, 360 mg sodium, 18 g carbohydrate, 1 g fiber, 4 g protein. **DIABETIC EXCHANGES:** 1/2 starch, 1/2 fat-free milk.

Saucy Poached Pears

(PICTURED BELOW)

PREP/TOTAL TIME: 30 Min.   **YIELD:** 6 Servings

These show-stopping poached pears are dressed up enough to serve with the fanciest meal. Make them ahead of time for added convenience. —Audrey Thibodeau, Mesa, Arizona

> 6 medium pears
> 1/4 cup minced fresh mint
> 1 can (11 ounces) mandarin oranges, drained
> 1 package (10 ounces) frozen unsweetened strawberries, thawed
> 2 teaspoons sugar
> 2 tablespoons finely chopped pistachios

Peel pears, leaving stem attached. Place in a Dutch oven and cover with water; add mint. Bring to a boil. Reduce heat; cover and simmer for 8-12 minutes or until pears are tender but firm. Remove with a slotted spoon. Refrigerate until serving.

For sauce, in a blender, combine the oranges, strawberries and sugar; cover and process until blended. Serve with poached pears; sprinkle with pistachios.

NUTRITION FACTS: 1 pear with 1/3 cup sauce equals 159 calories, 2 g fat (trace saturated fat), 0 cholesterol, 12 mg sodium, 37 g carbohydrate, 5 g fiber, 2 g protein. **DIABETIC EXCHANGES:** 2-1/2 fruit, 1/2 fat.

Fudgy Chocolate Dessert

(PICTURED ABOVE)

PREP: 25 Min.   **BAKE:** 20 Min. + Chilling   **YIELD:** 20 Servings

With a cake-like brownie and hot fudge topping, this scrumptious treat is a chocolate-lover's dream come true. It is my most-requested recipe. —Bonnie Bowen, Adrian, Michigan

> 1 package (18-1/4 ounces) chocolate cake mix
> 1 can (15 ounces) solid-pack pumpkin
> 3 cups cold fat-free milk
> 2 packages (1.4 ounces *each*) sugar-free instant chocolate pudding mix
> 1 package (8 ounces) fat-free cream cheese
> 1 carton (8 ounces) reduced-fat whipped topping
> 1/4 cup fat-free hot fudge ice cream topping
> 1/4 cup fat-free caramel ice cream topping
> 1/4 cup sliced almonds, toasted

In a large bowl, combine cake mix and pumpkin (mixture will be thick). Spread evenly into a 13-in. x 9-in. x 2-in. baking dish coated with nonstick cooking spray. Bake at 375° for 20-25 minutes or until a toothpick inserted near the center comes out clean. Cool completely on a wire rack.

In a large bowl, whisk milk and pudding mixes for 2 minutes. Let stand for 5 minutes or until soft-set. In a small mixing bowl, beat cream cheese until smooth. Add pudding; beat until well blended. Spread over cake. Cover and refrigerate for at least 2 hours.

Just before serving, spread whipped topping over dessert. Drizzle with fudge and caramel toppings; sprinkle with almonds. Refrigerate leftovers.

NUTRITION FACTS: 1 piece equals 200 calories, 5 g fat (2 g saturated fat), 2 mg cholesterol, 376 mg sodium, 35 g carbohydrate, 2 g fiber, 5 g protein. **DIABETIC EXCHANGES:** 2 starch, 1/2 fat.

Favorite Recipe Made Lighter

THE DESSERT TABLE is a special place for *L&T* home economist Anne Addesso and her family. "It brings us together for lively conversation at get-togethers," she explains. "My sister-in-law's Traditional Cheesecake reminds me of the times we've shared.

"The rich cheesecake goes equally well with a cup of coffee or a glass of wine," Anne assures. The makeover team couldn't agree more, but they wanted to make the yummy cake a less guilty pleasure.

They halved the crust's ingredients, and to prevent the thinner crust from absorbing the filling's moisture, they substituted confectioners' sugar for granulated sugar.

They also cut back on the filling's sugar and cream cheese, using a combination of reduced-fat cream cheese and 1% cottage cheese puree instead.

Makeover Traditional Cheesecake is a mouth-watering success. With 229 fewer calories and 21 fewer fat grams per serving, it's a surefire dessert-table favorite.

Makeover Traditional Cheesecake
(PICTURED ABOVE)

PREP: 40 Min. **BAKE:** 1-1/2 Hours + Chilling **YIELD:** 16 Servings

1-3/4 cups graham cracker crumbs
   2 tablespoons confectioners' sugar
   1/4 cup butter, melted
FILLING:
   1 tablespoon lemon juice
   1 tablespoon vanilla extract
   2 cups (16 ounces) 1% cottage cheese
   2 cups (16 ounces) reduced-fat sour cream, *divided*
   2 packages (8 ounces *each*) reduced-fat cream cheese
1-1/4 cups sugar
   2 tablespoons all-purpose flour
   4 eggs, lightly beaten
   1 tablespoon fat-free caramel ice cream topping
   2 Heath candy bars (1.4 ounces *each*), chopped

In a small bowl, combine graham cracker crumbs and confectioners' sugar; stir in butter. Press onto the bottom and 1 in. up the sides of a 9-in. springform pan coated with nonstick cooking spray. Place on a baking sheet. Bake at 325° for 18-22 minutes or until lightly browned. Cool on a wire rack.

Place the lemon juice, vanilla, cottage cheese and 1 cup sour cream in a blender; cover and process for 2 minutes or until smooth. In a large mixing bowl, beat cream cheese and sugar until smooth. Beat in the remaining sour cream. Add flour and pureed cottage cheese mixture; mix well. Beat in eggs on low speed just until combined. Pour into crust. Place pan on a double thickness of heavy-duty foil (about 18 in. square). Securely wrap foil around pan.

Place in a larger baking pan; add 3/4 in. of hot water to larger pan. Bake at 325° for 1-1/2 hours or until surface is no longer shiny and center is almost set. Remove pan from water bath. Cool on a wire rack for 10 minutes.

Carefully run a knife around edge of pan to loosen; cool 1 hour longer. Refrigerate overnight. Remove sides of pan. Garnish with caramel topping and candy bar pieces.

NUTRITION FACTS: 1 slice equals 311 calories, 15 g fat (9 g saturated fat), 93 mg cholesterol, 369 mg sodium, 32 g carbohydrate, trace fiber, 11 g protein.

Traditional Cheesecake

PREP: 40 Min. **BAKE:** 1-1/2 Hours + Chilling **YIELD:** 16 Servings

2-1/2 cups graham cracker crumbs
   1/4 cup sugar
   1/2 cup butter, melted
FILLING:
   4 packages (8 ounces *each)* cream cheese, softened
1-3/4 cups sugar
   2 cups (16 ounces) sour cream
   1 tablespoon lemon juice
   1 tablespoon vanilla extract
   4 eggs, lightly beaten
   2 tablespoons caramel ice cream topping
   4 Heath candy bars (1.4 ounces *each*), chopped

In a small bowl, combine the graham cracker crumbs and sugar; stir in butter. Press onto the bottom and up the sides of a greased 9-in. springform pan. Place on a baking sheet. Bake at 325° for 18-22 minutes or until lightly browned. Cool on a wire rack.

In a large mixing bowl, beat cream cheese and sugar until smooth. Beat in the sour cream, lemon juice and vanilla. Beat in eggs on low speed just until combined. Pour into crust. Place pan on a double thickness of heavy-duty foil (about 18 in. square). Securely wrap foil around pan.

Place in a larger baking pan; add 1 in. of hot water to larger pan. Bake at 325° for 1-1/2 hours or until surface is no longer shiny and center is almost set. Remove pan from water bath. Cool on a wire rack for 10 minutes.

Carefully run a knife around edge of pan to loosen; cool 1 hour longer. Refrigerate overnight. Remove sides of pan. Garnish with caramel topping and candy bar pieces.

NUTRITION FACTS: 1 slice equals 540 calories, 36 g fat (22 g saturated fat), 153 mg cholesterol, 369 mg sodium, 46 g carbohydrate, 1 g fiber, 8 g protein.

Cinnamon Blueberry Sauce

(PICTURED BELOW)

FAT SALT CARB

PREP/TOTAL TIME: 20 Min. **YIELD:** 1 Cup

Having frozen yogurt for dessert? Top it with this vitamin-packed sauce. It's tasty over pancakes, too.
—Linda Johnson, Montesano, Washington

Sugar substitute equivalent to 1/4 cup sugar
   2 teaspoons cornstarch
   2 cups frozen unsweetened blueberries
1/4 cup water
   2 tablespoons lemon juice
1/2 teaspoon ground cinnamon

In a small saucepan, combine sugar substitute and corn-starch. Add the blueberries, water, lemon juice and cinnamon. Cook and stir until mixture comes to a boil. Reduce heat; simmer, uncovered, for 5 minutes, stirring frequently. Serve warm. Refrigerate leftovers.

NUTRITION FACTS: 1/4 cup equals 50 calories, 1 g fat (trace saturated fat), 0 cholesterol, 1 mg sodium, 12 g carbohydrate, 2 g fiber, trace protein. **DIABETIC EXCHANGE:** 1 fruit.

Editor's Note: This recipe was tested with Splenda No Calorie Sweetener.

Cappuccino Trifle

FAT

PREP/TOTAL TIME: 30 Min. **YIELD:** 12 Servings

Hints of cinnamon and coffee flavor my lighter-than-air treat. Cool, quick and easy, it's also guilt-free and satisfies a crowd.
—Sherry Hulsman, Louisville, Kentucky

   1 package (8 ounces) fat-free cream cheese
1/2 cup cold strong brewed coffee
1-1/2 cups cold fat-free milk
   1 package (3.4 ounces) instant vanilla pudding mix
   1 teaspoon ground cinnamon
   1 carton (8 ounces) frozen reduced-fat whipped topping, thawed
   1 package (13.6 ounces) fat-free pound cake, cut into 1/2-inch cubes

In a mixing bowl, beat cream cheese until softened. Beat in coffee. In a small bowl, whisk milk, pudding mix and cinnamon for 2 minutes; let stand for 5 minutes. Stir into coffee mixture.

Set aside 1/4 cup whipped topping. Fold remaining whipped topping into coffee mixture. In a 2-1/2-qt. serving bowl, layer a third of cake cubes and a third of coffee mixture; repeat layers twice. Garnish with reserved whipped topping. Refrigerate until serving.

NUTRITION FACTS: 3/4 cup equals 193 calories, 3 g fat (2 g saturated fat), 2 mg cholesterol, 342 mg sodium, 34 g carbohydrate, trace fiber, 6 g protein. **DIABETIC EXCHANGES:** 2 starch, 1/2 fat.

Editor's Note: This recipe was tested with Entenmann's brand pound cake. You may substitute 6 cups cubed angel food cake if desired.

Apple Skewers

FAT SALT

PREP/TOTAL TIME: 30 Min. **YIELD:** 4 Servings

We enjoy these flavorful grilled apples with a lightly spiced coating all year. Best of all, they're a cinch to grill or broil, and cleanup's a breeze.
—Doris Sowers, Hutchinson, Kansas

   4 medium apples, peeled and quartered
   4 teaspoons sugar
1-1/4 teaspoons ground cinnamon

If grilling the apples, coat grill rack with nonstick cooking spray before starting the grill. Thread apples on four metal or soaked wooden skewers. Lightly spray with nonstick cooking spray. Combine sugar and cinnamon; sprinkle over apples.

Grill, covered, over medium heat or broil 4 in. from the heat for 6-8 minutes or until golden. Turn; cook 8-10 minutes longer or until golden and tender. Serve warm.

NUTRITION FACTS: 1 skewer equals 80 calories, trace fat (trace saturated fat), 0 cholesterol, trace sodium, 21 g carbohydrate, 2 g fiber, trace protein. **DIABETIC EXCHANGE:** 1 fruit.

HEALTHY OUTLOOK

Even though Cinnamon Blueberry Sauce is a sweet treat, it makes a smart food choice for diabetics because it takes advantage of a sugar substitute. In addition, the sauce offers plenty of nutrients for the calories by taking advantage of blueberries.

Cherry Cranberry Pinwheels
(PICTURED ABOVE)

PREP: 1 Hour + Chilling **BAKE:** 10 Min. per Batch + Cooling
YIELD: 4-1/2 to 5 Dozen

Flavored with a combination of cranberries, cherries, orange zest and cinnamon, these festive cookies are as fragrant as they are delicious.   —Deb Perry, Bluffton, Indiana

1-1/2 cups dried cranberries
    1 jar (10 ounces) cherry spreadable fruit
    1/4 cup water
    1/2 teaspoon ground cinnamon
DOUGH:
    1/4 cup butter, softened
1-1/4 cups sugar
    3 egg whites
    3 tablespoons canola oil
    2 tablespoons fat-free milk
    2 teaspoons vanilla extract
1-1/2 teaspoons grated orange peel
3-1/3 cups all-purpose flour
    3/4 teaspoon baking powder
    1/2 teaspoon ground cinnamon
    1/8 teaspoon baking soda

For the filling, combine the cranberries, spreadable fruit, water and cinnamon in a small saucepan. Cook and stir over medium heat for 8 minutes or until liquid is absorbed and cranberries have softened.

Remove from the heat; cool slightly. Transfer to a blender; cover and process until smooth. Transfer to a bowl; cover and refrigerate until chilled.

For the dough, in a large mixing bowl, beat butter and sugar for 2 minutes or until crumbly. Add egg whites, oil, milk, vanilla and orange peel; mix well. Combine the flour, baking powder, cinnamon and baking soda; gradually add to the sugar mixture.

Divide dough in half. On a floured surface, roll one portion of dough into a 14-in. x 9-in. rectangle. Spread with half of the filling. Roll up jelly-roll style, starting with a long side. Repeat with remaining dough and filling.

Wrap each of the rolls in plastic wrap, and refrigerate for at least 4 hours.

Unwrap dough; cut into 1/2-in. slices. Place 2 in. apart on baking sheets coated with nonstick cooking spray. Bake at 375° for 10-12 minutes or until bottoms are lightly browned (do not overbake). Remove to wire racks to cool.

NUTRITION FACTS: 1 cookie equals 83 calories, 2 g fat (1 g saturated fat), 2 mg cholesterol, 21 mg sodium, 16 g carbohydrate, trace fiber, 1 g protein. **DIABETIC EXCHANGES:** 1 starch, 1/2 fat.

Favorite Recipe Made Lighter

BANANA CAKE is a standby for many family bakers, but Jacqueline Kudron jazzes up her version with crushed pineapple and maraschino cherries.

"It's a delicious cake," she writes from her home in Dracut, Massachusetts. "Do you think there is any way that you could make it lighter while keeping its moist texture and its delicious taste?"

There sure is, Jacqueline! The original cake was very moist due to the 1-1/2 cups of oil the recipe called for. However, the banana, pineapple and maraschino cherries also contributed to the moisture. That's why our makeover team decreased the oil significantly and replaced a portion of it with applesauce. In addition, they decided to switch the oil from vegetable oil to heart-healthy canola oil.

Decreasing the sugar and the walnuts and swapping out a whole egg for two egg whites helped turn Makeover Old-Fashioned Banana Cake into a tasty sensation.

With 171 fewer calories per slice, it's a wonderful accompaniment to cups of hot coffee or glasses of cold milk. Best of all, 63% of the fat has been removed, yet the moist texture remains.

Old-Fashioned Banana Cake

PREP: 25 Min.   BAKE: 50 Min. + Cooling   YIELD: 16 Servings

- 3 cups all-purpose flour
- 2 cups sugar
- 3 teaspoons baking powder
- 1 teaspoon salt
- 1 teaspoon ground cinnamon
- 1/4 teaspoon baking soda
- 3 eggs, lightly beaten
- 1-1/2 cups vegetable oil
- 1-1/2 teaspoons vanilla extract
- 1 can (8 ounces) unsweetened crushed pineapple, undrained
- 2 cups cubed firm bananas
- 1 jar (10 ounces) maraschino cherries, drained
- 1 cup chopped walnuts
- 1-1/2 teaspoons confectioners' sugar

In a large mixing bowl, combine the first six ingredients. In a small bowl, combine the eggs, oil and vanilla. Beat into dry ingredients just until combined (batter will be thick). Stir in pineapple. Fold in the bananas, cherries and walnuts.

Transfer to a greased and floured 10-in. fluted tube pan. Bake at 350° for 60-70 minutes or until a toothpick inserted near the center comes out clean.

Cool for 10 minutes before removing from pan to a wire rack to cool completely. Dust with confectioners' sugar.

NUTRITION FACTS: 1 slice equals 475 calories, 27 g fat (2 g saturated fat), 40 mg cholesterol, 255 mg sodium, 57 g carbohydrate, 2 g fiber, 6 g protein.

Makeover Old-Fashioned Banana Cake

(PICTURED ABOVE)

PREP: 25 Min.   BAKE: 50 Min. + Cooling   YIELD: 16 Servings

- 3 cups all-purpose flour
- 1-1/2 cups sugar
- 3 teaspoons baking powder
- 1 teaspoon salt
- 1 teaspoon ground cinnamon
- 1/4 teaspoon baking soda
- 2 eggs
- 2 egg whites
- 1/2 cup unsweetened applesauce
- 1/2 cup canola oil
- 1-1/2 teaspoons vanilla extract
- 1 can (8 ounces) unsweetened crushed pineapple, undrained
- 2 cups cubed firm bananas
- 1 jar (10 ounces) maraschino cherries, drained
- 1/2 cup chopped walnuts
- 1-1/2 teaspoons confectioners' sugar

In a large mixing bowl, combine the first six ingredients. In a small bowl, combine the eggs, egg whites, applesauce, oil and vanilla. Beat into dry ingredients just until combined. Stir in pineapple. Fold in the bananas, cherries and walnuts.

Coat a 10-in. fluted tube pan with nonstick cooking spray and dust with flour. Add the batter. Bake at 350° for 50-60 minutes or until a toothpick inserted near the center comes out clean. Cool for 10 minutes before removing from pan to a wire rack to cool completely. Dust with confectioners' sugar.

NUTRITION FACTS: 1 slice equals 304 calories, 10 g fat (1 g saturated fat), 27 mg cholesterol, 258 mg sodium, 51 g carbohydrate, 1 g fiber, 5 g protein.

Watermelon Berry Sorbet

FAT ⬇ SALT ⬇

(PICTURED BELOW)

PREP: 30 Min. + Freezing   **YIELD:** 6 Servings

Strawberries, watermelon and three other items are all you need for this treat that's virtually fat-free. A friend gave me the recipe, promising it was the ultimate in refreshing summer desserts. I couldn't agree more.   —Jill Swavely, Green Lane, Pennsylvania

   1 cup water
1/2 cup sugar
   2 cups cubed seedless watermelon
   2 cups fresh strawberries, hulled
   1 tablespoon minced fresh mint

In a small heavy saucepan, bring the water and sugar to a boil. Cook and stir until sugar is dissolved. Remove from the heat; cool slightly.

Place the watermelon and strawberries in a blender or food processor; add sugar syrup. Cover and process for 2-3 minutes or until smooth. Strain and discard seeds and pulp. Transfer puree to a 13-in. x 9-in. x 2-in. dish. Freeze for 1 hour or until edges begin to firm.

Stir in mint. Freeze 2 hours longer or until firm. Just before serving, transfer to a blender or food processor; cover and process for 2-3 minutes or until smooth.

NUTRITION FACTS: 1/2 cup equals 95 calories, trace fat (trace saturated fat), 0 cholesterol, 3 mg sodium, 25 g carbohydrate, 2 g fiber, 1 g protein. **DIABETIC EXCHANGES:** 1 starch, 1/2 fruit.

> **TASTY TIP**
> Instead of using strawberries, Jill Swavely also suggests preparing Watermelon Berry Sorbet with raspberries, blueberries or a combination of both.

Caramel-Pecan Chocolate Cake

(PICTURED ABOVE)

PREP: 35 Min.   **BAKE:** 35 Min. + Cooling   **YIELD:** 24 Servings

No one will believe this ooey-gooey chocolate cake is actually light. The decadent dessert features two chocolate cake layers with creamy caramel between them.   —Ruth Lee, Troy, Ontario

       1 package (14 ounces) caramels
       1 can (14 ounces) fat-free sweetened condensed milk
   1/3 cup butter
       4 squares (1 ounce *each*) unsweetened chocolate, melted
   1/3 cup canola oil
1-1/2 cups water
   1/3 cup unsweetened applesauce
       2 egg whites
       1 egg
       2 teaspoons vanilla extract
2-1/2 cups all-purpose flour
1-1/3 cups sugar
   1/3 cup sugar blend for baking
       1 teaspoon baking soda
       1 teaspoon salt
   3/4 cup chopped pecans, toasted
       1 teaspoon confectioners' sugar

In a small heavy saucepan, heat the caramels, milk and butter over low heat until caramels are melted and mixture is smooth, stirring frequently; set aside and keep warm.

In a large mixing bowl, combine chocolate and oil. Beat in the water, applesauce, egg whites, egg and vanilla. Combine the flour, sugar, sugar blend, baking soda and salt; gradually add to chocolate mixture until blended.

Pour half of batter into a 13-in. x 9-in. x 2-in. baking pan coated with nonstick cooking spray. Bake at 350° for 14-18 minutes or until center is set. Spread caramel mixture evenly over cake; top with remaining batter. Sprinkle with pecans.

Bake 18-23 minutes longer or until a toothpick inserted near the center of the top layer comes out clean. Cool on a wire rack. Sprinkle with confectioners' sugar.

NUTRITION FACTS: 1 piece equals 318 calories, 13 g fat (5 g saturated fat), 18 mg cholesterol, 243 mg sodium, 49 g carbohydrate, 2 g fiber, 5 g protein.

Editor's Note: This recipe was tested with Splenda Sugar Blend for Baking.

Florida Pie
(PICTURED ABOVE)

PREP: 25 Min. **BAKE:** 15 Min. + Chilling **YIELD:** 8 Servings

Here's an orange meringue pie that tastes just as sun-kissed as it looks. It's a wonderful dessert for anyone watching their weight.
—Muriel Boyd, Roscoe, Illinois

    1 cup sugar
    5 tablespoons cornstarch
1-1/2 cups orange juice
    3 egg yolks, beaten
    2 large navel oranges, peeled, sectioned and finely chopped
    2 tablespoons butter
    1 tablespoon grated orange peel
    1 tablespoon lemon juice
    1 pastry shell (9 inches), baked
MERINGUE:
    3 egg whites
    2 tablespoons sugar

In a small saucepan, combine sugar and cornstarch. Stir in orange juice until smooth. Cook and stir over medium-high heat until thickened and bubbly. Reduce heat; cook and stir 2 minutes longer.

Remove from the heat. Stir a small amount of hot filling in-to egg yolks; return all to the pan, stirring constantly. Bring to a gentle boil; cook and stir for 2 minutes. Remove from the heat. Stir in the oranges, butter and orange peel. Gently stir in lemon juice. Pour into pastry shell.

In a small mixing bowl, beat egg whites on medium speed until soft peaks form. Gradually add sugar, 1 teaspoon at a time, beating on high until stiff glossy peaks form and sugar is dissolved. Spread evenly over hot filling, sealing edges to crust.

Bake at 350° for 15 minutes or until meringue is golden brown. Cool on a wire rack for 1 hour. Refrigerate for at least 3 hours before serving. Refrigerate leftovers.

NUTRITION FACTS: 1 piece equals 345 calories, 12 g fat (5 g saturated fat), 92 mg cholesterol, 153 mg sodium, 57 g carbohydrate, 1 g fiber, 4 g protein.

Cherry-Chocolate Chip Biscotti

PREP: 20 Min. **BAKE:** 25 Min. + Cooling **YIELD:** 2-1/2 Dozen

Delicious "dunkers," our Test Kitchen's biscotti are chock-full of dried cherries and chocolate chips. Wrapped in cellophane tied with ribbons, they make lovely gifts.

    2 eggs
    2 egg whites
    1 tablespoon canola oil
    2 teaspoons vanilla extract
1/4 teaspoon almond extract

3/4 cup sugar
2-3/4 cups all-purpose flour
1 teaspoon baking powder
1/4 teaspoon baking soda
1/4 teaspoon salt
2/3 cup dried cherries, chopped
1/2 cup miniature semisweet chocolate chips

In a small mixing bowl, beat the eggs, egg whites, oil and extracts; beat in sugar. Combine flour, baking powder, baking soda and salt; beat into egg mixture. Stir in cherries and chocolate chips.

Divide dough in half. With lightly floured hands, shape each portion into a 12-in. x 3-in. rectangle; place each on a baking sheet coated with nonstick cooking spray. Bake at 350° for 15-20 minutes or until lightly browned. Carefully remove to wire racks; cool for 5 minutes.

Transfer to a cutting board; cut with a serrated knife into 3/4-in. slices. Place cut side down on ungreased baking sheets. Bake for 5 minutes. Turn and bake 5-7 minutes longer or until firm. Remove to wire racks to cool. Store in an airtight container.

NUTRITION FACTS: 1 cookie equals 95 calories, 2 g fat (1 g saturated fat), 14 mg cholesterol, 55 mg sodium, 18 g carbohydrate, 1 g fiber, 2 g protein. **DIABETIC EXCHANGE:** 1 starch.

Rosemary Pineapple Upside-Down Cake

PREP: 20 Min. **BAKE:** 35 Min. + Cooling **YIELD:** 8 Servings

Rosemary and pineapple make an unexpectedly superb combination in this delicious cake. It's been such a hit, I usually have to bring two or three cakes to church functions.
              —Paula Marchesi, Lenhartsville, Pennsylvania

1 tablespoon plus 1/4 cup butter, softened, *divided*
1/3 cup packed brown sugar
1 teaspoon minced fresh rosemary
6 canned unsweetened pineapple slices, drained
2/3 cup sugar
1 egg
1 teaspoon vanilla extract
1-1/4 cups all-purpose flour
1-1/4 teaspoons baking powder
1/8 teaspoon salt
1/2 cup fat-free milk
Fresh rosemary sprigs, optional

Melt 1 tablespoon butter; pour into 9-in. round baking pan. Sprinkle with brown sugar and rosemary. Top with pineapple slices; set aside.

In a small mixing bowl, cream sugar and remaining butter. Beat in egg and vanilla. Combine the flour, baking powder and salt; add to creamed mixture alternately with milk. Spoon over pineapple.

Bake at 350° for 35-40 minutes or until a toothpick inserted near the center comes out clean. Cool on a wire rack for 5 minutes. Run a knife around edge of pan; invert cake onto a serving plate. Cool completely. Garnish with rosemary sprigs if desired.

NUTRITION FACTS: 1 slice equals 264 calories, 8 g fat (5 g saturated fat), 46 mg cholesterol, 207 mg sodium, 45 g carbohydrate, 1 g fiber, 3 g protein.

Frozen Almond-Cream Desserts
(PICTURED BELOW)

PREP: 30 Min. + Freezing **YIELD:** 12 Servings

These little, frozen cheesecakes are a surefire crowd-pleaser, particularly when served with the peach sauce. They're even great when made with a sugar substitute. —Eva Wright, Grant, Alabama

3/4 cup ground almonds
1 tablespoon butter, melted
1 envelope unflavored gelatin
1/4 cup cold water
12 ounces reduced-fat cream cheese
1/3 cup sugar
3/4 cup fat-free milk
1/4 teaspoon almond extract
PEACH SAUCE:
3 cups sliced peeled peaches
2 tablespoons sugar
1/8 teaspoon salt

In a small bowl, combine almonds and butter. Press onto the bottom of 12 paper- or foil-lined muffin cups. Cover and freeze for 10 minutes.

Meanwhile, in a small saucepan, sprinkle gelatin over cold water; let stand for 1 minute. Cook over low heat, stirring until gelatin is completely dissolved; set aside.

In a small mixing bowl, beat cream cheese and sugar until smooth. Gradually beat in milk and extract. Stir in gelatin mixture. Spoon into muffin cups; freeze until firm.

Remove desserts from the freezer 10 minutes before serving. Place the sauce ingredients in a blender or food processor; cover and process until pureed. Spoon onto dessert plates. Peel liners off desserts; invert onto peach sauce.

NUTRITION FACTS: 1 dessert with 3 tablespoons sauce equals 170 calories, 10 g fat (5 g saturated fat), 23 mg cholesterol, 163 mg sodium, 16 g carbohydrate, 2 g fiber, 6 g protein. **DIABETIC EXCHANGES:** 2 fat, 1/2 starch, 1/2 fruit.

nonstick cooking spray. Arrange nectarines on top; sprinkle with remaining sugar. Drop remaining batter by teaspoonfuls over nectarines. Sprinkle with raspberries, blackberries and reserved topping.

Bake at 350° for 35-40 minutes or until a toothpick inserted near the center comes out clean. Serve warm.

NUTRITION FACTS: 1 piece equals 177 calories, 6 g fat (3 g saturated fat), 35 mg cholesterol, 172 mg sodium, 28 g carbohydrate, 1 g fiber, 3 g protein. **DIABETIC EXCHANGES:** 2 starch, 1 fat.

Berry Nectarine Buckle
(PICTURED ABOVE)

PREP: 25 Min.   **BAKE:** 35 Min.   **YIELD:** 20 Servings

I found this recipe in a magazine but modified it over the years. We enjoy its fresh assortment of blueberries, raspberries, blackberries and nectarines. —Lisa Darling, Rochester, New York

> 1/3 cup all-purpose flour
> 1/3 cup packed brown sugar
> 1 teaspoon ground cinnamon
> 3 tablespoons cold butter

BATTER:

> 6 tablespoons butter, softened
> 3/4 cup plus 1 tablespoon sugar, *divided*
> 2 eggs
> 1-1/2 teaspoons vanilla extract
> 2-1/4 cups all-purpose flour
> 2-1/2 teaspoons baking powder
> 1/2 teaspoon salt
> 1/2 cup fat-free milk
> 1 cup fresh blueberries
> 1 pound medium nectarines, peeled, sliced and patted dry *or* 1 package (16 ounces) frozen unsweetened sliced peaches, thawed and patted dry
> 1/2 cup fresh raspberries
> 1/2 cup fresh blackberries

For topping, in a small bowl, combine the flour, brown sugar and cinnamon; cut in butter until crumbly. Set aside.

In a large mixing bowl, cream the butter and 3/4 cup sugar. Add eggs, one at a time, beating well after each addition. Beat in vanilla. Combine the flour, baking powder and salt; add to creamed mixture alternately with milk. Set aside 3/4 cup batter. Fold blueberries into remaining batter.

Spoon into a 13-in. x 9-in. x 2-in. baking dish coated with

Cranberry Fudge

(PICTURED BELOW)

PREP: 20 Min. + Chilling   **YIELD:** 1-1/3 Pounds (81 pieces)

This creamy, crunchy fudge is packed with walnuts and cranberries to satisfy all who try it. Though they may seem decadent, each little bite is filled with tons of fabulous, guilt-free flavor.
—Delia Kennedy, Deer Park, Washington

> 2 cups (12 ounces) semisweet chocolate chips
> 1/4 cup light corn syrup
> 1/2 cup confectioners' sugar
> 1/4 cup reduced-fat evaporated milk
> 1 teaspoon vanilla extract
> 1 package (6 ounces) dried cranberries
> 1/3 cup chopped walnuts

Line a 9-in. square pan with foil. Coat the foil with nonstick cooking spray; set aside.

In a heavy saucepan, combine chocolate chips and corn syrup. Cook and stir over low heat until melted. Remove from the heat. Stir in the confectioners' sugar, milk and vanilla. Beat with a wooden spoon until thickened and glossy, about 5 minutes. Stir in cranberries and walnuts. Spread into prepared pan; refrigerate until firm.

Using foil, lift fudge out of pan; discard foil. Cut fudge into 1-in. squares. Store in an airtight container in the refrigerator.

NUTRITION FACTS: 1 piece equals 36 calories, 2 g fat (1 g saturated fat), trace cholesterol, 3 mg sodium, 6 g carbohydrate, trace fiber, trace protein. **DIABETIC EXCHANGE:** 1/2 starch.

Blueberry Pound Cake

PREP: 20 Min.   **BAKE:** 65 Min. + Cooling   **YIELD:** 16 Servings

A lemony glaze tops off the old-fashioned flavor of this Bundt cake. Guests will have a hard time believing that the blueberry treat is lower in sugar and fat than traditional pound cake, so be ready to share the recipe. —Maxine Pierce, Biloxi, Mississippi

 2 cups fresh *or* frozen blueberries
 3 cups all-purpose flour, *divided*
1/2 cup reduced-fat butter, softened
 4 ounces reduced-fat cream cheese, cubed
 2 cups sugar
 2 teaspoons vanilla extract
 3 eggs
 1 egg white
 1 teaspoon baking soda
1/2 teaspoon salt
 1 carton (6 ounces) reduced-fat lemon yogurt
GLAZE:
1/2 cup confectioners' sugar
 4 teaspoons lemon juice

In a small bowl, combine blueberries and 2 tablespoons flour; set aside. In a large mixing bowl, cream the butter, cream cheese, sugar and vanilla until light and fluffy. Add eggs and egg white, one at a time, beating well after each addition.

Combine the baking soda, salt and remaining flour; add to creamed mixture alternately with yogurt. Fold in the reserved blueberries.

Transfer to a 10-in. fluted tube pan coated with nonstick cooking spray. Bake at 350° for 65-70 minutes or until a toothpick inserted near the center comes out clean. Cool for 10 minutes before removing from pan to a wire rack. In a bowl, whisk glaze ingredients until smooth. Drizzle over warm cake.

NUTRITION FACTS: 1 slice equals 276 calories, 6 g fat (3 g saturated fat), 55 mg cholesterol, 241 mg sodium, 52 g carbohydrate, 1 g fiber, 6 g protein.

Editor's Note: *If using frozen blueberries, do not thaw. This recipe was tested with Land O'Lakes light stick butter.*

Ginger Plum Tart   SALT
(PICTURED ABOVE)

PREP: 15 Min.   **BAKE:** 20 Min. + Cooling   **YIELD:** 8 Servings

Looking for a quick, easy dessert that's pretty as a picture? Try this mouth-watering tart. For an extra-special effect, our home economists suggest topping it with a scoop of low-fat ice cream or a dollop of reduced-fat whipped topping.

Pastry for single-crust pie (9 inches)
3-1/2 cups sliced unpeeled fresh plums
 3 tablespoons plus 1 teaspoon coarse sugar, *divided*
 1 tablespoon cornstarch
 2 teaspoons finely chopped crystallized ginger
 1 egg white
 1 tablespoon water

Roll pastry into a 12-in. circle. Transfer to a large baking sheet lined with parchment paper. In a large bowl, combine plums, 3 tablespoons sugar and cornstarch. Arrange plums in a pinwheel pattern over pastry to within 2 in. of edges; sprinkle with ginger. Fold edges of pastry over plums.

Beat egg white and water; brush over pastry. Sprinkle with remaining sugar. Bake at 400° for 20-25 minutes or until crust is lightly browned. Cool for 15 minutes before removing from pan to a serving platter.

NUTRITION FACTS: 1 piece equals 190 calories, 7 g fat (3 g saturated fat), 5 mg cholesterol, 108 mg sodium, 30 g carbohydrate, 1 g fiber, 2 g protein. **DIABETIC EXCHANGES:** 1-1/2 starch, 1 fat, 1/2 fruit.

Glossy Chocolate Frosting

PREP/TOTAL TIME: 15 Min.   **YIELD:** 1-1/4 Cups

I lightened up my grandmother's recipe for this thick, rich frosting.
—Melissa Wentz, Harrisburg, Pennsylvania

   1/2 cup sugar
Sugar substitute equivalent to 1/2 cup sugar
   1/2 cup baking cocoa
    3 tablespoons cornstarch
    1 cup cold water
4-1/2 teaspoons butter
    1 teaspoon vanilla extract

In a saucepan, combine the sugar, sugar substitute, cocoa and cornstarch. Add water and stir until smooth. Bring to a boil; cook and stir for 1 minute or until thickened. Remove from the heat; stir in butter and vanilla until smooth. Spread over cupcakes or cake while frosting is still warm.

NUTRITION FACTS: 4 teaspoons equals 54 calories, 1 g fat (1 g saturated fat), 3 mg cholesterol, 12 mg sodium, 11 g carbohydrate, 1 g fiber, 1 g protein. **DIABETIC EXCHANGES:** 1/2 starch, 1/2 fat.

Editor's Note: This recipe makes enough to frost 12 cupcakes or the top of a 13-inch x 9-inch cake. It was tested with Splenda No Calorie Sweetener.

Ruby Razz Dessert Squares

PREP: 20 Min.   **BAKE:** 45 Min. + Cooling   **YIELD:** 18 Servings

I rely on rhubarb and frozen raspberries for these crimson treats. The squares are perfect any time of year.
—Pauline Murray, Cleveland, Ohio

    1 package (10 ounces) frozen sweetened raspberries, thawed
    1 cup sugar
  1/4 cup cornstarch
    4 cups sliced fresh *or* frozen rhubarb
CRUST:
1-1/3 cups quick-cooking oats
    1 cup all-purpose flour
  2/3 cup packed brown sugar
  1/2 teaspoon ground cinnamon
  1/8 teaspoon salt
  2/3 cup butter, melted

Drain raspberries, reserving juice. Add enough water to reserved juice to measure 1-1/2 cups; set berries aside. In a small saucepan, combine the sugar and cornstarch. Gradually stir in raspberry juice mixture until smooth. Bring to a boil; cook and stir for 1-2 minutes or until thickened. Stir in the berries and rhubarb; set aside.

In a bowl, combine the crust ingredients until blended. Set aside 1/4 cup for topping. Press remaining crumb mixture into a 13-in. x 9-in. x 2-in. baking pan coated with nonstick cooking spray. Bake at 350° for 8-10 minutes or until set.

Top with fruit mixture. Sprinkle with reserved crumb mixture. Bake 35-40 minutes longer or until bubbly and rhubarb is tender. Cool on a wire rack. Cut into squares.

NUTRITION FACTS: 1 square equals 210 calories, 7 g fat (4 g saturated fat), 18 mg cholesterol, 90 mg sodium, 35 g carbohydrate, 2 g fiber, 2 g protein. **DIABETIC EXCHANGES:** 2 starch, 1 fat.

Pear Crumble Pie

(PICTURED ABOVE)

PREP: 20 Min.   **BAKE:** 45 Min. + Cooling   **YIELD:** 8 Servings

I couldn't imagine a pear pie until I bit into this succulent dessert. The sweet crumb topping is wonderful, and the filling is a nice change from apple. Try it with a scoop of low-fat frozen yogurt.
—Ruth Ann Stelfox, Raymond, Alberta

  1/3 cup sugar
    3 tablespoons all-purpose flour
    6 cups sliced peeled fresh pears
    1 unbaked pastry shell (9 inches)
CRUMBLE TOPPING:
  1/3 cup all-purpose flour
    3 tablespoons brown sugar
  1/4 teaspoon ground cinnamon
    2 tablespoons cold butter

In a large bowl, combine sugar and flour; add the pears and toss gently to coat. Spoon into pastry shell. In a small bowl, combine the flour, brown sugar and cinnamon; cut in butter until crumbly. Sprinkle over the pie.

Bake at 400° for 45-50 minutes or until pears are tender and topping is golden brown. Cover edges loosely with foil during the last 30 minutes to prevent overbrowning. Cool on a wire rack.

NUTRITION FACTS: 1 piece equals 300 calories, 10 g fat (5 g saturated fat), 13 mg cholesterol, 131 mg sodium, 51 g carbohydrate, 3 g fiber, 2 g protein.

Chocolate Dream Pie

(PICTURED AT RIGHT)

PREP: 45 Min. + Chilling **BAKE:** 15 Min. + Chilling **YIELD:** 8 Servings

What an impressive finish our Test Kitchen whipped up with this creamy chocolate pie topped with peaks of golden meringue!

- 1-1/4 cups all-purpose flour
- 2 tablespoons sugar
- 1/4 teaspoon baking powder
- 1/4 teaspoon salt
- 3 tablespoons cold butter
- 2 tablespoons canola oil
- 2 tablespoons buttermilk
- 6 to 7 teaspoons cold water

FILLING:

- 1/3 cup sugar
- 3 tablespoons baking cocoa
- 2 tablespoons cornstarch
- 1/4 teaspoon salt
- 2 cups fat-free evaporated milk
- 1/4 cup water
- 1 egg, beaten
- 2 squares (1 ounce *each*) semisweet chocolate, coarsely chopped
- 1 teaspoon vanilla extract
- 1/4 teaspoon almond extract

MERINGUE:

- 3 egg whites
- 1/4 teaspoon cream of tartar
- 6 tablespoons sugar

In a small bowl, combine the flour, sugar, baking powder and salt. Cut in butter until crumbly. Add oil and buttermilk; toss with a fork. Gradually add water, tossing with a fork, until a ball forms. Cover and refrigerate for 1 hour.

On a lightly floured surface, roll out dough to fit a 9-in. pie plate. Transfer pastry to a pie plate coated with nonstick cooking spray. Trim pastry to 1/2 in. beyond edge of plate; flute edges. With a fork, prick bottom and sides of pastry. Line with a double thickness of heavy-duty foil. Bake at 450° for 8 minutes. Remove foil; bake 6-8 minutes longer or until light golden. Cool on a wire rack.

In a small saucepan, combine the sugar, cocoa, cornstarch and salt. Stir in milk and water until smooth. Cook and stir over medium-high heat until thickened and bubbly. Reduce heat; cook and stir 2 minutes longer. Remove from the heat.

Stir a small amount of hot filling into egg; return all to the pan, stirring constantly. Bring to a gentle boil; cook and stir 2 minutes longer. Remove from the heat. Stir in chocolate until smooth; stir in extracts. Pour into pastry shell; set aside.

For meringue, in a small mixing bowl, beat egg whites and cream of tartar on medium speed until soft peaks form. Gradually beat in sugar, 1 tablespoon at a time, on high until stiff peaks form. Spread evenly over filling, sealing edges to crust.

Bake at 350° for 12-15 minutes or until golden brown. Cool on a wire rack for 1 hour; refrigerate for at least 3 hours before serving.

NUTRITION FACTS: 1 piece equals 337 calories, 11 g fat (4 g saturated fat), 41 mg cholesterol, 311 mg sodium, 51 g carbohydrate, 1 g fiber, 10 g protein.

Peanut Butter Swirl Cake

PREP: 35 Min. **BAKE:** 35 Min. + Cooling **YIELD:** 18 Servings

Pretty swirls of cream cheese and peanut butter dress up a chocolate cake mix in this recipe.   —Cheryl Paulsen, Omro, Wisconsin

- 1 package (18-1/4 ounces) chocolate cake mix
- 1-1/4 cups water
- 1/2 cup reduced-fat sour cream
- 2 egg whites
- 1 package (8 ounces) reduced-fat cream cheese
- 1 egg, lightly beaten
- 1/2 cup sugar
- 1/2 cup reduced-fat creamy peanut butter
- 1/4 cup fat-free milk

In a large mixing bowl, beat the cake mix, water, sour cream and egg whites on medium speed for 2 minutes. Coat a 13-in. x 9-in. x 2-in. baking pan with nonstick cooking spray and dust with flour. Pour batter into pan.

In a small mixing bowl, beat the cream cheese, egg, sugar, peanut butter and milk until smooth. Drop by tablespoonfuls over batter and swirl with a knife. Bake at 350° for 35-40 minutes or until a toothpick inserted near the center comes out clean. Cool on a wire rack. Refrigerate leftovers.

NUTRITION FACTS: 1 piece equals 225 calories, 9 g fat (4 g saturated fat), 23 mg cholesterol, 289 mg sodium, 32 g carbohydrate, 1 g fiber, 6 g protein. **DIABETIC EXCHANGES:** 2 starch, 1 fat.

> **TASTY TIP**
> Peanut Butter Swirl Cake is a very rich treat. Extra-small servings make great additions to cookie platters.

Favorite Recipe Made Lighter

SWEET cream cheese frostings served atop tender cakes make luscious desserts. And Joanne Brininstool's take on classic Italian Cream Cake is a perfect example. The moist treat from the Austin, Texas cook features a hint of coconut and nutty pecans.

But with all of the butter, shortening and sugar, Joanne's favorite dessert is not at all light. "Could you make over this wonderful recipe?" she asks.

The *L& T* staff was determined to keep the original's flavor while cutting calories, fat and cholesterol, so they replaced the shortening with unsweetened applesauce. They also decreased the egg yolks, cut back on coconut, decreased the nuts and lightened up the frosting.

Makeover Italian Cream Cake saves calories without a noticeable difference in flavor. With nearly half the fat, lowered trans fat and 34% less cholesterol per serving, it's a heart-healthy, happy ending to any meal.

Italian Cream Cake

PREP: 30 Min. **BAKE:** 25 Min. + Cooling **YIELD:** 18 Servings

- 1/2 cup butter, softened
- 1/2 cup shortening
- 1-1/2 cups sugar
- 5 eggs, *separated*
- 1 teaspoon vanilla extract
- 2 cups all-purpose flour
- 1 teaspoon baking soda
- 1/2 teaspoon salt
- 1 cup buttermilk
- 1 cup flaked coconut
- 1 cup chopped pecans

FROSTING:

- 1 package (8 ounces) cream cheese, softened
- 1/4 cup butter, softened
- 1 teaspoon vanilla extract
- 3-3/4 cups confectioners' sugar
- 1/2 cup chopped pecans, toasted

In a large mixing bowl, beat butter and shortening. Gradually add sugar; beat 2 minutes longer. Add egg yolks and vanilla; beat for 1 minute. Combine the flour, baking soda and salt; add to creamed mixture alternately with buttermilk.

In another mixing bowl, beat egg whites until stiff peaks form. Fold into batter. Fold in coconut and pecans. Transfer to a greased 13-in. x 9-in. x 2-in. baking pan. Bake at 350° for 30-35 minutes or until a toothpick inserted near the center comes out clean. Cool on a wire rack.

For frosting, in a bowl, combine the cream cheese, butter and vanilla. Gradually beat in confectioners' sugar. Spread over cake. Sprinkle with pecans. Store in the refrigerator.

NUTRITION FACTS: 1 piece equals 494 calories, 28 g fat (12 g saturated fat), 94 mg cholesterol, 296 mg sodium, 57 g carbohydrate, 2 g fiber, 6 g protein.

Makeover Italian Cream Cake
(PICTURED ABOVE)

PREP: 30 Min. **BAKE:** 25 Min. + Cooling **YIELD:** 18 Servings

- 1/2 cup butter, softened
- 1-1/2 cups sugar
- 1/2 cup unsweetened applesauce
- 3 egg yolks
- 1 teaspoon vanilla extract
- 2 cups all-purpose flour
- 1 teaspoon baking soda
- 1/2 teaspoon salt
- 1 cup buttermilk
- 5 egg whites
- 1/2 cup flaked coconut
- 1/2 cup chopped pecans

FROSTING:

- 1 package (8 ounces) reduced-fat cream cheese
- 2 tablespoons butter, softened
- 1 teaspoon vanilla extract
- 2-1/2 cups confectioners' sugar
- 1/4 cup chopped pecans, toasted

In a large mixing bowl, beat butter and sugar for 2 minutes. Stir in applesauce. Add egg yolks and vanilla; beat for 1 minute. Combine the flour, baking soda and salt; add to butter mixture alternately with buttermilk.

In another mixing bowl, beat egg whites until stiff peaks form. Fold into batter. Fold in coconut and pecans. Transfer to a 13-in. x 9-in. x 2-in. baking pan coated with nonstick cooking spray. Bake at 350° for 25-30 minutes or until a toothpick inserted near the center comes out clean. Cool on a wire rack.

For frosting, in a small mixing bowl, combine the cream cheese, butter and vanilla. Gradually beat in confectioners' sugar. Spread over cake; sprinkle with pecans. Store in the refrigerator.

NUTRITION FACTS: 1 piece equals 338 calories, 15 g fat (7 g saturated fat), 62 mg cholesterol, 291 mg sodium, 48 g carbohydrate, 1 g fiber, 5 g protein.

Autumn Surprise Pie
(PICTURED ABOVE)

PREP: 30 Min. **BAKE:** 45 Min. + Cooling **YIELD:** 8 Servings

This scrumptious apple pie calls for apples, pears and raisins tossed with sugar and spice for a treat that's definitely nice.
—Karen Gauvreau, Clearwater, Florida

1-1/2 cups all-purpose flour
  3 tablespoons sugar
1/4 teaspoon plus 1/8 teaspoon baking powder
1/4 teaspoon plus 1/8 teaspoon salt
  6 tablespoons cold butter
1/4 cup fat-free milk
1-1/2 teaspoons cider vinegar
FILLING:
  5 cups sliced peeled tart apples
  2 cups sliced peeled ripe pears
1/3 cup raisins
1/2 cup plus 1 teaspoon sugar, *divided*
1/4 cup all-purpose flour
  1 teaspoon ground cinnamon
1/4 teaspoon ground nutmeg
1/4 teaspoon ground cloves
3/4 teaspoon rum extract
  1 egg white

In a bowl, combine the flour, sugar, baking powder and salt; cut in butter until mixture resembles coarse crumbs. Combine milk and vinegar; gradually add to crumb mixture, tossing with a fork until dough forms a ball.

Divide dough into two balls, one slightly larger than the other. On a lightly floured surface, roll larger ball to fit a 9-in. pie plate. Coat pie plate with nonstick cooking spray; transfer pastry to plate.

In a large bowl, combine apples, pears and raisins. Combine 1/2 cup sugar, flour, cinnamon, nutmeg and cloves; add to fruit mixture and toss. Sprinkle with extract; toss well. Spoon into crust.

Roll out remaining pastry; make a lattice crust. Trim, seal and flute edges. Brush lattice with egg white; sprinkle with remaining sugar. Bake at 425° for 15 minutes. Reduce heat to 350°; bake 30-35 minutes longer or until crust is golden and filling is bubbly. Cool on a wire rack.

NUTRITION FACTS: 1 piece equals 331 calories, 10 g fat (5 g saturated fat), 23 mg cholesterol, 241 mg sodium, 60 g carbohydrate, 4 g fiber, 4 g protein.

Ladyfinger Cream Sandwiches
(PICTURED ABOVE)

SALT

PREP: 25 Min. + Chilling   **YIELD:** 2 Dozen

Dainty and delicious, these elegant finger sandwiches were created by our home economists and make the perfect finish to a ladies' luncheon or afternoon tea.

    1/4 cup all-purpose flour
    1/4 cup sugar
Sugar substitute equivalent to 1/4 cup sugar
    1/4 teaspoon salt
 2-3/4 cups 2% milk, *divided*
      3 eggs
    3/4 teaspoon vanilla extract
      2 packages (3 ounces *each*) ladyfingers, split
      2 teaspoons coarse sugar

In a small saucepan, combine the flour, sugar, sugar substitute, salt and 2-1/2 cups milk until smooth. Cook and stir over medium-high heat until thickened and bubbly. Reduce heat; cook and stir 2 minutes longer. Remove from the heat.

In a small bowl, whisk 2 eggs. Stir a small amount of hot filling into eggs; return all to the pan, stirring constantly. Bring to a gentle boil; cook and stir 2 minutes longer. Remove from the heat. Gently stir in vanilla. Transfer to a bowl; press plastic wrap onto surface of custard. Refrigerate until chilled.

Place tops of ladyfingers on an ungreased baking sheet. In a small bowl, whisk remaining egg and milk; lightly brush over ladyfingers. Sprinkle with coarse sugar. Broil 4 in. from the heat for 1-2 minutes or until golden brown.

Spread custard over the bottoms of ladyfingers. Replace tops. Serve immediately. Refrigerate leftovers.

NUTRITION FACTS: 2 filled ladyfingers equals 129 calories, 4 g fat (2 g saturated fat), 109 mg cholesterol, 114 mg sodium, 19 g carbohydrate, trace fiber, 5 g protein. **DIABETIC EXCHANGES:** 1 starch, 1/2 fat.

Editor's Note: This recipe was tested with Splenda No Calorie Sweetener.

Tropical Meringue Tarts
(PICTURED ABOVE)

FAT

PREP: 30 Min. + Standing   **BAKE:** 50 Min. + Cooling   **YIELD:** 10 Servings

What a special treat! As fun as an Easter basket, these tender meringue shells are filled with creamy pudding, then topped with fresh fruit and toasted coconut. The Test Kitchen staff thinks the low-fat showstoppers are a perfect way to welcome spring.

      4 egg whites
      1 teaspoon white vinegar
      1 teaspoon vanilla extract
      1 teaspoon cornstarch
      1 cup sugar
 1-1/4 cups cold fat-free milk
      1 package (1 ounce) sugar-free instant vanilla pudding mix
      1 cup reduced-fat whipped topping
      1 cup cubed fresh pineapple

2 kiwifruit, peeled and sliced
2 tablespoons flaked coconut, toasted

Place egg whites in a large mixing bowl; let stand at room temperature for 30 minutes. Meanwhile, line a baking sheet with parchment paper or foil. Draw ten 3-in. circles on paper; set aside.

Add vinegar and vanilla to egg whites; beat on medium speed until soft peaks form. Beat in cornstarch. Gradually beat in sugar, 2 tablespoons at a time, on high until stiff glossy peaks form and sugar is dissolved.

Cut a small hole in the corner of pastry or plastic bag; insert a large star pastry tip (#6B). Fill the bag with meringue. Pipe meringue in a spiral fashion to fill in circles on prepared pan. Pipe twice around the base of each shell in a spiral fashion to make the sides.

Bake at 275° for 50-60 minutes or until set and dry. Turn oven off and leave door closed; leave meringues in oven for 1 hour.

For filling, in a large bowl, whisk milk and pudding mix for 2 minutes. Let stand for 2 minutes or until soft-set. Fold in whipped topping. Spoon into meringue shells. Top with pineapple, kiwi and coconut.

NUTRITION FACTS: 1 tart equals 145 calories, 2 g fat (1 g saturated fat), 1 mg cholesterol, 157 mg sodium, 30 g carbohydrate, 1 g fiber, 3 g protein. **DIABETIC EXCHANGE:** 2 starch.

Tart 'n' Frosty Limeade Dessert

SALT ▼

PREP: 30 Min. + Chilling   **BAKE:** 10 Min. + Freezing   **YIELD:** 20 Servings

Luscious with lime flavor, this frozen treat is so lovely, it melts all resistance to dessert—even after hearty meals!
—Pam Peirce, Pewaukee, Wisconsin

1-2/3 cups quick-cooking oats
1/3 cup packed brown sugar
1/3 cup chopped pecans
1/4 cup butter, melted
FILLING:
1 can (12 ounces) reduced-fat evaporated milk
1 can (6 ounces) frozen limeade concentrate, thawed
1/4 cup sugar
1 teaspoon grated lime peel
1 teaspoon vanilla extract
4 to 6 drops green food coloring, optional
1 carton (8 ounces) frozen reduced-fat whipped topping, thawed

In a small bowl, combine the oats, brown sugar and pecans; stir in butter. Press into a 13-in. x 9-in. x 2-in. baking dish coated with nonstick cooking spray. Bake at 350° for 8-10 minutes or until lightly browned. Cool on a wire rack.

Pour the milk into a metal mixing bowl; place mixer beaters in bowl. Cover and refrigerate for at least 2 hours.

Beat milk until soft peaks form. Fold in limeade concentrate, sugar, lime peel, vanilla and food coloring if desired. Fold in whipped topping. Pour over the crust. Cover; freeze for 4 hours or until firm. Remove from the freezer 15 minutes before serving.

NUTRITION FACTS: 1 piece equals 145 calories, 6 g fat (3 g saturated fat), 8 mg cholesterol, 44 mg sodium, 21 g carbohydrate, 1 g fiber, 3 g protein. **DIABETIC EXCHANGES:** 1-1/2 starch, 1/2 fat.

Classic Yellow Cupcakes
(PICTURED BELOW)

PREP: 15 Min.   **BAKE:** 20 Min. + Cooling   **YIELD:** 1-1/2 Dozen

From the L&T team, these golden cupcakes are a perfect contribution to a baby shower or casual lunch.

2/3 cup butter, softened
3/4 cup sugar blend for baking
3 eggs
1-1/2 teaspoons vanilla extract
2-1/4 cups cake flour
2 teaspoons baking powder
1/4 teaspoon salt
3/4 cup fat-free milk
Fat-free whipped topping, optional
1 teaspoon confectioners' sugar

In a large mixing bowl, cream butter and sugar substitute. Add eggs, one at a time, beating well after each addition. Beat in vanilla. Combine the flour, baking powder and salt; add to creamed mixture alternately with milk.

Fill paper-lined muffin cups three-fourths full. Bake at 350° for 20-25 minutes or until lightly browned and a toothpick comes out clean. Cool for 5 minutes before removing from pans to wire racks to cool completely. Top with a dollop of whipped topping if desired, then dust with confectioners' sugar.

NUTRITION FACTS: 1 cupcake (calculated without whipped topping) equals 171 calories, 8 g fat (4 g saturated fat), 54 mg cholesterol, 171 mg sodium, 22 g carbohydrate, trace fiber, 3 g protein. **DIABETIC EXCHANGES:** 1-1/2 starch, 1-1/2 fat.

Editor's Note: This recipe was tested with Splenda Sugar Blend for Baking.

Icy Fruit Pops

(PICTURED BELOW)

PREP: 20 Min. + Freezing   **YIELD:** 2 Dozen

My grandmother made these pineapple treats for my brother and me when we were little. The pops are still cool snacks that delight kids of all ages.   —LeAnn Kane, Forsyth, Illinois

    1 **can (20 ounces) crushed pineapple, undrained**
    1 **cup water**
  3/4 **cup orange juice concentrate**
  3/4 **cup lemonade concentrate**
Sugar substitute equivalent to 1/2 cup sugar
    5 **medium firm bananas, cut into 1/4-inch slices and quartered**
    1 **can (12 ounces) diet ginger ale**
  24 **maraschino cherries *or* fresh strawberries**

In a large bowl, combine the pineapple, water, orange juice concentrate, lemonade concentrate and sugar substitute. Stir in the bananas and ginger ale.

    Place a cherry in each of twenty-four 3-oz. paper cups; fill with pineapple mixture. Insert wooden sticks. Cover and freeze until firm.

NUTRITION FACTS: 1 serving equals 66 calories, trace fat (trace saturated fat), 0 cholesterol, 5 mg sodium, 17 g carbohydrate, 1 g fiber, 1 g protein. **DIABETIC EXCHANGE:** 1 fruit.

Editor's Note: This recipe was tested with Splenda No Calorie Sweetener.

Raspberry Angel Cake

(PICTURED ABOVE)

PREP: 15 Min.   **BAKE:** 45 Min. + Cooling   **YIELD:** 12 Servings

Not only is this a refreshing dessert, but it's virtually fat-free. The cake's vibrant, red swirls make it a special and delicious treat that comes together easily.   —Sheri Erickson, Montrose, Iowa

    1 **package (16 ounces) one-step angel food cake mix**
  1/2 **teaspoon almond extract**
  1/2 **teaspoon vanilla extract**
    1 **package (.3 ounce) sugar-free raspberry gelatin**
    1 **package (12 ounces) frozen unsweetened raspberries, thawed**
    1 **tablespoon sugar**

Prepare cake batter according to package directions. Fold in extracts. Spoon two-thirds of the batter into an ungreased 10-in. tube pan. Add gelatin powder to remaining batter; drop by tablespoonfuls over batter in pan. Cut through with a knife to swirl.

    Bake according to package directions. Immediately invert pan onto a wire rack; cool completely, about 1 hour. Carefully run a knife around sides of pan to remove cake. Cut into slices. Combine raspberries and sugar; serve over cake.

NUTRITION FACTS: 1 slice with 2 tablespoons sauce equals 155 calories, trace fat (0 saturated fat), 0 cholesterol, 224 mg sodium, 35 g carbohydrate, 1 g fiber, 4 g protein. **DIABETIC EXCHANGE:** 2 starch.

> **TASTY TIP**
> Sheri Erickson likes to top servings of Raspberry Angel Cake with dollops of reduced-fat whipped topping.

Favorite Recipe Made Lighter

EVERYTHING'S SWEETER with fruit and berries. After all, colorful produce is a perfectly healthy choice for sprucing up after-dinner surprises.

Among the large variety of fresh-produce treats, colorful fruit pizzas are gaining popularity, making a splash in large bakeries as well as specialty shops and even with home bakers.

The pizzas showcase shortbread crusts that hold up beneath creamy spreads, ripe fruits and sweet sauces. But while they are delicious, the crusts contain loads of butter. That's why we made over a traditional fruit pizza.

It's difficult to reproduce classic shortbread with low-fat ingredients, so our home economists halved the crust, making it thinner. The result was a less-fat version that remained crispy regardless of the pizza's toppings.

The dessert's citrus glaze is flavored with pineapple juice. The juice was rather sweet on its own, allowing our team to eliminate the glaze's sugar.

Makeover Fruit Pizza is a delightful summer sensation. With nearly half the calories, fat and cholesterol of a traditional version, it's one dessert you can afford to enjoy.

Fruit Pizza

PREP: 30 Min. + Chilling   **YIELD:** 16 Servings

>   2 cups all-purpose flour
> 1/2 cup confectioners' sugar
>   1 cup cold butter
>   1 package (8 ounces) cream cheese, softened
> 1/3 cup sugar
>   1 teaspoon vanilla extract
>   2 cups halved fresh strawberries
>   1 can (11 ounces) mandarin oranges, drained
>   1 cup fresh blueberries

GLAZE:
> 1/2 cup sugar
>   2 tablespoons cornstarch
>   1 cup unsweetened pineapple juice
>   1 teaspoon lemon juice

In a large bowl, combine flour and confectioners' sugar. Cut in butter until crumbly. Press onto an ungreased 12-in. pizza pan. Bake at 350° for 12-15 minutes or until very lightly browned. Cool on a wire rack.

In a small mixing bowl, beat the cream cheese, sugar and vanilla until smooth. Spread over crust. Arrange the strawberries, oranges and blueberries on top.

For glaze, in a small saucepan, combine sugar and cornstarch. Stir in pineapple juice and lemon juice until smooth. Bring to a boil; cook and stir for 2 minutes or until thickened. Cool slightly. Drizzle over fruit. Refrigerate until chilled.

NUTRITION FACTS: 1 slice equals 294 calories, 17 g fat (10 g saturated fat), 46 mg cholesterol, 159 mg sodium, 34 g carbohydrate, 1 g fiber, 3 g protein.

Makeover Fruit Pizza
(PICTURED ABOVE)

SALT

PREP: 30 Min. + Chilling   **YIELD:** 16 Servings

>   1 cup all-purpose flour
> 1/4 cup confectioners' sugar
> 1/2 cup cold butter
>   1 package (8 ounces) reduced-fat cream cheese
> 1/3 cup sugar
>   1 teaspoon vanilla extract
>   2 cups halved fresh strawberries
>   1 can (11 ounces) reduced-sugar mandarin oranges, drained
>   1 cup fresh blueberries

GLAZE:
>   5 teaspoons cornstarch
> 1-1/4 cups unsweetened pineapple juice
>   1 teaspoon lemon juice

In a large bowl, combine flour and confectioners' sugar. Cut in butter until crumbly. Press onto an ungreased 12-in. pizza pan. Bake at 350° for 10-12 minutes or until very lightly browned. Cool on a wire rack.

In a small mixing bowl, beat cream cheese, sugar and vanilla until smooth. Spread over crust. Arrange the strawberries, oranges and blueberries on top.

For glaze, in a small saucepan, combine the cornstarch, pineapple juice and lemon juice until smooth. Bring to a boil; cook and stir for 2 minutes or until thickened. Cool slightly. Drizzle over fruit. Refrigerate until chilled.

NUTRITION FACTS: 1 slice equals 170 calories, 9 g fat (6 g saturated fat), 25 mg cholesterol, 120 mg sodium, 20 g carbohydrate, 1 g fiber, 3 g protein. **DIABETIC EXCHANGES:** 1-1/2 fat, 1 starch, 1/2 fruit.

Cranberry Pear Crisp Pie

(PICTURED ABOVE)

PREP: 25 Min. **BAKE:** 55 Min. + Cooling **YIELD:** 8 Servings

Filled with a bubbling combination of cranberries and pears, this crumb-topped dessert is a wonderful change of pace from traditional pies. —Priscilla Gilbert, Indian Harbour Beach, Florida

　　5 cups sliced peeled fresh pears
　　1 tablespoon lemon juice
　　1 teaspoon vanilla extract
1-2/3 cups fresh *or* frozen cranberries
　　1/2 cup packed brown sugar
　　1/3 cup all-purpose flour
　　1 unbaked pastry shell (9 inches)
TOPPING:
　　1/4 cup all-purpose flour

SALT ▼

　　1/4 cup quick-cooking oats
　　3 tablespoons packed brown sugar
3/4 teaspoon ground cinnamon
　　2 tablespoons cold butter

Place the pears in a large bowl; sprinkle with lemon juice and vanilla. Add cranberries. Combine the brown sugar and flour; sprinkle over fruit and gently toss to coat. Spoon into pastry shell.

For the toppining, in a small bowl, combine the flour, oats, brown sugar and cinnamon. Cut in butter until crumbly. Sprinkle over filling.

Cover edges of pastry loosely with foil. Bake at 375° for 30 minutes. Remove foil; bake 25-30 minutes longer or until filling is bubbly. Cool on a wire rack.

NUTRITION FACTS: 1 piece equals 332 calories, 11 g fat (5 g saturated fat), 13 mg cholesterol, 137 mg sodium, 58 g carbohydrate, 4 g fiber, 3 g protein.

Custard Berry Parfaits

FAT SALT

(PICTURED BELOW)

PREP: 25 Min. + Chilling   **YIELD:** 6 Servings

Here's a low-fat dessert that captures the flavors of summer. The homemade custard comes together in minutes but tasted like you fussed.   —Trisha Kruse, Eagle, Idaho

- 1/4 cup sugar
- 4 teaspoons cornstarch
- 1/4 teaspoon salt
- 1-2/3 cups 1% milk
- 2 egg yolks, lightly beaten
- 3/4 teaspoon vanilla extract
- 3 cups mixed fresh berries

In a small saucepan, combine the sugar, cornstarch and salt. Stir in milk until smooth. Cook and stir over medium-high heat until thickened and bubbly. Reduce heat; cook and stir 2 minutes longer.

Remove from the heat. Stir a small amount of hot filling into egg yolks; return all to the pan, stirring constantly. Bring to a gentle boil; cook and stir 2 minutes longer. Remove from the heat. Gently stir in vanilla. Cool to room temperature without stirring. Transfer to a bowl; press plastic wrap onto surface of custard. Refrigerate for at least 1 hour.

Just before serving, spoon 1/4 cup of berries into each parfait glass; top with 2 tablespoons of custard. Repeat layers.

NUTRITION FACTS: 1/2 cup berries with 1/4 cup custard equals 119 calories, 3 g fat (1 g saturated fat), 74 mg cholesterol, 137 mg sodium, 21 g carbohydrate, 3 g fiber, 4 g protein. **DIABETIC EXCHANGES:** 1 fruit, 1/2 starch, 1/2 fat.

Chocolate Pudding Cake

FAT

(PICTURED ABOVE)

PREP: 15 Min.   **BAKE:** 40 Min.   **YIELD:** 9 Servings

It's almost impossible to believe that this warm delicacy is low in fat. The moist cake bakes in the same dish as the chocolate sauce for an impressive dessert that you just can't beat. I serve the easy finale with ice cream but it is wonderful on its own, too.
    —Sue Ross, Casa Grande, Arizona

- 1/2 cup sugar
- Sugar substitute equivalent to 1/4 cup sugar
- 2 tablespoons butter, melted
- 1 teaspoon vanilla extract
- 1 cup all-purpose flour
- 2 tablespoons baking cocoa
- 2 teaspoons baking powder
- 1/8 teaspoon salt
- 1/2 cup fat-free milk

TOPPING:

- 1/2 cup packed brown sugar
- 1/4 cup sugar
- Sugar substitute equivalent to 1/4 cup sugar
- 2 tablespoons baking cocoa
- 1 cup cold water
- 3 cups fat-free vanilla ice cream

In a large mixing bowl, beat the sugar, sugar substitute, butter and vanilla. Combine the flour, cocoa, baking powder and salt; add to sugar mixture alternately with milk. Spread into an 8-in. square baking dish coated with nonstick cooking spray.

For topping, in a small bowl, combine the sugars, sugar substitute and cocoa. Sprinkle over batter. Pour water over topping. Bake at 350° for 37-42 minutes or until top is set and edges pull away from sides of dish. Serve warm with ice cream.

NUTRITION FACTS: 1 piece with 1/3 cup ice cream equals 261 calories, 3 g fat (2 g saturated fat), 7 mg cholesterol, 203 mg sodium, 55 g carbohydrate, 1 g fiber, 4 g protein.

Editor's Note: This recipe was tested with Splenda No Calorie Sweetener.

Colorful Frozen Yogurt

(PICTURED BELOW)

PREP: 20 Min. + Freezing   **YIELD:** 12 Servings

Here's a low-fat recipe for sunny days. Not only is it pretty, but blending the berries into the frozen yogurt is simple. I serve the honey-topped dessert in martini glasses with mint leaves for garnishes.   —Tiffany Blepp, Olathe, Kansas

        3 pints reduced-fat vanilla frozen yogurt, softened, *divided*
 1-1/2 cups frozen unsweetened sliced peaches, thawed
 1-1/4 cups frozen unsweetened blueberries, thawed
 1-1/4 cups frozen unsweetened strawberries, thawed
       12 teaspoons honey

Place one pint of frozen yogurt in a blender; add peaches. Cover and process until smooth. Transfer to a freezer-safe container; cover and freeze.

Repeat the same process twice, making a batch of blueberry frozen yogurt as well as a batch of strawberry frozen yogurt.

Using a small scoop or melon baller, scoop each flavor of yogurt onto a waxed paper-lined baking sheet. Freeze until firm.

For each serving, place two scoops of each flavor in individual dessert dishes. Drizzle each with 1 teaspoon honey.

NUTRITION FACTS: 1/2 cup equals 143 calories, 1 g fat (1 g saturated fat), 5 mg cholesterol, 60 mg sodium, 29 g carbohydrate, 1 g fiber, 5 g protein. **DIABETIC EXCHANGES:** 2 starch, 1/2 fat.

Lemon Drop Cookies

PREP: 20 Min.   **BAKE:** 10 Min. per Batch + Cooling   **YIELD:** 3-1/2 Dozen

No one would suspect that these adorable, little cookies are actually low in fat.   —Jalayne Luckett, Marion, Illinois

        2 eggs
        1 cup sugar
        2 teaspoons grated lemon peel
        2 teaspoons lemon extract
 1-1/3 cups all-purpose flour
        1 teaspoon baking powder
GLAZE:
 1-1/2 cups confectioners' sugar
        1 to 2 tablespoons lemon juice

In a small mixing bowl, beat eggs until frothy. Beat in the sugar, lemon peel and extract. Combine flour and baking powder; gradually add to sugar mixture.

Drop by teaspoonfuls 2 in. apart onto baking sheets coated with nonstick cooking spray. Bake at 325° for 10-12 minutes or until lightly browned. Cool completely on baking sheets before removing.

For glaze, in a small bowl, combine confectioners' sugar and enough of the lemon juice to achieve desired consistency; drizzle over the cookies.

NUTRITION FACTS: 2 cookies equals 107 calories, 1 g fat (trace saturated fat), 20 mg cholesterol, 17 mg sodium, 24 g carbohydrate, trace fiber, 1 g protein. **DIABETIC EXCHANGE:** 1-1/2 starch.

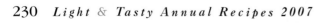

Favorite Recipe Made Lighter

HEAVENLY cakes are a hallmark of dessert time, and Coconut Supreme Torte is no exception. "My neighbor gave me the recipe," shares Vernelle Lazzarini of Upland, California. "Do you think you can adjust it so the cake is just as delicious but with fewer calories?"

Part of the cake's no-fuss appeal is that it starts with a mix. As such, our staff members lightening up the ingredients that are added to the mix. Egg whites replaced whole eggs and applesauce was swapped in for the oil.

By toasting the walnuts, our experts were able to capture the nutty flavor of the original cake and halve the amount of nuts called for. They were also able to achieve the flavor and texture of Vernelle's submission with less coconut and confectioners' sugar.

These steps created an impressive edible offering less than half the fat of the original. With nearly 200 calories trimmed from each slice, Makeover Coconut Supreme Torte is as easy on the waistline as it is on the taste buds.

Coconut Supreme Torte

PREP: 25 Min. BAKE: 25 Min. + Cooling YIELD: 16 Servings

- 1 package (18-1/4 ounces) yellow cake mix
- 1-1/3 cups water
- 4 eggs
- 1 package (3.4 ounces) instant vanilla pudding mix
- 1/2 cup vegetable oil
- 1-1/2 cups flaked coconut, toasted
- 1 cup chopped walnuts

FROSTING:

- 1 package (8 ounces) cream cheese, softened
- 2 teaspoons milk
- 1 teaspoon vanilla extract
- 3-1/2 cups confectioners' sugar
- 2 cups flaked coconut, toasted, *divided*

In a large mixing bowl, combine the cake mix, water, eggs, pudding mix and oil. Beat on medium speed for 4 minutes, scraping sides of bowl occasionally. Stir in the coconut and the walnuts.

Pour into three greased and floured 9-in. round cake pans. Bake at 350° for 23-27 minutes or until a toothpick inserted near the center comes out clean. Cool for 10 minutes before removing from pans to wire racks to cool completely.

For frosting, in a large mixing bowl, beat cream cheese, milk and vanilla until smooth. Gradually beat in confectioners' sugar. Stir in 1-1/2 cups coconut.

Place bottom cake layer on a serving plate; spread with 3/4 cup frosting. Repeat layers. Top with the remaining layer and frosting; sprinkle with the remaining coconut. Store in the refrigerator.

NUTRITION FACTS: 1 piece equals 542 calories, 28 g fat (12 g saturated fat), 69 mg cholesterol, 405 mg sodium, 69 g carbohydrate, 2 g fiber, 7 g protein.

Makeover Coconut Supreme Torte
(PICTURED ABOVE)

PREP: 25 Min. BAKE: 25 Min. + Cooling YIELD: 16 Servings

- 1 package (18-1/4 ounces) yellow cake mix
- 1-1/3 cups water
- 2 eggs
- 4 egg whites
- 1/2 cup unsweetened applesauce
- 1 package (1 ounce) sugar-free instant vanilla pudding mix
- 1 cup flaked coconut, toasted
- 1/2 cup chopped walnuts, toasted

FROSTING:

- 1 package (8 ounces) reduced-fat cream cheese
- 2 teaspoons fat-free milk
- 1 teaspoon vanilla extract
- 2-3/4 cups confectioners' sugar
- 1 cup flaked coconut, toasted, *divided*

Coat three 9-in. round cake pans with nonstick cooking spray and dust with flour; set aside. In a large mixing bowl, combine cake mix, water, eggs, egg whites, applesauce and pudding mix. Beat on medium speed for 4 minutes, scraping sides of bowl occasionally. Stir in coconut and walnuts.

Pour into prepared pans. Bake at 350° for 23-27 minutes or until a toothpick inserted near the center comes out clean. Cool for 10 minutes before removing from pans to wire racks to cool completely.

For frosting, in a large mixing bowl, beat cream cheese, milk and vanilla until smooth. Gradually beat in confectioners' sugar. Stir in 1/2 cup coconut.

Place bottom cake layer on a serving plate; spread with 2/3 cup frosting. Repeat layers. Top with remaining layer and frosting; sprinkle with remaining coconut. Store in the refrigerator.

NUTRITION FACTS: 1 piece equals 350 calories, 13 g fat (7 g saturated fat), 37 mg cholesterol, 316 mg sodium, 54 g carbohydrate, 2 g fiber, 6 g protein.

Luscious Fudgy Brownies

(PICTURED ABOVE)

 SALT

PREP: 15 Min. **BAKE:** 20 Min. + Cooling **YIELD:** 16 Brownies

This is a favorite after-dinner treat. I'm always very careful not to overbake these brownies because I love the ooey-gooey center.
— Krista Frank, Rhododendron, Oregon

    1 cup sugar
    3 tablespoons butter, melted
    3 tablespoons reduced-fat vanilla yogurt
    1 teaspoon vanilla extract
    1 egg, lightly beaten
  3/4 cup all-purpose flour
  1/3 cup baking cocoa
  1/8 teaspoon salt

In a small bowl, combine the sugar, butter, yogurt and vanilla. Stir in egg until blended. Combine the flour, cocoa and salt; stir into sugar mixture. Transfer to an 8-in. square baking dish coated with nonstick cooking spray.

Bake at 350° for 20-25 minutes or until a toothpick inserted near the center comes out clean and brownies begin to pull away from sides of pan. Cool on a wire rack. Cut into eight pieces, then cut each diagonally in half.

NUTRITION FACTS: 2 brownies equals 201 calories, 5 g fat (3 g saturated fat), 38 mg cholesterol, 93 mg sodium, 36 g carbohydrate, 1 g fiber, 3 g protein. **DIABETIC EXCHANGES:** 2 starch, 1 fat.

TASTY TIP
"I've made double batches of the fudge brownies to fit a 13- by 9- by 2-inch pan, added various chip flavors and even used the brownies as a base for a giant ice cream cake with very good results," Krista Frank notes.

Swirled Mint Cookies

(PICTURED BELOW)

FAT SALT

PREP: 40 Min. + Chilling **BAKE:** 10 Min. per Batch **YIELD:** 4 Dozen

No one will believe that these rich and buttery cookies are light, but they are! With their colorful red and green swirls, the minty bites are sure to add a festive touch to any dessert table.
— Lois Hill, Thomasville, North Carolina

  1/2 cup butter, softened
  1/2 cup reduced-fat butter, softened
  3/4 cup plus 1 tablespoon sugar, *divided*
    1 egg
    1 teaspoon vanilla extract
  1/2 teaspoon peppermint extract
    2 cups all-purpose flour
  1/2 teaspoon baking powder
  1/4 teaspoon salt
 10 to 20 drops red food coloring
 10 to 20 drops green food coloring

In a large mixing bowl, cream butters and 3/4 cup sugar. Beat in egg and extracts. Combine the flour, baking powder and salt; gradually add to creamed mixture.

Divide dough into thirds. Stir red food coloring into one portion of dough; stir green food coloring into another portion. Leave remaining dough plain. Cover and refrigerate for at least 1 hour.

Divide each portion of dough into four equal pieces. With lightly floured hands, roll each piece into a 12-in. rope. Place a red, a green and a plain rope next to each other. Cut through all three ropes at 1-in. intervals, forming sets of three differently colored doughs. Repeat.

Roll each set of doughs into a ball; place balls 3 in. apart on ungreased baking sheets. Flatten to 1/8-in. thickness with a glass dipped in remaining sugar. Bake at 375° for 8-10 minutes or until bottoms are lightly browned. Remove to wire racks.

NUTRITION FACTS: 1 cookie equals 59 calories, 3 g fat (2 g saturated fat), 13 mg cholesterol, 49 mg sodium, 7 g carbohydrate, trace fiber, 1 g protein. **DIABETIC EXCHANGES:** 1/2 starch, 1/2 fat.

Editor's Note: This recipe was tested with Land O'Lakes light stick butter.

Strawberry Sorbet Sensation

(PICTURED AT RIGHT)

FAT ⬇

PREP: 20 Min. + Freezing   **YIELD:** 8 Servings

With just five ingredients, this delightful frozen dessert will keep you cool and refreshed on hot late-summer days.
                                    —Kendra Doss, Smithville, Missouri

  2 cups strawberry sorbet, softened
  1 cup cold fat-free milk
  1 package (1 ounce) sugar-free instant vanilla pudding mix
  1 carton (8 ounces) frozen reduced-fat whipped topping, thawed
  1 cup sliced fresh strawberries

Line an 8-in. x 4-in. x 2-in. loaf pan with heavy-duty foil. Spoon sorbet into pan; freeze for 15 minutes.

In a small bowl, whisk milk and pudding mix for 2 minutes. Let stand for 2 minutes or until soft-set. Set aside 1/2 cup whipped topping for garnish; refrigerate until serving. Fold remaining whipped topping into pudding; spoon over sorbet. Cover and freeze for 4 hours or overnight.

Remove from the freezer 10-15 minutes before serving; unmold onto a serving plate and remove foil. Serve with the strawberries and the reserved whipped topping.

NUTRITION FACTS: 1 slice equals 153 calories, 3 g fat (3 g saturated fat), 1 mg cholesterol, 163 mg sodium, 27 g carbohydrate, 2 g fiber, 1 g protein. **DIABETIC EXCHANGES:** 2 starch, 1/2 fat.

Chocolate-Glazed Raspberry Torte

PREP: 25 Min.   **BAKE:** 20 Min. + Cooling   **YIELD:** 20 Servings

Guests won't believe a dessert so decadent and delicious could be low in fat. Our Test Kitchen can take a bow for this heavenly recipe with its fresh-fruit flavor, cake-mix convenience and impressive presentation.

     1 package (18-1/4 ounces) white cake mix
     1 cup water
     4 egg whites
  1/3 cup unsweetened applesauce
     1 carton (8 ounces) frozen reduced-fat whipped topping, thawed
 1-1/2 cups fresh raspberries, *divided*
  1/2 cup sugar
  1/4 cup baking cocoa
  1/2 cup fat-free milk
     4 squares (1 ounce *each*) semisweet chocolate, chopped

Coat a 15-in. x 10-in. x 1-in. baking pan with nonstick cooking spray. Line with waxed paper and coat the paper with nonstick cooking spray; set aside. In a large mixing bowl, combine the cake mix, water, egg whites and applesauce. Beat on medium speed for 2 minutes. Pour into prepared pan.

Bake at 350° for 18-20 minutes or until a toothpick inserted near the center comes out clean. Cool for 5 minutes before removing from pan to a wire rack to cool completely.

In a bowl, combine the whipped topping and 1-1/4 cups raspberries. Cut cake into three 10-in. x 5-in. rectangles. Place one layer on a serving plate; top with half of the berry mixture. Repeat layers. Top with remaining cake.

For glaze, in a small saucepan, combine the sugar, cocoa

and milk until smooth. Bring to a boil. Remove from the heat. Stir in chocolate until melted; cool slightly. Pour over cake. Refrigerate until serving. Garnish with remaining raspberries.

NUTRITION FACTS: 1 piece equals 196 calories, 6 g fat (3 g saturated fat), trace cholesterol, 177 mg sodium, 34 g carbohydrate, 2 g fiber, 3 g protein. **DIABETIC EXCHANGES:** 2 starch, 1/2 fat.

TASTY TIP
"You can use just about any combination of sorbet and fresh berries in this Strawberry Sorbet Sensation," Kendra Doss points out.

Coconut-Frosted Chocolate Cupcakes

PREP: 30 Min + Cooling **BAKE:** 15 Min. **YIELD:** 1 Dozen

These cute cupcakes have a wonderful German chocolate flavor. Created by our Test Kitchen, they'll appease any sweet tooth.

> 2 tablespoons butter, softened
> 3/4 cup sugar
> 1 egg
> 1 egg white
> 1/3 cup 1% buttermilk
> 1/3 cup water
> 1 teaspoon vanilla extract
> 1-1/2 cups all-purpose flour
> 1/3 cup baking cocoa
> 3/4 teaspoon baking soda
> 1/2 teaspoon salt
> FROSTING:
> 1 egg yolk
> 1/2 cup fat-free evaporated milk
> 1/2 cup sugar
> 1/4 cup marshmallow creme
> 1/2 teaspoon vanilla extract
> 1/2 cup flaked coconut
> 1/4 cup chopped pecans

In a large mixing bowl, beat butter and sugar until crumbly. Beat in egg and egg white. Beat in the buttermilk, water and vanilla. Combine the flour, cocoa, baking soda and salt; add to batter just until moistened.

Fill foil- or paper-lined muffin cups two-thirds full. Bake at 375° for 13-15 minutes or until a toothpick comes out clean. Cool for 5 minutes before removing from pan to a wire rack.

For frosting, in a saucepan, combine the egg yolk, milk, sugar and marshmallow creme. Cook and stir over medium heat until thickened, about 15 minutes (do not boil). Remove from the heat; stir in vanilla. Fold in coconut and pecans. Cool completely at room temperature. Frost cupcakes.

NUTRITION FACTS: 1 cupcake equals 229 calories, 6 g fat (3 g saturated fat), 41 mg cholesterol, 238 mg sodium, 40 g carbohydrate, 1 g fiber, 4 g protein.

Peanut Butter Chocolate Cake

(PICTURED ABOVE)

PREP: 25 Min. **BAKE:** 20 Min. + Cooling **YIELD:** 18 Servings

When my mom was told to avoid sugar and fats, I immediately got to work in my kitchen, creating something she could enjoy. I whipped up this delectable dessert. Now, Mom can indulge her sweet tooth while following doctor's orders.
—Annette Abbott, Charlotte, North Carolina

> 1 package (18-1/4 ounces) devil's food cake mix
> 1 cup water
> 3 eggs
> 1/3 cup unsweetened applesauce
> 1/4 cup reduced-fat creamy peanut butter
> FROSTING:
> 1/2 cup cold fat-free milk
> 1 package (1.4 ounces) sugar-free instant chocolate pudding mix
> 1 package (8 ounces) reduced-fat cream cheese
> 1/2 cup reduced-fat creamy peanut butter
> 1 carton (8 ounces) frozen reduced-fat whipped topping, thawed

In a large mixing bowl, combine the cake mix, water, eggs and applesauce. Beat on medium speed for 2 minutes. Transfer to a 13-in. x 9-in. x 2-in. baking dish coated with nonstick cooking spray. Bake at 350° for 20-25 minutes or until a toothpick inserted near the center comes out clean.

Immediately drop small amounts of peanut butter over hot cake; return to the oven for 1 minute. Carefully spread peanut butter over cake. Cool on a wire rack.

For frosting, in a small bowl, whisk milk and pudding mix for 1 minute. In a small mixing bowl, beat cream cheese and peanut butter until smooth. Gradually beat in pudding. Beat in half of the whipped topping; fold in remaining whipped topping. Frost cake. Store in the refrigerator.

NUTRITION FACTS: 1 piece equals 257 calories, 11 g fat (5 g saturated fat), 44 mg cholesterol, 413 mg sodium, 31 g carbohydrate, 1 g fiber, 7 g protein. **DIABETIC EXCHANGES:** 2 starch, 2 fat.

trimmed-down treats

Looking to scale-back the calories, fat or sugar of your favorite dessert? Keep the following ideas in mind and you'll see just how easy revamping a recipe can be!

- Many family cooks know that applesauce makes a smart replacement for the oil in certain baked goods. Keep in mind, that the sweet flavor the applesauce contributes means that the sugar in the recipe can often be decreased as well.

- Toasting nuts helps bring out their earthy flavor. This means that you need fewer of them to obtain a wonderfully nutty taste.

- Try mini chocolate chips in your cookies. You can cut calories by using less of them, but due to their size, you'll likely find a chocolate taste in every bite.

Favorite Recipe Made Lighter

SPRINGTIME sweets aren't any more appealing than Lemon Raspberry Cake shared by Eden Atkerson of Atlanta, Georgia. Sporting pretty raspberry ribbons and a creamy frosting, the layer cake is a delightful treat.

Want to celebrate with Eden's elegant cake but wish it were lighter? Our home economists trimmed it down.

Replacing some of the butter with applesauce lowered the fat. This also sweetened the cake, so the amount of sugar could be decreased as well.

Keeping one of the cake rounds whole, as opposed to splitting all three, meant one less layer and, therefore, less jam. We also used jam made with 100% fruit, as opposed to those sweetened with sugar.

Makeover Lemon Raspberry Cake is a tooth-tingling success. It has 184 fewer calories, 50% less fat and nearly half the cholesterol of the original, but it's still the perfect way to cap off spring get-togethers.

Lemon Raspberry Cake

PREP: 45 Min.   **BAKE:** 15 Min. + Cooling   **YIELD:** 16 Servings

- 1 cup butter, softened
- 2 cups sugar
- 4 eggs
- 3 cups all-purpose flour
- 3 teaspoons baking powder
- 1 teaspoon salt
- 1 cup milk
- 1 teaspoon vanilla extract
- 1 teaspoon almond extract
- 1 jar (12 ounces) seedless raspberry jam

FROSTING:
- 1-1/4 cups butter, softened
- 3 cups confectioners' sugar
- 3 tablespoons lemon juice
- 2 teaspoons grated lemon peel

In a large mixing bowl, cream butter and sugar. Add eggs, one at a time, beating well after each addition. Combine the flour, baking powder and salt. Combine milk and extracts; add to creamed mixture alternately with dry ingredients. Transfer to three greased and floured 9-in. round baking pans.

Bake at 375° for 18-22 minutes or until a toothpick inserted near the center comes out clean. Cool for 10 minutes before removing from pans to wire racks to cool completely.

Split each cake into two horizontal layers. Place a bottom layer on a serving plate; spread with a fifth of the jam. Repeat layers four times. Top with remaining cake. For frosting, in a mixing bowl, beat butter until smooth. Gradually beat in the confectioners' sugar, lemon juice and peel. Frost top and sides of cake.

NUTRITION FACTS: 1 slice equals 579 calories, 28 g fat (17 g saturated fat), 124 mg cholesterol, 507 mg sodium, 80 g carbohydrate, 1 g fiber, 5 g protein.

Makeover Lemon Raspberry Cake
(PICTURED AT RIGHT)

PREP: 45 Min.
BAKE: 15 Min. + Cooling
YIELD: 16 Servings

- 1/2 cup butter, softened
- 1-1/2 cups sugar
- 2 eggs
- 4 egg whites
- 3 cups all-purpose flour
- 3 teaspoons baking powder
- 1 teaspoon salt
- 1 cup fat-free milk
- 1/2 cup unsweetened applesauce
- 1 teaspoon vanilla extract
- 1 teaspoon almond extract
- 1 jar (10 ounces) seedless raspberry spreadable fruit

FROSTING:
- 1/2 cup butter, softened
- 1/3 cup reduced-fat butter, softened
- 2 cups confectioners' sugar
- 2 tablespoons lemon juice
- 1-1/2 teaspoons grated lemon peel

In a large mixing bowl, cream butter and sugar. Add eggs, one at a time, beating well after each addition. Beat in egg whites just until blended. Combine the flour, baking powder and salt. Combine the milk, applesauce and extracts; add to creamed mixture alternately with dry ingredients.

Coat three 9-in. round baking pans with nonstick cooking spray and dust with flour; add batter. Bake at 375° for 14-18 minutes or until a toothpick inserted near the center comes out clean. Cool for 10 minutes before removing from pans to wire racks to cool completely.

Split one cake in half horizontally. Place bottom layer on a serving plate; spread with a fourth of the spreadable fruit. Replace top; spread with another fourth of the spreadable fruit. Top with whole cake; spread with spreadable fruit.

Split remaining cake in half horizontally; place bottom layer over fruit. Spread with remaining spreadable fruit. Top with last layer.

For frosting, in a mixing bowl, beat butters until smooth. Gradually beat in the confectioners' sugar, lemon juice and peel. Frost top and sides of cake.

NUTRITION FACTS: 1 slice equals 395 calories, 14 g fat (9 g saturated fat), 64 mg cholesterol, 392 mg sodium, 63 g carbohydrate, 1 g fiber, 5 g protein.

Editor's Note: This recipe was tested with Land O'Lakes light stick butter.

Pineapple Poke Cake
(PICTURED ABOVE)

PREP: 20 Min. **BAKE:** 25 Min. + Cooling **YIELD:** 20 Servings

This delicious dessert with a creamy frosting and pineapple flavor refreshes all year round. With several store-bought ingredients, it's a snap to prepare anytime. —Sandra Etelamaki, Ishpeming, Michigan

- 1 package (18-1/4 ounces) yellow cake mix
- 1 package (1 ounce) sugar-free instant vanilla pudding mix
- 1/2 cup water
- 2 eggs, lightly beaten
- 1/2 cup egg substitute
- 1/2 cup fat-free milk
- 1/4 cup unsweetened applesauce
- 1 can (8 ounces) unsweetened crushed pineapple, undrained
- 1/4 cup packed brown sugar

FROSTING:
- 1-1/2 cups cold fat-free milk
- 1 package (1 ounce) sugar-free instant vanilla pudding mix
- 1 carton (8 ounces) frozen reduced-fat whipped topping, thawed

In a large mixing bowl, combine the first seven ingredients. Beat on medium speed for 2 minutes. Pour into a 13-in. x 9-in. x 2-in. baking pan coated with nonstick cooking spray. Bake at 350° for 25-30 minutes or until a toothpick inserted near the center comes out clean.

Meanwhile, in a small saucepan, combine pineapple and brown sugar. Cook and stir until mixture comes to a boil. Boil for 4-5 minutes or until most of the liquid is evaporated; cool slightly. Remove cake from the oven; place pan on a wire rack. Poke holes in warm cake with a fork. Spoon pineapple mixture evenly over cake; cool completely.

For frosting, in a small bowl, whisk milk and pudding mix for 2 minutes. Let stand for 2 minutes or until soft-set. Spread over cake. Spread whipped topping over pudding. Store in the refrigerator.

NUTRITION FACTS: 1 piece equals 180 calories, 4 g fat (2 g saturated fat), 22 mg cholesterol, 313 mg sodium, 31 g carbohydrate, 1 g fiber, 3 g protein. **DIABETIC EXCHANGES:** 2 starch, 1/2 fat.

Raspberry Key Lime Crepes
(PICTURED BELOW)

PREP: 20 Min. + Chilling **YIELD:** 6 Servings

Key lime juice turns cream cheese into a refreshing filling for these delicate crepes. Sometimes, I even pipe the mixture into crispy phyllo-dough cones that I bake ahead of time.
—Wolfgang Hanau, West Palm Beach, Florida

- 3 tablespoons key lime juice
- 1 package (12.3 ounces) firm silken tofu, drained and crumbled
- 6 ounces reduced-fat cream cheese, cubed
- 2/3 cup confectioners' sugar, *divided*
- 2-1/2 teaspoons grated lime peel
- Dash salt
- Dash ground nutmeg
- 6 prepared crepes (9 inches)
- 1-1/2 cups fresh raspberries

In a blender or food processor, combine the lime juice, tofu and cream cheese; cover and process until blended. Set aside 1 teaspoon confectioners' sugar. Add the lime peel, salt, nutmeg and remaining confectioners' sugar to the blender; cover and process until smooth. Cover and refrigerate for at least 1 hour.

Spread cream cheese mixture over crepes. Sprinkle with raspberries; roll up. Dust with reserved confectioners' sugar. Serve immediately.

NUTRITION FACTS: 1 filled crepe equals 222 calories, 9 g fat (5 g saturated fat), 26 mg cholesterol, 247 mg sodium, 28 g carbohydrate, 3 g fiber, 8 g protein. **DIABETIC EXCHANGES:** 1-1/2 starch, 1 lean meat, 1 fat, 1/2 fruit.

SHOP SMART
In the supermarket, look for key lime juice with the lemon and lime juices or in the baking aisle. Packages of prepared crepes can usually be found in the produce department.

Pineapple Breeze Torte
(PICTURED ABOVE)

PREP: 35 Min. + Chilling   **YIELD:** 12 Servings

This light and lovely torte with a creamy filling and crushed pineapple topping is a special treat for my large family. It's a must at Christmas and Easter.   —Barbara Joyner, Franklin, Virginia

  1 package (8 ounces) fat-free cream cheese
  1 package (3 ounces) cream cheese, softened
1/3 cup sugar
  2 teaspoons vanilla extract
  1 carton (8 ounces) frozen reduced-fat whipped topping, thawed
  3 packages (3 ounces *each*) ladyfingers, split

TOPPING:
1/3 cup sugar
  3 tablespoons cornstarch
  1 can (20 ounces) unsweetened crushed pineapple, undrained

In a mixing bowl, beat the cream cheeses, sugar and vanilla until smooth. Fold in whipped topping. Arrange ladyfingers on the bottom and around the edge of an ungreased 9-in. springform pan.

Spread bottom layer with half of cream cheese mixture. Top with remaining ladyfingers (ladyfingers may overlap); spread with remaining filling. Cover and chill.

In a small saucepan, combine sugar and cornstarch. Stir in pineapple. Bring to a boil over medium heat, stirring constantly. Cook and stir for 1-2 minutes or until thickened. Cool to room temperature; gently spread over torte. Cover and refrigerate for at least 4 hours or until set. Remove sides of pan.

NUTRITION FACTS: 1 slice equals 243 calories, 7 g fat (5 g saturated fat), 87 mg cholesterol, 156 mg sodium, 39 g carbohydrate, 1 g fiber, 6 g protein. **DIABETIC EXCHANGES:** 2 starch, 1-1/2 fat, 1/2 fruit.

Frozen Chocolate Delight

(PICTURED ABOVE)

FAT

PREP: 15 Min. + Freezing   **YIELD:** 9 Servings

My daughter shared this chocolaty treat with me, and we both think it's a hit. I took it to an office party, and no one could believe this rich, frosty dessert was light.

—Debbie Johnson, Centertown, Missouri

   3/4 cup cold fat-free milk
     1 package (1.4 ounces) sugar-free instant chocolate
        pudding mix
     2 cups fat-free vanilla frozen yogurt, softened
   1/4 cup reduced-fat chunky peanut butter
     2 cups plus 2 tablespoons fat-free whipped topping,
        divided

In a large bowl, whisk milk and pudding mix for 2 minutes. Stir in the frozen yogurt and peanut butter until blended. Fold in 1 cup whipped topping. Transfer to an 8-in. square dish coated with nonstick cooking spray. Cover and freeze until firm.

Remove from the freezer 10 minutes before serving. Cut into nine squares. Garnish each with 2 tablespoons whipped topping.

NUTRITION FACTS: 1 piece equals 134 calories, 3 g fat (1 g saturated fat), 1 mg cholesterol, 230 mg sodium, 22 g carbohydrate, 1 g fiber, 5 g protein. **DIABETIC EXCHANGES:** 1-1/2 starch, 1/2 fat.

Old-Fashioned Cheesecake

PREP: 35 Min.   **BAKE:** 40 Min. + Chilling   **YIELD:** 12 Servings

We love this light and luscious cheesecake. The creamy dessert has a mild lemon flavor that offers a refreshing twist to a long-standing favorite.
—Jean Castle, Comer, Georgia

     1 cup reduced-fat graham cracker crumbs (about 14
        squares)
   1/4 cup packed brown sugar
     1 teaspoon ground cinnamon
     2 tablespoons butter, melted

FILLING:
     2 cups (16 ounces) 2% cottage cheese
     1 cup (8 ounces) reduced-fat plain yogurt
     4 ounces reduced-fat cream cheese
   3/4 cup sugar
   1/2 cup egg substitute
     3 tablespoons cake flour
     2 tablespoons lemon juice
   1/2 teaspoon grated lemon peel
     1 teaspoon vanilla extract

In a small bowl, combine the graham cracker crumbs, brown sugar and cinnamon; stir in butter. Press onto the bottom and 1 in. up the sides of a 9-in. springform pan coated with non-stick cooking spray. Place on a baking sheet. Bake at 325° for 10 minutes. Cool on a wire rack.

In a blender or food processor, combine cottage cheese and yogurt. Cover and process until smooth; set aside. In a large mixing bowl, beat cream cheese and sugar until smooth. Add egg substitute; beat on low speed just until combined. Stir in the flour, lemon juice, lemon peel and vanilla. Fold in cottage cheese mixture. Pour into crust.

Return pan to baking sheet. Bake at 325° for 40-45 minutes or until center is almost set. Cool on a wire rack for 10 minutes. Carefully run a knife around edge of pan to loosen; cool 1 hour longer. Refrigerate overnight. Remove sides of pan. Refrigerate leftovers.

NUTRITION FACTS: 1 slice equals 197 calories, 5 g fat (3 g saturated fat), 18 mg cholesterol, 284 mg sodium, 29 g carbohydrate, trace fiber, 8 g protein. **DIABETIC EXCHANGES:** 2 starch, 1 fat.

White Chocolate Cranberry Cookies

SALT

PREP: 20 Min.   **BAKE:** 10 Min. per Batch   **YIELD:** 2 Dozen

I send these delectable cookies. With white chocolate and bright cranberries, they're a special addition to any holiday cookie tray.
—Donna Beck, Scottdale, Pennsylvania

   1/3 cup butter, softened
   1/2 cup packed brown sugar
   1/3 cup sugar
     1 egg
     1 teaspoon vanilla extract
 1-1/2 cups all-purpose flour
   1/2 teaspoon salt
   1/2 teaspoon baking soda
   3/4 cup dried cranberries
   1/2 cup vanilla *or* white chips

In a large mixing bowl, beat butter and sugars until crumbly, about 2 minutes. Beat in egg and vanilla. Combine the flour, salt and baking soda; gradually add to butter mixture and mix well. Stir in cranberries and chips.

Drop by heaping tablespoonfuls 2 in. apart onto baking sheets coated with nonstick cooking spray. Bake at 375° for 8-10 minutes or until lightly browned. Cool for 1 minute before removing to wire racks.

NUTRITION FACTS: 1 cookie equals 113 calories, 4 g fat (2 g saturated fat), 16 mg cholesterol, 109 mg sodium, 18 g carbohydrate, trace fiber, 1 g protein. **DIABETIC EXCHANGES:** 1 starch, 1/2 fat.

Family-Style Suppers

"Dinner's ready!" That's what you'll happily announce when you whip up any of the seven complete menus found in this chapter. Not only do the tried-and-true recipes come together easily, but each meal puts a healthy spin on family-friendly suppers.

Garlic Butter Green Beans, p. 247
Orange Pork Chops, p. 247

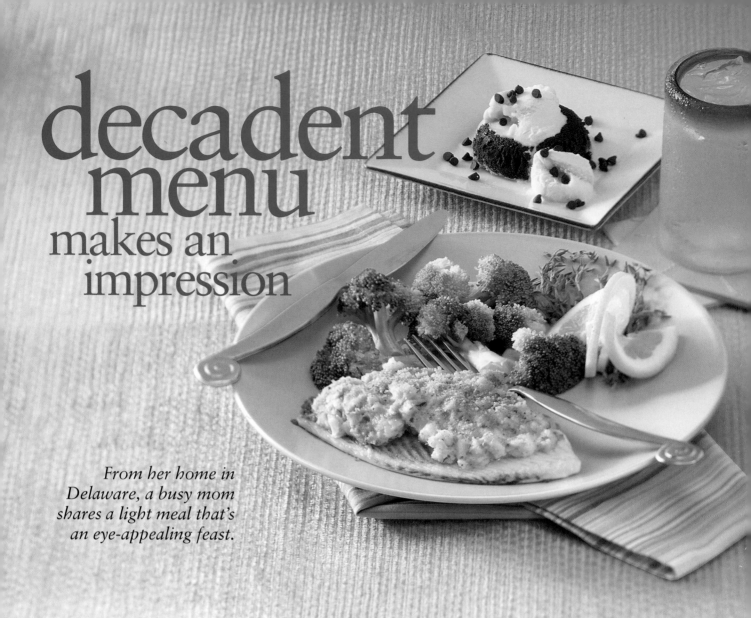

decadent menu
makes an impression

From her home in Delaware, a busy mom shares a light meal that's an eye-appealing feast.

As a former physical education teacher, Laura Merkle knows a thing or two about maintaining a healthy lifestyle. "My husband, Andy, and I enjoy being active with our kids," the Dover, Delaware mom notes.

And physical activity isn't hard to come by chasing after her two boys, Jacob, 3, and Jonathan, 1, on the Air Force base where Andy is a pilot. "We take walks to the park, go for bike rides and play games outside," she says. But, as Laura will tell you, exercise is only one part of the equation.

"I want my gang to be healthy," she relates. "My father survived a heart attack at age 45, and that gave me great incentive to create a better diet."

By keeping an eye on the groceries she buys, Laura has lightened up meals and taught her kids to enjoy many foods. "My boys are both great eaters and always surprise people with the dishes they love."

To keep meals interesting, Laura plans several menus at once. "I try to select new recipes that contain fat-free or re-duced-fat ingredients, as well as lean meats, vegetables, fish, poultry and whole grains," she notes.

When not cooking or spending time with the boys, Laura is busy pursuing her master's degree in education and hopes to return to teaching when the boys are older. But she always makes mealtime a priority. "Our family makes every effort to sit down together and take time eating, enjoying the food and conversation," she says.

SPECIAL SEAFOOD DINNER
The menu Laura shares here is filled with flavors her gang loves, yet special enough to share with guests. "I took the crab filling for Crab-Topped Tilapia from a stuffed mush-room recipe that's been in my family for many years and served it on tilapia fillets for a wonderful special-occasion entree," she explains.

She pairs the flaky fish with vibrant Garlic-Scented Broc-coli Florets. "Fresh broccoli is full of nutrients and so readily available," Laura comments. "This is a great accompani-ment to just about any dish."

To top it all off, she serves delectable Warm Chocolate Cakes. "'Scrumptious' and 'Wow' are the comments this dessert often receives," she raves. "It's hard to believe that something this rich is actually light!"

Crab-Topped Tilapia

(PICTURED AT LEFT)

CARB

PREP: 15 Min.   BAKE: 25 Min.   YIELD: 4 Servings

- 4 tilapia fillets (5 ounces *each*)
- 1/4 teaspoon pepper
- 1/8 teaspoon salt
- 1/3 cup finely chopped celery
- 2 tablespoons finely chopped onion
- 1 garlic clove, minced
- 2-1/2 teaspoons butter, melted, *divided*
- 2 teaspoons all-purpose flour
- 1/8 teaspoon dried thyme
- 1/4 cup fat-free milk
- 1-1/2 teaspoons lemon juice
- 3/4 teaspoon Worcestershire sauce for chicken

Dash hot pepper sauce

- 1/4 cup reduced-fat mayonnaise
- 1 pouch (6 ounces) premium crabmeat, drained
- 4 tablespoons seasoned bread crumbs, *divided*

Sprinkle tilapia with pepper and salt. Place in a 13-in. x 9-in. x 2-in. baking dish coated with nonstick cooking spray; set aside.

In a small nonstick skillet coated with nonstick cooking spray, cook the celery, onion and garlic in 2 teaspoons butter until tender. Stir in flour and thyme until blended. Gradually whisk in milk. Bring to a boil; cook and stir for 1-2 minutes or until thickened. Stir in the lemon juice, Worcestershire sauce and hot pepper sauce.

Remove from the heat; stir in mayonnaise until blended. Stir in crab and 3 tablespoons bread crumbs. Spoon onto fillets. Toss remaining bread crumbs and butter; sprinkle over crab mixture.

Cover and bake at 350° for 18 minutes. Uncover; bake 5-10 minutes longer or until fish flakes easily with a fork.

NUTRITION FACTS: 1 fillet equals 248 calories, 9 g fat (3 g saturated fat), 106 mg cholesterol, 618 mg sodium, 10 g carbohydrate, 1 g fiber, 32 g protein. DIABETIC EXCHANGES: 5 very lean meat, 1 fat, 1/2 starch.

Garlic-Scented Broccoli Florets

(PICTURED AT LEFT)

CARB   MEAT-LESS

PREP/TOTAL TIME: 25 Min.   YIELD: 4 Servings

- 3 cups water
- 6 cups fresh broccoli florets
- 4 garlic cloves, peeled and sliced
- 4-1/2 teaspoons olive oil
- 1/2 teaspoon salt

In a large saucepan, bring water to a boil. Add broccoli; cover and cook for 3 minutes. Drain and immediately place broccoli in ice water; drain.

In a large nonstick skillet coated with nonstick cooking spray, cook garlic in oil until lightly browned. Discard garlic. Add broccoli and salt to skillet; cook and stir until crisp-tender.

NUTRITION FACTS: 3/4 cup equals 75 calories, 5 g fat (1 g saturated fat), 0 cholesterol, 324 mg sodium, 6 g carbohydrate, 3 g fiber, 3 g protein. DIABETIC EXCHANGES: 1 vegetable, 1 fat.

Warm Chocolate Cakes

(PICTURED AT FAR LEFT)

PREP: 20 Min.   BAKE: 20 Min. + Cooling   YIELD: 4 Servings

- 2 teaspoons plus 1/2 cup sugar, *divided*
- 1/4 cup baking cocoa
- 1/4 cup fat-free milk
- 2 tablespoons butter
- 1 teaspoon canola oil
- 1 egg white
- 1/2 teaspoon vanilla extract
- 1/3 cup all-purpose flour
- 1/8 teaspoon salt
- 10 teaspoons miniature semisweet chocolate chips, *divided*
- 1/2 cup reduced-fat vanilla ice cream

Coat four 4-oz. ramekins or custard cups with nonstick cooking spray. Sprinkle sides and bottom of each ramekin with 1/2 teaspoon sugar; set aside.

In a small saucepan, combine the cocoa and remaining sugar; stir in milk until smooth. Cook and stir until sugar is dissolved and mixture comes to a boil. Remove from the heat; stir in butter and oil until butter is melted. Cool for 10 minutes.

Stir in egg white and vanilla until blended. Add flour and salt; stir just until combined. Place 2 tablespoons cocoa mixture in each prepared ramekin. Layer each with 2 teaspoons chocolate chips and remaining cocoa mixture. Bake at 350° for 17-22 minutes or just until centers are set (centers may appear moist). Cool on a wire rack for 10 minutes.

Carefully run a knife around edges of ramekins. Invert cakes onto dessert plates. Top with ice cream; sprinkle with the remaining chocolate chips. Serve immediately.

NUTRITION FACTS: 1 cake with 2 tablespoons ice cream equals 291 calories, 11 g fat (6 g saturated fat), 18 mg cholesterol, 169 mg sodium, 48 g carbohydrate, 2 g fiber, 5 g protein.

QUOTE FROM THE COOK

"When cooking light, think about the cooking method you use," Laura advises. "Cook foods in a nonstick skillet, and you won't need additional oil or butter. Eat a variety of foods, and follow the 'rainbow' philosophy. For instance, enjoy items that vary in color from purple cabbage and red tomatoes to orange carrots and yellow squash. Eating from the different food groups is important, too."

spice it up

An Oklahoma mom serves up a sizzling Southwestern menu and eating habits to last a lifetime.

After several older family members and friends began having diet-related health problems, Leah Lyon of Ada, Oklahoma decided to take a closer look at the foods she was feeding her husband and four girls, ages 5 to 14.

"I love rich, hearty meals and had always cooked mostly natural food with nutritious ingredients," Leah recalls. "But I often served too much or added too much fat and sugar.

"I wanted to ensure our future health and quality of life—not only by lightening up our diet, but also by adding more fresh foods," Leah explains.

It was a gradual process, and one that Leah says isn't finished by a long shot, but the changes are beginning to add up. "Small substitutions and reductions, made over time, have given my family time to adjust without realizing things are different," she notes.

In addition to enjoying both her full-time work at a local university and spending time with husband Bryan and the girls at sporting events, Leah says she loves to cook

and entertain. One of her favorite types of cuisine is definitely Mexican. "I've always said I could eat a rock if it had cheese and jalapenos on it," Leah laughs, "and my family agrees."

GREAT GRILLED MENU
One of her family's favorites is the simple and scrumptious combination Leah shares here.

For the main course, she serves Grilled Chicken and Veggies. "People are always asking me how to make this easy chicken entree," Leah comments. "I often substitute adobo seasoning for the blended spices."

She pairs this quick dish with Ranchero Soup. "This is delicious and vitamin-packed," Leah notes. "Filled with garden-fresh veggies, it goes with any grilled meat."

Leah rounds out dinner with versatile Southwest Iceberg Slaw. "This makes a cool, light side dish, and friends rave about it no matter what vegetables I add," she relates.

Grilled Chicken and Veggies

(PICTURED AT LEFT)

CARB

PREP: 20 Min. **GRILL:** 15 Min. **YIELD:** 6 Servings

- 3/4 teaspoon dried oregano
- 1/2 teaspoon garlic salt
- 1/2 teaspoon garlic powder
- 1/2 teaspoon onion powder
- 1/2 teaspoon ground turmeric
- 1/4 teaspoon ground cumin
- 6 boneless skinless chicken breast halves (6 ounces *each*)
- 1 medium green pepper, cut into strips
- 1 medium sweet red pepper, cut into strips
- 2 medium onions, halved and sliced
- 1 tablespoon canola oil

Combine the seasonings; sprinkle over chicken and set aside. In a bowl, toss the peppers and onions with oil; transfer to a grill wok or basket.

Coat grill rack with nonstick cooking spray before starting the grill. Place chicken and grill wok on grill. Grill, covered, over medium heat for 6 minutes.

Turn chicken and stir vegetables. Grill 5-8 minutes longer or until chicken juices run clear and vegetables are tender.

NUTRITION FACTS: 1 chicken breast half with 1/3 cup vegetables equals 237 calories, 6 g fat (1 g saturated fat), 94 mg cholesterol, 236 mg sodium, 8 g carbohydrate, 2 g fiber, 35 g protein. **DIABETIC EXCHANGES:** 5 very lean meat, 1 vegetable, 1/2 fat.

Editor's Note: If you do not have a grill wok or basket, consider using a disposable foil pan found at most supermarkets or the grilling area of many large discount department stores. Simply poke holes in the bottom of the pan with a meat fork to allow the liquid to drain.

Southwest Iceberg Slaw

(PICTURED ABOVE LEFT)

CARB MEAT-
LESS

PREP/TOTAL TIME: 20 Min. **YIELD:** 6 Servings

- 1/2 cup fat-free sour cream
- 3 tablespoons lime juice
- 2 tablespoons finely chopped onion
- 1 teaspoon finely chopped jalapeno pepper
- 3/4 teaspoon salt
- 1/2 teaspoon pepper
- 6 cups shredded iceberg lettuce
- 1 cup cubed avocado
- 1/2 cup chopped plum tomatoes
- 1/4 cup shredded carrot

For the salad dressing, in a small bowl, whisk together the sour cream, lime juice, onion, jalapeno, salt and pepper. In a large bowl, combine the lettuce, avocado, tomatoes and carrot. Add dressing and toss to coat. Serve immediately.

NUTRITION FACTS: 1 cup equals 83 calories, 4 g fat (1 g saturated fat), 3 mg cholesterol, 322 mg sodium, 10 g carbohydrate, 3 g fiber, 3 g protein. **DIABETIC EXCHANGES:** 1 vegetable, 1 fat.

Editor's Note: When cutting or seeding hot peppers, use rubber or plastic gloves to protect your hands. Avoid touching your face.

Ranchero Soup

(PICTURED ABOVE)

FAT MEAT-
LESS

PREP: 40 Min. + Standing **COOK:** 15 Min. **YIELD:** 8 Servings (2-1/2 quarts)

- 1 large onion, quartered
- 3 celery ribs
- 1 medium zucchini, halved lengthwise
- 1 large sweet red pepper, quartered and seeded
- 1 poblano pepper, quartered and seeded
- 1 tablespoon olive oil
- 2 cans (14-1/2 ounces *each*) diced tomatoes, undrained
- 2 cans (14-1/2 ounces *each*) vegetable broth
- 1 cup frozen sliced carrots
- 1 cup cooked rice
- 1/2 teaspoon lemon-pepper seasoning

Brush the onion, celery, zucchini and peppers with oil. Coat grill rack with nonstick cooking spray before starting the grill. Grill vegetables, uncovered, over medium heat for 7-8 minutes on each side or until tender (pepper skins will char). Immediately place peppers in a bowl; cover and let stand for 15-20 minutes. Peel off and discard charred skin. Coarsely chop grilled vegetables.

In a large saucepan, combine the tomatoes, broth and carrots. Bring to a boil. Reduce heat. Stir in grilled vegetables, rice and lemon-pepper; heat through.

NUTRITION FACTS: 1-1/4 cups equals 99 calories, 2 g fat (trace saturated fat), 0 cholesterol, 623 mg sodium, 18 g carbohydrate, 4 g fiber, 3 g protein. **DIABETIC EXCHANGES:** 2 vegetable, 1/2 starch, 1/2 fat.

Editor's Note: When cutting or seeding hot peppers, use rubber or plastic gloves to protect your hands. Avoid touching your face.

QUOTE FROM THE COOK

"I wanted to ensure our future health and quality of life—not only by lightening up our diet, but also by adding more fresh foods."
—Leah Lyon

pasta dinner surely satisfies

Light and refreshing, this meal is bound to become a fast favorite.

As Elaine Sweet of Dallas, Texas witnessed first-hand, eating nutritiously can have a profound effect. Elaine and her husband, Milton, adopted Andrei and Irina from Northern Russia who were ages 13 and 9 at the time.

"When they first arrived, the children weren't accustomed to healthy eating," Elaine explains. Positive changes in their eating habits as well as the warm Dallas sun helped the children thrive. Enjoying Elaine's light and delectable meals, Andrei has grown 8 inches and gained 35 pounds, and Irina has grown 6-½ inches and gained 25 pounds in the past year.

"They're still a little smaller than their peers, but they're gaining on them," Elaine says proudly.

"During the week, my goal is to put a healthy dinner on the table as quickly as possible," she shares. The fast suppers allow the family to keep up with their busy lifestyle.

In addition to working full-time as a financial manager, Elaine volunteers for several organizations. "We also love to cycle, hike, skate and do just about anything outdoors," she notes.

GARDEN-FRESH MADE FAST

For a light bite, Elaine serves pretty Asparagus Bruschetta. "I really like asparagus, so I'm always trying it in different things," she says.

Elaine teams the summery starter with Italian-style Fancy Chopped Salad. The tasty salad with a tangy homemade dressing is sure to become a dinner staple in your home.

For the main course, Elaine serves Shrimp and Olive Rigatoni. "This pasta dish is one of my gang's favorite recipes," she relates. "My little girl refers to shrimp as 'curly fish' and gets very excited when she sees them in the kitchen. I hope your family enjoys this meal as much as we do."

TASTY TIP

Turn the rigatoni into a "pizza" by spreading the cooked pasta mixture onto a pizza pan. Top with the Parmesan cheese and basil and bake until warmed through.

Fancy Chopped Salad
(PICTURED AT LEFT)

CARB MEAT-LESS

PREP/TOTAL TIME: 30 Min.   YIELD: 6 Servings

   3 cups torn romaine
   1 cup finely chopped cabbage
   1 cup garbanzo beans *or* chickpeas, rinsed and drained
   2 celery ribs, chopped
 1/2 cup chopped sweet red pepper
 1/2 cup chopped red onion
 1/2 small fennel bulb, thinly sliced
 1/2 cup chopped green pepper
   2 tablespoons Greek olives, halved
DRESSING:
   2 tablespoons red wine vinegar
   1 tablespoon olive oil
   2 teaspoons lemon juice
1-1/2 teaspoons Dijon mustard
   1 garlic clove, minced
1-1/2 teaspoons minced fresh oregano *or* 1/2 teaspoon dried oregano
 1/4 teaspoon salt
 1/4 teaspoon pepper
Fennel fronds for garnish, optional

In a large bowl, combine the first nine ingredients. For dressing, in a small bowl, whisk the vinegar, oil, lemon juice, mustard, garlic, oregano, salt and pepper. Pour over salad and toss to coat. Garnish with fennel fronds if desired. Serve immediately.

NUTRITION FACTS: 1 cup equals 98 calories, 4 g fat (trace saturated fat), 0 cholesterol, 259 mg sodium, 14 g carbohydrate, 4 g fiber, 3 g protein. DIABETIC EXCHANGES: 1 vegetable, 1/2 starch, 1/2 fat.

Asparagus Bruschetta
(PICTURED BELOW RIGHT)

MEAT-LESS

PREP/TOTAL TIME: 30 Min.   YIELD: 6 Servings

   3 cups water
 1/2 pound fresh asparagus, trimmed and cut into 1/2-inch pieces
   2 cups grape tomatoes, halved
 1/4 cup minced fresh basil
   3 green onions, chopped
   3 tablespoons lime juice
   1 tablespoon olive oil
   3 garlic cloves, minced
1-1/2 teaspoons grated lime peel
 1/4 teaspoon salt
 1/4 teaspoon pepper
   1 French bread baguette (8 ounces), cut into 12 slices and toasted
 1/2 cup crumbled blue cheese

In a large saucepan, bring water to a boil. Add the asparagus; cover and boil for 2-4 minutes. Drain and immediately place asparagus in ice water. Drain and pat dry.

   In a bowl, combine the asparagus, tomatoes, basil, onions, lime juice, oil, garlic, lime peel, salt and pepper. Using a slotted spoon, spoon asparagus mixture onto bread. Sprinkle with blue cheese.

NUTRITION FACTS: 2 slices equals 243 calories, 10 g fat (3 g saturated fat), 8 mg cholesterol, 490 mg sodium, 34 g carbohydrate, 4 g fiber, 7 g protein. DIABETIC EXCHANGES: 2 starch, 1-1/2 fat, 1 vegetable.

Shrimp and Olive Rigatoni
(PICTURED AT FAR LEFT)

PREP: 20 Min.   COOK: 20 Min.   YIELD: 6 Servings

 12 ounces uncooked rigatoni *or* large tube pasta
   3 garlic cloves, minced
   2 green onions, chopped
   1 tablespoon olive oil
   1 pound uncooked medium shrimp, peeled and deveined
   3 tablespoons white wine *or* reduced-sodium chicken broth
 1/4 cup minced fresh basil
   2 tablespoons minced fresh parsley
   1 teaspoon grated lemon peel
 1/2 teaspoon salt
 1/4 teaspoon coarsely ground pepper
 1/4 teaspoon crushed red pepper flakes
   1 can (2-1/4 ounces) sliced ripe olives, drained
 1/2 cup sliced pimiento-stuffed olives
   2 anchovy fillets, rinsed, drained and chopped
   5 plum tomatoes, seeded and chopped
   1 jar (2 ounces) sliced pimientos, drained
 1/3 cup shredded Parmesan cheese
Additional fresh basil, optional

Cook pasta according to package directions. Meanwhile, in a large nonstick skillet coated with nonstick cooking spray, saute garlic and onions in oil for 1 minute. Add shrimp and wine or broth; cook for 3-5 minutes or until shrimp turn pink.

   Remove from the heat; stir in the basil, parsley, lemon peel, salt, pepper and red pepper flakes. Add olives and anchovies.

   Drain the pasta; stir into skillet. Add tomatoes and pimientos; return to the heat and heat through. Sprinkle with Parmesan cheese. Garnish with basil leaves if desired.

NUTRITION FACTS: 1-2/3 cups equals 359 calories, 9 g fat (2 g saturated fat), 116 mg cholesterol, 793 mg sodium, 47 g carbohydrate, 3 g fiber, 23 g protein. DIABETIC EXCHANGES: 3 starch, 2 very lean meat, 1-1/2 fat.

SURPRISE YOUR FAMILY WITH THIS HEARTWARMING AUTUMN DELIGHT

Creamy Chicken 'n' Wild Rice Soup
(PICTURED ABOVE)

PREP: 15 Min.   **COOK:** 1 Hour   **YIELD:** 8 Servings (2-1/2 quarts)

This cool-weather soup is chock-full of homey, harvest goodness.
—Bonnie Erickson, Hinckley, Minnesota

- 2/3 cup uncooked wild rice
- 2/3 cup chopped onion
- 2/3 cup chopped carrot
- 2 tablespoons butter
- 6 cups reduced-sodium chicken broth
- 2 medium potatoes, peeled and cubed
- 1/2 teaspoon salt
- 1/2 teaspoon pepper
- 1 cup chopped fresh broccoli
- 3 cups cubed cooked chicken breast
- 1/2 cup all-purpose flour
- 1 cup fat-free half-and-half

Cook rice according to package directions. Meanwhile, in a large saucepan coated with nonstick cooking spray, cook onion and carrot in butter for 2 minutes. Stir in the broth, potatoes, salt and pepper. Bring to a boil. Reduce heat; cover and simmer for 10 minutes. Add broccoli; cook 3-7 minutes longer or until potatoes are tender.

Drain rice if necessary; fluff with a fork. Stir chicken and rice into potato mixture; heat through. In a small bowl, combine flour and half-and-half until smooth. Gradually stir into soup. Bring to a boil; cook and stir for 2 minutes or until thickened.

NUTRITION FACTS: 1-1/4 cups equals 251 calories, 5 g fat (2 g saturated fat), 48 mg cholesterol, 707 mg sodium, 29 g carbohydrate, 2 g fiber, 22 g protein. **DIABETIC EXCHANGES:** 2 starch, 2 very lean meat, 1/2 fat.

Roasted Pumpkin Seeds
(PICTURED AT LEFT)

PREP: 10 Min.   **BAKE:** 45 Min. + Cooling   **YIELD:** 2 Cups

Here, the Light & Tasty home economists offer a fun, new twist on an all-time classic.

- 2 cups pumpkin seeds
- 5 teaspoons butter, melted
- 1 teaspoon Worcestershire sauce
- 1 teaspoon sugar
- 1/2 teaspoon salt
- 1/4 teaspoon garlic powder
- 1/8 to 1/4 teaspoon cayenne pepper

Toss pumpkin seeds with butter and Worcestershire sauce. Combine the sugar, salt, garlic powder and cayenne; sprinkle over seeds and toss to coat. Line a 15-in. x 10-in. x 1-in. baking pan with foil; coat the foil with nonstick cooking spray. Spread seeds in pan. Bake at 250° for 45-60 minutes or until seeds are dry and lightly browned, stirring every 15 minutes. Cool completely. Store in an airtight container.

NUTRITION FACTS: 1/4 cup equals 95 calories, 5 g fat (2 g saturated fat), 6 mg cholesterol, 181 mg sodium, 9 g carbohydrate, 1 g fiber, 3 g protein. **DIABETIC EXCHANGES:** 1 fat, 1/2 starch.

Pumpkin Chip Cake
(PICTURED ABOVE LEFT)

PREP: 30 Min.   **BAKE:** 55 Min. + Cooling   **YIELD:** 16 Servings

Moist and delicious, this is a great dessert for fall meals.
—Barbara Lindberg, Portland, Oregon

- 1 cup egg substitute
- 1 can (15 ounces) solid-pack pumpkin
- 1/3 cup unsweetened applesauce
- 1 cup All-Bran
- 2 cups all-purpose flour
- 2 cups sugar
- 2 teaspoons baking powder
- 1 teaspoon baking soda
- 1/2 teaspoon salt
- 1-1/2 teaspoons ground cinnamon
- 1/2 teaspoon ground cloves
- 1/4 teaspoon ground ginger
- 1 cup chopped pecans
- 1 cup miniature semisweet chocolate chips
- 2 teaspoons confectioners' sugar

In a mixing bowl, beat egg substitute until frothy. Add the pumpkin, applesauce and bran; mix well. Combine the flour, sugar, baking powder, baking soda, salt and spices; gradually add to pumpkin mixture and mix well. Stir in pecans and chocolate chips.

Pour into a 10-in. fluted tube pan coated with nonstick cooking spray. Bake at 350° for 55-65 minutes or until a toothpick inserted near the center comes out clean. Cool for 10 minutes before removing from pan to a wire rack to cool completely. Dust with confectioners' sugar.

NUTRITION FACTS: 1 piece equals 287 calories, 9 g fat (2 g saturated fat), 0 cholesterol, 247 mg sodium, 51 g carbohydrate, 4 g fiber, 5 g protein.

GARDEN FRESH & FABULOUS!

FOR Erika Niehoff of Eveleth, Minnesota, the decision to lighten up meals came after a wake-up call. "I'd fallen into a rut of fast-food dinners and pre-packaged convenience items," she explains. "I went from a size 12 to a 22 in about 6 months.

"One morning as I watched my young daughter, Gracie, struggle to get into a pair of jeans, I realized I needed to change our lifestyle before it was too late."

Attacking the task with gusto, the single mom cleaned out the family's fridge, freezer and cupboards and began planning heart-smart menus and making shopping lists.

In no time, Erika and her three children, Gracie, T.J., and Branden, took to the change. "T.J. enjoys shopping and helping me prepare meals," Erika says.

Erika also says that eating nutritiously has not only helped the family budget, but it's allowed her to teach her children about cooking and making healthy food choices.

REFRESHING FAVORITE

The menu she shares here is loaded with tastes her whole gang enjoys, yet it's simple enough for a weeknight meal.

As the main course, Erika serves Orange Pork Chops. "The recipe came from my dad," she says. "The pork chops are so easy to prepare and have a nice, not-too-sweet citrus flavor.

"I created Garlic Butter Green Beans after my parents harvested a huge crop of beans from their garden," Erika recalls.

For the finale, the busy reader whips up Frosted Fruit Gelatin Dessert. "The bright color and creamy topping are appealing to kids even though the dessert is low in sugar," she confirms.

Orange Pork Chops
(PICTURED BELOW RIGHT)

PREP: 20 Min.   BAKE: 20 Min.   YIELD: 4 Servings

- 4 boneless pork loin chops (3/4 inch thick and 5 ounces *each*)
- 1/4 teaspoon salt
- 1/8 teaspoon pepper
- 1 garlic clove, minced
- 1 can (6 ounces) frozen orange juice concentrate, thawed
- 1/2 cup reduced-sodium chicken broth
- 1-1/2 teaspoons Worcestershire sauce
- 2 cups cooked brown rice

Sprinkle both sides of pork chops with salt and pepper. In a nonstick skillet coated with nonstick cooking spray, cook chops for 3-4 minutes on each side or until browned. Transfer to an 8-in. square baking dish coated with nonstick cooking spray.

In the same skillet, cook garlic for 1 minute. Stir in orange juice concentrate, broth and Worcestershire sauce; bring to a boil. Remove from heat. Pour 1/4 cup sauce over pork.

Bake, uncovered, at 350° for 20-25 minutes or until meat thermometer reads 160°, basting twice with sauce.

Bring remaining sauce to a boil. Reduce heat; simmer, uncovered, for 5 minutes or until reduced to 1/2 cup. Serve pork chops with sauce and rice.

NUTRITION FACTS: 1 pork chop with 2 tablespoons sauce and 1/2 cup rice equals 369 calories, 9 g fat (3 g saturated fat), 68 mg cholesterol, 291 mg sodium, 39 g carbohydrate, 2 g fiber, 31 g protein. **DIABETIC EXCHANGES:** 4 lean meat, 1-1/2 starch, 1 fruit.

Garlic Butter Green Beans
(PICTURED BELOW)

FAT SALT CARB MEAT-LESS

PREP/TOTAL TIME: 25 Min.   YIELD: 4 Servings

- 1 pound fresh green beans
- 1 garlic clove, minced
- 1 tablespoon butter
- 2 teaspoons lemon juice
- 1/2 teaspoon sugar
- 1/8 teaspoon pepper

Place beans in a steamer basket; place in a large saucepan over 1 in. of water. Bring to a boil; cover and steam for 7-9 minutes or until crisp-tender. Meanwhile, in a small nonstick saucepan, cook garlic in butter until tender. Remove from the heat; stir in the lemon juice, sugar and pepper.

Transfer beans to serving bowl; add garlic butter and stir to coat.

NUTRITION FACTS: 3/4 cup equals 60 calories, 3 g fat (2 g saturated fat), 8 mg cholesterol, 35 mg sodium, 8 g carbohydrate, 3 g fiber, 2 g protein. **DIABETIC EXCHANGES:** 1 vegetable, 1/2 fat.

Frosted Fruit Gelatin Dessert

FAT SALT

PREP: 30 Min. + Chilling   YIELD: 9 Servings

- 2 envelopes unflavored gelatin
- 1/3 cup cold water
- 2 cups plus 2 tablespoons cranberry juice, *divided*
- 3/4 cup orange juice
- 1 can (20 ounces) unsweetened pineapple tidbits, drained
- 1-1/2 cups sliced firm bananas
- 2 tablespoons sugar
- 1 cup (8 ounces) fat-free plain yogurt

Measure 1-1/8 teaspoons gelatin; set aside for topping. In a small saucepan, sprinkle remaining gelatin over cold water; let stand for 1 minute. Cook over low heat, stirring until gelatin is completely dissolved. Remove from the heat; stir in 2 cups cranberry juice and orange juice.

Place the pineapple and bananas in an 8-in. square dish coated with nonstick cooking spray. Pour juice mixture over fruit. Cover and refrigerate for 45-60 minutes or until firm.

For topping, in a small saucepan, sprinkle reserved gelatin over remaining cranberry juice; let stand for 1 minute. Stir in sugar. Cook over low heat, stirring until completely dissolved. Place the yogurt in a bowl; stir in cranberry mixture. Spread over gelatin. Cover and refrigerate for at least 2 hours.

NUTRITION FACTS: 1 piece equals 114 calories, trace fat (trace saturated fat), 1 mg cholesterol, 25 mg sodium, 29 g carbohydrate, 1 g fiber, 3 g protein. **DIABETIC EXCHANGE:** 1-1/2 fruit.

light, satisfying
and loaded with flavor

Tasty, nutritious meals are a cinch for Ellen Thompson of Springfield, Ohio. As a registered dietitian, she works with folks of all ages to fit menus to their dietary needs. But a few years ago, she realized it was time to follow her own advice.

"I decided that if I was going to tell people how to eat healthy, I needed to do it, too," explains Ellen.

The busy mom to pre-teens John, Samuel, and Naomi made small changes to the recipes she served. "I wanted to feed my family nutritious foods, cutting calories and fat wherever possible," she says.

"We've done things gradually, but my family loves most anything I prepare. My kids eat very well and aren't picky, so that's definitely helped."

In addition to homeschooling her children, Ellen is a part-time dietitian, consulting for an assisted living company. She also advises students and teaches a class at Cedarville University, where her husband, Tom, is an engineering professor.

"As a consultant, I often suggest recipes to clients," Ellen notes, "but I always try these dishes at home first. I like to as-semble the recipe the way that it's written, making small changes over time to lighten it and to create a flavor I feel that most people would like."

CASUAL COMFORT

The delicious dinner Ellen shares here is a favorite with her bunch. For the main course, she whips up hearty Spaghetti Pie, a classic Italian combination prepared as a casserole. "The recipe was given to me a long time ago, and I've served it over and over again," Ellen relates. "My family doesn't seem to grow tired of it, and I appreciate how easily it comes together. It's a great weeknight dish."

With a hint of herb flavor, warm Dilly Spoon Rolls are the perfect accompaniment to the hearty entree. "I often make big batches of these rolls and freeze the extras so they're always on hand," shares Ellen.

As a supper-time finale, Ellen's five-ingredient Frozen Yogurt Cookie Dessert is an ooey-gooey hit. "This earns raves both with company and my family," Ellen says. "We hope it becomes one of your favorites, too."

Spaghetti Pie
(PICTURED AT LEFT)

Prep: 25 Min.   Bake: 25 Min.   Yield: 6 Servings

    1 pound lean ground beef
1/2 cup finely chopped onion
1/4 cup chopped green pepper
    1 cup canned diced tomatoes, undrained
    1 can (6 ounces) tomato paste
    1 teaspoon dried oregano
3/4 teaspoon salt
1/2 teaspoon garlic powder
1/4 teaspoon sugar
1/4 teaspoon pepper
    6 ounces spaghetti, cooked and drained
    1 tablespoon butter, melted
    2 egg whites, lightly beaten
1/4 cup grated Parmesan cheese
    1 cup (8 ounces) fat-free cottage cheese
1/2 cup shredded part-skim mozzarella cheese

In a nonstick skillet, cook the beef, onion and green pepper over medium heat until meat is no longer pink; drain. Stir in the tomatoes, tomato paste, oregano, salt, garlic powder, sugar and pepper; set aside.

In a large bowl, combine the spaghetti, butter, egg whites and Parmesan cheese. Press onto the bottom and up the sides of a 9-in. deep-dish pie plate coated with nonstick cooking spray. Top with cottage cheese and ground beef mixture.

Bake, uncovered, at 350° for 20 minutes. Sprinkle with mozzarella cheese. Bake 5-10 minutes longer or until cheese is melted and filling is heated through.

NUTRITION FACTS: 1 slice equals 348 calories, 10 g fat (5 g saturated fat), 52 mg cholesterol, 690 mg sodium, 33 g carbohydrate, 4 g fiber, 29 g protein. DIABETIC EXCHANGES: 3 lean meat, 2 vegetable, 1-1/2 starch, 1 fat.

Frozen Yogurt Cookie Dessert
(PICTURED AT RIGHT)

Prep: 20 Min. + Freezing   Yield: 12 Servings

12 reduced-fat cream-filled chocolate sandwich cookies, crushed
    1 quart reduced-fat frozen vanilla yogurt, softened
1/3 cup chocolate syrup
1/4 cup dry roasted peanuts
    1 carton (8 ounces) frozen fat-free whipped topping, thawed

Set aside 1 tablespoon cookie crumbs. Sprinkle remaining crumbs in an 11-in. x 7-in. x 2-in. dish coated with nonstick cooking spray. Freeze for 10 minutes.

Carefully spread yogurt over crumbs. Drizzle with chocolate syrup and sprinkle with peanuts. Spread with whipped topping; sprinkle with reserved crumbs. Cover and freeze. Remove from freezer 10 minutes before serving.

NUTRITION FACTS: 1 piece equals 220 calories, 7 g fat (2 g saturated fat), 3 mg cholesterol, 193 mg sodium, 34 g carbohydrate, 1 g fiber, 6 g protein. DIABETIC EXCHANGES: 2 starch, 1 fat.

Dilly Spoon Rolls
(PICTURED AT FAR LEFT)

SALT MEAT-LESS

Prep: 30 Min. + Rising   Bake: 15 Min.   Yield: 1-1/2 Dozen

    1 package (1/4 ounce) active dry yeast
1-1/2 cups warm fat-free milk (110° to 115°)
    3 to 3-1/2 cups all-purpose flour
1/4 cup sugar
    1 teaspoon dill weed
3/4 teaspoon salt
    1 egg, lightly beaten
1/4 cup canola oil

In a large mixing bowl, dissolve yeast in warm milk. Stir in 1-1/2 cups flour, sugar, dill, salt, egg and oil. Beat until smooth. Beat in enough of the remaining flour to achieve a slightly sticky, thick batter. Do not knead. Cover and let rise in a warm place until doubled, about 45 minutes.

Spoon batter into muffin cups coated with nonstick cooking spray. Cover and let rise in a warm place until doubled, about 30 minutes. Bake at 400° for 13-18 minutes or until golden brown. Remove from pans to wire racks. Serve warm.

NUTRITION FACTS: 1 roll equals 127 calories, 4 g fat (trace saturated fat), 12 mg cholesterol, 113 mg sodium, 20 g carbohydrate, 1 g fiber, 3 g protein. DIABETIC EXCHANGES: 1 starch, 1 fat.

QUOTE FROM THE COOK

"I wanted to feed my family nutritious foods, cutting calories and fat wherever possible. We've done things gradually, but my family loves most anything I prepare."

—Ellen Thompson

A Pennsylvania family enjoys a delicious meal that pares down fat and calories.

healthy fare with a home-style taste

Necessity is what started Melissa Newman looking for ways to lighten up her family's daily menus after 12 years. "My husband, Jeff, daughter, Christine, and I are all trying to lose weight," she explains.

When Jeff's cholesterol also began creeping up, Melissa got busy—and creative—cooking up lighter meals for her family in Danville, Pennsylvania. Her modifications not only helped lower his cholesterol 40 points, but are also brightening the health outlook for them all!

"It's an ongoing process," Melissa notes. "Some things are obvious and easy, such as switching from whole to skim milk, removing the skin from chicken and turkey, and baking or broiling instead of frying foods." Other things, like introducing new healthy foods to her family, aren't.

"I'm still tackling this issue," she laughs. "Jeff is more open to trying new things than my daughter is. For instance, when we were first married, he vowed up and down that he'd never drink anything but whole milk. For the last 4 years, he's been drinking fat-free."

Although a part-time job as office manager for a local

church and occasional volunteer work keep Melissa busy, she takes time to study and compare labels when she shops. "I try to select products that are lower in both fat and sodium—and that's not always easy!"

Of course, good nutrition is always easier to swallow when the meals are as delicious as the family favorites that Melissa shares here.

SMART AND SCRUMPTIOUS
Her mother's treasured recipe for heartwarming Rustic Apple-Raisin Bread makes a toasty accompaniment to Jeff's specialty: Spicy Hearty Chili, which is just chock-full of veggies.

"My husband makes *the best* chili," Melissa pronounces. "And since he's a hunter, we often prepare this recipe with ground venison or a mix of ground beef and venison. Regardless of how we make, it's perfect with the bread."

She finishes off this simple fall menu with Peanut Butter Freezer Pie, a dessert so cool, creamy and melt-in-your-mouth wonderful that even her own family has a hard time believing it's lower in fat and calories. So will yours!

Spicy Hearty Chili
(PICTURED AT LEFT)

PREP: 35 Min.   COOK: 1-1/2 Hours   YIELD: 10 Servings (about 4 quarts)

  1 pound lean ground beef
  1 cup chopped onion
  10 garlic cloves, minced
  2 cups chopped green peppers
  1-1/2 cups chopped sweet red peppers
  1-1/2 cups chopped celery
  3 jalapeno peppers, seeded and chopped
  3 cans (14-1/2 ounces *each*) petite diced tomatoes, undrained
  2 cans (16 ounces *each*) kidney beans, rinsed and drained
  1 can (28 ounces) tomato sauce
  1 can (12 ounces) tomato paste
  1 cup water
  1/2 cup light beer *or* nonalcoholic beer
  3 tablespoons chili powder
  1 teaspoon crushed red pepper flakes

In a large saucepan or Dutch oven coated with nonstick cooking spray, cook the beef, onion and garlic over medium heat until meat is no longer pink; drain. Stir in the peppers, celery and jalapenos. Cook and stir for 8 minutes or until vegetables are crisp-tender.

Stir in the remaining ingredients. Bring to a boil. Reduce heat; simmer, uncovered, for 1 hour, stirring occasionally.

NUTRITION FACTS: 1-3/4 cups equals 261 calories, 4 g fat (1 g saturated fat), 22 mg cholesterol, 764 mg sodium, 39 g carbohydrate, 12 g fiber, 19 g protein. DIABETIC EXCHANGES: 3 vegetable, 2 lean meat, 1 starch.

Editor's Note: When cutting or seeding hot peppers, use rubber or plastic gloves to protect your hands. Avoid touching your face.

Peanut Butter Freezer Pie
(PICTURED AT RIGHT)

PREP: 15 Min. + Freezing   YIELD: 8 Servings

  1 package (8 ounces) fat-free cream cheese
  3 tablespoons fat-free milk
  2/3 cup confectioners' sugar
  1/2 cup reduced-fat creamy peanut butter
  1 carton (8 ounces) frozen reduced-fat whipped topping, thawed, *divided*
  3/4 cup miniature semisweet chocolate chips, *divided*
  1 chocolate crumb crust (8 inches)

In a large mixing bowl, beat cream cheese and milk until smooth. Beat in confectioners' sugar and peanut butter. Refrigerate 1/2 cup whipped topping for garnish. Beat 1/2 cup whipped topping into peanut butter mixture; fold in remaining whipped topping. Set aside 8 teaspoons chocolate chips for garnish; fold remaining chips into filling.

Spoon filling into crust. Cover and freeze for 3-4 hours or until firm. Remove from the freezer 20 minutes before serving. Garnish each slice with 1 tablespoon whipped topping and 1 teaspoon chocolate chips.

NUTRITION FACTS: 1 piece equals 393 calories, 18 g fat (8 g saturated fat), 3 mg cholesterol, 350 mg sodium, 48 g carbohydrate, 3 g fiber, 11 g protein.

Rustic Apple-Raisin Bread
(PICTURED AT FAR LEFT)

FAT ▼

PREP: 30 Min. + Rising   BAKE: 30 Min. + Cooling
YIELD: 2 Loaves (8 slices each)

  1 package (1/4 ounce) active dry yeast
  1/4 cup warm water (110° to 115°)
  1 cup unsweetened applesauce
  1/2 cup warm fat-free milk (110° to 115°)
  2 tablespoons sugar
  2 tablespoons butter, softened
  1 teaspoon salt
  1 egg, *separated*
  4 to 4-1/2 cups all-purpose flour
  1 cup raisins
  1 teaspoon caraway seeds
  1 tablespoon cold water

In a large mixing bowl, dissolve yeast in warm water. Add the applesauce, milk, sugar, butter, salt, egg yolk and 2 cups flour; beat until smooth. Stir in enough remaining flour to form a firm dough. Stir in raisins and caraway seeds.

Turn onto a lightly floured surface; knead until smooth and elastic, about 6-8 minutes. Place in a bowl coated with nonstick cooking spray, turning once to coat top. Cover and let rise in a warm place until doubled, about 1 hour.

Punch dough down. Turn onto a lightly floured surface; divide in half. Shape each portion into a ball. Place 4 in. apart on a baking sheet coated with nonstick cooking spray. Pat into 6-in. round loaves. Cover and let rise until almost doubled, about 45 minutes.

In a small bowl, beat egg white and cold water; brush over loaves. Bake at 375° for 30-35 minutes or until golden brown. Cool on a wire rack.

NUTRITION FACTS: 1 slice equals 175 calories, 2 g fat (1 g saturated fat), 17 mg cholesterol, 172 mg sodium, 35 g carbohydrate, 2 g fiber, 4 g protein. DIABETIC EXCHANGES: 2 starch, 1/2 fat.

Trimmed-Down Dishes for Two

Setting a table for two has never been easier or healthier than it is with this chapter's delicious duets. Whether you're a newlywed or empty nester, you'll find plenty to choose from with these dishes, each sized-right for a pair.

Snow Pea Medley, p. 257
Curry Citrus Chicken, p. 257

Warm Seafood Salad

CARB

PREP/TOTAL TIME: 20 Min.   YIELD: 2 Servings

Here's a recipe that's perfect for two seafood lovers. It features sauteed scallops and shrimp that get flavor from garlic and a simple, from-scratch vinaigrette.   —Lillian Julow, Gainesville, Florida

- 1/4 cup chopped red onion
- 2 tablespoons water
- 2 tablespoons white vinegar
- 1/2 teaspoon sugar
- 1/2 teaspoon salt
- 1/4 teaspoon paprika
- 1/4 teaspoon pepper
- 4 teaspoons olive oil, *divided*
- 1/2 pound uncooked medium shrimp, peeled and deveined
- 1/3 pound bay scallops
- 1/2 teaspoon minced garlic
- 4 cups spring mix salad greens

In a jar with a lid, combine the first seven ingredients; add 2 teaspoons oil. Shake well. In a large skillet, cook the shrimp, scallops and garlic in remaining oil over medium heat for 5-6 minutes or until shrimp turn pink and scallops are firm and opaque. Divide the greens between two plates; top with seafood mixture. Shake dressing and drizzle over salads.

NUTRITION FACTS: 1 serving equals 264 calories, 11 g fat (2 g saturated fat), 193 mg cholesterol, 934 mg sodium, 8 g carbohydrate, 3 g fiber, 33 g protein. **DIABETIC EXCHANGES:** 4 very lean meat, 2 fat, 1 vegetable.

Artichoke-Stuffed Portobellos

MEAT-LESS

PREP/TOTAL TIME: 20 Min.   YIELD: 2 Servings

For a tasty change of pace, try these tangy portobello mushrooms filled with artichoke hearts and roasted red peppers. They are a sheer delight.   —Robert Beck, Springfield, New Jersey

- 1 tablespoon olive oil
- 1 tablespoon balsamic vinegar
- 4 large portobello mushrooms, stems removed
- 1 cup canned water-packed artichoke hearts, rinsed, drained and coarsely chopped
- 1 jar (7 ounces) roasted sweet red peppers, drained and coarsely chopped
- 1/2 teaspoon dried oregano
- 1/2 teaspoon salt
- 1/4 teaspoon pepper
- 2 tablespoons fat-free Italian salad dressing
- 3 tablespoons shredded part-skim mozzarella cheese

In a small bowl, combine the oil and vinegar; brush over both sides of mushrooms. Place mushrooms stem side down on a broiler pan coated with nonstick cooking spray. Broil 4-6 in. from the heat for 4 minutes.

Meanwhile, in a small bowl, combine the artichokes, roasted peppers, oregano, salt and pepper. Turn mushrooms over; broil 2 minutes longer. Fill with artichoke mixture; drizzle with dressing. Broil for 2-3 minutes or until heated through. Sprinkle with cheese; broil 1-2 minutes longer or until cheese is melted.

NUTRITION FACTS: 2 stuffed mushrooms equals 225 calories, 9 g fat (2 g saturated fat), 9 mg cholesterol, 952 mg sodium, 28 g carbohydrate, 3 g fiber, 8 g protein. **DIABETIC EXCHANGES:** 5 vegetable, 2 fat.

Chicken with Citrus Salsa

FAT

(PICTURED ABOVE)

PREP: 25 Min.   GRILL: 15 Min.   YIELD: 2 Servings

Topped with a salsa that has tart citrus and sweet honey flavors, this tender grilled chicken makes an attractive entree.   —Molly Slosson, Westport, Washington

- 1 cup pink grapefruit sections
- 2/3 cup peeled orange sections
- 1/2 medium lemon, peeled and cut into sections
- 1 tablespoon minced fresh cilantro
- 1 tablespoon lime juice
- 3/4 teaspoon honey
- 1/4 teaspoon grated lime peel
- 1/8 teaspoon cayenne pepper
- 1/2 teaspoon ground cumin
- 1/2 teaspoon chili powder
- 1/4 teaspoon salt
- Dash onion powder
- Dash garlic powder
- Dash dried oregano
- 2 boneless skinless chicken breast halves (4 ounces *each*)

For salsa, in a small bowl, combine the grapefruit, orange and lemon. Combine the cilantro, lime juice, honey, lime peel and cayenne; stir into fruit mixture. Cover and refrigerate until serving.

Combine the cumin, chili powder, salt, onion powder, garlic powder and oregano; sprinkle over chicken. Coat grill rack with nonstick cooking spray before starting the grill. Grill chicken, covered, over medium heat for 6-8 minutes on each side or until juices run clear. Serve with salsa.

NUTRITION FACTS: 1 chicken breast half with 1/2 cup salsa equals 206 calories, 3 g fat (1 g saturated fat), 63 mg cholesterol, 359 mg sodium, 21 g carbohydrate, 3 g fiber, 24 g protein. **DIABETIC EXCHANGES:** 3 very lean meat, 1-1/2 fruit.

Creole Chicken
(PICTURED ABOVE)

PREP: 15 Min. **COOK:** 25 Min. **YIELD:** 2 Servings

Chili powder lends a touch of heat to this full-flavored and oh-so-easy chicken entree. —Susan Shields, Arcadia, Florida

- 2 boneless skinless chicken breast halves (4 ounces *each*)
- 1 teaspoon canola oil
- 1 can (14-1/2 ounces) stewed tomatoes, cut up
- 1/3 cup julienned green pepper
- 1/4 cup chopped celery
- 1/4 cup sliced onion
- 1/2 to 1 teaspoon chili powder
- 1/2 teaspoon dried thyme
- 1/8 teaspoon pepper
- 1 cup hot cooked rice

In a small nonstick skillet coated with nonstick cooking spray, cook chicken in oil over medium heat for 5-6 minutes on each side or until juices run clear. Remove and keep warm.

In the same skillet, combine the tomatoes, green pepper, celery, onion, chili powder, thyme and pepper. Bring to a boil. Reduce heat; cover and simmer for 10 minutes or until vegetables are crisp-tender. Return chicken to pan; heat through. Serve with rice.

NUTRITION FACTS: 1 chicken breast half with 2/3 cup sauce and 1/2 cup rice equals 320 calories, 5 g fat (1 g saturated fat), 63 mg cholesterol, 447 mg sodium, 41 g carbohydrate, 3 g fiber, 27 g protein. **DIABETIC EXCHANGES:** 3 very lean meat, 3 vegetable, 1-1/2 starch, 1/2 fat.

Gingered Cucumber-Carrot Salad

CARB MEAT-LESS

(PICTURED AT RIGHT)

PREP/TOTAL TIME: 15 Min. **YIELD:** 2 Servings

This delicious salad with vegetables and gingerroot is quick, simple and a little different from the usual tossed greens.
—Alexandra Armitage, Nottingham, New Hampshire

- 1 medium cucumber, peeled, halved lengthwise, seeded and thinly sliced
- 2 small carrots, thinly sliced
- 2 tablespoons minced fresh parsley
- 1 tablespoon olive oil
- 2 teaspoons white balsamic vinegar
- 3/4 teaspoon minced fresh gingerroot
- 1/4 teaspoon salt
- 1/8 teaspoon pepper

In a bowl, combine the cucumber, carrots and parsley. In a small bowl, whisk the oil, vinegar, ginger, salt and pepper. Pour over cucumber mixture and toss to coat. Refrigerate until serving. Serve with a slotted spoon.

NUTRITION FACTS: 1 cup equals 95 calories, 7 g fat (1 g saturated fat), 0 cholesterol, 321 mg sodium, 8 g carbohydrate, 2 g fiber, 1 g protein. **DIABETIC EXCHANGES:** 1-1/2 fat, 1 vegetable.

Tuna Artichoke Melts
(PICTURED AT RIGHT)

PREP/TOTAL TIME: 15 Min. **YIELD:** 2 Servings

After sampling a similar open-faced sandwich at a restaurant, I created a lovely lemon-seasoned tuna salad with artichoke hearts. Serve it on the patio for lunch with a friend.
—Evelyn Basinger, Linville, Virginia

- 1 can (6 ounces) light water-packed tuna, drained and flaked
- 1/3 cup coarsely chopped water-packed artichoke hearts
- 2 tablespoons fat-free mayonnaise
- 1/2 cup shredded reduced-fat Mexican cheese blend, *divided*
- 1/4 teaspoon salt-free lemon-pepper seasoning
- 1/8 teaspoon dried oregano
- 2 English muffins, split and toasted

In a small bowl, combine the tuna, artichokes, mayonnaise, 1/4 cup cheese, lemon-pepper and oregano. Spread over English muffin halves.

Place on a baking sheet. Broil 4-6 in. from the heat for 3-5 minutes or until heated through. Sprinkle with remaining cheese; broil 1-2 minutes longer or until cheese is melted.

NUTRITION FACTS: 2 open-faced sandwiches equals 335 calories, 8 g fat (4 g saturated fat), 47 mg cholesterol, 989 mg sodium, 31 g carbohydrate, 2 g fiber, 34 g protein. **DIABETIC EXCHANGES:** 4 very lean meat, 2 starch, 1 fat.

HEALTHY OUTLOOK

■ Due to its taste and wellness benefits, fresh gingerroot makes regular appearances in Alexandra Armitage's recipes such as Gingered Cucumber-Carrot Salad. "Healthy gingerroot adds wonderful flavor, so I use it whenever possible," she writes.

■ For extra fiber, Evelyn Basinger often prepares her tuna melts on toasted whole wheat bread instead of English muffins.

Beef Strip Salad

CARB

(PICTURED ABOVE)

PREP: 20 Min. + Chilling   **YIELD:** 2 Servings

For a refreshing meal in minutes, I add chilled beef tenderloin to salad greens with a tangy sour cream and lemon dressing.
—Betty Gregoire, Austin, Texas

- 1/2 pound beef tenderloin
- 1 small red onion, thinly sliced and separated into rings
- 1/4 teaspoon salt
- Dash coarsely ground pepper
- 1 cup torn leaf lettuce
- 1/4 cup chopped green pepper
- 2 tablespoons sliced pimientos
- 3 pitted ripe olives, sliced
- 1/4 cup reduced-fat sour cream
- 4-1/2 teaspoons lemon juice

In a large nonstick skillet coated with nonstick cooking spray, cook beef over medium heat for 5-7 minutes on each side or until meat reaches desired doneness (for medium-rare, a meat thermometer should read 145°; medium, 160°; well-done, 170°). Refrigerate until chilled.

Thinly slice the beef; place in a bowl. Add onion, salt and pepper; toss to combine. Divide the lettuce and beef mixture between two serving plates; top with green pepper, pimientos and olives. Combine sour cream and lemon juice; serve alongside the salad.

NUTRITION FACTS: 1 serving equals 251 calories, 11 g fat (5 g saturated fat), 81 mg cholesterol, 432 mg sodium, 9 g carbohydrate, 2 g fiber, 27 g protein. **DIABETIC EXCHANGES:** 3 lean meat, 1 vegetable, 1/2 starch, 1/2 fat.

Egg 'n' Bacon Sandwiches

CARB

(PICTURED BELOW)

PREP/TOTAL TIME: 5 Min.   **YIELD:** 2 Servings

This healthy, ultra-fast take on a drive-thru favorite was created by my son-in-law so he could quickly make breakfast for my grandchildren before they went to school.
—Sharon Pickett, Aurora, Indiana

- 2 eggs
- 1 teaspoon fat-free milk
- 1/4 teaspoon salt
- 1/8 teaspoon pepper
- 2 slices Canadian bacon (1/2 ounce *each*)
- 1 English muffin, split and toasted
- 2 tablespoons shredded reduced-fat cheddar cheese

In a small bowl, whisk the eggs, milk, salt and pepper. Divide between two 10-oz. microwave-safe custard cups coated with nonstick cooking spray. Microwave, uncovered, on high for 20 seconds. Stir; microwave 20-25 seconds longer or until center of egg is almost set.

Place a slice of bacon on each muffin half; top with egg and sprinkle with cheese. Microwave, uncovered, for 10-13 seconds or until cheese is melted. Let stand for 20-30 seconds before serving.

NUTRITION FACTS: 1 sandwich equals 179 calories, 8 g fat (3 g saturated fat), 223 mg cholesterol, 673 mg sodium, 14 g carbohydrate, 1 g fiber, 12 g protein. **DIABETIC EXCHANGES:** 1 starch, 1 lean meat.

Editor's Note: This recipe was tested in a 1,100-watt microwave.

Curry Citrus Chicken

(PICTURED AT RIGHT)

CARB

PREP/TOTAL TIME: 20 Min. **YIELD:** 2 Servings

To brighten dark winter days, I rely on this mouth-watering, microwave chicken. Flavored with a sunny splash of citrus and a warm dash of curry and cumin, it's always a hit in my home. Best of all, there are never any leftovers to deal with!
 —Marcy Hall, Visalia, California

  4 boneless skinless chicken thighs (3 ounces *each*)
  2 tablespoons finely chopped onion
  2 tablespoons lemon juice
  2 tablespoons orange juice
  2 tablespoons reduced-sodium soy sauce
  1/2 teaspoon curry powder
  1/2 teaspoon ground cumin
  1/4 teaspoon poultry seasoning
1-1/2 teaspoons cornstarch
  1 tablespoon water

Place the chicken in a microwave-safe dish coated with non-stick cooking spray. Combine the onion, juices, soy sauce, curry powder, cumin and poultry seasoning; pour over chicken.

Cover and microwave on high for 3 minutes; turn chicken over. Cover and microwave 2-4 minutes longer or until the chicken is no longer pink and a meat thermometer reads 180°. Remove chicken and let stand for 1-2 minutes.

Combine cornstarch and water until smooth; stir into the cooking juices. Microwave, uncovered, on high for 1 to 1-1/2 minutes or until thickened, stirring every 30 seconds. Serve over chicken.

NUTRITION FACTS: 2 chicken thighs with 3 tablespoons sauce equals 186 calories, 8 g fat (2 g saturated fat), 69 mg cholesterol, 665 mg sodium, 7 g carbohydrate, 1 g fiber, 21 g protein. **DIABETIC EXCHANGES:** 3 lean meat, 1/2 starch.

Editor's Note: This recipe was tested in a 1,100-watt microwave.

Snow Pea Medley

(PICTURED ABOVE RIGHT)

MEAT-LESS

PREP/TOTAL TIME: 20 Min. **YIELD:** 2 Servings

Even in frosty weather, I serve garden-fresh fare thanks to my colorful stir-fry. The crisp-tender side dish goes with a variety of entrees and is ready in minutes. —Lucille Mead, Ilion, New York

1/3 cup chopped red onion
  2 teaspoons canola oil
1/3 cup julienned sweet red pepper
1/3 cup julienned sweet yellow pepper
1/2 cup fresh snow peas
1/2 cup sliced fresh mushrooms
1/3 teaspoon salt

In a nonstick skillet coated with nonstick cooking spray, saute onion in oil for 1-2 minutes. Add peppers; cook for 2 minutes. Stir in the peas and mushrooms; saute 3-4 minutes longer or until vegetables are crisp-tender. Sprinkle with salt.

NUTRITION FACTS: 3/4 cup equals 83 calories, 5 g fat (trace saturated fat), 0 cholesterol, 299 mg sodium, 8 g carbohydrate, 2 g fiber, 3 g protein. **DIABETIC EXCHANGES:** 2 vegetable, 1 fat.

reducing ingredients

Looking to scale back the serving quantity of some of your favorite recipes? Doing so is a snap! Just remember these common calculations to make things easy.

ORIGINAL AMOUNT	HALF	ONE-THIRD
1 cup	1/2 cup	1/3 cup
3/4 cup	6 tablespoons	1/4 cup
2/3 cup	1/3 cup	3 tablespoons + 1-1/2 teaspoons*
1/3 cup	2 tablespoons + 2 teaspoons	1 tablespoon + 2-1/4 teaspoons*
1/4 cup	2 tablespoons	1 tablespoon + 1 teaspoon
1 tablespoon	1-1/2 teaspoons	1 teaspoon
1 teaspoon	1/2 teaspoon	1/4 teaspoon*
1/2 teaspoon	1/4 teaspoon	1/8 teaspoon*
1/4 teaspoon	1/8 teaspoon	dash

amount is rounded down

Stuffed Ranch Chicken

(PICTURED AT LEFT)

CARB

PREP: 15 Min.   **BAKE:** 25 Min.   **YIELD:** 2 Servings

My husband and I are trying to eat healthier, so I watch for light, flavorful foods that serve two. Stuffed with red pepper, green onion and creamy ranch dressing, this supper is a winner.
—LaDonna Reed, Ponca City, Oklahoma

    1 bacon strip, cut in half lengthwise
    2 boneless skinless chicken breast halves (4 ounces *each*)
    2 tablespoons fat-free ranch salad dressing
    3 tablespoons finely chopped fresh mushrooms
    3 tablespoons finely chopped sweet red pepper
    3 tablespoons finely chopped green onions
    6 tablespoons fat-free evaporated milk
    2 teaspoons cornstarch

In a small nonstick skillet, cook bacon over medium heat until cooked but not crisp. Drain on paper towel. Flatten chicken to 1/4-in. thickness; spread with ranch dressing. Top with mushrooms, red pepper and onions. Roll up and wrap a piece of bacon around each; secure with a toothpick if needed.

Place in a shallow 1-qt. baking dish coated with nonstick cooking spray. Bake, uncovered, at 350° for 25-30 minutes or chicken juices run clear. Remove and keep warm. Remove toothpicks before serving.

Strain pan juices. In a small saucepan, combine milk and cornstarch until smooth; stir in pan juices. Bring to a boil; cook and stir for 1 minute or until thickened. Serve over chicken.

NUTRITION FACTS: 1 chicken breast half with 2 tablespoons sauce equals 220 calories, 5 g fat (1 g saturated fat), 67 mg cholesterol, 339 mg sodium, 15 g carbohydrate, 1 g fiber, 28 g protein. **DIABETIC EXCHANGES:** 3 very lean meat, 1 starch, 1 fat.

Chive Scalloped Potatoes

MEAT-LESS

PREP: 15 Min.   **BAKE:** 40 Min.   **YIELD:** 2 Servings

I'd been wanting scalloped potatoes for some time, but wasn't able to find a downsized recipe until I came across this yummy version with a hint of chives. —Kathleen Bailey, Penetanguishene, Ontario

    2 teaspoons butter
    1 tablespoon all-purpose flour
1/2 teaspoon salt
1/4 teaspoon pepper
1/4 teaspoon ground mustard
3/4 cup 2% milk
    1 teaspoon minced chives
    2 medium potatoes, peeled and thinly sliced

In a small saucepan, melt butter. Stir in the flour, salt, pepper and mustard until smooth; gradually stir in milk. Bring to a boil; cook and stir for 2 minutes or until thickened. Remove from the heat; stir in chives.

In a 3-cup baking dish coated with nonstick cooking spray, layer half of the potatoes, 1/3 cup white sauce, remaining potatoes and remaining sauce. Cover and bake at 350° for 35 minutes. Uncover; bake 5-10 minutes longer or until potatoes are tender.

NUTRITION FACTS: 3/4 cup equals 197 calories, 6 g fat (3 g saturated fat), 17 mg cholesterol, 679 mg sodium, 31 g carbohydrate, 2 g fiber, 6 g protein. **DIABETIC EXCHANGES:** 2 starch, 1 fat.

Phyllo-Wrapped Halibut

(PICTURED BELOW)

PREP: 20 Min.   **BAKE:** 20 Min.   **YIELD:** 2 Servings

I created this to convince my husband that seafood doesn't always taste "fishy." He likes the flaky, phyllo wrapping and the vegetables hidden inside of the company-worthy dish.   —Carrie Vazzano
Rolling Meadows, Illinois

    4 cups fresh baby spinach
3/4 cup chopped sweet red pepper
3/4 teaspoon salt-free lemon-pepper seasoning, *divided*
1/2 teaspoon lemon juice
    6 sheets phyllo dough (14 inches x 9 inches)
    2 tablespoons reduced-fat butter, melted
    2 halibut fillets (4 ounces *each*)
1/4 teaspoon salt
1/8 teaspoon pepper
1/4 cup shredded part-skim mozzarella cheese

In a large nonstick skillet lightly coated with nonstick cooking spray, saute spinach and red pepper until tender. Add 1/2 teaspoon lemon-pepper and lemon juice. Remove from the heat; cool.

Line a baking sheet with foil and coat the foil with nonstick cooking spray; set aside. Place one sheet of phyllo dough on a work surface; brush with butter. (Until ready to use, keep phyllo dough covered with plastic wrap and a damp towel to prevent it from drying out.) Layer remaining phyllo over first sheet, brushing each with butter. Cut stack in half widthwise.

Place a halibut fillet in the center of each square; sprinkle with salt and pepper. Top with cheese and spinach mixture. Fold sides and bottom edge over fillet and roll up to enclose it; trim end of phyllo if necessary. Brush with remaining butter; sprinkle with remaining lemon-pepper.

Place seam side down on prepared baking sheet. Bake at 375° for 20-25 minutes or until golden brown.

NUTRITION FACTS: 1 serving equals 330 calories, 12 g fat (6 g saturated fat), 64 mg cholesterol, 676 mg sodium, 26 g carbohydrate, 4 g fiber, 33 g protein. **DIABETIC EXCHANGES:** 4 very lean meat, 2 vegetable, 1-1/2 fat, 1 starch.

Editor's Note: This recipe was tested with Land O'Lakes light stick butter.

Spicy Chicken Spaghetti
(PICTURED ABOVE)

PREP/TOTAL TIME: 25 Min.   YIELD: 2 Servings

I keep on the lookout for recipes that serve two. We're also watching our fat grams, so this main course was a great find. Adjust the spice level by decreasing the Cajun seasoning.
—LaDonna Reed, Ponca City, Oklahoma

      3 ounces uncooked spaghetti
  1/2 pound boneless skinless chicken breast,
         cut into 3/4-inch cubes
1-1/2 teaspoons Cajun seasoning
      1 cup sliced fresh mushrooms
  1/2 cup chopped green pepper
      2 green onions, thinly sliced
      1 garlic clove, minced
      1 tablespoon cornstarch
  1/8 teaspoon salt
  1/8 teaspoon pepper
      1 cup fat-free half-and-half

Cook spaghetti according to package directions. Meanwhile, sprinkle chicken with Cajun seasoning. In a nonstick skillet coated with nonstick cooking spray, cook chicken for 7-9 minutes or until lightly browned and juices run clear. Remove and keep warm.

In the same skillet, saute mushrooms, green pepper, onions and garlic until almost tender. Combine cornstarch, salt and pepper; sprinkle over vegetables. Cook and stir for 1 minute. Gradually stir in half-and-half. Bring to a boil over medium heat; cook and stir for 1-2 minutes or until thickened.

Return chicken to the pan; heat through. Drain spaghetti; top with chicken mixture.

NUTRITION FACTS: 1 cup chicken mixture with 3/4 cup spaghetti equals 401 calories, 4 g fat (1 g saturated fat), 63 mg cholesterol, 808 mg sodium, 53 g carbohydrate, 3 g fiber, 34 g protein. **DIABETIC EXCHANGES:** 3 very lean meat, 2 starch, 1 vegetable, 1 fat-free milk.

Apple Cranberry Crisp

PREP/TOTAL TIME: 10 Min.   YIELD: 2 Servings

You can't beat the convenience of a packet of oatmeal to create this delicious dessert.   —Charlotte Davidson, Batesville, Arkansas

      2 medium Golden Delicious apples, chopped
      1 cup chopped fresh *or* frozen cranberries
Sugar substitute equivalent to 2 tablespoons sugar
      1 tablespoon cold butter
      1 package (1.6 ounces) instant cinnamon and spice oatmeal

In a small bowl, combine the apples, cranberries and sugar substitute. Transfer to two 10-oz. ramekins or custard cups coated with nonstick cooking spray. Microwave, uncovered, on high for 3-1/2 to 4-1/2 minutes or until apples are almost tender.

In a bowl, cut butter into oatmeal until crumbly; sprinkle over apple mixture. Microwave, uncovered, on high 1-2 minutes longer or until butter is melted and topping is golden. Serve warm.

NUTRITION FACTS: 1 serving equals 246 calories, 7 g fat (4 g saturated fat), 15 mg cholesterol, 178 mg sodium, 46 g carbohydrate, 7 g fiber, 3 g protein.

Editor's Note: This recipe was tested with Splenda No Calorie Sweetener in a 1,100-watt microwave.

Turkey 'n' Swiss Sandwiches
(PICTURED BELOW)

PREP/TOTAL TIME: 15 Min.   YIELD: 2 Servings

Perfect for two, these toasted sandwiches turn boring lunches into exciting affairs. They offer a wonderful combination of flavors.
—Leah Starnes, Bedford, Texas

      4 slices sourdough bread, lightly toasted
      2 teaspoons Dijon mustard
      4 slices jellied cranberry sauce (1/4 inch thick)
      6 ounces thinly sliced deli smoked turkey
      2 slices reduced-fat Swiss cheese

Spread two slices of bread with mustard. Top with cranberry sauce, turkey and cheese. Broil 3-4 in. from the heat for 1-2 minutes or until cheese is melted. Top with remaining bread.

NUTRITION FACTS: 1 sandwich equals 384 calories, 8 g fat (2 g saturated fat), 43 mg cholesterol, 1,315 mg sodium, 54 g carbohydrate, 3 g fiber, 27 g protein.

Fine Dining Pared Down

Nothing brings family and friends closer together than celebrating special moments over a fine meal; however, pampering guests doesn't mean adding to their waistlines. Assemble a simply elegant menu with the dinners found here, then share a toast to the joy of healthy living.

Marinated Mushrooms, p. 269
Glazed Beef Tournedos, p. 269

feast on steak alfresco!

Grilled Marinated Sirloin

CARB ▼

(PICTURED AT LEFT)

PREP: 10 Min. + Marinating   **GRILL:** 20 Min.   **YIELD:** 6 Servings

A tasty marinade laced with lime juice is the secret behind this hearty sirloin recipe from our Test Kitchen. You'll enjoy warm-weather entertaining and stay out of a hot kitchen with this classic summer standout.

       1/4 cup lime juice
         1 green onion, finely chopped
         2 tablespoons paprika
         2 tablespoons canola oil
         1 tablespoon finely chopped jalapeno pepper
     1-1/2 teaspoons sugar
         2 garlic cloves, minced
         1 teaspoon dried oregano
         1 teaspoon grated lime peel
       1/2 teaspoon salt
         1 boneless beef sirloin steak (about 1-1/2 pounds)

In a bowl, combine the first 10 ingredients; mix well. Pour half of the marinade into a large resealable plastic bag; add steak. Seal bag and turn to coat; refrigerate for up to 4 hours. Cover and refrigerate remaining marinade for basting.

Coat grill rack with nonstick cooking spray before starting the grill. Grill steak, covered, over medium heat for 8-10 minutes on each side or until meat reaches desired doneness (for medium-rare, a meat thermometer should read 145°; medium, 160°; well-done, 170°). Baste with reserved marinade during the last 2 minutes of cooking.

NUTRITION FACTS: 3 ounces cooked beef equals 200 calories, 11 g fat (3 g saturated fat), 63 mg cholesterol, 245 mg sodium, 4 g carbohydrate, 1 g fiber, 22 g protein. **DIABETIC EXCHANGES:** 3 lean meat, 1/2 fat.

Editor's Note: When cutting or seeding hot peppers, use rubber or plastic gloves to protect your hands. Avoid touching your face.

Sweet 'n' Spicy Roasted Corn

SALT   MEAT-LESS ▼

(PICTURED AT FAR LEFT)

PREP: 5 Min. + Soaking   **GRILL:** 25 Min.   **YIELD:** 6 Servings

I spice up the corn I bring to get-togethers with this scrumptious idea. My husband came up with this flavorful glaze. It tastes really good, looks beautiful and requires far less butter than people generally use.
                                        —Erin Littlefield, Bryan, Texas

         6 large ears sweet corn in husks
         2 tablespoons butter
         4 garlic cloves, minced
         1 teaspoon brown sugar
       1/4 teaspoon crushed red pepper flakes
       1/4 teaspoon chili powder

Carefully peel back corn husks to within 1 in. of bottom; remove silk. Rewrap corn in husks and secure with kitchen string. Soak corn in cold water for 1 hour.

Coat grill rack with nonstick cooking spray before starting the grill. Grill corn, covered, over medium heat for 25-30 minutes or until tender, turning occasionally. Remove string before serving.

Meanwhile, in a small saucepan, melt butter. Add garlic, brown sugar, red pepper flakes and chili powder. Brush over grilled corn.

NUTRITION FACTS: 1 ear of corn equals 163 calories, 6 g fat (3 g saturated fat), 10 mg cholesterol, 62 mg sodium, 29 g carbohydrate, 4 g fiber, 5 g protein. **DIABETIC EXCHANGES:** 2 starch, 1 fat.

Greens with Pears and Blue Cheese

(PICTURED AT LEFT)

PREP/TOTAL TIME: 15 Min.   **YIELD:** 6 Servings

Fresh greens, pears, blue cheese, walnuts and a creamy citrus dressing make this healthy salad a refreshing delight. I concocted it 3 years ago and it was an instant sensation. We think that it is wonderful with grilled foods.
                                —Leanne Mocker, Fall River, Massachusetts

         3 tablespoons orange juice
         2 tablespoons plus 1 teaspoon cider vinegar
     4-1/2 teaspoons fat-free mayonnaise
         1 tablespoon honey
     2-1/4 teaspoons lemon juice
     2-1/4 teaspoons olive oil
       1/4 teaspoon salt
       1/4 teaspoon coarsely ground pepper
        12 cups spring mix salad greens
         3 medium pears, thinly sliced
       1/3 cup crumbled blue cheese
       1/3 cup chopped walnuts, toasted

For dressing, in a small bowl, whisk the first eight ingredients. Divide the greens, pear slices, blue cheese and walnuts between six salad plates. Drizzle each with 2 tablespoons dressing.

NUTRITION FACTS: 1 serving equals 169 calories, 8 g fat (2 g saturated fat), 6 mg cholesterol, 261 mg sodium, 22 g carbohydrate, 5 g fiber, 5 g protein. **DIABETIC EXCHANGES:** 1-1/2 fat, 1 vegetable, 1 fruit.

easy, impressive & elegant

Tenderloin with Herb Sauce
(PICTURED BELOW)

CARB ⬇

PREP/TOTAL TIME: 25 Min.   **YIELD:** 6 Servings

Juicy pork tenderloins are dressed up with a rich, slightly spicy sauce in this lovely, half-hour entree. It's tasty and very simple to prepare.   —Monica Shipley, Tulare, California

    2 pork tenderloins (1 pound *each*)
1/2 teaspoon salt
    4 teaspoons butter
2/3 cup half-and-half cream
    2 tablespoons minced fresh parsley
    2 teaspoons herbes de Provence
    2 teaspoons reduced-sodium soy sauce
    1 teaspoon beef bouillon granules
1/2 to 3/4 teaspoon crushed red pepper flakes

Cut each tenderloin into 12 slices; sprinkle with salt. In a large nonstick skillet coated with nonstick cooking spray, brown pork in batches in butter over medium heat for 3-4 minutes on each side. Return all pork to the skillet.

Combine the remaining ingredients; pour over pork. Cook and stir over low heat for 2-3 minutes or until sauce is thickened.

NUTRITION FACTS: 3-1/2 ounces cooked pork with 2 tablespoons sauce equals 238 calories, 10 g fat (5 g saturated fat), 104 mg cholesterol, 495 mg sodium, 2 g carbohydrate, trace fiber, 31 g protein. **DIABETIC EXCHANGES:** 4 lean meat, 1 fat.

Rosemary Red Potatoes

(PICTURED BELOW LEFT)

MEAT-LESS

PREP: 15 Min.   BAKE: 20 Min.   YIELD: 6 Servings

This delicious combination of roasted garlic, rosemary and potatoes makes the whole house smell wonderful. Try the side dish with grilled steak or roasted chicken. It's perfect for fall but just as tasty at a summer barbecue. —Sally Ridenour, Salem, Oregon

   1 large whole garlic bulb
   2 pounds small red potatoes, quartered
 1/2 medium onion, cut into chunks
   4 teaspoons olive oil
 1/2 teaspoon salt
   4 to 5 fresh rosemary sprigs
   3 tablespoons Dijon mustard
4-1/2 teaspoons balsamic vinegar

Remove papery outer skin from garlic; separate into cloves, leaving them unpeeled. In a large bowl, combine potatoes, onion and garlic. Add oil and salt; toss to coat.

Arrange potato mixture in a single layer in a 15-in. x 10-in. x 1-in. baking pan coated with nonstick cooking spray. Top with rosemary sprigs. Bake at 450° for 15-17 minutes or until garlic is tender.

Remove garlic cloves; cool. Stir potato mixture; bake 5-8 minutes longer or until potatoes are tender, stirring occasionally. Discard rosemary. Squeeze softened garlic into a large bowl; mash with a fork. Add mustard and vinegar; mix well. Add potato mixture and stir gently to coat.

NUTRITION FACTS: 3/4 cup equals 153 calories, 4 g fat (trace saturated fat), 0 cholesterol, 397 mg sodium, 27 g carbohydrate, 3 g fiber, 4 g protein. DIABETIC EXCHANGES: 2 starch, 1/2 fat.

Caramel Cream Crepes

(PICTURED ABOVE)

PREP: 20 Min. + Chilling   COOK: 15 Min.   YIELD: 6 Servings

Guests will rave about these lovely crepes that were created by our home economists. They have a creamy caramel filling and a topping of white wine and raspberries.

   6 tablespoons fat-free milk
   6 tablespoons egg substitute
1-1/2 teaspoons butter, melted
 1/2 teaspoon vanilla extract
   6 tablespoons all-purpose flour
   6 ounces fat-free cream cheese
   3 tablespoons plus 6 teaspoons fat-free caramel ice cream topping, *divided*
2-1/4 cups reduced-fat whipped topping
1-1/2 cups fresh raspberries
 1/3 cup white wine *or* unsweetened apple juice
   3 tablespoons sliced almonds, toasted

In a blender, combine the milk, egg substitute, butter and vanilla; cover and process until blended. Add the flour; cover and process until blended. Cover and refrigerate for 1 hour.

Lightly coat a 6-in. nonstick skillet with nonstick cooking spray; heat over medium heat. Pour about 2 tablespoons of batter into center of skillet; lift and tilt pan to evenly coat bottom. Cook until top appears dry and bottom is golden; turn and cook 15-20 seconds longer. Remove to a wire rack. Repeat with remaining batter. Stack cooled crepes with waxed paper or paper towels in between.

In a small mixing bowl, beat cream cheese and 3 tablespoons caramel topping until smooth. Fold in whipped topping. Spoon down the center of each crepe. Drizzle with remaining caramel topping; roll up.

In a small microwave-safe bowl, combine raspberries and wine or juice. Microwave on high for 30-60 seconds or until warm. Using a slotted spoon, place berries over crepes. Sprinkle with almonds.

NUTRITION FACTS: 1 serving equals 206 calories, 6 g fat (4 g saturated fat), 5 mg cholesterol, 227 mg sodium, 25 g carbohydrate, 3 g fiber, 8 g protein. DIABETIC EXCHANGES: 1-1/2 starch, 1 very lean meat, 1 fat.

Elegant Crepes Are Easy!

- Save on fat by omitting butter and coating a nonstick skillet with nonstick cooking spray. Heat the skillet over medium heat, and pour the batter into the center of the skillet.

- Carefully lift and slowly tilt the skillet to evenly coat the bottom with the crepe batter. Cook until the top of the crepe appears to be dry and the bottom is golden.

- Gently turn the crepe and cook another 15 to 20 seconds. Remove to a wire rack to cool. Stack cooled crepes on the rack with waxed paper in between each.

crowd-pleasing classics

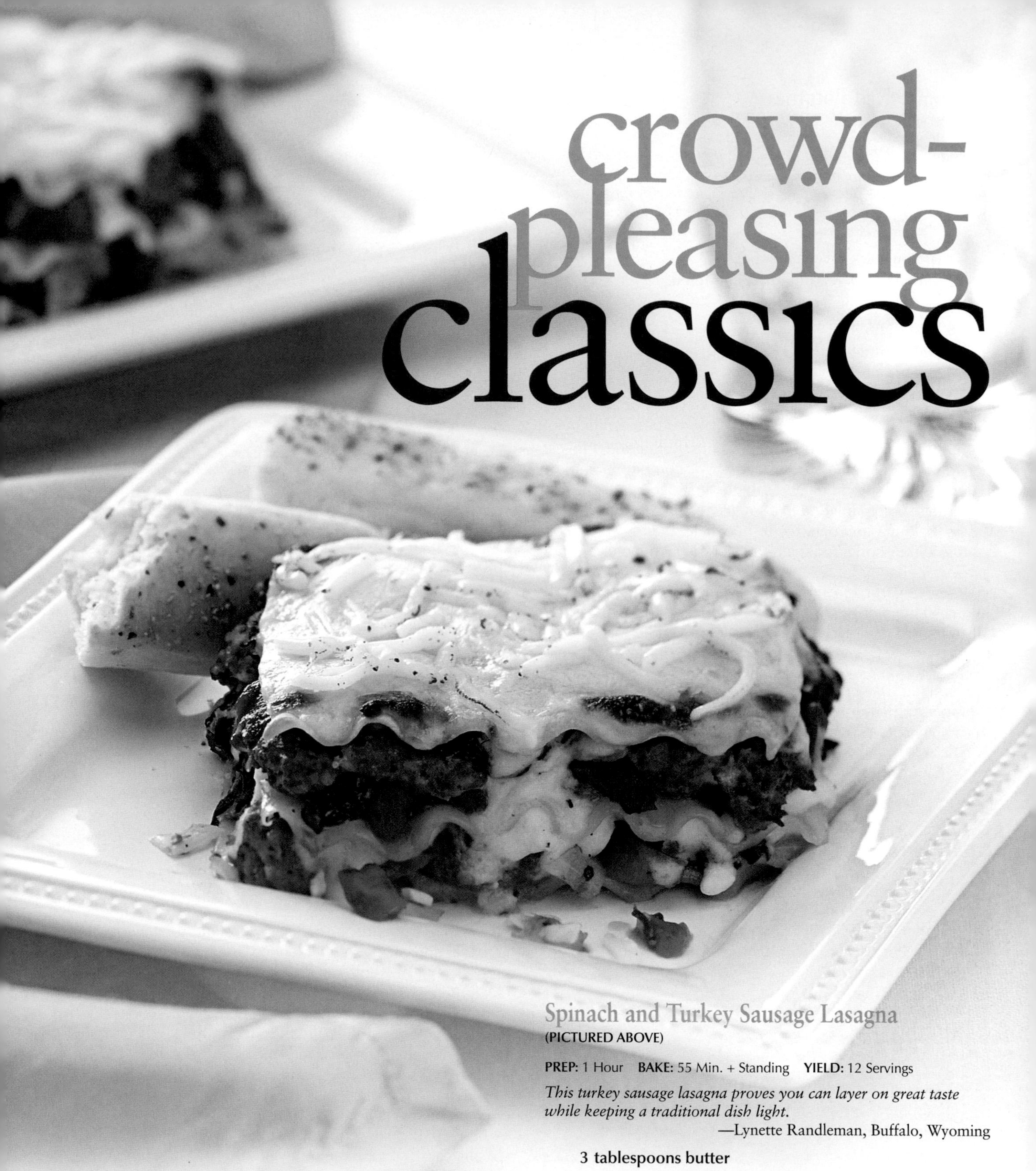

Spinach and Turkey Sausage Lasagna
(PICTURED ABOVE)

PREP: 1 Hour **BAKE:** 55 Min. + Standing **YIELD:** 12 Servings

This turkey sausage lasagna proves you can layer on great taste while keeping a traditional dish light.

—Lynette Randleman, Buffalo, Wyoming

- 3 tablespoons butter
- 1/3 cup all-purpose flour
- 1/2 teaspoon salt
- 1/4 teaspoon pepper
- 3 cups fat-free milk
- 3 ounces reduced-fat cream cheese, cubed
- 3/4 cup grated Parmesan cheese
- 1 pound Italian turkey sausage links, casings removed and crumbled
- 1 medium onion, chopped

4 garlic cloves, minced
1 teaspoon dried oregano
1 teaspoon dried marjoram
1/2 teaspoon fennel seed, crushed
1 jar (7-1/4 ounces) roasted sweet red peppers, drained and chopped
1/2 cup white wine *or* reduced-sodium chicken broth
2 packages (10 ounces *each*) frozen chopped spinach, thawed and squeezed dry
3/4 cup small-curd 2% cottage cheese
1/4 teaspoon ground nutmeg
9 lasagna noodles, cooked, rinsed and drained
1/2 cup shredded part-skim mozzarella cheese

In a saucepan, melt butter. Stir in flour, salt and pepper until smooth. Gradually stir in milk. Bring to a boil; cook and stir for 1-2 minutes or until thickened. Stir in cream cheese until melted. Stir in Parmesan cheese just until melted. Remove from the heat; set aside.

In a large nonstick skillet coated with nonstick cooking spray, cook sausage, onion and garlic over medium heat until sausage is no longer pink; drain. Stir in oregano, marjoram and fennel; cook for 1 minute.

Add roasted peppers and wine or broth. Bring to a boil. Reduce heat; simmer, uncovered, for 3-5 minutes or until liquid is reduced to 3 tablespoons. Remove from the heat; set aside. In a small bowl, combine spinach, cottage cheese and nutmeg; set aside.

Spread 1/2 cup reserved cheese sauce in a 13-in. x 9-in. x 2-in. baking dish coated with nonstick cooking spray. Top with three noodles, half of the sausage mixture, half of the spinach mixture and 1 cup sauce; repeat layers. Top with remaining noodles and sauce. Sprinkle with mozzarella cheese.

Cover and bake at 375° for 40 minutes. Uncover; bake 15-20 minutes longer or until heated through and top is lightly browned. Let stand for 10 minutes before cutting.

NUTRITION FACTS: 1 piece equals 279 calories, 11 g fat (6 g saturated fat), 43 mg cholesterol, 664 mg sodium, 27 g carbohydrate, 3 g fiber, 19 g protein. DIABETIC EXCHANGES: 2 lean meat, 1-1/2 starch, 1 vegetable, 1 fat.

Herbed Soft Breadsticks
FAT MEAT-LESS
(PICTURED ON PAGE 266)

PREP: 30 Min. + Rising   BAKE: 10 Min.   YIELD: 32 Breadsticks

Be prepared to refill the bread basket often when you put out these irresistible breadsticks. They were very popular with customers at the bakery where I once worked.
—Laneta Culp, Cazenovia, Wisconsin

1 package (1/4 ounce) active dry yeast
1/4 cup warm water (110° to 115°)
1-3/4 cups 2% milk
1 egg, lightly beaten
2-1/2 teaspoons canola oil
2 tablespoons plus 1-1/2 teaspoons sugar
2 teaspoons salt
3/4 teaspoon *each* dried oregano, marjoram and thyme
1/2 teaspoon garlic powder
5 to 5-1/2 cups all-purpose flour

TOPPING:
1 egg, lightly beaten
1 teaspoon salt-free Italian herb seasoning

In a large mixing bowl, dissolve yeast in warm water. Add the milk, egg, oil, sugar, salt, oregano, marjoram, thyme, garlic powder and 3 cups flour. Beat on medium speed until smooth. Stir in enough remaining flour to form a firm dough.

Turn onto a lightly floured surface; knead until smooth and elastic, about 6-8 minutes. Place in a bowl coated with nonstick cooking spray, turning once to coat the top.

Cover and let rise in a warm place until doubled, about 1 hour.

Punch dough down. Turn onto a lightly floured surface. Roll into a 16-in. x 12-in. rectangle. Cut into 6-in. x 1-in. strips. Place on baking sheets coated with nonstick cooking spray. Cover and let rise until doubled, about 30 minutes.

Brush with egg; sprinkle with herb seasoning. Bake at 400° for 9-12 minutes or until golden brown. Remove to wire racks.

NUTRITION FACTS: 2 breadsticks equals 181 calories, 2 g fat (1 g saturated fat), 29 mg cholesterol, 317 mg sodium, 33 g carbohydrate, 1 g fiber, 6 g protein. DIABETIC EXCHANGE: 2 starch.

Cranberry Blue Cheese Salad

SALT CARB MEAT-LESS
(PICTURED BELOW)

PREP/TOTAL TIME: 15 Min.   YIELD: 12 Servings

For a light and refreshing first course, turn to this fruity salad. Sweet apple, dried cranberries, blue cheese and a homemade vinaigrette give it a delightful punch of flavor.
—Lori McLaughlin, Pittsford, New York

6 cups torn Bibb *or* Boston lettuce
6 cups torn red leaf lettuce
1 large apple, chopped
1/2 cup dried cranberries
1/3 cup olive oil
1/4 cup rice wine vinegar
1-1/2 teaspoons Dijon mustard
1 garlic clove, minced
1/2 cup crumbled blue cheese

In a large bowl, combine the lettuces, apple and cranberries. In a small bowl, whisk the oil, vinegar, mustard and garlic. Pour over salad and toss to coat. Sprinkle with the blue cheese. Serve immediately.

NUTRITION FACTS: 3/4 cup equals 111 calories, 8 g fat (2 g saturated fat), 4 mg cholesterol, 98 mg sodium, 9 g carbohydrate, 2 g fiber, 2 g protein. DIABETIC EXCHANGES: 1-1/2 fat, 1 vegetable, 1/2 fruit.

easy
elegance

Glazed Beef Tournedos

CARB

(PICTURED AT LEFT)

PREP/TOTAL TIME: 20 Min.　YIELD: 4 Servings

I found this wonderful, quick recipe years ago. It's been a favorite for special occasions ever since. —Janet Singleton, Bellevue, Ohio

　　3 tablespoons steak sauce
　　2 tablespoons ketchup
　　2 tablespoons orange marmalade
　　1 tablespoon lemon juice
　　1 tablespoon finely chopped onion
　　1 garlic clove, minced
　　4 beef tenderloin steaks (6 ounces *each*)

In a small bowl, combine steak sauce, ketchup, marmalade, lemon juice, onion and garlic. Set aside 1/4 cup for serving.

　　Coat grill rack with nonstick cooking spray before starting the grill. Grill steaks, uncovered, over medium heat or broil 4-6 in. from the heat for 5-7 minutes on each side or until meat reaches desired doneness (for medium-rare, a meat thermometer should read 145°; medium, 160°; well-done, 170°), basting frequently with remaining sauce. Just before serving, brush steaks with reserved sauce.

NUTRITION FACTS: 1 serving equals 308 calories, 12 g fat (5 g saturated fat), 106 mg cholesterol, 385 mg sodium, 12 g carbohydrate, trace fiber, 36 g protein. **DIABETIC EXCHANGES:** 5 lean meat, 1 starch.

Marinated Mushrooms

SALT CARB MEAT-LESS

(PICTURED AT LEFT)

PREP: 10 Min. + Marinating　YIELD: 4 Servings

Guests will never guess a dish so flavorful could take only 10 minutes of hands-on prep and no cooking! They're great as a side dish or tempting as tidbits on a relish tray.
　　　　　　　　　　　—Billie Moss, Walnut Creek, California

　　2 cups small fresh mushrooms
　　3 tablespoons rice wine vinegar
　　2 tablespoons olive oil
　1/2 teaspoon dried basil
　1/2 teaspoon dried marjoram
　1/2 teaspoon mustard seed
　1/4 teaspoon onion salt

Place the mushrooms in a bowl. In another bowl, whisk the remaining ingredients. Pour over mushrooms and toss to coat. Cover and refrigerate for 8 hours or overnight. Drain and discard marinade before serving.

NUTRITION FACTS: 1/2 cup equals 46 calories, 4 g fat (trace saturated fat), 0 cholesterol, 115 mg sodium, 3 g carbohydrate, 1 g fiber, 1 g protein. **DIABETIC EXCHANGE:** 1 fat.

TASTY TIP

Try spinach tortellini for half of the pasta in the appetizer. The green color is eye-fetching placed near the bright dip. When serving the tortellini, consider using beaded or frilled party pics, or skewer several pieces on long wooden kabobs for a dramatic-looking dish.

Tortellini with Roasted Red Pepper Dip

MEAT-LESS

(PICTURED BELOW)

PREP/TOTAL TIME: 25 Min.　YIELD: 10 Servings

Looking to add a dash of color to your appetizer mix? This unique, savory treat and quick dip is sure to be a hit with any hungry crowd!　　　—Michelle Boucher, Milford, New Hampshire

　　1 package (19 ounces) frozen cheese tortellini
　　1 jar (7 ounces) roasted sweet red peppers, drained
　　3 garlic cloves, minced
　1/2 cup fat-free mayonnaise
　1/2 teaspoon balsamic vinegar
　1/4 teaspoon salt
　1/8 teaspoon pepper
　　1 tablespoon olive oil
　　1 large zucchini, cut into strips

Prepare tortellini according to package directions. Meanwhile, place red peppers and garlic in a food processor; cover and process until combined. Add the mayonnaise, vinegar, salt and pepper; cover and process until blended. Transfer to a small bowl.

　　Drain tortellini; toss with oil. Serve with zucchini strips and red pepper dip.

NUTRITION FACTS: 14 tortellini and 4 zucchini strips with 4-1/2 teaspoons dip equals 142 calories, 5 g fat (2 g saturated fat), 10 mg cholesterol, 333 mg sodium, 19 g carbohydrate, 1 g fiber, 6 g protein. **DIABETIC EXCHANGES:** 1 starch, 1 lean meat.

a taste of
tropical
sophistication

Pineapple Shrimp Kabobs
(PICTURED AT LEFT)

FAT

PREP: 30 Min. + Marinating   GRILL: 10 Min.   YIELD: 8 Servings

I don't remember where I found this wonderful recipe, but my husband and I just love it. It couldn't be easier and always makes an impression on dinner guests.   —Terry Hammond, Grabill, Indiana

  2 cans (20 ounces *each*) pineapple chunks
  2 cups fat-free Italian salad dressing
  2 cans (8 ounces *each*) tomato sauce
  1/4 cup packed brown sugar
  2 teaspoons prepared mustard
  2 pounds uncooked medium shrimp, peeled and deveined (about 64)
  4 large sweet red peppers, cut into chunks
  2 large onions, cut into chunks

Drain pineapple, reserving 1/2 cup juice; refrigerate pineapple. In a small bowl, combine the salad dressing, tomato sauce, brown sugar, mustard and reserved juice. Pour 3 cups into a large resealable plastic bag; add the shrimp. Seal bag and turn to coat; refrigerate for 3 hours. Cover and refrigerate remaining marinade for basting.

Coat grill rack with nonstick cooking spray before starting the grill. Drain and discard marinade from shrimp. On 16 metal or soaked wooden skewers, alternately thread the shrimp, red peppers, onions and pineapple. Grill, covered, over medium heat for 3-5 minutes on each side or until shrimp turn pink and vegetables are tender, basting occasionally with reserved marinade.

NUTRITION FACTS: 2 kabobs equals 221 calories, 2 g fat (trace saturated fat), 169 mg cholesterol, 629 mg sodium, 32 g carbohydrate, 4 g fiber, 20 g protein. DIABETIC EXCHANGES: 3 very lean meat, 2 vegetable, 1 fruit.

Orange Couscous
(PICTURED AT LEFT)

MEAT-LESS

PREP/TOTAL TIME: 15 Min.   YIELD: 8 Servings

Here is a fabulous, chilled side dish that features a delightful blend of fresh herbs and sunny, citrus flavors. Anytime I take this to a picnic, the bowl is always the first one emptied.
                    —Kathleen Martin, Medford, New York

  1 cup orange juice
  1 cup water
  1 teaspoon ground cumin
  1 package (10 ounces) couscous
  2 tablespoons olive oil
  2 tablespoons lime juice
  2 tablespoons reduced-sodium soy sauce
  1/4 cup minced fresh cilantro *or* parsley
  2 tablespoons minced fresh basil *or* 2 teaspoons dried basil
  2 tablespoons minced chives
  1 teaspoon minced fresh gingerroot
  1/4 teaspoon salt
  1 can (11 ounces) mandarin oranges, drained
  1/4 cup slivered almonds, toasted

In a saucepan, bring orange juice, water and cumin to a boil. Stir in couscous; remove from the heat. Cover and let stand for 5 minutes or until liquid is absorbed. Transfer to a large bowl; cool.

In a small bowl, whisk the oil, lime juice and soy sauce. Stir in the cilantro, basil, chives, ginger and salt. Pour over couscous and toss to coat. Add oranges and almonds; toss gently. Refrigerate until serving.

NUTRITION FACTS: 3/4 cup equals 206 calories, 6 g fat (1 g saturated fat), 0 cholesterol, 231 mg sodium, 34 g carbohydrate, 2 g fiber, 6 g protein. DIABETIC EXCHANGES: 1-1/2 starch, 1 fat, 1/2 fruit.

Fruity Coconut Cake Roll
(PICTURED BELOW)

FAT

PREP: 30 Min.   BAKE: 20 Min. + Chilling   YIELD: 12 Servings

Kiwi and coconut add tropical flair to this light, refreshing and simply delicious dessert. It makes a stunning finale to the fanciest of meals.   —Nancy Granaman, Burlington, Iowa

  1 package (16 ounces) angel food cake mix
  1/2 teaspoon plus 3 tablespoons confectioners' sugar, *divided*
  3/4 cup cold fat-free milk
  1 package (1 ounce) sugar-free instant white chocolate pudding mix
  1 carton (8 ounces) frozen fat-free whipped topping, thawed
  1/2 teaspoon coconut extract
  2 medium kiwifruit, peeled and thinly sliced
  2 cups fresh strawberries, sliced
  1/3 cup plus 2 tablespoons flaked coconut, *divided*
  2 tablespoons apricot spreadable fruit
  1/2 teaspoon hot water

Line a 15-in. x 10-in. x 1-in. baking pan with waxed paper; coat the paper with nonstick cooking spray and set aside.

Prepare cake batter according to package directions. Spread evenly in prepared pan. Bake at 350° for 16-20 minutes or until golden brown. Turn cake onto a kitchen towel dusted with 1/2 teaspoon confectioners' sugar. Gently peel off waxed paper. Dust with remaining confectioners' sugar. Roll up cake in the towel jelly-roll style, starting with a short side. Cool completely on a wire rack.

For filling, in a large bowl, whisk milk and pudding mix for 2 minutes. Let stand for 2 minutes or until soft-set. Stir in 1 cup whipped topping. Fold in remaining whipped topping; stir in extract.

Unroll cake; spread with filling to within 1 in. of edges. Arrange kiwi and strawberries over filling. Sprinkle with 1/3 cup coconut. Roll up again. Refrigerate for 1-2 hours.

Toast the remaining coconut. In a small bowl, whisk spreadable fruit and water until smooth. Drizzle over cake. Sprinkle with toasted coconut. Cut into slices. Refrigerate leftovers.

NUTRITION FACTS: 1 slice equals 233 calories, 2 g fat (1 g saturated fat), trace cholesterol, 378 mg sodium, 50 g carbohydrate, 1 g fiber, 4 g protein.

General Recipe Index

This handy index lists every recipe by food category, major ingredient and/or cooking method, so you can easily locate recipes to suit your needs.

● Table-ready in 30 minutes or less.

Alphabetical Index

*This handy index lists every recipe in alphabetical order
so you can easily find your favorite dish.*

● Table-ready in 30 minutes or less.

Skillet Pork Chops, 141
Slow Cooker Fajitas, 106
Smoked Salmon Pinwheels, 20
● Smoked Turkey Cranberry
    Salad, 44
● Snow Pea Medley, 257
● Soft Fish Tacos, 159
South-of-the-Border Stuffed
    Peppers, 104
● Southwest Iceberg Slaw, 243
Southwest Lasagna Rolls, 175
● Southwestern Bean Patties, 183
Southwestern Beef Stew, 97
Southwestern Stuffed Turkey
    Breast, 134
Spaghetti Pie, 249
Spaghetti with Italian Meatballs, 105
● Special Turkey Sandwiches, 125
Spiced Cranberry Wheat Bread, 191
● Spiced Oatmeal Mix, 93
● Spicy Beans and Rice, 169
● Spicy Buffalo Chicken Wraps, 120
● Spicy Chicken Spaghetti, 260
Spicy Hearty Chili, 251
Spicy Peanut Chicken Kabobs, 18
Spinach and Turkey Sausage
    Lasagna, 266
Spinach Meatball Subs, 100
Spinach Phyllo Triangles, 24
● Spinach-Pine Nut Pasta, 181
Spinach-Stuffed Portobello
    Mushrooms, 171
● Spinach with Hot Bacon
    Dressing, 51
Spring Green Guacamole, 28
● Stir-Fried Vegetables, 79
Stir-Fried Walnut Chicken, 125
● Strawberry Banana Smoothies, 94
● Strawberry Salad with Cinnamon
    Vinaigrette, 46
Strawberry Sorbet Sensation, 233
Stuffed Ranch Chicken, 259
Stuffed Steak Spirals, 103
Stuffed Sweet Onions, 78
Stuffing from the Slow Cooker, 84
Summer Squash Casserole, 82
Summer Squash Chicken
    Casserole, 120
Sun-Dried Tomato 'n' Basil
    Wreath, 198
Sun-Dried Tomato Chicken, 122
Swedish Tea Ring, 192
● Sweet 'n' Sour Pork Stir-Fry, 144
Sweet 'n' Spicy Roasted Corn, 263
● Sweet Potato Bean Soup, 176
Sweet Potato Crisp, 208
Sweet Potato Scones, 197
● Sweet-Sour Spinach Salad, 53
Swirled Mint Cookies, 232
Swordfish Skewers, 160

T

Tabbouleh, 63
Taco Oven-Fried Chicken, 132
Tamale Veggie Pie, 171
Tangy Pulled Pork Sandwiches, 145
● Tangy Vegetable Dip, 19
Tarragon Chops with
    Mushrooms, 144
● Tarragon Tuna Salad Wraps, 158
Tart 'n' Frosty Limeade
    Dessert, 225
Tempting Shrimp Phyllo Tarts, 19
● Tenderloin with Herb Sauce, 264
Teriyaki Flank Steak, 98
Terrific Tomato Tart, 32
Texas Beef Barbecue, 107
Toffee Crunch Dessert, 206
Tofu Manicotti, 180
Tomato Artichoke Salad, 52
Tomato Crab Soup, 40
Tortellini Minestrone, 42
● Tortellini with Roasted Red Pepper
    Dip, 269
Traditional Cheesecake, 211
Tropical Meringue Tarts, 224
● Tuna Artichoke Melts, 254
Tuna-Stuffed Potatoes, 159
● Turkey Alfredo Pizza, 134
● Turkey 'n' Swiss Sandwiches, 260
● Turkey Burgers with Jalapeno
    Cheese Sauce, 122
Turkey Fettuccine Skillet, 132
Turkey Quesadillas with Cranberry
    Salsa, 133
Turkey Roulades, 123
Turkey Wild Rice Casserole, 130
Turkey Wonton Cups, 25
Two-Cheese Turkey Enchiladas, 118

U

Ultimate Corn Bread, 195

V

Vanilla Tapioca Pudding, 29
● Vegetable Beef Stir-Fry, 98
Vegetable Crab Soup, 156
Vegetable Soup with Dumplings, 39
● Veggie Cheese Sandwiches, 174
Veggie Pasta Salad, 53
Veggie Shrimp Egg Rolls, 22
● Veggies from the Grill, 84
Velvet Shrimp, 157

W

Warm Broccoli Spinach Dip, 18
Warm Chocolate Cakes, 241
● Warm Seafood Salad, 253
Warm Spinach Spread, 31
Watermelon Berry Sorbet, 215
Watermelon Salsa, 20
Weekday Lasagna, 101
● White and Black Bean Salad, 57
White Chocolate Cranberry
    Cookies, 238
Whole Wheat Blueberry
    Scones, 196
Whole Wheat Buttermilk Rolls, 191
Wholesome Veggie Burgers, 168
Wild Mushroom Ravioli, 177
Wild Rice Turkey Salad, 54
Winter Squash Muffins, 190

Y

Yogurt-Herb Salad Dressing, 52
Yummy Pizza Bake, 110

Z

Zesty Vegetable Dip, 27
● Zippy Chicken Soup, 40
Zippy Raspberry Roast Pork, 146
Zucchini Chocolate Cake, 205
Zucchini-Wrapped Scallops, 164

Reference Index

Use this index to locate the many healthy cooking hints (by chapter) located throughout this book.